THE BOOK OF
SAINTS

A DAY-BY-DAY ILLUSTRATED ENCYCLOPEDIA

THE BOOK OF
SAINTS

A DAY-BY-DAY ILLUSTRATED ENCYCLOPEDIA

weldon**owen**

weldon**owen**

415 Jackson Street
San Francisco, CA 94111
Telephone: 415 291 0100
Fax: 415 291 8841
www.weldonowen.com

WELDON OWEN INC.
President, CEO Terry Newell
VP, Sales and New Business Development Amy Kaneko
VP, Publisher Roger Shaw
Associate Creative Director Kelly Booth
Editorial Assistant Katharine Moore
Production Director Chris Hemesath
Production Manager Michelle Duggan
Color Manager Teri Bell

**Weldon Owen would like to thank the following designers
for their contributions:**
Adrienne Aquino, Meghan Hildebrand, Marisa Kwek, Astrea White, Angela Williams

**Conceived and produced for Weldon Owen Inc.
by Heritage Editorial**
General Editor Andrew Heritage
Editorial Direction Andrew Heritage, Ailsa C. Heritage
Design and Illustration Philippa Baile at Oil Often (www.oiloften.co.uk)
Contributing Editors Laura Cowan, Thomas Cussans, Catherine Day, Elizabeth Wyse

**The Publishers would also like to thank the following consultants
for their help and advice in planning this book:**
Rev. Neil Brice; Frederick Mathewson Denny, Professor Emeritus of Religious Studies,
University of Colorado at Boulder; Fr. Rupert McHardy, The Brompton Oratory, London

Weldon Owen is a division of
BONNIER

A WELDON OWEN PRODUCTION
© 2012 Weldon Owen Inc.

ISBN 10: 1-61628-451-X
ISBN 13: 978-1-61628-451-0

Printed and bound in China

10 9 8 7 6 5 4 3 2

CONTENTS

This book is organized chronologically, divided into monthly sections, following the calendar year. In order to find a particular saint's feast day, readers should consult the Index, which references each saint by date.

FOREWORD

When this book was first conceived, a decade or so ago, many consultants said it would be impossible to achieve. The problems of reconciling the dating of feast days between the various liturgical calendars alone seemed insurmountable, as did the problem of quite simply who to include. The editors have attempted to feature the most significant saints from all quarters, and have included as a foundation all those listed on the General Roman Calendar, the Liturgical Calendar for the Dioceses of the United States of America, and those on the Lectionary of the Church of England. On this solid basis many more have been added, including many Eastern Orthodox, local, and modern saints. In order to accommodate as many saints as possible, a two-tier system has been adopted – in many instances determined by adequate illustrative or biographical material. This is by no means intended to be seen as a value or quality judgment.

Where appropriate, a few individuals who are not saints, but whose lives significantly contributed to the corpus of saintly activity and achievement (and who might currently be under consideration for beatification or canonization), have also been included in the book.

With some 20,000 saints to choose from, the editors may well be guilty of omissions that many might deem significant. However, within the scope and confines of the current volume, we hope we have done justice, in the spirit of ecumenism, to the many and various facets of what is now a truly global faith.

What Makes a Saint?

Three decades ago, *The Catholic Encyclopedia* included around 5,000 saints. Some of their lives were recorded in detail, while some remained barely identifiable from mere scraps of information, hearsay, and legend. During the pontificates of Pope John Paul II and Benedict XVI, the roster has grown exponentially and, with the loosening of atheistic Communist control in the countries of the former Soviet Union and China, a tidal wave of saints has been admitted to the canon, swelling the total to around 20,000. In addition, the Church of England, while carefully treading an ecumenical line in its selection of saints old and new alongside many worthy characters in its list of observances, has admitted a new list of 20th-century martyrs.

The first Christian saints were those immediately involved with the life and ministry of Christ – in effect His family members, first disciples, and immediate associates. As Christianity grew and spread within both the Eastern and Western Roman empires – driven by the missionary impetus of Christ's Apostles – a new and practically innumerable host of 'martyrs' were created as the new creed collided with long-standing pagan beliefs and traditions and the imperial persecution of Christians. The practice of inviting martyrdom, sadly not unfamiliar in the modern world, was almost certainly part of the Christian regimen at the time. Martyrdom has continued into the present day: missionary activity produced a huge number of martyrs, as did the global expansion of Christianity in the wake of European colonialism and the European wars of religion sparked by the Reformation.

A new category of saint, the 'confessor,' emerged after the emperor Constantine decreed Christianity to be the official religion of the Roman empire in 323. Many of these saints came to prominence as theologians, bishops, archbishops, and patriarchs involved in steering the passage, development, outreach, and consolidation of the Church. In more recent years, many worthy people have been added to the canon of sainthood by their sheer selfless good work, and their foundation of, and support for, religious orders dedicated to the care and education of the less fortunate.

Hagiography

The urge to record and celebrate the achievements and sacrifices of saints dates back to at least the 3rd century AD. One of the most important hagiographers was St. Jerome (Sept. 30), although his was only one of a wide range of martyrologies and calendars of saints' feast days. The *Martyrologium* of Usuard, dating from the mid-9th century, attempted an encyclopedic listing. From the early Middle Ages, a literary tradition of recounting the lives of the more lively and popular saints emerged. Perhaps the most famous example was Jacobus de Voragine's *Legenda Aurea* (*The Golden Legend*), completed in around 1266.

The most important list of saints is *The Roman Martyrology*. It was assembled from a wide range of sources with a sense of scientific and historical purpose in 1583 under the auspices of Pope Gregory XIII. It has been revised several times over the last four centuries and remains the main repository of information concerning the canon of saints, at least for the Western churches.

The Path to Sainthood

Saints tended to be adopted and recognized on a local level for the first thousand years or so of Christianity. Often sainthood was a product of veneration by a saint's contemporaries, peers, and successors, although increasingly the recognition of a saint was in the gift of the local bishop. During this period, relics (and the possession of them) also became an important aspect of veneration.

The many saints who entered the canon in the first millennium of Christian history are referred to as doing so 'Pre-Congregation.' The more formal process of recognition evolved from the 10th century as successive bishops of Rome began to assert their exclusive right to recognize saints. Pope Alexander III (d.1181) began a more formal process for the papal recognition of sainthood; this came to involve an advisory 'congregation' of senior churchmen. However, the earliest version of the modern rigorous examination of a candidate's worthiness for papal consideration or approval was only introduced in 1634. Today, this involves three main processes:

veneration, beatification, and canonization. Central to these processes is the Congregation for the Causes of Saints, which originated in the 17th century as the Congregation of Sacred Rites, but was reformed in 1969 with the specific task of carefully assessing all the evidence and providing the pontiff with reliable advice in making a decision.

Veneration The first stage is usually petitioned at a local or parochial level. The title 'Venerable' is applied to those whose beatification has been accepted in principle if not fully decreed, pending further investigation.

Beatification The second level involves a deeper testing of the evidence of the candidate's sanctity, and at least one attested miracle as a result of the individual's intercession is required. Exceptions may be made in the case of martyrdom or exceptional sanctity. A person who has been beatified acquires the title 'Blessed.'

Canonization The third and final stage of elevation to sainthood is the outcome of a long evaluation of evidence – biographical, testimonial, and otherwise – and the detailed appraisal of whether God has indeed performed miracles due to the saint's intercession. In recent years, this has relied increasingly on medically approved 'miracles,' such as the scientifically inexplicable recovery from an untreatable or terminal condition. The 'incorruption' of a saint's remains, a convincing qualification in previous centuries, is now regarded as less reliable.

Liturgical Calendars

Each denomination has its own liturgical calendar that lists particular days of observance for major feasts, many of which include saints' days. They do not always accord, and on an annual basis saints' feast days may be shifted or ignored if they coincide with a more important fixture on the calendar.

In addition, the calendars themselves may be affected by considerations like the paschal feast days linked to Easter.

For the purposes of this volume, the editors have included all those saints (canonized, beatified, or listed as significant contributors to the body of Christian faith) that are included on the following liturgical calendars (although there are provisions within these calendars for local observances, many of which have also been included):

The General Roman Calendar Established in 1969, and only minimally revised since then, the Calendar lists Optional Memorials, Obligatory Memorials, Feasts, and Solemnities. It allocates only about half of the days in a year to feasts for specific saints, although many more appear on *The Roman Martyrology (see previous page)*.

The General Roman Calendar also provides appendices for local feast days that it approves in various countries around the world (for example, St. Patrick in Ireland, or St. Elizabeth Ann Seton in the United States).

The Lectionary of the Church of England In many instances this accords with the General Roman Calendar, but it also includes teachers of the Faith, bishops and other pastors, members of religious communities, missionaries, Christian rulers, reformers, and others recognized uniquely by the Church of England.

The Liturgical Calendar for the Dioceses of the United States of America Based upon the General Roman Calendar, this includes a number of saints unique to North America.

KEY TO SYMBOLS AND ABBREVIATIONS

Date The entries in this volume are organized by calendar date. Where variations exist between the liturgical calendars they are often noted, but not exhaustively.

♣ These symbols indicate whether or not a saint is listed
☁ on the three main liturgical calendars. A filled-in symbol indicates inclusion on:

GRC   The General Roman Calendar

CofE   The Lectionary of the Church of England

LCDUS   The Liturgical Calendar for the Dioceses of the United States of America

Pre-Congregation Saint recognized before the formal process of pontifical beatification and canonization had been introduced (*see above*).

Other Where, or by whom, the particular cult is recognized.

♥ This indicates the date, if known, of beatification.

◯ This indicates the date, if known, of canonization.

✝ Emblem, symbol, or style of representation most frequently associated with the saint.

🙏 Patronage, or causes for which the saint's intercession may be most effectively pleaded.

Other abbreviations:

c.   *Circa*, approximate date

b.   Born

d.   Died

r.   Dates reigned/ruled

SS.   Used to refer to a church dedicated to multiple saints

Sts. Used when referring to more than one saint in a general context

JANUARY

The first month of the Julian and Gregorian calendars, January is associated with winter in the northern hemisphere and summer in the southern. It is named after the double-faced Roman deity Janus, god of the doorway.

Christian festivals during this month include the Circumcision, falling on the eighth day after the Nativity, and Epiphany which, on January 6, celebrates the Adoration of the Magi on the twelfth day of Christmas. For the Eastern Churches, where it is known as Theophany, the date is associated with the Baptism of Christ (and was the day upon which Christ's Nativity was originally celebrated). In some traditions, Epiphany forms a period of the liturgical calendar lasting until the beginning of Lent. In the West, it marks the beginning of the first period of Ordinary Time.

The Adoration of the Magi *by Pieter Brueghel the Younger (1564–1638) initially seems a familiar wintry, snow-clad Christmas scene. But the painter emphasizes the humility of Christ's birth in a stable by tucking it away in a corner of the painting, while the majority of the population continues with their everyday chores, unaware of the miraculous event.*

JANUARY 1 THE BLESSED VIRGIN MARY

STATUS Virgin, Mother of God, Queen of Heaven

BORN 1st century BC

DIED After AD 33

GRC ♣

CofE ♧

LCDUS ♣

OTHER Eastern Orthodox churches

⊙ Pre-Congregation

✝ The color blue, lily, fleur-de-lis, sword passing through a heart, mystic rose, crescent moon

⚜ Innumerable dioceses, places of worship, convents, schools, place names around the world

Mary's grieving 'Mater Dolorosa' symbol was suggested by Simeon; "Yea, a sword shall pass through thy own soul also." (Luke 2:35).

Mary's monogram combines all the letters of the name 'Maria.' Medieval artists would often surmount it with a crown.

The most important and widely revered saint in the Christian canon, the Blessed Virgin Mary is celebrated on the first day of the year, known formally as the Solemnity of Mary, Mother of God.

The hitherto numerous days in the ecclesiastical calendar devoted to the Blessed Virgin Mary were rationalized at the Second Vatican Council (1962–65), and in 1969 the General Roman Calendar assigned this day as hers alone. The Naming of Christ and the Circumcision, long associated with January 1, are still observed by the Orthodox churches and the Church of England.

However, the Blessed Virgin Mary (Miriam in Hebrew, and often referred to as 'Madonna' or 'Our Lady of … ') still reappears throughout the Christian calendar. Today there are major feast days associated with key events in her life (her Nativity on September 8; the Annunciation of Our Lord on March 25; the Nativity of Christ on December 25; the Presentation of the Lord on February 2; her Assumption on August 15, her principal feast day; and her Enthronement as the Queen of Heaven on August 22). Her mourning for her lost Son and the various trials she had to endure on His behalf are commemorated on September 15 as Our Lady of Sorrows (*Mater Dolorosa*). She has been adopted by innumerable local churches and cults worldwide, the most significant of these including pilgrimage centers where Marian apparitions have occurred, such as Lourdes in France (Feb. 11), Guadalupe in Mexico (Dec. 12), and Fátima in Portugal (May 13). The extraordinary monastery of Montserrat in Catalonia even has a black Virgin (*La Moreneta*), as does the major pilgrimage center of Czestochowa in Poland.

The Life of Mary

Nevertheless, underlying all this majesty is the enduring image of a humble girl from Nazareth. The apocryphal *Protoevangelium of James* gives an account of her birth to aging parents Anne and Joachim (July 26). In the New Testament, Mary — a girl selected by God to give birth to His Son — first appears already betrothed to Joseph, a local carpenter. Both were of the line of David. Although Mary only occasionally appears in the Gospels during the ministry of Jesus, she is understood to have been a continuing presence throughout His life, through to the Crucifixion and Resurrection. She is often regarded as His first disciple, and was with the Apostles when they were visited by the Holy Spirit on Pentecost.

Mary is believed to have lived to the end of her natural life, whereupon she was immediately taken up to Heaven to be enthroned. Her example of purity, chastity, humility, and devotion is one that nuns of every sort ('Sisters') are enjoined to emulate.

One particular dogmatic issue regarding Mary was debated at the Second Council of Ephesus in 449: if Jesus Christ is an indivisible part of the Holy Trinity, should Mary not therefore be acclaimed as the Mother of God? Nestorius believed not, but was overruled. For the Orthodox churches, Mary became *Theotokos* (the God-bearer); for the West, the Mother of God. As a result, an outburst of Marian cults spread across the Christian world. Later, this linked to the question of whether Mary herself was the product of an Immaculate Conception; this was promulgated as doctrine by Pope Pius IX in 1854, again provoking a wave of Marian fervor.

Despite this, the Blessed Virgin Mary remains the most accessible, approachable, and beloved of all the saints.

> "Behold the handmaid of the Lord; be it unto me according to thy word."
>
> THE BLESSED VIRGIN MARY, UPON THE ANNUNCIATION OF CHRIST (LUKE 1:38).

The Blessed Virgin Mary is the single most popular figure in Western art. Often glorified, often overwhelmed by attendants, here Giovanni Battista Salvi da Sassoferrato's simple vision of a devoted woman (c.1650) reflects her essential purity.

JANUARY 2 | BASIL THE GREAT

STATUS	Bishop, Doctor of the Church
BORN	c.330, Caesarea, Cappadocia, modern Turkey
DIED	379, Caesarea, Cappadocia, modern Turkey
GRC	♣
CofE	♣
LCDUS	♣
OTHER	Eastern Orthodox churches
⬯	Pre-Congregation

Born to a strongly Christian family, Basil's parents are revered as saints in the Eastern Orthodox churches, and he was brother to Gregory of Nyssa (Jan. 10) and Peter of Sebaste. He was educated at home, and then studied in Constantinople and Athens, where he met Gregory Nazianzen (*see below*). They both entered a Christian community at Pontus, where Basil developed his teachings concerning monasticism. Eventually ordained in around 362, he returned to Caesarea, where he developed a theological argument against Arianism (*see below*), then the creed of the Roman emperor, Valens. Basil succeeded Eusebius as bishop of Caesarea in 370. His arguments in support of the Council of Nicaea of 325 were successfully put forward by Gregory Nazianzen at the Council of Constantinople in 381 after Basil's untimely death.

Basil's emblem reflects his importance in building up the strong theological foundations of the Church.

The Three Holy Hierarchs (from the left), *Basil the Great, John Chrysostom (Sept. 13), and Gregory Nazianzen.*

JANUARY 2 | GREGORY NAZIANZEN (NAZIANZUS)

STATUS	Bishop, Doctor of the Church
BORN	c.329, Nazianzus, Cappadocia, modern Turkey
DIED	390, Nazianzus, Cappadocia, modern Turkey
GRC	♣
CofE	♣
LCDUS	♣
OTHER	Eastern Orthodox churches
⬯	Pre-Congregation

Gregory was the son of the bishop of Nazianzus in Cappadocia. He studied in Constantinople, Alexandria, and Athens, where he met Basil the Great (*see above*). Both he and Basil did much to develop the theological arguments in favor of Trinitarianism, and although their relationship was often fraught, Gregory responded to an appeal to aid the Orthodox Christian community at Constantinople, which had suffered during the rule of the Arian emperor Valens. Gregory was appointed bishop of Constantinople and was prominent in establishing the Trinitarian, or Nicene, Creed at the Council of Constantinople in 381.

Gregory's emblem is an epigonation, the richly embroidered vestment representing the 'sword of the spirit' worn by bishops of the Eastern Orthodox churches.

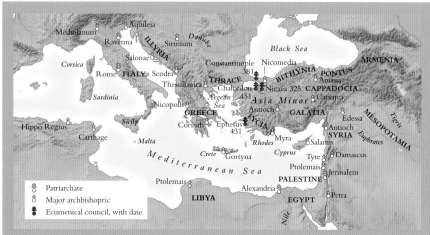

THE ARIAN HERESY

The Greek theologian Arius (c.250–336) promulgated a doctrine in which Jesus Christ was seen not as an indivisible part of the Holy Trinity, but rather as a separate being created by God, whose task was to establish the Kingdom of God on Earth. This belief, in direct contrast to the doctrine of Trinitarianism in which the Creator, the Holy Spirit, and Christ are seen as an indivisible whole, spread rapidly, threatening a major doctrinal rift in the Roman church.

Arius's ideas were condemned at the Council of Nicaea in 325. Both St. Basil and St. Gregory (*above*) argued for the Trinitarian or Nicene Creed, and at the Council of Constantinople in 381, Arian views were declared heretical. Nevertheless, the Roman emperor Valens (r.364–78), adopted the Arian view, and persecuted its opponents. His successor, Theodosius, adopted the Nicene Creed, which was to become a central tenet in all the major churches.

JANUARY 2 · SERAPHIM OF SAROV

STATUS Hermit
BORN 1759, Kursk, Russia
DIED 1833, Sarov, Russia
GRC ○
CofE ♣
LCDUS ○
OTHER Russian Orthodox Church
○ 1903, Russian Orthodox Church
† Often shown with a bear

Seraphim was born Prokhor Moshnin, the son of a builder. In 1779 Seraphim entered the monastery at Sarov, and was ordained in 1793. He adopted a hermit's lifestyle, dwelling in a hut in the forest, growing his own food, and praying continuously. In 1804 he was attacked by vagabonds, and was cared for in the monastery for some years before returning to the forest. However, in 1810 failing health forced him to accept the offer of a solitary cell in the monastery, where he lived as a hermit within the community, although he received visitors. Noted for his humility, compassion, and wisdom, Seraphim was said to have received visions of the Blessed Virgin Mary, and performed several curing miracles. He freed Nicholas Motovilov from years of rheumatic pains, and Motovilov recorded conversations he had with Seraphim, which have been widely translated. Seraphim died in his cell in 1833. His relics were hidden during the Bolshevik Revolution, and only rediscovered in 1991.

> **"Acquire a peaceful spirit, and thousands around you will be saved."**
> SERAPHIM, QUOTED BY NICHOLAS MOTOVILOV.

JANUARY 3 · GENEVIÈVE

STATUS Virgin
BORN c.422, Nanterre, France
DIED c.500, Paris, France
GRC ○
CofE ○
LCDUS ○
OTHER In France
○ Pre-Congregation
† Often shown tending sheep
⚕ Sufferers from fever; Paris

Born into a shepherding family in Nanterre, France, Geneviève moved to Paris after her parents died. She entered a nunnery there, apparently inspired to do so by St. Germanus of Auxerre (July 31). When the city was besieged by the Franks under Childeric in 464, she led a party from the city to gather food, her dedication winning the respect of Childeric and saving many lives. She subsequently is said to have converted his son, Clovis, in 496, who built the Church of the Holy Apostles in Paris in her memory. Earlier, in 451, her advocacy of peace and the power of prayer was also said to have saved Paris from the depredations of Attila the Hun's marauding army.

Geneviève's influence survived her: in 1129 an outbreak of ergot poisoning in Paris was brought to an end when her relics were taken in procession to Notre-Dame Cathedral, an event still celebrated today. Her relics were destroyed during the French Revolution; the Panthéon in Paris was originally built in her honor, but was later dedicated to secular heroes.

Date	Name	Status	Venerated	Life
Jan. 2	Munchin (d.7th century)	Bishop ○ Pre-Congregation	In Limerick, Ireland	Believed to have been first bishop of Limerick; known as 'the Wise.' Granted an island retreat on Ireland's west coast by local prince in return for withdrawing claim to throne.
Jan. 2	Vedanayagam Samuel Azariah (1874–1945)	Evangelist, Bishop, Founder	CofE In South Asia	First Indian Anglican bishop. Born in poor area of Andhra Pradesh. Recognized need for indigenous leadership in establishing Christian faith in South Asia. Founded Indian Missionary Society (1903) and National Missionary Society (1905). Ordained (1909); became bishop of Dornakal (1912). Avowed ecumenicalist. Died two years before inauguration of United Church of South India, which he had done much to create.

JANUARY 4 | ELIZABETH ANN SETON (MOTHER SETON)

STATUS Widow, Founder
BORN 1774, New York, USA
DIED 1821, Emmitsburg, Maryland, USA
GRC ☁
CofE ☁
LCDUS ♣
⬭ 1975
🙏 Regarded as creator of the US Catholic parochial school system

Elizabeth Ann Seton is the earliest American-born saint. Elizabeth (*née* Bayley) was raised in a wealthy Episcopalian family, and married a merchant when she was 20, raising five children. She became involved in charitable social work and set up the Society for the Relief of Poor Widows and Children in 1797, but her husband suddenly became bankrupt, and then she herself was widowed.

She converted to Catholicism in 1805, and was invited to establish a girls' school in Baltimore. In 1809, she founded the Sisters of Charity of St. Joseph, the first homegrown American religious society. This led to the founding of another school for poor children in Emmitsburg, Maryland. She was elected Superior and, with 18 companions, took her vows in 1810.

JANUARY 5 | JOHN NEPOMUCENE NEUMANN

STATUS Bishop
BORN 1811, Bohemia, modern Czech Republic
DIED 1860, Philadelphia, Pennsylvania, USA
GRC ☁
CofE ☁
LCDUS ♣
OTHER In Bohemia (March 5)
❤ 1963
⬭ 1977

The National Shrine of St. John Neumann lies under the altar of St. Peter the Apostle in Philadelphia, his remains encased in a glass reliquary.

Born to German/Czech parents, John Nepomucene was named after the patron saint of Bohemia, and was destined to enter the church. However, the Austro-Hungarian government suspended ordinations so, in 1836, John emigrated to the United States intending to undertake missionary work. He was ordained within three weeks of arriving in Manhattan, and joined the Redemptorist Order – the first American priest to do so – in 1842, meanwhile preaching to fellow immigrants in New York State, Pittsburgh, and Baltimore.

John was naturalized in 1848, and appointed bishop of Philadelphia in 1852. Under his tenure a massive program of building was inaugurated (despite resistance from the 'Know-Nothing' anti-Catholic movement), resulting in the completion of Baltimore's cathedral and the creation of almost 100 churches and 80 schools in Pennsylvania and Delaware.

Date	Name	Status	Venerated	Life
Jan. 5	Roger (Ruggiero) of Todi (d.1237)	⬭ Pre-Congregation	By Franciscans In Todi and Rieti, Italy	Received into Franciscan Order by St. Francis himself. Appointed spiritual director of community of nuns at Rieti in 1236; died the following year before fulfilling his true promise.
Jan. 5	Charles of Sezze (1613–70)	Monk, Stigmatist ❤ 1882 ⬭ 1959	By Franciscans † Shown with stigmata	Rural Roman peasant, poorly educated. Became Franciscan lay brother (1622), working at various priories near Rome. Extremely pious, received the stigmata and open wound in his side from beam of light deflected from the Host during Mass. Nursed plague victims (1656). Wrote popular spiritual autobiography, *The Grandeurs of the Mercies of God*.

JANUARY 5 — SIMEON (SIMON) STYLITES

STATUS Hermit

BORN c.390, Cilicia, modern Turkey

DIED 459, Telanissus (Dair Sem'an), Syria

GRC ☁

CofE ☁

LCDUS ☁

OTHER Eastern Orthodox churches (Sept. 1), Coptic Orthodox Church

○ Pre-Congregation

† A pillar; often shown in monk's robes

A 6th-century relief shows Christ blessing Simeon, while a serpent representing temptation attempts to scale the column.

Simeon's story attracted the interest of the anti-clerical Spanish Surrealist filmmaker Luis Buñuel. Simon of the Desert (1965) examines absurdity and faith.

Simeon is remembered as one of the more eccentric hermits who undertook various acts of intense self-mortification in the Near East, effectively inventing pillar asceticism. The son of a shepherd, from an early age Simeon undertook fasts and other rituals of self-mortification in a number of hermitages and monasteries in northern Syria. He was noted for his wisdom, sympathy, and practical advice but, seeking more privacy for meditation, he decided in around 423 to live on top of a pillar in the desert near Aleppo. Originally this pillar was quite small, but it was eventually extended to reach some 60 feet (18 m) in height, with a balustraded platform some 12 feet (3.5 m) square. He remained there for 37 years.

A Source of Wonder

Despite Simeon's yearning for seclusion, his unusual method of removal from the world had the opposite effect: so noted was he for his extreme asceticism that he was constantly visited by pilgrims and seekers of wisdom and solace. He made himself available to visitors every afternoon — they ascended to his platform by ladder — and was credited with converting many, especially among the Bedouin Arabs. He also corresponded with admirers from further afield and delivered addresses condemning usury and profanity. He refused to entertain women, including his mother.

Among his imitators were Daniel the Stylite and the apparently insane Simeon Stylites the Younger (May 24).

> " ... despairing of escaping the world horizontally, he tried to escape it vertically."
>
> UNATTRIBUTED, QUOTED IN *THE PENGUIN DICTIONARY OF SAINTS*, ATTWATER.

A monastery was built at the site of Simeon's pillar, the base of which can still be seen among the ruins.

Date	Name	Status	Venerated	Life
Jan. 6	Peter of Canterbury (d.607)	Abbot ○ Pre-Congregation	In Canterbury, England; Boulogne, France	One of St. Augustine's companions on his mission to Britain. Became first abbot of St. Augustine's (then SS. Peter and Paul), Canterbury. Drowned while crossing English Channel on mission to Gaul. His remains were translated to Boulogne, France.
Jan. 6	André (Alfred) Bessette (1845–1937)	Healer ♥ 1982	In Montreal, Canada	Born poor, orphaned young, and plagued by pain. Failed to hold down a job or become educated until admitted to Congregation of the Holy Cross at Notre Dame College, Montreal (1870). Remained doorkeeper there for 40 years. Devoted to St. Joseph. Acquired reputation for healing.

JANUARY 7 | RAYMOND OF PEÑAFORT

STATUS	Priest, Canonist
BORN	c.1175, Vilafranca del Penedès, Catalonia, Spain
DIED	1275, Barcelona, Spain
GRC	♣
CofE	○
LCDUS	♣
OTHER	By Dominicans
⊘	1601
†	Dominican robes
🙏	Canon lawyers

Raymond's importance in the development of the Catholic Church in Iberia made him a popular subject for visionary paintings during the Counter-Reformation period.

Raymond's arms reflect his learning and devotion, the hammer meaning 'enforcer of the faith.'

This long-lived and distinguished churchman was born to a noble family in Catalonia, then part of the kingdom of Aragon, and received a doctorate in canon and civil law at the University of Bologna. He then returned to Barcelona, joining the Dominican Order to preach and study. He was called to Rome in 1230 by Pope Gregory IX, and began the task of collating conciliar and papal decrees into a standard reference work for canonical lawyers. Raymond returned to Catalonia in 1236, becoming general of the Dominicans (1238–40), and was instrumental in establishing the Inquisition in Iberia, focusing on the conversion of Muslims and Jews. He supported Thomas Aquinas (Jan. 28) in writing his *Summa contra Gentiles*, and he seems to have been involved, with St. Peter Nolasco and James of Aragon, in the founding of the Mercedarian Order (established to rescue ransomed Christians during the Spanish *Reconquista*).

JANUARY 8 | LAURENCE GIUSTINIANI

STATUS	Bishop
BORN	1381, Venice, Italy
DIED	1456, Venice, Italy
GRC	○
CofE	○
LCDUS	○
OTHER	In Venice (Sept. 5); by Augustinians
⊘	1690

Laurence was admired for his humble piety, a trait he seems to have inherited from his mother, although the Giustinianis were a senior patrician family in 14th-century Venice. He eschewed a secular career, joining the congregation of canons regular of St. George at age 19. He wore sackcloth and begged for food. He was ordained in 1406, at a time when the congregation was being transformed into one with an active role in the community, and he rose to become general, reorganizing their constitution. In 1433 he was made bishop of Castello, part of the diocese of Venice, and his organizational skills meant that in 1451 (against his will) he was proclaimed the first Patriarch of Venice. His ascetic writings were widely published.

Laurence blesses the Adoration of the Lamb by St. Francis and John the Baptist.

JANUARY 9 | ADRIAN (HADRIAN) OF CANTERBURY

STATUS	Abbot
BORN	c.640, Africa
DIED	c.710, Canterbury, England
GRC	○
CofE	○
LCDUS	○
⊘	Pre-Congregation

The Venerable Bede (May 25) attests that Adrian was a Greek-speaking North African Berber, who became abbot of a monastery near Monte Cassino. He was twice offered, and twice declined, the archbishopric of Canterbury, but suggested a Greek monk, Theodore of Tarsus (Sept. 19), for the job. Papal assent was given, on condition that Adrian accompany Theodore to England. They arrived in 668, and Adrian became the abbot of SS. Peter and Paul (now St. Augustine's) in Canterbury, where he remained for the rest of his life. His great theological and linguistic knowledge helped to build the Canterbury monastic foundation into a major educational and missionary force in Britain.

During restoration work in 1091, Adrian's body was disinterred and found to be uncorrupted. His tomb became a major pilgrimage site, and many miraculous cures were claimed.

JANUARY 9 — PHILIP II OF MOSCOW

STATUS Metropolitan, Martyr
BORN 1507, Galich, Russia
DIED 1569, Tver, Russia
GRC ⬭
CofE ⬭
LCDUS ⬭
OTHER Eastern Orthodox
churches
⬭ 1652

Although Ivan IV did much to unify the Muscovite Russian state, he was noted for his ruthlessness and cruelty.

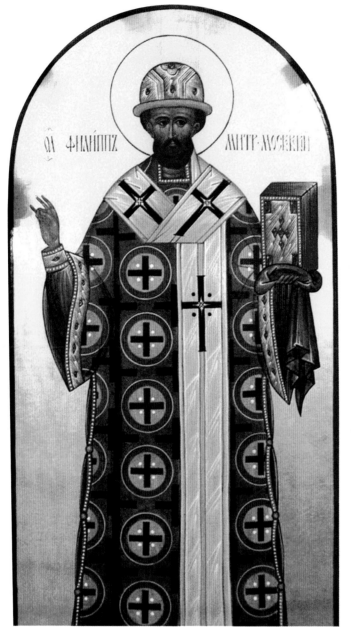

The story of Philip of Moscow is one that resonates with the frequent clashes between church and state that marked the Middle Ages. Born to an aristocratic family, Feodor Kolychev was taken into the Russian royal family circle as a boy, and was friendly with the crown prince, who was later, in 1533, to become Czar Ivan IV, 'the Terrible.' Feodor probably saw active service as a soldier. Around 1537, he somehow became implicated in a coup conspiracy and was forced to flee, taking refuge in Solovetsky Monastery on the White Sea. He rose to become abbot in 1547, adopting the name Philip, and inaugurated many building, drainage, and agricultural engineering projects on the monastic lands.

Church versus State

In 1565 Philip was elected metropolitan of Moscow, which made him the primate of the Orthodox Church in Russia, and the second most powerful man in Ivan IV's Muscovite kingdom. Ivan had supported his election. Ivan was a profoundly paranoid and fickle ruler, who would go on to kill his own son in a fit of rage. He sought to suppress any signs of dissent, and coerced the Church into supporting his creation of a brutal secret police (the Oprichnina) to implement this. Philip withdrew this support, and then openly criticized Ivan's vicious pogroms against Moscow's rival city, Novgorod. Philip urged Ivan to desist in private, and then, in despair, openly admonished the czar when he attended Mass at Moscow's cathedral. It was only a matter of time before Ivan concocted charges of sorcery and corruption against Philip; he was arrested during a liturgy at the Cathedral of Dormitian, Moscow, was incarcerated and starved in various monastic institutions, and eventually chained in a cell in Otroch Monastery. Philip was finally suffocated in his cell by an agent of Ivan's.

During the translation of Philip's relics from Otroch to Solovki in 1590, his remains were found to be uncorrupted. Miracles began to be reported, and in 1652 Czar Alexis was encouraged to translate the relics to Moscow.

"God rejects him who does not love his neighbor. I have to tell you this though I die for it."

PHILIP REBUKING IVAN IV DURING A SERMON IN MOSCOW CATHEDRAL.

Date	Name	Status	Venerated	Life
Jan. 7	Angela of Foligno (1248–1309)	Nun, Mystic	In Foligno, Italy By Franciscans	Wealthy woman. Married and had children. Began to have ecstatic visions (1285). Became Franciscan tertiary; after her husband's death gave away her wealth; founded community of tertiary nuns tending the poor. Her tomb in St. Francis, Foligno, is the site of numerous miracles.
Jan. 8	Pega of Peakirk (d.c.719)	Nun, Hermit ⬭ Pre-Congregation	In East Anglia, England	Sister of St. Guthlac. Lived as hermit in the Fens. The devil imitated her to tempt Guthlac from his fasting vows, forcing him to leave the area. Cured a blind man from Wisbech on way to Guthlac's funeral. Died on pilgrimage to Rome.

JANUARY 10

GREGORY OF NYSSA

STATUS Bishop

BORN c.330, Caesarea, modern Turkey

DIED c.395, Nyssa, modern Turkey

GRC ⬡

CofE ⬡

LCDUS ⬡

OTHER Eastern Orthodox churches; by Benedictines and Cistercians

⬭ Pre-Congregation

✝ Vested as a bishop

Gregory came from a notable family of early Christians in Asia Minor. With his older brother, Basil the Great, and the theologian Gregory Nazianzus (both Jan. 2), he is remembered as one of the Cappadocian Fathers. They asserted the superiority of Christian teachings over those of traditional Greek philosophy. In 372, he was consecrated Bishop of Nyssa, a remote city in eastern Anatolia near Armenia, where Arianism had taken hold. His most enduring contributions concerned the indivisible nature of the Trinity (central to the Nicene Creed, adopted at the Council of Constantinople, which Gregory attended in 381), the necessity of unquestioning faith in seeking to understand the infinity of God, the emulation of God through the example of Christ, and the importance of achieving this within a monastic community.

Gregory of Nyssa was of paramount importance to the development of the doctrines of the early Church. Here, he is depicted in an 11th-century mosaic, halo prominent, bearded face placidly serene, with a jewel-studded gospel in his left hand.

JANUARY 10

WILLIAM LAUD

STATUS Archbishop, Martyr

BORN 1573, Reading, England

DIED 1645, London, England

GRC ♧

CofE ♠

LCDUS ♧

OTHER US Episcopal Church

In 17th-century Europe, political and religious conflict were in effect the same. To the vast majority of English and Scots, for example, to threaten Protestant supremacy was to strike at the very roots of reformed Christian worship in Britain, and at the State itself. Laud, for all his grandeur, became a victim of these cross-currents.

The humbly-born William Laud attended Oxford and rose rapidly to become the most brilliant English churchman of his day, highly intellectual and an able administrator. In 1630 he was appointed Chancellor of Oxford University, and in 1633 he was made Archbishop of Canterbury by Charles I (Jan. 30). His legacy is, however, disputed. He has been called a "humorless dwarf," while the historian Macaulay dismissed him as a "ridiculous old bigot." Laud was unashamedly 'High Church,' and an implacable opponent of Puritanism. His determination, backed by the king, to impose High Church practices across all forms of Protestant worship in Britain, aroused fury in almost every quarter. For the Puritans, Laud's initiatives amounted to a clear attempt to reintroduce popery, and probably contributed to the eventual execution of Charles I. Parliament had Laud arrested in 1641 and beheaded four years later.

JANUARY 11

THEODOSIUS THE CENOBIARCH

STATUS Abbot

BORN c.423, Cappadocia, modern Turkey

DIED 529, near Bethlehem, modern Israel

GRC ⬡

CofE ⬡

LCDUS ⬡

OTHER Eastern Orthodox churches

⬭ Pre-Congregation

⚶ File-makers; the sick and insane

'Cenobiarch' means the head of those living together. It was as abbot of the monastery at Cathismus, near Bethlehem, that Theodosius achieved his greatest fame. Though he had spent the previous 30 years as a hermit, largely under the inspiration of St. Simeon Stylites (Jan. 5), Theodosius's holiness drew such crowds that he founded the monastery for his followers. Enthusiasm grew rapidly, attracting Armenians, Greeks, and Persians, each in separate

communities. Each placed a premium on charitable works, especially tending the sick and deranged. Theodosius fiercely opposed the Eutychian or Monophysite heresy and no less fiercely championed Orthodoxy. Numerous miracles were attributed to him. It was claimed that he was 105 when he died, "his skin as dry as stone."

This icon shows Theodosius surrounded by scenes reflecting his work with the sick.

JANUARY 12 — BENEDICT BISCOP

STATUS Bishop
BORN c.628, Northumbria, England
DIED 690, Wearmouth, England
GRC ♧
CofE ♣
LCDUS ♧
OTHER By Benedictines
⬭ Pre-Congregation
🙏 Musicians, painters

Biscop was among the leading Christian churchmen of early Anglo-Saxon England. Like most early Anglo-Saxon churchmen, he was high-born, raised at the court of King Oswy of Northumbria. He made five visits to Rome, each significantly helping the spread of Roman rites in his homeland. Among his most lasting legacies were the foundations, in 674 and 682 respectively, of the monasteries at Wearmouth and Jarrow. Both became major centers of Christian learning.

Benedict Biscop is here shown literally carrying a Roman basilica to England. In fact, the key moment in the Roman supremacy, actively pushed forward by Oswy and Benedict, was the Synod of Whitby in 664, which confirmed the primacy of Roman Christian practice over that of early Irish monastic observances.

JANUARY 12 — MARGUERITE BOURGEOYS

STATUS Missionary
BORN 1620, Troyes, France
DIED 1700, Montreal, Canada
GRC ♧
CofE ♧
LCDUS ♧
OTHER Anglican Church of Canada
♥ 1950
⬭ 1982
🙏 Orphans; those in poverty

European colonial endeavors in the 17th century may have been imperialist at heart, but they did at least partly spring from a desire to bring Western values to 'heathen' peoples. Marguerite Bourgeoys was 33 when she sailed for New France – Canada – in 1653, recruited by the governor of the new land to became a teacher as much as a missionary. It was a role Bourgeoys embraced with piety and energy. She not only built churches and schools, she recruited more high-minded French women to join her mission. She founded the Congregation of Notre-Dame in Montreal.

Marguerite Bourgeoys epitomized the combination of tough-mindedness and sanctity that has been the hallmark of successful female missionaries down the ages.

JANUARY 12 — AELRED

STATUS Abbot
BORN 1110, Hexham, England
DIED 1167, Rievaulx, Yorkshire, England
GRC ♧
CofE ♣
LCDUS ♧
⬭ 1476

In 1146, St. Aelred, only 36, was made abbot of the Cistercian abbey of Rievaulx, Yorkshire. In an age when the monastic ideal was thriving, his position made him remarkably powerful. He was a gifted historian and was exceptionally long-suffering – whether contending with the imperious Henry II, dealing with junior monks, or struggling with the succession of debilitating illnesses that eventually killed him. In his last years he was said to have been "more like a ghost than a man."

By the mid-12th century, a succession of exceptionally powerful monasteries had been established across Christendom. Their abbots were necessarily figures of influence. St. Aelred was among the most appealing: sympathetic, calm, and scholarly.

Date	Name	Status	Venerated	Life
Jan. 11	Mary Slessor (1848–1915)	Missionary	CofE, in Nigeria	Born in poverty in Scotland. Inspired by Dr. David Livingstone, traveled to Africa (1873) as a Presbyterian missionary. Went to Calabar, modern Nigeria, literally venturing into the unknown. Spent 39 years there, alternately cajoling and caring for the Efik people. Died of malaria.
Jan. 11	Francis Rogaczewski (1892–1940)	Priest, Martyr ♥ 1999	In Poland	Polish priest, ordained 1918. Arrested by Nazis on first day of invasion of Poland (1939). Imprisoned and tortured for several months, then shot. One of the 108 Polish Martyrs of World War II (group memorial day June 12).

JANUARY 13 — HILARY OF POITIERS

STATUS	Bishop, Doctor of the Church
BORN	c.300, Poitiers, France
DIED	c.368, Poitiers, France
GRC	♣
CofE	♣
LCDUS	♣
OTHER	Eastern Orthodox churches, Lutheran Church
⬭	Pre-Congregation
✝	Book
🙏	Many English legal and educational institutions refer to the spring semester, beginning in January, as the Hilary Term

Hilary was born to a patrician but pagan family in southwest France. He was educated in Latin and, unusually, Greek, at that point the almost exclusive language of Christian texts. It was his reading in both languages that led to his conversion to Christianity. He was baptized in around 345. Eight years later he was made bishop of Poitiers. His significance was as a champion of Nicene Trinitarianism, which was widely accepted in the Eastern Church and then making rapid inroads in the West where Arianism was still rife. Where Trinitarianism held that God the Father, God the Son, and God the Holy Spirit were 'eternally co-existent,' the Arians contended that Jesus, the son of God, not only had a separate existence, but had been 'created' rather than having always existed (*see* page 12).

Inevitably, the dispute had a political element. In 356, St. Hilary's forceful arguments led to his exile, on the orders of the emperor Constantius II, to Phrygia in Asia Minor. Here, again arguing in favor of Trinitarianism, he wrote *De Trinitate*, one of the earliest Christian texts in Latin. Returning to Poitiers in 361, Hilary, the 'Hammer of the Arians,' continued his campaign against Arianism, not just in France, but in many parts of Christendom.

A 14th-century manuscript showing the canonization of St. Hilary.

> "Obtain, O Lord ... that I may worship you, our Father, and with you, your Son; that I may deserve your Holy Spirit, who proceeds from you through your Only Begotten Son."
>
> HILARY OF POITIERS, *DE TRINITATE.*

JANUARY 13 — KENTIGERN (MUNGO)

STATUS	Bishop
BORN	c.515
DIED	c.600, Glasgow, Scotland
GRC	♢
CofE	♣
LCDUS	♢
OTHER	Eastern Orthodox churches
⬭	Pre-Congregation
✝	Salmon and ring
🙏	Salmon; Glasgow

Missionary, first bishop of Strathclyde, and founder of Glasgow, Kentigern was reputedly the illegitimate son of a Celtic princess – Kentigern means 'chief prince.' Mungo is derived from the Gaelic for 'dear one.' He was made bishop of Strathclyde in 540; later a substantial community – known as 'Clas-cu' or 'dear family' – settled around him. Numerous miracles were attributed to him.

It is clear that Kentigern was trained in the Irish missionary tradition, and there is one story that he exchanged pastoral staffs with Columba (June 9). There is also evidence that political turmoil in Strathclyde effectively banished him for a period to either Cumbria (where several churches are dedicated to him) or, less likely, to Wales, where he is said to have founded a monastery of 1,000 monks and become the first bishop of St. Asaph's. However, he certainly returned to Strathclyde, and his relics are claimed by Glasgow Cathedral.

Kentigern's curious symbol reflects a legend in which an indiscreet Celtic queen had thrown her wedding ring into a river. As a result of Kentigern's intervention, the ring was recovered from the gut of a salmon. Today, the city of Glasgow's coat of arms incorporates the fish and the ring.

Date	Name	Status	Venerated	Life
Jan. 14	John the Gardener (d.1501)	Monk	In Portugal, and Salamanca, Spain 🙏 Gardeners	Portuguese orphan. Worked as shepherd before being invited to work in gardens of Franciscan monastery in Salamanca. Subsequently took holy orders. Put in charge of the gardens. Exceptionally devout and sweet-natured; said to have gift for prophecy.
Jan. 14	Felix of Nola (d.c.255)	⬭ Pre-Congregation	In Nola, Italy	Son of Syrian Roman soldier. Gave most of inheritance to the poor. Ordained by Maximus of Nola. The latter fled when Decian persecutions began; Felix arrested in his place. Apparently released from jail by an angel. Retreated to small farm; shared produce with the poor. His tomb at Nola has miraculous properties.

JANUARY 13 · GEORGE FOX

STATUS Preacher, Founder
BORN 1624, Leicestershire, England
DIED 1691, London, England
GRC ○
CofE ♠
LCDUS ○
OTHER By Quakers

As the founder of the Religious Society of Friends, or 'Quakers' as they came to be known, George Fox was the most influential of the Nonconformists thrown up by the reformist religious turmoil that plagued 17th-century England. The core of Fox's belief was that Christianity did not depend on any organized, let alone hierarchic, church; nor did it need elaborate liturgies. Rather, he maintained that Christ was everywhere and available to everyone in whatever way they chose, provided they adhered to the basic Christian tenets of humility, charity, and faith. Fox, widely distrusted by the government (though admired by Oliver Cromwell), preached almost continuously across Britain. He was accordingly thrown into prison on numerous occasions, mostly on charges of blasphemy.

Fox was described as "graceful in countenance, manly in personage, grave in gesture, courteous in conversation." The name 'Quaker' came from a judge who imprisoned Fox in 1650. The judge taunted Fox as a 'Quaker' after Fox had exhorted him to "tremble at the word of the Lord." Fox's influence was particularly pronounced among the early English settlers of North America.

The wholesome nature of Fox's thinking has proved very successful in promoting both religion and the first 'organic' foodstuffs.

Quakers in Pennsylvania with Native Americans, signing a land-transfer agreement that formed the basis of the state of Pennsylvania. William Penn was a staunch Quaker, and the movement's ideals underpinned the foundation of his colony.

"The Lord showed me, so that I did see clearly, that he did not dwell in these temples which men had commanded and set up, but in people's hearts."

GEORGE FOX.

JANUARY 14 · SABAS (SAVA) OF SERBIA

STATUS Bishop
BORN c.1174, Rastko, Serbia
DIED c.1237, Trnovo, Bulgaria
GRC ○
CofE ○
LCDUS ○
OTHER Eastern Orthodox churches
♙ The Serbs, Serbian schoolchildren

Sabas was a central figure in the emergence of the independent Serbian Orthodox Church. He was born Prince Rastko Nemanjic, youngest son of Prince Stefan I Nemanjic, subsequently St. Simeon (Feb. 13), who had exploited waning Byzantine power to force through Serbian independence. To avoid marriage, Sabas spent much of his early manhood as a monk at Mt. Athos in Greece, where he and his father (who had abdicated) founded the Serbian monastery of Hilander. In 1207 he returned to Serbia, ending the civil war that had broken out between his brothers. In 1219, he was made the first archbishop of Zica and head of the newly independent Serbian church after persuading the patriarch of Constantinople that the Serbian and Bulgarian churches should both be granted autonomy. After resigning as archbishop in about 1230, he traveled widely, twice visiting Jerusalem. He died of pneumonia in Bulgaria.

St. Sabas crucially reinforced the sense of Serbian identity and bolstered Orthodoxy in the Balkans at a time when the Latin Church was threatening the Eastern churches – notably during the Fourth Crusade, when Constantinople was occupied and ransacked by the Franks in 1204.

JANUARY 15 · MARTIN LUTHER KING JR.

STATUS Martyr

BORN 1929, Atlanta, Georgia, USA

DIED 1968, Memphis, Tennessee, USA

GRC

CofE

LCDUS

OTHER US Episcopal Church (April 4), Lutheran Church

King and Lyndon Johnson. Johnson was a consistent advocate of the Civil Rights movement and a key ally of King, who was present when the president ceremonially signed the Civil Rights Act.

Dr. Martin Luther King Jr. remains by some distance the most influential figure of the American Civil Rights movement of the 1950s and '60s. He brought a potent combination of deeply held Christian faith, shrewd political awareness, and stirring oratory to the struggle against the racism of huge swaths of American society, above all in the South. Directly inspired by Gandhi (*see page 35*), King recognized early on that nonviolent protest on the largest possible scale was an effective weapon in forcing governments at state and federal levels to end the 'separate but equal' segregation of African Americans enshrined in the so-called 'Jim Crow' laws of the South. The passing of the Civil Rights Act of 1964 and the Voting Rights Act the following year was the direct consequence of King's tireless campaigning. He is still the youngest recipient of the Nobel Peace Prize, which he was awarded in 1964. In 1986, Martin Luther King Day was established as a national holiday in the United States.

King, a Baptist minister like his father, sprang to prominence with the year-long Montgomery bus boycott in 1955. Two years later, with fellow campaigner Ralph Abernathy, he founded the Southern Christian Leadership Conference, which he led until his assassination in 1968. Under its banner, King organized campaigns across the South, twice leading to his arrest. In 1966, he took the struggle to the North, specifically to Chicago.

King was killed at the Lorraine Motel in Memphis, shot by a petty criminal, James Earl Ray. His death provoked several conspiracy theories, including the claim that the FBI, which had kept King under surveillance since 1957, was responsible.

The March on Washington

The triumphant climax of King's campaign was the March on Washington for Jobs and Freedom, held on August 28, 1963. Despite government opposition – President Kennedy was against the march, fearing that it would merely antagonize white opinion – it was a striking success, the largest such civil demonstration in American history to that date. The police put the number of demonstrators at 200,000; the organizers claimed 300,000. The march ended at the Lincoln Memorial and it was there that King delivered his most memorable speech – "I have a dream" – claimed by many as the equal of Lincoln's Gettysburg Address.

> "One has not only a legal but a moral responsibility to obey just laws. Conversely, one has a moral responsibility to disobey unjust laws. I would agree with St. Augustine that 'an unjust law is no law at all.'"
>
> LETTER FROM BIRMINGHAM JAIL, APRIL 1963.

Ten planes, 2,000 buses, and 21 trains – as well as an unknown number of cars – carried the demonstrators to Washington. Despite fears the march would turn violent, it passed off entirely peacefully.

JANUARY 15 — PAUL THE HERMIT

STATUS Hermit
BORN c.228, Egypt
DIED c.341, Thebes, Egypt
GRC ⬭
CofE ⬭
LCDUS ⬭
OTHER Eastern Orthodox churches
⬯ Pre-Congregation
✝ Raven, cave
🙏 San Pablo City, Philippines

Paul the Hermit, also known as Paul of Thebes, is said to have been the first Christian hermit. A high-born Greek-Egyptian Christian, Paul fled to the desert at age 22 to escape a round of Christian persecutions launched by the emperor Decius. There he remained, gaunt and bearded, living in a cave, clad in rags, until he died at the age of 113. A raven was said to have fed him, bringing him half a loaf of bread a day (a story reminiscent of Elijah in the Old Testament). The best-known account of Paul's life was written by St. Jerome. It was Jerome who claimed that a later Egyptian monk, Antony of Egypt (Jan. 17), buried Paul with the help of two lions. Paul's retreat to a life of pious contemplation and hardship has also been regarded as a response to the increasingly comfortable life in the service of God enjoyed by many Christians after Constantine's adoption of Christianity as the official faith of the Roman empire.

Seer and holy man, his life given over to fasting and prayer, Paul the Hermit exerted a potent influence on later generations. He remains the archetypal Christian ascetic, depicted (below) by Mattia Preti (c.1660).

JANUARY 16 — BERARD OF CARBIO AND COMPANIONS

STATUS Martyr
BORN 12th century, Carbio, Italy
DIED 1220, Marrakesh, Morocco
GRC ⬭
CofE ⬭
LCDUS ⬭
OTHER By Franciscans
⬯ 1481

Berard was a Franciscan who, with two other monks, Peter and Otho, and two lay brothers, Adjustus and Accursius, was sent by St. Francis himself to Muslim Morocco as a missionary. Only Berard could speak any Arabic. They visited Seville, Spain (still in Moorish hands) on the way, but were arrested and expelled. In Morocco, they made their way to Marrakesh and preached in the streets, denouncing Muhammad. At first thought simply insane, they were eventually arrested and executed, apparently personally by the sultan. They were the first martyrs of the Franciscan Order, but their calling reveals much about the Christian perception of Islam at the time.

JANUARY 16 — HONORATUS OF ARLES

STATUS Bishop
BORN c.350, Lorraine, France
DIED 429, Arles, France
GRC ⬭
CofE ⬭
LCDUS ⬭
OTHER In Provence
⬯ Pre-Congregation
🙏 Lérins, Arles, France

Honoratus, a member of a Roman consular family, converted to Christianity and with his brother, Venantius, traveled to Greece intending to establish a monastic community. Venantius died, however, and Honoratus returned to France, setting up the small monastery and retreat of Lérins on the deserted Ile St.-Honorat, just off the coast near modern Cannes. He was joined by Hilary of Poitiers (Jan. 13) and others. The monastery is today a Cistercian foundation. Against his will, Honoratus was appointed archbishop of Arles in 427.

JANUARY 17　ANTONY OF EGYPT (THE GREAT)

STATUS	Abbot
BORN	251, near Memphis, Egypt
DIED	356, Mt. Kolzim, Egypt
GRC	♣
CofE	♣
LCDUS	♣
OTHER	Eastern Orthodox churches, Coptic churches
⊘	Pre-Congregation
✝	Tau Cross, pig, bell; often shown being tempted by demons
🙏	Basketmakers, gravediggers, hermits, monks, pigs; sufferers from skin disease, epileptics, ergotism ('St. Antony's Fire'), amputees

Antony's emblem, the Tau Cross, is an ancient Greco-Egyptian device also used within the Coptic Church.

Martin Schongauer (c.1435–91) provided an apocalyptic vision of Antony's struggle with demons.

Antony is widely regarded as the father of monasticism. He was born a Greek in Egypt to a wealthy family, but upon his parents' death in about 270, he sold their estates and gave the proceeds to the poor. He became a hermit, initially under the guidance of an older mentor. Egyptian hermits tended to live in ancient, empty rock-cut tombs, caves, or ruined buildings in the desert. Antony assembled a number of followers and established the first monastery around 306 – not the dedicated building for communal living we are familiar with today, but a loose community of mystics living in whatever shelter they could find. The Desert Fathers would undertake manual labor or weave palm baskets to pay for food and clothing, but physical deprivation and relative isolation would often lead to hallucinatory torments. Despite this, Antony lived to a great age. A biography of him written by St. Athanasius was influential in spreading the concept of monasticism.

The Temptation of St. Antony was a popular subject in medieval art. Hieronymus Bosch (c.1453–1516) returned to the theme several times: in this restrained painting (left) the hermit and his pig are shown in a not very isolated wilderness, while a strange assortment of demons begin to invade his surroundings.

JANUARY 18 · MARGARET OF HUNGARY

STATUS Princess
BORN 1242, Klis, Hungary
DIED 1271, Margaret Island, Hungary
GRC ○
CofE ○
LCDUS ○
OTHER By Dominicans
♥ 1789
○ 1943
✝ With a book or a lily, wearing a crown
🙏 Hungary, Budapest

When Hungary was liberated from Tatar domination in 1241, King Bela IV and his wife swore that their next daughter would be devoted to God. They kept their promise, and Princess Margaret was placed in the Dominican convent at Veszprem at the age of three; a decade later she transferred to the Convent of the Blessed Virgin, built by her parents on an island (now named after her) on the Danube at Buda.

Despite, or possibly because of, her early commitment to convent life, Margaret refused the offer of a diplomatic marriage to King Ottokar of Bohemia in 1260. Margaret was known for her humility and kindness to others. She died at only 28, possibly as a result of her self-imposed deprivations, but some 27 miracles were attributed to her, including raising someone from the dead.

Margaret, being of royal descent, is always shown wearing a crown.

JANUARY 19 · WULFSTAN

STATUS Bishop
BORN c.1008, Worcester, England
DIED 1095
GRC ○
CofE ♣
LCDUS ○
OTHER US Episcopal Church
○ 1203

A noble Anglo-Saxon who entered the Benedictine priory at Worcester, Wulfstan rapidly became prior of the community, and then Bishop of Worcester. He regularly visited the parishes of the diocese, and promoted church-building and restoration there, also rebuilding Worcester Cathedral. He was the only English bishop to remain in office after the Norman invasion in 1066. Wulfstan managed to halt the slave trade operated by the Vikings between Bristol and Ireland, and he was canonized by Innocent III.

Great Malvern Priory in Worcestershire, England, was one of Wulfstan's more important monastic foundations. It was begun in 1085 on lands owned by Westminster Abbey. Its patrons are Sts. Mary and Michael.

Date	Name	Status	Venerated	Life
Jan. 17	Sulpice (Pius) (d.646)	Bishop ○ Pre-Congregation	In France	Decided upon a celibate life at a young age. Devoted to charity. Became Bishop of Bourges (624). Said to have converted his entire diocese. Defended his citizens' rights against Dagobert, King of the Franks. Retired to serve the poor.
Jan. 17	Charles Gore (1853–1932)	Bishop	CofE	Bishop of Worcester, then Birmingham. Founder of the Community of the Resurrection in 1892.
Jan. 19	Gudula (Gudule/Goule) (c.650–c.712)	Virgin ○ Pre-Congregation	In Belgium ✝ Candle, lantern 🙏 Unmarried laywomen; Belgium, Brussels	Daughter of Count Wiger. From a family of Belgian saints. Studied under St. Gertrude of Nivelle. During morning visits to the church at Moorsel, the devil would attempt to extinguish her candle but it would remain alight. The winter-flowering *Tremella deliquescens* is known as 'St. Gudula's lantern.'
Jan. 19	Canute or Knud IV (d.1086)	King ○ 1101	In Denmark ✝ Lance, arrow 🙏 Denmark	Illegitimate son of King Sven II Estridson, nephew of Canute of England. Ascended to Danish throne c.1080; attempted to evangelize his kingdom. Defeated in attempt to claim the kingdom of England. Retreated to the island of Fünen. Murdered with his brother and 17 companions in church.

JANUARY 20 ✣ SEBASTIAN

STATUS Martyr

BORN c.265

DIED c.300

GRC ♣

CofE ♧

LCDUS ♣

OTHER Eastern Orthodox churches

⊘ Pre-Congregation

✝ Nearly nude, shot with arrows, or simply an arrow

🙏 Archers, soldiers, athletes, plague victims

A single arrow, or a group of them, is commonly used to represent St. Sebastian.

Most accounts describe Sebastian as a Gaul (although St. Ambrose says he came from Milan) who volunteered to join the Roman army in around 283. He was promoted to captain in the Praetorian Guard, the imperial bodyguards. When, during the persecutions under the emperor Diocletian, it was discovered that Sebastian had comforted some of the Christian martyrs, was himself a Christian, and had actively converted others, Diocletian condemned him to be shot to death by his fellow archers. He was buried at a cemetery on the Appian Way, and the first church dedicated to him is nearby.

The reason Sebastian is invariably represented alive, despite being pierced by innumerable arrows, is simple: the arrows didn't kill him. Left for dead by his executioners, Sebastian was apparently healed by St. Irene, the wife of a fellow martyr, St. Castulus. Unfortunately, Diocletian was not to be denied, and Sebastian was subsequently clubbed to death. Sebastian's fate, and the fact that so little is known about him, indicates that his story is probably an amalgam of several incidents during the persecutions of Diocletian, but it has become iconic.

The sinister appeal of the tortured saint continues to attract modern artists, such as the film director Derek Jarman (left).

The representation of Sebastian is immediately recognizable; the agony of his attempted execution, as a nearly nude youth, bound to a tree or column, pierced by arrows, became a popular subject for Renaissance painters such as Andrea Mantegna (c.1430–1506, right).

JANUARY 21 | AGNES

STATUS Virgin, Martyr

BORN c.291

DIED c.304, Rome, Italy

GRC ♣

CofE ♣

LCDUS ♣

OTHER Eastern Orthodox churches

◯ Pre-Congregation

✝ Book, lamb (due to the similarity of her name to *agnus*, Latin for lamb, although her name derives from the Greek term *hagne*, meaning chaste or pure)

🙏 Gardeners, crops, young girls, the betrothed, rape victims, chastity

Like Sebastian (*left*), there is more legend than fact associated with Agnes. Despite this, the story of the child martyr retains a great resonance, and her feast day is widely celebrated. The story is simple: little more than a girl, she refused marriage to the son of the Prefect Sempronius due to her dedication to Christ. As this was during the Diocletian persecutions, she was sentenced to death and taken to a brothel to be defiled before her execution. When she was stripped, her hair miraculously grew to hide her nakedness, and those who attempted to assault her were struck blind. Tied to a stake, the wood would not burn, so she was stabbed in the neck.

She remains one of the best known of the early Roman martyrs, and is particularly popular in the Spanish-speaking world, where she is called Inés.

The lamb and the book remain Agnes's emblems, although she neither wrote nor was associated with lambs.

Gruesome reconstructions of the fates of many early Christian martyrs were dwelt upon by Catholic artists from the Renaissance onwards.

St. Agnes was martyred in the Circus of Domitian, which is the modern-day site of the popular Piazza Navona in Rome. The west side of the piazza today is dominated by the basilica of Sant'Agnese in Agone (right), built by Rainaldi and Borromini (1653–57).

Date	Name	Status	Venerated	Life
Jan. 20	Fabian (d.250)	Pope, Martyr	GRC	Elected Pope in 236 despite humble origins. Reorganized Roman dioceses into seven deaconries. First martyr to be killed during persecutions of the Roman emperor Decius. His tomb is in the church of St. Sebastian, Rome.
Jan. 20	Richard Rolle (1290–1349)	Spiritual Writer	CofE	Studied at Oxford, but left, feeling subject to venal temptation. Read theology at the Sorbonne, Paris; possibly ordained. Returned to his native Yorkshire, living as a hermit. From 1340, director of Cistercian nunnery at Hampole. Described mystical experiences in *The Fire of Love*.

JANUARY 22 | VINCENT OF SARAGOSSA

STATUS Deacon, Martyr

BORN 3rd century, Huesca, Spain

DIED 304, Valencia, Spain

GRC ♣

CofE ♣

LCDUS ♣

OTHER Eastern Orthodox churches (Nov. 11); in Portugal

○ Pre-Congregation

† Gridiron/griddle, ravens

🙏 Vine growers (because he offers protection from frosts, common in January), wine and vinegar merchants; violations, abortions; Portugal, Lisbon

St. Vincent's emblem combines a gridiron with a dalmatic robe.

The image of the boat transporting Vincent's remains from Valencia to Lisbon, with the funerary ravens, forms part of the city of Lisbon's coat of arms.

A 16th-century image of Vincent bearing the palm of martyrdom while trampling a Moor.

Having trained under Bishop Valerius at Saragossa, Vincent was appointed deacon of the city but, like St. Lawrence (Aug. 10), was arrested in Valencia during the persecutions of Diocletian in 304. He managed to convert his jailer, but when asked to throw the Scriptures into a fire, he refused, and was then roasted on a gridiron (again like St. Lawrence). Before Vincent was buried in Valencia, ravens apparently guarded his body. His cult developed while Iberia was under Visigothic control from 589–715; a basilica named after him was built on the river Guadalquivir at Córdoba that was later replaced by a mosque, now converted to a cathedral. His remains were later transported by sea to what is now Cape St. Vincent in Portugal, and they were transferred to Lisbon in 1173. Portuguese navigators in the 16th century named an island for him in the Cape Verde group.

JANUARY 23 | ILDEFONSO (ILDEPHONSUS) OF TOLEDO

STATUS Bishop

BORN c.607, Toledo, Spain

DIED 667, Toledo, Spain

GRC ☁

CofE ☁

LCDUS ☁

OTHER In Spain

† Pen, book, miter, staff

A Visigothic cleric, Ildefonso became one of the major figures of the Church in 7th-century Iberia, due largely to his writing. This emphasized the Nicene Creed, and the importance of regular and profound preparation for Communion. His most important contribution was the promotion of Marian devotion in Spain. He was ordained and became Abbot of Agalia around 650, attended the councils of Toledo in 653 and 657, and was appointed Archbishop of Toledo in 657.

Ildefonso was known principally as a writer, and his continuing influence was marked by El Greco 900 years after his death.

Date	Name	Status	Venerated	Life
Jan. 22	Anastasius the Persian (Magundat) (c.600–28)	Martyr ○ Pre-Congregation	In Jerusalem and Persia 🙏 Goldsmiths, sufferers from headaches	Soldier in Persian army that looted the Holy Cross from Jerusalem. Converted, became a monk in Jerusalem, then returned to evangelize Persia. Beheaded, along with around 70 others, for refusing to deny his faith.
Jan. 23	John the Almsgiver (or Almoner) (c.550–c.616)	Patriarch ○ Pre-Congregation	Eastern Orthodox churches 🙏 Knights Hospitaller	Cypriot who became Patriarch of Alexandria (608). After a vision, became dedicated to compassion and gave much to the poor. Protected refugees from the Holy Land. Relics housed in the cathedral at Pressburg (now Bratislava), Slovakia.

JANUARY 23 — MARIANNE COPE

STATUS Nun, Missionary
BORN 1838, Heppenheim, Germany
DIED 1918, Kalaupapa, Hawaii
GRC ☁
CofE ☁
LCDUS ☁
OTHER In Hawaii (Aug. 9)
♥ 2005
☫ Leprosy sufferers, HIV/AIDS sufferers, outcasts; Hawaii

Christened Maria Anna Barbara Koob in Hesse, Germany, Marianne Cope's family emigrated to the United States when she was three, and settled in Utica, New York. After working as a factory hand, she entered the Sister Order of St. Francis as a tertiary. She taught German immigrants for a decade, then became involved with hospital work in Syracuse, New York.

In 1883, responding to a call for help from King David Kalakaua, she and six other nuns traveled to Honolulu to care for sufferers from leprosy (Hansen's Disease). She initially worked in a hospital on Oahu, but in 1888 moved to the leper colony at Kalaupapa, where she cared for the victims and their families with Father Damien of Molokai (May 10). When he died she took over control of the colony. Several miraculous cures from the disease have been attributed to her intercession.

> "I wish with all my heart to be one of the Chosen Ones, whose privilege it will be to sacrifice themselves for the salvation of the souls of the poor Islanders."
>
> THE BLESSED MARIANNE COPE.

JANUARY 24 — FRANCIS DE SALES

STATUS Bishop, Doctor of the Church
BORN 1567, Annecy, France
DIED 1622, Lyon, France
GRC ♣
CofE ♣
LCDUS ♣
♥ 1622
◯ 1665
☫ Journalists, the deaf

Having studied in Paris, de Sales became a Doctor of Law at Padua, and was destined for a glittering diplomatic career. Instead, in 1593 he insisted on becoming ordained, despite his father's resistance. His first task was hazardous: to convert the Calvinists of his native Chablais country in Savoy. He largely succeeded, becoming Bishop of Geneva in 1602. He was famed for the skill, gentleness, and persuasiveness of his preaching. He was an excellent administrator and writer; his *Treatise on the Love of God* and the *Introduction to the Devout Life* (intended for lay readers) were widely translated and remain in print today. He wrote many informal tracts. De Sales became friendly with Jane Frances de Chantal (Aug. 12), and helped her found the Order of the Visitation in 1610. His insistence that the devout life should be integrated with everyday life, and should be accessible to all, led to several congregations being established under his patronage, notably the Oblates of St. Francis de Sales and the Salesians of John Bosco.

> "More flies are attracted by a spoonful of honey than by a whole barrel of vinegar."
>
> FRANCIS DE SALES.

De Sales is usually represented as balding and bearded in bishop's robes, and he appears on the coat of arms of the Salesian Society (left).

Date	Name	Status	Venerated	Life
Jan. 23	Henry Suso (Amandus) (1295–1366)	Monk, Mystic ♥ 1831	In Germany and Switzerland By Dominicans	German noble. Entered Dominican Order (1308); studied under controversial Meister Eckhart at Cologne; subsequently imprisoned. Later taught in Constance and the Rhine valley. For 16 years wore a barbed girdle, until an angel told him to stop. Threw girdle into the Rhine.
Jan. 24	Bartholomew Osypiuk (1843–74)	Martyr ♥ 1996	In Poland	Married layman. One of the 13 Polish Martyrs of Podlasie shot by Russian soldiers during Czar Alexander II's campaign to convert his Eastern Rite subjects to the Russian Orthodox church. Did not die immediately; prayed for his killers before expiring.

JANUARY 25

THE CONVERSION OF PAUL THE APOSTLE

STATUS Apostle of the
Gentiles

BORN c. AD 5, Tarsus,
modern Turkey

DIED c. AD 67, Rome, Italy

GRC ♣

CofE ♣

LCDUS ♣

OTHER US Episcopal Church

⊘ Pre-Congregation

✝ Often represented
by crossed swords, or
with paper and quill,
or book

🙏 Gentiles

An important feast day for most of the main churches, Paul's conversion signifies the overwhelming power of the Christian faith to cross the boundaries of belief and nationality. Born to a Greco-Jewish family in Cilicia, he was originally named Saul. He was raised as a Pharisee, but was also a Roman citizen and became an ardent persecutor of the first Christians, participating in the stoning of St. Stephen (Dec. 26), the first martyr. Traveling to Damascus around AD 35, he had a revelatory vision and was temporarily blinded. He was baptized and then retired to the Arabian Desert, and realized there that his task was to bring Christianity to the Gentile (non-Jewish) world. He returned to Damascus, was met with hostility, then proceeded to Jerusalem, where he convinced the Apostle Barnabas (June 11) of his intentions.

For the decade between AD 38–48, Paul traveled through Syria and Asia Minor, preaching and establishing the missionary tradition. Thereafter he traveled around the eastern Mediterranean, writing the enormously influential letters that form part of the New Testament and setting up numerous Christian communities. Returning to Jerusalem in AD 57 he was arrested and held for two years. He appealed to Caesar as a Roman citizen and was sent to Rome for trial, but was stranded for two years in Malta after a shipwreck. In Rome he was imprisoned for a further two years, but he appears to have visited Ephesus and possibly Iberia, presumably after his trial. Returning to Rome, he was beheaded during the persecutions of Nero, and is buried at St. Paul's 'Outside the Walls.'

Paul also shares a feast day with St. Peter, on June 29.

JANUARY 26

TIMOTHY AND TITUS

STATUS Bishops (Timothy
also a Martyr)

BORN 1st century AD

DIED 1st century AD
(Timothy c. AD 97)

GRC ♣

CofE ♣

LCDUS ♣

OTHER US Evangelical
Lutheran Church

⊘ Pre-Congregation

✝ Usually shown with
miters

Known as Companions of St. Paul, very little is known about these two early bishops. They emerge as recipients of letters from Paul in the New Testament. Timothy was born at Lystra in Asia Minor, and like Paul was of Greco-Jewish parentage. He met Paul on the latter's second missionary journey, and accompanied him to its conclusion. Timothy also traveled with Paul on his third missionary journey. Thereafter Paul tasked him with encouraging Greek Christian communities in Thessalonica, Corinth, and Philippi; he is often referred to as the first bishop of

Ephesus. One 4th-century account has him clubbed and stoned to death by worshippers of Artemis for objecting to one of their festivals.

Titus was a Greek, probably born at Antioch, and he traveled with Paul and Barnabas (June 11) to Jerusalem to discuss with Peter (June 29) whether Gentile converts to Christianity should be circumcised. He then accompanied Paul to Ephesus, and interceded in Paul's dispute with the Christians of Corinth. Paul instructed him to organize Christian communities in Crete; Titus is regarded as the first bishop of Gortyna in Crete.

Timothy's martyrdom is reflected in his arms which combine a club with rocks.

The Conversion of St. Paul (1601) by Caravaggio (left) dramatically captures the moment of revelation, using the painter's characteristic directness and mastery of light and dark. However, it is clear that the light is only seen by Paul, as his horse and companion seem unaware of it.

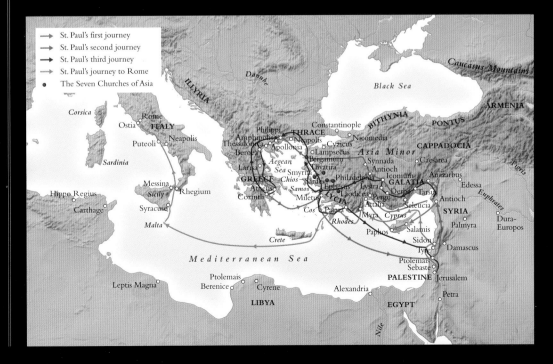

JANUARY 27 | ANGELA (ANGELICA) MERICI

STATUS Virgin, Founder
BORN c.1470, Desenzano del Garda (then in the Republic of Venice), near Brescia, Italy
DIED 1540, Brescia, Italy
GRC ♣
CofE ♧
LCDUS ♣
❤ 1768
◯ 1807
✝ Cloak, ladder
🙏 Orphans, the handicapped, sickness

Angela and her sister were orphaned when young and moved to Brescia. After her sister's death, Angela entered the Tertiary Franciscan Order, and became devoted to educating poor girls in the Christian tradition. Legend tells of her journeying to the Holy Land around 1524, losing her sight in Crete on the way, but regaining it at the same place upon her return. In 1535, having selected 12 other nuns, she established a house in Brescia under the patronage of St. Ursula (Oct. 21). The Ursulines wore lay clothing and continued Angela's work in educating girls and tending the poor. She was buried in the church of St. Afra, Brescia, which was destroyed by Allied bombing in WWII, but has now been restored as the Merician Centre.

JANUARY 27 | GEORGE MATULAITIS

STATUS Bishop, Founder
BORN 1871, Lugine, Lithuania
DIED 1927, Kaunas, Lithuania
GRC ♧
CofE ♧
LCDUS ♧
❤ 1987

Matulaitis was born in Lithuania when it was under Czarist Russian control. His family was poor, he was one of eight children, and as a teenager he developed tuberculosis, leaving him with a limp. He studied in Warsaw, and read theology at St. Petersburg and Fribourg, Switzerland. He returned to St. Petersburg as a teacher, preacher, and spiritual adviser and was the reformer and founder of a number of Marian institutions in eastern Europe.

Matulaitis was elected bishop of Vilnius in 1918 when the city was divided by German and Russian forces during WWI, and he defended the independence of the Church and the freedom of its citizens. He was made an archbishop in 1925, and restored diplomatic relations between the Vatican and Lithuania.

Although often portrayed teaching young girls, here Angela is shown in her glory, with Franciscan priests attending the Christ Child.

Date	Name	Status	Venerated	Life
Jan. 29	Gildas (c.500–70)	Abbot ◯ Pre-Congregation	In Scotland, Ireland, and Morbihan in Brittany, France	Scottish priest who influenced monasticism in Ireland. Wrote *De Excidio Britanniae* (*On the Ruin of Britain*) blaming Anglo-Saxon invasions on the lassitude of British ruling class and clerics. Founded a monastery on an island in Morbihan Bay, Brittany.
Jan. 29	Juniper (c.1200–58)	Missionary ◯ Pre-Congregation	By Franciscans	Lowly friar, received into Franciscan Order by Francis himself. Established various missions. Tending to a sick man who craved stewed pig's foot, angered a farmer by removing the item from one of his piglets. Apologizing, managed to secure the rest of the beast for the table.

JANUARY 28 | THOMAS AQUINAS

STATUS Priest, Doctor of the Church

BORN c.1225, Aquino, near Naples, Italy

DIED 1274, Fossanova, Terracina, Italy

GRC ♣

CofE ♣

LCDUS ♣

⭕ 1323

🙏 Catholic universities

The 'Sun in Splendor' combined with the 'All-Seeing Eye' refers directly to God, and thus to Thomas's divine inspiration in compiling his enormous Summa Theologica.

"All I have written seems to me like so much straw compared with what I have seen and what has been revealed to me."

THOMAS AQUINAS
UPON ABANDONING HIS
SUMMA THEOLOGICA, 1273.

The importance of Thomas Aquinas is difficult to overestimate. He was, and remains, a wonderful communicator and sharer of ideas. Principally known as a theologian, writer, and teacher, his great work, *Summa Theologica*, set down between 1268 and 1273, presented a considered appraisal of the work of many previous theologians and philosophers and set an agenda for the Catholic Church at a time of considerable doctrinal and political instability. In many ways, his concentration upon the central articles of Christian faith and their interpretation, and his openly ecumenical approach (often drawing on the work of Jewish or pre-Christian thinkers such as Aristotle), might have forestalled the tumult of the Reformation three centuries later. It is no accident that his writings were acclaimed by both factions at that historic moment of division.

Education and Writings

Aquinas was educated at the Benedictine monastery of Monte Cassino, north of Naples, then at Naples University. Despite his noble family's opposition, he entered the Dominican Order of the Preachers in 1244. He continued his studies in Paris and Cologne (under Albertus Magnus), and in 1256 was appointed a Master of Theology. Between 1259 and 1268 he taught, studied, and wrote variously at Naples, Orvieto, Viterbo, and Rome, returning in his later years to Paris (between 1269 and 1272) and Naples. In 1259 he began *Summa contra Gentiles*, a discussion of how Christianity might be argued to pagans or those of other faiths. This became a key text centuries later when overseas Christian missions began in earnest. His sheer output of writing was enormous (the unfinished *Summa Theologica* was translated into English in 22 volumes), but in 1273 he suddenly stopped writing — whether this was due to illness is not known. Nevertheless, in a relatively short life he wrote more than most would in a long one.

St. Thomas Aquinas Dedicating his Works to Christ *(1593) by Santi di Tito, in San Marco, Florence, has an extraordinary quality: Aquinas's vision of the Crucifixion, attended by the Blessed Virgin Mary, Mary Magdalene, St. John, and St. Catherine, is presented as if tangibly before him.*

JANUARY 30 · HYACINTHA MARISCOTTI

STATUS Nun, Founder
BORN 1585, Vignanello, near Viterbo, Italy
DIED 1640, Rome, Italy
GRC ☁
CofE ☁
LCDUS ☁
♥ 1726
⬭ 1807
🙏 Franciscans

From a noble family, Hyacintha was a notably pious girl who was educated as a tertiary at the Franciscan Convent of St. Bernardine in Viterbo. There a more frivolous streak emerged. In 1605 she hoped to marry the Marquess Cassizucchi, but she was passed over in favor of her younger sister. She entered the community at St. Bernardine, but was self-indulgent, wore only rich materials, and cooked fine meals for herself, living a life of considerable freedom and luxury, despite her vows.

After a period of ten years, following illness and pressure from her Franciscan confessor, she made an open confession to the convent, adopted a standard habit, slept on boards, and entered a life of extreme self-mortification; she fasted on bread and water, went barefoot, and undertook vigils and scourging. She gained a considerable reputation for sagacity and devotion to the Blessed Virgin Mary, and established the Sacconi, or Oblates of Mary, who were dedicated to collecting alms for the poor and sick.

The emblem of the Franciscan Sacconi, or Oblates of Mary, combines the initials C and M, the C deriving from Hyacintha's baptismal name, Clarice.

JANUARY 30 · CHARLES STUART

STATUS King, Martyr
BORN 1600, Dunfermline, Scotland
DIED 1649, London, England
GRC ☁
CofE ♣
LCDUS ☁
⬭ 1660 (CofE)

The second son of James I of England, Charles came to the throne of England, Scotland, and Ireland on March 25, 1625. Nominally also the head of the Church of England, he was an advocate of the Divine Right of Kings, believing that his power and rights came directly from God. Consequently, he increasingly ignored the English Parliament, raising his own taxes, and was supported in this by the Archbishop of Canterbury, William Laud, (Jan. 10). He further upset many by marrying a Catholic, Henrietta Maria of France. Although not a practicing Catholic, he had High Church tastes in art and decorum. Eventually, tension erupted into two phases of civil war, with Royalists confronting largely Puritan reformers. After the first phase (1642–45), the Royalists in defeat, Charles remained reluctant to cede power to Parliament. He sought support from Scotland and overseas, provoking a second phase of hostilities from 1648–49. Finally defeated and imprisoned, Charles was arraigned as a traitor, and Parliament pushed through a death sentence. The first instance of regicide in early modern Europe was Charles's public beheading in Whitehall, London, on January 30, 1649. The monarchy was abolished, while the 'Commonwealth' led by Oliver Cromwell, an experiment in popular democratic idealism, ended after Cromwell's death in 1658. Charles's son, Charles II, was restored to the throne in 1660, and on the same day his father was canonized by the Church of England.

Charles Stuart's 'High Church' or Catholic leanings and his belief in the Divine Right of Kings is here exemplified as the monarch receives the gift of regal power from on high.

On a chilly January morning, on a scaffold erected in front of a building he had commissioned (Inigo Jones's Banqueting Hall in London), Charles I met his execution with great dignity before an enormous crowd.

MODERN SAINTLINESS

Occasionally, figures emerge whose spirituality and self-sacrifice inspire worldwide admiration. Some of these extraordinary individuals will be profiled throughout this book in sidebars like this one, to recognize their contributions to saintly activity outside of the Christian tradition. The Indian leader Mohandas K. Gandhi (1869–1948) was born and remained a Hindu. He trained as a lawyer in London, and practiced in South Africa. After returning to British India in 1915, he developed his ideas about non-violent civil disobedience, organizing campaigns and marches against injustices imposed by the British. This culminated in his 'Quit India' campaign for independence. Despite a number of lengthy incarcerations, Gandhi stuck to his principles, and lived a simple, peaceful life. He was a practitioner of *ahimsa* (non-violence), insisted on telling the truth, fasted regularly, lived in a simple house in a self-sufficient community, and wore a traditional *dhoti* of cloth he made himself on a spinning wheel. The honorific 'Mahatma' means Great Soul. Gandhi was assassinated on January 30, 1948, by Hindu fanatics, only months after independence was achieved. He is widely remembered on the day of his death, although in India the 'Father of the Nation's' birthday, October 2, is a national holiday and the International Day of Non-Violence.

The Indian flag must, by law, be made of khadi, *a type of hand-spun cloth popularized by Gandhi.*

JANUARY 31

JOHN (DON) BOSCO

STATUS Priest, Founder
BORN 1815, Becchi, near Castelnuovo, Italy
DIED 1888, Turin, Italy
GRC ♣
CofE ♣
LCDUS ♣
♥ 1929
◯ 1934
⚜ Catholic publishers and editors, schoolchildren, apprentices, laborers

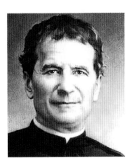

Raised in poverty, and one of three brothers, Bosco lost his father at age two. Good with his hands, Bosco practiced magical tricks, and worked at various crafts to help fund his studies. He was ordained in 1841 and worked constantly with the young and poor. Regarded as a wild card, he didn't enhance his reputation in 1854 when the Kingdom of Sardinia threatened to close down monasteries; Bosco sent the court messages saying he had visions of many funerals if they did so. The prime minister, Cavour, had to intervene. Bosco established the Society of St. Francis de Sales in 1859, and set up workshops to educate impoverished boys and youths based on a Christian artisanal vocational training, teaching such skills as bookbinding, printing, shoemaking, ironworking, and tailoring. The Salesian Teaching Order was formally approved in 1874 and has spread around the world. The first mission was to Argentina in 1875, where Salesians also evangelized the Patagonian Indians. He was canonized by Pope Pius XI who, in his youth, had encountered Bosco.

The influence of the Salesian Society is now global, and is particularly strong in South America, but the impressive mother church, the Basilica Don Bosco, is in Castelnuovo, Italy.

Date	Name	Status	Venerated	Life
Jan. 31	Charles Mackenzie (1825–62)	Missionary	CofE	Born in Scotland. Attended Cambridge University. In 1855 went to Natal, southern Africa, serving as archdeacon, then as bishop of Cape Town (1861). Fellow Scottish missionary Dr. David Livingstone appealed to Cambridge for support, and Mackenzie was appointed missionary bishop to Nyasaland (modern Malawi). Traveled up Zambezi to interior; set up a mission. Staunchly opposed to slavery. Died of blackwater fever on January 31. Grave marked by Livingstone.

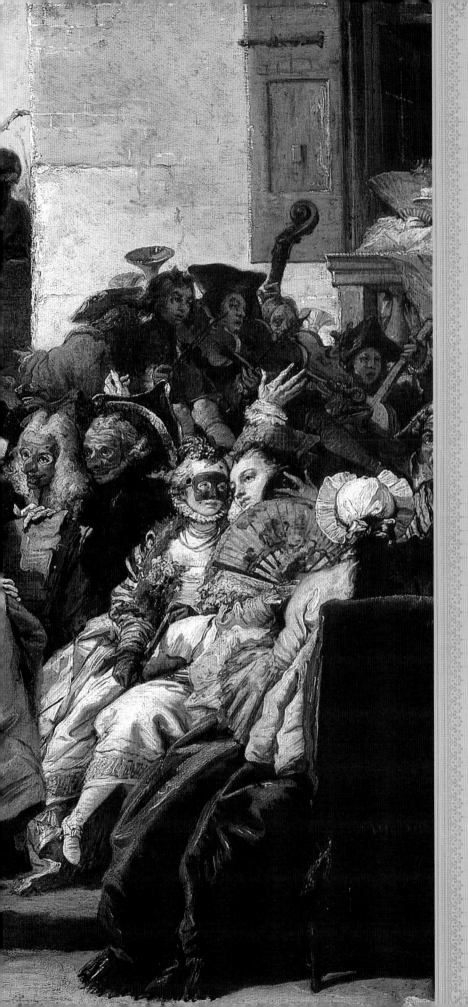

FEBRUARY

The second month of the year, and often the coldest in northern climes, February is traditionally associated with purification. February 2 is Candlemas when, tradition has it, if the weather is fair and frosty, there are severe wintry conditions yet to come before spring. A high point in the month occurs on February 14, when Saint Valentine's Day is almost universally recognized as a day celebrating love and romance.

Shrove Tuesday, the day before Ash Wednesday, which inaugurates the 40-day pre-Easter Lenten fast, also frequently falls in February. The day is one of confession and atonement, 'shrove' deriving from the act of shrivening – the absolution of sin. In much of the Christian world this is celebrated as Mardi Gras, Carnival, or 'Fat Tuesday,' a joyous festival often including masked dancing and a final culinary indulgence before Holy Month.

Carnival or The Minuet *by the Venetian painter Tiepolo (1727–1804) wonderfully captures the spirit of release, liveliness, and frivolity associated with the moment of absolution from sin on Shrove Tuesday.*

FEBRUARY 1 | BRIGID (BRIDE) OF KILDARE

STATUS Virgin, Abbess

BORN c.453, County Louth, Ireland

DIED c.525, Kildare, Ireland

GRC ♧

CofE ♣

LCDUS ♧

OTHER Irish Catholic Church, Eastern Orthodox churches

⌾ Pre-Congregation

✝ Abbess; with a lamp or candle

🙏 Ireland

Brigid's emblem combines the flame of knowledge with acorns.

With Patrick (March 17) and Columba (June 9), Brigid is one of three patron saints of Ireland, a figure venerated across the country. Yet, despite the proliferation of legends surrounding her and the large number of accounts of her life, she may never have existed at all. If she did, it is possible she was a pagan goddess rather than a Christian saint. At any event, her life overlaps closely with a number of pagan traditions from Ireland's pre-Christian Druidic past. Even her name is a variant of Brid, 'the poetess' and the greatest of the Druid goddesses, whose symbol, like Brigid's, was fire, 'the flame of knowledge.' Her feast day was also an important pagan celebration, Imbolc, which heralded the coming of spring. The oldest written account of her life, largely concerned with the many miracles she performed, dates from at least a century after her presumed death.

Brigid is said to have been the illegitimate daughter of a pagan chief called Dubhthach, her mother one of his slaves. From an early age she was known not just for her sweet disposition but for her piety, inspired in part by having heard the elderly St. Patrick preach. She became a nun and set about founding a series of convents. The most celebrated, founded perhaps in 470, was at what became Kildare, or *Cill-Dara* – 'the church of the oak.' The land on which the convent and a later monastery were built was given to Brigid by the king of Leinster, who told Brigid she could have as much land as her cloak would cover. Once placed on the ground, the cloak miraculously grew to a vast size.

St. Brigid's Cross is as recognizable a symbol of early Christian Ireland as St. Patrick's shamrock. It is said that Brigid first made the cross when visiting a dying pagan man, weaving it from rushes on his floor. When he saw it, the man (in some versions her father) asked to be baptized.

FEBRUARY 2 | ALFRED DELP

STATUS Priest, Martyr

BORN 1907, Mannheim, Germany

DIED 1945, Berlin, Germany

GRC ♧

CofE ♧

LCDUS ♧

OTHER By Jesuits

Alfred Delp, a Jesuit priest ordained in 1937, was hanged by the Nazis in February 1945, having been arrested the previous July on suspicion that he had been involved in the unsuccessful plot to kill Hitler on July 20, 1944. In fact, as even the court was forced to acknowledge, he had played no part in the attempt – although Delp was an active member of the Kreisau Circle, one of the small number of German anti-Nazi groups during the war. But his opposition to the Nazis, whom he regarded as a profound perversion of Christian and German values, was never in doubt. Since at least 1941, as rector of the church of St. Georg in Munich, Delp had been active in helping Jews to escape Germany. His faith never wavered during his imprisonment. The Gestapo offered to spare him if he would resign from the Jesuits. As Delp understood only too well, his refusal was his death warrant.

Delp at his trial in Berlin, January 1945. In a letter written by him in December 1944 and smuggled out of prison, he wrote: "I'm going to try hard not to break down, even if I have to go to the gallows. I know that God's strength is with me."

Date	Name	Status	Venerated	Life
Feb. 3	Blaise (d.c.316)	Bishop, Martyr ⌾ Pre-Congregation	Eastern Orthodox churches, Armenian Apostolic Church 🙏 Wild animals, infants	Born to patrician family; raised as Christian. Took refuge in mountains of Armenia to escape persecutions; cured number of wild animals and boy with bone stuck in his throat. Said to have been bishop of Sebastea, Asia Minor. One of Fourteen Holy Helpers (*see* page 302).
Feb. 3	Margaret of England (d.1192)	Nun ⌾ Pre-Congregation	In southwest France	Cistercian nun, born in Hungary to an English mother. With her mother, visited the Holy Land, where her mother died. Subsequently settled in convent of Sauve-Benite near Puy in southwest France.

FEBRUARY 2 — THE PRESENTATION OF THE LORD

Luke the Evangelist describes Mary and Joseph bringing the young Jesus to the Temple at Jerusalem, as demanded by Mosaic Law, to be purified and dedicated to the Lord (Luke 2:22–38). During the ceremony they encounter two aged prophets, Simeon and Anna, who both recognize the child as the Messiah, and the full meaning of the miraculous birth of Jesus is revealed to His parents. This day is recognized by all the major churches.

The Presentation, always featuring the prophets Simeon and Anna, was a popular subject in medieval devotional art in both the Eastern (top left) and Western churches. This altarpiece (right) was painted by the Sienese artist Ambrogio Lorenzetti in 1342.

"Lord, now lettest thou thy servant depart in peace, according to thy word; For mine eyes have seen thy salvation … "

SIMEON, UPON RECOGNIZING JESUS (LUKE 2:29–30).

FEBRUARY 3 — ANSGAR (ANSKAR, OSCAR)

STATUS	Evangelist, Bishop
BORN	801, Picardy, France
DIED	865, Bremen, Germany
GRC	♣
CofE	♣
LCDUS	♣
OTHER	Eastern Orthodox churches, Lutheran Church
○	Pre-Congregation
†	Bishop's miter and clothing
⚘	Denmark; a crater on the Moon, Ansgarius, named after him

Ansgar, the 'Apostle of the North,' was a key figure in the dramatic expansion of Christianity from the 8th century onward to those parts of northern and central Europe beyond the frontiers of what had been the Roman empire.

On the back of Charlemagne's brutal conquest of Saxony, extensive efforts were made to convert the lands further north and east. As early as 820, Ansgar was sent to Jutland (modern Denmark). In 822, he helped establish a monastery at Corvey in Westphalia. In 829, he ventured farther afield again, to Birka in Sweden, where he built the country's first church and to which he would return in 848 and again in 854. Meanwhile, in 831, he was appointed archbishop of Hamburg, and given responsibility for all further missionary work in Denmark. Following a devastating Danish raid on Hamburg in 845, Ansgar was made bishop of Bremen, from where he continued his fearless missionary work until his death.

A consistent feature of Ansgar's life was a series of visions he had, urging him, as he believed, to ensure that 'salvation reached the ends of the earth.' In reality, Ansgar's achievements proved short-lived, with much of Denmark and Sweden reverting to paganism after his death. It was only in the 12th century that the region became predominantly Christian.

The 19th-century statue of Ansgar in Hamburg, Germany.

FEBRUARY 4   GILBERT OF SEMPRINGHAM

STATUS Founder

BORN c.1083, Lincolnshire, England

DIED 1189, Lincolnshire, England

GRC ⚬

CofE ♣

LCDUS ⚬

⬭ 1202

Gilbert, noted for his austerity and charitable works, was the son of a minor Norman magnate. On his father's death in 1131, Gilbert used his inheritance to found what became known as the Gilbertine Order, the only native monastic community established in England in the Middle Ages. It was unusual, too, in accepting both men and women. By the time of Gilbert's death at the improbably old age of 105, there were 13 foundations.

Gilbert fell out of favor with the king, Henry II, for his supposed support of Thomas Becket (Dec. 29). In his old age, Gilbert also had to confront a revolt by lay brothers of the order, who complained of being overworked and underfed. By the time of its dissolution by Henry VIII, the order comprised 26 monasteries.

FEBRUARY 4   RABANUS MAURUS

STATUS Bishop

BORN c.780, Mainz, Germany

DIED 856, Winkel, Germany

GRC ⚬

CofE ⚬

LCDUS ⚬

⬭ Pre-Congregation

Rabanus played a key role in the great diffusion of knowledge begun under the Frankish emperor Charlemagne and his leading scholar, the Northumbrian Alcuin (May 20), who was Rabanus's teacher. Rabanus embarked on an impressive program of building and teaching when he was elected abbot of Fulda in 822. In 847, he was appointed archbishop of Mainz. Rabanus was the author of a large number of theological and philosophical works.

Rabanus, on the left, with the elderly Alcuin, presents a copy of one of his works to the long-dead Martin of Tours (Nov. 11). The revival of learning at the court of Charlemagne was one of its most crucial features.

FEBRUARY 5   AGATHA

STATUS Virgin, Martyr

BORN c.231, Sicily

DIED c.251, Sicily

GRC ♣

CofE ⚬

LCDUS ♣

OTHER Eastern Orthodox churches

⬭ Pre-Congregation

✝ Disembodied breasts, loaves of bread

🙏 Nurses, firefighters, sufferers from breast cancer

Although the circumstances of her life remain almost entirely obscure, Agatha was one of the most venerated of the early Christian martyrs, the object of a cult that by the 6th century had become widespread.

According to legend, she was born to a noble family and dedicated herself to God from a young age, rejecting all men. A Roman magistrate, Quintian, furious at having his advances spurned by the young and beautiful Agatha, first forced her to work in a brothel, then had her tortured, variously rolling her over live coals — in the process setting off an earthquake — and ordering that her breasts be hacked off. St. Peter himself is said to have healed her.

Agatha was frequently depicted carrying her sundered breasts on a tray. This heroic image of her mutilation was painted in around 1756 by the Venetian painter Giovanni Battista Tiepolo.

Date	Name	Status	Venerated	Life
Feb. 4	Joseph of Leonissa (1556–1612)	Monk ⬭ 1746	In Lazio and Umbria, Italy	Italian Capuchin monk. Indefatigable preacher. Given to extremes of abstinence. Visited Constantinople (1587) to tend Christian slaves in Ottoman galleys. Attempted to preach to the sultan; thrown into prison and hung for three days by hooks through his right foot and hand. An angel is claimed to have released him.
Feb. 4	Manche Masemola (1913–28)	Martyr	Anglican Church of Southern Africa	Born into Pedi tribe of Transvaal, South Africa. Drawn to distrusted minority Christian converts. Attended classes for baptism; parents thought her possessed. Forced to consume a spirit doctor remedy, died at age 15 after continual parental beatings. Mother denied culpability; was baptized herself decades later.

STATUS Martyrs

DIED 1597, Nagasaki, Japan

GRC ♣

CofE ♣

LCDUS ♣

♥ 1627

◯ 1862

The 26 Martyrs of Nagasaki included a notable Franciscan missionary, Peter Baptist, shown at the center of this painting of the event.

"After Christ's example I forgive my persecutors. I do not hate them. I ask God to have pity on all, and I hope my blood will fall on my fellow men as a fruitful rain."

ST. PAUL MIKI.

In 1549, seven years after the first Europeans had reached Japan, the Jesuit priest St. Francis Xavier (Dec. 3) led a mission to the country. The Japanese authorities were warily welcoming, seeing contact with the West as a means of increasing trade. A series of small Christian communities were founded. In time, other missionaries arrived. Paul Miki, the son of a high-ranking Japanese soldier, was among their converts and in 1582 entered the Jesuit seminary in Azuchi. He would emerge as a forceful and energetic preacher.

Attitudes toward the Christians hardened, however, once the country's ruler, Toyotomi Hideyoshi, became convinced that the West intended to colonize Japan and was merely exploiting Christianity as a means of infiltrating the country. In 1587, he outlawed the religion, although initially the ban was only partially enforced. But in December 1596, Miki and six Franciscan missionaries, seventeen Japanese laymen, and two other Japanese Jesuits were arrested in Osaka and condemned to be crucified in Nagasaki, site of the country's largest Christian community, 600 miles (966 km) away. As a traditional Japanese symbol of shame, each had the lobe of his left ear sliced off before beginning a month-long forced march through the snow to Nagasaki.

They were crucified on February 5 on a hill overlooking the city, strapped to the crosses with ropes and chains, and then speared to death. The martyrs were defiant to the last. They chanted the *Te Deum* as they were led to their deaths. Paul Miki continued to preach to the assembled crowds even from his cross.

Date	Name	Status	Venerated	Life
Feb. 6	Amand (584–675)	Missionary, Bishop ◯ Pre-Congregation	Winemakers, brewers	French-born. Founded first monasteries in Belgium. Spearheaded first efforts to spread Christianity into modern-day Slovakia. Briefly bishop of Maastricht, imposing discipline on clerics across the Low Countries.
Feb. 6	Dorothy (d.c.311)	Virgin, Martyr ◯ Pre-Congregation	Florists, brides	Early Christian persecuted under Diocletian, apparently tortured to death. Before she died, a lawyer, Theopohilus, demanded she send him "apples or roses from the gardens of her spouse [God]." When an angel brought them to him, he converted to Christianity and was also martyred.

FEBRUARY 7 | COLETTE

STATUS Virgin, Founder
BORN 1381, Corbie, France
DIED 1447, Ghent, Belgium
GRC ☁
CofE ☁
LCDUS ☁
OTHER By Franciscans
♥ 1740
⬭ 1807

Colette combined the worldly and the unworldly in unusual ways. Her chief claim to fame was as the founder of the Colettine Poor Clares, an order of nuns that attempted to restore the austerity of the original order of the Poor Clares, founded in 1212 by Sts. Clare and Francis of Assisi. That she was imbued with a deep spirituality is clear. At only 21, having become a Franciscan tertiary, she became a hermit. It was then that she had a vision in which St. Francis instructed her to reform the Poor Clares. To do this, in 1406 she walked to Nice to petition the schismatic French pope, Benedict XIII, to support her. She founded 17 convents, the nuns enjoined to practice not merely 'extreme poverty' but 'perpetual fast and abstinence.' She also had a formidably potent personality. Her rejection of Benedict XIII at the Council of Constance (1414–18) was an important step toward healing the papal schism that split the Church between 1378 and 1417.

Even in an age when intense devotion was hardly unusual, St. Colette had an all-consuming spirituality, most obviously manifested by prolonged bouts of prayer.

FEBRUARY 8 | JOSEPHINE BAKHITA

STATUS Nun
BORN 1869, Darfur, Sudan
DIED 1947, Schio, Italy
GRC ♣
CofE ☁
LCDUS ♣
♥ 1992
⬭ 2000
🙏 Sudan

At about the age of seven, Josephine Bakhita was kidnapped and sold into slavery. For perhaps the next nine years, she was not merely regularly sold and re-sold to a variety of masters, she was as regularly tortured and abused. One owner, an Ottoman soldier, had 60 separate patterns cut into her torso, leaving her scarred for life. It was a life of appalling, routine degradation. It was then that she was given the name Bakhita (in later life she was unable to remember her real name). It meant 'lucky.'

In 1883, she was sold to an Italian diplomat, Callisto Legnani. He was the only one of her owners not to mistreat her. Two years later he returned to Italy, taking Bakhita with him. There she was passed to a second family, the Michielis, and became nanny to their daughter, Mimmina. In 1888 or 1889, Bakhita and Mimmina were left in the care of an order of nuns, the Canossian Sisters or Daughters of Charity, in Venice, when the Michielis traveled to the Red Sea. In 1890, Bakhita was baptized into the Catholic Church. She would remain with the order for the rest of her life –

Since her canonization on October 1, 2000, the tomb of Josephine Bakhita in the church at Schio has become a place of regular pilgrimage for increasing numbers of Catholics. She is the only Sudanese saint.

initially much against the wishes of the Michielis, who wanted her to join them in the Middle East – and was received by them as a nun in 1896, when she took the name Josephine.

In 1902, the order sent Josephine to Schio, north of Venice. It was here she developed her reputation for sanctity. Her humility, her willingness to please, and her extreme devotion were widely recognized, so much so that, despite her modesty, her fame spread across Italy. It was at Schio that she was given the name 'La Nostra Madre Moretta' or 'Our Little Brown Mother.'

For much of the final years of her life, Josephine was severely ill, wracked by pains. She retained her demure cheerfulness to the end, however, always content to act "as the Master [God] desires." There were calls for her canonization almost from the moment of her death.

As befits the modesty that was so striking a part of her life at Schio, there are few images of St. Josephine Bakhita. This is the best known.

"Seeing the sun, the moon, and the stars, I said to myself: 'Who could be the Master of these beautiful things?' And I felt a great desire to see Him, to know Him, and to pay Him homage ... "

JOSEPHINE BAKHITA.

FEBRUARY 8 | JEROME EMILIANI

STATUS Priest, Founder
BORN 1481, Venice, Italy
DIED 1537, Somascha, Italy
GRC ♣
CofE ♧
LCDUS ♣
OTHER In France
♥ 1747
◯ 1767
🙏 Orphans, abandoned children

It was as a prisoner in 1511 that Jerome, a high-born Venetian and soldier, underwent a conversion that transformed his life. In 1518, he was ordained and thereafter devoted himself selflessly to helping the disadvantaged and dispossessed, and above all plague victims and orphans. Starting in Venice, he built a series of hospitals, orphanages, and homes for fallen women across much of northern Italy. In 1532, at Somascha, he began a religious order, later known as the Somaschi Fathers, to carry out the work on a larger scale. Jerome was himself a survivor of the plague.

Jerome Emiliani has remained a popular folk hero in the Veneto and Alpine regions.

FEBRUARY 9 | APOLLONIA

STATUS Virgin, Martyr
BORN c.200
DIED c.249, Alexandria, Egypt
GRC ♧
CofE ♧
LCDUS ♧
OTHER Eastern Orthodox and Coptic churches
◯ Pre-Congregation
✝ Tongs for pulling teeth
🙏 Dentists; sufferers from toothache

If little is known about her life, the circumstances of Apollonia's martyrdom are well documented for an early Christian saint. She died during a series of riots in Alexandria that turned into an anti-Christian massacre. With others, Apollonia was seized and her teeth were knocked out after a number of blows to her face. The rioters then threatened to burn her alive if she would not renounce Christianity. In response she flung herself into the flames. Given that she died of her own volition, concerns remained that she had committed suicide – a mortal sin – rather than suffering martyrdom. The matter was decisively settled in Apollonia's favor by St. Augustine of Hippo (Aug. 28) in the 5th century.

Apollonia was particularly venerated in the German-speaking world, where she was one of the original Fourteen Holy Helpers (see page 302). Here she holds a martyr's palm in her left hand, a set of tongs clasping a tooth in her right. This striking rococo statue was carved in 1742 by Franz Anton Koch and is in Mondsee Church in Austria.

Date	Name	Status	Venerated	Life
Feb. 9	Miguel Febres Cordero (1854–1910)	Educator ♥1977 ◯1984	In Ecuador	First Ecuadorean saint. Member of Institute of the Brothers of the Christian Schools.
Feb. 9	Teilo (c.500–c.560)	Bishop ◯ Pre-Congregation	In Wales	Member of one of earliest Christian families in Wales. Associated with abbey at Llandeilo Fawr. Tomb in Llandaff Cathedral.
Feb. 10	Scholastica (c.480–543)	Virgin, Founder ◯ Pre-Congregation	GRC, CofE, Eastern Orthodox churches 🙏 Benedictine nuns; children suffering convulsions	Best known as twin sister of St. Benedict (July 11), the founder of Western monasticism. Said to have played a leading role in helping her brother realize his vocation. Founded own order of nuns at Plombariola, Italy.

FEBRUARY 11   OUR LADY OF LOURDES

Marian Apparitions

More than 500 accounts of appearances by the Blessed Virgin Mary have been recorded, although only ten, including Our Lady of Lourdes, have been granted papal approval as 'worthy of belief:'

Our Lady of Guadalupe (Mexico)
1531 (see Dec. 12)

Our Lady of Laus (France)
1664–1718

Our Lady of the Miraculous Medal (France)
1830 (see Nov. 28)

Our Lady of La Salette (France)
1846

Our Lady of Pontmain (France)
1871

Our Lady of Fátima (Portugal)
1917 (see May 13)

Our Lady of Beauraing (Belgium)
1932–33

Our Lady of Banneux (Belgium)
1933

Our Lady of Akita (Japan)
1973

" ... we remain convinced that the Apparitions are supernatural and divine, and that by consequence, what Bernadette saw was the Most Blessed Virgin."

LAURENCE, BISHOP OF TARBES, 1862.

Between February 11 and July 16, 1858, in a grotto just outside the town of Lourdes in the French Pyrenees, 'a small young lady' appeared 18 times to a 14-year-old French peasant girl, Bernadette Soubirous. Bernadette, subsequently canonized (April 16), claimed the woman asked her to return to the grotto every day for 15 days. Her startled parents forbade her. She continued nonetheless. In March, the apparition announced herself to Bernadette as the Immaculate Conception, or Mary, the mother of Jesus. The following month, on Easter Sunday, Bernadette, now in a state of religious ecstasy, held her hands over a candle flame without burning them. By much the same time, the muddy trickle of water in the grotto had become sparklingly clear. The 'small young lady' last appeared to Bernadette on July 16. "I have never seen her so beautiful before," claimed Bernadette.

As the news leaked out, it caused a sensation. Almost from the start, the water in the grotto was held to have miraculous powers. The Church, fearful of being seen to support a kind of credulous witchcraft, refused to be drawn. No less alarmed, the local authorities closed the grotto. It was reopened on the personal orders of Napoleon III.

In 1862, swayed by evidence that the waters of the grotto genuinely appeared to have healing powers, the Church threw its official weight behind Bernadette's claims. Lourdes was confirmed as the focus of an intense Christian cult.

Lourdes Today

'Marian apparitions' have occurred in a number of places (see left), but none has enjoyed the same enduring allure as that at Lourdes. Every pope since Benedict XV has visited the shrine, John Paul II no less than three times. Benedict XVI made a pilgrimage to Lourdes for the first time in 2008.

The appeal of Lourdes as a place of pilgrimage has moved beyond the Catholic Church. In September 2008, Rowan Williams, the Archbishop of Canterbury, gave a sermon under the Marian statue in the grotto where the Virgin Mary appeared to Bernadette.

Bernadette was emphatic that the apparition she saw was dressed in flowing white robes with a blue sash, with a pink rose on either foot. Subsequent representations of Bernadette and the Virgin Mary have remained faithful to this vision.

The town, otherwise nondescript and with a population of 15,000, has more hotels than anywhere in France other than Paris. Approximately five million people visit it every year. A Mass held on February 11, 2008, the 150th anniversary of the first apparition, drew 45,000 people. Since 1862, 200 million people are claimed to have visited Lourdes. The Roman Catholic Church has officially recognized 67 'miraculous healings' there.

Date	Name	Status	Venerated	Life
Feb. 11	Benedict of Aniane (c.747–821)	Abbot, Founder ⬭ Pre-Congregation		Leading reformer of monastic life within Carolingian empire, vigorously championing and imposing Rule of St. Benedict, whose name he took (c.775). Founded monasteries at Aniane and Kornelimünster. Commissioned by Charlemagne's successor, Louis the Pious, to reform monasteries across empire.
Feb. 12	Julian the Hospitaller (no known date)	Penitent ⬭ Pre-Congregation	⚓ Ferrymen, innkeepers, circus people	Early medieval courtier; accidentally murdered his parents. In expiation built hostel with his wife by river, helping travelers; almost froze when he gave his bed to a leper, who revealed himself to be an angel, forgiving Julian.

CATHERINE DE' RICCI

STATUS Prioress, Virgin

BORN 1522, Florence, Italy

DIED 1590, Prato, Italy

GRC ☁

CofE ☁

LCDUS ☁

OTHER In Tuscany, Italy

♥ 1732

◯ 1746

✝ Usually represented in ecstasy

⚶ The sick; against illness

The ecstasy experienced by saints such as Catherine was almost always seen in terms of a marriage with Christ, a mystical union between Jesus and His virgin bride. In this 1740 painting by Pierre Subleyras, the betrothal is made explicit, Christ placing a wedding ring on Catherine's finger as the Blessed Virgin Mary presents her to her Son.

Catherine de' Ricci was among the most devout, even extreme, saints in a period notable for a series of extraordinary saints. As young as age six, she manifested an acute desire for prayer and contemplation. When she was 13, she became a member of the exactingly strict Dominican convent of San Vincenzo in Tuscany, at the same time adopting the name Catherine. She would remain at San Vincenzo for the rest of her life, in 1547 becoming perpetual prioress.

She is best known as a mystic. For 12 years from the age of 20, at precisely noon on every Thursday, she experienced a state of religious ecstasy, which lasted for exactly 28 hours, in which she relived Christ's Passion. This mystical marriage, as it was known, was sufficiently extreme for Catherine to exhibit stigmata, the physical wounds suffered by Christ during His crucifixion, although these may have been self-inflicted. That said, it is also claimed that in order to increase her own physical suffering, Catherine wore a 'sharp iron chain' around her neck. She was also given to bouts of rigorous fasting. St. Philip Neri (May 26), then in Rome and with whom she corresponded regularly, asserted that she appeared to him in a vision that lasted several hours. Catherine de' Ricci is one of the 'incorruptibles,' those saints whose bodies exhibited no sign of decay after their death.

SIMEON

STATUS Monk, Founder

BORN 1109, Serbia

DIED 1199, Mt. Athos, Greece

GRC ☁

CofE ☁

LCDUS ☁

OTHER Eastern Orthodox churches

◯ 1200

Simeon, father of St. Sabas (Jan. 14), was otherwise known as the Grand Prince Stefan I Nemanjić, the first ruler of a unified Serbian state. In 1196 he abdicated, decreeing that the kingdom pass to his second son, Stefan (in the process sparking a civil war between Stefan and his elder brother Vukan) and retired to the monastery of Studenica, which he had founded himself in 1190, taking the name Simeon. His wife Ana simultaneously became a nun, under the name Anastasia, in the Monastery of the Mother of Christ in Kuršumlija.

In 1199, Simeon joined Sabas at Mt. Athos in Greece where together they rebuilt the Serbian monastery of Hilandar. Simeon died the same year. He was canonized after holy oil, claimed to have miraculous powers, seeped from his tomb. In 1207, he was re-buried at Studenica, when again oil emerged from his tomb. Cults devoted to him are still in existence at Studenica and at Mt. Athos.

Simeon, variously known as Monk Simeon and St. Simeon the Myrrh-flowing (a reference to the oil that escaped from his tomb), was called by his son and successor, Stefan, 'The Gatherer of the Lost Pieces of the Land of his Grandfathers.'

FEBRUARY 14 | CYRIL AND METHODIUS

CYRIL

STATUS Monk, Confessor

BORN c.826, Thessalonica, Greece

DIED 869, Rome, Italy

GRC ♣

CofE ♣

LCDUS ♣

OTHER Eastern Orthodox churches (May 11), Czech Republic and Slovakia (July 5), Macedonia (May 24)

⊖ Pre-Congregation

✝ Monk's habit, often holding scroll with Cyrillic letters on it

🙏 Ecumenism, unity of Eastern and Western churches; Bulgaria, Macedonia, Czech Republic, Slovakia, Europe

METHODIUS

STATUS Bishop, Confessor

BORN c.815, Thessalonica, Greece

DIED 885, Velehred, Czech Republic

GRC ♣

CofE ♣

LCDUS ♣

OTHER Eastern Orthodox churches (May 11), Czech Republic and Slovakia (July 5), Macedonia (May 24)

⊖ Pre-Congregation

✝ Bishop's habit with omophorion

🙏 Ecumenism, unity of Eastern and Western churches; Bulgaria, Macedonia, Czech Republic, Slovakia, Europe

Cyril and Methodius, the 'Apostles of the Slavs,' remain among the most important missionary saints in the history of Christianity. Their endeavors to bring the Christian message to eastern Europe and Russia involved arduous missionary journeys, political infighting, and the creation of a new Slavic-Greek alphabet that could be used to translate the Gospels and scriptures, a version of which is still in general use today.

Cyril and Methodius were brothers, raised in a senatorial family in Thessalonica, northern Greece, which was also settled by Slavic peoples from the north, and the brothers were raised speaking both Greek and Slavonic. Cyril (originally named Constantine) became a librarian at Santa Sophia in Constantinople, while his elder brother Methodius became a local public official before entering a monastery. In 860, they were sent on an evangelical mission to Ukraine. They became convinced that attempting to teach the Christian message in Latin or Greek was less effective than using the vernacular tongues of their potential converts.

Cyril presents his new alphabet in a damaged Orthodox illumination. The Cyrillic alphabet is now used to write some 50 eastern European and central Asian languages.

New Alphabets

Following the success of the Ukrainian mission, in about 863 Cyril and Methodius were sent to Moravia (modern Czech Republic) by Emperor Michael III, at the request of the local ruler Rostislav, who wished to align with the Eastern church. They preached in the vernacular Slavonic, and it was there that Cyril began to use an alphabet he developed for transcribing the scriptures. This would later be developed into the Cyrillic alphabet by disciples of the missionary brothers. Pope Hadrian II approved the Slavonic liturgy, and went on to ordain Methodius and some of his assistants. Cyril sadly died at age 42, and was buried in San Clemente, Rome.

Methodius was made archbishop of Sirmium (in modern Serbia) in 870, but was still resisted by local bishops, who imprisoned, exiled, and made charges of heresy against him. The papal court absolved Methodius in 879, and he returned to Moravia as archbishop. He went on to translate most of the Bible into Slavonic, using his brother's alphabet.

Pope John Paul II declared Cyril and Methodius, along with Benedict of Nursia (July 11), patron saints of Europe.

Date	Name	Status	Venerated	Life
Feb. 14	Antoninus of Sorrento (d.830)	Abbot ⊖ Pre-Congregation	In Sorrento, Italy	Italian Benedictine monk. Became a hermit after his monastery threatened by attacks (possibly from Saracen or Viking raiders). Received vision of St. Michael the Archangel on Monte Angelo. Became abbot of St. Agrippinus. His relics miraculously repelled later assault on Sorrento by Saracen pirates.
Feb. 14	Maro (4th century)	Abbot ⊖ Pre-Congregation	By Maronites	Disciple of St. Zebinus. Lived in wilderness near Cyrrhus, northern Syria. Converted pagan temple into church. Trained other hermits; founded monasteries; corresponded with St. John Chrysostom. Maronite Order takes its name from Maro's burial place at monastery of Bait-Marun, Turkey.

FEBRUARY 14 | VALENTINE

STATUS Martyr
BORN c.235
DIED c.270
GRC ☁
CofE ♣
LCDUS ☁
OTHER Eastern Orthodox churches
○ Pre-Congregation
✝ Heart, heart pierced by arrow, pairs of birds
🙏 Beekeepers, lovers, the betrothed, those courting; Terni, Italy

This Orthodox image (above) shows Valentine blessing newlyweds, with their wedding gifts of farm animals.

Although it seems unusual for Christianity to celebrate carnal love, Valentine provides a link to earlier mythologies on the subject, such as that of Cupid and Ariadne (right).

Despite his almost global recognition as the patron saint of love and romance, remarkably little is known about Valentine. He was a Roman (possibly a soldier or priest) who converted to Christianity and helped Christians to escape during the persecutions of Claudius or Valerian. He is said to have been martyred on the Flaminian Way in Rome, probably by crucifixion or burning.

Ancient martyrologies cite two Valentines on this day. The other was a bishop of Terni, Italy, who was also martyred in Rome, although his remains were translated to Terni. They may be one and the same person.

Valentine's cult date may relate to an ancient and widespread belief that, in the northern hemisphere, pairs of birds mate on February 14. Some scholars believe that the date relates to the Roman festival of Lupercalia, which occurred on the ides of February (mid-month), a springtime feast of purification, health, and fertility. The tradition of choosing a Valentine, and sending a card anonymously, can be traced back (in England at least) to the 16th century.

St. Valentine's Day, although suppressed by the revision of the General Roman Calendar in 1969, remains an outstanding example of an obscure ancient belief that has been thoroughly adopted into modern popular culture, likely encouraged by the commercial interests of printers, flower vendors, and restaurant owners.

The commercialization of St. Valentine's Day, especially the mailing of anonymous cards, dates from the end of the 19th century.

With a surefire name for a romantic superstar, Italian-American actor Rudolph Valentino (1895–1926), was the heartthrob star of such smoldering epic silent movies as The Sheik *(1921), and* Blood and Sand *(1922). He epitomized the noble Latin lover. His enormous popularity, eerily enhanced by his death from peritonitis at the age of only 31, did much to propel the cult of St. Valentine into the modern world.*

FEBRUARY 15 | SIGFRID OF SWEDEN

STATUS Bishop

BORN Late 10th century, England

DIED c.1045, Växjö, Sweden

GRC ○

CofE ♠

LCDUS ○

OTHER In Sweden, Norway, Denmark

✝ In bishop's attire, bearing the three severed heads of his companions (sometimes confused as three loaves of bread)

🙏 Sweden

Sigfrid was an English Benedictine monk from the abbey at Glastonbury who was selected by King Ethelred to evangelize Norway and Sweden. He baptized King Olaf of Sweden and became bishop of Växjö in southern Sweden. He enjoyed some success in Gothland, and established two further bishoprics. While away on a missionary journey, Sigfrid's three helpers (his cousins) were slain by pagans. As a measure of his devotion, Sigfrid successfully pleaded that Olaf should not have the murderers executed. They were fined, but Sigfrid refused to accept the money.

A medieval wall painting from Växjö showing Sigfrid (right) bearing the heads of his companions, with Olaf of Sweden bearing an axe and a fish, a common early symbol of Christianity.

FEBRUARY 15 | CLAUDE DE LA COLOMBIÈRE

STATUS Priest, Founder

BORN 1641, near Lyon, France

DIED 1682, Paray, France

GRC ○

CofE ○

LCDUS ○

OTHER By Jesuits

❤ 1929

⬭ 1992

The aristocratic Colombière was a noted rhetorician and preacher.

Colombière was the Jesuit confessor of Margaret Mary Alacoque (Oct. 16) and, with her, helped to establish the Feast of the Sacred Heart of Jesus. He had entered the Society of Jesus in 1658 and was ordained in 1675. He deployed devotion to the Sacred Heart against the growing French taste for Jansenism, a movement that drew on Calvinist and Lutheran doctrines. He met Alacoque at the convent at Paray-le-Monial, Burgundy, and promoted the validity of her visions. Later he was active in Restoration England, as confessor to the future King James II's wife, but was arrested for preaching treachery and imprisoned in appalling conditions. An appeal from King Louis XIV saved him from execution, but he died from his deprivations shortly after returning to France.

A stained glass window from the Jesuit church in Milwaukee, Wisconsin, showing Colombière with Margaret Mary Alacoque.

FEBRUARY 16 · JULIANA

STATUS Virgin, Martyr

BORN c.285

DIED c.305

GRC ☁

CofE ☁

LCDUS ☁

OTHER Eastern Orthodox churches

⬯ Pre-Congregation

✝ Shown with a winged devil, often on a chain, or fighting a dragon

⚚ Childbirth

In this Greek icon, Juliana is shown bearing the distinctive cross of the Orthodox Church.

A medieval copper reliquary of Juliana produced in the Netherlands.

Martyred in Nicomedia (modern Turkey) or near Naples, Italy, during the persecutions of Maximian, Juliana is remembered for her extended debate with the Devil, who encouraged her to honor her pagan father's wishes and marry a Roman prefect. She refused, and having survived burning in a furnace and immersion in boiling oil, she was eventually decapitated. Like others with similar hagiographies (such as Agnes, Jan. 21, or Parasceva, July 26) her cult became popular across Europe from the 7th century and was particularly popular in the Netherlands.

FEBRUARY 17 · SEVEN FOUNDERS OF THE SERVITES

STATUS Founders

BORN Early 13th century

DIED Mid-late 13th century

GRC ♣

CofE ☁

LCDUS ♣

OTHER In Florence, Italy

⬯ 1887 (jointly)

NAMES Buonfiglio (Bonfilius) Monaldi
Giovanni Bonaiuncta
Benedict dell'Antello
Amadeus degli Amidei (Bartholomew)
Ricovere Uguccione (Hugh)
Geraldino Sostegni
Alexis Falconieri

In 1233, seven well-born Florentines founded the Order of Friar Servants of Mary, popularly known as the Servites. They were against the growing moral depravity of Florence, a rapidly expanding mercantile center. The confraternity retreated to a humble house outside the city and, devoting themselves to the Seven Sorrows of the Blessed Virgin, they practiced solitude, penance, and prayer. An abundance of visitors forced them to retreat further from Florence, and they built a hermitage and simple church at Monte Senario. The confraternity claimed direct inspiration and instruction from the Blessed Virgin Mary. They later emerged from isolation as friars, actively working within the community.

Despite near-suppression in 1274, the Servites were officially approved by Pope Benedict XI in 1304, and became over the centuries one of the most vigorous and far-reaching of the five original mendicant orders.

Santissima Annunziata, Florence, is the mother church of the Servite Order. It was designed by Leon Battista Alberti.

Date	Name	Status	Venerated	Life
Feb. 15	Thomas Bray (1658–1730)	Missionary	CofE	Oxford-educated English clergyman. In 1696 selected by bishop of London to undertake mission to Maryland. Became involved in evangelizing Native Americans. Laid foundations for Society for the Propagation of the Gospels (SPG, founded 1701). Established parish library system, designed to spread Anglican faith in Britain's colonies, which developed into Society for Promoting Christian Knowledge (founded 1699). Returned to England 1700; vicar of St. Botolph's, Aldgate, London, until his death.

FEBRUARY 18 — COLMAN OF LINDISFARNE

STATUS Bishop
BORN c.600, Ireland
DIED 676, Inishbofin, Ireland
GRC ○
CofE ○
LCDUS ○
○ Pre-Congregation

Colman was an important but controversial figure in the establishment of the Irish (Celtic) missionary church in northern England. He became a monk at Iona and succeeded St. Finan as bishop of Lindisfarne, Northumberland, in around 661. He became embroiled in a controversy between the Celtic and Roman churches concerning the dating of Easter and, supporting the Celtic argument at the Synod of Whitby in 664, he was defeated by the pro-Roman St. Wilfrid (Oct. 12). Colman immediately resigned and retired to Inishbofin off the Connacht coast of Ireland, accompanied by many sympathetic Irish and English monks from Iona. The monks fell out concerning work allocation, so Colman established a foundation on the mainland for the English faction, the 'Mayo of the Saxons.' Colman's brief rule at Lindisfarne was much admired by the Venerable Bede (May 25).

FEBRUARY 18 — JOHN (GIOVANNI) OF FIESOLE (FRA ANGELICO)

STATUS Friar, Artist
BORN c.1395, Tuscany, Italy
DIED 1455, Rome, Italy
GRC ○
CofE ○
LCDUS ○
♥ 1982
🙏 Catholic painters

Born Guido di Pietro, this extraordinarily gifted painter is known to us today as Fra Angelico. After training as a painter, Guido entered the Dominican Order in Fiesole in around 1418, taking the name Giovanni. He continued painting initially in the service of the order in Florence and Tuscany. He soon became an important figure in the development of early Renaissance religious narrative painting, with a style marked by compassion and luminosity. He was an outstanding colorist and mastered perspective representation. He painted many Annunciations, created extensive cycles of paintings for San Marco, Florence, and in 1445 was called to Rome by Pope Eugene IV, but worked mainly for his successor Nicolas V, providing cycles of the lives of St. Stephen and St. Lawrence for Nicolas's chapel. He then worked in Orvieto, and returned to Florence in 1450, where he was by then the most celebrated painter of his age. He was given the sobriquet 'Angelico' posthumously.

Working at a time when most were illiterate and the liturgy was recited in Latin, painters such as Fra Angelico realized the almost cinematic power of narrative painting – providing, effectively, visual sermons. It was at this point that the importance of saintly 'attributes' emerged, allowing individuals in a composition such as The Crucifixion with Saints (1441–42, San Marco, Florence) to be readily identified. Here, among others, we can see Lawrence in front of his griddle, Mark the Evangelist with his gospel, the bearded, rough-hewn John the Baptist and, with her back to us showing her flowing hair, Mary Magdalene.

FEBRUARY 18 | MARTIN LUTHER

STATUS	Monk, Priest, Church Reformer
BORN	1483, Eisleben, Germany
DIED	1546, Eisleben, Germany
GRC	☁
CofE	♣ (Oct. 31)
LCDUS	☁
OTHER	Lutheran Church, US Episcopal Church, Church of Scotland

The Reformation transformed Europe. For the first time, the Roman Church's central role as the focus and wellspring of a resurgent continent, unquestioned for a millennium, was challenged. Played out well into the 18th century, the Reformation detonated both the political and the religious map of the continent. A direct consequence was a series of strikingly savage wars, and its effects are still felt today.

The man who unleashed this transformation was a German, Martin Luther, an Augustinian monk from 1505, ordained in 1507, and made professor of theology at Wittenberg University in 1508. He was tormented by the gulf between the "abject wickedness of man" and the "dazzling goodness of God." For over a decade, Luther wrestled with this conundrum. His eventual, painful realization was that salvation was not something to be obtained via the official mechanisms of the Church, but could only be a matter of faith. And faith could only be the result of knowledge of, and trust in, the source of Christian truth: the Bible. From this realization, Luther came to the conclusion that the Roman Church's claim to be the sole guardian of Christian teaching must be false.

The 95 Theses

Luther went on to argue that the Church itself was an imposter — "Babylon and Sodom" in his words. These were not simply matters of doctrine. By the end of the 15th century, the Catholic Church was complacently exploiting its claims to spiritual authority in ways that were actively corrupt. Clerics were buying their way to high office (simony); popes were spawning children and amassing mistresses; brothels established specifically for priests were commonplace. More shocking still to Luther was the selling of indulgences, in effect the handing over of cash to the Church as a means of buying off sins. In 1517, Luther nailed his 95 theses regarding indulgences to the door of the Castle Chapel in Wittenberg, thus sparking the Reformation.

Luther's relentless assertion of Rome's falsity was crucially aided by a recent invention: printing. For the first time, the Bible, newly and controversially translated into languages other than Latin, was becoming widely available. Anyone literate could read for themselves what God had actually revealed. Who then needed priests?

A number of rulers were quick to exploit this dramatic division in the Christian world, renouncing Rome to take over former church properties that would enhance their own revenues. Luther found himself something of a pawn in these political positionings. But his aggressive criticism of Rome remained unwavering, and he was excommunicated by Pope Leo X in 1521. When Charles V, the Holy Roman Emperor, demanded that Luther retract his criticisms of Rome at the Diet of Worms later the same year, Luther flatly refused.

Luther never intended to overthrow the primacy of Rome in the Catholic world. He meant only to return it to the purity of its origins. He ended by convulsing Christian Europe.

IO ET SPE ERIT   FORTITVDO VE

The thin-lipped, unrelenting Luther, painted by Lucas Cranach in 1533.

"I am born to fight innumerable monsters and devils."

MARTIN LUTHER.

Date	Name	Status	Venerated	Life
Feb. 19	Conrad of Piacenza (c.1290–1351)	Hermit	By Franciscans In Noto, Italy ♣ Against hernias	Nobleman who, while hunting, gave orders that a fire be lit to flush out game from scrubland. Resulting conflagration wrongly blamed on a local peasant. When the innocent man was condemned to death, Conrad revealed himself as the guilty party. Consumed by remorse, gave away all his possessions and lived as Franciscan hermit for his last 35 years. Had gift of healing.
Feb. 20	Wulfric (c.1080–1154)	Priest, Hermit		Noted English hermit and miracle worker, famed for his sanctity and self-denial. Said to have gift of prophecy.

THE REFORMED CHURCHES

The reformed churches may have begun with a common purpose to 'protest' (hence Protestant) against Rome's corruption of Christ's teaching, but they rapidly split into a variety of rival groupings. In 1522, for example, Huldrych (Ulrich) Zwingli (1484–1531), a pastor in Zurich, began a reform movement that broadly followed Luther's doctrines, though the two were never able to agree whether the Eucharist – the transformation of bread and wine into Christ's body and blood during Mass – should be interpreted literally or symbolically. At much the same time, an even more radical grouping appeared in central Europe: the Anabaptists. Their insistence that baptism required a conscientious acceptance of Christianity led to their continued persecution. By the end of the 17th century, they had splintered into even more fundamentalist groupings: Amish, Hutterites, and Mennonites.

The main thrust of Lutheranism was continued in Geneva by a Frenchman, John Calvin (1509–64). Where Calvinism generally established itself in parts of Switzerland, most of northern Germany, much of Hungary, scattered areas of France (as the Huguenots), the Netherlands, and in Scotland (under the name Presbyterianism), Lutheranism was most successful in Scandinavia.

In England, the Anglican Church established by Henry VIII in 1536 was an entirely political construction. At least initially, its forms of worship remained Roman, but by the accession of Elizabeth I in 1558, the Anglican Church was much more obviously in line with reform movements elsewhere. In the 17th century it was then wrenched firmly toward Calvinism by the Puritans, this in turn giving rise to non-conformist movements such as Quakerism and Methodism, later still to Pentecostalism, which itself split into various branches, which in turn led to Adventism. The broader Anglican Communion across the world is often also generally described as Episcopalian, meaning its branches are directed by independent bishops. All the reformed churches were and are actively Christian.

One of the first reformist measures was the dissolution of the monasteries, ordered by England's Henry VIII in 1536. Monasteries were looted and destroyed and their income appropriated by the crown. The Cistercian abbey of Rievaulx, Yorkshire, is one of many whose spectacular ruins survive.

FEBRUARY 20

JACINTA AND FRANCISCO MARTO

STATUS Visionaries

BORN Francisco 1908, Jacinta 1910, Portugal

DIED Francisco 1919, Jacinta 1920, Portugal

GRC ☁

CofE ☁

LCDUS ☁

OTHER In Portugal

♥ 2000

✝ As children

🙏 The sick

With their cousin, Lúcia dos Santos, Jacinta and Francisco Marto, brother and sister, were the peasant children to whom the Virgin Mary is said to have appeared in 1917 at Fátima in Portugal (May 13). Instantly deluged by a wave of global notoriety, Jacinta and Francisco spent what remained of their young lives in a daze of sanctity. Francisco plunged himself into rounds of solitary prayer, "to console Jesus for the sins of the world." The seven-year-old Jacinta, tormented by a vision of Hell revealed to her by the Virgin, became convinced she had a duty to sacrifice herself in order to save sinners everywhere.

Both died in the global influenza epidemic. Francisco died almost at once. Jacinta, who eventually developed pleurisy, lingered for several months before succumbing to a death she had already predicted. Both were exhumed in 1935 and in 1951. Jacinta's face was subsequently pronounced to be incorrupt.

A statue of Jacinta and Francisco at the site where the Virgin was revealed to them, now one of the Catholic world's major places of pilgrimage. Both were buried at Fátima. Lúcia died in 2005, at age 97. She, too, is buried at Fátima.

FEBRUARY 21

SAINTS, MARTYRS, AND MISSIONARIES OF AFRICA

The Coptic Church was well established in Ethiopia around 700. It became an outpost of Christianity isolated by the spread of Islam, but its fervor is attested to by the impressive rock-cut shrines in centers such as Lalibela.

The early Christian church took root in Africa very rapidly, among the Ptolemaic Greeks who lived in Egypt, and in parts of the North African coast that fell within the Roman empire. The Monophysite Church that emerged in Egypt developed the first monastic communities, and spread south along the Nile Valley. Linked to this was the establishment of the Coptic Church in Abyssinia (modern Ethiopia).

The rise of Islam in the 7th century, although by no means initially eradicating Christianity in the conquered areas, had the effect after the Crusades of isolating Western Christendom from the African continent, while trading routes disseminated the Islamic faith across the Sahara and down the East African coast. Nevertheless, medieval Europeans were fascinated by tales of 'Prester John,' an isolated Christian ruler in Abyssinia.

European Inroads

From the 15th century, European adventurers seemed more interested in feeding the trans-Atlantic slave trade, and plundering gold and ivory, than in saving souls, although Portuguese Catholic missions made some inroads in coastal trading areas by 1700, while Dutch and German settlers introduced Calvinism to the Cape Colony from 1652 onward.

Only in the 19th century did missionary activity really take off. This was often accompanied by brutality (on both sides) on an unimaginable scale. Resistance to what were perceived as covert imperialist strategies often provoked violent backlashes, as in the slaughter of the missionaries and local converts enacted by Mwanga II of Buganda (*see* June 3). Queen Ranavalona of Madagascar (r.1828–61),

while mimicking European courtly manners, banished Christian missionaries, and was known to take delight in boiling Christian converts alive or hurling them off cliffs. On the other hand, at the end of the 19th century, in what was to become today's Democratic Republic of the Congo, the region's inhabitants and resources were mercilessly exploited by Leopold II of Belgium in a singularly unchristian manner.

Obstacles to Conversion

Among the native rulers, conversion was often little more than a political and economic expedient. Catholic missionaries struggled to convert royal families that still favored polygamy and ancestor and spirit worship. Protestant missionaries sought less to proselytize, but instead to win potential converts with their organizational, agricultural, and medical skills.

Independent churches, mainly in West Africa, began to develop in the late 19th century, drawing together Christian and native spiritist ideas, in a parallel with some of the African-American saint-based cults that developed in Brazil and the Caribbean.

Unfortunately, the persecution of Christians in Africa persists, notably in Egypt and Sudan, while modern martyrs can be found in many post-independent states, often reflecting persistent tribalism as much as religious conflict. This was the case in the unhappy fate of Apolo Kivebulaya (May 30).

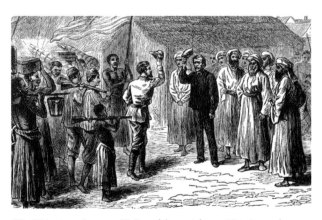

"Dr. Livingstone, I presume?" One of the most famous Victorian explorers and missionaries was the Scottish Congregationalist Dr. David Livingstone (1813–73), whose dedication to his task in a remote region of modern Zambia resulted in his eventual death from malaria. Here he is, being famously greeted by the American journalist Sir Henry Morton Stanley, whose quest to track down the 'lost' Scottish doctor created a huge upsurge of support for missionary activity.

FEBRUARY 21 ✣ # PETER DAMIAN

STATUS Bishop, Doctor of the Church

BORN 1007, Ravenna, Italy

DIED 1072, Faenza, Italy

GRC ♣

CofE ◌

LCDUS ♣

♥ 1828

✝ As a cardinal or a pilgrim holding a papal bull

Peter Damian portrayed by Francesco del Rossi (Il Saviati, 1510–63) in Sta. Maria delle Carceri, Italy. The saint is shown bearing a book and a whip for self-flagellation. The Italian poet Dante ranked Damian as a significant predecessor of St. Francis of Assisi in his Divine Comedy.

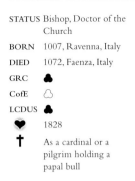

In the absence of opportunities for martyrdom, Peter Damian promoted self-harming activities such as flagellation as a means of demonstrating both faith and penance.

Peter Damian was one of the outstanding reformers of the early medieval church. He was born into a large, poor family and at age 28 he entered the Camaldolese Benedictine monastery at Fonte Avellana, noted for its austerity. By 1043 he had been appointed abbot. Appalled by the behavior of many in the clergy, he began a campaign of reform, particularly addressing simony (the buying, or selling, of ecclesiastical offices) and the widespread abuse of the vows of celibacy; he also called for a strict evaluation of the role of the papacy. In 1057, he was made a cardinal by Gregory VII (May 25) and appointed bishop of Ostia, but he nevertheless continued his reform work. He eventually appealed to be relieved of his episcopate and returned to Fonte Avellana to end his life in retreat and contemplation.

If indeed a harsh critic of others, Damian was certainly also severe on himself, and it may be that he found the temptations of the flesh almost too great to resist. He wore a hair shirt, fasted frequently, and did much to promote the benefits of self-flagellation as a means of mortification. His recommendation that gay men be barred from the Church has meant that his reputation and work (notably *The Book of Gomorrah*, c.1049) have been frequent matters of debate in recent years.

FEBRUARY 22 | THE CHAIR OF ST. PETER

This day was set aside on the General Roman Calendar to celebrate the first pope, St. Peter (June 29). Although not originally classified as a 'pope,' Peter was the preeminent Apostle and he has become the foremost father of the Church. Peter's relics have long been associated with Rome, and a portable wooden chair, preserved in the Vatican, is regarded as one of the physical links with the birth of the Roman Church. It is believed to have been used when Peter presided over his first Mass in Rome, although it is likely that it dates from the 2nd century. This feast effectively marks the beginning of the Roman papal tradition.

The cathedra at St. Peter's, Rome (right), designed by Bernini in 1650 to surmount the main altar, makes the most of a number of Baroque devices, including a grandiose representation of the 'chair.' With an unusual orientation toward the west ('occidental' rather than 'oriental'), the afternoon light shines through the glazed image of a dove, itself surrounded by a gilded sunburst. Around this, Bernini assembled a spectacular polychromatic sculptural group of angels supporting the black marble papal throne. The feast is also celebrated on January 18.

FEBRUARY 22 | MARGARET OF CORTONA

STATUS Penitent

BORN 1247, Laviano, Italy

DIED 1297, Cortona, Italy

GRC ☁

CofE ☁

LCDUS ☁

OTHER In Cortona

♥ 1515

◯ 1728

✝ Lapdog

⚚ Single mothers, penitent prostitutes, sexual temptation, the falsely accused, the homeless, the insane

Margaret was, by all accounts, a beautiful woman, born a peasant, whose mother died when she was young. She did not get on with her stepmother. She enjoyed the favors of a young knight and lived with him at Montepulciano for some ten years, bearing him a son out of wedlock. He was murdered when she was 26 and, rejected by her family, she was taken in by two women who offered Margaret and her son a home in the Etruscan hilltop town of Cortona. Pursued by poisonous gossip, she became repentant and took to very public acts of extreme self-mortification, including starvation, mutilation, and punishment of her son. Eventually, she was accepted as a Franciscan tertiary, devoting herself to acts of charity until her son grew up. He then became a Franciscan novitiate. Thereafter, Margaret became increasingly reclusive, and moved to the ruined church of St. Basil's outside the city walls. Here she gained a reputation as a savior of sinners through counseling and prayer. She was active in founding a paupers' hospital in Cortona. A number of ecstatic visions, miraculous cures, and other unusual occurrences were recorded by her confessor. Her apparently incorrupt remains can still be seen in the church built for her over the ruins of St. Basil's at Cortona.

Lapdogs were a frequent symbol of lust in medieval and Renaissance art; thus Margaret's frequent representation with such a beast means that, despite her fervent penitence, her former sins are not forgotten.

FEBRUARY 23   POLYCARP

STATUS Bishop, Martyr

BORN c. AD 69

DIED c.155, Smyrna, modern Turkey

GRC ♣

CofE ♣

LCDUS ♣

OTHER Eastern Orthodox churches

⬭ Pre-Congregation

✝ Wearing a pallium, often holding a book; frequently surrounded by flames

🙏 Those suffering earache or dysentery

Polycarp's miraculous survival when initially burnt at the stake is commemorated in his emblem.

Polycarp was a very significant figure in the development of the Early Church in Greek Asia Minor. He was a disciple of John the Evangelist (Dec. 27), and as such is regarded as one of the few direct links between the Apostles of the New Testament and the early Christian bishops. With Pope Clement I (Nov. 23), and Ignatius of Antioch (Oct. 17), Polycarp is regarded as one of the Apostolic Fathers of the Church. He became bishop of Smyrna, where he defended the Christian orthodoxy against the various heresies of Gnosticism *(see below)*, especially those promulgated by Marcion and Valentinus. His sole surviving written work is his *Letter to the Philippians*, recorded by Irenaeus (June 28), which was used as a liturgical text for several centuries.

At a considerable age (probably in his eighties) Polycarp was invited to Rome by Pope Anicetus (r.c.155–66) to discuss the dating of Easter. Polycarp advocated the traditional (Eastern) link to the dating of the Jewish Passover; until then, Rome had no specific date, celebrating the Resurrection effectively every Sunday. The two could not agree, but parted on good terms.

Shortly after his return to Smyrna (according to Irenaeus), a Roman youth, Germanicus, was killed at a 'pagan' ceremony. Whether this was 'pagan' in the Roman or Christian sense remains unclear, but in the ensuing confusion Polycarp was arrested and asked to denounce his faith. He refused, and was sent to the amphitheater for public execution. Attempts were made to burn him at the stake, but surrounded by an ethereal blue light, the flames failed to vanquish him. He was eventually stabbed to death by a Roman attendant, and his corpse was then successfully cremated.

Polycarp's theological importance is somewhat overshadowed by his valiant approach to martyrdom. When his accusers arrived at a solitary farm to arrest him, he offered them supper, and quietly denied their demands that he apostatize.

> "For 86 years I have been His servant and He has never done me wrong: how can I blaspheme my King who saved me?"

POLYCARP RESPONDING TO HIS ACCUSERS UPON ARREST.

Even the Bible provides evidence of unorthodoxy and magic: in 1 Samuel 28, Saul invites the witch of Endor to summon the spirit of the prophet Samuel to advise him (right). The suggestion that there might be alternative paths to communion with the spirit world beyond or outside the Christian liturgy has consistently beset the Church. Images of witches' sabbaths (above) bear witness to this.

GNOSTICISM

As the early Christian church progressed toward the east, so it encountered other beliefs and cults that proved capable of introducing alternative interpretations of what were seen as core Christian doctrines. One of the most significant of these was Gnosticism, which was a shadowy cult in which the Supreme Being, or 'Demiurge,' might be interpreted as good or evil. The Christian Gnostics, notably Marcion (who denied the inspiration of the Old Testament, probably on anti-Semitic grounds) and Valentinus (who denied both the humanity of Christ and the notion of the Holy Trinity as an impossibility), also promoted the image of revelation being only accessible to a chosen few. This legacy echoed through the ages, attracting many to the concept of an elite, select group of 'Illuminati' and providing much succor for subsequent secret societies and others fascinated by hermeticism, alchemy, necromancy, and other arcane traditions.

FEBRUARY 24 | ETHELBERT OF KENT

STATUS King

BORN c.560, Kent, England

DIED 616, Kent, England

GRC ⛢

CofE ⛢

LCDUS ⛢

⬭ Pre-Congregation

The ruins of St. Augustine's Abbey (formerly SS. Peter and Paul) in Canterbury, Kent. It was the first Christian foundation in England, endorsed by Ethelbert, and is his final resting place.

Ethelbert, ruler of the ill-defined kingdom of Kent in southeast England, was the first English Anglo-Saxon king to convert to Christianity. It is not known whether his conversion came as a result of St. Augustine's mission to England in 597 (May 27), or whether Ethelbert had already been converted as a condition of marrying his queen, Bertha, daughter of the king of Paris and herself a Christian. Either way, his embrace of Christianity was critical not just in re-introducing Christianity to England, but in facilitating the spread of Roman notions of law and literacy, which were at that point the almost exclusive preserves of the Church.

A mid-15th century stained-glass image of Ethelbert in the chapel of All Souls College, Oxford. Ethelbert was canonized because of his role in aiding the spread of Christianity in an otherwise pagan England.

Date	Name	Status	Venerated	Life
Feb. 25	Sebastian of Aparicio (1502–1600)	Friar ♥ 1787	⚓ Travelers	Known as the 'Angel of Mexico.' Spanish peasant who traveled to Mexico (1533). Oversaw construction of road between Mexico City and Zacatecas. Made fortune as a rancher. Married twice, though neither marriage consummated. Became Franciscan monk; gave away all his money. More than 300 miracles attributed to him.
Feb. 26	Porphyry of Gaza (c.347–421)	Hermit, Bishop ⬭ Pre-Congregation		Greek-born hermit; later bishop of Gaza, Palestine. Renowned for destruction of Gaza's pagan temples. Built large Christian basilica on site of largest – that of Zeus Marnas. Most of what is known of him comes from single contemporary source, the *Vita Pophyrii*, largely dismissed by scholars as unreliable.
Feb. 27	George Herbert (1593–1633)	Priest, Poet, Hymnist	CofE, US Evangelical Lutheran Church (March 1)	Welsh-born scholar, metaphysical poet, parliamentarian. Entered priesthood at age 36. Rector of Fugglestone St. Peter near Salisbury, England. Famed for good works and his religious verses, a number of which were later used as hymns.
Feb. 28	Daniel Brottier (1876–1936)	Priest, Missionary ♥ 1984	In France	Ordained in 1899. Member of French missionary order Congregation of the Holy Spirit. Worked in Senegal (1903–11), then a French colony. Served as chaplain to French forces in World War I. Director and fund-raiser for Foundation for Apprenticed Orphans in Auteuil, Paris (1923). Built chapel at Auteuil to newly canonized St. Thérèse of Lisieux (Oct.1), whose intercession he believed saved his life in the war.

WALBURGA

STATUS Abbess, Missionary
BORN c.710, Devon, England
DIED 777, Heidenheim, Germany
GRC ☁
CofE ☁
LCDUS ☁
OTHER By Benedictines; in Germany
⊖ Pre-Congregation
✝ Crown, crosier, phial of oil, three ears of corn
🙏 Storms, sailors, rabies; protection of crops

Walburga was the daughter of St. Richard, a West Saxon king. Not only was her father canonized, but both of her brothers, Willibald (July 7) and Winibald, were also saints, as was her uncle, Boniface (June 5), who was the foremost Anglo-Saxon missionary of the period, largely responsible for bringing Christianity to Germany. It was in response to a plea from Boniface that Walburga went to Germany in around 748, where she became abbess of both the monastery and the convent at Heidenheim. She became trained in medicine, and was notable for writing, in Latin, lives of her brothers, who were also active in Germany.

In 870, her remains were removed from Heidenheim and reburied in the Benedictine convent, today the abbey of St. Walburg, at Eichstätt in Bavaria. There, it was discovered that holy oil — in reality water produced naturally — was running from her tomb. It has continued to flow and is still bottled by the nuns at Eichstätt.

Walburga is conventionally represented with a crosier, indicating her role as an abbess, and holding a phial containing holy oil. The crown in this image highlights her royal birth.

GABRIEL OF OUR LADY OF SORROWS

STATUS Priest
BORN 1838, Assisi, Italy
DIED 1862, Isola, Italy
GRC ☁
CofE ☁
LCDUS ☁
♥ 1908
⊖ 1920
✝ Passionist habit and sign
🙏 Students, seminarians; Abruzzi, Italy

Gabriel of Our Lady of Sorrows, born Francis Possenti, was unusually vain as a youth and much given to dancing, but discovered his vocation, fiercely resisted by his father, after a series of illnesses. In 1856, he joined the Passionists, an Italian contemplative and missionary congregation founded in 1720 by St. Paul of the Cross (Oct. 19). From the start, he was a model novitiate, exceptionally studious, and scrupulous in the execution of his spiritual duties. Three years later, he fell ill with tuberculosis. The certainty that he would die young only increased his already profound sanctity. Two miracles are ascribed to him.

In the United States, a campaign, apparently based on a story in which Gabriel is said to have chased a band of gun-waving bandits out of the town of Isola, was launched to have him declared the patron saint of handguns.

Throughout his brief career as a Passionist, St. Gabriel's spiritual mentor was Father Norbert, here seen with St. Gabriel (center). He was present at Gabriel's beatification in Rome by Pius X in 1908. The distinctive white symbol of the Passionists is clearly visible on Gabriel's robes.

OSWALD OF WORCESTER

STATUS Bishop
BORN c.925, England
DIED 992, Worcester, England
GRC ☁
CofE ☁
LCDUS ☁
⊖ Pre-Congregation

Oswald was of Danish military descent, and related to St. Odo of Canterbury. The latter sent him to study at the Cluniac monastery at Fleury, France. After returning to England, he became bishop of Worcester in 962, and from 972 was archbishop of York, the second-most senior churchman in the country. Despite these high offices, however, he did much to introduce monastic practices in England, founding Westbury-on-Trym near Bristol, and Ramsey, Huntingdonshire. From these, several other houses were founded in the diocese of Worcester. Oswald thus played a key role in the consolidation of Christianity in Anglo-Saxon England, itself threatened since the early 980s by a series of formidable Danish invasions. Numerous miracles were attributed to him and a vigorous cult developed after his death.

MARCH

Named for Mars, the Roman god of war, March is the third month of the Gregorian calendar and can be a suitably harsh and unforgiving period. It includes two key festivals in the British Isles: Saint David's Day for the patron saint of Wales (March 1), and Saint Patrick's Day for the patron saint of Ireland (March 17). Both are robustly celebrated in feasting, drink, and song. A more solemn festival is the Annunciation of the Blessed Virgin Mary on March 25, which is especially important in the Eastern Orthodox calendar. In Europe, Mother's Day traditionally falls on the fourth Sunday in Lent, and was originally an occasion upon which workers and domestic servants could travel home to their mother churches and visit their families.

The festival of Easter does, on occasion, fall within March, when it may neatly coincide with the beginning of spring at the northern hemisphere's vernal equinox.

The Annunciation, the revelation to the Blessed Virgin Mary by the Archangel Gabriel that she had been chosen to be the mother of Christ, is one of the central episodes in the Christian story. It was a popular subject among Renaissance artists, including Fra Angelico (Feb. 18), who painted several variations of the scene.

MARCH 1 | DAVID

STATUS Bishop

BORN c.500, Pembrokeshire, Wales

DIED c.589, St. David's, Wales

GRC ◌

CofE ♠

LCDUS ◌

OTHER US Episcopal Church

⊘ 1120

✝ In abbot's robes, usually accompanied by a dove

🙏 Poets, vegetarians; Wales, Pembrokeshire

Unlike the patron saints of England (George, April 23) and Scotland (Andrew, Nov. 30), David has only an incidental link to the national flag: some legends have him, like St. George, defeating dragons.

The Welsh national emblems, the daffodil and the leek, are traditionally worn on St. David's Day. Like the saint himself, the origins of this symbolism are now lost.

St. David (*Dewi Sant* in Welsh) is patron saint of Wales. With more than 50 churches dedicated to him in the south of the country, including that of the monastery he founded at Menevia or Mynyw, today simply called St. David's, he is among the best known of all saints. While he clearly existed and appears to have been a forceful preacher, teacher, and missionary, his life remains almost entirely legendary. The earliest account of David was compiled some 500 years after his presumed death, and seems largely to have been produced to justify the independence of the Welsh Church from that of England. Later accounts are more fanciful still, improbable confections of miracles, prophecies, and fabulous beasts.

Mythic Origins

David was said to have been the son of a Welsh prince, Sandde, and a woman, Non, variously described as an Irish nun or a Welsh princess, who had been raped by Sandde. David, in some accounts King Arthur's nephew, in others his uncle, was claimed to have been born on a cliff top in Pembrokeshire in a violent storm. The site was later marked by the ancient and ruined Chapel of St. Non. An angel is said to have foretold the saint's birth to St. Patrick (March 17) thirty years earlier. For ten years, David studied scripture under the venerable St. Paulinus of Wales, who the youthful David cured of blindness brought on by "excessive weeping through prayer."

David later traveled widely across the Celtic world, including Brittany in northern France, establishing 12 monasteries, among them those at Glastonbury and Bath. He instituted an exceptionally austere regime for his monks: all were expected to engage in manual labor; speech was largely forbidden; personal possessions were not allowed; no meat was to be eaten (hence David's adoption as the patron saint of vegetarians); and only water was to be drunk. David was nicknamed 'Aquaticus' ('water drinker') and was claimed to immerse himself regularly in freezing water up to his neck as an aid to contemplation.

David is reputed to have made pilgrimages to Jerusalem, where the patriarch himself is said to have appointed him an archbishop, and to Rome.

Early images of David are rare. Here the saint is depicted with a dove in a fine 19th-century stained-glass window in the church of Great St. Mary's, Cambridge, England.

St. David's Cathedral, in the county of Pembrokeshire in the far southwest of Wales, is a Romanesque building founded in 1181. It has been restored several times, with a major refitting in the 19th century.

David and the Dove

At a date sometimes given as 545 (or, according to some accounts, 512), David, still no more than a minor abbot, was persuaded to attend a synod called to condemn Pelagianism at the central Welsh town of Llanddewi Brefi. Here the most famous miracle associated with him occurred. Addressing a crowd that could neither hear nor see him well, the ground on which David stood is said to have spontaneously risen into the air so that he towered over the assembled masses. A white dove, symbol of divine grace, then settled on his shoulder. St. Dubric, the senior Welsh bishop present, was so struck by this that he resigned to live as a hermit, insisting David be appointed in his place. It was after the synod that David, apparently with the blessing of King Arthur, founded his monastery at Menevia, making it the prime focus of Christianity in Wales. It later became a leading place of pilgrimage, visited by William the Conqueror and Henry II, in whose reign the cathedral was begun. David was buried at St. David's, though his relics were looted in Viking raids in the 9th century.

MARCH 2   AGNES OF BOHEMIA

STATUS	Nun, Abbess
BORN	1205, Prague, modern Czech Republic
DIED	1282, Prague, modern Czech Republic
GRC	☁
CofE	☁
LCDUS	☁
♥	1874
⬭	1989
⚚	Bohemia

Agnes is still celebrated in the Czech Republic.

Agnes was among the most notable of medieval central European saints, the daughter of Ottokar I of Bohemia, who spurned her royal background to embrace a life of what Pope John Paul II, who canonized her, called "heroic charity." Despite having been engaged to a number of princes and other rulers, Agnes had early decided to dedicate herself to God and to live a life of "austerity and virginity" as "a spouse of Christ." After a lengthy correspondence with St. Clare herself (Aug. 11), in 1231 she founded a branch of the Poor Clares in Prague, and a Franciscan monastery and a hospital, also dedicated to St. Francis (Oct. 4). Her willing embrace of poverty and her habit of tending to the poor and the sick herself, with no menial task beneath her, encouraged large numbers of high-born Bohemian women to dedicate themselves to similar good works. Agnes was claimed to have the gift of prophecy and was said to have been much given to religious ecstasies.

A primitive late 15th-century Bohemian painting of St. Agnes tending the sick. Even once she had been appointed Mother Superior of the Prague Clares in 1234, St. Agnes personally cooked for the sick in her hospital.

Date	Name	Status	Venerated	Life
March 2	Chad (c.634–72)	Bishop ⬭ Pre-Congregation	CofE	Chad and his brother St. Cedd were significant figures in the spreading of Christianity in early medieval England. Ordained in Ireland; successively bishop of Northumbria and of Mercia, credited, chiefly by Bede (May 25), with converting Mercia to Christianity. Died of plague. Numerous churches dedicated to him, including the Roman Catholic cathedral in Birmingham, where his relics are preserved.

MARCH 3 | KATHARINE DREXEL

STATUS Missionary, Founder

BORN 1858, Philadelphia, USA

DIED 1955, Bensalem, USA

GRC ○

CofE ○

LCDUS ♠

○ 2000

🙏 Philanthropists, racial justice

This life-size statue of Katharine accompanied by an African-American boy and a Native American girl is in the Basilica of the National Shrine of the Immaculate Conception in Washington, D.C.

Born in Philadelphia, Pennsylvania, of Dutch descent, Katharine Drexel was a pioneer in providing education and justice for Native Americans and African Americans in the first half of the 20th century. She began life as a society heiress; her wealthy father, a successful and philanthropic banker, left her a legacy worth in excess of $100 million (by today's values). Under the influence of Pope Leo XIII, Katharine became a nun and, in 1891, founded the Sisters of the Blessed Sacrament as an order dedicated to missionary work within the Native American and black communities.

She established her first missionary school in Santa Fe, New Mexico, in 1894, and went on to found a further eleven such schools on various Indian reservations. In addition, Katharine used her wealth to found, staff, and support nearly 60 schools, as well as orphanages, across the rural areas and inner cities of the Deep South, at a time when African Americans did not have access to a basic education. She was instrumental in establishing the school that would evolve into Xavier University, in New Orleans, Louisiana, the only black Roman Catholic college in the United States. This work led her to become the second American-born saint.

An idealized image of Katharine bringing children of various races to Jesus (above). The reality, in the deserts of New Mexico in the 1890s, was somewhat harsher (below).

Date	Name	Status	Venerated	Life
March 6	Baldred (Balther) of Tyninghame (d.c.764)	Hermit ○ Pre-Congregation	In Northumbria	Priest from the Northumbria/south Scotland area. According to legend, moved a dangerous shoal in Firth of Forth to save sailors from shipwreck. Lived as hermit on desolate Bass Rock off the coast from Berwick, currently home to 40,000 pairs of gannets.
March 6	Sylvester of Assisi (d.1240)	Priest ○ Pre-Congregation	By Franciscans	Companion of St. Francis of Assisi and first priest in Franciscan Order. Buried near the tomb of St. Francis.

MARCH 4 · CASIMIR 'THE PEACEMAKER'

STATUS Prince

BORN 1458, Kraków, Poland

DIED 1484, Grodno, Lithuania (now in Belarus)

GRC ♣

CofE ○

LCDUS ♣

○ 1521

† Lily, crown, absence of sword

🙏 Bachelors, kings, princes, youth; Poland, Lithuania

The cult of Casimir is particularly strong among the Polish and Lithuanian immigrant communities of North America. This elaborate altar dedicated to him is in St. Casimir Church, Cleveland, Ohio.

Casimir was the second son of Casimir IV, king of Poland. In 1471, at the request of Hungarian nobles, Casimir's father sent him to Hungary at the head of a large army. The Hungarians were unhappy with their king, Matthias Corvinus, and wanted Casimir to replace him. However, Casimir would not wage war and returned home. He refused to fight against fellow Christians and remained a lifelong conscientious objector (*see also* Maximilian, March 12). Pacifism was not the only unusual aspect of Casimir's royal life: he turned away from all kingly pursuits, and turned down an arranged marriage with the Holy Roman Emperor Frederick III's daughter, preferring to dedicate himself to a life of prayer, humility, and chastity. Suffering from illness throughout his life, Casimir finally succumbed to tuberculosis. Miracles were reported at Casimir's tomb in Vilnius, the Lithuanian capital, where his relics still rest today.

MARCH 5 · JOHN JOSEPH OF THE CROSS

STATUS Priest, Confessor

BORN 1654, Ischia, Italy

DIED 1734, Naples, Italy

GRC ○

CofE ○

LCDUS ○

OTHER By Franciscans

♥ 1789

○ 1839

† Sometimes represented levitating

🙏 Naples, Ischia

Born Carlo Gaetano, he entered the Franciscan Order at age 16, taking the name John Joseph of the Cross. He seemed to take to the contemplative life, and was ordained a monk in 1677. Although John Joseph preferred to live the modest life of his order, he held several positions of authority, including vicar provincial of the Alcantarine Reform in Naples. He was appointed to the latter position at a time when there was tension between the Italians and Spanish in the province, as the Italian religious orders were suppressed by the Spanish.

John Joseph is known as one of the 'flying saints': some of the many miracles ascribed to him include levitation and levitation of his walking stick, apparently witnessed by a church full of people.

MARCH 6 · CHRODEGANG OF METZ

STATUS Bishop

BORN c.712 near Liège, modern Belgium

DIED 766, Metz, Germany

GRC ○

CofE ○

LCDUS ○

○ Pre-Congregation

🙏 Metz, Germany

Chrodegang was born to a noble Frankish family, and rose to become chief minister under the kings Charles Martel and Pepin III. He was named bishop of Metz in 742, at a time when such offices were important administrative and political appointments. Following the murder of Boniface (June 5) he became responsible for church reform throughout the Frankish empire. He introduced Roman liturgy and Gregorian chant to the Frankish church, and is responsible for the Rule of Chrodegang, a guide for how Catholic secular clergy and canons – those priests attached to a diocese – should live in the community.

This 19th-century stained-glass window celebrating Chrodegang's importance as a bishop is in Metz Cathedral.

MARCH 7 · PERPETUA, FELICITY, AND COMPANIONS

STATUS Martyrs

BORN c.180, Carthage, modern Tunisia

DIED 203, Carthage, modern Tunisia

GRC ♣

CofE ♣

LCDUS ♣

OTHER Eastern Orthodox churches, US Episcopal Church, Lutheran Church

⬭ Pre-Congregation

✝ Wild cows, spiked ladder, Perpetua often guarded by a dragon

🙏 Perpetua: death of children, sterility, birth of sons, widows Felicity: cattle, death of children

Perpetua's dreams, concerning dragons and ladders to Heaven, form her symbolic representation.

The religious significance of Perpetua and Felicity has endured for almost two millennia: their feast day can be found in a Roman calendar dating from 354 and their names are still recited in the Roman Canon in Catholic churches today. In fact, four men, Saturus, Saturninus, Secundus, and Revocatus, were martyred with them, but it is the names of the two women that are remembered most vividly.

Both were married catechumens (new initiates to the Church), imprisoned together for their beliefs during the persecutions of Septimius Severus. The 22-year-old Perpetua was a respectable matron with a son only a few months old; Felicity was her slave, heavily pregnant, who gave birth in prison. When the prisoners were finally brought to trial, Perpetua, Felicity, and the others were sentenced to die in the arena, fighting wild animals.

Leopards and bears attacked the men. A heifer tossed Perpetua and Felicity on its horns, goring Perpetua and crushing Felicity. Perpetua is said to have been in such a religious ecstasy that she did not realize that she had been wounded and pulled herself and Felicity to their feet. As the crowd called for their deaths, Perpetua and Felicity, and the surviving men, Saturninus and Revocatus, were killed by gladiators. When the sword intended for Perpetua did not kill her, she guided it to her throat herself.

A modern stained-glass window showing Perpetua and Felicity confronted by the heifer, with a gladiator lurking in the background.

A 19th-century mosaic showing Perpetua and Felicity being awarded the palms of martyrdom.

Perpetua's Dreams

During her imprisonment, Perpetua wrote *Ad Passionem*, describing several significant dreams or visions: in one she followed Saturus up a ladder, guarded by a dragon and covered in swords; in another she saw herself wrestle with an Egyptian, treading on his head. In one she turned into a man. She also saw her brother, Dinocrates, who had died as a child, but was still suffering. After she had prayed for God to help him, she dreamed about her brother again: this time, he was happy. She also described the conditions of her imprisonment, referring to her prison as a 'palace.' This document, completed by a witness to Perpetua's martyrdom, is an important source concerning early Christian women and persecutions, and has also fascinated psychoanalysts.

Date	Name	Status	Venerated	Life
March 8	Felix of Dunwich (of Burgundy) (d.c.647)	Bishop ⬭ Pre-Congregation	Felixstowe, Suffolk, England	Burgundian bishop sent as missionary to East Anglia at behest of King Sigebert of the Angles. Introduced liturgical Gallic practices in his see. Dunwich then a thriving port, but today sunk in the North Sea due to coastal erosion.

MARCH 8 | # JOHN OF GOD

STATUS Priest, Founder

BORN 1495, Montemoro Novo, Portugal

DIED 1550, Granada, Spain

GRC ♣

CofE ♧

LCDUS ♣

OTHER US Episcopal Church, US Evangelical Lutheran Church

♥ 1630

○ 1690

† Crown of thorns, heart, an alms box, holding a pomegranate, two bowls hung around his neck and a basket

🙏 Nurses, hospitals, booksellers, publishers, printers, alcoholics, firefighters, the sick, the dying; Tultepec (Mexico) and Montemoro Novo (Portugal)

As a child, John worked as a shepherd, his mother having died and his father having entered a monastery. As a youth he moved to Spain, joining a band of mercenaries and fighting in several campaigns for Charles V.

At around age 40, he experienced a religious revelation and traveled south, determined to work among Christian slaves in Moorish North Africa, inviting martyrdom. He was deterred by a Franciscan monk, and turned to an itinerant life distributing printed religious texts and images in Andalusia. He finally settled in Granada. He heard a sermon by John of Ávila (May 10), which provoked in him such an extreme fervor for religious penitence that John was committed to an insane asylum.

It would be John of Ávila, once again, who visited and saved him, encouraging John to care for the poor and sick, given his experience with his fellow inmates in the asylum. He went on to establish a hospital in Granada, and formed the Hospitaller Order of St. John of God, which attracted many voluntary supporters. The order today cares for the health of the pope, while the St. John Ambulance service is named after him.

This extraordinarily lifelike bust of St. John by Alonso Cano, c. 1655, is a fine example of devotional Andalusian art. It is made of painted wood with applied fibers representing hair, eyelashes, and a beard. The eyes are of painted glass. It was made about a century after the saint's death.

John's symbol combines a cross with the legendary healing properties of the pomegranate.

A dramatic painting of St. John of God receiving inspiration from an angel, by the Spanish Baroque painter Murillo (c.1617–82).

SPANISH DEVOTIONAL SCULPTURE

A unique style of statuary, a blend of folk art, superb craftsmanship, and high art developed in post-Renaissance Spain, and continues today. The tradition was rooted in the creation of life-sized and lifelike polychromatic representations of Christ, His Passion, and the saints, often to be processed through the streets during fiestas. Separate craftsmen would do the carving and painting. The imagery is often intense and painfully realistic, designed to induce contemplation and awe.

The principal relic of St. Teresa of Ávila is one of her fingers, preserved in the convent at Ávila, Spain. This early 17th-century devotional statue in painted wood (right) was probably created to display the finger during processions, the saint's digit lodging in her locket for the event. Her face is wet with resin tears.

This head of St. Paul in painted wood (right), by Juan Alonso Villabrille y Ron, dates from 1707 and epitomizes the Spanish style of heightened realism. The sculpture's eyes are made of painted glass, the teeth crafted of bone.

MARCH 9 | # FRANCES (FRANCESCA) OF ROME

STATUS Nun, Founder

BORN 1384, Rome, Italy

DIED 1440, Rome, Italy

GRC ♣

CofE ○

LCDUS ♣

○ 1608

✝ In Benedictine robes, often carrying basket of food with guardian angel bearing a branch of oranges or a lamp

🙏 Automobile drivers, cab drivers, death of children, lay people, people ridiculed for their piety, widows

Francesca dei Roffredeschi was born to a noble family in Trastevere, Rome. Although keen to become a nun, she was married at age 13 by her parents to a soldier, who was often away campaigning. They had six children, but lost two to plague, after which Frances adopted a vow of continence, reduced her diet to bread and occasional vegetables, and helped the poor and sick.

It was the time of the Great Schism; the papacy was divided, and Rome was largely in ruins, filled with bandits. In this hostile city, Frances is said to have been guided through the streets by her guardian angel, bearing a lamp. She eventually founded the Benedictine Oblates of Mary. Following her husband's death, Frances became the superior of the community. Possibly due to her restricted diet, Frances is said to have enjoyed ecstasies and visions, and predicted the end of the Schism and the restoration of papal supremacy. Her remains are now near her convent, in the church of Santa Francesca Romana, overlooking the Forum in Rome.

Frances receiving approval for her community from Pope Eugene IV in 1433.

MARCH 10 | # JOHN OGILVIE

STATUS Martyr

BORN 1579, Banffshire, Scotland

DIED 1615, Glasgow, Scotland

GRC ○

CofE ○

LCDUS ○

OTHER By Jesuits

❤ 1929

○ 1976

Upon ascending the scaffold, Ogilvie is said to have thrown his rosary to the assembled crowd. The man who caught it is said to have instantly converted to Catholicism.

Until the accession in 1603 to the English throne of Mary Queen of Scots' son, James VI of Scotland (who then became James I of England), Scotland had remained quite tolerant of Catholicism, despite the growing strength of Calvinism. But King James was now the formal head of the Church of England, and matters of faith became matters of state.

John Ogilvie was a Scottish Calvinist who converted to Catholicism while attending the Scottish College at Louvain in 1596, and he joined the Jesuits in 1608. He returned in disguise to Scotland in 1613, and celebrated Mass in private for Catholic families there, but within a year he was arrested for treason. He was held for eight days and nights. During this time he was tortured and prevented from sleeping, but refused to reveal the names of other Catholics in Scotland. He did not change his mind, even when he was offered his freedom in exchange for a reversion to Protestantism. He was hanged and disemboweled in Glasgow, becoming the only Catholic martyr of the Scottish Reformation.

Date	Name	Status	Venerated	Life
March 9	Dominic Savio (1842–57)	Novice ○ 1954	By Salesians 🙏 Children's choirs, juvenile delinquents, the falsely accused	Son of a blacksmith and early follower of John Bosco (Jan. 31). Noted for his extreme devotion, and encouragement of joint youth activities such as choir singing. Died at only age 14. The youngest non-martyr to have been canonized.
March 11	Eulogius of Córdoba (d.859)	Martyr ○ Pre-Congregation	In Córdoba	One of the Martyrs of Córdoba, Christians who suffered in Moorish Andalusia. Wrote an account of Christians who courted martyrdom by publicly denouncing Islam. Encouraged voluntary martyrdom. Eventually executed for protecting St. Leocritia, a convert from Islam.

THE 40 MARTYRS OF SEBASTE

STATUS Martyrs

BORN Late 3rd century

DIED 320, Sebaste, modern Turkey

GRC ⚪

CofE ⚪

LCDUS ⚪

OTHER Eastern Orthodox churches

⚪ Pre-Congregation

✝ Normally shown naked, en masse, freezing

The Roman emperor Licinius ordered that every Christian in the Roman army should renounce his religion on pain of death, but 40 soldiers at Sebaste in Cappadocia (modern Turkey) refused to sacrifice to Roman idols. In the middle of winter, these soldiers were stripped naked and left overnight on a frozen lake. A heated bathhouse was built at the lake's edge as an incentive to apostatize. One of the 40 did, but he was replaced by one of the men guarding the soldiers who underwent a religious conversion during the night. By morning, all except one, St. Melito, were dead. Melito's mother carried her son behind the cart full of the soldiers' bodies until he died, and then she placed him with the others. The bodies of the soldiers were burned and their ashes thrown into the waters.

This superb bas-relief ivory carving conveys the chilly fate of the soldiers of Sebaste.

Date	Name	Status	Venerated	Life
March 12	Maximilian of Thebeste (d.295)	Martyr ⚪ Pre-Congregation		Son of a Roman army veteran at Thebeste, Numidia, North Africa. Refused to be conscripted and bear arms due to his Christian faith, saying "I cannot fight for this world." Beheaded, and buried at Carthage.
March 12	Angela Salawa (1881–1922)	Virgin ♥ 1991	In Poland	Polish servant girl who took a private vow of chastity and used spare time to perform acts of charity, particularly for the sick and wounded during World War I. Devoted last five years of her life to a solitary existence of prayer and poverty.

MARCH 15 | LONGINUS

STATUS Penitent, Martyr

BORN Early 1st century AD

DIED Mid-1st century AD

GRC ☁

CofE ☁

LCDUS ☁

OTHER Eastern Orthodox churches (Oct. 16); Armenian Apostolic Church (Oct. 22)

○ Pre-Congregation

✝ In centurion's uniform, or on horseback, in knight's armor bearing a spear

Longinus is the unnamed Roman soldier who pierced Christ's side with his spear at the Crucifixion. Although the event is mentioned only in the Gospel of St. John, all three other Gospels describe a centurion who, upon Christ's death, proclaims that He must have been the Son of God.

The spearman and the centurion have become fused in the apocryphal legend of Longinus.

The name Longinus is probably derived from the Greek *longche*, a spear. The story of Longinus remains almost completely legendary and was embellished in many different accounts, including Voragine's *Golden Legend.* It seems that Longinus's revelation on Golgotha immediately converted him, and in some accounts he helped the women depose Christ's body from the Cross, and was involved in washing and anointing Him before burial.

Thereafter, he is variously described, much like St. George, as a traveling Christian knight errant, bearing his spear. In some accounts he was martyred in Cappadocia (modern Turkey).

His cult emerged in the 6th century, as did the cult of the 'Spear of Destiny' in Jerusalem. A number of stories concerning his relics developed during the Middle Ages, and claims to hold them have been made in Mantua, Bologna, Rome, and Prague. The 'Lance of Longinus' is a feature of several Holy Grail legends, and a fragment of a spearhead discovered in the Holy Land during the Crusades is a revered relic in St. Peter's, Rome.

"Truly this was the Son of God."

THE CENTURION,
MATTHEW, 27:54.

In the Holy See the importance of Longinus and his spear was taken sufficiently seriously for Bernini to be commissioned to create a monumental sculpture (right), one of four under the crossing of St. Peter's, Rome.

In Mantegna's Crucifixion *(c. 1500, right) we recognize immediately the scene we are looking at, but who is Longinus? The cut-off spearman in the foreground, or the centurion chatting to onlookers to the right of the Cross? As is usual in Mantegna's paintings, there is a strong narrative quality undercut by an almost cinematic framing and ambiguity.*

Date	Name	Status	Venerated	Life
March 13	Euphrasia of Constantinople (d.c.420)	Virgin ○ Pre-Congregation	Eastern Orthodox churches	Daughter of nobleman, and related to Theodosius I. Although betrothed at age seven, went to Egypt with mother, both becoming nuns. After mother's death, returned to Constantinople to plead with Theodosius to be excused from her marriage contract. Gave her inheritance to charity, to remain a nun. Emperor approved her petition.
March 14	Matilda (Mechtildis, Maud) (c.895–968)	Queen ○ c.970	In Germany	Married to Henry I of Germany, bearing him 5 children. Performed acts of mercy, but criticized and briefly exiled by her sons Otto and Henry. Returned to found three convents and a monastery.

Date	Name	Status	Venerated	Life
March 15	Louise de Marillac (1591–1660)	Widow, Founder ⬭ 1934	By Daughters of Charity In France	Parisian aristocrat, widowed young. Under influence of Vincent de Paul (Sept. 27) trained lower-class widows and girls to care for the poor. Founded influential Daughters of Charity of St. Vincent de Paul (1633).
March 15	Clement Maria Hofbauer (1751–1820)	Priest ⬭ 1909	In Austria 🙏 Vienna	Moravian baker who entered Redemptorist congregation while traveling in southern Europe. Worked for them in Poland until Napoleon dispersed religious communities. Became influential voice in reform and détente with German Protestantism.
March 16	Abraham Kidunaia (possibly 4th century)	⬭ Pre-Congregation	Eastern Orthodox churches	Well-born in either Cappadocia or Mesopotamia (accounts vary). Escaped marriage to live as a hermit. Ordained to undertake conversion of local pagans, but for three years constantly driven back and persecuted. Finally succeeded. Highly venerated in Eastern Orthodox churches.

MARCH 17 | PATRICK

STATUS	Bishop, Missionary
BORN	c.387/390, Britain
DIED	c.463/469, Ireland
GRC	♣
CofE	♣
LCDUS	♣
OTHER	Lutheran Church
⬭	Pre-Congregation
🙏	Engineers; Ireland, New York, Boston, Nigeria

St. Patrick's arms are a simple variant on the saltire design, similar to those of St. Andrew.

Patrick's feast day has become associated with a general celebration of Irishness, when leprechauns, a prevalence of shamrock green, and the generous consumption of Guinness all but overshadow the significance of the saint himself.

The Christianization of Celtic Ireland, an island never colonized by Rome, is generally assumed to have been the work of St. Patrick. Patrick is not merely the patron saint of Ireland alongside Sts. Columba and Brigid (June 9, Feb. 1), but is perhaps the best known of all such national patron saints, his fame exported around the world by generations of Irish migrants. As with many Dark Age saints, historical truth, where it is known at all, is embroidered with more or less fantastical later legends. In St. Patrick's case, the two most enduring such legends were his use of a shamrock — subsequently the country's national symbol — to illustrate the three-in-one nature of the Trinity, and his expulsion of snakes, obvious symbols of evil, from Ireland, though in reality they had never existed there at all. Patrick undoubtedly existed, even if an earlier emissary, Palladius, was the first explicitly Christian missionary in Ireland, sent around 430 by the same pope, Celestine I. The major source of Patrick's life is his own account, *The Confession*, written in Latin, and apparently intended to refute charges that he had used his Irish mission as a means of financial gain.

A Legendary Life

Patrick was born a Christian in Britain, either in Wales or Scotland, and at age 16 was abducted by Irish raiders, who removed him to Ireland. Perhaps symbolically, he was forced to work as a shepherd, in the process not only nurturing a desire to escape, but discovering a latent spirituality. Having duly fled after six years of slavery in Ireland, he traveled to France, where he was ordained and spent some years on missionary work before Celestine I, who declared him a bishop, sent him to Ireland, perhaps in 432, to "gather the Irish into the one fold of Christ."

His work in Ireland necessarily brought Patrick into conflict not just with local chiefs and kings, but also with Druids and other religious leaders. He claimed once to have been beaten, robbed, and set in chains. He asserted not only that he had "baptized thousands of people," but had established numerous chapels and, in particular, convents. No existing religious foundation has ever been shown to have definitely been established by Patrick, however. He is said to have been buried in the grounds of what is now Down Cathedral in Ulster.

The appeal of St. Patrick is especially acute in North America. His feast day is widely celebrated. This stained-glass window of the saint in full bishop's regalia is in the Cathedral of Christ the Light in Oakland, California.

IRISH MISSIONARIES

However energetic St. Patrick's efforts in Ireland, Christianity's early hold there was tenuous. Despite clinging to the margins of Europe in a series of remote and tiny foundations, a distinctive brand of Celtic Christianity not only survived but in time was exported to Britain — chiefly to Scotland and Wales — by a series of intrepid Irish missionaries, among them Columba (June 9) and Aidan (Aug. 31).

The conversion of pagan Northumbria, a kingdom straddling Scotland and England, and the establishment of monasteries in northeast England such as Lindisfarne, Jarrow, and Wearmouth, beginning in 627, was the outcome of these arduous enterprises. From here, Irish missionaries pushed on into England — to Mercia, East Anglia, Essex, and eventually London. Here they were faced with those missionaries, led by Augustine (May 27) who had been charged by Pope Gregory (Sept. 3) with spreading Roman Christianity northward into England. The doctrinal differences between them, chiefly regarding the date of Easter, were settled in Rome's favor at the Synod of Whitby in 644.

Other Irish missionaries traveled further afield still. At the end of the 6th century, Columban (Nov. 23) led evangelizing missions into the Frankish empire. In the 8th century, Irish missionaries ventured deep into Switzerland and Germany, contributing to a general initiative to spread Christianity beyond the limits of what had been the Roman empire.

Patrick allegedly used the trefoil shamrock as a way of illustrating the Holy Trinity.

JOSEPH OF ARIMATHEA AND NICODEMUS

STATUS	Disciples of Jesus
BORN	1st century BC, Palestine
DIED	1st century AD
GRC	♣
CofE	♣
LCDUS	♣
OTHER	Eastern Orthodox churches
⬭	Pre-Congregation

Joseph's arms combine the thorned cross and the Holy Grail. The background of drops of water represents the sweat he collected at the Crucifixion and his tears at the burial of Christ.

The ruins of Glastonbury Abbey, destroyed during the Reformation, remain one of the most mystical sites in England for Druids, New Age mystics, and Christians alike.

Joseph of Arimathea, a Jew of substantial wealth and possibly a member of the Jewish legislative court in Palestine, the Sanhedrin, was a follower of Jesus who gave up the tomb he had planned for himself — carved into rock in the garden of his house — so that it could be used by Christ after His crucifixion. According to John 19:38, Joseph "besought [Pontius] Pilate that he might take away the body of Jesus." This was a highly unusual act given the social disparity between the two: Jesus officially a common criminal; Joseph a figure of considerable standing. Assisted by Nicodemus, a rabbi and also a member of the Sanhedrin, Joseph removed Jesus's body from the Cross, bathed it, and wrapped it in "fine linen," anointing it with myrrh and aloe. A heavy stone was then rolled against the opening of the tomb. This same stone apparently miraculously rolled aside when Jesus, in accordance with the Scriptures, rose on the third day after His Crucifixion.

The Legend of the Holy Grail

An elaborate series of myths grew up much later about Joseph, among them that he had traveled to Britain, eventually reaching Glastonbury in the English West Country, taking with him for safekeeping the Holy Grail. This was the cup that Jesus had used to celebrate the Last Supper and in which, later legends asserted, Joseph had caught the last drops of blood and sweat to fall from the dying Jesus. William of Malmesbury claimed that Joseph was among the 12 evangelists dispatched to Britain by Philip the Apostle (May 3). Writing in the 13th century, the French poet Robert de

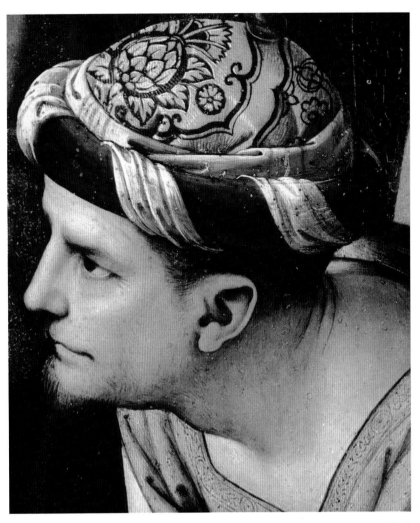

Boron conflated these tales with the burgeoning Arthurian legend, much of which centered on Glastonbury, then, as now, venerated by some as a place of mystical significance. It was also later asserted that Joseph was the Virgin Mary's uncle, and thus Jesus's great-uncle, and had journeyed to Britain with Jesus when He was a boy.

A detail of The Lamentation over the Dead Christ *by Pietro Perugino, painted in 1495 and now in the Pitti Palace in Florence, showing Joseph of Arimathea.*

Date	Name	Status	Venerated	Life
March 18	Cyril of Jerusalem (c.313–86)	Bishop, Doctor of the Church ⬭ Pre-Congregation	GRC, CofE, Eastern Orthodox churches	Bishop of Jerusalem from c.350. Forceful early Christian theologian; consistent opponent of Arianism; enthusiastic supporter of the Nicene belief in the indivisible nature of the Trinity. His learned championship of what would become the orthodox Roman view was of enduring importance. Declared a Doctor of the Church in 1883.

MARCH 19 | JOSEPH

STATUS Foster-Father of
Jesus Christ

BORN 1st century BC,
Bethlehem, modern
Israel

DIED 1st century AD,
Nazareth, modern
Israel

GRC ♣

CofE ♣

LCDUS ♣

OTHER The Coptic Church,
Eastern Orthodox
churches, US
Episcopal Church,
US Evangelical
Lutheran Church

○ Pre-Congregation

† A flowering rod,
sometimes with
a perched dove,
a symbol of his
betrothal to the
Blessed Virgin Mary;
various carpenter's
tools, ladder; often
shown as an old
man with the Christ
Child

🙏 Carpenters and
those who work
with wood, laborers
generally; fatherhood,
pregnant women,
migrants, pioneers,
those in doubt;
patron saint of
innumerable towns,
cities, and countries
including Austria,
Canada, China,
South Korea, Mexico,
Vietnam; patron of
the Universal Church

*Joseph's arms combine a
carpenter's square with the lily
of the Madonna.*

The husband of the Blessed Virgin Mary, and therefore Jesus Christ's foster-father, Joseph appears in the gospels of St. Luke, St. John, and St. Matthew. He is described as being a descendant of the House of David, and a carpenter or builder by trade. Undoubtedly a kindly man, the divine pregnancy of his betrothed was revealed in an angelic vision, and he humbly accepted his future role. After marrying Mary, they moved to Nazareth in Galilee, returning to Bethlehem a few months later to register for a tax census, where Mary gave birth. Aware of his burden of responsibility, he took his wife and her newborn son to Egypt to escape the wrath of Herod. Upon the latter's death, Joseph took his family back to Nazareth where, as a caring and nurturing father, he raised Jesus and trained Him as a carpenter.

Later Traditions

Joseph disappears from the New Testament before Christ's ministry. It is assumed he died of natural causes before Christ's crucifixion, probably at about 45, although he is frequently portrayed as an old man. Details of his biography were fancifully extended in the apocryphal Greek narrative *The History of Joseph the Carpenter*, written some 500 years later. This document appears to have sparked Joseph's cult status in the Egyptian Coptic and Eastern Orthodox churches, although a separate, and still thriving, cult became established in the West around the 10th century.

As the patron saint of workers, Joseph is also celebrated on May 1, Labor Day in many nations.

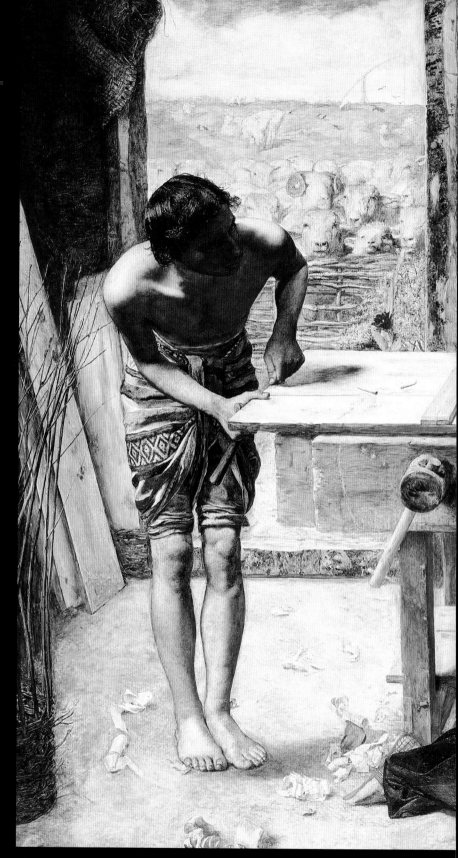

Christ in the House of His Parents *was painted between 1849 and 1850 by the Pre-Raphaelite master John Everett Millais, and is sometimes called simply* The Carpenter's Shop. *Joseph and Mary are shown tending her son, who has a splinter in his hand, presaging His crucifixion, which is also echoed by the cruciform composition, the drops of blood on His foot, and the ladder, wood, nails, and woodworking tools of Joseph's trade. To the right is a young John the Baptist bearing water, reminding us that he will go on to baptize Jesus some years later.*

"Then Joseph, being raised from sleep, did as the angel of the Lord
had bidden him, and took unto him his wife: And knew her not till
she had brought her firstborn son; and he called his name Jesus."

MARCH 19 | CLEMENT OF DUNBLANE

STATUS Bishop
BORN c.1200, Scotland
DIED 1258, Dunblane, Scotland
GRC ☁
CofE ☁
LCDUS ☁
OTHER In Scotland

Clement, made bishop of Dunblane in central Scotland in 1233, was the first Dominican bishop in Britain. He had joined the Dominicans, themselves founded only in 1216, in Paris in 1219. The order was actively wooed by Alexander II of Scotland, anxious to expand Christianity across his still feebly ruled realm and seeing a vigorous new Christian order as a possible means of doing so. But Dunblane itself had not only had no bishop since 1230, it was among the most impoverished dioceses in the country, its meager revenues illicitly siphoned off by local magnates. The situation was so desperate that Clement was obliged to travel to Rome in 1237 to ask Pope Gregory IX for his personal help. That this paid off is made plain by the fact that by about 1240 Clement was able to begin work on what is today Dunblane Cathedral.

Clement's success at Dunblane was such that, by 1247, he had been appointed bishop of the even more impoverished bishopric of Argyll, in reality a vaguely defined area stretching over the highlands and islands of the west coast and only nominally subject to royal rule. Clement also worked actively to secure the canonization in 1250 of the 11th-century queen of Scotland, Margaret (Nov. 16).

By Clement's death in 1258, it seems likely that the choir, nave, and chapter house of Dunblane Cathedral had largely been completed. Clement is buried in the choir. By 1600, the church had fallen into disrepair. Today's sturdy structure was largely rebuilt in the 19th century. Since the Reformation it has been a Presbyterian church and, as it has no bishop, is not technically a cathedral.

Date	Name	Status	Venerated	Life
March 19	Alkmund of Derby (c.770–c.800)	⬭ Pre-Congregation	⚲ Derby, England	Son of a Northumbrian king, Alchred, who was deposed and killed c.775 by a rival, Eardwulf. Alkmund, known for his charity to the poor and orphaned, also murdered by Eardwulf after attempting to wrest the throne back from him. Buried first in Derby, then in Shrewsbury, and finally in Derby again (1140). It was claimed his remains exuded perfume when returned to Derby. Numerous miracles associated with his relics.

MARCH 20 · CUTHBERT

STATUS Bishop
BORN c.634, Scotland
DIED 687, Farne, England
GRC ○
CofE ♣
LCDUS ○
OTHER US Episcopal Church
♏ Northumbria

Cuthbert's arms are linked to those of the city of Durham, England, with the addition of a unique form of a fleurée cross.

Cuthbert enjoys a reputation for sanctity and miracle working unmatched by any other early medieval British saint. In part this was a result of a sympathetic account of his life written in the century after his death by Bede (May 25). Cuthbert, part mystic, part man of the world, had a kind of charismatic saintliness capable of inspiring immense devotion among his followers.

Cuthbert was a product of the Irish Christian tradition exported to Scotland and thence to England, above all by Aidan (Aug. 31), beginning in about 635. Appropriately, it was a vision of St. Aidan being carried to Heaven that inspired Cuthbert, tending sheep at night as a boy, to become a monk at the monastery at Melrose in Scotland.

In 664, Cuthbert was made prior of Melrose. This was a critical year in the development of early Christian Britain. Put simply, the question was whether Irish Christian practices or those of Rome should have priority. The differences were not great — how to calculate the date of Easter, for example — but they were real enough and were debated at the Synod of Whitby in 664. Rome prevailed. If this was a defeat for the likes of Cuthbert, it was one taken in excellent spirit. Both at Melrose, then at Lindisfarne, where Cuthbert was made prior the same year, he reconciled his fellow monks to their new doctrinal practices with characteristic patience, humility, and tact.

In 676, Cuthbert, long since given to standing knee-deep in the sea and declaiming psalms, left Lindisfarne to become a hermit, eventually settling on the tiny island of Farne, at one with the seabirds and the grey wastes of the North Sea. Though he reluctantly agreed to become bishop of Lindisfarne in 685, by the following year he was back on Farne, again a hermit, where he died.

The Relics of St. Cuthbert

Numerous miracles were ascribed to Cuthbert during his life. Vastly more were ascribed to the tomb and relics of the 'Wonder-Worker of England,' as he became known. He was buried first at Lindisfarne. In 875, fearful of yet another round of Viking invasions, the monks on the island removed his body and, eight years later, re-buried it at Chester-le-Street. In the late 10th century his relics were taken to Ripon and from there to Durham, where a church, forerunner of today's great Norman cathedral, was begun over the site of his new tomb. In 1069, as William the Conqueror laid waste the north of England, Cuthbert's remains were removed again before, finally, being brought back to Durham in 1104. There they remained, the focus of an intense cult, until the cathedral was plundered in 1542 during the Reformation. Though a body was discovered at Durham in 1827 that many assumed was St. Cuthbert, no positive identification has been possible.

A 12th-century fresco of Cuthbert in Durham Cathedral. Cuthbert's tomb was second only to that of Thomas Beckett (Dec. 29) as a place of pilgrimage in medieval England.

Lindisfarne, Holy Island, accessible only at low water, is among the most hauntingly beautiful of England's Christian sites.

Date	Name	Status	Venerated	Life
March 19	Andrea Gallerani (d.c.1236)	Founder		Devoted to 'penitential acts of mercy' after he killed a blasphemer, for which he was banished from his native Siena. Allowed to return, founded a hospital and order, the Brothers of Mercy, which expired in 1308. A new order, the Brothers of Our Lady of Mercy, established in 1839, was dedicated largely to welfare of prisoners.
March 20	John of Parma (1209–89)	Priest ♥ 1777	By Franciscans	Renowned scholar and preacher. Minister General of Franciscans (or Friars Minor) 1247–57. Task was reform of the order, rent by divisions since death of St. Francis (1226). To this end, visited England, France, and Spain. Having resigned his post, ended his days as a hermit.

THOMAS CRANMER

STATUS	Bishop, Protestant Martyr
BORN	1489, Nottinghamshire, England
DIED	1556, Oxford, England
GRC	♧
CofE	♣
LCDUS	♧

Thomas Cranmer was one of the most distinguished and able churchmen in Tudor England. To a huge extent, the Church of England was his creation.

As archbishop of Canterbury under Henry VIII, he was responsible for arranging for Henry's divorce from his first wife, Catherine of Aragon. He not only provided the legal and theological justifications for Henry's renunciation of papal authority, but also laid the groundwork for the establishment of a new, reformed Anglican Church, with the monarch as its head. In fact, with Henry remaining essentially a practicing Catholic until his death — his defiance of Rome was a matter of state, not of personal piety — the scope for Cranmer to introduce more radical Protestant reforms was limited. By contrast, Henry's heir, Edward VI, age nine on his accession in 1547, was a fervent, not to say rabid, Protestant. Under him, Cranmer was able to recast the forms of Anglican worship almost entirely, above all with the introduction in 1549 of *The Book of Common Prayer*, written by Cranmer himself. Its use was compulsory.

The Catholic Revival

The accession of Henry's elder daughter, Mary, after Edward's death in 1553 from tuberculosis, brought this ambitious enterprise to a shuddering halt. Determined to reintroduce not just Catholicism but to reinstate the position of the pope, Mary (r.1553–58) had Cranmer arrested almost as soon as she came to the throne. He was imprisoned for two years before being tried for heresy and treason and burned at the stake at Oxford in March 1556.

Cranmer had initially attempted to reconcile himself to Mary's re-introduction of Catholicism. On the day of his death, he defiantly reasserted his Protestantism. Two years later, after Mary's death and the accession of Elizabeth I, Protestantism was restored.

However practiced — and ambitious — a courtier, Cranmer, seen here in a 1545 portrait by Gerlach Flicke, was a convinced Protestant, his espousal of the new forms of worship shaped by extensive contacts with reformers elsewhere in Europe.

THE MARIAN MARTYRS

The troubled reign of Mary I of England *(left)* has generally been seen as one of fanatical Catholic persecution of innocent, principled English Protestants. This view was crucially reinforced by the publication in 1563, five years after Mary's death, of John Foxe's *Acts and Monuments*, popularly known as 'Foxe's Book of Martyrs.' It was the publishing sensation of the age, its crude but explicit woodcuts of the deaths of the so-called Marian martyrs – among them Cranmer, as well as Hugh Latimer and Nicholas Ridley (Oct. 16), respectively the bishops of Worcester and London – definitively demonizing Mary in the later Protestant national imagination. The book was clearly propaganda. Foxe double-counted some of the victims. He made no mention of those executed no less horribly under Henry VIII. But its impact was enormous. In reality, by the standards of the mass executions of those deemed 'heretics' by either Catholics or Protestants elsewhere in continental Europe, there was little unusual in the deaths of the 284 martyrs executed under Mary. In addition, the more vindictive aspects of the program were largely driven forward by the new archbishop of Canterbury, Reginald Pole, rather than the queen herself.

Successive editions of 'Foxe's Book of Martyrs' were illustrated with lurid woodcuts.

MARCH 21 | NICHOLAS VON FLÜE

STATUS Hermit

BORN 1417, Sachseln, Switzerland

DIED 1487, Ranft, Switzerland

GRC ☁

CofE ☁

LCDUS ☁

❤ 1669

⬭ 1947

🙏 Switzerland

In 1467, at the age of 50, Nicholas, married and the father of 10 children, with a notable career as a soldier and civic leader in the still emerging Swiss Confederation behind him, declared himself a hermit. For 19 years, it is said, St. Nicholas, 'Brother Klaus' to the Swiss, survived exclusively on the Eucharist, the wafer-like hosts distributed at Holy Communion. His reputation for sanctity grew to such an extent that, with the support of the pope, his cell at Ranft in central Switzerland became a recognized place of pilgrimage as well as a stop on one of the many roads to Santiago. But his chief claim to fame came in 1481, when he successfully brokered a compromise deal between those rural Swiss cantons determined that the Swiss Confederation should not be expanded and the cities of Zürich and Lucerne, equally determined that it should – it was a dispute that had posed a serious prospect of civil war.

St. Nicholas is consulted by a priest, Heini am Grund, desperate for help in solving the crisis that threatened to tear the country apart in 1481. The illustration is from the Amtliche Luzerner Chronicle *of 1513.*

Date	Name	Status	Venerated	Life
March 22	Clemens August Graf von Galen (1878–1946)	Bishop, Cardinal ❤ 2005	In Germany	Count of Galen; ordained in 1904. Appointed bishop of Münster in 1933. Launched persistent and outspoken attacks on Nazi regime. Also vehement critic of Soviet Union under Stalin. In February 1946, elevated to College of Cardinals by Pope Pius XII.

MARCH 23 — TURIBIUS (TORIBIO) OF MOGROVEJO

STATUS Bishop
BORN 1538, Mayorga, Spain
DIED 1606, Saña, Peru
GRC ♣
CofE ♢
LCDUS ♣
OTHER In Peru
⊖ 1726

Toribio Alfonso de Mogrovejo, with Rose of Lima (Aug. 23), whom he confirmed, was one of the first two Catholic South American saints. He was a lawyer at the University of Salamanca whose evident abilities were such that he was first appointed Grand Inquisitor of Spain, and then, though not even a priest, archbishop of Lima in Peru. He arrived in South America in 1581 after having been hurriedly ordained. In what was still a recent as well as a remote Spanish colony, he immediately brought order to the Church there, as well as proving a stern defender of native rights in the face of widespread Spanish oppression. In 1591, he established the first seminary in the New World and, in 1604, he began the building of the cathedral in Lima.

MARCH 24 — OSCAR ROMERO

STATUS Bishop, Martyr
BORN 1917, Ciudad Barrios, El Salvador
DIED 1980, San Salvador, El Salvador
GRC ♢
CofE ♣
LCDUS ♢
OTHER In El Salvador

Oscar Romero, appointed archbishop of San Salvador in 1977, was the most high-profile victim of the struggle between Left and Right that destabilized so much of Central America from the early

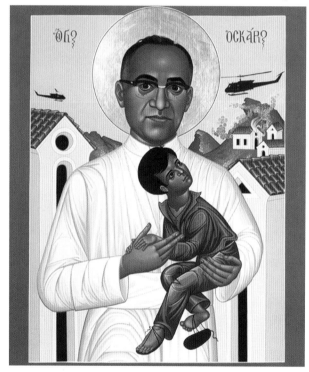

American military aid, Romero contended, would "undoubtedly sharpen the injustice and the repression inflicted on the people, whose struggle has often been for their most basic human rights."

1980s onward. On March 24, 1980, while conducting Mass in San Salvador, he was shot and killed by a lone gunman. The shock of his death sparked a civil war that lasted 12 years and left an estimated 75,000 dead. Even at the archbishop's funeral, attended by perhaps 250,000, as many as 50 people were killed as shots, said to have been fired by security forces, rang out from the roof of the National Palace.

It was not surprising that the Church would be sucked into so wide-ranging a conflict. Even during the three years when Romero was archbishop, six Catholic priests had been murdered. Nine months after Romero's death, four American nuns were raped and murdered by a death squad (Dec. 2). Yet to many in the Salvadorean church, the appointment of Romero as archbishop had been a matter of dismay. He was a distinctly conservative priest, his views anathema to the Left-leaning advocates of Liberation Theology, who were widespread in many parts of Latin America. Yet Romero, who had been ordained in Rome in 1942, would prove himself a staunch opponent of oppression in his country. It was his appeal in February 1980 to the American president, Jimmy Carter, to halt military aid to the government of El Salvador that led directly to his death. In 1997, a campaign for his canonization was launched. Pope John Paul II declared him a Servant of God. Romero was included as one of the ten 20th-century martyrs whose statues, unveiled in 1998, stand above the west door of Westminster Abbey in London.

MARCH 24 — CATHERINE OF SWEDEN

STATUS Abbess
BORN c.1331, Sweden
DIED 1381, Vadstena, Sweden
GRC ♢
CofE ♢
LCDUS ♢
OTHER In Sweden
🙏 Miscarriages; against abortion

Catherine of Sweden, sometimes known as Catherine of Vadstena, was the daughter of St. Bridget, founder in around 1350 of the Brigittine Order of nuns (July 23). Though Catherine was married at age 13 to a German nobleman, husband and wife both took vows of chastity. In 1348, she journeyed to Rome with her mother. The two women remained there for the next 25 years, living in extreme poverty, interrupted only by a pilgrimage to the Holy Land in 1372. On her mother's death in 1373, Catherine returned to Sweden, bringing her mother's body with her for burial at the convent Bridget had founded at Vadstena, and of which Catherine was now made head. She returned to Rome the next year to argue for her mother's canonization. Though Innocent VIII gave permission for Catherine's veneration in 1484, she was never formally beatified, the process being halted by the spread of the Reformation within Sweden.

MARCH 25

THE ANNUNCIATION OF THE BLESSED VIRGIN MARY

One of the symbols associated with the Blessed Virgin Mary as the Mother of God is the Mater Dei, expressed in an abbreviated form.

The Annunciation of the Blessed Virgin Mary, or more commonly simply the Annunciation, is one of the 12 Great Feasts of the Christian year. It commemorates the miraculous appearance of the Archangel Gabriel in Nazareth to Mary, the future mother of Jesus. In the only biblical account of the event, that of Luke, Gabriel greeted a startled Mary. He then explained that she would give birth to a son and that: "thou shalt call his name Jesus. He shall be great, and shall be called the Son of the Highest; and the Lord God shall give unto him the throne of his father David." To her reply that "I know not a man," meaning that she was a virgin, the Archangel explained that hers was an immaculate conception, made possible by the grace of God and of the Holy Spirit. Mary replied modestly: "Behold the handmaid of the Lord; be it unto me according to thy word."

The significance of the Annunciation in Christian theology is hard to overstate. As the tender embodiment of motherhood, the Blessed Virgin Mary rapidly became the most revered of all the major saints. By the same token, the Annunciation itself, the moment when her divine role was revealed to her, became, with the Nativity and the Crucifixion, one of the most important subjects of Gothic and Renaissance art.

Perugino's Annunciation of 1489 encapsulates the conventional late 15th-century Italian view of the event: a demure Mary, a kneeling Gabriel offering her lilies, symbols of purity, a hovering dove to represent the Holy Spirit, and, over all, a benign God encircled by cherubs, the whole in an idealized architectural setting, itself placed in a haunting landscape.

"Hail, thou that art highly favored, the Lord is with thee; blessed art thou among women."

LUKE 1:28.

Date	Name	Status	Venerated	Life
March 24	Walter Hilton (1340–96)	Mystic	CofE	English Augustinian abbot. Writings, specifically *Scala Perfectionis* or 'Ladder of Perfection,' reveal a profoundly spiritual mystic, concerned above all to come closer to God through prayer and contemplation. Wrote most lucid and highly influential treatises on interior life of Middle Ages.

MARCH 26 | LUDGER (LIUDGER) OF MÜNSTER

STATUS Bishop, Missionary
BORN c.744, Zuilen, Netherlands
DIED 809, Westphalia, Germany
GRC ☁
CofE ☁
LCDUS ☁
OTHER In the Low Countries and Saxony
⊘ Pre-Congregation
✝ Flanked by swans; holding a book or cathedral
🙏 East Frisia, Münster

Ludger was a missionary to Frisia and Saxony in northwest Germany, areas outside the Roman empire and, in the 8th century, still fiercely resistant to Christianity. In 753, he met Boniface (June 5) and, after studying under Gregory at Utrecht and Alcuin at York (May 20), he was ordained in 777 in Cologne before beginning an arduous seven-year missionary program in Frisia, which ended with only partial success. He visited Rome before retiring to Monte Cassino. In 787, he returned to Frisia, this time with more success. In 793, Charlemagne charged him with missionary work in Saxony. It was now that Ludger began what would become Münster Cathedral (*münster* means monastery),

as well as a number of other churches. In about 803, he was also instrumental in the establishment of an early convent in Westphalia, at Nottuln, headed by his sister, St. Gerburgis. At one point he was charged by Charlemagne with excessively distributing alms to the detriment of funds meant for building churches. By 805, he had also been made bishop of Münster.

MARCH 27 | RUPERT OF SALZBURG

STATUS Bishop, Missionary
BORN c.660
DIED 710, Salzburg, Austria
GRC ☁
CofE ☁
LCDUS ☁
OTHER Eastern Orthodox churches
⊘ Pre-Congregation
✝ With a container of salt
🙏 Salzburg

Rupert of Salzburg was a member of the Merovingian royal family and, until around 697, bishop of Worms in Germany. He was then sent to Regensburg in Bavaria as a missionary. There he won numerous converts, among them Duke Theodo of Bavaria, who in around 700 granted Rupert land in the ruined Roman city of Juvavum, modern Salzburg. There he began the building of the church and abbey of St. Peter, today the site of Salzburg Cathedral, a monastery at Mönchberg, and Nonnburg Convent.

Rupert promoted the mining of salt in the region to support the religious houses and his missionary work.

Today's Baroque cathedral in Salzburg, built between 1614 and 1628 by an Italian architect, Santino Solari, is a far cry from the simple structure begun by Bishop Rupert. But the enduring faith it represents makes clear how deeply rooted is Christianity in the region, as it also is across much of southern Germany.

Date	Name	Status	Venerated	Life
March 26	Didacus of Cadiz (1743–1801)	Capuchin Preacher ❤ 1894	By Capuchins	Known as the 'Dunce of Cadiz' in his childhood due to his slowness at school. Once ordained as Capuchin monk, proved to have remarkable gifts as a preacher. Traveled widely across Spain, drawing ever-larger crowds; increasingly admired for his evident simplicity and unquenchable faith.
March 26	Harriet Monsell (1811–83)	Abbess	CofE	With Canon T. T. Carter, founded Community of St. John the Baptist that also supported hospitals and orphanages. Opened the Clewer House of Mercy outside Windsor, England, to care for fallen women. Became a Religious (1881).

MARCH 28 — SIXTUS III

STATUS Pope
BORN 4th century, Italy
DIED 440, Rome, Italy
GRC ☁
CofE ☁
LCDUS ☁
◯ Pre-Congregation

Sixtus III was pope not merely at a time of doctrinal dispute, chiefly over the nature of the Virgin Mary, but when papal authority was under threat from a number of directions. He succeeded in significantly strengthening the latter, above all in Illyria in Greece, which the Eastern emperors had long sought to bring under their direct control. His acceptance of the Council of Ephesus of 431 made it clear that the Virgin was henceforth to be regarded as the Mother of God and not merely as the Mother of Christ. It was in commemoration of her new status that Sixtus III began the construction of Santa Maria Maggiore, one of the four papal basilicas.

As one of the four most important churches in Rome, Santa Maria Maggiore has necessarily been extensively remodeled since the 5th century. The façade dates from the early 18th century; towering over it is a 14th-century bell tower, the tallest in the city.

MARCH 28 — PATRICK FORBES

STATUS Bishop
BORN 1564, Aberdeenshire, Scotland
DIED 1635, Aberdeen, Scotland
GRC ☁
CofE ☁
LCDUS ☁
OTHER In Scotland

As uncompromisingly puritanical as he may have been, even Forbes's opponents recognized both his piety and his substantial theological learning. This is a contemporary portrait.

Patrick Forbes, ferociously puritanical, was among the most influential early post-Reformation churchmen in Scotland, virulently anti-Catholic and a fearsomely effective preacher. He was ordained only in 1612 at age 48. Within six years he had been appointed bishop of Aberdeen. He continued his anti-papist diatribes – in 1613 he had contended that the Roman church had been hopelessly corrupted by the avarice of its bishops at almost the moment it was declared the official religion of the Roman empire by Constantine in 313. Forbes also largely reorganized Aberdeen University. This was highly significant: Aberdeen became a key center of opposition to attempts by Charles I (Jan. 30) and his archbishop of Canterbury, William Laud (Jan. 10), to impose uniformity of worship across England and Scotland. It was this opposition, in the form of the 'Great Covenant,' that led in 1639 to an invasion of England by a Covenanter army, in effect sparking the English Civil War.

Date	Name	Status	Venerated	Life
March 27	Francesco Faà di Bruno (1825–88)	Priest, Founder ❤ 1988	Roman Catholic Church	Ordained only in 1876 at age 51 after Pope Pius IX intervened on his behalf, overriding opposition of archbishops who objected to any priest entering Holy Orders so late in life. Born into aristocracy; trained first as a soldier, then as a mathematician and astronomer, in Paris, then in Turin where, already a priest, later became professor of mathematics. Spent much of life working with the oppressed, above all domestic servants and prostitutes, founding Society of St. Zita, which opened hostels for them.

MARCH 30 — JOHN CLIMACUS

STATUS Abbot, Hermit
BORN c.579, Syria
DIED 649, Mount Sinai, Egypt
GRC ⬡
CofE ⬡
LCDUS ⬡
OTHER Eastern Orthodox churches
⬭ Pre-Congregation
✝ Abbot's crosier

John Climacus joined St. Catherine's Monastery on Mt. Sinai — one of the two oldest monasteries in the world — at age 16. In his fifties, he removed himself from the monastery, living instead at its foot as a hermit, in the process becoming one of the great scholars of the early Church. His reputation for sanctity was such that he was eventually persuaded to return to the monastery as abbot, or 'igumen' as it is known in the Orthodox Church. He remained at the monastery for a further four years before resuming his life as a hermit and preparing himself for death.

He is best known as the author of two theological works, *The Ladder of Divine Ascent* and *To the Pastor*, both still widely read in the Orthodox world.

The Ladder of Divine Ascent, here depicted in a 12th-century icon, describes the attainment of spirituality in 30 steps, the final rung of the ladder being union with Christ, who can be seen welcoming those who have reached the summit. At any stage, devils are on hand to pluck the unworthy from the ladder. John Climacus is shown with monks behind him (bottom right).

MARCH 31 — JOHN DONNE

STATUS Priest, Poet
BORN 1572, London, England
DIED 1631, London, England
GRC ⬡
CofE ♣
LCDUS ⬡
OTHER US Episcopal Church, US Evangelical Lutheran Church

John Donne is known chiefly as one of the principal Metaphysical poets of the late Elizabethan and Jacobean periods in England. Despite being born into a strongly Catholic family, from 1615 he was an Anglican priest, and from 1621 until his death held the prestigious position of Dean of St. Paul's Cathedral in London. The extent to which his conversion was a purely pragmatic response to the increased persecution of Catholics — in 1593, for example, his brother, Henry, had been tortured for sheltering a Catholic priest — or the result of more deeply held doctrinal beliefs, has always been hard to say. On the other hand, his increasing focus on death no less than his interest in mysticism seem to have driven his last, gloomy years closer to a belief in traditional High Church teachings. He was acutely conscious of the impermanence of life.

Donne had this engraving of himself wearing his death shroud made shortly before his demise. It was how he expected himself to appear when roused from his tomb at the Last Judgment. It hung on the wall of his study.

Date	Name	Status	Venerated	Life
March 29	Jonas and Barachisius (d.327)	Monks, Martyrs ⬭ Pre-Congregation	Eastern Orthodox churches	Interceded on behalf of Christians persecuted by King Sapor of Persia. Arrested but refused to renounce their faith. Barachisius killed when pitch poured down his throat. Jonas beaten with clubs; stake thrust through his abdomen; left overnight in freezing water; crushed to death in wine press.
March 30	Peter Regulatus (1390–1456)	Monk ⬭ 1746	By Franciscans	Franciscan from an early age. Devoted life to poverty and penance. Said to have lived on only bread and water and observed Lent nine times every year. Became abbot of Franciscan monasteries at Tribulos (1422) and Aguilera (1442). When his body exhumed in 1782, found not to have decayed.

ANNE FRANK – VOICE OF THE HOLOCAUST

Anne Frank remains perhaps the most moving embodiment of the Holocaust, a deeply human, always engaging, and precociously self-aware Jewish girl. She was born a German in Frankfurt am Main in 1929. Her family moved to the Netherlands in 1933, and as a result of Nazi anti-Semitic policies they became officially stateless. She was only 13 when her family was forced into hiding in Nazi-occupied Amsterdam, only 15 when she died in Bergen-Belsen concentration camp. Her memory is preserved in the diary she kept of the 25 months the family endured in a cramped three-story hiding place above her father's offices in Amsterdam. As Nazi round-ups of Jews intensified, the Franks had fled – father Otto, mother Edith, and daughters Margot and Anne – to their 'secret annex,' or *Achterhuis*, on July 6, 1942. A week later they were joined by the van Pels family – Herman, Auguste, and their teenage son Peter. In November, they were joined by an eighth member, a dentist, Fritz Pfeffer.

> "One single Anne Frank moves us more than the countless others who suffered just as she did but whose faces have remained in the shadows."
>
> PRIMO LEVI.

Anne's diary, given to her on her 13th birthday, less than a month before going into hiding, meticulously records the increasing strains of this unnatural existence, none of the group able to venture outside, being given diminishing amounts of food by the six Dutch men and women who sustained them (and provided their only link with the world), and the growing fear of eventual discovery and death. Throughout, Anne's own response to this nightmare – her hopes of becoming a writer, her frequently tense relationship with her mother, her growing relationship with her sister, her irritation with Pfeffer – are recorded in remarkable and, in retrospect, harrowing detail. The last entry is dated August 1, 1944. Three days later, they were arrested.

That the Franks were betrayed is clear. By whom has never been established but, on August 4, 1944, all the members of the *Achterhuis* were rounded up and taken to various holding camps before being transported in September to Auschwitz in Poland. In late October, Anne, her sister, and Auguste van Pels, all three severely ill, were then moved to Bergen-Belsen concentration camp in Saxony. Anne's parents remained in Auschwitz, where her mother died of starvation. Her father survived. Anne was last reported in Bergen-Belsen as 'bald, shivering, and emaciated.' Margot seems simply to have faded away. Anne probably died on March 31, 1945, from a typhus epidemic that carried off 17,000 of the prisoners. The foundation set up by her father distributes funds to many charities.

The memorial statue to Anne Frank stands outside the house where the Frank family hid in Amsterdam.

Anne's diary, rescued from the Achterhuis by Miep Gies, one of the Dutch women who had sustained the family, was returned to her father in 1945. It was published first in Holland, in 1947. It appeared in Germany and France in 1950, in Britain and the United States in 1952.

Date	Name	Status	Venerated	Life
March 30	Ludovico of Casoria (1814–85)	Monk, Founder ♥ 1993	In Naples, Florence, Assisi, Italy	Franciscan monk. Devoted life to poor and dispossessed. In Naples, started two schools for African children and dispensary for the poor, as well as institutions for orphans, the deaf and mute, and the elderly. Founded Gray Friars of Charity (1859), and Franciscan Sisters of St. Elizabeth (1862).
March 31	Stephen of Mar Saba (c.725–94)	Monk, Hermit ○ Pre-Congregation	Eastern Orthodox churches	At age 10 admitted to monastery of Mar Saba (St. Sabas) in Palestine, then ruled by his uncle, St. John of Damascus. Ordained 14 years later. A 'brilliant light' said to have emanated from his person when he celebrated Mass. Became hermit devoted to prayer and caring for animals. Doves and deer were claimed to feed from his hand.

APRIL

A month inaugurated by an outburst of practical jokes on April Fools' Day, April's name derives from the Latin *aperire*, to open, reflecting the period when many plants spring into bloom. April is most frequently when the festival of Easter occurs, the most important event in the liturgical calendar, commemorating the Passion and celebrating Christ's Resurrection.

The important weeklong Jewish festival of Passover also usually occurs in April, starting on the first full moon after the vernal equinox in the Hebrew month of Nisan.

In England, April 23 commemorates the national patron, Saint George. Although it is not a public holiday, his distinctive flag of a red cross on a white background is flown from many churches and other buildings. The flag is also traditionally flown on English churches on other major religious feast days.

Christ's agonizing death on the Cross on Good Friday is portrayed here on the Sayen Panel (1470) by the unnamed German Master of the Story of St. George. The attendants at the scene are neatly divided, with saints on the left (the Blessed Virgin Mary, John, and Mary Magdalene), and the noble patron of the painting kneeling in prayer.

APRIL 2 | FRANCIS OF PAOLA

STATUS Friar, Founder

BORN 1416, Paola, Italy

DIED 1507, Plessis, France

GRC ♣

CofE ♧

LCDUS ♣

OTHER By Franciscans

⬭ 1519

✝ Usually depicted with staff and cloak

⚓ Boatmen, mariners, naval officers; Calabria, Italy

A pious and abstemious friar who founded the Order of Minims, Francis was born in Paola, southern Italy, and was educated by the Franciscans. When still a baby, he had suffered a condition that threatened the sight in one of his eyes, and his frantic parents sought the intercession of Francis of Assisi (Oct. 4), vowing that their son would spend an entire year in a Franciscan convent – the baby was immediately cured. At age 13 Francis entered a convent of the Franciscan Order. Following pilgrimages to Assisi and Rome, he lived in seclusion, giving himself up to prayer and mortification. One story describes how, in 1464, a boatman refused to ferry him across the Strait of Messina to Sicily. Francis laid his cloak on the water, tied one end to his staff to make a sail, and navigated his own way across.

By the age of 20 he had acquired two followers and formed a movement that was to become the Hermits of St. Francis of Assisi, later renamed the Minim Friars. The Minim Friars led a harsh and severe life, seeking poverty, emphasizing penance, charity, chastity, and humility, and abstaining from meat. Francis went on to found new monasteries throughout Calabria and Sicily, as well as establishing a convent of nuns.

Francis was famous for miraculous healings and prophesies; he is said to have foretold the capture of Otranto by Ottoman Turks in 1480, and its subsequent recovery.

Francis and France

King Louis XI of France begged the increasingly celebrated saint to attend him at his last illness, and the pope ordered Francis to travel to Plessis. Francis remained at the French court, much revered by Charles VIII, Louis's successor, and subsequently by Louis XII. Despite his eagerness to return to Italy, Francis remained in Plessis, spending the last three months of his life in total solitude, preparing for death. He was buried in Plessis and when, in 1562, a group of Huguenots broke open his tomb, they found an incorrupt body. They dragged it out, burned it, and scattered the bones, although some relics were recovered.

Francis of Paola in many ways represents the ideal of the mendicant Franciscan friar, humble, self-denying, and devout, yet capable of inspiring awe and reverence among the upper echelons of society. He became a popular subject for Catholic artists such as Prospero Fontana (c.1512–97) during the early Counter-Reformation period.

Date	Name	Status	Venerated	Life
April 1	Hugh of Grenoble (d.1132)	Bishop ⬭ 1134	In Grenoble, France	Brilliant and capable man; unanimously elected bishop of Grenoble at age 27. Appalled by disorder of his diocese, devoted life to reform of both clergy and laity. In latter years suffered a painful, chronic illness with great fortitude.
April 1	Frederick Denison Maurice (1805–72)	Priest, Educator, Founder	CofE	Born a Unitarian. Attended Cambridge University; ordained in Anglican Church (1834). Prolific writer and editor. Founded Queen's College, London, for women (1848), and the Working Men's College (1854). Socialist leanings made him controversial figure.

APRIL 3 | MARY OF EGYPT

STATUS Penitent, Hermit

BORN c.344, Egypt

DIED c.421, Sinai Desert, Palestine

GRC ☁

CofE ☁

LCDUS ☁

OTHER Eastern Orthodox churches (April 1)

○ Pre-Congregation

✝ Depicted as naked, grey-haired, being handed a cloak by Zosimas; often shown with three loaves of bread

⚭ Chastity, fevers, skin diseases; deliverance from demons, temptations of the flesh

The starkness of Mary's 47 years of penitence in the desert attracted Counter-Reformation artists such as José de Ribera (1591–1652), although here, with her simple crusts and evident contemplation of mortality, she could be a contemporary peasant from southern Italy.

Scenes from the life of Mary of Egypt in an elaborate 16th-century Eastern Orthodox panel (right).

A celebrated penitent and hermit, what we know of Mary of Egypt is derived from a biography of her by the 6th-century Patriarch of Jerusalem, St. Sophronius. Mary's later piety was thrown into sharp relief by the dissolution of her early life. Born in Egypt, Mary ran away from home at age 12, and went to the cosmopolitan city of Alexandria, where she is said to have worked as a prostitute. After 17 years of this life she joined a pilgrimage to Jerusalem for the Feast of the Exaltation of the Holy Cross. This was not the journey of a devout believer – she saw the trip as an ideal opportunity to exploit fellow pilgrims. She paid for the journey by offering sexual favors to fellow travelers.

However, when she attempted to enter the Church of the Holy Sepulchre in Jerusalem she felt that she was being held back by a mysterious force, and concluded that it was her impurity that was barring her entry. When she prayed for forgiveness and vowed to become an ascetic, she was able to enter. Praying in front of an icon, she heard a voice telling her "If you cross the Jordan, you will find glorious rest." She hurried to the Monastery of St. John the Baptist on the banks of the river, and received absolution and Holy Communion. The next morning she crossed the river, carrying just three loaves of bread, and vowed to spend the rest of her life as a hermit in the wilderness.

A Desert Encounter

As an old woman Mary encountered St. Zosimas of Palestine, who had traveled to the desert for a period of fasting and contemplation. She was naked, wild-haired, emaciated, and barely recognizable as a human being, yet she appeared to know Zosimas, who handed her a cloak, and she told him her life story. She asked if she could meet him on the river Jordan on Holy Thursday the following year, so that she could take Holy Communion. When he saw her on the opposite bank, she walked on the surface of the water to reach him. She asked him to come, during the following Lent, to the spot in the desert where they had first met. Zosimas made his way there, but found her lying dead, her body incorrupt. An inscription in the sand above her head stated that she had died the very same night that he had given her Holy Communion, and had been miraculously transported back to her desert home. Zosimas then enlisted the help of a passing lion and buried the body, before returning to his monastery where he told her story to the brethren.

Relics of the saint are venerated at Rome, Naples, Cremona, and Antwerp. There is also a chapel devoted to her in the Church of the Holy Sepulchre, Jerusalem. Her story has been seen as a local interpretation of the story of Mary Magdalene (July 22), which it in part resembles.

Date	Name	Status	Venerated	Life
April 2	John Paul II ('The Great') (1920–2005)	Pope (r.1978–2005) Declared Venerable 2009		Polish Karol Jozef Wojtyla was first non-Italian pope for over 450 years, and second-longest ruling in history. Survived assassination attempt. Enormously popular, great ecumenicist. Beatified record-beating 1,338 candidates, and canonized 482 saints.
April 3	Benedict the African (1526–89)	Franciscan Friar ○ 1807	In Sicily By Franciscans	Son of Nubian slaves transported to Sicily. Widely known for his piety, modesty, and humility – especially when subjected to racist taunts. Gained reputation as healer of the sick.

APRIL 4 | ISIDORE OF SEVILLE

STATUS Bishop, Doctor of the Church

BORN c.560, Cartagena, Spain

DIED 636, Seville, Spain

GRC ♣

CofE ☁

LCDUS ♣

◯ 1598

† Bees (surrounded by a swarm or standing near a beehive); pen and book; associated with Sts. Leander, Fulgentius, Florentina

🙏 Proposed as patron saint of the Internet

The Etymologiae *was the first encyclopedia to be compiled in the post-classical world. Its 20 volumes form a repository of classical learning, which would otherwise have been lost. Isidore's work also led to a florescence of encyclopedic writing over the following centuries.*

> "The extraordinary doctor, the latest ornament of the Catholic Church, the most learned man of the latter ages, always to be named with reverence, Isidore."
>
> EIGHTH COUNCIL OF TOLEDO (653).

A medieval scholar, whose histories of the Iberian peninsula were the primary source for later medieval histories, Isidore was also a Catholic bulwark against the cultural depredations of the Visigoths.

Isidore was born to an influential Catholic family in Cartagena, Spain. Educated in the cathedral school in Seville, he mastered Latin, Greek, and Hebrew. He succeeded his brother St. Leander as bishop of Seville, and on his elevation, he immediately became a protector of the monastic orders.

As bishop of Seville, he presided over a period of great upheaval. The great institutions of the classical world were rapidly disintegrating under the pressure of barbarian invasions, and the intellectual legacy of Rome was under threat. The Visigoths – invaders from the steppes of eastern Europe – had been in control of Iberia for almost two centuries, and their contempt for learning was threatening to undermine Hispanic civilization. Isidore set about the ambitious task of creating a sense of national unity by assimilating the various foreign elements that were tearing Hispania apart. The Visigothic kings had adopted the Arian heresy, which taught that Jesus is not of one substance with God the Father. They were persuaded to abandon the heresy, which was eradicated. Religious discipline was thus strengthened, becoming a formidable unifying force.

Educational Legacy

From 619, Isidore presided over a series of councils at Seville and Toledo, which formulated the stance of the Church in relation to the Arian heresy, as well as clarifying the allegiance that a free and independent Church bore to the king. At the Fourth Council of Toledo in 633, it was agreed that bishops would establish seminaries in their cathedral cities, ensuring that an enlightened education would counteract the dangers of barbarism. The study of Greek and Hebrew was compulsory, but interest in law and medicine was also encouraged.

Isidore, a prolific and wide-ranging writer, is also remarkable in that he undertook the epic task of compiling a summation of universal knowledge. His most important and ambitious work was the *Etymologiae*. Isidore was considered the most learned man of his age, and his influence on education in medieval Spain was incalculable. He was declared a Doctor of the Church in 1722.

APRIL 5 — VINCENT FERRER

STATUS Missionary
BORN 1350, Valencia, Spain
DIED 1419, Vannes, France
GRC ♣
CofE ♧
LCDUS ♣
⬭ 1455
✝ Pulpit, cardinal's hat, trumpet, captives, the Bible
🙏 Builders, construction workers, plumbers

A dedicated missionary and preacher at a time when the Catholic Church was being undermined by internal dissent, Vincent traveled all over western Europe, a tireless proponent of the Christian message.

Vincent's birth is surrounded by legend. It is said that his father learned in a dream that his son would be famous throughout the world, and his mother experienced no pain in childbirth. Vincent grew up a pious and charitable child. He entered the Dominican Order at age 18, studying philosophy and theology, and became a Master of Sacred Theology.

Vincent refused all the dignities the Church sought to bestow on him, preferring to spread the Christian message; he traveled throughout Spain, Switzerland, France, Italy, and the British Isles, preaching the message of the Gospels. He is said to have converted many Jews to Catholicism in his homeland.

During the troubled period of the Avignon papacy from 1309–78, when seven popes resided in Avignon, reflecting the increasing dominance of the French kings over Rome, Vincent remained loyal to the Avignonese pope, Benedict XIII, encouraging him to end the division. He lived to see the end of the Great Schism, with the election of Pope Martin V in Rome in 1417. Vincent died in 1419 in

Brittany, and is buried in Vannes Cathedral.

Vincent is patron saint of builders, because he is celebrated for 'building up' faith in the Catholic Church.

APRIL 7 — JOHN BAPTIST DE LA SALLE

STATUS Priest, Educator, Founder
BORN 1651, Reims, France
DIED 1719, Rouen, France
GRC ♣
CofE ♧
LCDUS ♣
♥ 1888
⬭ 1900
✝ Instructing children; books
🙏 Teachers, educators, La Sallian schools

D e la Salle was born in Reims and became a canon of the cathedral at only 16. He was a notable and devout scholar, but when his parents died he abandoned his education to take care of his family. He was not ordained as a Dominican until age 27, receiving a Doctorate in Theology two years later.

He helped establish a school for the poor in Reims, and then founded the Institute of the Brothers of the Christian Schools (also known as the Christian Brothers). Moved by the plight of children born in poverty, with little hope of an education, he renounced his own wealth and formed a new community of lay religious teachers, the first Catholic teaching order that did not include clergymen. The use of lay teachers brought him into conflict with the ecclesiastical authorities. Despite this, he succeeded in creating a network of excellent schools throughout France, noted for the integration of religious instruction with secular subjects.

De la Salle pioneered training programs for lay teachers, founding a teacher training seminary in Reims in 1685, and introduced Sunday courses for working men, secondary schools for modern languages, institutions dedicated to the care of delinquents, and schools specializing in arts, sciences, and technical skills. Realizing the absurdity of using Latin texts to teach reading, he made the vernacular the language of instruction. De la Salle's pedagogical system is outlined in *The Conduct of Schools* (1695).

De la Salle died at age 67, but his work quickly spread around the globe, and led to the foundation of many other teaching orders throughout the 18th and 19th centuries that still flourish today.

Date	Name	Status	Venerated	Life
April 6	Crescentia Hoess (1682–1744)	Mother Superior ♥ 1900 ⬭ 2001	In Germany	Known in hometown of Augsburg as 'the little angel.' Devout daughter of a poor weaver. Became a nun and mother superior. Gained reputation in spiritual matters; advised bishops, cardinals, princes, and princesses. Crippled by ill health, but bore her sufferings with great stoicism.
April 8	Julie Billiart (1751–1816)	Nun, Founder ♥ 1906 ⬭ 1969	In France 🙏 Poverty, the sick	Paralyzed in her youth. Well known for her quiet, devout contemplation. Founded Institute of the Sisters of Notre Dame in Namur, Belgium, dedicated to salvation of poor children and Christian education of girls. Went on to found 15 further convents.

APRIL 9   DIETRICH BONHOEFFER

STATUS Martyr

BORN 1906, Breslau, Germany

DIED 1945, Flossenbürg concentration camp, Germany

GRC ⬯

CofE ♣

LCDUS ⬯

OTHER US Evangelical Lutheran Church

> "Action springs not from thought, but from a readiness for responsibility."
>
> DIETRICH BONHOEFFER, *ETHICS.*

Bonhoeffer's ideas continue to be regarded as central to the revitalization of Christianity in Germany following the failure of the Church to confront Nazism.

Born to a wealthy German middle-class family, Bonhoeffer showed academic promise from an early age. It was assumed that he would follow his father's profession as a neurologist and psychiatrist, but at age 14 he announced that he wanted to study theology.

He attended university at Tübingen and Berlin, achieving his doctorate in 1927 with his thesis *Sanctorum Communio* (Communion of Saints). He traveled to Rome, Barcelona, and New York, then visited Mexico and Cuba. He returned to Berlin University to lecture, and was ordained as a pastor in 1931. With Hitler's coming to power, Bonhoeffer took an anti-Nazi stance, broadcasting warnings about Hitler. He eventually formed the Confessing Church based at a seminary in Finkenwalde, in opposition to the acquiescent German Evangelical Church, and the Nazi-sponsored German Christian movement.

The Confessing Church

From 1933–35 Bonhoeffer worked in London, furthering the Confessing Church through his ecumenical contacts, but upon his return to Germany the organization had been suppressed; it was outlawed in 1937. He spent two years traveling in eastern Germany, covertly sponsoring the Confessing Church, before leaving once again for New York in 1939. Prior to this he made contact with members of the German resistance via his brother-in-law, Hans von Dohnanyi, who worked for Abwehr. Abwehr was the German military intelligence organization, and a center of the anti-Nazi Kreisau Circle. He remained in New York for only a few weeks, but feeling that war was almost certain, he returned to Germany.

The Failure of Resistance

Bonhoeffer's activities were monitored by the Gestapo, and he was forbidden to speak in public or publish. From 1941 he worked closely with Dohnanyi at Abwehr, using military and diplomatic channels to enable Jews to escape to Switzerland, and acting as a courier for the anti-Nazi resistance movement. However, the Gestapo brought charges of 'anti-Nazi activities' against Abwehr. In April 1943 Bonhoeffer was arrested and interned at Tegel military prison in Berlin. He conducted extensive correspondence during his 18 months in Tegel (later published as *Letters and Papers from Prison*), and continued his Christian outreach activities among his fellow inmates. Throughout the war Bonhoeffer

The commemorative plaque to Bonhoeffer at St. Matthias Church, Berlin, where he was ordained.

continued to work on his most famous book, *Ethics*, which was never completed.

After the failure of the attempt to assassinate Hitler on July 20, 1944, Bonhoeffer's connections with the conspirators led to him being transferred from Tegel to the Gestapo's top-security prison in September 1944. In February 1945 he was moved to Buchenwald concentration camp, and then to the camp at Flossenbürg. In April, Hitler ordered that all conspirators be executed. On April 8, Bonhoeffer was condemned by an SS judge and on the following day he was hanged. His brother and two brothers-in-law were also executed.

Bonhoeffer's legacy as an example of selfless resistance to tyranny and his belief in ecumenicalism remain enormously powerful, and did much to reinstate the Church as a central pillar of German society in the reconstruction years following World War II.

Date	Name	Status	Venerated	Life
April 9	Waldetrude (d.688)	Founder ⬭ Pre-Congregation	† In Belgium	Daughter of St. Walbert and St. Bertilia; sister to St. Aldegunus of Maubeuge. Her husband, St. Vincent Madelgarius, founded a monastery (c.643) at Hautrnont, France, and became a monk. She then founded a convent at Chateaulieu, in Mons, Belgium. Her four children, Landericus, Madalberta, Adeltrudis, and Dentelin all revered as saints in Belgium.
April 9	Casilda (d.1050)	Martyr ⬭ Pre-Congregation	† In Burgos and Toledo, Spain	Born in Toledo, of Moorish descent. Converted to Christianity. Became hermit at Briviesca, near Burgos, Spain.

APRIL 9 ♣ SAINTS, MARTYRS, AND MISSIONARIES OF SOUTH AMERICA

The evangelization of South America by the Spanish and Portuguese during their colonization of the continent was seen as one of the principal opportunities for the Catholic Counter-Reformation church. The division of the continent into Spanish and Portuguese spheres of influence was ratified by Pope Alexander VI under the Treaty of Tordesillas in 1494, giving Portugal control of Brazil.

Although some priests accompanied Columbus and the first expeditions by the conquistadores, organized attempts at evangelization only began in 1500 when groups of Franciscan friars arrived on the northwest coast of the continent. It would not be until almost 50 years later that they would be followed by missions of Dominicans, Augustinians, and other orders.

The responsibility for converting the native peoples fell to the rulers of Spain and Portugal, although Pope Alexander stressed that the natives should not be coerced, but should convert of their own free will. The relationship between church and state was not easy in the New World. The rapacity of the empire-builders, and the diseases they carried with them, saw the two main civilizations of the time, the Aztecs of Mexico and the Incas of Peru, destroyed. Some priests, such as the Dominican Bartolomé de las Casas (July 20), spoke out against the colonial policies, but to little effect.

In the 17th century, the Jesuits established missionary 'states' or 'reductions' in the South American interior, the most notable being Paraguay. These were Christian settlements that offered protection from the colonists to the native population. They persisted until the Jesuits were banished from Spanish and Portuguese dominions in the late 18th century.

Success and Syncretism

Unlike in Africa and the Far East, there were relatively few instances of native populations revolting against their new Christian rulers, or martyring missionaries, and in comparison the introduction of Christianity to the continent can be seen as a major success.

The first American saint was Rose of Lima (1586–1618, Aug. 23). The cult of saints came to be widely embraced throughout Latin America, often blending with native gods and traditions. This persists today, for example, in an array of syncretist saints in Guatemala. The importation of slaves from Africa also resulted in curious admixtures of Christian saints with African traditions, especially in the development of cults such as Santeria, Voodoo, and Candomblé.

The Latin American church came under attack in the 20th century as a result of radical political movements. Violent anti-clericalism persisted for many years in revolutionary Mexico, and provoked the outrage of the assassination of Archbishop Oscar Romero and his followers in El Salvador in 1980 (March 24, Dec. 2).

Christ, in Franciscan robes, guides a Catholic soul through the perils of the wilderness in this typical example of the simplified Baroque style of painting that developed in Latin America.

APRIL 11 | STANISLAUS (STANISLAW) OF SZCZEPANÓW

STATUS Bishop, Martyr

BORN 1030, Szczepanów, Poland

DIED 1079, Kraków, Poland

GRC ♣

CofE ⬭

LCDUS ♣

⬯ 1253

✝ Episcopal insignia, sword, Piotr rising from the dead at his feet

⚖ Moral order; Poland, Kraków

Stanislaus was born in rural Poland, the only son of a nobleman, and was educated at the cathedral school at Gniezno (then Poland's capital). He traveled to France and Belgium, and on his return was ordained by the bishop of Kraków.

When the bishop died in 1072, Stanislaus was elected as his successor, with strong papal support. At a time when Poland was only beginning to adopt Christianity, Stanislaus built firm relations with Rome. When Duke Boleslaw was crowned king in 1076, Stanislaus made it a condition that the metropolitan see of Gniezno would be reinstated. He also encouraged the new king to establish Benedictine monasteries throughout the country.

Stanislaus's first confrontation with Boleslaw concerned a trivial dispute about land. Stanislaus had purchased some land for the diocese on the banks of the Vistula from a man named Piotr, who subsequently died. The family then laid claim to the land, and the king ruled in their favor. Stanislaus spent three days fasting and praying and then visited Piotr's grave, which was opened. When Stanislaus summoned Piotr back to life, Piotr obliged, and was dressed in a cloak for his appearance before the king and the dumbfounded court. The king dismissed the suit against the bishop. When Piotr was asked if he wanted to remain alive, he declined, returned to his grave, and was re-buried.

A Moral Crusader

A more serious clash between Boleslaw and Stanislaus arose after a prolonged war in Ruthenia. Warriors were returning home, often to find that their family estates and their wives had been taken by overseers. The king inflicted harsh punishments on the faithless wives, and Stanislaus intervened, criticizing the king for his severity. It has been suggested that Stanislaus had also become involved with discontented nobles, who were plotting to overthrow the king. At this point Stanislaus excommunicated King Boleslaw,

The gruesome dismemberment of Stanislaus by Boleslaw and his knights has been seen as a prophetic metaphor for the successive division and partition of the Polish state between the 17th and 20th centuries.

a gesture that proved helpful to the king's political opponents.

The king retaliated by accusing Stanislaus of treason, and condemned him to death. The men he sent to carry out the sentence dared not touch the bishop, and the king decided to kill the bishop himself. It is said that he attacked the bishop as he was conducting Mass in Kraków. Stanislaw was hacked apart, and his remains were thrown into a pool outside the church. According to legend, eagles guarded the pool, and the dismembered body was miraculously reintegrated.

The murder of Stanislaus led to the dethronement of Boleslaw, who fled to Hungary, and Stanislaus almost immediately became the focus of a cult. In 1245, his relics were removed to Kraków's Wawel Cathedral, and within eight years he had been canonized. Wawel Cathedral became a principal national shrine; Polish kings were crowned kneeling before Stanislaus's sarcophagus in the cathedral.

The reintegration of Stanislaus's body came to symbolize the reunification of the repeatedly fragmented Polish polity. When the Polish constitution was framed in 1791, it was dedicated to Stanislaus.

APRIL 11 · GEORGE AUGUSTUS SELWYN

STATUS Missionary, Bishop
BORN 1809, London, England
DIED 1878, Lichfield, England
GRC ○
CofE ♣
LCDUS ○
OTHER In New Zealand; Cambridge, England

Selwyn was born into a distinguished English family and studied at Cambridge University. He was ordained deacon in 1833, and a mere eight years later was appointed bishop of New Zealand. He set sail with his wife in 1841, and they set up residence at the Waimate Mission Station in 1842. Selwyn immediately made a number of arduous journeys to mission stations and native settlements throughout the North Island. In 1844 he bought 450 acres of land near Auckland, which he named Bishop's Auckland.

An energetic and adventurous Anglican, Selwyn was a pioneering founder of the 'colonial see,' and his administration of the diocese was to become an Anglican model worldwide. In 1854, he returned to England to seek permission to institute a system of self-governance in the Anglican Church of New Zealand, allowing him to consecrate four bishops and establish the legal constitution. But the increasing tension over the acquisition of Maori lands by British colonists, culminating in the Taranaki War in 1860, alienated the Maoris. Selwyn attempted to mediate, only to be met by hostility on both sides.

In 1867, he was offered the see of Lichfield, Staffordshire, where he died.

APRIL 12 · SABAS THE GOTH

STATUS Martyr
BORN 334, Wallachia, Romania
DIED 372, Wallachia, Romania
GRC ○
CofE ○
LCDUS ○
OTHER Eastern Orthodox churches
○ Pre-Congregation

A Goth by blood, Sabas was born to Christian parents, and became a 'cantor' (reader) to the Christian community in Romania, or Dacia (which had been part of the Roman empire until 271, when it fell to Goth invaders from the eastern steppes). In 371, the Goths began the suppression of the Christians in the Wallachian region of Romania. Christians in Sabas's village were forced to eat pagan sacrificial meat. Sabas publicly proclaimed his Christian faith, and refused to eat the meat. Because he was a man of little account, the Goth leader dismissed him.

The following year, Sabas celebrated Easter with a priest, Sansala. Spies reported this news to the authorities, and three days later Athanaric, son of the Goth king, arrested Sansala. More punishment was meted out to Sabas, who was dragged naked through thorn bushes, bound to a tree, and again forced to eat defiled meat. Once again Sabas refused, and was condemned to death by drowning in the river Musaeus, a tributary of the Danube. He met his death declaiming his Christian religion and denouncing the idolatry of his captors, as he was bound to a wooden pole with a rock tied around his neck and thrown into the river.

Christian supporters salvaged his relics and sent them to Thessalonica. In around 374 the relics were translated by Basil the Great (Jan. 2) to Caesarea, Cappadocia (modern Turkey). Basil proclaimed Sabas an "athlete of Christ" and "martyr for the truth."

Date	Name	Status	Venerated	Life
April 10	Fulbert of Chartres (d.c.1028)	Bishop ○ Pre-Congregation	In Chartres and Poitiers, France	Attended cathedral school in Reims. Founded school in Chartres; appointed bishop there (1007). Rebuilt the cathedral after a fire. Prolific writer of epistles; composer of hymns. Active proponent of cult of the Blessed Virgin Mary. Developed many ideas that led to 12th-century Gregorian church reforms.
April 12	Alferius de la Cava (c.930–1050)	Abbot, Hermit ♥ 1893	In Salerno, Italy † Shown in old age	Italian nobleman. Following illness, entered monastery at Cluny. Recalled to Salerno to reform monasteries. Failed; became a hermit (1011). Later established network of Cluniac Benedictine monasteries in southern Italy and Sicily. Lived an improbably long time.

APRIL 13 — MARTIN I

STATUS Pope, Martyr
BORN Late 6th century, Umbria, Italy
DIED 655, Cherson, Crimea, Russia
GRC ♣
CofE ○
LCDUS ○
OTHER Russian Orthodox Church
⬭ Pre-Congregation

The period between 537 and 752 is generally described as that of the Byzantine papacy. This was the direct consequence of the attempted reconquest of the barbarian West, above all Italy, launched by the Byzantine emperor Justinian in 533. Though Justinian's conquests proved short-lived, they nonetheless greatly strengthened Byzantium's hold over the papacy. Martin I, elected pope in 649, had been papal ambassador in Byzantium and might therefore have been expected to favor Byzantium. The opposite proved to be the case. What in the 11th century would become a definitive split between the Western and the Eastern Christian churches was prefigured during Martin's papacy. The issue was Monothelitism, enthusiastically embraced in the East, as energetically rejected in the West. Much like Arianism, it was a dispute over the extent to which Jesus could have been simultaneously human and divine.

Almost Martin's first action on becoming pope was to call in 649 what became known as the Lateran Council to resolve the issue. It overwhelmingly dismissed Monothelitism as heresy. In revenge, though it took him almost four years to arrange, the emperor, Constans II, subsequently had Martin seized. Martin was taken to the island of Naxos, where he was starved, and then brought in chains to Byzantium for trial as a 'heretic, rebel, enemy of God, and of the state.' Throughout the hearing, Martin was beaten, abused, and humiliated. He was then publicly flogged, but rather than executing him, Constans exiled Martin to Cherson in the Crimea, where in effect he was starved to death.

APRIL 14 — PEDRO GONZÁLEZ

STATUS Monk
BORN 1190, Astorga, Spain
DIED 1246, Tuy, Spain
GRC ○
CofE ○
LCDUS ○
♥ 1254
⬭ 1741
✝ Holding a ship
⚓ Spanish and Portuguese sailors

A nephew of the bishop of Astorga, Pedro González was an unlikely candidate for sainthood, in his youth energetically devoting himself to the pursuit of aristocratic pleasure. Appointed dean of Astorga Cathedral by his uncle in what seems to have been an act of open nepotism, Pedro arrived in the city in splendor, cheered by the assembled crowds. His horse apparently threw him, however, and he landed either in a puddle or a dunghill. Humiliated, Pedro was made instantly aware of the fickleness of acclaim and the consequences of vanity. He renounced all worldly ambitions, joined the Dominicans, and gained fame as a preacher. Summoned to the court of Ferdinand III (May 30), in 1236 he accompanied the king to the siege of Córdoba, still a major Moorish stronghold. When the city fell, Pedro is said to have urged compassion toward the defeated Muslim forces. The rest of his life was spent in Galicia, Spain, preaching to fishermen and sailors. His patronage of sailors explains his occasional identification with St. Elmo, the patron saint of seafarers, more properly the 3rd-century St. Erasmus of Formiae.

APRIL 15 — CÉSAR DE BUS

STATUS Catechist
BORN 1544, Cavaillon, France
DIED 1607, Avignon, France
GRC ○
CofE ○
LCDUS ○
♥ 1975

If less obviously indolent and pleasure seeking in his youth than St. Pedro González (see above), César de Bus was affected by no less sudden a conversion. Having been ordained in 1582, he became the pre-eminent representative of the Counter-Reformation in France, a relentless and determined champion of Catholic belief in the face of the religious convulsions sparked by the Reformation. Inspired by Charles Borromeo (Nov. 4), he was seized by a "spirit of repentance," determined to

César was in the vanguard of the Counter-Reformation in France.

"seek and love sacrifice." He became a leading champion of catechesis. This was essentially religious instruction, aimed particularly at the young, generally framed in the form of questions and answers to be memorized. It was conceived to reinforce official Church teaching. To this end, de Bus not only wrote widely, but also established an order for men, the Fathers of Christian Doctrine. He subsequently founded a short-lived order for women, the Ursulines of Provence.

APRIL 16 | # MAGNUS OF ORKNEY

STATUS Martyr
BORN 1075, Norway
DIED c.1115, Orkney Islands, Scotland
GRC ☁
CofE ☁
LCDUS ☁
⬭ 1135

The extent to which Magnus can properly be considered a martyr is moot. He died – his head split open by an axe – less in defending his faith than in a power struggle between himself and his cousin, Haakon Paulsson, for control of the Orkney Islands, nominally Christian since 995, and a Norwegian possession since 875. What is known of Magnus comes almost entirely from the *Orkneyinga Saga*. According to the saga, both Magnus and Haakon were sons of the joint rulers of the Orkneys. In 1098, both accompanied the Norwegian king, Magnus Barefoot (or Barelegs), on a raiding mission in the Irish Sea. St. Magnus, having no quarrel with his intended victims, preferred to stand in the sea chanting psalms. Thus disgraced in the king's eyes, he was forced to flee to Scotland. By 1105, having argued his case in Norway, Magnus was confirmed as joint earl of the Orkneys with Haakon, but in 1114, goaded by disaffected magnates, Haakon determined on a showdown. He had his cousin slain, apparently by his cook. Magnus, pious to the last, forgave his assassin.

Miracles were reported where Magnus was first buried, at Birsay; almost at once, barren ground became suddenly fertile. When the bishop of Orkney, William the Old, dismissed the claims, he was struck blind, his sight restored only when he prayed to Magnus. In 1137, a cathedral was begun at Kirkwall, where St. Magnus's remains were transferred. It is the most northerly cathedral in the British Isles.

APRIL 16 | # BERNADETTE SOUBIROUS

STATUS Visionary
BORN 1844, Lourdes, France
DIED 1879, Nevers, France
GRC ☁
CofE ☁
LCDUS ☁
♥ 1925
⬭ 1933

Bernadette enjoys the singular distinction of being the first saint to be photographed.

Bernadette was the peasant girl to whom, between February 11 and July 16, 1858, the Blessed Virgin Mary appeared 18 times at a spring at Lourdes in southwest France (*see also* Feb. 11). Her father was a miller, her mother a laundress. She had five siblings, and all lived in a single room. Even before the visions had stopped, Bernadette had become one of the most famous figures in France, endlessly quizzed, relentlessly interrogated. For an illiterate 16-year-old, it was a distressing experience in which she was variously dismissed as insane and hailed as a mystic. It seems clear that she was, at best, slow and simple-minded. She was subsequently taken in by the Sisters of Charity in Nevers in central France. They taught her to read; she also became an accomplished seamstress. Bernadette had always been sickly and died at only 35 from tuberculosis.

Bernadette's canonization was confirmed after three medical examinations of her corpse – in 1910, 1919, and 1925 – agreed that her body was incorrupt. The wax death mask made of her in 1925 has since been displayed on her actual body, on display in an elaborate glass reliquary in the chapel named after her in the Sisters' mother house in Nevers. Her hands, too, are made of wax.

MODERN SAINTS

The long tradition of creating and representing saints continues today. Both recent popes, John Paul II (r.1978–2005) and Benedict XVI (r.2005–), beatified and canonized larger numbers of saints than any of their predecessors (over 1,500 beatifications and more than 500 canonizations between them), while the Church of England has also added many recent martyrs to its calendar. The roles of many traditional saints also continue to be reinterpreted in contemporary society.

> "My hope is to enkindle and enlighten through painting."
>
> FRED VILLANUEVA, 2008.

Pope Benedict XVI at Prayer with the Holy Theologians. *This painting in the National Museum for Catholic Art and History, New York, was painted by Mexican-American artist Fred Villanueva to celebrate Pope Benedict XVI's visit to the United States in 2008. It presents a particularly modern vision, albeit one based on earlier representations of several major saints. Pope Benedict (praying right of center) is accompanied by (top row from left) Josemaría Escrivá (founder of Opus Dei, June 26), Augustine of Hippo (Aug. 28, after Botticelli), Bridget of Sweden (July 23), The Blessed Virgin Mary (after Raphael), Albertus Magnus (Nov. 15), Gregory the Great (Sept. 3), and Irenaeus (June 28); (bottom row, from left) Catherine of Siena (April 29, after Beccafumi), John of the Cross (Dec. 14), Teresa of Ávila (Oct. 15, after Rubens), Thomas Aquinas (Jan. 28, after Crivelli), and Bonaventure (July 15, after Murillo). The cat at the center is based on a drawing by Leonardo da Vinci.*

APRIL 16 | BENEDICT JOSEPH LABRE

STATUS Mendicant

BORN 1748, Amettes, France

DIED 1783, Rome, Italy

GRC ☁

CofE ☁

LCDUS ☁

⬭ 1881

⚘ Bachelors, the mentally ill, beggars, the homeless

The eldest of a family of 15, born to a prosperous shopkeeper, Benedict was notable from an early age for his piety. At age 16 he applied, successively, to join the Trappists, Carthusians, and Cistercians, but was rejected by all three orders: they detected signs of mental instability, which they deemed would make him unsuitable for the rigors of communal, cloistered life.

Labre was overwhelmed by a desire to leave his home and family and seek out a new life as a devout pilgrim and penitent. He set out for Rome on foot, subsisting on charitable donations. He went on to travel to most of the major shrines of Europe, a punishing itinerary that took him to Santiago de Compostela in Spain, Paray-le-Monial in France, Einsiedeln in Switzerland, and Loreto, Assisi, Naples, and Bari in Italy. He always traveled on foot, slept outdoors, dressed in rags, and lived on what little he was given. He was prone to heightened spirituality, frequently swooning when lost in prayer or contemplation, and was reputed to levitate. He was also said to have cured some of the other homeless people he met on his travels.

He spent the last years of his life living in the Colosseum in Rome, making an annual pilgrimage to Loreto. He became a familiar figure in Rome, well known for his asceticism, piety, and devotion. He died of malnutrition during Holy Week, 1783, and was buried in the church of Santa Maria dei Monti, near the Colosseum. Soon after his death, a cult began to build up around him, and 136 separate cures were attributed to his intercession in the first three months after he died.

Benedict Joseph Labre is usually depicted in a pose of humility and piety. His dedication to a life of extreme poverty, pilgrimage, and penitence may be related to the mental instability detected when he attempted to join successive reclusive orders.

Date	Name	Status	Venerated	Life
April 18	James Oldo (1364–1404)	Priest ❤ 1933	In Italy	Wealthy, self-indulgent man, but after death of two daughters from the plague resolved to dedicate himself to good works. Became priest; dedicated himself to looking after the sick and prisoners of civil war that devastated Lombardy. Died after contracting a disease from one of his patients.
April 18	Apollonius the Apologist (d.185)	Martyr ⬭ Pre-Congregation		Roman senator who was denounced as a Christian by his slave. Arrested but refused to renounce his faith. Forced to debate merits of Christianity before the Senate; made eloquent defense of the faith, but was nevertheless condemned and beheaded.

APRIL 17

DONNAN (DONAN) AND COMPANIONS

STATUS Missionary, Martyr

BORN Ireland

DIED c.617, Eigg, Scotland

GRC ⬭

CofE ⬭

LCDUS ⬭

OTHER Church of Scotland

⬮ Pre-Congregation

🙏 Eigg, Scotland

One of the wave of Christian Irish missionaries who sailed to Scotland in the last two decades of the 6th century, Donnan was a friend and disciple of St. Columba (June 9). Accompanied by a band of disciples, he started to work among the Picts of Galloway. An indefatigable apostle of the Christian faith, he founded churches as he moved through northern Scotland: at Colmonell, Carrick, Kintyre, Loch Garry, Sutherland, Loch Broom, Uist, and on the Isle of Arran. The headquarters of Donnan's 'family' of monks and missionaries was eventually established on the island of Eigg (Inner Hebrides).

It is said that the arrival of the missionaries provoked the resentment of a Pictish noblewoman who grazed her livestock on the island, who was determined to obliterate the monastic community. Lacking local support, she turned to the services of 'pirates.' These could have been an early group of marauders from Jutland (Denmark), precursors of the pagan Vikings who later terrorized the British Isles. The assassins arrived as Donnan was celebrating Mass. They allowed him to finish the service, and then gathered together the missionaries and shut them into the refectory, which they set alight. The entire community, numbering 52, perished in the flames.

The places of worship that missionaries such as Donnan founded, like this one at Auchterless, were relatively humble structures built of locally sourced stone.

APRIL 18

MARY OF THE INCARNATION

STATUS Nun

BORN 1566, Paris, France

DIED 1618, Pontoise, France

GRC ⬭

CofE ⬭

LCDUS ⬭

OTHER By Carmelites

❤ 1791

🙏 Poor people, widows, orphans; against poverty

A variant on the Carmelite arms, reflecting their brown-colored scapular.

Born to wealthy parents in Paris, Barbe Avrillot was a student in a religious house of the Order of Saint Clare, near Paris, from the age of 11 to 14. She was devout and unworldly, and determined to enter a religious order, but her parents opposed her plan. On her 16th birthday she was married to Pierre Acarie, a wealthy nobleman, and went on to have six children. She dedicated herself to their spiritual upbringing, and her three daughters all went on to become Carmelites. Her three sons entered the magistracy, the priesthood, and the military. Her husband, who supported the Catholic League against Henry IV, was beset by political difficulties when Henry became king. His house and possessions were seized and he was exiled from Paris. She was a stalwart defender of her husband, writing letters to people of influence and tracking down proof of his innocence. He was eventually acquitted and was then allowed to return to Paris.

Barbe became well known throughout Paris for her good works. There was a renaissance in religious piety during this period in France, and Barbe became deeply involved in reforms of the religious orders and foundations of new congregations. Inspired by a biography of Teresa of Ávila, she founded the first Discalced Carmelite house in France, at rue St. Jacques, Paris, in 1602. When her husband died in 1613, she entered the order, taking the name Mary of the Incarnation. She lived in a Carmelite house in Amiens, where her daughter was the superior, and subsequently at Pontoise, taking on the humblest duties, working in the kitchens. Her remains are in the chapel of the Carmelites of Pontoise.

A contemporary portrait of Barbe Acarie wearing the distinctive black and white robes of the Carmelite Order.

APRIL 19 | LEO IX

STATUS Pope
BORN 1002, Egisheim, Holy Roman Empire
DIED 1054, Rome, Italy
GRC ○
CofE ○
LCDUS ○
◉ 1087

Born Bruno von Egisheim-Dagsburg to a family of noble rank, Bruno was educated at Toul, and became a bishop in 1027. During his tenure he established a firm peace between France and the Holy Roman Empire, helped to bring the kingdom of Burgundy into the empire, and built up a reputation as a reforming cleric, who enthusiastically spread the rule of the monastic order of Cluny.

In 1048, he was selected as successor to Pope Damasus II by an assembly at Worms. He had ecclesiastical and imperial approval, but insisted that he should also be elected by the people and clergy of Rome. He arrived in Rome two months later in humble pilgrim's clothing, and was duly accepted and consecrated as pope in 1049, taking the name Leo IX.

A traditionalist by temperament, Leo reasserted the doctrine of celibacy at the Easter Synod of 1049. He also stated his abhorrence of simony. He then embarked on the first of a series of papal progresses through Italy, France, and Germany that were to become a characteristic feature of his papacy. During these journeys he presided over a number of synods, met with the higher clergy, reasserted his fundamental beliefs, and engaged in various diplomatic initiatives.

In 1053, after many failed attempts at diplomatic mediation, Leo set out with an army of Italian and German volunteers to confront Norman invaders in the south of Italy. His forces suffered a terrible defeat at the battle of Civitate in 1053, although he immediately secured the loyalty of the enemy. Despite this, he was held in captivity in Benevento, and did not long survive his return to Rome, dying in 1054. Not long before, Leo IX had written to Michael Caerularius, Patriarch of Constantinople, who was campaigning to loosen ties with the Roman Church. Leo asserted his belief that only the apostolic successor to Peter was the rightful head of the Church. The Patriarch rejected these claims of papal primacy, and the Catholic Church was split in two with the East–West Schism of 1054.

APRIL 19 | ALPHEGE (ALFEGE) OF ABINGDON

STATUS Bishop
BORN 954, Weston, England
DIED 1012, Greenwich, England
GRC ○
CofE ♣
LCDUS ○
◉ Pre-Congregation
✝ Archbishop; sometimes with an axe cleaving his skull
🙏 Victims of kidnapping; Greenwich, England

Born on the outskirts of Bath, Alphege became a monk while still young, and was praised for his devotion and asceticism. He rose to become abbot of Bath, and was elected bishop of Winchester in 984. He promoted the cult of St. Swithun (July 15), and was famous for the construction of an impressive organ in the cathedral, audible from at least a mile away.

In 1006, Alphege became archbishop of Canterbury, and duly arrived there with the relic of St. Swithun's head. He traveled to Rome to receive his pallium, symbolic of his ties to the Roman Catholic see, and promoted the cult of St. Dunstan (May 19). In 1011, Danish raiders laid siege to Canterbury, sacked the city, and plundered and burned Canterbury Cathedral. Alphege was taken prisoner and held captive for seven months. His captors demanded a ransom for his freedom, but he refused to allow this, and as a result he was murdered on April 19 at Greenwich, reputedly on the site of St. Alphege's Church. The *Anglo-Saxon Chronicle* relates that he was pelted with bones and heads of cattle, and then decapitated with the blow of an axe.

Alphege was buried in St. Paul's Cathedral, London, but in 1023 his body was removed to Canterbury. An incised paving slab to the north of the high altar marks the spot where the medieval shrine is believed to have stood.

Alphege's symbol is the axe that killed him.

Date	Name	Status	Venerated	Life
April 19	Luchesio and Buonadonna (d.1260)	Secular Franciscans ♥ 1273 (Luchesio)	By Franciscans	Luchesio a wealthy merchant. Met Francis of Assisi (c.1213), and dedicated himself to acts of charity, aided by his wife Buonadonna. Couple wanted to share in religious life, but outside the cloister, so Francis set up Secular Franciscan Order. Lived life of austerity and charity.
April 20	Agnes of Montepulciano (c.1268–1317)	Nun, Founder ○ 1726	By Dominicans In Tuscany	Lived in convent from age nine. Sent to Proceno (1281), to found new convent, which then moved to Viterbo. Gained reputation for performing miracles and was reported to have 'multiplied loaves.' Established convent of Dominican nuns near Montepulciano. Her incorrupted remains attracted many pilgrims.

APRIL 21 — ANSELM OF CANTERBURY

STATUS Bishop, Doctor of the Church

BORN 1033, Aosta, Italy

DIED 1109, Canterbury, England

GRC ♣

CofE ♣

LCDUS ♣

⊘ 1492

✝ With a ship

Anselm's arms include a ship, symbol of spiritual independence.

Anselm was born in Alpine Italy to a noble family. His father was a violent man, who refused to consent to Anselm entering a monastery. At age 23, Anselm escaped his oppressive father and crossed the Alps, traveling through Burgundy and Normandy. Four years later he submitted himself to the Rule of St. Benedict at Avranches, and in 1078 he was consecrated abbot of Bec. Under him the abbey became a center of learning famous throughout Europe. Anselm began to develop his reputation as a Christian philosopher, while also asserting the abbey's independence from episcopal control.

Anselm established links with Benedictines in England and, in 1089, he was seen as the natural successor to the archbishop of Canterbury, Lanfranc. However, Lanfranc's death was seen by King William II as a chance to seize the revenues of the see, and no appointment was made. In 1092, Anselm made his way to England and prolonged negotiations took place between monarch and churchman. Eventually, William agreed to return Canterbury's lands, and Anselm was consecrated.

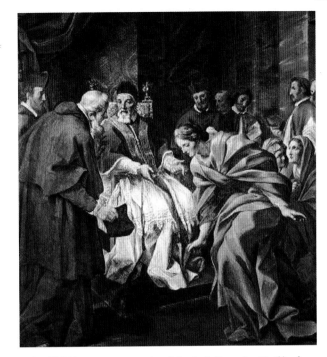

A fanciful 16th-century representation of Anselm (left) greeting Matilda of Canossa before Pope Urban II.

An Independent Churchman

Anselm remained a thorn in William's side, continuing to canvass for church reform and asserting the rights and interests of Canterbury, resisting William's desire to impose royal control over both church and state. Eventually the arguments between them became so entrenched that William offered Anselm an ultimatum: the choice of exile or total submission. Anselm opted for exile in Normandy, and William promptly seized the revenues of the see.

When William was killed in 1100, his successor Henry I invited Anselm to return, but Anselm once again came into conflict over the right, asserted by the English kings, to invest high-ranking churchmen. The dispute was eventually laid before the pope, who ruled in Anselm's favor. Henry turned against Anselm, and the saint once again went into exile. Following Anselm's threats of excommunication, Henry arranged a compromise at Laigle in 1106. But Anselm insisted on having the agreement sanctioned by the pope before returning to England, and was able to extract further concessions from the king, who restored to Anselm all the churches that had been seized by William. These promises, announced in the Concordat of London in 1107, were a major step in establishing the rights of the Church over the king.

Philosopher and Theologian

Anselm's assertion of the independence of the Church was highly effective, but he is primarily remembered as the first scholastic philosopher of Christian theology. He sought to understand doctrine through reason, and is famous for his attempts to prove the existence of God. In *De Veritate* (Of Truth) he argued that all creatures owe their being and value to God as the source of all truth. In the *Monologion* he described deity as the one most truly good thing, from which all real moral values derive and whose existence is required by the reality of those values. In his *Proslogion* Anselm proposed the famous 'Ontological Argument,' according to which God is understood as "that than which nothing greater can be conceived." The being so conceived must necessarily exist in reality as well as in thought, he argued, since otherwise it would in fact be possible to conceive something greater. Anselm was made a Doctor of the Church in 1734.

Date	Name	Status	Venerated	Life
April 21	Conrad of Parzham (1818–94)	Keeper of a Shrine ⊘ 1934	By Capuchins	Devout child, with a love of solitude, from farming family in Bavaria. Became lay brother among Capuchin Franciscans (1849). Sent to convent of St. Anne in Altötting, where held position of porter at shrine to the Mother of Mercy for 40 years. Known for his diligence, kindness, and devotion.
April 22	Theodore of Sykeon (d.613)	Hermit, Bishop ⊘ Pre-Congregation	Eastern Orthodox churches	Lived in a cave beneath a chapel, becoming noted exorcist. Later lived in a cage suspended over his cave, and established a monastery. Appointed bishop of Anastasiopolis (c.590), near Turkey's capital, Ankara. Said to have cured a royal prince of leprosy and performed many other healing miracles. Helped neglected children.

This depiction of George's combat with the dragon, by Lucas Cranach the Elder (1472–1553), takes place in a wild Germanic forest.

"Follow your spirit; and, upon this charge
Cry 'God for Harry, England, and St. George!'"

STATUS	Martyr
BORN	Late 3rd century
DIED	c.304, Lydda, modern Israel
GRC	♣
CofE	♣
LCDUS	♣
OTHER	Eastern Orthodox churches
○	Pre-Congregation
†	Usually shown mounted, wearing armor, bearing a sword and a lance, and his colors, a white cross on a red (or silver) field; occasionally, like St. Michael, shown trampling a dragon
⚕	Soldiers, knights, armorers, swordsmen, archers, farmers; sufferers from plague, leprosy, and syphilis; England, Portugal, Catalonia, Genoa, Venice

George's flag, comprising a red cross on a white or silver ground, is flown on English churches on his feast day and other important ecclesiastical festivals.

T his enormously popular saint is, like St. Christopher (July 25), an elusive if not entirely legendary character.

Much of what we know about George is recorded in Jacobus de Voragine's *The Golden Legend* (*Legenda Aurea*) – a lengthy martyrology completed in the mid-13th century, itself based on a survey of numerous sources. George was, however, a familiar figure throughout Europe by the 8th century. It seems likely that George was born in Cappadocia (Greek Anatolia, modern Turkey) toward the end of the 3rd century.

George and the Dragon

The most popular legend involving George tells of the pagan city of Silene in 'Libya' (a general term for North Africa at the time), which is beset by a dragon who dwells near a vast lake. The dragon's noxious breath (fire isn't mentioned by Voragine) forces the inhabitants to offer it two sheep a day. When they run out of sheep, they offer it their daughters. Finally, only one maiden is left, the king's daughter, who is led out to feed the beast. Fortunately for her, George appears on the scene and, ignoring her warnings that he is sure to be killed, he succeeds in stunning the dragon, which the princess and the knight proceed to take to the city. George says he will slay it if the thousands of inhabitants convert to Christianity, to which they agree. George refuses the king's offer of a huge reward, telling him to give it to the poor, and then goes on his way.

Possibly at Nicomedia in modern Turkey, although more probably at Lydda in Palestine, George became caught up in the persecutions of Diocletian and Maximinus. Proclaiming his Christianity, George was tortured, but miraculously survived; he then invoked God to destroy the local temple, after which he was rearrested, dragged through the streets, and finally beheaded.

George's popularity grew rapidly after the translation and printing (by Caxton) of *The Golden Legend* during the European Middle Ages, when his profile as a knight errant, traveling the countryside in pursuit of challenges, chimed with notions of chivalric idealism. His colors were adopted by Richard the Lionheart's forces during the Third Crusade (1187–92), which embedded George at the heart of English military endeavors and nationalism from that point on. But he was also adopted by other nations involved in the Crusades, including Portugal, and the powerful maritime city states of Genoa and Venice.

Supporters of English sporting teams tend to use the flag of St. George rather than the Union flag, even painting his cross on their faces, or dyeing

CRUSADER FOR THE COMMON PEOPLE

Born to a humble Mexican laboring family in Arizona in 1927, César Chávez did not become involved in social politics until the 1950s, when the Civil Rights movement began to gain some ground in the United States. He worked for the Latino Community Service Organization (CSO) from 1952, and soon became an active campaigner, becoming the CSO's director in 1958. Chávez went on to found (with Dolores Huerta) the National Farm Workers Association in 1962, which later became the United Farm Workers (UFW). He supported illegal immigrant control, but this was due to his implacable stance against the Bracero Program (1942–64), by which more than 4 million Mexican farm laborers left to work in the United States – he saw the program as a means of exploiting migrant laborers at the expense of farm workers in the United States.

His focus was not limited to the rights of Latinos, but extended to the conditions under which increasingly popular agricultural products, such as table grapes and lettuce, were being brought to the consumer. In contrast to the militant activities of many other pressure groups at the time, Chávez adopted a non-violent form of protest (including personal hunger strikes) to support campaigns urging consumers to boycott farm crops produced under slave-like conditions and those produced using hazardous pesticides. Chávez was a committed vegan.

Chávez died on April 23, 1993. He has acquired a cult following of such proportions that his canonization is very likely.

Chávez became an iconic figure for both farm workers and Latino Civil Rights groups throughout the southwest United States.

APRIL 23	ADALBERT OF PRAGUE

STATUS Bishop, Martyr

BORN c.956, Libice, Bohemia (modern Czech Republic)

DIED 997, Elbing, Germany, or Beregovoe, modern Russia

GRC ♣

CofE ◖

LCDUS ♣

OTHER Eastern Orthodox churches

◯ 999

✝ Bishop's vestments and miter

⚓ Bohemia, Prussia, Poland

The son of noble parents of the Slavnik clan, Adalbert was to become the first native Bohemian bishop. He studied in Magdeburg, Germany, and was inspired to undertake missionary work, but in 982 was appointed bishop of Prague. He was opposed by the nobility and so withdrew in 990 to Rome and became a Benedictine hermit. Two years later, the Vatican ordered him to return to Bohemia, where he reassumed his bishopric and established the abbey of Brevnov.

In 995, his hometown of Libice was attacked and four of Adalbert's five brothers were murdered on the orders of Duke Boleslav II of Bohemia. He fled to neighboring Hungary and then to Poland, where he attempted to evangelize the

there under armed guard with his remaining half-brother Radim, but their activities, which included chopping down oaks sacred to the pagans, resulted in Adalbert's assassination. It is not known what happened to Radim.

Some of Adalbert's remains were translated to Gniezno in Poland and then to Prague in 1039, but the former is still his major cult center, and was where Pope John Paul II celebrated the millennial anniversary of Adalbert's martyrdom in 1997. Like many early saints, several other locations retain some of his relics, including Beregovoe in Kaliningrad, while both Gniezno and Prague claim to have Adalbert's skull.

Adalbert and his half-brother Radim setting out to convert the Prussians immortalized in bronze at

APRIL 24 · FIDELIS OF SIGMARINGEN

STATUS Priest, Martyr

BORN 1578, Sigmaringen, Germany

DIED 1622, Seewis, Switzerland

GRC ♣

CofE ☁

LCDUS ♣

♥ 1729

○ 1746

✝ Often shown bearing a sword or nailed club, trampling heretics; often paired with Joseph of Leonissa (Feb. 4)

🙏 Lawyers and advocates; those who battle heresy

Born Mark Rey, the young Fidelis read philosophy and civil and canon law at Freiburg University. He was ordained in around 1610 and entered a Capuchin branch of the Franciscan Order in 1612, adopting the name Fidelis (faithful). A capable administrator, his career as superior of three successive houses was characterized by the intensity of his devotion and preaching, his skills as a confessor, and his compassion for the poor and sick. It also spanned the most turbulent and bloody time in early modern European history – the Thirty Years' War, which saw much of his homeland decimated in the struggle between Catholic and Protestant forces.

Fidelis was scrupulous in not admonishing those who veered in their adherence to the Christian faith. Among the more extreme Reformist movements were the followers of the Swiss preacher Ulrich Zwingli (d.1531), who denied the spiritual presence of the Host in Mass. In 1622, Fidelis went on a mission to attempt to reconcile the Zwinglians of Grisons canton to Catholicism, but after some initial success, he was assassinated by them, stabbed in church, having been accused of spying.

Fidelis, here shown trampling heresy in an uncharacteristically brutal manner by Giovanni Tiepolo (1696–1770), is accompanied by Joseph of Leonissa.

During the Thirty Years' War (1618–48) appalling atrocities were enacted in the name of religion. The French artist and engraver Jacques Callot (1592–1635) captured many scenes of abomination, such as The Hanging Tree *(above), where Catholic priests delivered Protestant prisoners to their doom.*

Date	Name	Status	Venerated	Life
April 23	Felix, Achilleus, and Fortunatus (d.212)	Martyrs ○ Pre-Congregation	In Vienne, France; Valencia, Spain	Felix was a Roman priest sent to evangelize region of Vienne, France. Accompanied by two deacons; all three martyred by local inhabitants after undergoing considerable torture.
April 24	Mellitus (d.624)	Bishop ○ Pre-Congregation	CofE	Missionary sent by Pope Gregory I to Britain (601) in wake of St. Augustine. Became first bishop of East Saxons, establishing first see in London. Converted Saxon king, Sabert, but met with hostility by his sons. Took refuge in France (618); returned to become archbishop of Canterbury (619).

APRIL 25 | MARK THE APOSTLE AND EVANGELIST

STATUS Evangelist

BORN Early 1st century AD, Jerusalem, modern Israel

DIED d.c. AD 74, Alexandria, Egypt

GRC ♣

CofE ♣

LCDUS ♣

OTHER Eastern Orthodox churches

◯ Pre-Congregation

✝ Winged lion, lions in general, writing or holding his Gospel, black hair and beard

🙏 Notaries, lawyers, glaziers, glassblowers, stained-glass window makers, the imprisoned, lions; sufferers from insect bites, scrofula, goiters; Venice, the Ionian Islands

The winged lion that forms Mark's emblem is said to refer to the regal dignity and supreme power of Christ. It has also become, by default, the symbol for the city of Venice.

Mark was born in Jerusalem, and raised by his mother, Mary, in a house where (according to Acts 12:12) the first Apostles would meet. He is often identified as the young man who briefly accompanied Christ after His arrest in the Garden of Gethsemane, narrowly escaping arrest himself by slipping out of his clothes and running for safety (Mark 14:51). He is sometimes referred to as John Mark. After their visit to Jerusalem, he traveled with Paul and Barnabas (who was Mark's cousin) back to Antioch; Barnabas and Mark then both accompanied Paul on his first missionary journey, although Mark decided to return to Jerusalem when they reached Perga (Pamphylia) in Anatolia. This caused something of a rift with the senior Apostle, although Barnabas and Mark later went on to evangelize Cyprus under Paul's guidance (Acts 14–15).

At a later date, Mark appears to be in Rome with both Paul and Peter, the latter referring to him as "my son," in the sense of a protégé rather than a blood relative. It is with Peter that Mark became most closely associated, seemingly acting as his secretary and as an 'interpreter' of Peter's ideas. This experience primed Mark well for his most important achievement – the compilation of the second Gospel. Later accounts describe Mark evangelizing Egypt and becoming the first bishop of Alexandria, and some also refer to his martyrdom there during Nero's reign.

The Gospel of St. Mark

Mark's Gospel has two notable features. First, much of his narrative account of Christ's life, especially the Passion, replicates (sometimes word for word) Matthew's Gospel. This subsequently led some to question which was composed first; the spareness of Mark's prose and the absence of elaboration of Christ's story lend some credence to Mark's being the first. The second feature is Mark's promotion of the teachings and recollections of St. Peter. Mark focuses closely on the ministry of Christ, and begins with His encounter with John the Baptist. The Gospel goes on to include an account of the death of John the Baptist, descriptions of several popular parables, the miraculous feeding of the five thousand, the story of the Gadarene swine, and numerous healings performed by Christ. Setting aside the unproved tradition of Mark's bishopric and martyrdom in Alexandria, it seems likely that the Gospel was written in Rome, shortly after St. Peter's death. It remains an outstanding source of instructive storytelling.

> ## "He that hath ears to hear, let him hear."
>
> FROM THE PARABLE OF THE SOWER, MARK 4:9.

Traditionally, Mark's remains were transported to Venice from Alexandria in around 828, after the conquest of Egypt by Arab armies; the relics were supposedly smuggled past Muslim guards under layers of pork. Venice became his principal cult center. The original church of San Marco was destroyed by fire in 976, and the rebuilt basilica (above) was completed in the 11th century. A series of mosaics was added to the façade, relating Mark's life, death, and translation to Venice.

In both Western and Orthodox art, Mark the Gospel writer is usually shown with dark hair and a flourishing beard.

The Theft of the Body of St. Mark from Alexandria *by Tintoretto was one of a cycle of paintings celebrating the life and sainthood of St. Mark, painted for the city of Venice between 1562–66. Mark's role is not dissimilar to that of James the Greater (July 25) in the Spanish Reconquista. Both became emblematic patrons of a series of campaigns against Islamic adversaries. In the case of Venice, Mark became the spiritual standard-bearer in the maritime city-state's power struggle with the Ottoman Turks.*

APRIL 26 | STEPHEN OF PERM

STATUS Missionary

BORN c.1340, Veliky Ustyug, Russia

DIED 1396, Moscow, Russia

GRC ☁

CofE ☁

LCDUS ☁

OTHER Eastern Orthodox churches

○ 1549

✝ Bearded, bearing Orthodox cross and book

⚜ Russian Orthodox missionaries

In the Russian Orthodox Church, Stephen is regarded as one of the most important missionaries. Born in northern Russia, he entered a monastery in Rostov where he was educated, learning Greek and manuscript copying. Deciding to become a missionary among the Komi Zyrians, he learned their customs and language, later inventing an alphabet in order to translate selected biblical texts and liturgy.

Stephen was appointed the first bishop of Perm in central Russia in 1383, and built churches, seminaries, and schools. Perm at the time was notionally under the control of Novgorod, Moscow's rival city state. Stephen's resistance to Novgorod's attempts to oust him brought the region

into Moscow's sphere of control at a critical point in the expansion of the Russian state.

Stephen is known as the 'Enlightener of Perm,' and is often cited as one of the leading figures in the rebirth of the Russian Orthodox Church *(see below)*.

The missionary journeys of Stephen in eastern Russia exemplify those of many such 'Enlighteners' who undertook arduous and dangerous expeditions – often on foot – to spread the word.

RENAISSANCE OF THE RUSSIAN ORTHODOX CHURCH

The late 14th and early 15th centuries saw a cultural and spiritual reinvigoration of the Russian Orthodox Church undertaken by missionaries such as Stephen of Perm *(see above)*, the writer Epiphanius the Wise (d.1420), the monastic reformer Sergei (Sergius) of Radonezh (Sept. 25), and the painter Andrei Rublev (d.c.1427).

Rublev remains the most important and influential of the late medieval Russian icon painters. The richness of his imaginative approach moves well beyond the restrictive confines of the traditional icon. His work in many ways parallels that of his Italian predecessors Duccio and Giotto in introducing a sense of naturalism and narrative to a long-established and highly stylized tradition of devotional painting. Where Duccio and Giotto were struggling to break free from the restrictions of the ornate International Gothic style of painting – paving the way for Renaissance masters such as Fra Angelico (Feb. 18) – Rublev set about injecting life into the formulaic and increasingly craft-based manner of Russian icon painting, itself a derivative of Greek/Byzantine Christian art.

Rublev is recorded as working in the Cathedral of the Annunciation in the Kremlin, Moscow, and providing murals for the Cathedral of the Domition at Vladimir. A number of other works are attributed to him, but his only firmly identified work is the *Icon of the Holy Trinity*, c.1411. Rublev is venerated as a saint by the Russian Orthodox Church. He was canonized in 1988.

The Icon of the Holy Trinity *combines three angelic personifications bearing their staves of office: God the Father is seated on the left, God the Son (Christ) sits in the middle, and God the Holy Spirit is on the right. In front of the three figures is a bowl containing a sacrificial calf, representing Christ.*

APRIL 26 | # PEDRO DE SAN JOSÉ BETANCUR

STATUS Missionary, Founder
BORN 1626, Tenerife, Canary Islands
DIED 1667, Guatemala City, Guatemala
GRC ☁
CofE ☁
LCDUS ☁
OTHER In the Canary Islands and in Guatemala
♥ 1980
⬭ 2002
✝ Holding a walking stick and bell

Born on the Spanish Canarian island of Tenerife, Pedro grew up working as a shepherd, and lived hermit-like in a cave (today a popular shrine). In 1649, he crossed the Atlantic hoping to work with a relative in Guatemala. Running out of money, he was forced to stop in Havana, Cuba, but after working there for a year arrived in Guatemala. He was keen to enter the Society of Jesus, but failed to complete his studies and became a Franciscan tertiary at a convent in Antigua Guatemala. He worked tirelessly for the poor, the unemployed, and prisoners, raising enough money to found a pauper's hospital and several other charitable shelters and schools.

Pedro's selflessness attracted a following of other Franciscan tertiaries, and he went on to found the Order of the Bethlemites, which included female tertiaries. His compassion for the poverty-stricken and underprivileged earned him enduring popularity in Guatemala, one of the poorest countries of Central America.

A shrine to Pedro in Antigua Guatemala.

APRIL 27 | # ZITA (CITHA, SITHA)

STATUS Virgin
BORN c.1218, Monsagrati, Italy
DIED c.1271, Lucca, Italy
GRC ☁
CofE ☁
LCDUS ☁
OTHER In Italy
⬭ 1696
✝ Shown tending children or the poor, barefoot, with rosary
♨ Domestic servants

Zita entered the service of the wealthy Fatinelli wool-merchant family in Lucca at age 12, where she worked for the rest of her life. Her simple devotion was initially scorned by the family and by other servants, but her persistence, piety, abilities as a nursemaid to the Fatinelli children, and kindness to the poor and needy transformed the household. Her incorrupt remains can be seen in the church of San Frediano in Lucca.

Folk images of Zita usually portray her barefoot, distributing leftovers from the Fatinelli household to the poor.

Date	Name	Status	Venerated	Life
April 26	Cletus (Anacletus) (d.c. AD 91)	Pope ⬭ Pre-Congregation		Third Roman pope. Credited with dividing Rome into 25 parishes and ordaining several priests. Feast removed from General Roman Calendar in 1969. Shares feast day with Marcellinus (see below).
April 26	Marcellinus (d.c.304)	Pope ⬭ Pre-Congregation		Bishop of Rome during reign of Diocletian. When the persecutions began in 303 he was arraigned, but accounts differ: he either refused to apostatize and was martyred, or succumbed. Shares joint feast day with Cletus (see above).
April 27	Maughold (Machalus) (d.c.488)	Bishop ⬭ Pre-Congregation	✝ Coracle ♨ Isle of Man	Irish pirate prince and robber, converted by St. Patrick. Sent by Patrick to evangelize the Isle of Man. Sailed there from Ireland in a wicker coracle with no oars in penance for his crimes, and to avoid returning to piracy.
April 27	Christina Rossetti (1830–94)	Poet, Visionary	CofE	From an artistically gifted family. Posed as Blessed Virgin Mary in paintings by her Pre-Raphaelite brother, Dante Gabriel Rossetti. Wrote mythological and devotional poetry. Dedicated much time to looking after fallen women. Regarded today as important proto-feminist.

APRIL 28 · PETER (PIERRE) CHANEL

STATUS Missionary, Martyr
BORN 1803, France
DIED 1841, Futuna, French
Polynesia
GRC ♣
CofE ♣
LCDUS ♣
OTHER By Marists
♥ 1889
○ 1954
🙏 Oceania

Chanel was born to a peasant family, and due to his piety was encouraged to enter the Church by the local priest. He was ordained in 1827 and joined a recently established missionary group, the Society of Mary (the Marists) in 1831. He was sent to French Polynesia in the Pacific in 1836, in the company of a number of other Marists, among them Jean Baptiste François Pompallier, who was later the first Catholic bishop of New Zealand.

Chanel's destination was the island of Futuna, which he reached in November 1837. Only recently had cannibalism been abolished by the local ruler, Niuliki. Chanel, warmly greeted and endlessly enthusiastic, made striking headway. He learned the indigenous language, and his care for the sick earned him many followers and converts. But his efforts fell foul of Niuliki, who saw Chanel as a direct threat to his authority — the more so when Niuliki's son asked to be baptized. In April 1841, Niuliki had Chanel clubbed, then killed with an ax. His body was then chopped up. Chanel became the first proto-martyr of the Pacific, and of the Marists.

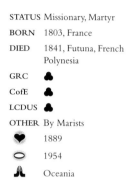

Peter Chanel's arms include the palm of martyrdom, the ax with which he was slain, the torch of truth, his mission hut, the black and white lily of the Marists, and the blue waters of the Pacific.

This stained-glass window from the Church of St. Louis, King of France in St. Paul, Minnesota, shows the warrior Musumusu executing Chanel, while others loot his hut.

Date	Name	Status	Venerated	Life
April 28	Louis de Montfort (1673–1716)	Priest, Confessor, Founder ♥ 1888 ○ 1947	GRC, LCDUS, CofE By Jesuits	Entered Jesuit college at Rennes, France, at age 12. Ordained in 1700, but became a Dominican tertiary (1710), wishing to travel and preach. Strong advocate of Mariology and influential writer of tracts and hymns. Founded the Daughters of Wisdom (1703).
April 30	Pandita Mary Ramabai (1858–1922)	Translator of the Scriptures Social Reformer	CofE In India	Indian women's rights activist, writer, and translator. Used a Christian stance to try to reform plight of Hindu women, arguing for female education, and against child marriage and *suttee*, the ritual suicide of widows. Traveled widely. Author of *The High-Caste Hindu Woman* (1888).

APRIL 29 | CATHERINE OF SIENA

STATUS Virgin, Mystic, Doctor of the Church

BORN c.1347, Siena, Italy

DIED 1380, Rome, Italy

GRC ♣

CofE ♣

LCDUS ♣

OTHER By Dominicans

✝ Dominican tertiary robes; in mystic marriage, ecstasy, or receiving stigmata; lily, book

🙏 Against illness and pestilence; Italy, Europe

Catherine was allegedly the 24th of 25 children of a wealthy Sienese dyer, and decided not to marry, vowing chastity after having a vision of Christ when she was only seven. Resisting her parents' attempts to marry her off, she became a Dominican tertiary at around age 20. She lived at home as a virtual hermit, but after experiencing a mystic marriage with Christ she received the stigmata, worked in a Sienese hospital, and began to preach reform and repentance. Preaching proved to be her forte, despite being a laywoman. A group of followers, the 'Caterinati,' formed around her. They attested to her persuasive powers and accompanied her on her travels.

By 1375, Catherine had become active on a broader canvas, preaching widely, campaigning for peace between the states and principalities of Italy, and traveling to Avignon to implore the pope, Gregory XI, to leave France and return to Rome. He did so, but died in 1378, whereupon his successor, Urban VI, was immediately opposed by a rival claimant. This was the beginning of the 'Great Schism' in the Western Church, lasting from 1378–1417. Catherine threw herself into support for Urban, dictating numerous letters and becoming Urban's

St. Catherine Receiving the Stigmata by Pompeo Batoni (1708–87). Apparently, although Catherine experienced the pain of stigmata, blood did not flow from the wounds.

Catherine dictating her influential work, The Dialogue (1377–78), while receiving divine inspiration. It is said that she never learned to write, which is probably untrue.

trusted advisor. She did not live to see a united Roman Church, however, dying of a stroke, probably induced by fasting or anorexia. According to her confessor, Raymond of Capua, in her later years she took to sucking pus and phlegm from the sick, this being her only food apart from the Communion Host. Her head and thumb were miraculously smuggled out of Rome after her death and taken back to Siena, where her incorrupt head can still be seen in the Basilica of San Domenico. Most of her remains lie in Santa Maria sopra Minerva, Rome. Her writings (over 300 letters survive) reveal a woman of simple but ardent faith, with a direct style unabashed by whomever she was addressing.

Catherine was declared the first female Doctor of the Church in 1970.

APRIL 30 | PIUS V

STATUS Pope

BORN 1504

DIED 1572

GRC ♣

CofE ♢

LCDUS ♣

Pope Pius, despite his promotion of the notorious Inquisition, regarded himself as rather too lenient in his treatment of non-Catholics.

Pius was born Antonio Ghislieri in northern Italy. He entered the Dominican Order at age 14, and was ordained in 1528, by which time the Reformation had already begun. He taught philosophy and theology, and then became an outstanding inquisitor at Bergamo. Under the patronage of Pope Paul IV he was appointed bishop, then cardinal, and finally head of the Roman Inquisition in 1558. Eight years later, in 1566, he was elected pope with the strong support of Charles Borromeo (Nov. 4).

It fell to Pius to implement the reforms of the Catholic Church announced at the Council of Trent in 1545, reforms inaugurated in response to the challenge of the Reformation. In his personal life Pius was stringent and disciplined, and he expected this of others, introducing strictly supervised standards. To back these up he relied heavily upon the Inquisition, installing it in a new palace and strengthening its rules and powers. Ironically, his excommunication of Queen Elizabeth I of England in 1570 proved disastrous for English Catholics, laying them open to widespread persecution.

MAY

In the Catholic Church, the entire month of May is dedicated to the Blessed Virgin Mary. May Day, the first day of the month, has long been associated with Beltane, a European pagan festival of fertility and rising spirits. It is also now widely identified as Labor (or International Workers') Day. Mother's Day is celebrated on the second Sunday in May in many countries.

Ascension Thursday frequently falls in this month, occurring 40 days after Easter, and Pentecost (or Whitsunday) follows ten days later. Pentecost celebrates the sending of the Holy Spirit to the Blessed Virgin Mary and the assembled Apostles. It marks the end of the Easter season. Pentecost is regarded as the original foundation day of the Christian Church, and is celebrated in the Eastern Orthodox churches by a three-day festival.

Having become aware of Christ's Resurrection, and witnessing His Ascension, the eleven original Apostles and Judas Iscariot's replacement, Matthias, were inspired by the Holy Spirit to follow their often hazardous missionary journeys on the day of Pentecost. This richly colored panel illustrating the event, from the 13th-century Umbrian school of painting, does not include Matthias.

MAY 1 · JOSEPH THE WORKER

Joseph's main feast day is March 19. This second feast was introduced by Pope Pius XII in 1955. It was allocated to May 1, widely celebrated as Labor Day or May Day, in direct response to the challenge of atheistic Communism.

Joseph had previously had a second feast day, celebrating his role as Patron of the Universal Church, which fell on the third Wednesday after Easter, but this was abandoned when the new feast was introduced.

Philip is usually shown as a long-haired, bearded young man, bearing a cross in the form of a stave, with which he is said to have cast a noxious dragon from a temple; a book; or often loaves of bread, reminding us of the Feeding of the Five Thousand.

MAY 2 · ATHANASIUS

STATUS Bishop, Doctor of the Church
BORN c.295, Alexandria, Egypt
DIED 373, Alexandria, Egypt
GRC ♣
CofE ♣
LCDUS ♣
OTHER Eastern Orthodox churches
⬭ Pre-Congregation

The emblem of Athanasius shows his defense of Trinitarianism (represented by the triangle) draped by the pallium of his office.

Athanasius ranks alongside Basil the Great, Gregory Nazianzen (both Jan. 2), and John Chrysostom (Sept. 13) as one of the four Doctors of the Church in the East. He was elected bishop of the powerful Eastern see of Alexandria in 328, at age 33. He was an energetically pastoral bishop, and a robust promoter of the recently promulgated Nicene Creed in the face of the Arian tendency (*see* page 12). As such, he earned powerful enemies, who persuaded Emperor Constantine to banish Athanasius to Augusta Treverorum (modern Trier) in northern Gaul.

In 346, Constantine's successor, Constantius II, allowed Athanasius to return to Alexandria following the death of a rival bishop, but Athanasius continued to be persecuted by his Arian peers. In 356 he had to flee to the Libyan desert when he was threatened by armed troops. There he continued his ministry, and wrote extensively, including a *Life of St. Antony* (Jan. 17). He returned to Alexandria in 366. Athanasius died only eight years before Arianism was declared definitively heretical at the Council of Constantinople in 381.

Date	Name	Status	Venerated	Life
May 3	Theodosius of the Caves (c.1009–74)	Abbot, Hermit ⬭ 1106	Eastern Orthodox churches	Ascetic and devoted to the poor when young. Joined the cave-dwelling hermits of Kiev (c.1132), becoming their second abbot. Did much to engage them in social works. Built a more conventional monastery where the sick, poor, and itinerant found succor, but resisted royal patronage.

THE APOSTLES PHILIP AND JAMES THE LESS

PHILIP

STATUS Apostle, Martyr

BORN 1st century AD, Bethsaida, modern Israel

DIED 1st century AD, Phrygia, modern Turkey

GRC ♣

CofE ♣ (May 1)

LCDUS ♣

OTHER Eastern Orthodox churches

⬭ Pre-Congregation

Philip's cross 'bottony' is accompanied by two roundels, said to represent the loaves of bread he distributed at the Feeding of the Five Thousand.

JAMES

STATUS Apostle, Martyr

BORN 1st century AD

DIED c. AD 53/62, Jerusalem

GRC ♣

CofE ♣ (May 1)

LCDUS ♣

OTHER Eastern Orthodox churches

⬭ Pre-Congregation

† Saw, club

🙏 The dying

James's symbol is the saw, the tool of his martyrdom.

Both Philip and James were among the original Twelve Apostles, though little is known about them.

Philip the Apostle
According to John 1:43–44, Philip was among the first to join Jesus, along with Peter (June 29) and Andrew (Nov. 30), and was from the same city, Bethsaida in Galilee. He introduced Nathaniel (later to become St. Bartholomew the Apostle, Aug. 24) to Jesus. Philip figures in the Feeding of the Five Thousand, when he helps distribute food among the throng. At the Last Supper, Philip asks Jesus to show God the Father to the assembled Apostles, eliciting a lengthy response in which Jesus not only reveals His indivisibility from God the Father, but provides comfort for the Apostles in the future (John 14:8–31). He was also present at Pentecost, and received the Holy Spirit. It seems that he may have traveled to Asia Minor (some sources cite Phrygia in the northwest, where Bartholomew also preached) spreading the Gospel, and he is said to have been martyred there. The means of his martyrdom is not clear, although stoning is commonly described. He is sometimes, probably mistakenly, identified as the same person as Philip the Deacon (June 6). Philip's remains were translated to Rome at an early date, and now reside in the Church of the Twelve Apostles, originally dedicated to Philip and James.

> ## "He that hath seen me hath seen the Father ... I am in the Father, and the Father in me."
> JESUS TO PHILIP, (JOHN 14:9–11).

James the Less ('the Just')
James the Less (so named to distinguish him from James the Greater, July 25) remains a more shadowy figure than Philip, although he is mentioned in three gospels: Matthew 10:3; Mark 3:18; and Luke 6:15. He is described as the son of Alphaeus. He has also been tentatively identified as 'James the Just,' cited as the brother of Jesus (Mark 15:40).

Unlike many of the Apostles, James seems to have remained within the Christian community in Jerusalem after Pentecost (he is listed among the Apostles at the event), and was apparently tried for sedition by the Jewish court, the Sanhedrin, and sentenced to death. He was cast from the parapets of the Temple and beaten to death.

S·IACOBVS MINOR·A

James is often represented clasping a fuller's club, with which he was beaten during his martyrdom.

Philip's fate remains very unclear, some sources saying he was crucified, some that he was stoned to death in Phrygia.

MAY 4   THE CATHOLIC MARTYRS OF ENGLAND AND WALES

STATUS Martyrs

BORN 16th–17th centuries

DIED 16th–17th centuries

GRC ☁

CofE ♠

LCDUS ☁

♥ 1886, 1895, 1929, 1987

◯ 1970

"In condemning us, you condemn all your own ancestors, all our ancient bishops and kings, all that was once the glory of England."

ST. EDMUND CAMPION.

Between 1535 and approximately 1690, thousands of English and Welsh Catholics died as a result of their faith. Two hundred eighty-five have since been beatified as martyrs, and of these, 42 have been canonized. All but two — St. John Fisher and St. Thomas More (June 22) — are now commemorated on May 4 in England, although previously there were several feast days for different groups.

The manner of their various deaths reflects not just the traumas of the Reformation in England and Wales, and the brutal uprooting of centuries of Catholic worship, but also the violent seesawing between Catholicism and Protestantism that occurred under Henry VIII's first two successors, Edward VI, implacably

This painting by Geoffrey Webb depicts 14 of the martyrs beatified in 1929. On the far left is Philip Howard (d.1595); in the center, in red, is the Jesuit John Southwell (d.1595); the monk kneeling on the left of the center group is John Jones (d.1598); the priest kneeling on the right of the center group is the Jesuit Edmund Arrowsmith (d.1628); the women on the right are, from left to right, Margaret Clitherow (d.1586), Anne Line (d.1601), and Margaret Ward (d.1588).

Protestant, and Mary I, no less fanatically but very much more bloodily Catholic.

Elizabeth I's accession in 1558 promised a middle way between these extremes. Officially, she reaffirmed Protestantism; unofficially, she turned a blind eye to the substantial surviving pockets of Catholicism. Yet her reign saw a new and even bloodier phase of Catholic persecution. In the face of the Reformation, the Roman Church, determined to eradicate Protestant heresies, adopted a new militancy — a Counter-Reformation. In 1570, Pope Pius V excommunicated Elizabeth and pronounced it a Catholic duty to assassinate her. Given that the country's most fervent enemies, led by Spain, were all Catholic, the consequence was that Protestantism and patriotism effectively became the same. The very survival of the nation demanded it, as the Spanish Armada of 1588 made clear. By extension, all English Catholics, even those professing loyalty to the queen, were automatically suspect. Not only were all Catholic priests made fugitives, anyone who consorted with them, let alone sheltered them, was to be executed.

Thus the brutal killings continued not just in Elizabeth's reign, but throughout those of her Stuart successors in the 17th century, despite their Catholic leanings.

THE 40 CATHOLIC MARTYRS

The stories of all 40 martyrs canonized in 1970 are harrowing. Margaret Clitherow (1566–86), for example, wife of a candle-maker in York and mother of three, was crushed to death after refusing to answer charges of having sheltered Catholic priests. Tied to the ground, she had a rock the size of a fist placed under her back. A door was placed on her and weights progressively added to it. It took her 15 minutes to die; her last words were "Jesu! Jesu! Jesu! Have mercy on me!"

Edmund Campion (1540–81) was a Jesuit priest sent on a clandestine mission to England in 1580 and arrested the following year. He was repeatedly racked in the Tower of London before being hanged, drawn, and quartered. Nicholas Owen (c.1550–1606), the most skilled builder of 'priest holes' and a lay Jesuit, suffered what were called 'examinations' on the 'Topcliffe' rack, named after a particularly sadistic persecutor of Catholics, Richard Topcliffe: Owen was hung by his arms, with weights suspended from his feet.

In the foreground, a Jesuit priest, Edward Oldcorne (c.1561–1606), is racked in the Tower of London. Behind him, weights at his feet, is Nicholas Owen. This mid-17th-century engraving is by the Dutch artist Gaspar Bouttats.

Date	Name	Status	Venerated	Life
May 4	Michael Giedroyc (1400–85)	Augustinian Hermit		Born a dwarf; later after an accident able to use only one foot. Trained as metalworker before becoming Augustinian monk and then hermit, living in simple cell adjoining Augustinian monastery in Krakow. Life thereafter one of extreme devotion to Christ. "The church," it was said, "was his home by day and by night."

MAY 4 · FLORIAN

STATUS Martyr

BORN c.250

DIED c.303, Lorch, Austria

GRC ⬭

CofE ⬭

LCDUS ⬭

⬭ Pre-Congregation

✝ Roman soldier with pitcher of water

🙏 Firefighters; invoked as a protector against fire and water; Linz, Poland

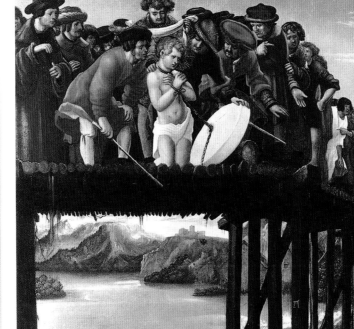

The Martyrdom of St. Florian, *one of seven panels depicting the life of the saint painted by Albrecht Altdorfer in around 1530.*

Florian was the Roman commander of the imperial forces in Noricum, modern-day Austria, who in around 284 converted to Christianity. He was rounded up by the governor of the province, Aquilinus, in a persecution ordered by the emperor Diocletian. Refusing to renounce his faith, he was repeatedly whipped, flayed, set alight, and then hurled into the river Enns with a rock tied to his neck. His body was later recovered after he appeared to a Christian woman in a dream asking to be reburied. He was interred on the site of what from 1071 became the abbey of St. Florian, today a commanding Baroque structure, near Linz. In 1138, the pope authorized that some of his relics be transferred to Poland, hence his patronage of that country. His became one of the most enduring traditions of early Christian martyrdom in central Europe.

MAY 4 · GOTTHARD (GODEHARD) OF HILDESHEIM

STATUS Abbot, Bishop

BORN 960, Bavaria, Germany

DIED 1038, Hildesheim, Germany

GRC ⬭

CofE ⬭

LCDUS ⬭

⬭ 1131

🙏 Traveling merchants; childbirth, sufferers from gout

Gotthard was a Benedictine monk at the abbey of Niederaltaich in Bavaria, where he was ordained in 993. In 996, he was made abbot, reviving the Rule of St. Benedict (July 11), which he subsequently helped spread to a series of other German abbeys. In 1022, he was made bishop of Hildesheim in northern Germany, where he oversaw the construction of 30 churches. Gotthard also established an important refuge for the poor in St. Moritz.

The St. Gotthard Pass in the Alps, named after him, reflects his role as patron saint of traveling merchants.

Numerous miracles were attributed to Gotthard's relics. His cult was spread widely over Scandinavia, Switzerland, and Eastern Europe.

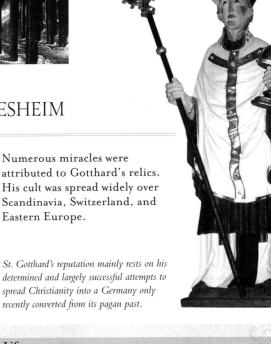

St. Gotthard's reputation mainly rests on his determined and largely successful attempts to spread Christianity into a Germany only recently converted from its pagan past.

Date	Name	Status	Venerated	Life
May 5	Hilary of Arles (c.403–49)	Bishop ⬭ Pre-Congregation		Monk at abbey of Lérins under his relation, St. Honoratus of Arles. Like St. Honoratus, became bishop of Arles (429). Best remembered for protracted power struggle with Pope Leo I the Great. Hilary, contending his authority, embraced sees outside his own diocese.
May 6	Marian and James (d.259)	Martyrs ⬭ Pre-Congregation	In Gubbio, Italy	Two active Christians, born in Numidia (modern Algeria). Imprisoned during Valerian persecutions. Unsuccessfully tortured on rack to apostatize. Both enjoyed inspirational dreams of martyrdom. Martyred at Lambaesis during mass decapitation.

MAY 7 — JOHN OF BEVERLEY

STATUS Bishop, Theologian
BORN 7th century, Yorkshire, England
DIED 721, Beverley, Yorkshire
GRC ○
CofE ○
LCDUS ○
◯ 1037

John was one of the most important churchmen in the period immediately following the conversion of Anglo-Saxon Northumbria to Christianity. He was known personally to the great historian of the early Church, the Venerable Bede (May 25), by whom he was in fact ordained. He was a priest first at Whitby before, in 687, he was made bishop of Hexham. In 705, he was made bishop of York, remaining in office until 717, when he retired to Beverley, where he founded a monastery. A substantial cult grew up around him after his death. His tomb developed into a major place of pilgrimage, a fact that largely accounts for Beverley's importance and prosperity in the Middle Ages. Edward I visited it three times, while Henry V claimed his victory at Agincourt was the result of John's 'miraculous intervention.' The sumptuous shrine containing his relics was destroyed in the Reformation.

John of Beverley in a 19th-century stained-glass window at Beverley Minster, commonly regarded as one of the most magnificent medieval churches in England.

MAY 8 — JULIAN OF NORWICH

STATUS Hermit, Mystic
BORN 1342, Norfolk, England
DIED c.1416, Norwich, England
GRC ○
CofE ●
LCDUS ○
OTHER US Evangelical Lutheran Church

Julian of Norwich — a woman, not a man: her name is sometimes given as Juliana — was among the most remarkable saints in medieval England, an anchoress (female hermit), seer, and mystic whose writings exercised a striking influence. At age 30, apparently near death, she had a series of intense visions of Christ. Though she wrote about them at the time, 20 years later she described them in much greater detail in a book, *Revelations of Divine Love*, which showed remarkable knowledge of theology as well as exceptional psychological insight. Unusually for the time, she conceived of God as a fount of intense, universal love that would save all humanity at the Last Judgment, whatever humanity's many frailties and inevitable sinfulness. Although never canonized, she is nonetheless generally regarded as a saint.

"All shall be well and all shall be well and all manner of things shall be well."

JULIAN OF NORWICH,
REVELATIONS OF DIVINE LOVE.

A modern statue of Julian of Norwich on the west front of Norwich Cathedral.

Date	Name	Status	Venerated	Life
May 7	Rose Venerini (1656–1728)	Educator, Founder ◯ 2006	By the Venerini Sisters	Destined to be a nun; abandoned vocation on death of father. Discovered calling as an educator. Opened school in Viterbo, Italy (1685), teaching peasant women religious instruction. Established further 40 schools across Italy. The Venerini Sisters have spread across the globe.
May 8	Peter of Tarentaise (1102–74)	Abbot, Bishop ◯ 1191	By Cistercians	Cistercian monk; abbot of monastery of Tamié in French Alps. Reluctantly became bishop of Tarentaise (1142). Known for liturgical reforms, building shelters for Alpine travelers, distributing free food.
May 9	George Preca (1880–1962)	Priest, Founder ♥ 2001 ◯ 2007	♠ Malta, Gozo, Society of Christian Doctrine	The first Maltese saint. Founder (1907) of controversial Society of Christian Doctrine (not formally approved until 1932), training lay preachers to spread Christian doctrine on Malta. Joined Carmelites (1918). Today society has spread around world, with 110 centers. Noted for simple, humble life.

MAY 9 · PACHOMIUS

STATUS Hermit, Abbot
BORN c.292, Thebes, Egypt
DIED c.346, Egypt
GRC ☁
CofE ☁
LCDUS ☁
OTHER Eastern Orthodox churches, Coptic Church, Lutheran Church; by Benedictines
○ Pre-Congregation
✝ Black-garbed hermit; often crossing the Nile on a crocodile

Pachomius was an Egyptian who converted to Christianity in 314, thereafter becoming a hermit in an attempt to imitate the example of Antony of Egypt (Jan. 17). His real significance was in the development of monastic, or cenobitic, life. Previously, holy men had almost always lived as hermits. It was Pachomius who conceived the idea of bringing them together in communities, in effect monasteries, dedicated to communal worship and communal work. He established his first such monastery around 320 in Tabennisi. Within a matter of years,

A medieval Byzantine mosaic of Pachomius.

it had attracted over 100 monks. Eight further monasteries followed. Pachomius subsequently spent most of his life at the monastery of Pabau. It has been estimated that 3,000 such monasteries were in existence in Egypt alone by the time of Pachomius's death. Within a further 20 years or so, the number had grown to 7,000. The monastic tradition thus established rapidly spread south beyond its Egyptian homelands with the Coptic Church to Ethiopia and to the Middle East, from where, in time, it would take root in Europe.

MAY 10 · DAMIEN OF MOLOKAI

STATUS Priest
BORN 1840, Tremelo, Belgium
DIED 1889, Molokai, Hawaii
GRC ☁
CofE ☁
LCDUS ♣
OTHER Some Lutheran churches
♥ 1995
○ 2009
🙏 Lepers, AIDS sufferers; Hawaii

Damien de Veuster, the 'Apostle of the Lepers,' was a Belgian Roman Catholic priest and member of the Congregation of the Sacred Hearts of Jesus and Mary. It was under the auspices of this missionary order that in March 1864 Damien went to Hawaii, then still an independent kingdom, where shortly afterwards he was ordained. The first European contact with Hawaii had come only in 1778, and in its wake came a series of diseases hitherto unknown on the islands that led to the deaths of thousands. Among these diseases was leprosy. In 1865, Hawaii's lepers were quarantined in two remote settlements on the island of Molokai. Within a few years, both

had degenerated into near chaos, the government unwilling to provide sufficient food and medical aid, the lepers unable to help themselves. The French vicar apostolic of Hawaii, in effect bishop of the islands, realized that at the very least a priest should be nominated to tend to the victims' spiritual needs. Damien volunteered. He arrived at the colony in May 1873. His presence almost immediately had as much practical as spiritual effect, bringing order and cohesion. Crops were planted, farms reorganized, and schools and a church built. Perhaps inevitably, in 1884 Damien himself contracted the disease and he died from its complications.

It is said that when he was training to be a priest, Damien (above) prayed every day before an image of St. Francis Xavier, patron saint of missionaries.

MAY 10 · JOHN OF ÁVILA

STATUS Preacher, Mystic
BORN 1500, Almodóvar del Campo, Spain
DIED 1569, Montilla, Spain
GRC ☁
CofE ☁
LCDUS ♣
♥ 1893
○ 1970
🙏 Andalusia, Spain

John of Ávila was among the most charismatic and successful preachers of 16th-century Spain. Trained first in law, then in philosophy and theology, once ordained in 1525 he had initially hoped to travel to Mexico, a Spanish colony only since 1521, as a missionary. Rather against his better judgment, John allowed himself to be persuaded by the archbishop of Seville, Don Alfonso Manrique, that his unusual sanctity could more

usefully be employed buttressing the faithful in Spain itself. So began a 40-year career of ceaseless travel and preaching across Spain. John's sermons regularly attracted thousands, drawn by his passion and mysticism. His rejection of worldly goods was such that he was charged by the Inquisition of unreasonable criticism of the rich and of asserting that their wealth denied them any hope of going to heaven. The charges were rapidly dropped.

Teresa of Ávila (Oct. 15) was among those swayed by John of Ávila's fierce denunciations of impiety.

MAY 11 | ODILO

STATUS Abbot

BORN 962, Auvergne, France

DIED 1049, Souvigny, France

GRC ⬭

CofE ⬭

LCDUS ⬭

OTHER By Benedictines

⬭ Pre-Congregation

✝ Benedictine abbot with skull and crossbones at his feet

🙏 Souls in purgatory

In 994, Odilo was made abbot of Cluny in Burgundy. At a stroke he became not merely one of the leading churchmen of his day but one of the greatest figures in Christendom. Cluny, founded in 910 by William I, Duke of Aquitaine, was the powerhouse of early medieval European monasticism. Under the generous terms of William's foundation, Cluny owed the monarch only prayer. What this meant in practice was that no temporal lord could assert any prior claim on the foundation; Cluny and its rapidly growing riches were answerable only to the pope. Directed by a series of exceptional abbots, of whom Odilo was among the greatest, Cluny became not merely immensely wealthy, but exerted an influence, part theological, part political, that was felt across Christendom. In a turbulent age it offered order, stability, and certainty.

Odilo, consort of kings and princes as well as of popes and bishops, took full advantage of his position. He was largely responsible for the introduction of All Souls' Day (Nov. 2) on the Christian calendar, and also attempted to impose a 'Truce of God' on the generally brutally warlike rivalries of European kings jockeying for supremacy, recalling them to their Christian duties. But perhaps most significantly, during his term as abbot the number of Cluniac houses grew from 37 to 65. By the 12th century, Cluny was waning, but at its peak it had been a startlingly forceful indicator of a resurgent Europe.

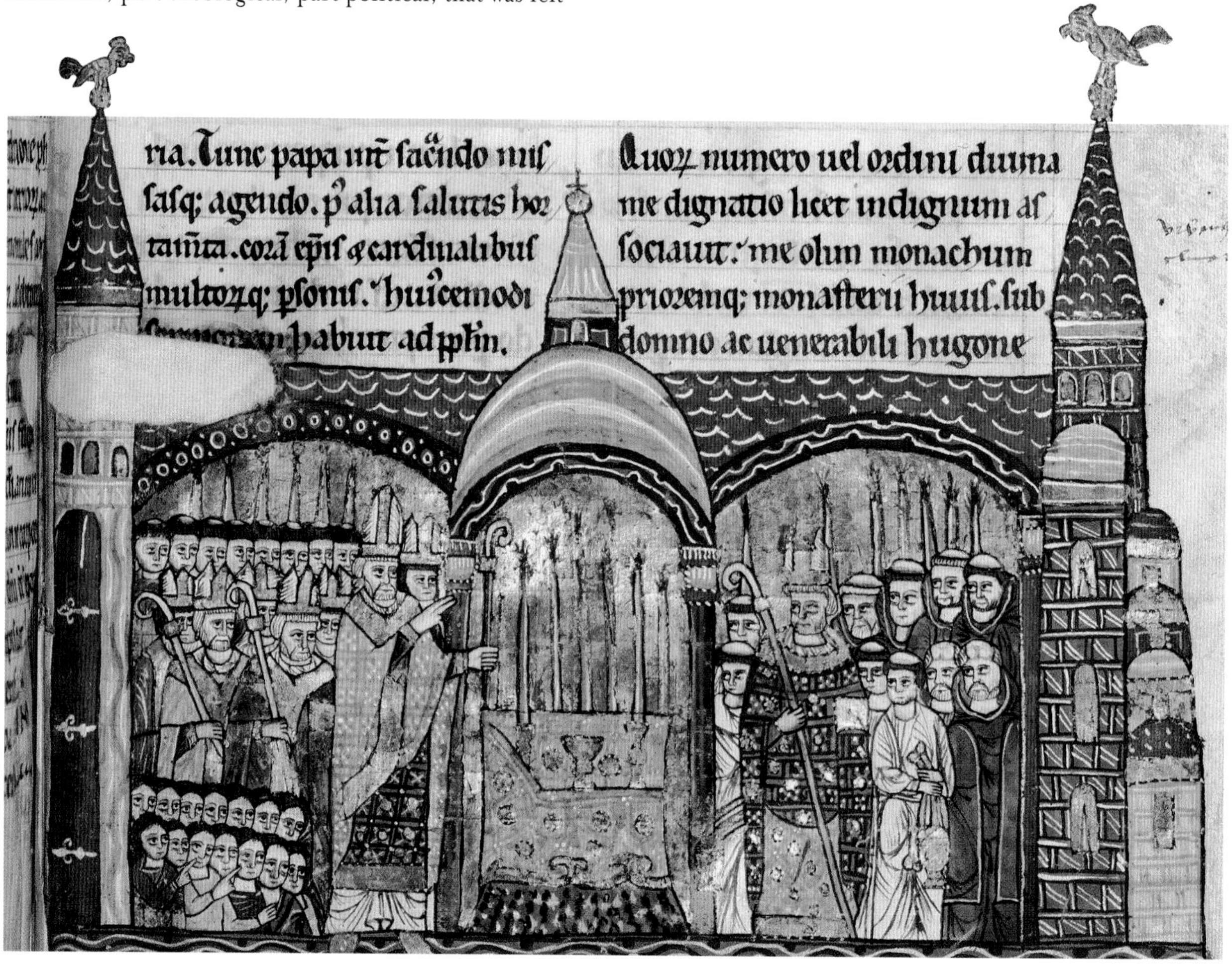

In its 11th-century heyday, Cluny easily outdistanced every other Christian institution, the papacy included: richer, larger, and vastly more sumptuous, it dwarfed its rivals. Its combination of piety and worldly hardheadedness has rarely been equaled.

Date	Name	Status	Venerated	Life
May 11	Ignatius of Laconi (1701–81)	Friar ❤ 1940 ⬭ 1951		Franciscan friar, dedicated to modesty, piety, obedience, and poverty. Chief duty was collection of alms for his monastery in Cagliari, but also helped with caring for the sick, educating the young, and urging religious observance on sinners. Blind for two years before he died, but sanctity and gentleness in no way diminished. Many miracles credited to his intercession after his death.

MAY 12 · PANCRAS OF ROME

STATUS Martyr
BORN c.290, Anatolia
DIED c.304, Rome, Italy
GRC ♣
CofE ♤
LCDUS ♣

⬭ Pre-Congregation

✝ Depicted as a young man and soldier

⚕ Children, headaches, perjury

Pancras, said to have been converted at only eight years old, was brought to Rome from Asia Minor by his uncle after the death of his parents. At age 14, during the Diocletian persecutions, he was brought before the emperor himself. He resolutely refused to renounce his faith and was beheaded. He was buried in the catacombs on the Aurelian Way. His head was later removed to the basilica of St. Pancras, built over the site of his burial in about 500 (though since substantially remodeled). A particularly strong cult devoted to him developed in England. St. Pancras Old Church in London stands on what is thought to be one of the oldest sites of Christian worship in England, dating from hardly more than ten years after the martyr's death. The abundance of myths that surrounded his martyrdom led to the firm conviction in the 19th century that Pancras had been killed in the Colosseum, first thrown to wild animals who, recognizing his sanctity, instead lay peacefully at his feet.

Pancras was frequently identified with Sts. Nereus and Achilleus (see below), themselves possibly soldiers. As such, despite his youth, he was frequently depicted as a soldier as well as holding a martyr's palm. This 19th-century stained-glass window is from St. Pancras New Church in London.

MAY 13 · OUR LADY OF FÁTIMA

Our Lady of Fátima remains the most significant Marian apparition of the 20th century. The Virgin Mary is said to have appeared on six successive occasions between May 13, 1917 and October 13, 1917 to three Portuguese children, Lúcia Santos, then age ten, and her cousins, Jacinta and Francisco Marto, respectively nine and seven years old (*see also* Feb. 20). The woman they saw was, according to Lúcia, "brighter than the sun ... pierced by the burning rays of the sun." Exactly as had happened to Bernadette Soubirous at Lourdes 70 years earlier (April 16), as the news leaked out, it caused a sensation. A crowd of 70,000 gathered to see what Lúcia had claimed would be the last appearance of the Virgin in October 1917.

Central to the children's claims was that the Virgin had given them three 'secrets,' prophecies of a world

Lúcia, Francisco, and Jacinta, photographed in 1917, the world closing in on them. They were only children, yet they sparked a bizarre frenzy of religious fervor. Rational Catholic belief was brought into headlong conflict with fervent mysticism.

variously wrenched between a form of Armageddon and salvation based on prayer and, oddly, a rejection of (soon to become Bolshevik) Russia. The first two secrets, never less than impenetrable, were released in 1941 and 1943; the third, more apocalyptic still, in 2000, five years before Lúcia's death in 2005. This last was no less obviously incoherent. While acknowledging that the children's vision is 'worthy of belief,' the Church has consistently maintained a discreet distance between these surprising visions of the future and its own official position.

None of this has stopped Our Lady of Fátima from becoming one of the major centers of Marian pilgrimage today. Francisco and Jacinta both died as children, in 1919 and 1920, victims of the Spanish flu. They were beatified in 2000. Lúcia, a Carmelite nun from 1928, later claimed to have been visited by the Virgin Mary on a series of occasions throughout her life.

Date	Name	Status	Venerated	Life
May 12	Nereus and Achilleus (d.c. AD 100)	Martyrs ⬭ Pre-Congregation		Among most celebrated of early Christian martyrs. Put to death during reign of Domitian in 1st century AD. Little known about them. Most reports claim they were members of Praetorian Guard charged with executing Christians; impressed by their victims' stalwart faith, they converted and were martyred. Alternative story claims they were eunuchs and chamberlains in household of Flavia Domitilla, herself a Christian. She was first exiled, then beheaded. Link with Domitilla, venerated as a saint until 1969, may be result of Nereus and Achilleus being buried in the Catacomb of Domitilla, the oldest in Rome.

MAY 14 — MATTHIAS THE APOSTLE

STATUS Apostle, Martyr

BORN Early 1st century AD

DIED c. AD 64

GRC ♠

CofE ♠

LCDUS ♠

OTHER Eastern Orthodox churches (Aug. 9)

⬭ Pre-Congregation

✝ In old age, carrying the supposed tools of his martyrdom, a halberd or an axe

🙏 Carpenters, tailors, reforming alcoholics; against smallpox

Matthias first appears in the Acts of the Apostles when, after the death of the treacherous Judas Iscariot, he is elected by lot rather than Joseph (called Barsabbas or Justus) by the remaining eleven to join their company (Acts 1:15–26). He was a witness to the very beginning of Christ's ministry — the baptism of Christ by St. John the Baptist (June 24) — and the Crucifixion.

Following the miracle of Pentecost, at which he was present, Matthias seems to have preached in Judea, and then went on a missionary journey to Cappadocia, in eastern Asia Minor, on the shores of the Caspian Sea. The site of his possible martyrdom is regarded as either Colchis, in the mountainous Caucasus region to the north of Cappadocia, Sebastopol in the Crimea, southern Russia, or Jerusalem.

Medieval artists tended to show Matthias being martyred using an ax or halberd. Here, from the Nuremberg Chronicle, *the Apostle has successfully toppled a demon from his shrine before meeting his end.*

MAY 15 — ISIDORE THE FARMER

STATUS Lay Visionary

BORN c.1070, near Madrid, Spain

DIED 1130, Madrid, Spain

GRC ◌

CofE ◌

LCDUS ♠

OTHER In Madrid

⬭ 1622

✝ Sickle

🙏 Farmers, laborers; Madrid

Isidore toiled as a peasant farmer all his life and married a peasant neighbor. Their only son died young, after which the couple lived in celibacy and helped the poor.

Due to the huge expansion of the original Moorish fortress city of Madrid after Philip II of Spain made it his capital in 1561, the local cult of Isidore was swept to national significance. Isidore is an outstanding example of a minor figure who achieved widespread popularity and recognition centuries after his death.

Isidore was canonized at the insistence of Philip III of Spain, who attributed his recovery from illness to the humble saint's intercession.

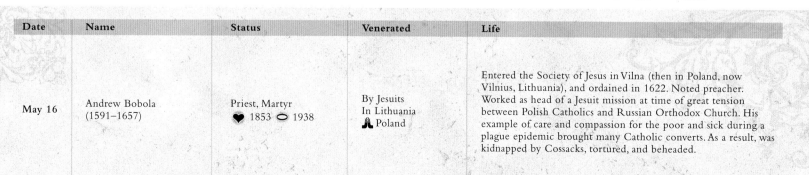

Date	Name	Status	Venerated	Life
May 16	Andrew Bobola (1591–1657)	Priest, Martyr ❤ 1853 ⬭ 1938	By Jesuits In Lithuania 🙏 Poland	Entered the Society of Jesus in Vilna (then in Poland, now Vilnius, Lithuania), and ordained in 1622. Noted preacher. Worked as head of a Jesuit mission at time of great tension between Polish Catholics and Russian Orthodox Church. His example of care and compassion for the poor and sick during a plague epidemic brought many Catholic converts. As a result, was kidnapped by Cossacks, tortured, and beheaded.

Matthias witnesses the baptism of Christ by John the Baptist in this painting by Piero della Francesca, c.1450.

MAY 16   BRENDAN (BRANDON) THE NAVIGATOR

STATUS Abbot

BORN c.489, Kerry, Ireland

DIED c.577, Galway, Ireland

GRC ☁

CofE ☁

LCDUS ☁

OTHER Eastern Orthodox churches; in Ireland

⊙   Pre-Congregation

✝   Whale, one of group of monks in boat

🙏   Sailors, whales; Clonfert, Kerry

Brendan, ordained perhaps in 512, was an Irish monk and abbot, one of the Twelve Apostles of Ireland, those 6th-century Irish monks said to have studied under St. Finian. In Ireland, he founded monasteries at Ardfert, Inishdadroum, Annadown, and most famously at Clonfert, where he is buried. Yet his name 'the Navigator' highlights the best-known aspect of his life: that he voyaged widely and regularly across the remote outposts of Christianity in northwest Europe. He certainly visited St. Columba (June 9) on the Scottish island of Iona; in Wales, he is claimed to have been the abbot of the monastery of Llancarvon, where he taught the Breton saint, Malo.

Other reports have Brendan visiting Brittany in northwest France, the Orkneys off the north coast of Scotland, the yet more remote Shetland Islands, and possibly even the Faroes, deep in the North Atlantic. Most famously of all, legend claims that with a group of monks (17 in most accounts, as many as 60 in others), he also made a seven-year voyage in a leather-skinned curragh across the Atlantic to the Americas, the 'Isle of the Blessed' or the 'Promised Land of the Saints.'

THE VOYAGE OF BRENDAN

What is known of Brendan's voyage to the New World is recorded in the *Navigatio Sancti Brendani Abbatis*, generally known simply as the *Navigatio*. Numerous versions exist, the oldest possibly dating from about 800, all certainly reflecting a much older oral tradition. Quite apart from the apparent impossibility of an open boat making so lengthy and arduous a voyage in such stormy northern seas, Brendan's adventures have so fantastical a quality that, superficially, they can only be seen as legend embroidered on legend. He encounters a huge pillar of crystal in the sea and an island where the inhabitants hurl flaming rocks at the monks. At one point he mistakes a sleeping whale for land and lights a fire on its back to cook a meal, waking the now enraged monster.

It is clear that had Brendan or any other group of Irish monks undertaken such a journey, they would necessarily have found themselves in waters where icebergs, easily imagined as crystal pillars, and volcanoes, above all in Iceland, are common. An underwater volcanic eruption could have easily been construed as a deliberate assault on the monks. Similarly, these are seas that teem with whales, the largest of which would have dwarfed Brendan's frail craft and might only slightly fancifully have been taken for an island.

Equally to the point, seafaring was a fact of life for Irish missionary monks such as Brendan. Contacts across the Irish Sea were not merely frequent and regular, they were essential. It is no less the case that the northerly route

possibly taken by Brendan across the Atlantic – via Scotland, the Faroes, Iceland, perhaps Greenland, and thence to Newfoundland – not merely broke the journey into manageable stages, but generally avoided the headwinds that blew farther south, while benefiting from favorable currents. A generally warmer climate at the time – the medieval 'warm period' – adds credence to such claims.

Whether Irish monks did cross the Atlantic 500 years before the Vikings and 1,000 years before Columbus is impossible to prove, but the balance of possibility tilts in Brendan's favor.

This 17th-century engraving shows St. Brendan and his monks celebrating Easter on the back of a vast whale. It also includes a mythical island, Brandano, named after the saint.

MAY 16 | CAROLINE CHISHOLM

STATUS Social Reformer
BORN 1808, Northamptonshire, England
DIED 1877, London, England
GRC ○
CofE ♣
LCDUS ○

Caroline Chisholm belongs to an easily recognized class of well-born Victorian humanitarians, many of them women. Beginning in 1832, she lived in India with her husband, a soldier and a Catholic (who encouraged her conversion to Roman Catholicism on their marriage). There, she was shocked by the destitution of many of the wives and daughters of ordinary British soldiers. Her response was to establish the Female School of Industry for the Daughters of European Soldiers. In 1838, she and her husband traveled to Australia. Young female immigrants, many unemployed, were being driven to crime and prostitution, so in 1841, Chisholm founded the Female Immigrants' Home. Among her other innovations was a fund to help immigrants pay for their passage and find employment upon their arrival.

By 1853, Caroline Chisholm was among the most famous figures in England, championed by Charles Dickens, among others. Yet she died impoverished and largely forgotten.

MAY 17 | PASCHAL OF BAYLON

STATUS Monk
BORN 1540, Aragón, Spain
DIED 1592, Valencia, Spain
GRC ○
CofE ○
LCDUS ○
OTHER In Spain
♥ 1618
○ 1690
✝ As a friar, with shepherd's crook
🙏 Eucharistic confraternities and devotions, shepherds

It is claimed that Paschal, a shepherd, taught himself to read while watching his flocks in order to further what, since childhood, seems to have been an exceptional spirituality. Having joined the reformed Franciscan Friars Minor of Peter of Alcántara as a lay brother in about 1564, he thereafter devoted his life to prayer and poverty.

Paschal developed a reputation as a mystic with a particular veneration for the Eucharist, the miraculous transformation of the host and wine into the body and blood of Christ.

On a mission to the Observant Franciscans in France, he was assaulted by Protestant Huguenots, and never fully recovered. His tomb in Villareal became a place of pilgrimage.

"I was born poor and am resolved to die in poverty and penance," declared Paschal. This stained-glass window is from the early 20th-century Polish basilica of St. Josaphat in Milwaukee, Wisconsin.

MAY 18 | JOHN I

STATUS Pope, Martyr
BORN 5th century, Siena, Italy
DIED 526, Ravenna, Italy
GRC ♣
CofE ○
LCDUS ♣
○ Pre-Congregation

Little is known about Pope John I (r.523–26), other than that in 525, already elderly, he was sent by King Theodoric the Great, the Ostrogoth ruler of Italy, to Byzantium to demand that the Byzantine emperor, Justinian, repeal his decree of 523 confirming the heresy of Arianism (*see page 12*). It was an impossible mission. Theodoric may have been an advocate of Arianism, but his reasons for dispatching the pope were more political than doctrinal. The Ostrogoths had ruled Italy only since 476. Nominally, they owed allegiance to Byzantium; in reality, they were at least its equal. Justinian's persecution of Arians was rightly seen by Theodoric as an attempt to reassert Byzantine supremacy in Italy. If John could scarcely hope to alter official Byzantine policy, at the same time, were he to support Justinian's decree, there was the risk he would invite reprisals by Theodoric against orthodox Christians in Italy; he would also be accused of betraying Theodoric. A tepid compromise was the best he could hope for. Unsurprisingly, he succeeded only in enraging Theodoric. On his return to Italy, he was arrested in Ravenna and thrown into prison, where he died. He was subsequently re-buried in St. Peter's in Rome.

MAY 19 · DUNSTAN

STATUS Bishop
BORN c.909, Somerset, England
DIED 988, Canterbury, England
GRC ☁
CofE ♣
LCDUS ☁
OTHER Eastern Orthodox churches
⊙ 1029
† Holding a pair of tongs; with a dove
⚒ Blacksmiths, locksmiths, musicians, silversmiths

Dunstan, archbishop of Canterbury from 960 to 978, was among the most important reformers of the Anglo-Saxon church, not merely enlarging England's monasteries and imposing on them much stricter adherence to the Rule of St. Benedict, but vigorously driving through improvements in education for the clergy. His goal was twofold: first, that better-administered monastic foundations and better-educated clergy would significantly increase the authority of the Church; second, that a more powerful Church would in turn reinforce the role of the state, which in practice meant that of the monarch. Among Dunstan's most lasting achievements was to recast the English coronation ceremony, making it an explicitly Christian

Dunstan was believed to have chased away the devil with a pair of red-hot tongs.

rite for the first time, in the process underlining the idea that the monarch was divinely sanctioned. Similarly, the impartial application of 'the king's justice' depended on there being a recognized and codified body of law. Much of it was Roman in origin and thereby tied the state yet more closely to the Roman Church.

Dunstan was ordained in 943 and became abbot of Glastonbury and bishop of Worcester before becoming archbishop of Canterbury under King Edgar. He spent his final years as a teacher in Canterbury. He was a skilled metalworker and craftsman as well as a noted musician. His tomb became the most popular place of pilgrimage in England until the murder of Thomas Becket (Dec. 29) in 1170.

MAY 20 · ALCUIN

STATUS Abbot, Scholar
BORN c.740, Northumbria, England
DIED 804, Tours, France
GRC ☁
CofE ♣
LCDUS ☁

The fall of Rome in the year 476 produced a Dark Age vacuum across Europe that a succession of rulers struggled to fill. When, on Christmas Day 800, Charlemagne was crowned Holy Roman Emperor by the pope, the decisive step was taken in the slow reconstruction of western Europe. Charlemagne, presiding over his expanding Frankish empire, intended to reinstitute not only the unity of Rome but also its learning. No figure was more important in this audacious quest than Alcuin.

Alcuin's origins were modest for so notable a churchman. He was educated at York, then a leading intellectual center. It was there that he was introduced to classical authors, even if he was perturbed by their pagan origins. In 781, then head of St. Peter's School in York, Alcuin was sent to Rome to petition the pope to allow the city to become an archbishopric. On his return journey, in Parma, he was recruited by Charlemagne to join those scholars already at the monarch's court in Aachen, today in Germany.

Among Alcuin's pupils were Charlemagne himself, with whom Alcuin formed a close relationship, and the emperor's sons, Pepin and Louis. He taught them first the Trivium – grammar, logic, and rhetoric – then the Quadrivium – arithmetic, geometry, music, and astronomy – before moving on to philosophy and theology. The restoration of Latin as a literary language was among Alcuin's most notable achievements. He returned to England in 790 but was back in Aachen again in 792, where he played a leading role in the fight against the Adoptionism heresy, the belief, widespread in Spain, that Christ became divine only after His

death. In 796, Charlemagne allowed Alcuin to retire to the monastery of St. Martin in Tours, where he was made abbot. Despite his reputation for sanctity, Alcuin seems never to have been ordained; neither has he been beatified or canonized.

The magnificent octagonal throne room at Aachen, center of the Carolingian renaissance, which was greatly influenced by Alcuin.

CAROLINGIAN SCRIPT

Central to Alcuin's endeavors at Aachen was the copying of huge numbers of manuscripts. To make these texts as accessible as possible, Alcuin insisted on the use of a uniform script, which has since been known as Carolingian, or minuscule, script. This is not only neat and thus easily legible, but for the first time upper and lower case letters were used, as in modern calligraphy. Other innovations included regular spacing between words, and descenders (as in the letter 'g,') and ascenders (as in the letter 'h').

Carolingian script from a 10th-century manuscript produced at Freising, Germany.

MAY 20 ✤ BERNARDINE OF SIENA

STATUS Priest
BORN 1380, Tuscany, Italy
DIED 1444, Aquila, Italy
GRC ♣
CofE ◌
LCDUS ♣
OTHER By Franciscans
○ 1450
✝ Tablet displaying the letters HIS; three miters for the three bishoprics he refused
🙏 Advertisers, gambling addicts, chest problems; San Bernardino, California

Bernardine, ordained in 1404, was perhaps the most famous preacher in Italy in the first half of the 15th century. He not only drew huge crowds, he preached at prodigious length, sometimes for as much as four hours. He was a fierce upholder of the Holy Name of Jesus and as fierce an opponent of homosexuality, urging violent deaths for its practitioners. From 1430, he wrote widely on theological matters and, recognizing the importance of educating the clergy, opened schools of theology at Perugia and Monteripido. He was not without his detractors: in Rome in 1427 he was charged with heresy, though acquitted. He subsequently preached in the city every day for 80 days. He turned down three bishoprics – Siena, Ferrara, and Urbino – and in 1436 was made vicar general of the Observant Franciscans and in 1438 vicar general of the Franciscans in Italy. In 1442, he resigned to return to preaching again.

Bernardine's success as vicar general of the Observants was such that he increased the numbers of those wanting to join the order by 30 times. This altarpiece, painted c.1450, is in the church of San Francesco della Vigna in Venice.

MAY 20 ✤ ARCANGELO TADINI

STATUS Priest, Founder
BORN 1846, Verolanuova, Italy
DIED 1912, Botticino Sera, Italy
GRC ◌
CofE ◌
LCDUS ◌
♥ 2001
○ 2009

Never more than a north Italian parish priest, Arcangelo Tadini, ordained in 1870, was a striking example of how the power of prayer combined with practicality can make a genuine difference to people's lives. As a young curate in a remote mountain village, he organized soup kitchens for villagers left homeless by flooding. As the parish priest in Botticino Sera near Brescia, where he remained from 1887 to his death, Arcangelo found a number of ways to bring help and relief to workers injured, ill, or made unemployed, creating a Workers' Mutual Aid Association as a form of social insurance. He also built a spinning factory with his own money to offer employment to young women, whom he also educated in his own foundation, the Congregation of Worker Sisters of the Holy House of Nazareth. He was a noted preacher.

Arcangelo Tadini was left lame as the result of an accident in his youth. This disability did nothing to halt a life that combined devotion and vigor to a striking degree.

Date	Name	Status	Venerated	Life
May 19	Theophilus of Corte (1676–1740)	Monk ○ 1930	By Franciscans In Corsica and Tuscany	Among most modest of saints but no less sanctified as a result. Born to noble Corsican family but joined Franciscans (1693), thereafter devoting life to austerity and contemplation, preaching widely and zealously. Established retreat houses to encourage others to devotion in many parts of Corsica and Tuscany.

MAY 21 | CHRISTOPHER MAGALLANES

STATUS Priest, Martyr
BORN 1869, Totatiche, Mexico
DIED 1927, Colotitlán, Mexico
GRC ♣
CofE ○
LCDUS ♣
OTHER In Mexico
♥ 1992
○ 2000

Christopher Magallanes, born to a family of shepherds, was ordained at age 30 and served as a parish priest in his native village in central Mexico. He was active in the conversion of the indigenous Huichol people, and in 1915 opened his own seminary. He was a convinced pacifist who was nevertheless falsely accused of supporting the Catholic Cristero rebellion. In May 1927, he was arrested and summarily shot. "I die innocent," he said, "and ask God that my blood may serve to unite my Mexican brethren." He gave his executioners absolution before he died.

THE CRISTERO WAR

The Cristero uprising (or Cristiada) lasted from 1926–1929. It was a reaction by mainly rural Mexican Catholics against the atheist President Calles's harsh reinterpretation of anti-clerical provisions of the secularizing 1917 Mexican Constitution. It began with peaceful protests, but broke into armed conflict in 1927. Eventually some 50,000 rebels were under arms, many of them women. The war ended with a US-brokered truce, but claimed around 90,000 lives, only a third of which were Cristeros, although about 5,500 were executed after the truce. At least 40 priests were killed. In 2000, Pope John Paul II canonized 25 victims of the rebellion, and a further 13 lay martyrs have been beatified.

MAY 21 | GODRIC OF FINCHALE

STATUS Hermit
BORN c.1065, Norfolk, England
DIED 1170, Finchale, England
GRC ○
CofE ○
LCDUS ○
○ Pre-Congregation
✝ Hermit

Godric of Finchale was an Anglo-Saxon peddler turned adventurer who, following a visit to the shrine of St. Cuthbert (March 20) on Lindisfarne, discovered a religious calling that would make him one of the best-known holy men in England. For 60 years, having traveled to Rome and Jerusalem, he lived as a hermit at Finchale, near Durham, on the banks of the river Wear, in repentance for his former sins. His writings remain among the earliest examples of Middle English verse. He also set them to music.

MAY 22 | RITA OF CASCIA

STATUS Nun
BORN c.1381, Perugia, Italy
DIED 1457, Cascia, Italy
GRC ♣
CofE ○
LCDUS ♣
OTHER By Augustinians
♥ 1627
○ 1900
✝ Forehead wound, roses, bees
🙏 Lost causes, marital difficulties

Rita ranks high among those medieval saints whose lives inspired great dedication among their followers as well as an improbably large number of miracles. At age 12, despite pleading to be allowed to enter a convent, she was married to a man who combined cruelty and dissipation in equal measure, and who was eventually murdered. Rita's two sons, determined to avenge their father's death, both died of natural causes after Rita prayed that God take their lives rather than allow them to commit a mortal sin. At 36, she was admitted to the convent of St. Mary Magdalene at Cascia in Perugia. The nuns had been reluctant to accept her as she was not a virgin. Their doubts were swept aside when she was miraculously brought to the convent one night by St. John the Baptist, St. Augustine, and St. Nicholas of Tolentino.

St. Rita is commonly depicted with a gash on her forehead; she fell and cut herself after she had prayed to be allowed to suffer like the Divine Savior.

Date	Name	Status	Venerated	Life
May 23	William of Rochester (William of Perth) (d.1201)	Martyr ○ 1256	🙏 Adopted children	Scottish baker. Gave to the poor every tenth loaf he baked. Adopted baby, which he took with him on pilgrimage to the Holy Land. In Rochester, Kent, the boy cut his benefactor's throat after clubbing him to the ground. Venerated as a martyr when a local madwoman, finding his body, was cured.
May 23	Felix of Cantalice (1515–87)	Monk ○ 1712	By Capuchins	Capuchin lay brother from 1543. Lived in Rome from 1547, where he remained until his death. Ardent advocate of social justice and no less effective a catechist. Especially revered by St. Philip Neri (May 26).

MAY 24 — SIMEON STYLITES THE YOUNGER

STATUS Hermit
BORN c.521, Antioch, Asia Minor
DIED c.597, Antioch, Asia Minor
GRC ☁
CofE ☁
LCDUS ☁
OTHER Eastern Orthodox churches
⊝ Pre-Congregation
✝ On a pillar

Simeon, directly inspired by (although unrelated to) Simeon Stylites the Elder (Jan. 5), devoted his life to similarly extreme religious asceticism. He was first, apparently at only age eight, a member of a community of pillar dwellers, or stylites, centered around another pillar hermit, John. Following John's death, Simeon, who spent a reported 68 years on a variety of pillars, embraced an

even more extreme life, eating only shrubs. He was ordained by the Patriarch of Antioch. Thereafter, numerous followers would ascend his pillar one by one to receive Holy Communion from him. He was noted for converting many pagans.

The number of miracles ascribed to Simeon Stylites the Younger was such that the site of his final pillar, near Antioch, was dubbed the 'Hill of Wonders.'

MAY 24 — JOHN WESLEY

STATUS Preacher, Founder
BORN 1703, Lincolnshire, England
DIED 1791, London, England
GRC ☁
CofE ♣
LCDUS ☁
OTHER Evangelical Lutheran Church, US Episcopal Church

John Wesley remains one of the most formidable of English churchmen, immensely high-minded, ferociously hardworking, and unwavering in his promotion of Methodism, the form of stern but merciful Anglicanism he pioneered. Today, Methodism has followers across the English-speaking world. The essence of Methodism, which Wesley was at pains to stress never deviated from the essential doctrines of the Anglican Church, was that the religion was open to all, because all are children of God. But salvation – "Christian perfection," to Wesley – could be achieved only through active Christian practice: not merely avoiding evil and doing good, but consistently following the "ordinances of God" as revealed in the Bible. Wesley described himself as "a man of one book" – by which he meant the Bible.

This amounted to a newly inclusive interpretation of Christian teaching. At least one direct consequence was that Wesley consistently sought out those on the margins of society, a society that was being transformed by the Industrial Revolution and mass urbanization. Wesley and his followers eschewed social blights such as alcoholism and prostitution. Methodism also played a crucial early role in prison reform and the abolition of slavery.

To achieve these aims, from 1739 onward Wesley set up a network of Methodist societies and chapels across England and Wales (and, from 1784, in Scotland and North America, too). This formidable organization, allied to Wesley's conviction that active preaching was essential to reach the largest possible numbers of

people, inevitably brought him into conflict with the established Anglican Church. His later belief that Methodist preachers could be ordained by him in a ceremony known as the 'laying on of hands' only increased these tensions. His brother Charles, a much more conventional churchman (and the author of over 2,000 hymns), was increasingly troubled by this unorthodoxy.

Wesley was a man of extraordinary energy: he traveled continuously, visiting, cajoling, and encouraging Methodist groups everywhere in England. He gave an estimated 40,000 sermons. When he died, he did so uttering the words: "The best of all is, God is with us." His impact, part mystical, much more importantly rational and humane, remains huge.

It was part of the strength of Wesley that he was never free of self-doubt.

Date	Name	Status	Venerated	Life
May 23	John Baptist de Rossi (1698–1764)	Priest ⊝ 1881	By Jesuits	Born to poor but pious parents in Voltaggio near Genoa. Though an epileptic, was accepted by the Jesuits in Rome in 1721 and ordained shortly thereafter. Rapidly acquired reputation as formidable champion of the poor and distressed. Especially venerated as a confessor.
May 25	Madeleine Sophie Barat (1779–1865)	Founder ♥ 1908 ⊝ 1925	By Society of the Sacred Heart In France	Planned to be Carmelite lay sister. Called by Joseph Varin to teach girls at convent school in Amiens, France (1801); became first house of the Society of the Sacred Heart. Remained superior there for rest of life, founding many successful convent schools throughout Europe and America.

MAY 25 | THE VENERABLE BEDE

STATUS	Monk, Scholar, Doctor of the Church
BORN	c.673, Northumbria, England
DIED	735, Jarrow, England
GRC	♣
CofE	♣
LCDUS	♣
OTHER	Eastern Orthodox churches, Lutheran Church
○	1899
†	Bearing writing implements
🙏	English writers and historians; Jarrow

Bede, known as 'the Venerable' from the 9th century, is the only English Doctor of the Church. He was perhaps the foremost scholar of the early medieval church, author of as many as 60 books on subjects including spelling, natural history, astronomy, poetry, the lives of saints, biblical commentaries — including the first Gospel in Old English (Bede otherwise wrote in Latin) — and history. His five-volume *Ecclesiastical History of the English People*, finished in 731, is the most complete and authoritative account of the Christianization of England.

Remarkably, this outpouring of knowledge was produced on the very margins of civilized, Christian Europe, in the twin monasteries of Monkwearmouth and Jarrow in remote and rugged Northumbria in the northeast of England. Uniting this lonely outpost with the wider Roman Church was Bede's constant goal. Among the many claims to fame of the man recognized as the 'Father of English History' was his use of AD, or *anno domini*, 'the year of our Lord,' to indicate all dates after Christ's birth.

No contemporary images of Bede exist. This portrait of the saintly monk dates from 1754.

MAY 25 | GREGORY VII

STATUS	Pope
BORN	c.1020, Tuscany, Italy
DIED	1085, Salerno, Italy
GRC	♣
CofE	♡
LCDUS	♣
♥	1584
○	1728

Gregory VII, pope from 1073, was among the most dynamic of the medieval popes. He was an unrelenting reformer and aggressive champion of the papacy's claims to spiritual superiority across Christendom at the expense of temporal rulers. He insisted on celibacy for all clergy and campaigned actively against simony, the buying of ecclesiastical offices. He challenged the right of the Holy Roman Emperor, Henry III, ruler of Germany and much of Italy, including Rome,

to appoint bishops in his territories. This, the 'Investiture Contest,' in which Gregory twice excommunicated Henry, and Henry in turn sought to overthrow Gregory (appointing an antipope in his place), profoundly destabilized Europe until well into the 16th century. Although Gregory died in exile in Salerno in southern Italy, he had decisively strengthened the temporal and political power of the papacy.

MAY 26 | JOHN CALVIN

STATUS	Reformer, Theologian
BORN	1509, Picardy, France
DIED	1564, Geneva, Switzerland
GRC	♡
CofE	♣
LCDUS	♡
OTHER	Lutheran Church

The erudite John Calvin, measured and scholarly, was almost the antithesis of his near contemporary, the excitable, irascible reformer Martin Luther (Feb. 18). Yet his influence on the Protestant Reformation was enduring. Hardworking, inspired by a ruthless determination to return the Church to its original simplicity and sanctity, Calvin galvanized the Reformation, making it intellectually respectable as well as spiritually pure. His central belief, which he expressed from his home in Geneva, where he moved in 1536, was that virtue was its own reward, and that only the virtuous could be properly Christian. He also expounded a belief in God's pre-determination of the fate of mankind and the universe.

Virtue for Calvin was a very narrowly defined and rigorously applied creed demanding exacting standards of probity. In Geneva he presided over a 'Protestant Sparta': adultery, blasphemy, and heresy were all punishable by death — Calvin tolerated no deviation from the path of godliness. His vision has inspired and terrified generations of Protestants.

An anonymous Flemish portrait of the young Calvin, today in the Library of Geneva, Switzerland.

MAY 26 PHILIP NERI

STATUS Oratorian
BORN 1515, Florence, Italy
DIED 1595, Rome, Italy
GRC ♣
CofE ♣
LCDUS ♣
OTHER By Oratorians
♥ 1615
⬭ 1622
🙏 US Special Forces;
Rome

Philip Neri, born to an impoverished noble family, was one of the towering figures of the Counter-Reformation, the Roman Church's response to the Reformation. He was much given to fasting and prayer, and devoted much of his early life to helping the poor, the sick, and the dispossessed of Rome, establishing the Confraternity of the Most Holy Trinity in 1548. He was ordained in 1551, and he then founded the Congregation of the Oratory, which was given papal sanction in 1575. This would, with the Jesuits, become one of the keystones of the newly militant Catholic Church. The Oratorians proved particularly successful in France, where by the mid-18th century there were 58 Oratorian communities. The order's Roman church, Santa Maria in Vallicella, built from 1575, became one of the most imitated of the city's new Baroque churches, a model of sumptuous ecclesiastical architecture. The Congregation of the Oratory closely reflected Neri's personality: informal, practical, and rather whimsically grand.

The Chiesa Nuova and the adjoining Oratorio dei Filippini are monuments to Philip Neri's endeavors to revive Rome during the Counter-Reformation.

Tiepolo's dramatic image (right) of the Virgin and Child appearing to Philip Neri, painted in 1740.

Date	Name	Status	Venerated	Life
May 25	Aldhelm (c.640–709)	Bishop ⬭ Pre-Congregation	CofE	Learned, prolific, and influential early English scholar. Abbot of Malmesbury and bishop of Sherborne, Dorset. Supporter of the Celtic liturgical tradition.
May 25	Mary Magdalene de' Pazzi (1566–1607)	Nun, Mystic ♥ 1626 ⬭ 1669	By Carmelites 🙏 Naples	Born Catherine de' Pazzi, one of most celebrated mystic saints of the Counter-Reformation. Reputedly had first mystic experience at age 12; at age 16 became a Carmelite nun in Florence, devoted to prayer, penance, and good works. Many miracles ascribed to her cult after her death, when she was also declared incorruptible.

MAY 27 · AUGUSTINE (AUSTIN) OF CANTERBURY

STATUS Bishop, Missionary

BORN Mid-6th century, Rome, Italy

DIED c.604, Canterbury, England

GRC ♣

CofE ♣ (May 26)

LCDUS ♣

○ Pre-Congregation

✝ Benedictine robes

🙏 Canterbury, England

This image of a Mediterranean-looking Augustine is probably more accurate than the later, bearded patriarch favored by the Victorians (right).

Augustine's arms remain those of Canterbury, the principal Anglican see, a crosier surmounting a white pall with four black crosses.

Augustine was born in Italy, and at a young age became prior of the monastery of St. Andrew on the Celian Hill in Rome. He was a contemporary and friend of Pope Gregory the Great (Sept. 3), who commissioned him to evangelize the seven Anglo-Saxon kingdoms of southern and eastern England, and to establish Roman liturgical rites among Christians already practicing in the British Isles (notably in Ireland, Wales, and Scotland). Augustine set out with 30 monks; the expedition was temporarily halted in Gaul over a leadership dispute, which Gregory settled by appointing Augustine bishop, and the party arrived at Ebbsfleet, Kent in 597. They were met by King Ethelbert of Kent, who initially confined them to the marshy Isle of Thanet, but who was sympathetic, as his French-born wife Bertha was a Christian. Eventually Ethelbert permitted the monks to establish a prayer house and preach in Canterbury.

Augustine proceeded carefully, aware of the political fragility of the Anglo-Saxon English polity, and Gregory granted him considerable freedom of liturgical movement. The policy produced fruit when Augustine established his see at Canterbury, building the first cathedral in the city, a cathedral school, and the monastery of SS. Peter and Paul just outside the city walls, now called St. Augustine's. He also created sees at Rochester in Kent and London, and planned the archbishopric of York, which remains second in importance only to Canterbury in the Anglican Church. The prevalence of Roman rites in Britain would not be established until the Synod of Whitby in 664, three generations after Augustine's death.

Date	Name	Status	Venerated	Life
May 26	Mariana Paredes y Flores (d.1645)	Virgin ♥ 1853 ○ 1950	In Ecuador ✝ Lily, whip, skull 🙏 Sickness, loss of parents; Ecuador	Story similar to that of Rose of Lima (Aug. 23). Sheltered poor and Indian children in parents' house in Quito. Healed many and raised some from the dead. Given to extreme self-mortification, eventually dying after an epidemic when she offered her life in expiation of others' sins. Lily bloomed from her remains upon death.

MAY 28 — GERMANUS (GERMAIN) OF PARIS

STATUS Bishop
BORN c.500, Autun, France
DIED 576, Paris, France
GRC ◌
CofE ◌
LCDUS ◌
OTHER In France
◯ 754
🙏 Prisoners, slaves; Paris

Having lived a monastic life in Burgundy, Germanus was ordained at around age 30, and was soon appointed abbot of the monastery church of St. Symphorien. His success there as an administrator and benefactor led the Frankish emperor Childebert I to support Germanus's popular appointment as bishop of Paris — imperial support that was extended to founding a cathedral and the church of St. Vincent and the Holy Cross, now known as St.-Germain-des-Prés. Germanus became embroiled in various dynastic intrigues following Childebert's death, but sought to bring peace to the opposing factions. Germanus was noted for his charity toward prisoners, and was an active participant in the church councils of Paris in 557 and 573, and Tours in 566.

A sculpture of Germanus outside the church of St.-Germain-des-Prés.

MAY 28 — BERNARD OF MONTJOUX (MENTHON)

STATUS Priest
BORN c.923, Menthon, France
DIED c.1081, Novara, Italy
GRC ◌
CofE ◌
LCDUS ◌
OTHER In the Alpine region
◯ 1681
✝ In black habit, often leading a devil on a chain, with a dog
🙏 Mountain climbers, Alpine travelers, skiers; the Alps, Aosta

A noble Savoyard who became archdeacon of Aosta in the western Alps, Bernard sought to protect travelers and pilgrims from bandits and extreme weather conditions in the treacherous passes of the Alps. As a result, he has two passes named after him, the Great St. Bernard and the Little St. Bernard, which link Aosta with Switzerland. At the summit of the first, Bernard built a monastery for Augustinian monks, and then established a hospice at the highest point of each pass to provide shelter for travelers. The monks are famed for rescuing travelers, aided by their herding dogs.

Monumental statues of Bernard perched on tall cairns guard the approaches to both passes that bear his name.

The St. Bernard is a hardy herding and rescue dog originally bred in the Alps.

Date	Name	Status	Venerated	Life
May 29	Maximinus of Trier (d.c.347)	Bishop ◯ Pre-Congregation	In Trier, Germany	Gallic bishop of Trier, one of the capitals of west Roman empire. Highly regarded by Sts. Jerome and Athanasius as an early bastion against Arian heresy.
May 29	Bona of Pisa (c.1156–1207)	◯ Pre-Congregation	In Pisa, Italy 🙏 Pilgrims, guides	Child mystic. Visionary Augustinian tertiary by age 12. Made pilgrimage to Holy Land to visit crusader father; captured by Muslim pirates on return; rescued, then led many pilgrimages in gratitude.

MAY 30 | JOAN OF ARC

STATUS Virgin

BORN c.1412, Domrémy, France

DIED 1431, Rouen, France

GRC ♧

CofE ♣

LCDUS ♧

OTHER In France

♥ 1909

◯ 1920

✝ Usually shown in male armor

🙏 France

Born to a peasant farmer during the Hundred Years' War between France and an alliance of England and Burgundy, Joan was illiterate but intelligent. She heard heavenly voices when she was 13 or 14, urging her to save France from its enemies. She later identified the voices as those of the Archangel Michael, Catherine of Alexandria, and Margaret of Antioch. In 1429, Joan was received by Charles, Dauphin of France, who appointed her to the army. She defeated English forces besieging Orléans, leading to her sobriquet, the 'Maid of Orléans.' She then enjoyed victories at Patay and Troyes. She encouraged the Dauphin to be crowned Charles VII at Rheims.

At the height of her success as an inspirational field commander, she led her forces to relieve Compiègne, which was surrounded by Burgundian troops. She was captured and sold to the English. Imprisoned for nine months, she was then charged with heresy and witchcraft — accusations she refuted with natural common sense and good humor. Refusing to confess or recant, she was burned at the stake in Rouen, and her ashes were scattered in the river Seine.

Charles VII attempted to have the judgment overturned, and in 1456 Pope Callistus III quashed the verdict, proclaiming her innocence. Nevertheless, it would be almost 500 years before she was beatified by Pius X, and canonized by Benedict XV.

Images of St. Joan are found throughout France, such as Frémiet's gilded statue on the Place des Pyramides, Paris.

> "Are you in the grace of God?"
> "If I am not, may God put me there; if I am, may He keep me there."

FROM THE TRANSCRIPT OF JOAN OF ARC'S TRIAL.

No life portraits of St. Joan exist, but this early representation (above) set the pattern. Shaw's play St. Joan (1923) and films by Dreyer (1928), Fleming (with Ingrid Bergman, right, 1948), Preminger (1957), and Bresson (1962) show the persisting allure of her story.

Date	Name	Status	Venerated	Life
May 30	Gabinus (d.c.130)	Martyr ◯ Pre-Congregation	In Sardinia	Sardinian preacher martyred under Hadrian.
May 30	Isaac of Constantinople (d.c.410)	Abbot ◯ Pre-Congregation	Eastern Orthodox churches	Critic of the Arian heresy under Valens.
May 30	Walston of Bawburgh (mid-10th century–c.1016)	Laborer ◯ Pre-Congregation	In Norfolk, England ✝ With a scythe, pair of calves 🙏 Farmers	Popular local saint in Norfolk, England. Closely involved with peasant community; included farm animals in church services. Offered land, he accepted a cow in calf; her two offspring bore his body at his funeral after he died praying in a field.

MAY 30 | FERDINAND III OF CASTILE

STATUS King
BORN 1198, Zamora, near Salamanca, Spain
DIED 1252, Seville, Spain
GRC ☁
CofE ☁
LCDUS ☁
OTHER In Spain, where he is often referred to as Fernando el Santo or San Fernando
♥ 1655
⬯ 1671
✝ Greyhound
🙏 Governors, magistrates, engineers, paupers, prisoners; Seville

One of the major kings of Spain, Ferdinand was the son of Alfonso IX of León and Princess Berenguela of Castile. Although his parents divorced, his mother allowed him to ascend to the throne of Castile in 1217, and he inherited the crown of León upon his father's death in 1230, uniting the two kingdoms. This created an important power base to continue the *Reconquista* – the Christian recapture of Muslim territories in Iberia. Between 1233 and 1248 Ferdinand took the cities of Ubeda, Córdoba, Jaén, and Seville, bringing Murcia and Andalusia under Castilian control.

Ferdinand expanded Salamanca University, and founded the cathedral at Burgos (where El Cid is buried). He founded Benedictine, Franciscan, Trinitarian, and Mercedarian monasteries in Andalusia, giving the region a religious character distinct from the many Cistercian and Cluniac foundations of northern Spain.

Following his reconquest of much of Moorish Andalusia, Ferdinand began the conversion of the mosque in Seville to one of the finest cathedrals in Europe (above). It contains his tomb, as well as that of Christopher Columbus.

A harsh but just ruler and negotiator, Ferdinand was described as gentle and retiring in his domestic life.

MAY 31 | THE VISITATION OF THE BLESSED VIRGIN MARY

The most significant emblem of Mary is the lily, symbolizing purity.

Set aside by the Roman church as an important feast, the Visitation celebrates Mary's sojourn with her cousin, Elizabeth, pregnant with St. John the Baptist, shortly after the Annunciation of Jesus.

Originally a Franciscan feast, it was adopted in 1389 by Pope Urban VI in an attempt to end the Great Schism, and was celebrated on July 2. However, as this date falls a few days after the feast of the Birth of St. John the Baptist (June 24) it was deemed anomalous, and in 1969 Pope Paul VI reassigned it to May 31. Anglicans still observe the feast on July 2, and the Eastern churches on March 30.

Representations of the Blessed Virgin Mary are not limited to fine art – devotional images can be found to suit almost any budget.

Date	Name	Status	Venerated	Life
May 30	Apolo Kivebulaya (c.1864–1933)	Missionary	In Central Africa CofE	Ugandan–born Muslim. Converted to the Anglican Church (1894). Became a leading missionary in the Belgian Congo.
May 31	Petronilla (1st century AD)	Martyr ⬯ Pre-Congregation	🙏 Fever victims, Dauphins, mountain travelers	Closely associated with St. Peter (her memorial is in St. Peter's, Rome). Celebrated for her beauty. Upon rejecting an offer of marriage from a pagan ruler, died for her faith after carrying out a hunger strike.
May 31	James Salomone (1231–1314)	Monk ♥ 1526	In Venice	Dominican monk. Tended the poor and sick of Venice. Many miraculous healings attributed to him.

JUNE

With the ecclesiastical calendar entering its second period of Ordinary Time following Pentecost, June also sees the longest day of the year in the northern hemisphere, usually on the 22nd of the month.

Several major saints' days are observed during June, including the birth of Saint John the Baptist on June 24, and the shared feast of Saints Peter and Paul on June 29. On the following day, the heroic sacrifices of the First Holy Martyrs are collectively remembered, commemorating those early Christians whose sufferings and persecution helped to establish the Church within the Roman empire.

The birth of John the Baptist predated that of Christ the Redeemer by only a few months. It remains a festival of outstanding importance in all churches, not least in the Orthodox Church. This painting of John preaching before Christ began his ministry in earnest is by the early 15th-century Italian artists Jacopo and Lorenzo Salimbeni.

JUNE 1 · JUSTIN

STATUS Martyr

BORN c. AD 100 Shechem (modern Nablus), Israel

DIED c.165

GRC ♣

CofE ♣

LCDUS ♣

OTHER Eastern Orthodox churches

○ Pre-Congregation

† Sword, quill

🙏 Philosophers

Justin's quill naturally signifies his importance as a writer; the sword represents his stout defense of Christianity, and was the tool of his martyrdom.

Born to Greek parents, Justin studied philosophy at Antioch and Alexandria. Through his reading, particularly of Plato, Justin sought a vision of the supreme Creator, and around 130 he converted to Christianity. He went on to become one of the most powerful and eloquent defenders of the early Church, using philosophical arguments rather than mysticism. He openly debated with Gnostics (*see* page 57), Jews, and others.

Justin traveled to Rome in about 150, opening a philosophical school in the city and writing his principal works, the two *Apologias* and the *Dialogue*. He and several colleagues were arrested in Rome during the persecution under Marcus Aurelius, and were tried by Rusticus (the account of their hearing is one of the few to survive). Invited to sacrifice to the Roman deities, Justin refused, saying "No right-minded man forsakes for falsehood … We are Christians, and we cannot sacrifice to idols." He and his companions were beheaded.

A 16th-century Greek icon of Justin in philosopher's robes, painted by Theophanes the Cretan for the walls of Stavronikita Monastery on Mount Athos, Greece.

JUNE 2 · BLANDINA AND COMPANIONS

STATUS Martyrs

BORN Mid-2nd century

DIED 177, Lyon, France

GRC ♤

CofE ♤

LCDUS ♤

OTHER In Lyon, France

† Often shown with a bull

"I am a Christian, and we do nothing vile."

BLANDINA, DEFENDING AGAINST FALSE ACCUSATIONS AT HER TRIAL.

Blandina was a Roman slave in Lyon who, like her mistress, was a Christian convert. She was tried during the persecutions under Marcus Aurelius, along with her mistress, the bishop of Lyon, St. Pothinus, and a fellow slave, Ponticus. All were accused of barbaric acts such as incest and cannibalism. Under severe torture, she refused to recant, and her accusers claimed they had never seen "a woman show such endurance." She and her fellows were eventually led to the amphitheater where Blandina was wrapped in a net, thrown to wild bulls, and finally gored to death – a punishment particularly popular at the time (*see also* Saturninus, Nov. 29, and Fermín, July 7).

Martyrdom involving bulls was particularly popular in southwest France and Iberia, and may be linked to the modern practice of bullfighting.

JUNE 2 — MARCELLINUS AND PETER

STATUS Martyrs
BORN Mid-4th century
DIED 304, Rome, Italy
GRC ♠
CofE ♧
LCDUS ♠
⊘ Pre-Congregation
✝ Tonsured, bearing the palm of martyrdom

Marcellinus was a senior Christian priest in Rome, Peter apparently an exorcist. They were beheaded outside Rome during the Diocletian persecutions. Although little verifiable is known of this pair of early Christian martyrs, they are notable for the catacombs dedicated to them in Rome, which were opened by Pope Damasus I (Dec. 11), who was largely responsible for their cult. The catacombs are decorated with wall paintings of key episodes from Christian history, providing a valuable insight into the way in which passages from both the Old and New Testaments were treasured and preserved among the early Christian community in Rome. The relics of Marcellinus and Peter were translated to (or possibly stolen by) the Frankish empire around 810. They now lie at Seligenstadt, Germany, although the cathedral at Cremona in Italy also claims to have them.

The catacombs of Marcellinus and Peter contain one of the earliest known depictions of Adam, Eve, and the Tree of Knowledge (Genesis 2:2–9).

JUNE 3 — JOHN XXIII

STATUS Pope
BORN 1881, Sotto il Monte, Italy
DIED 1963, Vatican City, Rome, Italy
GRC ♧
CofE ♧
LCDUS ♧
OTHER US Evangelical Lutheran Church, Anglican Church of Canada
❤ 2000

"Obedience and Peace."
POPE JOHN XXIII'S MOTTO.

John was born Angelo Giuseppe Roncalli, one of 14 children in a peasant family in northern Italy. He was ordained in 1904, and worked as secretary to the bishop of Bergamo and as a lecturer in Church history. He served as a stretcher-bearer and chaplain in the Italian army during World War I.

A memorial card showing John XXIII's original tomb in St. Peter's, Rome. He was later re-interred in a new tomb within the basilica.

In 1921, he was appointed director of the Council for the Propagation of the Faith by Pope Benedict XV. He served as a papal ambassador for Pope Pius XI, first to Bulgaria (1925–35), then as Apostolic Delegate to Turkey and Greece (1935–44); there, he worked with the Jewish underground, helping many to escape the Holocaust. In 1944, he was appointed Nuncio to France (resulting in his elevation to Cardinal) and, in 1953, became Patriarch of Venice.

His election to the papacy upon Pius XII's death in 1958 was unexpected. A keen ecumenicist, his greatest achievement was to convene the Second Vatican Council (1962–65), an opportunity to re-evaluate the role of the Catholic Church in the modern world, with a focus on social justice, human rights, and world peace. He also supported the World Council of Churches, opening dialogues across the Christian world. His unique and very active experience of two world wars undoubtedly drove his vision and sense of purpose.

John died of cancer on June 3, 1963, after a brief but hugely significant pontificate, universally admired and loved. He remains beatified but not canonized.

Date	Name	Status	Venerated	Life
June 2	Erasmus (Elmo) (d.c.303)	Martyr ⊘ Pre-Congregation	✝ Windlass, capstan ⚓ Mariners	Probably legendary Syrian bishop persecuted under Diocletian. His final torture involved his intestines being wound out of his body by a windlass, leading to his patronage of sailors. 'St. Elmo's Fire' – electric discharges in the rigging of sailing vessels – attributed to his protection of sailors. One of the 14 Holy Helpers.

JUNE 3   THE MARTYRS OF UGANDA

STATUS Martyrs
BORN Mid-19th century
DIED 1886, Uganda
GRC ♣
CofE ♣
LCDUS ♣
♥ 1920
◯ 1964
🙏 Protomartyrs of black Africa

King Mwanga II, the last ruler of independent Buganda (now Uganda), saw Christian missions as the advance guard of colonial rule. Among the first to attract his ire was James Hannington (Oct. 29), an Anglican missionary, who was murdered with his six assistants by Mwanga in 1885. When criticized for this by the head of his courtly pages, Joseph Mukasa, who had earlier converted to Catholicism, Mwanga had Mukasa beheaded. The following year, 22 followers of Mukasa, led by Charles Lwanga, were rounded up, marched to Lake Victoria, and were burned alive at Namugongo on June 3, 1886. A further 23 Anglicans were massacred. Mwanga eventually cut a deal with the British government: he handed over sovereignty and was exiled to the Seychelles, where he died of old age.

This tapestry features the 22 Catholic Martyrs of Uganda who were canonized by Pope Paul VI. In his address at their canonization, the pope also acknowledged the sacrifice of their Anglican companions.

JUNE 3   CLOTILDE (CLOTILDA)

STATUS Queen
BORN 475, France
DIED 545, Tours, France
GRC ◯
CofE ◯
LCDUS ◯
OTHER In France
◯ Pre-Congregation
✝ Crown with church
🙏 Children, parents, exiles

Wife of the Frankish king Clovis, Clotilde bore him three sons, and converted him to Christianity in 496. After Clovis's death in 511, her sons fought bitterly over the kingdom. She retreated to Tours, France, where she tended the sick and poor.

JUNE 4   PETROC (PEDROG)

STATUS Abbot
BORN 6th century
DIED c.594, Cornwall
GRC ◯
CofE ♣
LCDUS ◯
OTHER In Cornwall, Brittany
◯ Pre-Congregation

An important Celtic figure, Petroc was probably born in Wales, but set up a monastic community in Padstow on the Camel river estuary in Cornwall, England. Several local churches and coastal settlements bear variants of his name. He later became a hermit on nearby Bodmin Moor. His remains were lodged in Bodmin, but were stolen in 1117 and temporarily taken to Brittany in France.

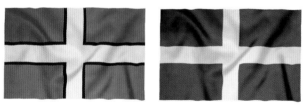

Although Petroc is the patron saint of Cornwall, his white saltire on a green ground has been adopted as the flag of the neighboring county of Devon.

The Cornish flag is based on the arms of St. Piran, a white saltire on a black ground. Ironically, St. Piran was an abbot most widely associated with Devon.

Date	Name	Status	Venerated	Life
June 3	Kevin of Glendalough (d.c.617)	Abbot ◯ 1903	In Ireland ✝ Blackbirds	Lived as a hermit in County Wicklow, Ireland, founding an abbey there. Close to nature and animals.
June 3	Isaac of Córdoba (c.825–52)	Martyr ◯ Pre-Congregation	In Córdoba, Spain	Christian civil servant at the Moorish court. Executed when he denounced Muhammad after retiring to a monastery at Tábanos.
June 4	Mary Elizabeth Hasselblad (1870–1957)	Nun ♥ 2000	In Sweden and US Brigittine Order	Swedish Lutheran. Converted to Catholicism (1902) after emigrating to New York. Sheltered Jews in Rome, Italy, in WWII.
June 5	Ferdinand of Portugal (1402–43)	Prince ♥ 1470	In Portugal	Led an expedition against the Moors in Morocco (1437). Defeated, he offered himself as a hostage, dying in prison.

JUNE 5   BONIFACE

STATUS Bishop, Martyr
BORN c.675, Crediton, Devon, England
DIED c.754, Frisia
GRC ♣
CofE ♣
LCDUS ♣
OTHER Eastern Orthodox churches (Dec. 19)
⬭ Pre-Congregation
✝ Axe, oak, raven, fox
🙏 Brewers; Germany

Effectively the founding father of Christianity in Germany, Boniface was born Wynfrith in Devon, England. He was educated in Benedictine monasteries in England and ordained in 705. Choosing a missionary vocation, he preached conversion in Frisia (northern Netherlands), before being directed to evangelize in Hesse, Thuringia, and Bavaria by Pope Gregory II. According to legend, he felled an oak tree near Fritzlar, Hesse, dedicated to the Nordic god Thor, to prove Christian superiority over local superstition. Supported by the Frankish ruler Charles Martel, Boniface established many Benedictine foundations in Hesse and went on to become head of the Frankish church. At the age of 80 he retired and returned to Frisia where, while preparing to confirm some converts at Dokkum, his camp was attacked by local pagans; forbidding any resistance, he was slain along with some 50 followers. His principal shrine is at Fulda in Germany.

The martyrdom of St. Boniface was only a temporary setback for the Church in the Low Countries.

JUNE 6   NORBERT

STATUS Bishop
BORN c.1080, Xanten, Germany
DIED 1134, Magdeburg, Germany
GRC ♣
CofE ♧
LCDUS ♣
⬭ 1582
✝ Monstrance, ciborium
🙏 Safe childbirth; Magdeburg

Norbert's emblems are either the ciborium (above) or the monstrance.

Born to an aristocratic Rhineland family, Norbert was given various clerical benefices while living the life of a courtier. After a brush with death, he was ordained in 1115, and in 1120 established a reformist Augustinian community in the valley of Prémontré near Laon. The Premonstratensian Order spread throughout France and the Holy Roman Empire. In 1126 Norbert was appointed Archbishop of Magdeburg, but his reformist zeal was not unopposed. Surviving several assassination attempts, he vigorously supported the exiled Pope Innocent II, and Holy Roman Emperor Lothair appointed Norbert Chancellor of Italy. In 1627 Norbert's remains were removed from Magdeburg to the abbey church of Strahov, Prague.

A statue on the Charles Bridge in Prague showing St. Norbert (with a monstrance) flanked by St. Wenceslaus (Sept. 28) and St. Sigismund, both patron saints of the Czech Republic.

Date	Name	Status	Venerated	Life
June 6	Philip the Deacon (d.c. AD 58)	Deacon ⬭ Pre-Congregation	One of the Seven Deacons of Jerusalem	Preached widely, converting many in Palestine and Samaria – including Simon Magus – and performed miracles.
June 6	Marcelino Champagnat (1789–1840)	Priest, Founder ♥ 1955 ⬭ 1999	By Marists	Founder of the Little Brothers of Mary (Marists). Several miraculous cures ascribed to him.
June 6	Mariam Thresia Chiramel Mankidiyan (1876–1926)	Nun, Founder ♥ 2000	In India	Born in Kerala, India. Cared for the poor, including the Untouchables. Founded the Congregation of the Holy Family (1914).
June 6	Ini Kopuria (c.1900–45)	Missionary	In Melanesia CofE	Police officer from Guadalcanal in the Solomon Islands. Founded the Melanesian Brotherhood (1925).

JUNE 8

WILLIAM OF YORK

STATUS Bishop
BORN c.1110, Yorkshire, England
DIED 1154, York, England
GRC ☁
CofE ☁
LCDUS ☁
⬭ 1227

William FitzHerbert was born to a wealthy landowning Norman family, which ensured his progress to a profitable ecclesiastical office. However, William fell foul of the sort of intrigues that beset church and state at the time, most famously in the case of the slightly younger Thomas Becket (Dec. 29). Although William was patronized by the English king, Stephen (William had been his private chaplain), his first election to the office of archbishop of York in 1141 faced some opposition, mainly by the powerful Cistercian Order, which owned extensive estates in Yorkshire. The Cistercians were supported by their founder, Bernard of Clairvaux (Aug. 20). Pope Eugenius III, himself a Cistercian, suspended and then deposed William following accusations of simony and incontinence. Despite powerful and violent supporters, William retired to Winchester. After the deaths of his successor at York, Henry Murdac (abbot of the Cistercian Fountains Abbey), Pope Eugenius, and St. Bernard, William was reinstated by Pope Anastasius IV in 1154. His triumphal re-entry to York was only marred by the bridge over the Ouse collapsing as he crossed it. Within weeks William was dead, possibly poisoned by wine administered at Mass. He was buried in York Minster and a strong local cult developed. His relics were regarded as miraculous.

York Minster is the largest Gothic cathedral in northern Europe apart from Cologne. A stained-glass window in the cathedral, dating from 1421, recounts the life of William and the many miracles associated with his relics.

Date	Name	Status	Venerated	Life
June 7	Robert of Newminster (1100–59)	Abbot ⬭ Pre-Congregation	In England	Born in Yorkshire and studied in Paris. Joined Benedictine Order and then the founders of the Cistercian Fountains Abbey. Went on to found Newminster Abbey, Northumberland (c.1138), among others. Many healing miracles associated with his relics.
June 8	Thomas Ken (1637–1711)	Bishop, Writer of Hymns	CofE	Oxford-educated Anglican clergyman. Reached high ecclesiastical office under Charles II, but was one of the Seven Bishops tried (but acquitted) by Charles's Catholic successor James II. Wrote a number of important hymns and *The Practice of Divine Love* (1685).
June 10	John Dominici (c.1356–1419)	Bishop, Theologian ♥ 1837	By Dominicans	Dominican prior. Founded monastery at Fiesole. Dominican reformer and vigorous preacher after speech impediment miraculously cured. Appointed archbishop of Ragusa and personal counselor to Pope Gregory XII, whom he persuaded to resign from the Papacy (1415), ending the Western Schism.

JUNE 9 — EPHRAEM (EPHREM)

STATUS Deacon, Doctor of the Church

BORN c.306, Nisibis, modern Turkey

DIED 373, near Edessa, modern Turkey

GRC ♣

CofE ○

LCDUS ♣

OTHER Eastern Orthodox churches, Syriac Orthodox Church

Ephraem entered the monastery at Nisibis after his baptism in around 324, and he taught at the cathedral school, eventually becoming its principal. Nisibis was overrun by the Persians in 363, and Ephraem retreated to become a hermit in a cave near the major theological center of learning at Edessa. There he found time to create one of the largest surviving bodies of early Christian writing, composing over 500 hymns and producing detailed commentaries on both the Old and New Testaments. His style is poetic and didactic, and often addressed the heresies that were current, especially in the Eastern churches, during his lifetime. Ephraem was proclaimed a Doctor of the Church in 1920.

A Syrian fresco of Ephraem from the 14th century.

JUNE 9 — COLUMBA OF IONA

STATUS Abbot, Missionary

BORN c.521, Donegal, Ireland

DIED 597, Iona, Scotland

GRC ○

CofE ♣

LCDUS ○

OTHER In Scotland

○ Pre-Congregation

One of the most famous of the Irish/Celtic missionaries, Columba was dispatched by the Irish Church to evangelize Scotland. Before this, Columba had established monastic foundations at Derry (modern Londonderry), Durrow, and Kells, all of which later emerged as centers of learning and artistic endeavor. He and twelve companions settled on the island of Iona off the southwest Scottish coast in 563, from where, it is said, he could still see his homeland. Under Columba's guidance, Iona became an influential center of missionary activity in Scotland and Northumbria, training monks, copying texts, and mediating in local affairs. Columba died in front of the altar of the abbey church.

The distinctive Iona cross, an elegant variant on the Celtic cross, was unique to Columba's community on the island.

Columba's stormy voyage north from Ireland to Iona, and his foundation there of a center of learning and missionary activity, has been celebrated in stamps and stained glass.

CELTIC ILLUMINATED GOSPELS

The skills of the copyists and illuminators of the Celtic Church remain unsurpassed. *The Book of Kells*, produced in around 800 at the monastery founded by Columba, is an outstanding example. The 12th-century Welsh chronicler Giraldus described the work of illumination as follows: "You will make out intricacies so delicate and so subtle, so full of knots and links, with colors so fresh and vivid, that you might say that all this were the work of an angel and not of a man."

The Book of Kells remains the preeminent example of the Celtic illuminated manuscript tradition. This facsimile has restored some of the luster of the original.

JUNE 11   BARNABAS THE APOSTLE

STATUS Apostle, Martyr

BORN 1st century AD, Cyprus

DIED c. AD 61, Salamis, Cyprus

GRC ♣

CofE ♣

LCDUS ♣

OTHER Eastern Orthodox churches

○ Pre-Congregation

✝ Often holding a book and olive branch; often with St. Paul

🙏 Peacemakers, against hailstorms; Cyprus

Barnabas, originally named Joseph, was a Jew ('Levite') from Cyprus. He was not listed among the original Twelve Apostles, but was added by Luke (Oct. 18), and features prominently in Acts. The name Barnabas, meaning 'son of consolation,' was given to him by the other Apostles, and he emerges as a good-natured man of persuasive powers. In Acts he is described as disposing of property and donating the proceeds to the Apostles (Acts 4:36–37), and then is sent to Antioch to consolidate the Christian community there. Barnabas calls on the support of St. Paul (Jan. 25), then travels with Paul to Jerusalem, and supports Paul during the debate with St. Peter concerning the admission of Gentiles to the Faith. His association with Paul continues when he accompanies Paul to Jerusalem, and then travels with Paul on his first missionary journey to Cyprus and Asia Minor.

Barnabas eventually fell out with Paul, and returned to Cyprus with the Apostle Mark (Acts 15:39), where he founded the Cypriot Church, but was then allegedly martyred by Greco-Roman pagans. The Epistle of Barnabas almost certainly was not actually written by him.

The martyrdom of Barnabas is not mentioned in the New Testament, but legends tell of him being stoned then burned, either at the Cypriot port of Salamis, or in Greece.

JUNE 11   METROPHANES, CHI SUNG

STATUS Martyr

BORN 1855, China

DIED 1900, Peking (Beijing), China

GRC △

CofE △

LCDUS △

OTHER Eastern Orthodox churches

○ 2000

By the time of the Boxer Rebellion (1900), Christianity had established a strong presence in the Chinese empire. This made its followers a prime target for the Boxers, who were keen to eradicate all traces of foreign influence. Metrophanes was a scholarly, unassuming Chinese man, with some Russian forebears. He was educated at the Russian Ecclesiastical Mission in Peking (modern Beijing) and was encouraged to become ordained, which he reluctantly was, by Nikolai, bishop of Japan, in 1880. He concentrated on the translation, printing, and publication of Russian religious texts into Chinese. During the Boxer uprising his print shop was ransacked and he was fatally stabbed. Seventy other Christians in his house and the adjacent Mission church were murdered, as were his wife, two sons (one only eight years old), and future daughter-in-law over the next few days. He is noted as the first Chinese Eastern Orthodox martyr, although some 222 Holy Chinese Martyrs, many killed by the Boxers, were glorified by the Eastern Orthodox Church in 2000.

An embroidered icon of the Holy Chinese Martyrs produced in 1917, with Metrophanes and his family in the foreground (right).

Date	Name	Status	Venerated	Life
June 12	Onouphrios (Onofrio) (d.c.400)	Hermit ○ Pre-Congregation	Eastern Orthodox churches	Egyptian monk who forsook collective monastic life at Thebes to wander the desert. Life recorded by Paphnoutios, who encountered the elderly, naked, bearded, unkempt hermit who promptly predicted his own death. Paphnoutios buried him on a hillside, and the grave immediately disappeared. Popular mythical figure in early Middle Ages, with a basilica, Sant Onofrio, dedicated to him on the Janiculum Hill in Rome.

JUNE 13 | ANTHONY OF PADUA

STATUS Monk, Preacher, Doctor of the Church

BORN c.1195, Lisbon, Portugal

DIED 1231, Arcella, Padua, Italy

GRC ♣

CofE ☁

LCDUS ♣

OTHER In Portugal

◯ 1232

✝ Book, bread, Infant Christ, lilies

♙ Animals, fishermen, horses, lost objects, the poor; Portugal, the Philippines, Lisbon, Padua

Born to one of the noblest families in Portugal, Anthony was one of the most celebrated saints of the Middle Ages, famed for his sanctity, gentleness, preaching, and miracles, which he performed in greater numbers than perhaps any other saint. At age 15, he joined the Augustinians, first in Lisbon, then at the more remote convent of Santa Croce in the north of the country. It was to Santa Croce in 1220 that the mutilated and headless corpses of St. Berard and his companions, Franciscan monks martyred in Morocco (Jan. 16), were brought. Anthony, determined to emulate them and fired by a zeal for martyrdom, joined the Franciscans. His desire was thwarted when he fell ill – his life was punctuated by sickness – and he was forced to return to Portugal. His ship, however, was then blown to Sicily, from where he eventually made his way to Assisi. There the Franciscans, unsure what to make of the sickly, waif-like Anthony, sent him to a rural hospice, San Paolo, in Romagna. It was there that he discovered his gift for preaching. In 1224, St. Francis himself sent Anthony to Lombardy and France, where he remained until 1226, a fierce opponent of heresy, his reputation as a charismatic preacher growing. The remaining years of his life were spent mostly in Padua, where he established a convent and where his fame as a preacher – he was said to have once preached to 30,000 people – as well as a peacemaker reached its height. Wracked with dropsy, he spent his last days as a hermit, living under a walnut tree, near Venice.

Anthony's reputation as a miracle worker, or thaumaturge, is central to his appeal. He is said to have preached to fish in a river, who dutifully gathered to hear him. A horse that refused to eat did so again only after Anthony blessed him. He reattached the foot of a

Both St. Francis and the Infant Christ are said to have appeared to St. Anthony. Representations of the saint commonly show him with the Infant Christ, such as this 17th-century painting by the Spanish painter Antonio de Pereda.

young man who, appalled at his behavior after kicking his mother, had hacked it off. He brought back to life a girl who had drowned. Poisoned food fed to him by heretics was rendered edible. When he died, church bells rang spontaneously – or possibly were rung by angels. His importance was such that he was canonized within a year of his death. In 1546, his body was exhumed. Though his body had decomposed, his tongue, a 'lively red,' remained intact as miraculous evidence of the purity of his words. In 1946, St. Anthony was declared a Doctor of the Church.

JUNE 14 | METHODIUS OF CONSTANTINOPLE

STATUS Patriarch

BORN c.790, Syracuse, Sicily

DIED 847, Constantinople, modern Turkey

GRC ☁

CofE ☁

LCDUS ☁

OTHER Eastern Orthodox churches

◯ Pre-Congregation

Methodius I (sometimes Methodios) played a key part in the final resolution of the violent split in the Eastern Church over iconoclasm, the bitter dispute as to whether the veneration of icons – images of God and his saints – was heretical. This had begun around 730, when the Byzantine emperor, Gregory III, sided with those who regarded icons as sinful – the iconoclasts, or image-breakers. In 821, Methodius, an iconodule, or staunch opponent of iconoclasm, already an abbot and returning from a mission to Rome, was arrested and exiled by the emperor Michael II. Michael's successor, Theophilos, an even more determined iconoclast, initially released Methodius, before in

A 14th-century icon of the 'Triumph of Orthodoxy.' It shows Methodius in the upper row of figures next to an icon of the Virgin and Child. Theodora and Michael III, in scarlet robes, stand on the other side of the icon.

turn re-arresting, torturing, and imprisoning him. On Theophilos's death in 842, Methodius was released on the orders of the Empress Theodora, mother of the new emperor, the two-year-old Michael III. Theodora was a fervent iconodule, like Methodius. Methodius was almost at once made patriarch. On March 11, 843, he symbolically restored the icons to the great church of Hagia Sophia in Constantinople. This, the 'Triumph of Orthodoxy,' has ever since been marked on the First Sunday of Great Lent, one of the holiest days in the Orthodox calendar.

JUNE 15   ALBERTINA BERKENBROCK

STATUS Martyr
BORN 1919, Santa Catarina, Brazil
DIED 1931, Santa Catarina, Brazil
GRC ☁
CofE ☁
LCDUS ☁
OTHER In Brazil
♥ 2007

Albertina Berkenbrock was only 12 when she died. She was a Brazilian girl, raised in a devoutly Catholic family. She was said to have been unusually spiritual. Her first Holy Communion was, she claimed, the most beautiful day of her life. She was killed by an employee of her father, who attempted to rape her. When she resisted, he slit her throat. It was claimed that over the following days whenever the killer, Maneco Palhoça, approached the room where her body was laid, blood seeped from her throat. She was almost instantly proclaimed a martyr by local people, and a substantial cult grew up around her as a result of her intercession on behalf of others.

Albertina was initially buried in the graveyard of a local church, São Luís. Her grave attracted so many visitors that she was re-buried in the church itself, where she is still venerated today.

JUNE 15   VITUS AND COMPANIONS

STATUS Martyr
BORN c.290, Sicily
DIED c.303, Lucania, Italy
GRC ☁
CofE ☁
LCDUS ☁
OTHER Eastern Orthodox churches
⊖ Pre-Congregation
† In a cauldron, with rooster or lion
⚕ Dancers, dogs, epileptics, oversleeping, snake-bites, storms; Prague

Vitus and his companions have almost no basis in historical fact. Yet Vitus has always been widely venerated, above all in Central Europe. A variety of legends about him exist. The most popular is that at the age of around seven, already a Christian, he was tortured by his father, a senator in Lucania in southern Italy, who demanded he give up his faith. Instead, he fled with his tutor, Modestus, and his nanny, Crescentia, the wife of Modestus, both also Christian. They eventually arrived in Rome, where Vitus expelled a demon from the son of the Roman emperor, Diocletian. Still refusing to renounce their Christianity, Vitus and his companions were tortured until an angel miraculously returned them to Lucania, where they died.

The cult of St. Vitus is in many ways more important than his life, assuming he existed at all. His remains were said to have been transferred to St.-Denis in France in 756 and from there to Corvey in western Germany. In 925, the king of East Francia, Henry I, presented one of the saint's hands to Wenceslas, the duke of Bohemia. The church he built to house it, St. Vitus's Cathedral, is today the largest Gothic church in the Czech lands. St. Vitus's Dance, the common name for a neurological disorder, chorea, whose sufferers move their hands and feet uncontrollably, comes from the habit of dancing wildly, even to the point of prostration, in front of representations of the saint. It was an activity especially widespread in medieval Germany.

St. Vitus's Cathedral in Prague (right) is one of the largest Gothic churches in Eastern Europe, and remains the principal center of his cult.

Date	Name	Status	Venerated	Life
June 15	Evelyn Underhill (1875–1941)	Writer, Mystic	CofE	English middle-class wife of a barrister, and perhaps the most intensely religious woman of her generation. Her book *Mysticism* (1911) was a potent argument in favor of spirituality – which she considered much more properly real than the apparent world – and "the quiet movement of the heart." In no sense unworldly, wrote journalism as well as books, taught, lectured, and performed an immense amount of charitable work. Became convinced pacifist, certain that only love could conquer evil.

ALTARPIECES

Altarpieces remain the focal point of many church or chapel layouts. In days when many of the congregation were illiterate, and the services were performed in Latin, altarpieces and wall paintings provided a visual sermon whereby the Christian message could be learned and discussed. Altarpieces provided an opportunity for celebrating the lives of saints, and often featured saints adoring Christ or the Virgin Mary, or being martyred.

This magnificent carved and painted altarpiece showing scenes from the life of the Blessed Virgin Mary was made in Germany in the 16th century.

JUNE 16 — LUTGARDIS

STATUS	Nun, Mystic
BORN	1182, Tongeren, Belgium
DIED	1246, Aywières, Belgium
GRC	☁
CofE	☁
LCDUS	☁
OTHER	By Cistercians; in Belgium
🙏	Blindness, childbirth, the disabled

Lutgardis was forced at age 12 to join a Benedictine convent after her family lost its money, meaning she could expect no dowry and hence no possibility of a suitable marriage. She quite soon began to experience extreme states of religious ecstasy, including reported levitations and blood emanating from her forehead in a form of stigmata said to have been acquired from Christ's Crown of Thorns.

Lutgardis consistently refused to become abbess and in 1216, seeking stricter religious discipline, joined a Cistercian convent at Aywières (modern Awirs). She was blind for the last 11 years of her life.

Lutgardis at prayer before the Crucifixion in a 1787 work by the Spanish painter Goya in the monastery of St. Joaquín and St. Ana, Valladolid, Spain.

JUNE 16 — QUIRICUS AND JULITTA

STATUS	Martyrs
BORN	3rd century, Syria
DIED	c.304, Tarsus, modern Turkey
GRC	☁
CofE	☁
LCDUS	☁
OTHER	Assyrian Church of the East, Coptic Church, Syriac Orthodox Church, Eastern Orthodox churches
⊘	Pre-Congregation
✝	A naked child on a boar
🙏	Family happiness, sick children

If, like so many early Christian martyrs, Quiricus, either three years or three months old at the time of his death, and Julitta, his mother, seem largely to exist in the realms of legend, they were nonetheless widely venerated in the Middle East, France, and Italy.

Reputedly, during the persecutions of Diocletian, they were brought before the governor of Tarsus and charged with being Christians. Quiricus then scratched the man's face; the governor responded by having the child thrown down steps, killing him. Julitta, rejoicing that her child would be honored as a martyr, was then torn apart by hooks on the orders of the governor. Their bodies were flung onto a heap of criminals' corpses. In other versions, both were decapitated.

Scenes from the life of Quiricus and Julitta from a 17th-century Russian icon.

JUNE 17 — BOTOLPH (BOTOLF)

STATUS	Abbot, Missionary
BORN	7th century, England
DIED	c. 680, England
GRC	☁
CofE	☁
LCDUS	☁
⊘	Pre-Congregation
✝	Often shown with a bridge in marshland
🙏	Travelers, farming

The facts of Botolph's life remain uncertain, but he remains a popular English saint. He trained as a Benedictine monk abroad, becoming 'full of the grace of the Holy Spirit.' In around 645, he founded a monastery, probably in Suffolk in East Anglia. He was also associated with a foundation at Ikanhoe (Icanhoh), set in the marshes near Boston in Lincolnshire. He was highly active as a missionary in England. Botolph's considerable influence

The chevron set against waves indicates Botolph's prowess as a builder.

is attested to by the establishment of perhaps as many as 70 churches in England bearing his name, four in London alone.

Botolph has a particular association with religious foundations and bridges, many of which are named after him in low-lying or reclaimed English lands such as the Fens or Romney Marsh.

JUNE 17 RAINERIUS OF PISA

STATUS Hermit, Monk
BORN c.1115, Pisa, Italy
DIED 1160, Pisa, Italy
GRC ⚬
CofE ⚬
LCDUS ⚬
⬭ Before 1181
✝ Bearded hermit in hair shirt
🙏 Travelers; Pisa, Italy

Rainerius spent a dissolute youth, mostly as a minstrel. He then became a successful merchant before giving away his fortune to live a life of extreme religious self-denial, first as a hermit in the Holy Land, which he visited several times, later as a monk in Pisa at the Benedictine abbeys of St. Peter and St. Vitus. Numerous miracles were ascribed to him, most involving holy water.

In 1632, Rainerius was declared patron saint of Pisa. In 1689, he was re-buried in Baroque splendor in the cathedral there.

JUNE 17 ALBERT CHMIELOWSKI

STATUS Founder
BORN 1845, Igolomia, Poland
DIED 1916, Kraków, Poland
GRC ⚬
CofE ⚬
LCDUS ⚬
OTHER In Poland
❤ 1983
⬭ 1989

Albert Chmielowski, more commonly Brother (or Brat) Albert, was a man who dedicated his life to charity. He was exceptionally well born, with a natural bent for the arts. When he was only 17, he lost a leg during riots against the Czarist Russian government of eastern Poland. He spent most of the next decade abroad as a painter before returning to his homeland. In 1880, he became a secular Franciscan and in 1887 founded the Albertine Brothers (more properly the Brothers of the Third

Order of St. Francis, Servants of the Poor), still active across Poland today. In 1891, he founded an equivalent order for women. He worked tirelessly for the poor and destitute. He died, on Christmas Day, in one of the shelters he had established for the homeless.

Brother Albert (left) had a lasting influence on the young Karol Wojtyla, later Pope John Paul II, who presided over his fellow Pole's beatification and canonization.

Date	Name	Status	Venerated	Life
June 16	Richard of Chichester (c.1197–1253)	Bishop ⬭ 1262	CofE	One of best-educated churchmen of his day. Key figure in ongoing dispute between papacy and rulers in many parts of Europe for primacy in church affairs. Appointed bishop of Chichester by the pope. King Henry III of England initially refused to allow Richard to take up position. Uneasy compromise that followed never fully resolved. Tomb in Chichester Cathedral became major place of medieval pilgrimage.
June 16	Joseph Butler (1692–1752)	Bishop, Theologian	CofE	Leading Anglican theologian and philosopher. Chaplain to Queen Caroline from 1736, bishop of Durham from 1750. Chiefly celebrated as forceful champion of deism, the belief that observation of natural world reinforces argument that it could only have been created by a divine being.
June 17	Samuel Barnett (1844–1913)	Priest, Social Reformer	CofE	Oxford-educated Anglican priest and leading social reformer. Vicar of St. Jude's in Whitechapel, a deprived area of London. With his wife, Henrietta Rowland, launched intensive program of good works. Most lasting achievement was Toynbee Hall, a 'settlement house' where middle-class students encouraged to live and work alongside members of working classes. Had substantial influence in the US, where, by 1913, 413 such settlements had been established.

JUNE 19 ROMUALD

STATUS Abbot, Hermit, Founder

BORN c.951, Ravenna, Italy

DIED c.1027, Val di Castro, Italy

GRC ♣

CofE ○

LCDUS ♣

○ 1582

Though a Benedictine monk himself, Romuald, born to an aristocratic family in Ravenna, reversed the general trend in medieval Europe toward the integration of monastic communities with the wider world. Instead he established the Camaldolese Order, which demanded what almost amounted to a return to hermit-like observance on the part of its members. The order's name comes from the monastery of Camaldoli in Tuscany, founded by Romuald. He admonished his monks to follow an extreme form of contemplation and went on to found a series of other monasteries in Italy, all enjoined to follow the same strict rule of prayer away from the distractions of the world.

JUNE 19 GERVASE AND PROTASE

STATUS Martyrs

BORN 2nd century

DIED 2nd century, Milan, Italy

GRC ○

CofE ○

LCDUS ○

OTHER Eastern Orthodox churches (Oct. 14)

○ Pre-Congregation

✝ Club, sword, scourge

🙏 Haymakers; discovery of thieves; Milan

The obscurity of Sts. Gervase and Protase, executed under either Nero or Diocletian, is almost total. Their cult, widespread in medieval Italy, even more so in medieval France, came about when the whereabouts of their bodies were revealed to St. Ambrose (Dec. 7) in a dream. "All the bones were perfect," he wrote. "There was much blood." The relics were taken to St. Ambrose's substantial basilica in Milan, completed in about 386, and laid to rest in the new church. Ambrose himself was later buried next to them.

The tombs of Sts. Gervase and Protase (left) in the crypt of the Basilica of St. Ambrose in Milan.

Romuald in an altarpiece of 1641 in the Church of San Romualdo in Ravenna. Beyond the gaunt figure of the saint, an angel fights off a demon.

Date	Name	Status	Venerated	Life
June 18	Gregorio Barbarigo (1625–97)	Cardinal, Scholar ❤ 1771 ○ 1960		Venetian noble, trained initially in law. Ordained in 1655. Became dominant figure in post-Counter-Reformation period. Worked heroically to help the sick during plague of 1657. Helped elect four popes.
June 18	Bernard Mizeki (c.1861–96)	Missionary, Martyr	CofE In southern Africa	Black Mozambiquan. At age 25 baptized an Anglican in Cape Town. Sent with new bishop of Mashonaland on mission to Shona peoples of modern Zimbabwe. Killed in anti-British Matabeleland Rebellion; dragged from his hut and speared to death.

JUNE 20 | # 17 IRISH CATHOLIC MARTYRS

Ireland remained a stronghold of Catholic resistance to the Reformation in the British Isles. Appallingly bloody events, such as the siege of Drogheda by Cromwell's Parliamentary forces in 1649 (above), did much to promote the antagonism between Catholics and Protestants that continues to this day.

While a number of those English and Welsh Catholics killed during and after the Reformation were recognized as martyrs relatively early by Rome (*see* May 4, June 22), the same was not so true of Ireland's Catholic martyrs, other than Oliver Plunkett (July 11). This was not the result of discrimination on the part of the Roman authorities, but almost no reliable information existed on the estimated 260 Irish men and women believed to have been killed for their faith. It was only in the second half of the 19th century that systematic efforts were made to investigate those known or thought to have died. In 1992, 17 were beatified. None has yet been canonized. They were chosen as representative of those who died: the list is in no sense definitive. Some, such as Bishop Dermot O'Hurley, tortured and hanged in Dublin in 1584, are relatively well documented. Of others, such as the Wexford sailors – three seamen executed in 1581 after a failed attempt to arrange the escape of the Catholic Viscount Baltinglass and his Jesuit chaplain – their names and the fact of their deaths are all that is known.

JUNE 21 | # ALOYSIUS GONZAGA

STATUS Religious

BORN 1568, Castiglione delle Stiviere, Italy

DIED 1591, Rome, Italy

GRC ♣

CofE ◯

LCDUS ♣

OTHER By Jesuits

♥ 1605

◯ 1726

✝ Rosary, lily, cross, skull

⚕ AIDS victims, Jesuit novices, the young

Aloysius, high-born but sickly from childhood, seems to have enjoyed a remarkable vocation from an early age. To the fury of his father, in 1585 he joined the Jesuits in Rome (though his death at only 23 meant that he was never ordained). Though a variety of ailments subsequently plagued him, his extreme piety and purity – he apparently never looked his mother in the face so as not to offend her – were evident. In 1590, he claimed to have had a vision of the Archangel Gabriel, who informed him that he would die in less than a year, as indeed he did, after caring for plague victims in the streets of Rome.

An 18th-century German image of Aloysius. He was buried in the Church of St. Ignatius in Rome, though his head was later transferred to the basilica in the town of his birth.

Date	Name	Status	Venerated	Life
June 19	Matt Talbot (c.1856–1925)	Ascetic	In Dublin, Ireland ⚕ Alcoholics	One of 12 children born and brought up in poverty in Dublin; all effectively uneducated. By his teens was an alcoholic. At 28 gave up drinking and discovered spirituality and self-denial. Died of a heart attack on way to Mass; body found bound in chains as self-mortification.
June 19	Sundar Singh (1889–1929)	Evangelist	CofE In India	High-born Sikh. Converted to Christianity at 14. Never wholly accepted by Anglican Church, yet shunned by own people. Professed a devout Christianity yet adopted life of a *sadhu* (Indian mystic). Preached extensively in Asia, Britain, US.

JUNE 22 · JOHN FISHER

STATUS Bishop, Cardinal, Martyr

BORN 1469, Yorkshire, England

DIED 1535, London, England

GRC ♣

CofE ♣ (July 6)

LCDUS ♣

♥ 1886

⬭ 1935

John Fisher remains the only member of the College of Cardinals to have been executed. Pope Paul III made Fisher a cardinal in order to protect him, calculating that Henry VIII would not dare execute Fisher once he was directly under papal protection. The move backfired disastrously, succeeding only in enraging Henry.

With Thomas More (*see below*), John Fisher, bishop of Rochester from 1504, and a member of the College of Cardinals from 1535, ranks as the most noteworthy of those Catholic martyrs executed under Henry VIII after refusing to acknowledge the king's supremacy as head of the newly created Church of England. Fisher was a leading scholar as well as a churchman. He played a central role in the founding of St. John's and Christ's colleges in Cambridge, where from 1504 to his death he was Chancellor.

Fisher is chiefly remembered as the primary advocate of Catherine of Aragon, Henry's first queen who, from 1527 and in direct defiance of the pope, Henry was determined to divorce in favor of the much younger Anne Boleyn. Unlike More, Fisher openly and repeatedly criticized the king. He was arrested for the first time in 1530, again in 1533, and for a final time in 1534. He was tried the following year on the charge that he did "openly declare in English that the king, our sovereign lord, is not supreme head on earth of the Church of England." Henry commuted the sentence, declaring that Fisher need not be hanged, drawn, and quartered – the usual fate of commoners sentenced to death – but could, more mercifully, be beheaded.

JUNE 22 · THOMAS MORE

STATUS Scholar, Martyr

BORN 1478, London, England

DIED 1535, London, England

GRC ♣

CofE ♣ (July 6)

LCDUS ♣

♥ 1886

⬭ 1935

🙏 Statesmen, Catholic lawyers

Thomas More, Lord Chancellor under Henry VIII of England from 1529 to 1532, has long enjoyed a reputation as a martyr for freedom of conscience, a staunch defender not just of Catholicism but also of Humanist values. The truth is murkier. He was one of the leading minds in Europe and a fearsome opponent of Reform movements. He called Lutheranism "the most pestiferous and pernicious poison." He not only oversaw the interrogation and torture of reformers, especially those suspected of distributing Tyndale's English Bible, but had a number burned at the stake and wrote a series of extraordinarily foul-mouthed tirades against Lutheranism. That said, his essential view that the Catholic Church was a central prop of England itself never wavered. To attack the Church, he contended, was little better than to declare war against the fundamental fabric of the state. It followed that any such assaults, even if instituted by the king himself, had to be resisted at all costs. It was this absolutely held belief that drove his refusal to acknowledge any authority in Church matters greater than the pope's.

More, imprisoned from April 1534 and tried on a charge of treason in July the following year, was a lawyer to the last. He never explicitly denied the king's self-asserted role as head of the Church, he simply refused to be drawn on the subject. It did him little good. Like Fisher before him (*see above*), he was found guilty and beheaded.

Thomas More, captured here in one of the most penetrating Tudor portraits, painted by Hans Holbein in 1527, may have been unforgiving in matters of state. But that he was a man of high intelligence, exceptionally well read, and no less exceptionally well connected, was always clear.

JUNE 22   ALBAN

STATUS Martyr

BORN Verulamium (now St. Albans), England

DIED c.209/c.304, St. Albans, England

GRC ○

CofE ♣

LCDUS ○

OTHER US Episcopalian Church

⬭ Pre-Congregation

🙏 Torture victims, converts, refugees

Among the many legends that grew up about the martyrdom of Alban is that his first executioner was so awed by Alban's faith that he converted instantly and was martyred himself. As the replacement executioner decapitated Alban, his eyes flew from his head, as this 13th-century manuscript illustration shows.

With Sts. Julius and Aaron, Alban is celebrated as one of the first three English martyrs. From the 6th century he became the focus of a substantial cult, of which the most obvious manifestation is St. Albans Cathedral itself.

Alban's life itself remains shrouded in obscurity. The best estimates as to when he died vary by almost a century. The cause of his martyrdom was his sheltering a Christian priest, who converted Alban. When a decree was issued for the arrest of the priest, Alban, donning the priest's cloak, offered himself instead, affirming his Christianity with the words: "I worship and adore the true and living God who created all things."

JUNE 22   PAULINUS OF NOLA

STATUS Bishop

BORN c.354, Bordeaux, France

DIED 431, Nola, Italy

GRC ♣

CofE ○

LCDUS ♣

⬭ Pre-Congregation

Paulinus was an aristocratic Roman senator, born in Gaul (modern France), who converted to Christianity in 389. Following the death of his only child, a boy, some years later, he was ordained a priest and embraced a much more thoroughgoing form of Christianity. Despite holding substantial estates in France and Spain, he moved to Nola in southern Italy. There, at his own expense, he set about commemorating a little-known Roman martyr, Felix (April 23), executed in the 3rd century, building a substantial complex, including a basilica, in his honor. Paulinus also formed a small monastic community. In 410 he was appointed bishop of Nola. Paulinus's life is unusually well documented, chiefly due to the survival of a substantial number of his letters and poems.

JUNE 23   ETHELDREDA (AETHELTHRYTH)

STATUS Abbess

BORN c.636, Suffolk, England

DIED 679, Ely, England

GRC ○

CofE ♣

LCDUS ○

⬭ Pre-Congregation

🙏 Sore throats

Etheldreda was one of the four daughters of the Anglo-Saxon king Anna of East Anglia, given in marriage to a local fenland prince, Tondbert. As she had already taken a vow of 'perpetual virginity,' the marriage was never consummated. On Tondbert's death, Etheldreda secluded herself in Ely in the Fens. However, her father married her off again, this time to the king of Northumbria, Ecgfrith. Not only did she again refuse to consummate this marriage, she became a nun. Escaping her husband's lust-filled wrath, she again fled to Ely, where she founded an abbey. Following her death, her sister Sexburga (July 6) succeeded her as abbess, as would her niece and great-niece. Etheldreda is also commemorated by the 13th-century church of St. Etheldreda in London, once part of the palace of the bishop of Ely. It is the only pre-Reformation church in England that has seen continuous Catholic worship, as well as one of only two surviving buildings in London from the reign of Edward I.

St. Etheldreda is seen here in a stained-glass window in the church of St. Etheldreda in London. The crosier in her left hand indicates her status as an abbess, the church in her right is evidence of her foundation of the abbey at Ely.

JUNE 24 THE BIRTH OF JOHN THE BAPTIST

STATUS Prophet, Martyr

BORN Late 1st century BC

DIED c. AD 29

GRC ♣

CofE ♣

LCDUS ♣

OTHER Eastern Orthodox churches

◯ Pre-Congregation

✝ With lamb, with cross, in animal skins, bearded and often unkempt

The cross of St. John was adopted by the powerful crusading order, the Knights Hospitaller, whose principal foundation in Jerusalem was built on the site of the Monastery of St. John. By the mid-12th century the order, originally created to provide succor to Christian pilgrims, had also become a formidable military force rivaling the Knights Templar.

This Syrian icon (right) shows John contemplating his fate (see page 219).

John the Baptist is among the few saints who enjoy two main feast days. This day, the more important of the two and one of the oldest feasts, celebrates his birth and ministry; his other (Aug. 29) celebrates his martyrdom. John is described with great consistency in all four Gospels.

John was born the son of Zechariah and Elizabeth (Nov. 5), thus making him a cousin of Jesus. Little is known of his early years, but Jesus acknowledged him as an important forebear of His ministry. John is generally recognized as the last in the line of Hebrew prophets that led directly to Jesus Christ. John appears to have withdrawn into the wilderness, wearing camel skins and subsisting on locusts and honey, an existence that became a very popular subject in art. He re-emerged as an itinerant preacher in the valley of the river Jordan in around AD 27. He proclaimed that the coming of the Messiah was imminent, and offered baptism in the Jordan in repentance of sins.

John gathered many followers, among them several who were to become Christ's Apostles; crucially, he also baptized Jesus. His function as a herald of Jesus is ambiguous. He was evidently something of a fire-and-brimstone preacher, impatient,

> "Among those who are born of women, there is not a greater prophet ... "
>
> JESUS CHRIST, LUKE 7:28.

irascible, and inspired – full of exhortation – and not afraid to use shock and awe to capture his audience. He called the Jewish officials, the Pharisees and Sadducees, who came to hear him "Ye offspring of vipers." John's was a very different approach to preaching, far from the gentleness, compassion, wisdom, and imagination we hear from the lips of Christ. Nevertheless, he was humble enough to insist that his followers immediately transfer their allegiance to Jesus once His ministry began. For all that,

Bernini's powerful statue of St. John, bursting out of his niche in St. Peter's, Rome, conforms to John's traditional iconography: dressed in animal skins, bearded and unkempt, bearing a cross, and accompanied by a lamb.

John's fate further presages that of Christ: his career was brought to an abrupt end when he was imprisoned and eventually executed on a whim, by Herod the Tetrarch, essentially for being a rabble-rouser.

Date	Name	Status	Venerated	Life
June 25	Prosper of Aquitaine (c.390–463)	Theologian ◯ Pre-Congregation		Lived in Provence, France; disciple of Augustine of Hippo (Aug. 28), and a moderate advocate of his views concerning Pelagianism, emphasizing power of God's grace and divine mercy, available to all. Secretary to Pope Leo the Great (Nov. 10) from c.440. Died in Rome.
June 25	Jutta of Thuringia (d.c.1264)	Nun ◯ Pre-Congregation		Jutta's legend similar to that of Elisabeth of Hungary (Nov. 17); a young noblewoman, happily married, whose husband died of plague on way to Holy Land. Retired as a hermit to nunnery in Kulmsee (modern Chelmza, Poland), then controlled by the Teutonic Knights, tending to the poor and needy.
June 26	John and Paul (d.c.362)	Martyrs ◯ Pre-Congregation		Brothers and faithful soldiers of the emperor Constantine. Martyred at their home on the Celian Hill in Rome, at the command of Constantine's successor Julian the Apostate.

In St. John in the Wilderness *(c. 1500), by the Dutch mystic painter Hieronymous Bosch, the prophet is shown transfixed by the lamb (symbolic of Christ), apparently unaware of the bizarre, sultry, and vaguely malevolent landscape that surrounds him.*

JOSEMARÍA ESCRIVÁ DE BALAGUER

STATUS Priest, Founder
BORN 1902, Barbastro, Spain
DIED 1975, Rome, Italy
GRC ◯
CofE ◯
LCDUS ◯
OTHER By Opus Dei
♥ 1992
◯ 2002

Escrivá was an enormously influential Aragonese doctor of law and theology who studied in Madrid and Rome after being ordained in 1925. He was forced into hiding during the Spanish Civil War (1936–39) due to the anti-clerical tendencies of the Popular Front government, and he supported Franco's Nationalists. He first developed the idea of Opus Dei (literally 'Work of God') in 1928. His vision was to fully incorporate the laity into the activities of the Church through the sanctification of their secular work.

He formally founded the Priestly Society of the Holy Cross, linked to Opus Dei, in 1943, and moved to Rome in 1946, where the movement was given papal approval in 1950. Much criticized, but supported by the highest ranks of the Catholic Church, Escrivá pursued his vision unswervingly, organizing conferences and workshops, encouraging vocations to the priesthood, and writing. His publications include the epigrammatic *The Way*, which has sold over five million copies in 43 languages. Opus Dei now has over 80,000 members worldwide, while Escrivá's overall book sales have topped eight million.

REPUBLICA DOMINICANA
Correos
CATEDRAL PRIMADA DE AMERICA
Josemaría Escrivá de Balaguer
(1902-2002)
Fundador del Opus Dei
$10 CENTENARIO DE SU NATALICIO

Escrivá's influence was felt all around the Catholic world.

RAMÓN LLULL – ALCHEMIST OR SAINT?

There are many who, despite their deep devotion to the Christian message, have been tainted by their involvement in practices regarded by the Church as 'unorthodox.' Outstanding among these is the Catalan philosopher, mystic, theologian, ecumenicist, missionary, and eventual martyr, Ramón Llull, condemned unfairly as an alchemist.

Llull (c.1232–1316) was an extraordinary polymath. Born to a wealthy family in Majorca, he was well educated and was conversant in Latin, Catalan, Occitan, and Arabic. He was tutor to James II and traveled extensively. He translated many works, and established chairs in many universities dedicated to the study of Hebrew and Arabic.

In his dictated autobiography, *Vita coaetanea*, he described a vision of the crucified Christ that appeared to him five times as he was composing a love poem in 1265. He became a lay Franciscan tertiary, particularly dedicated to converting Muslims to Christianity. At the same time he wrote treatises on botany, astrology, and mathematics, developed a system of information organization that prefigured the computer, and an analysis of how elections work. His wide-ranging interests led to accusations of alchemy and hermeticism.

Llull undertook three missionary journeys to Muslim North Africa, hoping to unite the three 'Religions of the Book' – Judaism, Christianity, and Islam. He was forcibly rebuffed and, on his last journey, to Bougie in modern Algeria at age 82, he was fatally stoned. He was conveyed back to his birthplace before he expired. His life is celebrated on June 26 in Catalonia.

Llull (left) was famed for his learning, facility with languages, and general erudition.

Llull's attempt to bridge the gap between Christianity, Judaism, and Islam was fiercely rejected by Algerian Muslims, who stoned him, causing his death.

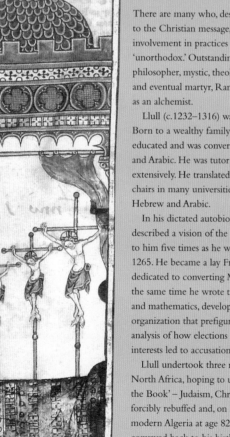

Llull's vision of five crucifixes (left) from an illuminated edition of Vita coaetanea.

JUNE 27 | CYRIL OF ALEXANDRIA

STATUS Bishop, Doctor of the Church

BORN c.376, Alexandria, Egypt

DIED 444, Alexandria, Egypt

GRC ♣

CofE ♣

LCDUS ♣

OTHER Eastern Orthodox and Nestorian churches

⬭ Pre-Congregation

† Bishop's miter, book

ΘΕΟΤΟΚΟΣ

Cyril was one of the outstanding theologians of the 5th century. He was the nephew of Theophilus, patriarch of Alexandria, and succeeded him in 412. He became a highly partisan defender of the supremacy of the see of Alexandria in the Eastern Church, a position bolstered by his argument against the doctrine that Christ existed in two forms – one divine and one human – as promulgated by Nestorius, the patriarch of Constantinople.

The Nestorian position implied that the Blessed Virgin Mary could only be the mother of Christ, not the mother of God. Presiding over the Council of Ephesus in 431, Cyril defeated Nestorius, and as a result the Nestorian Church split away from Eastern Orthodoxy (*see page 172*). In his less doctrinal (and political) writing, Cyril emphasized the presence of God in each and every human being. He was proclaimed a Doctor of the Church in 1882.

Cyril's emblem combines two quill pens and the Blessed Virgin Mary's title 'God-bearer' in Greek.

A mid-13th century wall painting of Cyril from the Church of the Holy Apostles in Peć, Serbia.

JUNE 28 | IRENAEUS

STATUS Bishop, Martyr

BORN c.130

DIED c.200, Lyon, France

GRC ♣

CofE ♣

LCDUS ♣

⬭ Pre-Congregation

Irenaeus's emblem unites a Bible with a crook and two crosses.

Irenaeus was probably of Greek origin, but studied in Rome, and after being ordained served at Lyon in Gaul (modern France). He acted as a negotiator during the persecutions under Marcus Aurelius, and succeeded the bishop of Lyon, one of the victims, in around 178. Only in the early 20th century did his writings come to light. They revealed a thoughtful analysis of the apostolic succession that embraced all of human history, and particularly that of the Hebrew and Christian traditions, which came to a zenith in the life of Christ.

Among the writings of St. Irenaeus was a forceful condemnation of Gnosticism in his Adversus Haereses (Against Heresies).

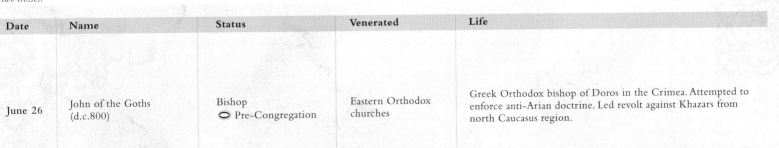

Date	Name	Status	Venerated	Life
June 26	John of the Goths (d.c.800)	Bishop ⬭ Pre-Congregation	Eastern Orthodox churches	Greek Orthodox bishop of Doros in the Crimea. Attempted to enforce anti-Arian doctrine. Led revolt against Khazars from north Caucasus region.

STATUS Apostle

BORN c. AD 1, Bethsaida, modern Israel

DIED c. AD 64, Rome, Italy

GRC ♣

CofE ♣

CDUS ♣

OTHER Eastern Orthodox churches, US Evangelical Lutheran Church

○ Pre-Congregation

✝ Two crossed keys, book, inverted cross. Often represented at the gates of Heaven

🙏 Fishermen, shipwrights, stonemasons; the Papacy, Rome

The 'First Apostle' doesn't have his own day in most calendars, but shares this significant day with Paul, who has his own feast day (Jan. 25).

Peter remains the most important of the original disciples, chosen by Christ to be the 'rock of the church.' He was born in Bethsaida, near the Sea of Galilee, to a family of fishermen, and was originally named Simon. His brother Andrew introduced him to Jesus, and they witnessed Christ walking on water. Jesus said that Peter would become a 'fisher of men' and renamed him Cephas (Peter in English, which means rock).

Peter emerges from the Gospels as strong but impetuous and fallible. He also attempted to walk on water, and briefly succeeded until his faith faltered; Jesus prayed that Peter's faith be strengthened, but immediately after Christ's crucifixion it would be Peter who denied knowledge of Him three times. Despite this, Peter was the first Apostle to whom Christ would appear after His resurrection, and after the Pentecost, Peter became the leader of the Christian community in Jerusalem, and the arbiter of debates, disputes, and matters of faith. Even St. Paul deferred to his judgment when discussing how Gentiles might enter the faith.

He was briefly imprisoned by Herod Agrippa, but was freed by an angel. Several miracles were attributed to him in Christ's name. He seems to have made missionary journeys to Samaria and Antioch, where he is regarded as the first bishop of the city.

Whether he traveled to Rome has been questioned, although archaeological evidence increasingly suggests that he did. The apocryphal *Acts of Peter* describes him fleeing from the persecutions of Nero, but encountering Christ on the way and returning to face martyrdom. The tradition of Peter being the first bishop of Rome has not been traced earlier than the end of the 2nd century, although it is universally accepted.

St. Peter's in Rome is the mother church of the Catholic faith. The modern basilica is part of the Vatican, and replaces an earlier cathedral, built over the tomb of St. Peter by Constantine in the 4th century. It was begun in 1503 and took more than a century to complete, drawing on the architectural skills of Bramante, Raphael, Antonio da Sangallo the Younger, Michelangelo, Maderno, and Bernini.

"Feed my lambs ... Feed my sheep."

JESUS TO PETER (JOHN 21:15–16).

The historian Eusebius describes Peter being crucified upside down, at his own request, to avoid imitation of Christ (right).

VARIETIES OF THE CROSS

Peter is usually represented by an inverted Cross, as he was crucified upside down. There are many variations on the basic form of the Cross, which since the 5th century has been the central symbol of Christianity. The most familiar is the Latin Cross, which may appear 'clothed' (with the Christ figure on it), 'unclothed,' or adorned with flowers signifying Easter. Early Christians sometimes used an anchor or trident symbol as a disguised reference to the Cross.

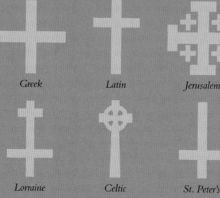

Greek   Latin   Jerusalem   Papal   Patriarchal   Russian Orthodox

Lorraine   Celtic   St. Peter's   St. Andrew's   St. Antony's   St. Chad's

JUNE 30 THE FIRST HOLY MARTYRS

During times of persecution, Christians in the Roman empire developed various ways of communicating their faith secretly. The plaque above containing a symmetric arrangement of 25 letters has been found on several houses. The Latin words, which read vertically or horizontally, translate as 'he who works the plow sows the seed.' However, the phrase forms an anagram of pater noster, meaning 'Our Father,' which can be rearranged as below, the spare As and Os meaning alpha (beginning) and omega (end).

This feast day was introduced to the revision of the General Roman Calendar in 1969 to compensate for the absence of the many – indeed hundreds – of Pre-Congregational saints (of whom very little is known, often little more than a name and a traditional feast day) who had been removed from the Calendar during the revision. The day particularly refers to those who suffered under the persecution of Nero (r. AD 54–68). These persecutions, according to the Roman historian Tacitus, were provoked by a great fire that broke out in Rome in AD 64, destroying about two-thirds of the city. Probably, like the Great Fire of London in 1666, it was simply the result of an accident waiting to happen in a rapidly expanding old city, but Nero selected the Christian community as a scapegoat, as they presented themselves as opponents of the traditional Roman pantheon of gods and protectors.

Hundreds of Christians were rounded up and subjected to appalling methods of torture and execution, often in public arenas, as a new attraction to satisfy the Roman populace's taste for spectacular but violent 'games.' Burnings at sunset, the victims covered in wax, were spectacular, but often over too quickly for the crowds, while crucifixions were popular but could drag on too long. More in line with the crowd's expectations were gladiatorial combats, and especially those in which Christian victims were smeared with animal scent or stitched into hides, and left to the mercy of wild beasts. Even hardened ticket-holders at the arenas were shocked by the spectacle.

Both Sts. Peter and Paul appear to have been among those who lost their lives during the persecutions of Nero.

A very secret Christian symbol was the anchor, a disguised Cross and a symbol of safety after the storms of life.

A simple symbol, which could be drawn in the sand to acknowledge one's faith, was the fish, which in Greek is ichthus, forming an acrostic:

Iesous	Jesus
CHristos	Christ
THeou	God's
Uios	Son
Soter	the Savior

A 19th-century vision of Roman barbarity by Henryk Siemiradzki shows a corpulent Nero inspecting a victim.

CHRISTIAN PERSECUTIONS UNDER ROME

Rome was largely tolerant of local religions, often absorbing interesting deities worshipped by conquered peoples into its own pantheon, and even tolerating Hebrew monotheism. But from its earliest days, during and immediately after Christ's ministry, Christianity was at best regarded as a superstition and at worst as a troublesome agitation movement. Where possible, legal means were brought to bear to suppress the faith, often with the collaboration of local authorities, courts, and priesthoods, who were keen not to upset their imperial masters (as happened in Jerusalem, with the trial and condemnation of Christ, among others).

The first Christian missionaries (such as Sts. Paul and Peter and their followers), traveling in Palestine, Syria, Mesopotamia, Anatolia, Greece, and the eastern Mediterranean, often encountered, and often greatly upset, established pagan communities. This frequently resulted in their ostracism or a grisly fate at the hands of outraged mobs. There is some evidence from Roman commentators

that certain Christian extremists actively sought martyrdom, and would provoke the authorities in order to achieve it.

The first organized Roman imperial persecution of the Christian community occurred in Rome under Nero, but this set a trend which was to recur on and off for the next 250 years. The persecutions were finally brought to an end by the emperor Constantine (r.306–37), who converted to the faith following a vision before the battle of Milvian Bridge in 312 and proclaimed Christian toleration throughout the empire with the Edict of Milan of 313.

EMPEROR	DATES OF PERSECUTION
Nero	c. AD 64–68, mainly in Rome
Domitian	c. AD 90–96, disputed
Trajan	c.109–11, Bithynia
Marcus Aurelius Antoninus	161–80, Italy, Gaul
Septimius Severus	c.202–11, Carthage, Rome, Corinth, Alexandria
Maximinus	235, directed against church leaders
Decius Trajan	250–51, throughout the empire
Valerian	253–60, throughout the empire
Diocletian	303–06, Eastern empire – the 'Great Persecution'
Galerius and Maximian	308–11, Eastern empire
Julian the Apostate	361–63, an attempt to restore pagan worship within the empire

THE 'GREAT PERSECUTION'

After centuries of centralized unity, but pressured on all fronts by 'barbarians,' the Roman empire was divided into various segments. The most important were the Western empire, still centered on Rome, and the Eastern empire, based in Byzantium, largely Greek in character. This division of the empire involved a new administrative structure, one in which each area had a supreme 'emperor' but with attendant senior 'caesars' who could often tip the decision-making balance. The burning of Emperor Diocletian's palace at Nicomedia was blamed on Christians by his deputy Galerius. Although many members of Diocletian's family and court were Christians, he issued four edicts demanding the burning of Christian texts and churches. Galerius and another caesar, Maximian, proved to be enthusiastic persecutors, perpetrating particularly gruesome atrocities in Bithynia, Syria, and Egypt. (*See also* Dec. 28).

The initial attempts of Diocletian (left) to bloodlessly suppress Christianity escalated into full-scale massacres under his deputies Galerius and Maximian.

JULY

Mark Antony named the seventh month of the Gregorian calendar, July, after another celebrated calendrical reformer, the Roman dictator Julius Caesar. July is traditionally a time of waiting while crops come to fruition. They may well be severely delayed if it rains on Saint Swithun's Day on July 15, in which case tradition holds it will rain for a further 40 days.

The celebrations of two great early modern theologians fall in July: Thomas à Kempis on July 24 and Ignatius of Loyola on July 31.

One of the towering figures of the Catholic Counter-Reformation, Ignatius of Loyola was a Spanish nobleman and soldier who went on to found the missionary order of the Society of Jesus, or the Jesuits. The casting out of devils from a possessed couple is the one miracle attributed to him, an act represented here by Peter Paul Rubens (1577–1640).

JULY 1 | JUNÍPERO SERRA

STATUS Friar, Founder
BORN 1713, Majorca, Spain
DIED 1784, Carmel, California
GRC ☁
CofE ☁
LCDUS ♣
⬯ 1988
✝ Usually shown in Franciscan robes, brandishing a cross, sometimes with a Native American
🙏 Vocations

Born Miquel Josep Serra i Ferrer (he took the name Junípero in honor of St. Juniper), Serra entered the Franciscan Order of Friars Minor in 1730. It soon became clear that he was academically gifted, and he became a professor of theology at age 24.

He joined the Missionary College of San Fernando in 1749 and journeyed to North America. He first arrived in Veracruz and, despite a crippling riding accident, then walked 200 arduous miles (320 km) to Mexico City. Thereafter, he traveled on foot wherever possible.

For the next 15 years he took on missionary work to be near the Indians, learning their languages, and helping to administer the College of San Fernando in Mexico City. He became famous as a passionate and volatile preacher. During his dramatic sermons he was said to scourge himself, beat his own chest with a stone, and apply a lit torch to his bare chest, and he refused any remedial treatment.

Building Missions

In 1768, the Spanish emperor expelled the Jesuits from Spain's colonies and Serra, with a group of Franciscans, was sent to take over the administration of the Jesuit missions in Baja California. This was the beginning of his extraordinary mission-building career. Under his presidency, nine California missions were established, stretching 600 miles (965 km) from San Diego in 1769 to San Francisco in 1776. Serra was a zealous and tireless missionary who walked vast distances, suffered from malnutrition and scurvy, and was prone to mortification of the flesh.

Serra's missionary efforts were disrupted when he fell foul of

An inspirational statue of Serra accompanied by a Native American child, in Mallorca, in the Balearic Islands, Spain. He once said of the Indians, whom he regarded as 'Gentiles' rather than pagans, that they had "stolen my heart away."

Serra died at the Mission San Carlos Borromeo at Carmel and is buried under the sanctuary floor. He has come to be seen as a pivotal figure in the colonization of California.

the military commander in California, and returned to Mexico City to argue successfully that the authority of the Franciscans over the army and baptized Indians should be increased. He encouraged Mexican officials to establish an overland route to Alta California, which encouraged colonizing expeditions and the foundation of civilian settlements in San Francisco in 1776 and Los Angeles in 1781. Serra's political influence was commensurate with the impact of the missions. With their populations of baptized Indians (Serra is said to have converted over 6,000), the missions kept the region within the Spanish political sphere. They also contributed economically, providing surpluses of cattle and grain.

Serra spent the rest of his life tirelessly traveling throughout California, confirming all those who had been baptized. Baptized Indians submitted completely to the authority of the Franciscans, but conditions of mission life were both harsh and oppressive, for which Serra has been occasionally criticized.

Date	Name	Status	Venerated	Life
July 2	Bernardino Realino (1530–1615)	Confessor ⬯ 1947	By Jesuits 🙏 Lecce, Italy	Born into noble Italian family. Studied both medicine and law, and was summoned to Naples as auditor and lieutenant general. When he realized his vocation, joined the Society of Jesus. Worked unstintingly – both in Naples and Lecce – in service of his community. Became rector of Jesuit college in Lecce. Celebrated for his charity to the poor and sick.
July 2	Francis Jerome (1642–1716)	Priest ♥ 1806 ⬯ 1839	By Jesuits 🙏 Naples	Italian Jesuit. Worked 40 years helping criminals, slaves, and the sick in Naples. Numerous miracles attributed to him.

JULY 1 — THE VENNS AND THE CLAPHAM SECT

STATUS Evangelists, Reformers

HENRY
BORN 1725, Barnes, England
DIED 1797, Yelling, England

JOHN
BORN 1750, London, England
DIED 1813, London, England

HENRY
BORN 1796, London, England
DIED 1873, London, England

JOHN
BORN 1834, Hull, England
DIED 1923, Cambridge, England

GRC ☁
CofE ♣
LCDUS ☁

The Venns were a dynasty of English Evangelical churchmen who pioneered self-reliant, self-governing church reform.

Henry Venn was educated at Cambridge before becoming an Anglican curate. He was considered a Methodist because of his propensity to teach scripture in his own home. He became curate of Clapham, London, in 1754, and a founding member of the Clapham Sect. In 1763, he published his popular *The Compleat Duty of Man*, a manual of doctrine and ethics for Christian families.

The Clapham Sect campaigned for religious and humanitarian causes, notably the abolition of the slave trade. They were greatly promoted by Henry's son John, a charismatic preacher who became rector of Clapham in 1792, and by William Wilberforce (July 30), whose cousin, John Thornton, funded the Sect.

Later, the Sect dedicated itself to philanthropy, supporting Sunday schools and schools for the poor, and campaigned to protect child workers. It became the nucleus of the Church Mission Society (founded 1799, under the co-leadership of John Venn), which sent many missionaries to Africa and Asia. John's son Henry was enormously influential in the development of missionary activity, and the encouragement of indigenous churches.

Henry's son John, ordained in 1858 after graduating from Cambridge, is more noted as a mathematician (he invented the Venn diagram), logician, philosopher, and historian.

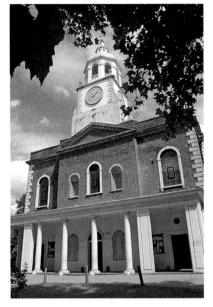

Holy Trinity Church, Clapham, London. This elegant neoclassical church was erected as the headquarters of the Clapham Sect by the wealthy Evangelical philanthropist John Thornton in 1776.

JULY 2 — JOHN FRANCIS REGIS

STATUS Confessor, Missionary
BORN 1597, Fontcouverte, France
DIED 1640, La Louvesc, France

GRC ☁
CofE ☁
LCDUS ☁
OTHER By Jesuits
◯ 1737
♙ Lacemakers, social workers, marriage

John Francis bearing the Christ Child in a stained-glass window in the Church of the Gesu, Wisconsin.

John Francis was educated at the Jesuit college of Béziers. At age 19 he entered the Jesuit novitiate at Toulouse, and took his vows two years later. His life as a newly ordained priest began in Toulouse, where he worked with victims of bubonic plague. He then moved to the Jesuit college at Montpellier, where he preached Catholic doctrine, worked with poor and fallen women, visited hospitals, and worked for the conversion of the Huguenots.

He organized charitable collections of donations from the wealthy, and established hostels for prostitutes, setting up destitute girls as lacemakers. John Francis's reputation for moral integrity and zealous good works began to spread and the local bishop invited him to the diocese of Viviers in the Ardèche, where he continued his missionary work.

Toward the end of his life he alternated periods when he pursued his good works in the city with long stretches of time when he undertook missionary work for the Society. These arduous journeys finally broke down his health. Immediately after his death, pilgrims began to visit his tomb. The place where he died was turned into a mortuary chapel, and waters of a nearby stream were attributed with miraculous cures, brought about by his intercession.

Date	Name	Status	Venerated	Life
July 2	Juvenaly of Alaska (1761–96)	Martyr	Eastern Orthodox churches	With St. Herman, member of first Russian Orthodox mission sent to proclaim Gospel in the New World. From 1794, mission worked in harsh conditions on Kodiak Island, moving to mainland in 1796. Mission baptized over 12,000 natives in Russian colony of Alaska. Martyred by enraged pagan Eskimos in 1796. According to Eskimo legend, rose from the dead to confront his assailants three times before being diced into small pieces.

JULY 3 | THOMAS THE APOSTLE

STATUS Apostle, Martyr

BORN Early 1st century AD

DIED c. AD 72

GRC ♣

CofE ♣

LCDUS ♣

OTHER Eastern Orthodox churches

○ Pre-Congregation

✝ Usually shown as a young man bearing a carpenter's square or spear

🙏 Surveyors, architects, construction workers, geometricians, theologians; India, Pakistan, the East Indies

Thomas's emblem combines a carpenter's square, reflecting the legend that he built a church with his own hands in India, and a spear, the tool of his martyrdom.

Thomas is also known as Didymus ('the twin'), and the fullest account of his role as one of the Twelve Apostles is found in the Gospel of St. John. Thomas has three key functions in the Gospels, and in the proof of Christian belief in the face of skepticism. He is mainly remembered for doubting the reports of Christ's Resurrection, until confronted by Jesus in the flesh (John 20:24–29); Jesus rebukes him, pointing out that Thomas now believes only because he has seen the evidence with his own eyes, but "blessed are they that have not seen, and yet have believed." Earlier, and by way of balance, Thomas's second important act was to confirm, during the raising of Lazarus (July 29), that he was ready to die alongside Jesus for his faith (John 11:16), thus providing a justification for innumerable subsequent martyrdoms. Thirdly, at the Last Supper, Thomas indicates that he doesn't understand where Christ is going, or how the Apostles can continue to follow Him, provoking the response "I am the way, and the truth, and the life: no man cometh unto the Father, but by me." (John 14:6).

"My Lord and my God."

THOMAS, UPON SEEING CHRIST'S WOUNDS AFTER THE RESURRECTION, JOHN 20:28.

The Nestorian Church

Following Pentecost, Thomas's biography becomes less clear and yet even more impressive. Eusebius attests that he went east and successfully preached to the Parthians of Mesopotamia (modern Iraq) and Persia (modern Iran), establishing the earliest of the Eastern churches in Asia. This has come to be known as the Nestorian Church, based first at Antioch in Syria, and then at Edessa. From the 3rd to the 13th centuries it remained an important bastion of Christianity in the region, trammeled only by the rise of Islam and the Mongol invasion. It developed into a distinct entity, quite separated by its theology from the Western and Monophysite (Egyptian) churches.

Either Thomas or his disciples are believed to have gone even further east, reaching southern India and Ceylon (modern Sri Lanka), founding the first Christian missionary centers in South Asia. The Syrian Christians of Malabar (or Mylapore, near Chennai), still referred to as Thomas Christians, believe the saint was martyred by a spear-thrower and that his relics reside there. The Nestorian Church also spread along the silk routes of Central Asia. Nestorians are today referred to as Chaldaean Christians.

'Doubting' Thomas examining the spear wound in the resurrected Christ's side, portrayed with unflinching realism by the Counter-Reformation master Caravaggio c.1602.

Month of July 173

JULY 4 | ELIZABETH OF PORTUGAL

STATUS Queen
BORN 1271, Saragossa, Spain
DIED 1336, Estremoz, Portugal
GRC ♣
CofE ○
LCDUS ♣
⬭ 1625
🙏 Brides, charity workers, victims of adultery; Coimbra, Portugal

Elizabeth, known as Isabella in Spain, was the daughter of the king of Aragon and became queen of Portugal by marriage to King Denis (Diniz). The union was not happy, and she turned to prayer and the care of the unfortunate. Denis died in 1325, and Elizabeth withdrew to become a Franciscan tertiary; her impressive pedigree meant, however, that she was drawn into negotiations to prevent a war between Portugal and Castile, which seemingly exhausted her to the point of death.

Elizabeth at her devotions, accompanied by an attendant nun, painted by the Flemish artist Petrus Christus approximately 120 years after Elizabeth's death.

JULY 5 | ANTHONY MARY ZACCARIA

STATUS Priest, Founder
BORN 1502, Cremona, Italy
DIED 1539, Cremona, Italy
GRC ♣
CofE ○
LCDUS ♣
OTHER By Barnabites
⬭ 1897

Initially trained as a doctor, Anthony was ordained in 1528 and, recruiting two Milanese noblemen as sponsors, established the Clerics Regular of St. Paul ('the Beheaded' was added later). It was a reformist order, dedicated to intense, open-air preaching and the correct administering of the sacraments based on the writings of St. Paul, while also attending the sick. The order received papal approval in 1533, and Anthony began negotiations to make its headquarters at the church of St. Barnabas in Milan, hence the order's popular name of 'Barnabites.'

JULY 6 | MARIA GORETTI

STATUS Virgin, Martyr
BORN 1890, Corinaldo, Italy
DIED 1902, Nettuno, Italy
GRC ♣
CofE ○
LCDUS ♣
♥ 1947
⬭ 1950
🙏 Chastity, teenage girls, rape victims, the Children of Mary

Born to a peasant family in the Marche in central Italy, after her father's death Maria was left to tend the house while her mother toiled in the fields. A local youth began to make romantic advances to her and, when rejected, attempted to rape her. She fiercely resisted, upon which he stabbed her repeatedly. She died the following day in the hospital, having forgiven her attacker. He was convicted, sentenced to 30 years imprisonment, and later repented of his actions. He lived to see her canonization almost half a century after her murder.

Maria Goretti has become a particularly popular modern folk saint in rural regions of central and southern Italy. She is normally shown carrying the knife that killed her, and bearing flowers symbolizing her youthful innocence.

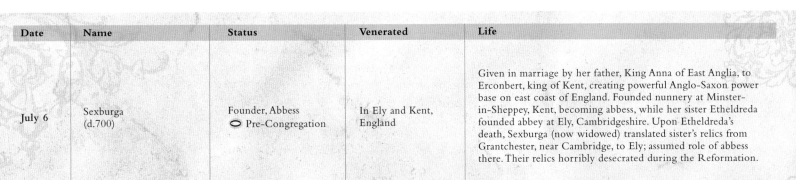

Date	Name	Status	Venerated	Life
July 6	Sexburga (d.700)	Founder, Abbess ⬭ Pre-Congregation	In Ely and Kent, England	Given in marriage by her father, King Anna of East Anglia, to Erconbert, king of Kent, creating powerful Anglo-Saxon power base on east coast of England. Founded nunnery at Minster-in-Sheppey, Kent, becoming abbess, while her sister Etheldreda founded abbey at Ely, Cambridgeshire. Upon Etheldreda's death, Sexburga (now widowed) translated sister's relics from Grantchester, near Cambridge, to Ely; assumed role of abbess there. Their relics horribly desecrated during the Reformation.

JULY 7 | BENEDICT XI

STATUS Pope
BORN 1240, Treviso, Italy
DIED 1304, Perugia, Italy
GRC ○
CofE ○
LCDUS ○
OTHER By Dominicans
♥ 1736

Nicola Boccasini entered the Dominican Order at age 14, and went on to become lector of theology and, in 1296, master general of the order. At that time, Pope Boniface VIII was attracting general hostility because of his determined assertion of the temporal, as well as spiritual, supremacy of the papacy. He restricted the powers of both the Dominican and Franciscan orders, while his conflict with Philip IV of France, where royal power was becoming increasingly consolidated, was particularly intense. Boccasini, however, remained unshakably loyal to the pope, issuing a general order to his Dominicans forbidding them from favoring opponents of the papacy. His loyalty was repaid with support from the pope: Boccasini became a cardinal in 1298, and then was appointed bishop of Ostia.

Hungary was being torn apart by civil war, and Boccasini was sent as a papal legate to expedite a peace agreement. By the time he returned to Rome, Boniface was locked in conflict with Philip of France. In a dramatic climax, the pontiff was confronted by France's chief minister Guillaume de Nogaret and the Italian Sciarra Colonna, who demanded that he resign and then imprisoned him. Boniface was threatened, beaten, and nearly executed; he committed suicide a month later.

Boccasini was unanimously elected pope in 1303, taking the name Benedict XI. He immediately worked to restore the shattered relations with the French court, absolving Philip of any censure, and restoring rights and privileges to the French king that had been removed by Boniface. His leniency did not extend to Nogaret and Colonna, who were excommunicated. After just eight months, Benedict died suddenly – some suspected he was poisoned by Nogaret. Clement V (r.1305–14), his immediate successor, removed the papal seat from Rome to Avignon, thus consolidating the dominance that the king of France would wield over the papacy in the 14th century.

JULY 7 | WILLIBALD

STATUS Bishop, Missionary
BORN c.700, Wessex, England
DIED 787, Eichstätt, Germany
GRC ○
CofE ○
LCDUS ○
⬭ Pre-Congregation
✝ Bishop overseeing building of a church

Willibald's arms combine arrows, a diagonal river, and lozenges representing travel and the holy sites he visited.

Believed to be one of the most widely traveled of all Anglo-Saxons, Willibald spent many years in Italy, the Holy Land, and Asia Minor. His lasting impact, however, was in Germany, where he co-founded a monastery and served as a bishop.

Willibald was brother to both St. Winnebald and St. Walburga (Feb. 25), and his mother was related to Boniface (June 5). He was educated at an abbey in Hampshire from the age of five. In 722 he set off on a pilgrimage to Rome with his father and brother, but his father died at Lucca in northern Italy. Willibald went on to Rome, and is said to have been laid low by the plague. After a miraculous recovery he traveled to Naples, Ephesus, and Cyprus. During his travels he was captured by Saracens who suspected him of being a spy. After he was released, he set out for the Holy Land with two companions. He arrived

Willibald is shown here supervising the construction of the monastery at Heidenheim, in a 15th-century engraving.

in Jerusalem in 725, and then traveled to Tyre, Constantinople, and back to Rome via Monte Cassino where he stayed at the monastery for ten years, working as a sacristan, dean, and porter.

In 740, Pope Gregory III sent him to Germany. He was ordained by his cousin Boniface on July 22, 741, and assigned to missionary work at Eichstätt. His brother Winnebald also made his way to Germany and, together, the two brothers founded the monastery at Heidenheim in southern Germany in 752. Winnebald was appointed the abbot, and his sister Walburga governed the female community. Willibald served as a bishop in Eichstätt for four decades. After his death, Willibald's body was found to be incorrupt, and a marble reliquary was constructed for his remains in 1269, now to be found in St. Willibald Cathedral in Eichstätt.

Date	Name	Status	Venerated	Life
July 7	Palladius (5th century)	Missionary, Bishop ⬭ Pre-Congregation	In Ireland, Scotland	Deacon from Auxerre sent by Pope Celestine to teach Roman Rite to Irish Christians. Met limited success; proceeded to Scotland. Sometimes identified with Germanus (May 28) and probably the first Apostle of Ireland, preceding Patrick (March 17).
July 8	Aquila and Priscilla (d. after AD 66)	Companions of Paul the Apostle ⬭ Pre-Congregation	Eastern Orthodox churches	Tentmakers by trade, of Jewish heritage. Among Jews expelled from Rome (c. AD 49). Escaped to Corinth, Greece, where they met St. Paul the Apostle. It is thought Paul stayed with them in Corinth, where their home became an early church. Accompanied Paul on his journey to Ephesus (modern Turkey).

JULY 7 ✣ FERMÍN (FIRMINIUS OF AMIENS)

STATUS Missionary, Bishop, Martyr

BORN c.272, Pamplona, Spain

DIED c.303, Amiens, France

GRC ☁

CofE ☁

LCDUS ☁

OTHER In France (Sept. 25), in Pamplona

⬯ Pre-Congregation

✝ In bishop's robes

🙏 Navarre, Amiens

An unattributed 18th-century painting of Fermín, now in Pamplona.

The story of St. Fermín (or Firminius) is a tangled one that confuses several early Christian missionary bishops active in the Roman empire. Fermín was born in the capital of Navarre, and he is said to have been baptized by St. Saturninus (Cernin in Spanish, Nov. 29). Saturninus went on to become bishop of Toulouse and was martyred by being tied to a bull and dragged through the streets of Toulouse. A church, Our Lady of the Bull (Notre-Dame-du-Taur) was erected to hold his relics. Fermín headed north and became the first bishop of Amiens. There he met his martyrdom by being beheaded. Fermín's feast day in Amiens is on September 25. His successor, another Firminius (the Confessor) built a church over Fermín's grave, named St. Acheul.

The Bull Run at Pamplona

The fate of Saturninus has somehow transferred to Fermín, at least in Pamplona, where the annual bull run (*encierro*) is held on this day, regarded as Fermín's feast day in Navarre.

Both the story of Saturninus and that of Fermín/Firminius is somewhat confounded by dates, as it is likely that Saturninus was martyred in 257, fifteen years before Fermín was traditionally born. Their mutual association with bulls may spring from the widespread Roman cult of Mithras, which involved bull sacrifice, and was particularly popular in Iberia and Gaul – probably also the origin of bullfighting *corridas* today.

The encierro at Pamplona was made popular by Ernest Hemingway's account of it in his novel The Sun Also Rises *(1926); the fiesta now attracts huge crowds of tourists. The participants run alongside the bulls through the narrow streets of the town on their way to the bullring.*

JULY 8 ✣ KILIAN

STATUS Missionary, Bishop, Martyr

BORN 640, Ireland

DIED 689, Würzburg, Germany

GRC ☁

CofE ☁

LCDUS ☁

⬯ Pre-Congregation

✝ Wearing a bishop's miter; wielding a sword

🙏 Sufferers of rheumatism; Würzburg, Germany, Tuosist, Ireland

The swords and cross of St. Kilian.

Kilian was a native of Ireland who, as an ordained 'traveling' bishop, journeyed to the pagan regions of Franconia and Thuringia with eleven companions, intent on missionary work. From 686 he adopted Würzburg as the base of his mission, and succeeded in converting the local lord, Duke Gozbert, and much of the local population to Christianity.

However, Kilian came into conflict with Gozbert when he told the duke that he was in violation of the teaching of the sacred scriptures, because Gozbert had chosen to marry his brother's widow, Geilana. Kilian persuaded Gozbert that he should promise to separate from his wife. Geilana had not converted to Christianity, and when she heard of Kilian's admonitions, she was so enraged that she arranged for Kilian and his companions, Colman and Totnan, to be murdered. The story has it that she concealed the murder from Gozbert, but subsequently went insane.

In 743, the first bishop of Würzburg, St. Burchard, transferred the relics of the three martyrs — after wonderful cures had brought fame to their burial place — to the Church of Our Lady. The skulls of the saints, inlaid with precious stones, were transferred to the newly finished Cathedral of the Savior in 752. The New Testament belonging to Kilian was preserved among the treasures belonging to the cathedral, and is currently housed in the university library. On St. Kilian's Day, a glass case containing the three skulls is paraded through the streets of Würzburg, and publicly displayed in the cathedral.

A statue of Kilian at Würzburg, brandishing his evangelizing sword.

GREGORY GRASSI

JULY 8

STATUS Missionary, Martyr

BORN 1823, Italy

DIED 1900, China

GRC ♧

CofE ♧

LCDUS ♧

OTHER In China; by Franciscans

⬯ 2000

AUGUSTINE ZHAO RONG

JULY 9

STATUS Martyr

BORN c.1746, Wuchuan, China

DIED 1815, Chengdu, China

GRC ♣

CofE ♧

LCDUS ♣

♥ 1900

⬯ 2000

A popular memorial card of Augustine Zhao Rong, bearing his palm of martyrdom.

These adjacent dates remember victims of Chinese persecutions of Christians. Most prominent among these were the Italian missionary Gregory Grassi and Augustine Zhao Rong.

Gregory Grassi

A Franciscan bishop and missionary, Gregory Grassi was ordained in 1856 and sent to China five years later, becoming the bishop of Shanxi. In 1898, the Boxer uprising had begun to spread across northern China. Anti-imperialist and anti-Christian, the Boxers wanted foreign influence to be expunged from China. At first they were ruthlessly suppressed, but in the summer of 1900 they besieged the foreign ministries in Beijing, holding diplomats and embassy staff hostage for 55 days, until the hostages were relieved by soldiers of the Eight-Nation Alliance (Austria-Hungary, Britain, France, Germany, Italy, Russia, the United States, and Japan).

On the night of July 5, Grassi, 11 other European missionaries, and 14 Chinese Christians were arrested, and imprisoned. Four days later, on July 9, the governor of Shanxi, an ardent supporter of the Boxers, ordered that the Christians should be killed on the spot. A

The Boxers, seen here under attack by British and other foreign troops, killed five bishops, 50 priests, two brothers, two nuns, and 40,000 Chinese Christian converts during their brief uprising.

terrible bloodbath ensued, as soldiers closed in on the prisoners and hacked at them with their swords.

The short, but bloody, Boxer Rebellion ended with the Boxer Protocol of September 1901 when, in turn, many of the rebels were publicly beheaded.

Augustine Zhao Rong

An unusual entry on the calendar, July 9 celebrates the martyrdoms of 33 Western missionaries and 87 Chinese Catholics killed during various periods of persecution in China between the beginning of the Manchu (Qing) dynasty in the mid-17th century and 1930. The persecutions before the Boxer Rebellion of 1900 were largely the result of imperial edicts, which normally granted clemency if the accused apostatized, but few agreed to do so. Some were simply ferocious attacks on Christians during recurrent periods of Sino-Western tension. This feast was inaugurated by Pope John Paul II in 2000.

Augustine Zhao Rong was the most notable of many Chinese converts who were turned upon by their fellow citizens. Augustine Zhao was a soldier who had escorted the Franciscan priest Gabriel John Tauin du-Fresse to Beijing, and he became so impressed by his ward's pacific saintliness that he asked to be baptized. He went on to continue missionary work, but was arrested in Chengdu in central China, and starved to death in prison.

Zhao Rong and his 119 Companions are memorialized here in a heady blend of contemporary Chinese and Italian Baroque styles.

JULY 9 — THE MARTYRS OF GORKUM

STATUS Martyrs

BORN Early 16th century, modern Netherlands

DIED 1572, Ruggen, modern Netherlands

GRC ☁

CofE ☁

LCDUS ☁

♥ 1675

◯ 1865

In an example of the intensity of hatred engendered during the wars of religion that followed the Reformation, this group of 19 Catholic (mainly parish) priests was arrested at Gorkum by Dutch Calvinists in the summer of 1572. The prisoners included 11 Franciscans, two Norbertines, a Dominican, an Augustinian, and four diocesan priests. They were tried at Brielle, and offered the chance to deny Catholicism. Refusing to do so, they were hanged. Their reliquary is housed in St. Nicholas Church in Brussels, Belgium.

A 19th-century memorial card for the Martyrs of Gorkum. The priests were not hanged in public as this suggests, but in a shed.

JULY 9 — VERONICA GIULIANI

STATUS Abbess, Mystic

BORN 1660, Urbino, Italy

DIED 1727, Città di Castello, Italy

GRC ☁

CofE ☁

LCDUS ☁

OTHER By Franciscans

♥ 1804

◯ 1839

✝ Crown of thorns, often embracing the Cross

Born to a middle-class family, Veronica joined the Capuchin Order of the Poor Clares at Città di Castello in 1677, against her father's wishes. Her novitiate was not easy, but she began to have visions, including one of Christ's Crown of Thorns, wherein bleeding wounds from the Crown appeared on her head. She went on to experience full stigmata on Good Friday, 1697. In a further vision she experienced profound pain in her heart upon witnessing Christ's Passion.

Veronica was elected abbess in 1716, and proved highly practical, discouraging her nuns from reading mystical texts, despite her own avowed mysticism. Upon her death, an impression of the Cross was found upon her heart. Her remains are at Città di Castello and are regarded as incorrupt.

Veronica Giuliani receiving the stigmata from a vision of the Crucifix.

Date	Name	Status	Venerated	Life
July 9	Rose Hawthorne (1851–1926)	Nun, Social Worker, Founder	By Dominicans In USA	Daughter of novelist Nathaniel Hawthorne. Married George Parsons Lathrop (1871); both converted to Catholicism (1891) but separated after death of son. Worked for cancer patients of Lower East Side, became a Dominican nun (1898), founded Dominican Sisters of Hawthorne (1900).
July 10	The Seven Brothers (d.2nd century)	Martyrs ◯ Pre-Congregation		The seven sons of the Roman widow Felicity (March 7), Felix, Philip, Martial, Vitalis, Alexander, Silvanus, Januarius. All followed their mother's example, refusing to apostatize during persecutions of Antoninus Pius and suffering various martyrdoms, preceding that of their mother. Probably legendary.
July 10	Emmanuel Ruiz & Companions (19th century)	Missionaries, Martyrs ♥ 1926	By Franciscans and Maronites	Ruiz (b.1804) was a Spanish Franciscan missionary to Lebanon. During Druze uprising, he and other Franciscan missionaries, plus three young Maronites, executed after refusing to apostatize and convert to Islam.

RELIQUARIES

The veneration of relics – body parts, clothing, possessions, or other objects associated with the life of a saint – is particularly pronounced in the Catholic Church. Relics, along with the tombs of saints, are often the subject of pilgrimages. Many richly decorated vessels, called reliquaries, have been created to house and preserve these valued items.

Reliquaries often take the form of the relic they are purported to contain, such as a head or bust for skull fragments, hair, or teeth. Arms were particularly common. This silver reliquary (left), containing part of St. George's arm or hand, dates from 13th-century France.

A late-16th century Mexican reliquary (right) designed to display bone fragments from Sts. Peter and Paul.

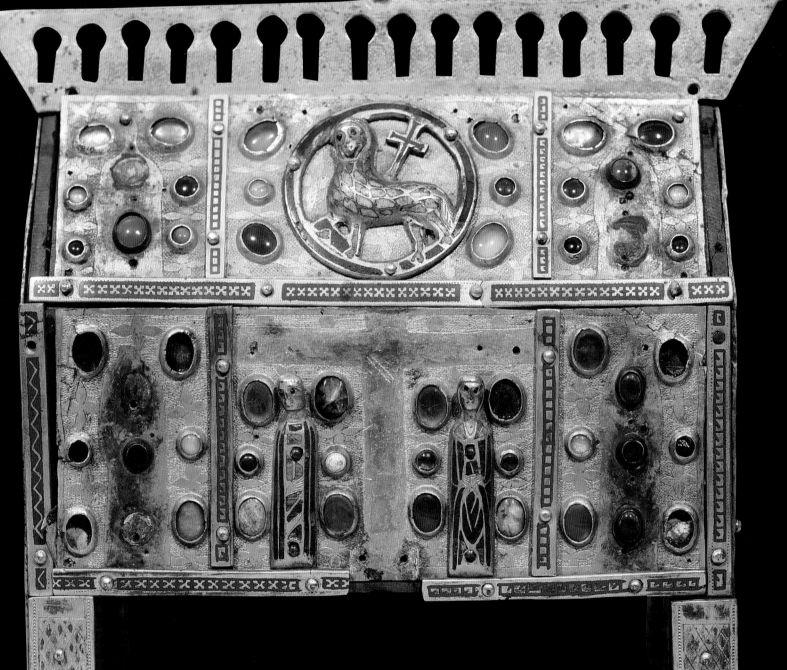

A 13th-century gold casket reliquary, probably French, inlaid with precious stones.

JULY 11   BENEDICT OF NURSIA

STATUS Abbot, Founder

BORN c.480, Nursia, Italy

DIED c.547, Monte Cassino, Italy

GRC ♣

CofE ♣

LCDUS ♣

OTHER Eastern Orthodox churches (March 14)

◯ 1220

✝ Broken cup, broken plate, crosier, raven

🙏 Agricultural workers, the dying, monks, cavers, schoolchildren, sufferers from gallstones, nettle rash, and temptation; Europe

An early Renaissance painting of St. Benedict, by Fra Angelico, c.1440, in the Dominican Convent of St. Mark in Florence.

This Austrian 50-euro coin celebrates Benedict as a patron saint of Europe. He is shown with his sister St. Scholastica.

Benedict of Nursia remains one of the towering figures of the Christian world, the man who more than any other established the practical means whereby monastic communities could best be organized. In almost every way, he was the guiding spirit behind Western monastic life. Even today, his influence is substantial — in the Middle Ages, it was immense. His designation by Pope Paul VI in 1964 as patron saint of Europe was a precise reflection of this eminence.

That said, neither in the 12 monasteries he founded and led in Subiaco, east of Rome, nor in his most celebrated monastery, Monte Cassino, did he attempt to establish an order in the later sense of specific religious communities bound by strict rules of behavior and worship. His goal was to create loose groupings united only by their worship of God and their desire to live together harmoniously, all following what was later known as the Rule of St. Benedict (*see below*).

Much of what is known of St. Benedict's life was written by Pope Gregory I towards the end of the 6th century. Inevitably, its reliability has been disputed, but it is generally accepted that St. Benedict was the son of a Roman noble and that, from the age of about 20, he spent three years as a hermit, attracting wide renown, before establishing the 12 monasteries at Subiaco, each with 12 monks and a superior, with Benedict as abbot of all 12. The monastery at Monte Cassino is conventionally said to have been founded by him in 529. It was here that he wrote the Rule of St. Benedict. Numerous miracles were ascribed to St. Benedict during and after his life. His sanctity and gentle wisdom have never been doubted.

THE RULE OF ST. BENEDICT

Written in 73 short chapters, Benedict's Rule stresses *pax* (peace), *ora* (prayer), and *labora* (work). It details how the monks' days should be divided — how much time should be given over to prayer and when; how much work they should do and of what type; what and when they should eat and drink; when they should sleep, and when they should wake; how they should best serve the communities in which they live; how recalcitrant members should be treated and, if necessary, chastised — but also how the abbot should seek to direct any such monastery. The tone throughout is moderate, encouraging, and wise.

Benedict was visited once a year by his equally devout twin sister, St. Scholastica (Feb. 10), who had founded a convent in nearby Plombariola. She died in 543 and was buried in the tomb in the monastery of Monte Cassino that Benedict had prepared for himself. In 547, Benedict died while standing at prayer, and he was buried with his sister. For many centuries his feast was kept on the day of his death (March 21), but the Roman calendar transferred his feast day to July 11, the day his relics were moved to the monastery of St.-Benoît-sur-Loire in France.

Benedict's major foundation, the monastery at Monte Cassino, southeast of Rome, was destroyed by Allied forces in 1944. It has since been reconstructed.

"Listen, O my son, to the precepts of thy master, and incline the ear of thy heart, and cheerfully receive and faithfully execute the admonitions of thy loving Father."

THE RULE OF ST. BENEDICT, CHAPTER 1.

JULY 11 · OLIVER PLUNKETT

STATUS Bishop. Martyr

BORN 1625, County Meath, Ireland

DIED 1681, London, England

GRC ○

CofE ○

LCDUS ○

OTHER Irish Catholic Church

○ 1975

☩ Peace and reconciliation in Ireland

Oliver Plunkett came from a comfortable Catholic background, and was related to many members of the Irish aristocracy. Educated by the abbot of St. Mary's, Dublin, he then set out for Rome, aspiring to the priesthood. He left a country that was being torn apart by the Confederate Wars – a religious conflict between Irish Roman Catholics, English and Irish Anglicans, and Protestants.

Plunkett was ordained in Rome in 1654, and acted as representative of the Irish bishops in the Holy See. Meanwhile, Oliver Cromwell's conquest of Ireland had driven Roman Catholicism underground, and Plunkett was forced to remain in Rome. He became a theological professor at the Jesuit college and, in 1669, became archbishop of Armagh.

He did not return to his native land until 1670. By this time the English Restoration had introduced greater religious tolerance. He set about rebuilding and reforming the Irish Catholic Church, establishing schools for clergy and laity, and founding a Jesuit college in Drogheda.

Defender of the Faith

In 1673, the Test Act was introduced. This was a penal law that forced those seeking public office to repudiate fundamental Catholic beliefs. Plunkett was implacably opposed to this and went into hiding. In England, the so-called Popish Plot of 1678 stoked up a febrile atmosphere of anti-Catholicism. Plunkett was arrested in Dublin in 1679, accused of conspiring against the state and plotting to bring 20,000 French soldiers into the country. A conviction in Ireland was impossible, so Plunkett was moved to Newgate Prison in London. Here, after a travesty of a trial, he was found guilty of high treason for "promoting the Roman faith."

Plunkett was the last Roman Catholic martyr to die in England.

Plunkett was hanged, drawn, and quartered at Tyburn. His remains, initially buried at St. Giles in London, were exhumed in 1683 and moved to the Benedictine monastery at Lamspringe in Germany. His head was brought to Rome, and eventually taken back to Armagh, and, in 1921, to Drogheda. Most of his body was taken back to Downside Abbey, England, but some parts still remain in Lamspringe.

Date	Name	Status	Venerated	Life
July 12	Veronica (d.1st century AD)	Early Disciple ○ Pre-Congregation	☩ Woman holding a veil with Christ's image ☩ Launderers, photographers	Veronica was moved by pity at sight of Jesus carrying His cross to Calvary, and gave Him her veil so that He could wipe His forehead. It is believed that an image of His face was miraculously impressed upon the cloth. Her charitable act commemorated in the Stations of the Cross.
July 12	John Gualbert (c.985–1073)	Monk, Founder ○ 1193	By Benedictines ☩ Foresters, park rangers, parks	Florentine noble. Experienced religious epiphany when, on Good Friday, his brother's murderer begged John to spare his life. Became Benedictine monk and founded own monastery at Vallumbrosa, Tuscany.
July 13	Henry II (973–1024)	Holy Roman Emperor, Founder ○ 1146	GRC, LCDUS In Germany ☩ Bamberg	Only German king to have been canonized. Last emperor of Ottonian dynasty. Consolidated imperial power in Poland and Italy through astute military campaigns. Supported bishops against monastic clergy and founded diocese of Bamberg.
July 13	Teresa of the Andes (1900–20)	Nun ♥ 1987 ○ 1993	☩ Against illness	Girl from an upper-class family in Santiago, Chile. Became Discalced Carmelite novice at age 19. Through series of letters shared her spiritual life with many people. Died of typhus just before her 20th birthday. Relics venerated at the Sanctuary of Auco-Rinconada, Chile.

JULY 14 | KATERI TEKAKWITHA

STATUS Mohawk Convert, Virgin

BORN 1656, Ossernenon, (modern Auriesville, New York), USA

DIED 1680, Kahnawake, Canada

GRC ♧

CofE ♧

LCDUS ♣

♥ 1980

✝ Lily, turtle

🙏 Ecologists, environmentalists, exiles

ST. KATERI
TEKAKWITHA

The daughter of a Mohawk chief, Kateri lost her entire family to a smallpox epidemic when she was only four, and she was left with unsightly facial scars and poor eyesight. She was adopted by an uncle, chief of the Turtle Clan, and began to show an interest in Christianity – her mother had been an Algonquin who had converted to Catholicism. At age 20, she was baptized by a Jesuit priest.

Kateri was a zealous convert, who consequently alienated fellow members of her tribe. Mistrust turned to persecution, and she was threatened with torture and death if she refused to renounce her newfound religion. Kateri was forced to flee from her own people to an established community of Native American Christians in Kahnawake, Quebec. She dedicated the rest of her life to prayer, penance, care of the elderly, and chastity. The self-imposed austerity of her life broke down her already fragile health and she died when she was only 24. Eyewitnesses reported that her disfiguring smallpox scars disappeared at the time of her death. Kateri was the first Native American to be beatified, and is especially revered by Native American Catholics.

JULY 15 | BONAVENTURE

STATUS Bishop, Confessor, Doctor of the Church

BORN 1221, Bagnoregio, Italy

DIED 1274, Lyon, France

GRC ♣

CofE ♣

LCDUS ♣

⬭ 1482

✝ Cardinal's hat, ciborium, in Franciscan robes

🙏 Lyon, Canary Islands

One of the greatest theologians and philosophers of the 13th century, Bonaventure was also an able minister general of the Franciscan Order.

Bonaventure, born John of Fidanza, is said to have acquired his name (meaning 'good fortune') when he was miraculously cured of a childhood illness through the intercession of Francis of Assisi (Oct. 4). He entered the Franciscan Order in 1243 and studied at the University of Paris alongside his contemporary, Thomas Aquinas (Jan. 28). He went on to become a master of theology in 1255, taking over leadership of the Franciscan School in Paris.

At age 35, Bonaventure was appointed minister general of the order, and was instrumental in restoring harmony to the Franciscans, who were bitterly divided about the nature of their religious order. Some argued that Franciscans should adhere to the traditional Rule, with its emphasis on self-denial and poverty; others supported a more worldly ideal, in which Franciscans played a leading role in universities and in political life. Bonaventure strove to heal the rift, and issued a rational treatise on the nature of the Franciscan Rule, the *Constitutiones Narbonenses*, which the order adopted as its new constitution. He also wrote a life of St. Francis, which became the officially approved biography of the saint – indeed, earlier biographies were required to be destroyed. His influence on the Franciscan Order in the 13th century was profound.

Influence beyond the Order

Although he was nominated for the post of Archbishop of York he begged not to be forced to accept the dignity. He was instrumental in procuring the election of Pope Gregory X, and was rewarded with the titles of cardinal and bishop of Albano in 1273. He was present at the Council of Lyon, and made a significant contribution to the union of the Greek and Latin Churches.

Along with Thomas Aquinas, Bonaventure is regarded as one of the greatest thinkers of the 13th century. His main memorial is his works, which include a *Commentary on the Sentences of Lombard* and a *Commentary on the Gospel of St. Luke*. He was familiar with the works of Aristotle and the Arab philosophers, but was also a traditional theologian, with strong ties to the works of Augustine of Hippo (Aug. 28). He was declared a Doctor of the Church in 1588.

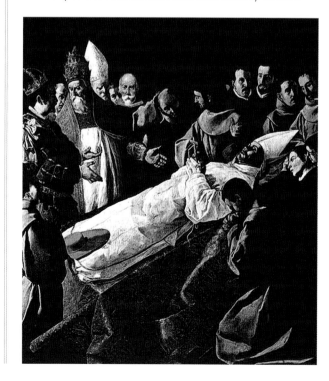

Bonaventure's death at age 52 cut short a brilliant career. It was also shrouded in mystery – it has been suggested that he was poisoned. While his position in the Franciscan Order was not controversial, his role in seeking a resolution of the schism between the Eastern and Western churches was hotly debated, and earned him enemies among the curia.

JULY 15 | SWITHUN

STATUS Bishop

BORN c.800, possibly Hampshire, England

DIED 862, Winchester, England

GRC ☁

CofE ♣

LCDUS ☁

⬭ Pre-Congregation

✝ Bishop holding a bridge, broken eggs at feet

⚘ The weather; Hampshire, Winchester

Swithun was bishop of Winchester from 852, but little is known about his life – the only tangible legacy is his signature, which appears appended to the witness lists of several Anglo-Saxon charters. A biography ascribed to Goscelin of St. Bertin, written in the mid-11th century, furnishes further details: it was said that his reputation as a learned, pious man and assiduous builder and restorer of churches reached the ears of King Aethelwulf, who appointed him tutor to his son Alfred the Great. When Swithun became bishop of Winchester, he requested that Aethelwulf tithe a tenth of royal lands to the Church. He was renowned for making arduous journeys throughout his diocese on foot, and for his practice of inviting the poor to banquets, but not the rich. During his lifetime, miracles were attributed to Swithun. The most famous was his restoration of a basket of unbroken eggs to an old woman in Winchester, after the original eggs had been maliciously broken by workmen who were building a new bridge.

When Swithun died in 862, he was buried outside the cathedral, as he had requested, where "passers-by might tread on his grave and where the rain from the eaves might fall on it." In 971, his remains were moved to an indoor shrine at Winchester and, according to contemporary writers, a number of miracles surrounded the move. His body was then divided and distributed to a number of shrines; his head was taken to Canterbury, his arm to Peterborough.

I CAN'T STAND THE RAIN

Swithun's name is associated with English weather lore. In the words of the proverb:

> "St. Swithun's day if thou dost rain
> For forty days it will remain … "

One legend traces this proverb to the day, in 971, when the saint's remains were moved. A heavy downpour was said to mark the saint's disapproval at the disregard of his wishes. It has also been postulated that days of incessant rainfall delayed the re-burial of the saint's body. However, it is more probable that the legend comes from a prehistoric pagan day of augury. In fact, there is some scientific evidence that if the jet stream lies across the south of Britain in mid-July, climatic conditions will remain consistent until the end of August.

JULY 16 | OUR LADY OF MOUNT CARMEL

The arms of the Carmelite Order incorporate three stars representing the Holy Trinity.

The Blessed Virgin Mary, in her role as patroness of the Carmelite Order, is celebrated on this day. The Carmelites were Christian hermits who lived on Mount Carmel (modern Israel) during the 12th and 13th centuries. The Scapular of Our Lady of Mount Carmel is a brown cape-like garment, or sacramental, and is associated with promises of Mary's special aid for the salvation of the wearer.

This liturgical feast evolved in England in the 14th century as thanksgiving to Mary for the protection she had given the Carmelite Order. The popularity of the feast has spread to most countries with a strong Christian tradition. The feast is known to many Catholics as the 'scapular feast,' and there is a tradition, attributed to the late 13th century, that St. Simon Stock, an early prior general of the Carmelite Order, had a vision of the Blessed Virgin Mary in which she gave him the brown scapular, which formed part of the Carmelite habit, as a symbol of salvation.

Date	Name	Status	Venerated	Life
July 14	John Keble (1792–1866)	Churchman, Poet, Leading member of the Oxford Movement	CofE	Academic, poet, and author of popular volume of verse *The Christian Year* (1827). Leading light of the Oxford Movement, a Catholic revival within Church of England. Spent much of life as vicar in Hampshire, England. Keble College, University of Oxford, founded in 1870 in his memory.
July 16	Osmund (d.1099)	Bishop ⬭ 1457	CofE	Counselor to William the Conqueror; Lord Chancellor of England c.1070. Involved in drawing up the Domesday Book. Consecrated as bishop of Old Sarum (modern Salisbury) in 1078. Developed 'Sarum Use,' which regulated the Divine Office, Mass, and Calendar in his diocese, and was soon adopted throughout British Isles.

JULY 18 · ELIZABETH OF RUSSIA

STATUS Abbess, Martyr

BORN 1864, Hesse, Germany

DIED 1918, Alapaevsk, Russia

GRC ⬡

CofE ⬡

LCDUS ⬡

⬭ 1981 (Russian Orthodox Church Outside Russia); 1992 (in Russia)

Born into European royalty, Elizabeth Alexandra Louise Alice was the daughter of Duke Ludwig IV of Hesse, and Princess Alice, daughter of Queen Victoria. When she was just 14, she lost both her mother and her younger sister to a diphtheria epidemic.

An outstanding beauty, Elizabeth soon caught the eye of many potential suitors, but finally lost her heart to a Russian grand duke, Sergei, the fifth son of Elizabeth's great-aunt, the Empress Maria Alexandrovna, and Tsar Alexander II of Russia. Like Elizabeth, Sergei was sensitive, artistic, and intensely religious. They married in 1884, in St. Petersburg, and she became Grand Duchess Elizabeth Feodorovna. She captivated both her immediate Russian family and the Russian people. Elizabeth had been brought up as a German Lutheran and, although not required to convert to Russian Orthodoxy, she chose to do so in 1891. Although Elizabeth and Sergei had no children, they eventually became the foster parents of Sergei's niece and nephew. Unfortunately, in 1905, Sergei, governor-general of Moscow, was assassinated in the Kremlin by an anarchist.

A pastel portrait of Elizabeth around the time of her wedding, by Friedrich August von Kaulbach (1850–1920).

A Martyr of the Revolution

Sergei's death changed Elizabeth's life. She wore mourning clothes, gave up eating meat, gave away her jewelry, sold her most valued possessions, and founded the Convent of SS. Martha and Mary in Moscow, becoming its abbess. She dedicated herself to charitable works, opening a hospital, an orphanage, and a pharmacy in the convent grounds, and helping the sick and poor of the city.

The Russian Revolution in 1917 was to bring a violent end to Elizabeth's spiritual aspirations. In 1918, the Bolshevik leader Lenin ordered the Cheka (secret police) to arrest Elizabeth, a much-loved representative of the old order. She was exiled first to Perm, then to Yekaterinburg, where she was joined by other members of her family, and a sister from the convent. They were taken to Alapaevsk and incarcerated in a school on the outskirts of the town.

On the night of July 17, Cheka men drove the prisoners to a village some 12 miles (19 km) from Alapaevsk. The prisoners were beaten and thrown into a mineshaft. Hand grenades were hurled into the mine, but one of the killers could still hear the prisoners singing a Russian hymn and, panicking, he thrust burning brushwood into the shaft. Nearly three months later, members of the White Army discovered the remains of Elizabeth and her companions. Her remains were eventually removed to Jerusalem, where they lie today in the Church of Mary Magdalene.

Elizabeth as abbess, photographed in about 1912.

Date	Name	Status	Venerated	Life
July 17	Hedwig of Poland (1374–99)	Queen ♥ 1986 ⬭ 1997	In Poland	Daughter of Louis Angevin of Poland and Hungary. Crowned at age ten, and married Jagiello of Lithuania at age 12. They endowed several monasteries, and she worked to reunify Latin and Orthodox churches. Died after unsuccessful childbirth.
July 18	Pambo (c.303–90)	Hermit, Founder ⬭ Pre-Congregation	Eastern Orthodox churches	Disciple of St. Antony (Jan. 17). Lived in Egypt as hermit in the desert. Founded many early monasteries. Renowned for wisdom and silence. Spiritual mentor of many hermits and monks.

JULY 18 · CAMILLUS DE LELLIS

STATUS Founder
BORN 1550, Abruzzi, Italy
DIED 1614, Rome, Italy
GRC ♠
CofE ♧
LCDUS ♠
♥ 1742
○ 1746
🙏 Nurses, the sick, hospitals; against gambling

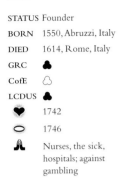

Born in the Kingdom of Naples, Camillus was largely abandoned by his mercenary father; he made his way to Venice and joined the army as a youth. He was known for his aggression and obsessive gambling, which eventually ruined him. In 1575, he experienced a revelation at a sermon, and tried unsuccessfully to join the Franciscans. After spending time working in a hospital for incurables, he rejoined the army, and fought against the Turks.

When his regiment was disbanded, he traveled to Rome and founded the Order of Clerks Regular, Ministers to the Sick (Camillians, a mixture of priests and lay brothers), drawing on his battlefield experience to care for wounded soldiers in the field and in recuperation. The order, bearing its distinctive red cross, became well known also for tending plague victims, and while working during a plague outbreak in Rome, Camillus was briefly hailed as patron saint of the city. He was responsible for many innovations in health care (giving patients fresh air, providing appropriate diets, and isolating contagious cases). He himself suffered almost continual ill health, forcing his resignation as head of the order in 1607, although he continued to visit and minister to the sick until his death.

Camillus, celebrated in marble in a typically Baroque manner, in St. Peter's in Rome.

JULY 19 · MACRINA THE YOUNGER

STATUS Virgin, Teacher
BORN 330, Caesarea, modern Turkey
DIED 379, Pontus, modern Turkey
GRC ♧
CofE ♧
LCDUS ♧
OTHER Eastern Orthodox churches
○ Pre-Congregation

Born into a leading religious family in Cappadocia, Macrina's parents were Basil the Elder and Emmelia, and her grandmother was St. Macrina the Elder. She had nine younger siblings, including brothers who went on to become Basil the Great (Jan. 2) and St. Gregory of Nyssa (Jan. 10).

Her father arranged her marriage at age 12, but when her fiancé died, she dedicated herself to a religious life, becoming a nun. A leading holy woman, scholar, and religious instructress, she is regarded as one of the most prominent nuns in the Eastern Church. Her brother Gregory's biography of his sister records that she had a major influence on her family after her mother died. Not only was her devout life an outstanding example to her younger siblings, she also provided a rigorous critique of their ideas, and a willingness to engage in penetrating philosophical discussions. Gregory recorded one such discussion with his sister in *On the Soul and the Resurrection.*

It was probably Macrina's example that inspired Basil to pursue the monastic ideal, and three of her brothers, Basil, Gregory, and Peter, went on to become bishops.

A very early Byzantine fresco of Macrina from St. Sophia Cathedral, Kiev.

Date	Name	Status	Venerated	Life
July 18	Elizabeth Ferard (d.1883)	Deaconess, Founder	CofE	First modern deaconess of the Church of England, ordained in 1862. Founded the Community of St. Andrew, deaconesses within a religious sisterhood, working in the King's Cross area of London.
July 19	Francisco Garcés and Companions (d.c.1781)	Missionaries, Martyrs	In Mexico and Arizona	Spanish Franciscan sent to Mexico, then to the missions of Arizona and New Mexico after expulsion of the Jesuits. Much revered by the indigenous peoples. Missions attacked during revolt among the Yumas; Garcés and companions killed.

JULY 20 — BARTOLOMÉ DE LAS CASAS

STATUS Bishop

BORN c.1474, Seville, Spain

DIED 1566, Madrid, Spain

GRC ⬡

CofE ♣

LCDUS ⬡

OTHER US Episcopal Church (July 18), US Evangelical Lutheran Church (July 17)

A controversial Dominican priest, Bartolomé remains highly revered in the Americas for his extraordinary work in advocating the Native American cause following the Spanish conquest of Central America. He witnessed the return of Christopher Columbus after his first voyage to the Americas, and Bartolomé's father accompanied Columbus on his second voyage. Bartolomé himself emigrated to Hispaniola in 1502, and was soon appalled by the way the Spanish colonists were treating the native peoples, which involved wholesale murder or enslavement. He joined the Dominican Order in an attempt to bring reform to the Spanish colonial administration, and went on to become bishop of Chiapas in Mexico. He was highly critical of the *encomienda* system, whereby the Spanish crown granted land and natives to European settlers. His *Short Account of the Destruction of the Indies* (1552) was one of several polemics designed to bring these injustices to public attention. His famed, if inconclusive, debate with Juan Ginés de Sepúlveda, who argued that the native peoples needed to be subsumed and controlled, laid the foundations for later human rights agreements. Some later accused Bartolomé of contributing to the dark reputation of Spanish, and by implication Catholic, rapacity and cruelty. Although Bartolomé was proposed for beatification in 2000, difficulties still remain over his criticism of the Catholic Church and his support for the importation of African slaves.

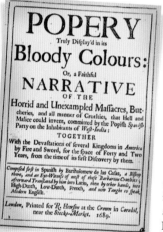

Despite being a devout Dominican, Bartolomé wrote a number of angry descriptions of the mistreatment of the Native American peoples by the Catholic invaders, as the title page of this book translated into English makes clear.

Bartolomé de las Casas is known as the 'Apostle to the Indies' for his work in protecting Native Americans.

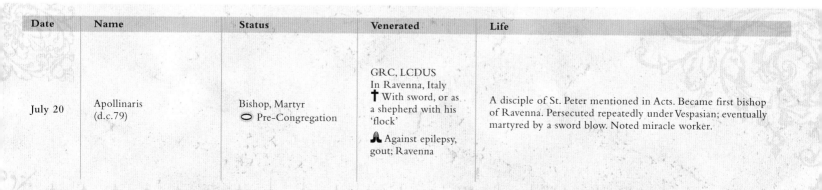

Date	Name	Status	Venerated	Life
July 20	Apollinaris (d.c.79)	Bishop, Martyr ⬯ Pre-Congregation	GRC, LCDUS In Ravenna, Italy ✝ With sword, or as a shepherd with his 'flock' ⚕ Against epilepsy, gout; Ravenna	A disciple of St. Peter mentioned in Acts. Became first bishop of Ravenna. Persecuted repeatedly under Vespasian; eventually martyred by a sword blow. Noted miracle worker.

JULY 20 — MARGARET (MARINA) OF ANTIOCH

STATUS Virgin, Martyr

BORN Late 3rd century, Antiochia, modern Turkey

DIED c.304, Antiochia, modern Turkey

GRC ○

CofE ♠

LCDUS ○

OTHER Eastern Orthodox churches

○ Pre-Congregation

✝ Usually shown with a vanquished dragon, often holding a cross

🙏 Childbirth, pregnant women, exiles, the falsely accused, the dying; against kidney disease

Margaret's arms show Satan, in the form of a dragon, trying to swallow her crucifix.

Most probably entirely legendary, Margaret remains a popular saint. According to Voragine's *Golden Legend*, she was the beautiful daughter of a pagan priest of Antiochia in Pisidia, central Turkey. Though her father derided her for her belief in Christianity, he nevertheless attempted to keep her from harm during the Diocletian persecutions by secreting her on his rural estate, tending sheep with her nanny.

Upon refusing an offer of marriage from the Roman governor, her faith was revealed, and she was summarily tortured in various ways, including being beaten, being raked with combs, and having her flesh torn with pincers. Miraculous interventions prevented her death, notably when she was swallowed by a dragon. The cross she was holding forced the beast to regurgitate her, although even *The Golden Legend* warns that this story may be apocryphal. As with so many of her contemporaries, she was eventually beheaded.

Margaret's cult was enormously popular in medieval Europe, and she was numbered as one of the Fourteen Holy Helpers.

Margaret is most frequently shown trampling a dragon.

JULY 21 — LAWRENCE OF BRINDISI

STATUS Priest, Doctor of the Church

BORN 1559, Brindisi, Italy

DIED 1619, Lisbon, Portugal

GRC ♣

CofE ○

LCDUS ♠

♥ 1783

○ 1881

✝ Shown leading an army, bearing a cross

🙏 Brindisi

Lawrence was born to a wealthy Venetian merchant family trading in Brindisi, then part of the Spanish Kingdom of Naples. He was educated in Venice, and entered the Capuchin Order in 1574, being ordained in 1582. An effective administrator and preacher, he rose swiftly, by 1596 becoming definitor-general of the Franciscan Order, with a special brief for converting Jews.

In many ways an arch example of a vigorous, career-building, Counter-Reformation priest, Lawrence was responsible for successfully establishing many Capuchin houses across central Europe at the time of the wars of religion, and he notoriously led a German Catholic army into battle against the Ottoman Turks in 1601, armed only with a crucifix.

In 1602, Lawrence was elected vicar-general of the Capuchins, but refused to renew the post three years later, preferring ambassadorial tasks and writing. He is noted for an important essay condemning Lutheranism. He retired to a monastery near Lisbon in 1618, and died on his birthday the following year.

Lawrence's rather placid demeanor in this contemporary likeness belied an enthusiastic and often martial commitment to confronting the challenges faced by the Catholic Church.

JULY 22 | MARY MAGDALENE

STATUS Virgin

BORN Early 1st century AD, Magdala, Holy Land

DIED Late 1st century AD, possibly in Provence, France

GRC ♠

CofE ♠

LCDUS ♠

OTHER Eastern Orthodox churches

⊘ Pre-Congregation

✝ Flowing auburn hair, a pot of ointment

🙏 Fallen women, the repentant

Mary's pot of ointment remains the central symbol in her emblem, the background of her tears falling on purple (for penitence) and black (for mourning).

The legend of Mary Magdalene escaping from the Holy Land to raise Jesus's child in southern France provides the unlikely theme to Dan Brown's 2003 best seller.

The Victorian obsession with 'fallen women' made Mary Magdalene a very popular subject in art. Pre-Raphaelite painters and others, such as George Frederic Watts (1817–1904, above), often rendered her in a sacred manner that nevertheless suggested a more profane interest on the part of the artist – and viewer.

Even reading between the lines in the Gospels, Mary Magdalene remains a difficult figure to pin down. Most Gospels agree that she prayed by the Cross at Christ's Crucifixion, she went to anoint Christ's body at the tomb and, according to both Mark and John, she was the first person to whom the resurrected Christ appeared on Easter Sunday. It is clear that she was one of the women who attended Christ during His ministry in Galilee, but her earlier life, and exactly which biblical 'Mary' she is, remains problematic.

Who was Mary Magdalene?
Mary Magdalene's name derives from Magdala, a town in northern Galilee. She has sometimes been identified as Mary the sister of Martha and Lazarus of Bethany (July 29), who is described anointing Christ's feet with expensive perfumed oil and wiping them with her hair (John 12:2–8). A similar scene occurs when an unnamed fallen woman anoints Christ's feet at the house of Simon the Pharisee (Luke 7:37–38). Later, both Luke and Mark refer to Mary Magdalene as someone whom Jesus had cured of possession by seven demons, which would seem to suggest that she was a repentant sinner.

Gregory the Great propounded that all these references were to the same woman, a proposal rejected during the revision of the General Roman Calendar in 1969, where she was acknowledged as the uncontentious sister of Martha and Lazarus. This revisionism did not stop Mary Magdalene from being revered as a fallen woman who nevertheless aspired to salvation through devotion, a theme that was attractive to artists down the centuries. Mary remains one of the few female subjects in Christian iconography who may be acceptably portrayed nude or semi-nude. Her modesty is, however, normally preserved by her flowing auburn hair.

Later Legends
Many legends accumulated around this enigmatic figure. Some cast her as betrothed to St. John the Evangelist, although she is equally frequently portrayed with John the Baptist. One popular myth relates how, some 14 years after the Crucifixion, she was cast adrift from Palestine in an oarless boat with Lazarus, Mary of Bethany, St. Maximin (who is said to have baptized her), St. Sidonius, her servant Sera, and the body of St. Anne. They improbably drifted to southern France, where Mary apparently ended her days as a hermit in a cave at Sainte-Baume, sustained only by angels feeding her the Eucharist daily. According to this story, she lived to age 72.

This bizarre French connection has endured, and her relics have been claimed by the abbey church at Vézelay. The church of La Madeleine in Paris, built in a striking neoclassical style, is one of the most prominent buildings in the city, while in nearby cafés, Madeleines (simple small sponge cakes) are often dipped in coffee.

Both Oxford and Cambridge universities have colleges named for her that date back to the Middle Ages, and some 187 churches in England are also dedicated to her.

Part of a 16th-century wooden altarpiece from Toruń Cathedral, Poland, showing Mary nude, but protected by her hair, being accompanied to Heaven by angels.

JULY 23 | BRIDGET (BIRGITTA) OF SWEDEN

STATUS Abbess, Mystic, Founder

BORN 1303, Uppland, Sweden

DIED 1373, Rome, Italy

GRC ♣

CofE ♣

LCDUS ♣

OTHER Lutheran Church

○ 1391

✝ Book, pilgrim's staff

🙏 Widows; Europe, Sweden

Bridget, mother of St. Catherine of Sweden (March 24) and founder in 1350 of the Brigittine Order of nuns, is Sweden's best-known saint. Though married at only 13 and the mother of eight children, religion dominated her life. Following a pilgrimage to Santiago de Compostela, in 1349 the widowed Bridget traveled to Rome with her daughter, Catherine, to seek papal permission for her proposed order. Other than a pilgrimage to the Holy Land in 1372, she remained in Rome until her death, where her obvious sanctity and gentle nature made a deep impression. She had a series of visions throughout her life, chiefly of the Nativity and of Purgatory. She claimed, too, that when she had been anxious to know the precise number of blows Christ had received during the Passion, Christ himself appeared to tell her that the number was 5,475. To honor his wounds, He instructed Bridget to say 15 Our Fathers, 15 Hail Marys, and 15 other prayers, which He then revealed to her every day for a year. In the later Middle Ages, this exercise became extremely popular. If faithfully honored, it was said to ensure the release of 15 souls from Purgatory. Though Bridget died in Rome, her body was brought back to Vadstena, headquarters of her order. The Brigittines, still thriving, spread across much of Europe and, much later, to the United States.

An image of St. Bridget produced in 1476 in a breviary intended for use by Brigittine nuns.

JULY 24 | CHARBEL MAKHLOUF

STATUS Monk, Hermit

BORN 1828, Bekaa Kafra, Lebanon

DIED 1898, Annaya, Lebanon

GRC ♣

CofE ○

LCDUS ♣

OTHER Eastern Orthodox churches

♥ 1965

○ 1977

Charbel Makhlouf, a Lebanese, or Maronite, Catholic monk, was among the most remarkable saints of the 19th century. He joined the Monastery of Our Lady of Lebanon at age 23, spending two years there before being sent to the monastery of St. Maron at Annaya. He was ordained in 1859, and spent a further 16 years at St. Maron, his embrace of poverty and humility as striking as his reverence for the Holy Eucharist. He early developed the habit of rising at midnight to contemplate the Blessed Sacrament. Only after 11 hours of such contemplation would he feel sufficiently spiritually purified to celebrate Mass. In 1875, he left St. Maron and spent the rest of his life as a hermit. He quickly gained a reputation for extreme sanctity. He died on Christmas Eve 1898, clutching the Eucharist. After he was buried at St. Maron, a large number of miracles were attributed to him, his grave rapidly attracting Muslims as well as Christians. In 1950, he was found to be incorruptible. A blood-like oil was said to trickle from his body. His exhumation in 1950 sparked a proliferation of new miracles. Between April and August alone that year, 350 miracles were claimed to have occurred at his grave, 20 of them to Muslims. His cult continues to thrive.

An illusionistic image of Charbel in his characteristic pose, at prayer.

Charbel Makhlouf's rejection of material possessions, his rigorous and frequent fasting, and his absorption in prayer gained him a reputation of extreme sanctity.

JULY 24 | # THOMAS À KEMPIS

STATUS Priest, Theologian, Mystic

BORN c.1380, Kempen, Germany

DIED 1471, Zwolle, Netherlands

GRC ☁

CofE ☁

LCDUS ☁

OTHER US Episcopal Church

♥ 1965

◯ 1977

The relics of St. Thomas à Kempis (below) in the Basilica of Our Lady of the Assumption in Zwolle, the Netherlands.

Though never formally beatified or canonized by the Roman Catholic Church, Thomas à Kempis was one of the most influential figures in the late medieval church, an author, mystic, preacher, and scholar. *The Imitation of Christ*, written by him in 1418 (though subsequently much expanded), is commonly claimed to have sold more copies than any Christian text other than the Bible. Almost his whole adult life was spent as a member of the Brethren of the Common Life at the order's Mount St. Agnes Monastery at Zwolle, today in the Netherlands. It was here that he was ordained, in either 1413 or 1414. The order had been founded at the end of the 14th century by Geert Groote who, shocked by the laxity and corruption of the clergy, was determined to return to the simple certainties of the early Christians.

It was a creed Thomas à Kempis, unworldly and contemplative, eagerly embraced. "In all things I sought quiet and found it not save in retirement and in books." His output was huge: he personally copied by hand — this in the final years before the introduction of printing in Europe — five copies of the Bible (one of which survives). To this immense labor, he added spiritual treatises, works of religious instruction, mystical reflections, prayers, and hymns. His tone throughout was modest, practical, devotional, and obviously human. "A poor peasant who serves God is better than a proud philosopher who ponders the courses of the stars," he said. Thomas was not to know it, but this insistence on unadorned, deeply felt faith would prove a key precursor of the Reformation in the next century.

"If, however, you seek Jesus in all things, you will surely find Him."

THOMAS À KEMPIS, *THE IMITATION OF CHRIST.*

Date	Name	Status	Venerated	Life
July 24	Declan (5th century)	Bishop, Missionary ◯ Pre-Congregation	In Ireland	Semi-mythical figure. One of first Christian missionaries in Ireland, pre-dating St. Patrick (March 17). Earliest account of his life dates from 12th century. According to legend, having journeyed to Rome, was made a bishop by the pope. Returned to Ireland, proving an energetic and enterprising preacher. Monastery of Ardmore in Waterford said to have been established by him. Numerous miracles associated with his life and tomb.

JULY 25 | JAMES THE GREATER

STATUS Apostle, Martyr

BORN 1st century AD, Galilee, modern Israel

DIED c. AD 44, Judaea, modern Israel

GRC ♣

CofE ♣

LCDUS ♣

OTHER Eastern Orthodox churches (April 30)

⬭ Pre-Congregation

✝ Scallop shell, pilgrim's cloak and broad-brimmed hat, a staff, black beard, sword

🙏 Pilgrims, horsemen, laborers, hatmakers, veterinarians, apothecaries; sufferers from rheumatism and arthritis; Spain

The cross of St. James was adopted by the elite crusading Spanish Order of Santiago, and takes the form of a red sword, signifying both his manner of martyrdom and his patronage of the Spanish army. Today promotion to the Order is in the gift of the Spanish royal family.

James, son of Zebedee, was one of the Twelve Apostles. James is the English form of the Hebrew name Jacob. Some traditions see him as the cousin of Jesus, with his mother as Mary's sister. He is referred to as 'the Greater' to distinguish him from the younger apostle named James, 'the Less' (May 3). The Gospel of St. Mark describes Jesus naming James and John 'the Sons of Thunder' for their evangelizing zeal. James followed his family's trade as a fisherman on the Sea of Galilee. He was among the three Apostles closest to Jesus (with his brother John, and Peter) and, according to the Gospel of St. Matthew, he was chosen to witness both Christ's Transfiguration and the Agony in the Garden. James was apparently physically very similar to Jesus — one of the reasons why Judas Iscariot had to identify Jesus to the Roman guards with a kiss in the Garden of Gethsemane.

James was the first Apostle to be martyred. He was beheaded at the order (and possibly by the hand) of Herod Agrippa I to appease Jewish critics of Christianity; his accuser repented at the last moment, and was executed alongside him.

The Spreading Cult

It is likely that James remained in Jerusalem after the Crucifixion to preach the gospel, although some legends from the 7th century have him traveling across the Mediterranean to the other end of the Roman empire to evangelize

→ pilgrimage route
⚲ major pilgrimage church

The main pilgrimage routes to Santiago de Compostela.

SANTIAGO DE COMPOSTELA

The shrine of St. James in the cathedral of Santiago de Compostela in northwest Spain has made the city one of the Christian world's most popular devotional centers. The pilgrimage tradition began in the 11th century, and often saw groups of over 200 devotees making their way across Europe to the city. Today it still attracts around 200,000 pilgrims each year, many still traveling on foot along the network of medieval routes which spread across Spain, Portugal, and southern France, known as the *Camino de Santiago* (the Way of St. James). An elaborate Baroque façade was attached to the Romanesque basilica in the 18th century.

Iberia. A column in the church of Nuestra Señora del Pilar at Zaragoza is venerated as the place where the Blessed Virgin Mary is said to have appeared while James was preaching on the banks of the Ebro on January 2, AD 40. Spanish tradition also has it that his remains were either transported by the Apostles to the port of Iria Flavia, or miraculously floated in a stone sarcophagus to the coastal village of Padrón, both landing places near Compostela in Galicia, northwest Spain, where his cult took root.

During the Christian reconquest of Spain from Islamic rule, St. James was adopted as patron by the Crusaders, becoming by default the patron saint of Spain. The expansion of the Iberian empires in the 16th century saw his cult spread overseas, not least by Portuguese missions to Congo in central Africa, where July 25 was proclaimed the main national holiday by the converted ruler. It remains a major feast day in Puerto Rico and Haiti, where many slaves from central Africa were transported.

St. James is said to have appeared at the battle of Clavijo (844), where the heavily outnumbered Christian forces under Ramiro I of Asturias defeated the Moorish army of the Emir of Córdoba. Thereafter St. James was called 'Matamoros' (the Moor-slayer).

"Santiago y cierra España – St. James and strike for Spain."

TRADITIONAL BATTLE CRY OF SPANISH SOLDIERS.

Galicia is noted for the quality and variety of its seafood. Early pilgrims to St. James's shrine at Santiago frequently took home a scallop shell as a souvenir, and this rapidly became a sign of one who had undertaken a pilgrimage. Scallop shell motifs may be found on many buildings throughout northern Spain, and the saint's name lives on today in the popular delicacy, coquilles St. Jacques. In Germany the scallop is called Jakobsmuschel.

Innumerable place names throughout the Christian world are named after St. James, including St. James's Park in London and St. James's Gate in Dublin, where Guinness is brewed. The name was also immortalized in the traditional song 'St. James Infirmary Blues,' popularized by Louis Armstrong (left) in 1928.

Date	Name	Status	Venerated	Life
July 25	Cucuphas (Cugat) (d.304)	Martyr ⬭ Pre-Congregation	In Spain, in Paris	Born in Africa. Martyred during Diocletian persecutions. Benedictine abbey of Sant Cugat del Vallès near Barcelona built on site of his death.
July 25	Rudolph Acquaviva (1550–83)	Martyr ♥ 1893	In India (July 26)	Jesuit missionary to India (1578). Evangelized the Mogul court at Agra at the invitation of Akbar. He and four other priests – the Martyrs of Cuncolim – slain during an anti-Portuguese uprising near Goa. Bodies thrown into a well, but after two days showed no signs of decomposition. Water from well believed miraculous.
July 25	Darío Acosta Zurita (1908–31)	Martyr ♥ 2005	In Mexico	Mexican priest from Veracruz. One of over 40 clerics assassinated during and after the Cristero revolt.

JULY 25   CHRISTOPHER

STATUS Martyr
BORN c.220
DIED c.250
GRC ☁
CofE ☁
LCDUS ☁
OTHER Eastern Orthodox churches
⬭ Pre-Congregation
† Often giant-like, bearing the Christ Child on his shoulders
🙏 Travelers, gardeners; sufferers from epilepsy and toothache; protection from sudden death

The Greek name Christophoros means 'bearer of Christ.' Little is known about this popular saint's life. Like St. George, his story seems to have developed from two different traditions stemming from his martyrdom in Asia Minor, possibly during the persecutions of the Roman emperor Decius (r.249–251).

The most well-known story is of a giant of a man who, keen to serve, but rejected by both a king and by Satan, lived as a hermit on a river's bank, helping travelers to cross the torrent. One stormy night a child appeared and, placing him on his shoulders, Christopher attempted to wade through the river. The child became unbearably heavy, and Christopher struggled to make it to the far bank. The child explained that Christopher had been carrying the whole world on his shoulders, and revealed himself to be Christ the Savior.

His feast was removed from the General Roman Calendar in 1969 due, like St. George, to lack of credible historical evidence. The Eastern Orthodox churches observe his feast day on May 9.

JULY 26   ANNE (ANN) & JOACHIM

STATUS Parents of Mary
BORN c.40 BC
DIED c. AD 10
GRC ♣
CofE ♣
LCDUS ♣
⬭ Pre-Congregation
† Anne wears red and green robes; often carries a book
🙏 Grandparents, housewives, the childless; Canada

The parents of the Blessed Virgin Mary do not appear in the Bible, but feature in the apocryphal *Protoevangelium of James*. They are described as being quite old, and childless. Joachim retreated to the desert to pray for offspring, and while he was away both he and Anne were informed by angels that indeed they could expect a child, and in due course Mary was born. In thanks for this gift from God, Anne and Joachim gave their three-year-old daughter to the Temple. Veneration for St. Anne began in the East (the Orthodox churches celebrate this feast on July 25), but she became a popular saint in the West, especially in Germany, by the 15th century.

St. Anne and her husband Joachim delivering Mary to the Temple by the Flemish Mannerist Denys Calvaert (1540–1619).

Date	Name	Status	Venerated	Life
July 26	Parasceva of Rome (c.135–180)	Martyr ⬭ Pre-Congregation/ 1584	🙏 The blind	During persecutions of Antoninus Pius she emerged unharmed after being thrown in burning oil. Antoninus accused her of witchcraft so she threw boiling oil in his eyes, blinding him. Her appeal to Jesus cured him, and he halted the persecutions. They were revived under Marcus Aurelius. His governor Asclepius cast her into a pit with a venomous snake. She made the sign of the Cross and the snake split in two. Asclepius and his court converted. Arrested again (180) and beheaded.
July 26	Andrew the Catechist (1625–44)	Martyr ♥ 2000	In Macao	Born in what is now Vietnam. Converted at age 15 to Christianity by the Jesuit Alexandre de Rhodes. Christianity was banned in Vietnam; in 1643 he was beaten and imprisoned. Invited to renounce his faith, refused, and was hanged. Father de Rhodes had his body shipped to Macao. Ship attacked by pirates and holed on a rock, but a large ballast stone miraculously plugged the gap until the ship reached Macao.
July 26	Antonio Lucci (1682–1752)	Bishop, Theologian ♥ 1989	By Franciscans	Influential Italian theologian. Joined Conventual Franciscans at age 16. Ordained in 1705. Taught at Ravello and Naples, then professor at St. Bonaventure College, Rome (1719). Appointed bishop of Bovino in 1729. Closely involved in pastoral teaching. Wrote hagiography of Franciscan saints and martyrs.

St. Christopher's patronage of travelers was extended in the early 20th century to include motorists – and his image, often bearing the Christ Child, appears on automobile key-fobs around the world (left). In Austria, donations to fund travel for overseas missionaries are collected annually on this day.

St. Christopher is celebrated as one of the Fourteen Holy Helpers (see page 302) – saints whose presence oversees our everyday lives. A medieval belief that simply looking at St. Christopher's image would save one from harm that day explains the frequent presence of his (often oversized) image in many Catholic churches and the enormous popularity of folk-art images for the home (right).

JULY 27 — PANTALEON (PANTELEIMON)

STATUS Martyr

BORN Mid-3rd century, Nicomedia, modern Turkey

DIED c.303, possibly Constantinople (modern Istanbul, Turkey)

GRC ☁

CofE ☁

LCDUS ☁

OTHER Eastern Orthodox churches

⊘ Pre-Congregation

✝ Box with medicines, spatula

⚕ Physicians, torture victims, bachelors; against tuberculosis

Pantaleon was born to a wealthy pagan father and a Christian mother, St. Eubula, in the Christian region of Nicomedia in western Asia Minor. He studied medicine and became personal physician to the future emperor Galerius Maximianus. During this period he abandoned his faith, but later reclaimed it under the influence of St. Hermolaus. There are a large number of accounts of Pantaleon's miraculous healing powers. One legend sees Pantaleon confronted by pagan doctors, with whom he competed to cure a paralytic; by mentioning Jesus's name, Pantaleon cured the man. During the persecutions of Diocletian, Pantaleon was denounced, tried, nailed to a tree in a mock crucifixion, and then beheaded.

Pantaleon's relics, mainly phials of dried blood, can be found in Istanbul, Madrid, Lyon, and Ravello in Italy. His blood in Ravello is said to miraculously liquefy on his feast day. The church dedicated to him in Venice is one of the most spectacular ever built for an early Christian martyr. Pantaleon is often cited as one of the Fourteen Holy Helpers.

This detail (right) is of an illusionistic ceiling fresco by Gian Antonio Fumiani in the church of San Pantaleon, Venice. Painted between 1684 and 1704, it is a grand example of Baroque exuberance, and shows a number of events from Pantaleon's story.

JULY 28 — PROCHORUS, NICANOR, TIMON, AND PARMENAS

STATUS Deacons, Martyrs

BORN Early 1st century AD

DIED Late 1st century AD

GRC ☁

CofE ☁

LCDUS ☁

OTHER Eastern Orthodox churches

⊘ Pre-Congregation

These are four of the seven men named in Acts 6:1–6 as the early Church's first deacons. The others were Stephen (Dec. 26), Philip (June 6), and Nicolas of Antioch. They were appointed during the period after Christ's Resurrection and Ascension, when St. Peter was organizing the early Church. Their function was to serve the Twelve Disciples, and to minister to the needs of Greek Christians, much as the Disciples did for Jewish Christians. They went on to become missionaries.

Various traditions recount their activities. Prochorus had been a companion of St. John the Baptist (June 24, Aug. 29) and became bishop of Nicomedia. He was eventually martyred at Antioch in Syria. Nicanor traveled to Cyprus, but was martyred during the persecutions of Vespasian. Timon turned east and was appointed bishop of Bostra in Arabia, but was burned to death by the Persians at Basra. Parmenas went on missionary journeys in Asia Minor, and then sailed to Cyprus where he became bishop of Soli. Later he retired to mainland Greece, and was martyred at Philippi during the persecutions under Trajan, in around AD 98.

Fra Angelico's fresco from the Niccoline Chapel (c.1448) in the Vatican shows St. Peter blessing the Seven Deacons. Stephen is kneeling, Philip is clad in blue.

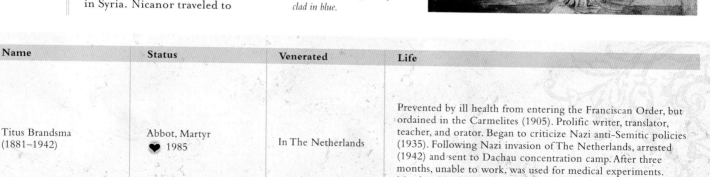

Date	Name	Status	Venerated	Life
July 27	Titus Brandsma (1881–1942)	Abbot, Martyr ♥ 1985	In The Netherlands	Prevented by ill health from entering the Franciscan Order, but ordained in the Carmelites (1905). Prolific writer, translator, teacher, and orator. Began to criticize Nazi anti-Semitic policies (1935). Following Nazi invasion of The Netherlands, arrested (1942) and sent to Dachau concentration camp. After three months, unable to work, was used for medical experiments. Murdered by lethal injection.

Date	Name	Status	Venerated	Life
July 27	Brooke Foss Westcott (1825–1901)	Bishop, Theologian	CofE	Cambridge-educated. Went on to become Professor of Divinity there after teaching at Harrow. Prolific author of scholarly studies of the New Testament, including *Introduction to the Study of the Gospels*, and *The Gospel of the Resurrection*. Bishop of Durham from 1890. Strong supporter of the Christian Social Movement and overseas missionary activity, especially in India.

Mary contemplating the realities of both life and death, by the French painter Georges de la Tour (c. 1593–1652).

JULY 29 · MARTHA, MARY, AND LAZARUS

STATUS Companions of Our Lord

BORN Early 1st century AD, Bethany, modern Israel

DIED c.mid-1st century AD, Bethany, modern Israel

GRC ♣

CofE ♣

LCDUS ♣

OTHER Eastern Orthodox churches

○ Pre-Congregation

> "I am the resurrection, and the life: he that believeth in me, though he were dead, yet shall he live."
>
> JESUS, UPON RAISING LAZARUS FROM THE DEAD (JOHN 11:25).

The sisters Martha and Mary, and their brother Lazarus, feature three times in the New Testament as friends of Jesus Christ. In the Gospel of Luke (10:38–42) Martha invites Jesus to her home in Bethany. While she prepares a meal, her sister Mary (possibly Mary Magdalene, July 22) kneels listening to Jesus; Martha rebukes her for not helping, but Jesus points out that Mary "has chosen the better part" by listening to Him.

The Raising of Lazarus

In John 11:1–44 Martha seeks out Jesus, as her brother Lazarus has died, a calamity that she claims would not have happened if Jesus had been present. In His most dramatic and controversial miracle, Jesus restores Lazarus to life, despite having been entombed for four days. Finally, with the events of the Passion gathering momentum, Martha and Mary again provide Christ with a meal at Bethany (John 12:1–18), where Lazarus joins them. Once again Martha cooks, and Mary anoints Christ's feet before His final return to Jerusalem. Although Mary (Magdalene) is regularly depicted as being at the Crucifixion, Martha and Lazarus are not mentioned again. Nevertheless, the importance of this family group as domestic and compassionate companions of Our Lord cannot be overestimated.

Lazarus is also celebrated separately on December 17 on certain liturgical calendars.

A late 19th-century illustration of the raising of Lazarus by Alexandre Bida.

Lazarus, in an unattributed Spanish painting from the 15th century, flanked by Mary (left) and Martha (right).

JULY 30 · PETER CHRYSOLOGUS

STATUS Bishop, Doctor of the Church

BORN c.406, Imola, Italy

DIED c.450, Imola, Italy

GRC ♣

CofE ♧

LCDUS ♣

OTHER Eastern Orthodox churches

○ Pre-Congregation

† Bishop's robes and miter

Peter was appointed archbishop of Ravenna, then the capital of the western Roman empire, by Valentinian III in around 435. His surviving sermons reveal common sense, warmth, and tolerance, especially toward Jews and pagans, which is unusual for the period. He was named 'Chrysologus' – meaning 'golden-worded' in Greek – in the 9th century, providing the Western Church with a counter-balance to the Orthodox Church's John Chrysostom ('golden-tongued,' Sept. 13). Peter was declared a Doctor of the Church in 1729.

Date	Name	Status	Venerated	Life
July 30	William Wilberforce (1759–1833)	Humanitarian	CofE	English politician and philanthropist. An Evangelical Christian from 1785, who forcefully promoted the Slave Trade Act (1807) and the Slavery Abolition Act, eventually passed by Parliament in 1833, months before his death. Also supported the Society for the Suppression of Vice, the Church Mission Society, the Society for the Prevention of Cruelty to Animals, and the creation of the free state of Sierra Leone.

JULY 31 | IGNATIUS OF LOYOLA

STATUS Priest, Founder

BORN 1491, Guipúzcoa, Spain

DIED 1556, Rome, Italy

GRC ♠

CofE ♠

LCDUS ♣

OTHER By Jesuits

♥ 1609

◉ 1622

✝ Eucharist, book, cross, chasuble

⚘ Society of Jesus (Jesuits), soldiers, educators; Basque country

Ignatius's leg wound while defending Pamplona was a turning point in his career.

Ignatius of Loyola remains one of the towering figures of the revitalization of the Catholic Church during the Counter-Reformation, a man whose martial background prepared him well for the battle to extend the faith in Europe and overseas. Like many of his most forceful contemporaries, his origins lay in Spain, where he was born to a noble family in the Basque country. He served in the Spanish army and was severely wounded during the siege of Pamplona by French forces. It was during his convalescence at Manresa near Barcelona that he discovered his vocation. He undertook a pilgrimage to Jerusalem, then studied in Paris.

It was in the French capital, in 1534, that he formed a group of enthusiasts (including Francis Xavier, Dec. 3) who determined to dedicate themselves to converting Muslims to Christianity. Although that venture never really developed, it was the essential seed that would eventually grow some six years later into the foundation of the Society (or Company) of Jesus, a group dedicated to missionary activity under the direct authority of Pope Paul III, more commonly known as the Jesuits. Ignatius devoted the last 15 years of his life to the vigorous growth of the missionary order, expanding its membership to over 1,000, and establishing schools and seminaries throughout Europe and the colonial world.

His major literary work, *Spiritual Exercises* (1548), begun during a period of convalescence, took 20 years to complete, and continues to be a seminal text. Ignatius's tomb is in the Jesuit mother church of Il Gesù in Rome, a remarkable Baroque confection.

JULY 31 | JUSTIN DE JACOBIS

STATUS Bishop

BORN 1800, San Fele, Italy

DIED 1860, Hebo, Ethiopia

GRC ○

CofE ○

LCDUS ○

♥ 1904

◉ 1975

Jacobis was born and raised in southern Italy, joining the Congregation of the Lazarists at age 18, and becoming ordained in 1824. He worked among the poor in Brindisi and Monopoli, and rose to become superior of the order at Lecce and then at Naples. In 1839, he was commissioned to establish Catholic missions in Ethiopia.

Jacobis was resisted by the local Coptic Christian community, and was persecuted, imprisoned, and at one point exiled. Nevertheless, he was appointed bishop of Nilopolis in 1847, and successfully founded several seminaries for training Catholic clergy in the country. Jacobis is regarded as the founder of the Ethiopian Catholic Church, and is today revered by both Christians and Muslims in Ethiopia.

After a long struggle, Justin became a towering figure in modern Ethiopian Christian development.

Date	Name	Status	Venerated	Life
July 31	Germanus of Auxerre (c.378–448)	Bishop ○ Pre-Congregation	In France	Bishop of Auxerre. Visited Britain around 429 to counter the Pelagian heresy. Appears to have led Britons in battle against Saxons and Picts; won by baptizing troops and shouting "Alleluia."
July 31	Neot (9th century)	Monk, Hermit ○ Pre-Congregation	In Cornwall and Huntingdonshire, England ⚘ Fish	Legendary monk from Glastonbury, possibly a former soldier. Became hermit in Cornwall. Remains transferred to Eynesbury. Monastery near Huntingdon.
July 31	John Colombini (c.1300–67)	Founder	In Siena	Tuscan businessman transformed into a religious philanthropist by reading a life of Mary of Egypt (April 3). Founded the Jesuati in the name of St. Jerome, the order dedicated to caring for others, silence, and scourging. Order was patronized by Urban V after his return from Avignon (1367), but ended in the 1870s.

Prayer cards for Ignatius are often based on Rubens's portrait of the saint receiving inspiration.

The original symbol of the Society of Jesus combines a sunburst with the letters IHS, a widely used early Christogram based on the first three letters of 'Jesus' in Greek (IHSOVS).

ADMAIO REMGLO RIAMDEI.

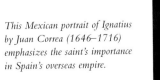

This Mexican portrait of Ignatius by Juan Correa (1646–1716) emphasizes the saint's importance in Spain's overseas empire.

AUGUST

Named by the Roman emperor Augustus after himself, the month of August is associated with vacations and holidays. However, some gruesome martyrdoms are also tied to August: Saint Lawrence's ordeal on the gridiron on August 10, the flaying of Saint Bartholomew the Apostle on August 24, and the beheading of Saint John the Baptist on August 29. From more recent times, the Nazis' execution of Teresa Benedicta of the Cross (Edith Stein), a Jewish convert to Roman Catholicism, is commemorated on August 9.

On a brighter note, the dedication of the great early medieval basilica of Santa Maria Maggiore in Rome occurs on August 5, the day before the feast of the Transfiguration, while the Blessed Virgin Mary's ascendance to the throne as Queen of Heaven is marked on August 22.

The ascent of the Blessed Virgin Mary to become the Queen of Heaven is here envisaged in an extraordinary manner by the unnamed German painter, the Master of Aachen, in around 1485.

AUGUST 1 — ALPHONSUS LIGUORI

STATUS Bishop, Founder, Doctor of the Church

BORN 1696, Campania, Italy

DIED 1787, Campania, Italy

GRC ♣

CofE ♢

LCDUS ♣

♥ 1816

⬭ 1839

🙏 Arthritis, confessors, moralists, theologians, vocations; Naples

Alphonsus was among the most significant and important churchmen in 18th-century Italy, a tireless missionary to the poor in Naples and the surrounding areas. He was founder in 1732 of the Congregation of the Most Holy Redeemer, still active today, and was bishop of Sant'Agata dei Goti from 1762. More lastingly, he was a noted theologian, the author of 111 works. He was trained as a lawyer but abandoned his career in 1723 to become a priest, and was ordained in 1726. In Naples, he opened what would eventually grow to become 72 'Evening Chapels' to minister to the young dispossessed of the city. He was subsequently to discover that conditions among the poor in rural areas were worse still, hence his foundation of what would become known as the Redemptorists. Their success was limited by local laws and customs and, although Alphonsus sold all he owned to help feed the rural poor during the famine of 1763, it was not until after his death that the Redemptorists had a major impact. His *Moral Theology*, perhaps the best known of his books, was one of the most robust and coherent defenses of Catholicism in an age of increasing anti-clericalism.

Alphonsus giving thanks to the Blessed Sacrament, from a mid-19th-century stained-glass window in Carlow Cathedral, Ireland.

AUGUST 2 — EUSEBIUS OF VERCELLI

STATUS Bishop

BORN c.283, Sardinia, Italy

DIED 371, Vercelli, Italy

GRC ♣

CofE ♢

LCDUS ♣

⬭ Pre-Congregation

🙏 Vercelli, Italy

Eusebius, bishop of Vercelli in Lombardy from 340, whose father had been martyred in Sardinia, was one of the most energetic defenders of the orthodox Christian belief in the divinity of Christ. This doctrine was officially affirmed at the Council of Nicaea in 325, in the face of the Arian heresy (*see* page 12). Following the Council of Milan in 355, called by the Arian-supporting Roman emperor, Constantius II, to rebuke those opposing Arianism, Eusebius was exiled, first to Syria, then to Asia Minor, and finally to Egypt. Freed in 362 by the new emperor, Julian, Eusebius remained in the East, cooperating with another great champion of orthodoxy, St. Athanasius of Alexandria (May 2), before returning to Vercelli the following year. There he worked closely with St. Hilary of Poitiers (Jan. 13) in the continuing struggle against Arianism.

AUGUST 2 — PETER JULIAN EYMARD

STATUS Priest, Founder

BORN 1811, Grenoble, France

DIED 1868, Rome, Italy

GRC ♣

CofE ♢

LCDUS ♣

♥ 1925

⬭ 1962

Eymard became a priest in the face of the rampant anti-clericalism in much of post-Revolutionary France, despite the ill health that dogged him throughout his life. Nonetheless, he was ordained in 1834 and in 1839 joined the Marist Fathers, becoming a senior member of the Society until 1856, when he founded the Congregation of the Blessed Sacrament in Paris. Two years later, he founded a lay order, the Servants of the Blessed Sacrament. Though beset by financial problems, both orders survived due to Eymard's fierce conviction of the need for spiritual renewal through active worship and the necessity of receiving Holy Communion regularly. He was declared 'Apostle of the Eucharist' by Pope John Paul II.

Eusebius, on the left, suitably bearded and gowned, with, from left to right, the Archangel Gabriel, the Blessed Virgin Mary, and Sts. Sebastian and Roch, from a painting (1724–25) by Sebastiano Ricci.

AUGUST 4 | JEAN-BAPTISTE VIANNEY

STATUS Priest
BORN 1786, Dadilly, France
DIED 1859, Ars, France
GRC ♣
CofE ♣
LCDUS ♣
♥ 1905
◯ 1925
🙏 Confessors, parish priests

Despite being no more than the parish priest of one of the smallest parishes in France, Ars-en-Dombes, close to Lyon, Jean-Baptiste Vianney was ordained in 1815, and became one of the most celebrated Catholic priests in Europe. Although an unsuccessful student (he found Latin difficult), he became known not just for his sanctity and piety, but as a confessor. By the 1850s, upwards of 20,000 people per year were descending on Ars for Vianney to hear their confessions. Vianney, who

generally rose at one in the morning and spent as much as 18 hours a day taking confession, asked frequently if he could leave Ars to live a quieter, more contemplative life, but was as frequently rebuffed by his bishop. He disapproved of frivolities like music and dancing, and was known for his 'fire and brimstone' sermons.

Pope Benedict XVI declared 2009, the 150th anniversary of the death of Vianney (the 'Curé d'Ars' – Priest of Ars – as he was universally known), a 'year for priests.'

AUGUST 5 | OSWALD OF NORTHUMBRIA

STATUS King, Martyr
BORN c.604, Northumbria, England
DIED 642, Shropshire, England
GRC ◯
CofE ♣
LCDUS ◯
OTHER Eastern Orthodox churches
◯ Pre-Congregation

Oswald, king of Northumbria from 634 to 642, then the most powerful of the kingdoms emerging in Dark Age Britain, played a crucial role in the spread of Christianity in England. He had been exiled in 616 to Iona after his father, Athelfrith, had been killed in battle by a Welsh prince, Cadwallon. On Iona, Oswald converted to Christianity. When, in turn, Oswald fought to regain his kingdom in 634 in what later became known as the Battle of Heavenfield, he claims to have been visited the night before by St. Columba (June 9). Before the battle, he had a wooden cross erected. His nobles swore to convert to Christianity if they were victorious. Oswald subsequently recruited an Irish monk

from Iona, Aidan (Aug. 31), to convert the Northumbrians. It was Aidan who established the monastery at Lindisfarne, Holy Island.

Oswald was killed at the Battle of Maserfield, fighting the pagan Mercians under their king, Penda. Almost at once, miracles were ascribed to the place of his death. When Oswald's body was later taken to be buried at Bardney Abbey in Lincolnshire, the monks agreed to accept it only after a column of light shone from it. In the 10th century, Oswald was re-buried at Gloucester Cathedral, though his head was taken to Durham Cathedral. One of his arms was later claimed to have been removed to Peterborough Cathedral in Cambridgeshire.

What little is known of Oswald, shown here in a 13th-century manuscript, comes almost entirely from Bede (May 25), the great historian of early Christian Britain.

AUGUST 5 | THE DEDICATION OF SANTA MARIA MAGGIORE

The basilica of Santa Maria Maggiore is the oldest of the four principal Roman basilicas, originally founded in the 4th century on the Esquiline Hill by Pope Liberius, but rebuilt a century later by Sixtus III. It was originally called Our Lady of the Snows, as it

was sited where the Blessed Virgin Mary left her footprints in an unusual Roman snowfall. It remains a masterpiece of richly mosaicked early medieval architecture, and is said to contain fragments of the manger from Bethlehem.

Date	Name	Status	Venerated	Life
Aug. 3	Lydia Purpuraria (1st century AD)	Early Christian Convert ◯ Pre-Congregation	🙏 Dyers	A dyer (*purpuraria* means 'purple dyer'). Has the distinction of having been first convert of St. Paul (Jan. 25), who visited her birthplace on his second missionary journey. Seems likely that Paul and his companions, Silas, Timothy, and Luke, stayed in her house.
Aug. 6	Maria Francesca Rubatto (1844–1904)	Nun, Missionary ♥ 1993	By Capuchins In Uruguay	Superior General of Capuchins in Italy. Went to Uruguay as missionary (1892). Returned to South America several times to continue missionary work, extending it into Argentina and Brazil (where, in 1901, number of Capuchin sisters murdered). Remains only Uruguayan to have been beatified.

AUGUST 6 — THE TRANSFIGURATION OF OUR LORD

This day celebrates the appearance in glorified form of Jesus Christ to the Apostles Peter, James, and John on either Mt. Tabor or Mt. Hermon. The event is detailed in the Gospels of Matthew, Mark, and Luke. Christ was accompanied by the Old Testament prophets Moses and Elijah, while a heavenly voice proclaimed Him the 'beloved son.'

AUGUST 7 — CAJETAN

STATUS Priest, Founder
BORN 1480, Vicenza, Italy
DIED 1547, Naples, Italy
GRC ♣
CofE ◌
LCDUS ♣
♥ 1629
◯ 1671
† Usually shown in Theatine robes
🙏 Gamblers, the unemployed; Albania, Argentina, Brazil, El Salvador, Guatemala

Cajetan was the principal founder of the Theatines in 1524, more properly the Congregation of Clerks Regular of the Divine Providence. Of aristocratic birth and trained initially as a lawyer before being ordained in 1516, he was a crucial early figure in the Catholic Church's attempts to counter Protestant teachings by means of a spiritual rebirth among clergy and laity alike. His own piety had earlier been underlined by his joining the Oratory of Divine Love, an order intended to alleviate poverty. In Vicenza, he also began a hospital for incurables. Though effectively disbanded after 1860, for two centuries the Theatines were among the most dynamic of Catholic orders, not just in Italy, but in many parts of Europe. Cajetan died, exhausted, suffering what has been called 'a mystical crucifixion.'

Though its members took vows of strict poverty, the Theatines nonetheless became one of the richest Catholic orders. Their chief church, Sant'Andrea della Valle, is among the most sumptuous of Rome's Baroque churches.

Date	Name	Status	Venerated	Life
Aug. 7	John Mason Neale (1818–66)	Priest, Hymn Writer	CofE, US Evangelical Lutheran Church	Cambridge-educated, member of the Oxford Movement. Ordained (1841), becoming warden of an almshouse in East Grinstead, Sussex (1846). Noted scholar and known for writing Christmas hymns such as 'Good King Wenceslas' and 'O Come, O Come Emmanuel.'
Aug. 8	Mary MacKillop (1842–1909)	Nun, Founder ♥ 1995 ◯ 2010	🙏 Australia, Brisbane	Energetic daughter of an unsuccessful immigrant. Worked as teacher and governess; founded Bayview College, Portland, Victoria, and co-founded Sisters of St. Joseph of the Sacred Heart (or Josephites, 1867). Briefly excommunicated (1871–72) for 'insubordination,' she remained a controversial figure while Josephite schools spread through South Australia, Victoria, Queensland, and to New Zealand. Visited Rome (1873). Re-elected Mother Superior-General even after debilitating stroke in 1902.
Aug. 9	Mary Sumner (1828–1921)	Founder	CofE, Church of Wales	Social improver, founder in 1876 of the Mothers' Union, intended to give practical support for mothers of all classes to enable them to provide not just for their children's physical needs but to raise them 'in the love of God.' "Those who rock the cradle rule the world," she declared. By 1892, the Mothers' Union had 60,000 members; by 1900, 169,000. Today it has 3.6m members in 76 countries.

AUGUST 8 | DOMINIC

STATUS   Monk, Preacher,
          Founder

BORN   1170, Caleruega,
          Spain

DIED   1221, Bologna, Italy

GRC   ♣

CofE   ♣

LCDUS   ♣

⬯   1234

✝   Chaplet, dog, black
          Dominican habit,
          lilies, star, tonsure

⚜   Astronomers, those
          falsely accused;
          Dominican Republic

The Dominicans, or Friars Preachers, were referred to as "the watchdogs of the Lord, defending the fold of the Church with the fire of the Holy Spirit."

With his almost exact contemporary St. Francis of Assisi (Oct. 4), St. Dominic, founder in 1216 of the Dominicans (Friars Preachers, or Black Friars), was among the most significant figures of the medieval church. His insistence on intellectual rigor, on preaching, on unquestioned faith, and on good works, helped revive a Church that was increasingly complacent and corrupt, but was facing a heretical movement – Catharism – that threatened its very foundations. Dominic, born to a noble family with an early reputation for sanctity and good works, was highly educated and, at the age of only 25, was made a canon of the cathedral of Osma in Burgos. In 1201, he was appointed its superior. It was in this capacity that in 1204 he accompanied a Spanish diplomatic mission to Denmark.

Having reached France on his way to Denmark, for the first time Dominic was brought face to face with the reality of the Cathars (*right*). He was as impressed by their evident sincerity and the effectiveness of their organization as he was appalled by their heresy, to say nothing of the feebleness of Rome's response. The Cathars, Dominic understood, could only be

Though the rosary pre-dates St. Dominic, the saint is widely credited with popularizing its use as an aid to prayer. The Virgin Presenting the Rosary to St. Dominic, *(1638–40), is by the Spaniard Bartolomé Murillo.*

directly confronted. "Zeal must be met by zeal, humility by humility, false sanctity by real sanctity, preaching falsehood by preaching truth," he asserted. This hardheaded, galvanic approach paid off only slowly, but it was critical in provoking the Church into a far more effective – and ultimately brutal – response to the Cathars. Though from 1218 the Dominicans were based in Bologna in northern Italy, Dominic continued to travel widely, generally barefoot, preaching, organizing, and cajoling with remarkable intensity.

CATHARISM

The Cathar or Albigensian heresy is named for the Greek word *katharos*, meaning 'pure,' and the city of Albi in southern France where Dominic debated with the Cathars. It seems to have begun in the mid-12th century. Generally associated with southwest France, it also occurred in the Rhineland and northern Italy. Catharism fused pre-Christian beliefs – notably Gnosticism and Dualism – with contempt for the moral laxity of the medieval Church. At its heart was the belief that the physical world is inherently evil and that divinity can consist only of pure spirit. If God had created the physical world, it followed that He, too, was evil, as was Jesus by having been made Man. The heresy was destroyed by the Albigensian Crusade of 1209–29, a savagely successful mission, backed in full by the papacy. Figures for those killed vary between 200,000 and one million.

Cathar imagery, shown on this Cathar coin, combined Christian and arcane magical symbols.

AUGUST 9 | TERESA BENEDICTA OF THE CROSS

STATUS   Nun, Martyr

BORN   1891, Breslau
          (Wrocław), Poland

DIED   1942, Auschwitz,
          Poland

GRC   ♣

CofE   ♡

LCDUS   ♣

OTHER   By Carmelites

❤   1987

⬯   1998

✝   Book, flames, Star of
          David

⚜   Martyrs, orphans;
          Europe

Teresa Benedicta was born Edith Stein in what is now Poland and was then part of the German empire. She was Jewish. She was an exceptionally bright child, academically very gifted, who at 13 declared herself an atheist. She gained a doctorate in philosophy from Göttingen University in 1916. A latent spirituality, inspired by reading the life of Teresa of Ávila (Oct. 15), subsequently developed. In 1922, she became a Catholic. In 1933, despite a brilliant career as a teacher and philosopher, she became a Discalced Carmelite nun in Cologne, the

order founded by Teresa of Ávila, appropriately taking the name Teresa. In 1938, recognizing that, Catholic convert or not, Teresa was still a Jew in the eyes of the Nazis, the Carmelites arranged for her to be smuggled to Holland and apparent safety. On August 2, 1942, she and her sister, Rosa, also a Carmelite, were rounded up. They were taken to Auschwitz and on August 9 were gassed. A colleague, Professor Jan Nota, memorably called her: "A witness to God's presence in a world where God is absent."

A stained-glass window of Teresa Benedicta by Alois Plum, installed in 1970 in Herz Jesu Church in Kassel, Germany. She holds a book, symbol of her learning, wears a Star of David, sign of her Jewish origins, and is consumed by flames, a reference to her murder.

AUGUST 10 | LAWRENCE

STATUS Deacon, Martyr
BORN Early 3rd century
DIED 258, Rome, Italy
GRC ♣
CofE ♣
LCDUS ♣
OTHER Eastern Orthodox churches, Lutheran Church
⬭ Pre-Congregation
✝ Gridiron, dalmatic (priest's tunic)
⚬ Chefs, roasters, comedians, librarians, students, tanners; Rome, Rotterdam

Little is known with certainty about Lawrence other than that he was one of seven deacons — in Lawrence's case charged with guarding the treasures of the Church, reputedly including the Holy Grail — under Pope Sixtus II. All seven were condemned to death along with Sixtus himself on the orders of the emperor Valerian. But Lawrence remains one of the most venerated of saints, with a cult dating at least from the 4th century. The church dedicated to him in Rome, San Lorenzo fuori le Mura, begun around 580 on the site where the saint was claimed to have been martyred, and substantially remodeled since, is one of the seven pilgrim churches in the city. Similarly, his name is commemorated in hundreds of towns, especially in France. According to legend, Lawrence was slowly roasted to death by Valerian, at one point asking to be turned over as "This side is done ... Have a bite."

A marble relief of the Martyrdom of St. Lawrence carved in 1758 by Juan de León for the Royal Palace in Madrid. Valerian is to the right, the martyr — and his gridiron — in the center.

AUGUST 11 | CLARE OF ASSISI

STATUS Nun, Founder
BORN 1194, Assisi, Italy
DIED 1253, Assisi, Italy
GRC ♣
CofE ♣
LCDUS ♣
OTHER US Lutheran Church
⬭ 1255
✝ Habit of Poor Clares, lamp, monstrance, pyx
⚬ Clairvoyance, embroiderers, eye diseases, goldsmiths, laundry workers, needle workers, television

Clare of Assisi was a devoted follower and pupil of St. Francis of Assisi (Oct. 4) who in 1212, to the consternation and dismay of her aristocratic parents, escaped an unwelcome marriage by running away from home to join an order of Benedictine nuns. She was soon joined by her sister, Agnes of Assisi. In 1216, the sisters moved to Francis's monastery at the church of San Damiano, outside Assisi. It was there on Palm Sunday of the same year, with the active encouragement of Francis, that Clare founded an order of nuns devoted to penance and poverty. It was known originally as the Order of Poor Ladies; after Clare's death, its name was changed to the Order of St. Clare, better known as the Poor Clares. The austerity Clare insisted on alarmed many in the Church, who considered such a wholehearted embrace of poverty shocking. Clare mounted a series of spirited defenses of her espousal of 'pure poverty.' It was only two days before her death in 1253 that Innocent IV gave papal sanction to her rule.

In 1260, her body was moved from its original burial place and transferred to the newly built Basilica of St. Clare in Assisi. In 1872, she was disinterred and is displayed in the crypt of the church.

Clare, painted c.1320 by Simone Martini, Basilica of St. Francis, Assisi. "They say that we are too poor," wrote St. Clare, "but can a heart which possesses the infinite God be truly called poor?"

Date	Name	Status	Venerated	Life
Aug. 12	Euplius (d.c.304)	Martyr ⬭ Pre-Congregation		Deacon in Catania, Sicily. Found guilty of possessing copy of the Bible during persecutions of Diocletian. After period of imprisonment, still refusing pleas to recant, was beheaded.
Aug. 12	Jane Frances de Chantal (1572–1641)	Nun, Founder ⬭ 1767	GRC	Burgundian noble, widowed when husband killed in hunting accident. Founded Congregation of the Visitation of Holy Mary, a quietly contemplative order. "We throw ourselves into God as a little drop of water into the sea," she wrote. Guided by her confessor Francis de Sales (Jan. 24).

AUGUST 11   JOHN HENRY NEWMAN

STATUS Theologian, Cardinal

BORN 1801, London, England

DIED 1890, Birmingham, England

GRC ○

CofE ♠

LCDUS ○

Newman was one of the most celebrated and controversial figures in Victorian Britain. He was an Oxford don and Anglican priest, and important in the so-called Oxford Movement in the 1830s that sought to bring the Church of England back to its Catholic roots. Sensationally for the time, this exotic, mesmerizing figure then became a Catholic convert and priest, founder of the English Oratorians. His profoundly held religious faith found expression in a vast quantity of written material that was highly personal and, for many, highly persuasive. His best-known book, *Apologia pro Vita Sua* (*A Defense of One's Life,* 1864) was among the literary sensations of its age, and played a critical role in diluting the assumption that Rome was bent on the sinister subjection of Protestant Britain. Newman didn't just make Catholicism in 19th-century Britain intellectually respectable, he made it almost fashionable.

He first sprang to prominence in 1833 with the publication of *Tracts for the Times,* the first of 90 such 'tracts' that gave the Oxford Movement – or Tractarians – its initial impulse. For the poetic, mystical Newman, it was clear that as Christ had made St. Peter His vicar on Earth, any rejection of Peter's direct successors, the popes, was effectively a rejection of Christ Himself. In practice, the Anglican Church in Victorian Britain was not just a branch of the state, it was an essential prop of it. If this meant that the Anglican Church could never be brought to re-embrace Rome, it also meant that the only valid response to this impasse for a Christian conscience as troubled as Newman's was to convert to Catholicism.

Newman's Conversion

Newman was received into the Catholic Church in 1845. The following year, ordained a Catholic priest, he was given permission by Pope Pius IX to establish a branch of the Oratorians in England, which he did first in Birmingham in 1848, then in London in 1849. These early Catholic years were not easy for Newman. In 1852, Newman was found guilty of libel against a de-frocked Italian Catholic priest Giovanni Achilli in a near-comical miscarriage of justice. In 1854, he began four largely fruitless years as rector of the newly established Catholic University of Ireland. In 1858, largely through the machinations of a fellow Catholic convert, Henry Manning, Newman was refused permission to establish an Oratory in Oxford.

Manning, archbishop of Westminster from 1865, a cardinal from 1875, was worldly where Newman was spiritual, scheming where Newman was only too ready to resign himself to God's will. Manning also had allies in Rome. In 1870, when Pius IX called the First Vatican Council principally to assert the Doctrine of Papal Infallibility, Manning was able to exploit Newman's skepticism of the pope's self-aggrandizement to marginalize him yet further in the eyes of Rome.

Yet in the end, made a cardinal by the new pope, Leo XIII, in 1879, it was the aged Newman who would be vindicated. He was declared 'venerable' in 1991, the first step on the road to his beatification and canonization.

Cardinal Newman, painted by John Everett Millais in 1881. That Newman reveled in his fame was always clear. His piety, filtered through a distinctive English poetic tradition, was no less so.

| AUGUST 13 | # PONTIAN AND HIPPOLYTUS |

STATUS Pontian: Pope, Martyr; Hippolytus: Priest, Anti-pope, Martyr

BORN Late 2nd century, Italy

DIED 236, Sardinia, Italy

GRC ♣

CofE ♧

LCDUS ♣

OTHER Eastern Orthodox churches, Lutheran Church

◯ Pre-Congregation

♙ Horses, prison guards (Hippolytus)

Pontian, pope from 230–35, and Hippolytus, so-called anti-pope, embody both the doctrinal differences that bedeviled the early Christian church and the almost constant threat of persecution its members faced within the Roman empire. Hippolytus, presumed to have been born in Rome, was among the most important writers of the early Christian Church, though only fragments of his works survive. His opposition to a series of popes – Callixtus (r.217–222), Urban I (r.222–230), and then Pontian himself – was based partly on a dispute, not unlike Arianism (*see* page 12), concerning the divinity of Christ and His exact relationship to His father. Hippolytus also rejected Callixtus's ruling that sinners should be allowed back into the Church if they were genuinely repentant, a judgment that in fact did much to broaden the appeal of the Church. As a result, around 220 he appears to have set himself up as a rival bishop of Rome, or 'anti-pope.' Nonetheless, Hippolytus seems to have become reconciled to the pope when he and Pontian were arrested on the orders of the emperor Maximinus Thrax, who exiled them to Sardinia, where both died in the island's mines. A later legend, based on a misreading, claimed that Hippolytus had been torn apart by horses. The bodies of both men were returned to Rome shortly after their deaths and buried there, honored as martyrs.

| AUGUST 13 | # JEREMY TAYLOR |

STATUS Bishop, Theologian

BORN 1613, Cambridge, England

DIED 1667, Lisburn, Ireland

GRC ♧

CofE ♣

LCDUS ♧

Jeremy Taylor, the 'Shakespeare of the Divines' and the 'Spenser of the pulpit,' was among the best known theologians of 17th-century England, famed for the eloquence and obvious learning of his copious writing. Much of his life was turbulent, however, disrupted by the upheavals of the English Civil War and the religious as well as political disputes that followed in its wake. In 1638, William Laud, archbishop of Canterbury (Jan. 10), appointed Taylor chaplain-in-ordinary to Charles I (Jan. 30). Thus associated with the royalist cause, Taylor, who would be imprisoned three times, was inevitably suspect in Parliamentarian eyes. But with the Restoration in 1660, he was appointed bishop of Down and Connor in Ireland as well as vice-chancellor of Trinity College in Dublin. His struggles with an obdurate, mostly Presbyterian clergy and the "perfect disorder" of the university proved unrewarding. His

A characteristic 17th-century obsession with the transience of life: Jeremy Taylor with a child, a young woman, and an old man – representatives of the three stages of life – points to a figure of death, the inevitable fate of us all.

theology, the majority produced at Golden Grove, home of the Earl of Carbery, after 1646, presents a very different face. His two best known works, *The Rule and Exercise of Holy Living* (1650) and *The Rule and Exercise of Holy Dying* (1651), had an influence well into the 20th century, the result of their poetry as much as of the compassion they urge.

Date	Name	Status	Venerated	Life
Aug. 13	Radegund (c.520–87)	Nun ◯ Pre-Congregation	In Poitiers, France ♙ Jesus College, Cambridge, England	Daughter of Thuringian king, Berthar. Forced to marry Clotaire, brother of Frankish king. She subsequently founded convent in Poitiers; devoted rest of life to prayer. Particularly venerated in England in 15th century.
Aug. 13	Octavia Hill (1838–1912)	Social Reformer	CofE	English social reformer. Worked to preserve open spaces for urban poor to enjoy, a movement that led to her co-founding UK's National Trust (1895). Best known for work in providing housing – much of it bought and paid for by herself – for the dispossessed, above all in London.

AUGUST 13 | FLORENCE NIGHTINGALE

STATUS Nurse, Social Reformer

BORN 1820, Florence, Italy

DIED 1910, London, England

GRC ○

CofE ♣

LCDUS ○

Florence Nightingale was perhaps the greatest social reformer of her age, a high-born woman of relentless energy and single-mindedness who, first during the Crimean War of 1853–56, then from the seclusion of her Mayfair drawing room, drew up and implemented the modern business of hygienic nursing. Her *Notes on Nursing*, published in 1859, remains its foundation stone. She had no hesitation in making full use of her influential contacts. It was the Secretary at War himself, Sidney Herbert, a close friend of Nightingale's, who arranged for her to be sent to the Crimea after she had badgered him to do so. And it was via Herbert that Nightingale subsequently instituted a complete overhaul of the medical care of soldiers in the British Army.

Her fame rests nonetheless on her work in the Barrack Hospital at Scutari, where she arrived in 1854, ten days after the battle of Balaclava and one day before the battle of Inkerman. Its four miles of beds amounted to a kind of inferno of dead and dying men. There were almost no facilities. Most of the wounded were abandoned to a squalor in which ten times more died of infections contracted at Scutari than of their actual wounds. In the face of persistent official complacency and obstruction, Florence Nightingale effected an entire transformation of this monument to filth, sweeping aside obstacles, imposing herself by sheer force of will.

When she returned home in July 1856, she was perhaps the most famous woman in England. In 1859, she oversaw the opening of the Nightingale Training School, the first dedicated teaching establishment for nurses in the world. Her influence on nursing in the US Civil War was decisive. It seemed that almost nothing was beyond this extraordinary woman.

The 'Lady with the Lamp,' as Florence became known, did more to transform standards of hospital care in the 19th century than any other figure.

AUGUST 14 | MAXIMILIAN KOLBE

STATUS Priest, Founder, Martyr

BORN 1894, Zdunska Wola, Poland

DIED 1941, Auschwitz, Poland

GRC ♣

CofE ♣

LCDUS ♣

OTHER Lutheran Church

♥ 1971

○ 1982

⚓ Drug addicts, families, journalists, prisoners, pro-life movement; the 20th century

Kolbe was born in part of what was at the time the Russian empire. Inspired in his childhood by a vision of the Virgin Mary, in 1907 he escaped to Austria and joined the Franciscans. He was ordained in 1918, returning to what was then a newly independent Poland. He was a remarkably active priest. During his training in Rome, he had already established the Militia Immaculata, (the 'Army of Mary'), an organization that vigorously promoted Catholicism, principally through veneration of the Virgin. He was no less energetic in Poland, founding Catholic newspapers and a radio station as well as the monastery of Niepokalanów. Between 1930 and 1936, he also undertook a series of missionary journeys to Japan, where he established a monastery outside Nagasaki.

With the German invasion of Poland in 1939, Kolbe instantly became a rallying point for resistance to the Nazis, using his radio station to broadcast anti-Nazi messages. More particularly, he took in and sheltered huge numbers of refugees at the monastery in Niepokalanów. Among them were 2,000 Jews. Catholic priest or not, in February 1941 he was rounded up by the Gestapo. By May he had been sent to Auschwitz. There, he volunteered to take the place of one of ten men arbitrarily selected by the camp commandant to be starved to death after one of the prisoners disappeared. Kolbe survived with no food or drink for three weeks before, eventually, he was given a lethal injection of carbolic acid.

When he was canonized in 1982, Kolbe was declared 'the patron saint of our difficult century' by his fellow Pole, Pope John Paul II. He is depicted here in a stained-glass window in the Franciscan church in Szombathely, Hungary, his prison number at Auschwitz accurately represented.

AUGUST 15 | ASSUMPTION OF THE BLESSED VIRGIN MARY

The Assumption of the Blessed Virgin Mary has long been one of the most popular subjects in Christian art.

The Assumption is one of the most notable dates in the Christian calendar, a Holy Day of Obligation in the Catholic Church and a national holiday in many countries. This most resonant of Catholic feasts is one that is shared nevertheless by many of the reformist churches.

The feast commemorates the ascent of Mary, the mother of God, to Heaven "having completed the course of her earthly life." But, not only is the Assumption unrecorded in the Bible (other than in an ambiguous reference in the Book of Revelation), there is also no scriptural record of how or where the Virgin Mary ascended to Heaven. The earliest account of her Assumption is Ethiopian, and dates from the 4th century. Even so, by the 7th century, the event was generally recognized across the whole Christian world, rapidly becoming a major feast. Mary's Ascension is variously said to have occurred at Ephesus in Turkey and at Jerusalem. The Apostles themselves were claimed to have been present, all having been transported there at the moment of her Ascension, though it is also asserted that St. Thomas arrived only later, opening her tomb to find it empty. There is also considerable uncertainty as to whether her Assumption occurred after her death, as the Orthodox Church holds, or whether the Virgin rose to Heaven and eternal life without dying at all. The Catholic Church is vague on the point. This uncertainty, whatever the central role of the Virgin's Assumption in Christian belief and its obvious symbolism (if the Virgin Mary, born human, could ascend to Heaven, so in time can all Christians, having repented of their sins), is reflected in the fact that it was only in 1950 that Pope Pius XII asserted unequivocally that the Assumption was an unchallengeable point of Catholic dogma.

Date	Name	Status	Venerated	Life
Aug. 16	Charles Inglis (1734–1816)	Bishop	CofE, LCDUS	First Anglican bishop in North America. In 1787, appointed by George III as bishop of Nova Scotia in Canada – a purely political appointment, in reward for staunch loyalty to British crown Inglis had demonstrated during American Revolution, when he was an Anglican priest in America. Appears to have made little effort to visit much of his vast if sparsely populated diocese.
Aug. 17	Jeanne Delanoue (1666–1736)	Nun, Founder ♥ 1947 ◯ 1982		Lived entire life in Saumur, France. Consistent champion of the poor. Founder of the Congregation of St. Anne of Providence. Zealous worker on behalf of the dispossessed. Established series of communities on behalf of the old, the aged, and the impoverished. Led life of self-mortification and prayer. The Sisters of St. Jeanne Delanoue remain active in France, Sumatra, and Madagascar.
Aug. 19	Jean Eudes (1601–80)	Priest, Founder ♥ 1909 ◯ 1925		Founder of the Sisters of Our Lady of Charity of the Refuge (1641) and the Society of Jesus and Mary (1643). Among most forceful and tireless propagandists of the Catholic Church in 17th-century France. Wrote widely in support of Counter-Reformation and preached no less aggressively. Had active support of Cardinal Richelieu. Also established the Society of the Heart of the Mother Most Admirable (1648).

AUGUST 16

STEPHEN OF HUNGARY

STATUS King

BORN c.970, Esztergom, Hungary

DIED 1038, Esztergom, Hungary

GRC ♠

CofE ○

LCDUS ♠

OTHER Eastern Orthodox churches

◯ 1083

🙏 Hungary

Not unlike Charlemagne two centuries earlier, Stephen used Christianity as a means of forging a more or less coherent political entity, the kingdom of Hungary, of which he was the first king. Stephen may well have been a devout Christian – he later founded a monastery in Jerusalem as well as hospices in Rome, Ravenna, and Constantinople – but it is evident that for him the prime attraction of Christianity was political. Marriage to the sister of the future Holy

Roman Emperor, Henry II (July 13), ensured a crucial military alliance with the most powerful Christian ruler in Europe. No less important, Stephen also secured the backing of the papacy at a time when its status had never been greater. Early medieval Hungary was a fragile construct at best. That it existed at all was clearly due to Stephen.

A statue of Stephen in his birthplace of Esztergom. He emerged as a potent symbol of Hungarian nationalism in the 19th century.

AUGUST 16

ROCH (ROCCO)

STATUS Pilgrim

BORN c.1295, Montpellier, France

DIED c.1327, Montpellier, France/Voghera, Italy

GRC ○

CofE ○

LCDUS ○

OTHER Episcopalian churches

◯ 1591

✝ Thigh plague wound, dog offering bread

🙏 Sufferers from plague, apothecaries, bachelors, dogs, pilgrims

Although one of the most popular saints of the Middle Ages, especially as the patron saint of plague sufferers – whose intercession against the devastating ravages of the disease was consistently invoked – it seems unlikely that Roch ever existed. Traditionally, he is said to have been born to a barren mother who conceived him only after she prayed to the Virgin. Roch himself was claimed to have had a red cross on his chest from birth. At age 20, he embarked on a pilgrimage to Rome. Encountering plague sufferers, he miraculously cured them by making the sign of the cross. When Roch himself contracted the plague, he took himself off to a forest where a spring miraculously gushed, and a dog brought him bread and cured him by licking his wounds. He died either in his native Montpellier or

in Voghera in Italy. Following the spread of the Black Death in Europe in 1347, his cult grew dramatically, above all in Venice, where in 1478 the opulent Confraternity of St. Roch (Rocco) was established.

In a time when the plague could descend without warning on entire communities, the medieval popularity of St. Roch is easily understood. Mythical or not, he loomed large in imaginations struggling to come to terms with apocalyptic-seeming disasters.

AUGUST 18

HELENA (HELEN), MOTHER OF CONSTANTINE

STATUS Empress

BORN c.248, Drepanum, modern Turkey

DIED c.328, Constantinople, modern Turkey

GRC ○

CofE ○

LCDUS ○

OTHER Eastern Orthodox churches

◯ Pre-Congregation

✝ Often represented in her quest to find the 'True Cross'

Helena was the mother of Constantine, the East Roman emperor from 306 who, in 313, by the Edict of Milan, made Christianity the official religion of the empire. She became an exceptionally devout Christian. As well as establishing a series of lavish religious foundations in the Holy Land, in 325 in Jerusalem, on the site of what was said to have been Calvary, the place of Christ's crucifixion, Helena apparently discovered the remains of the Cross on which Christ had died, as well as the nails that had held Him to it. These almost instantly became the most prized relics in Christendom, brought back to Rome by Helena and housed in what today is the church of Santa Croce in Gerusalemme. They remain there today, tiny slivers of wood, whose authenticity remains tantalizingly unknowable.

St. Helena's search for the 'True Cross' was celebrated by the artist Piero della Francesca (c.1460).

AUGUST 20 ✤ BERNARD OF CLAIRVAUX

STATUS Abbot, Founder, Doctor of the Church

BORN 1090, Fontaines, France

DIED 1153, Clairvaux, France

GRC ♠

CofE ♠

LCDUS ♣

◯ 1174

✝ White Cistercian habit, often shown carrying three miters, or bearing book and pen, trampling a demon

⚖ Beekeepers, wax-makers

A stained-glass window showing Bernard at prayer.

Bernard was one of the most active and influential churchmen of his day. He was born to a wealthy Burgundian landowning family, but at age 23 he decided to join the monastery at Cîteaux, accompanied by four of his brothers and some 27 friends. It was a time when the Rule of Benedict, which guided monastic communities for around 500 years, was falling into misuse, and Bernard did much to restore and reform its use. Such was Bernard's ability and enthusiasm that he was ordered to found a new monastery at Clairvaux, where he became abbot, a position he retained for the rest of his life – refusing three offers of bishoprics. It was from Clairvaux that a new monastic vigor emanated, carried by the Cistercians, who by the time of Bernard's death had founded or converted over 300 monastic communities throughout Europe and the British Isles.

A Man of Influence

In spite of his preference for a withdrawn life of contemplation, Bernard was very active in public affairs, mediating between the Cluniac and Cistercian monks, and in the controversial papal election of 1130. He argued vigorously against the teachings of Peter Abelard, preaching against the Albigensian heresy in its Languedoc heartland, and promoting the Second Crusade. He was also involved in securing papal approval for founding the Knights Templar.

Bernard was a prolific writer, writing *De consideratione*, a treatise on the papal office and the curia for one of his former monks who was elected Pope Eugenius III in 1145. His *On Loving God* and *On the Song of Songs* remain widely read today, his eloquence earning him the sobriquet 'Doctor Mellifluous.' He was made a Doctor of the Church in 1830.

MONASTICISM IN EUROPE

Monasticism – the gathering of devout men and women in discrete communities for the common observance and celebration of their religion – is characteristic of many faiths. The initial impetus in the Christian world for monasticism was provided by Pachomius in Egypt in the 4th century (May 9). In western Europe the key figure was Benedict in Italy in the 6th century (July 11). The 'Rule of Benedict' dominated almost every subsequent monastic movement. Cluny, the most influential monastic community in early medieval Europe, was avowedly Benedictine and came to be the model for the monastery – a substantial foundation, independent of the king or state, sustained by huge holdings of land worked by peasants, and its monks able to devote themselves to lives of prayer, contemplation, and learning.

The Cistercians were formed in 1098 by St. Bernard, just as Cluny was losing its influence, in order to reinvigorate the precepts of Benedict. Similar monastic reforms provoked the foundation in the 13th century of three further orders: the

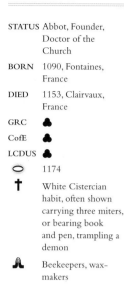

The ruins of Fountains Abbey in Yorkshire, England, a spectacular example of a Cistercian monastery, destroyed by Henry VIII.

Franciscans, the Dominicans, and the Augustinians. These orders loomed large over later medieval Europe. The crucial difference, most obviously espoused by Francis of Assisi, founder of the Franciscans (Oct. 4), was their embrace of poverty; these were mendicant monks (friars), dependent not on well-endowed foundations to sustain them, but on their acceptance of poverty and a willingness to preach.

Monasticism in medieval Europe, subject only to God and the papacy, was a vital prop of society, guarding learning, providing succor, and offering redemption. For 500 years or more, it was a constant of life. In northern Europe, the Reformation brought it to a sudden end, uprooting centuries of tradition. During the French Revolution, what was left of Cluny was obliterated in the name of a new deity: Rationalism. Monastic foundations still exist, but they are now peripheral to most European societies.

AUGUST 21 | PIUS X

STATUS Pope
BORN 1835, Riese, Italy
DIED 1914, Rome, Italy
GRC ♣
CofE ♧
LCDUS ♠
♥ 1951
◯ 1954

Giuseppe Melchiorre Sarto was born to a poor family in the northern Veneto; entering the church was a good option at the time, and he was ordained in 1858. He served as a rural pastor until he was appointed chancellor to the bishop of Mantua in 1875, succeeding to the see nine years later, and reviving the city's fortunes. In 1893 he was appointed patriarch of Venice, often an indication of a future papacy, and indeed he was elected pope in 1903.

His principal concerns involved reform of the Church to combat modernist tendencies. He is seen as an extreme conservative, weeding out dissent and disobedience within the clergy. However, he reorganized the Roman curia, developed a revised Code of Canon Law, and encouraged greater cooperation between the Church and the laity. His death almost exactly coincided with the outbreak of World War I in Europe and, like many things during that period, his ideological legacy was largely swept away by this tumultuous event.

AUGUST 22 | QUEENSHIP OF THE BLESSED VIRGIN MARY

This relatively recent Marian feast, celebrating the Virgin's crowning as Queen of Heaven, follows rapidly (and logically) after the feast of the Assumption of the Blessed Virgin Mary (Aug. 15). Formerly celebrated on May 31, it was instituted by Pope Pius XII in 1954.

AUGUST 23 | ROSE OF LIMA

STATUS Virgin
BORN 1586, Lima, Peru
DIED 1617, Lima, Peru
GRC ♠
CofE ♧
LCDUS ♠
◯ 1671
🙏 Florists, Peruvian social services; Peru, South and Central America, the West Indies, the Philippines

Born to a middle-class but poor Spanish colonial family, Rose was baptized Isabel de Flores, but an Indian servant remarked that as a baby Isabel was *"como una rosa,"* (like a rose) and the name was adopted. As a girl she worked hard to help support her family, taking in needlework and selling dried flowers. At the same time, she took Catherine of Siena (April 29) as a spiritual mentor, undertaking severe penances of self-flagellation and extreme fasting, which induced visions; like Catherine, her penances also provoked vomiting, and she was probably bulimic. Rose became a Dominican tertiary at age 20, and retreated to a hermitage in her parents' garden, where she slept on broken tiles. She took over some rooms in the family home to create an infirmary for the destitute, children, Indians, slaves, and the elderly, which boosted her cult in Lima. She died at age 31, probably as a result of her deprivations. Rose was the first canonized saint of the Americas. Her story is similar to that of her close contemporary St. Mariana Paredes y Flores (d.1645) from Quito in Ecuador.

Date	Name	Status	Venerated	Life
Aug. 20	William Booth (1829–1912)	Founder	CofE	With his wife Catherine, founded the Salvation Army (1878), British evangelical movement targeting the burgeoning urban poor. Spread gospel on the street through sermons and music, and provided hostels for the homeless. Movement became global in early 20th century.

AUGUST 24 | BARTHOLOMEW

STATUS Apostle

BORN Early 1st century AD

DIED Mid-1st century AD

GRC ♣

CofE ♣

LCDUS ♣

OTHER Eastern Orthodox churches

○ Pre-Congregation

✝ Being flayed, bearing a flaying knife, sometimes flayed and carrying his skin

🙏 Tanners and leatherworkers

Bartholomew's emblem is a flaying knife, referring to his presumed manner of martyrdom. He is often shown carrying his skin (below).

In truth, little is known about Bartholomew, except that he is mentioned in all the lists of the Twelve Apostles that appear in the New Testament. Some analysts identify him as the man Nathaniel, who is introduced to Jesus by the Apostle Philip.

Bartholomew is later thought to have preached in Mesopotamia, Persia, and possibly India, although accounts of his particularly gruesome martyrdom — being flayed before decapitation — place the event at Derbend (Albanopolis) in upper Armenia, on the shores of the Caspian Sea.

His relics were translated eventually to Rome, and are claimed by the church of St. Bartholomew on the Tiber. King Canute's wife apparently donated one of Bartholomew's arms to the see of Canterbury in the 11th century, which explains the enormous popularity of his cult in medieval England, where over 160 churches were dedicated to him. St. Bartholomew's Hospital in London is one of the world's leading medical training centers.

Bartholomew is often represented after being flayed, and sometimes bearing his own skin.

THE FATE OF THE HUGUENOTS

St. Bartholomew's Day is now more frequently associated with the massacre of Huguenot Protestants in France on August 24, 1572, one of the first and most brutal incidents in the Reformation wars of religion. The massacre started as a series of targeted assassinations of leading Huguenots on St. Bartholomew's eve, planned by Catherine de' Medici, the mother of the French king, Charles IX. Only a few days earlier, Charles's sister, Margaret, had married Henry III of Navarre, a leading Protestant. The bloodshed spread throughout France, lasting some three weeks, and resulted in the deaths of between 3,000 and 5,000 Huguenots. The survivors fled to the Netherlands and England.

Date	Name	Status	Venerated	Life
Aug. 25	José de Calasanz (1557–1648)	Educator, Founder ♥ 1748 ○ 1767	GRC By Piarists 🙏 Schools, students	Ordained in 1583. Served in several administrative roles in Spain before moving to Rome (1592) where he set up free schools for the poor. Founded Congregation of the Pious Schools (Piarists) dedicated to teaching for all. Support for philosophers Galileo and Campanella led, in part, to downfall in 1646. Great influence on St. John Bosco (Jan. 31).

AUGUST 25 — LOUIS IX OF FRANCE

STATUS King
BORN 1214, Poissy, France
DIED 1270, Tunis, North Africa
GRC ♣
CofE ○
LCDUS ♣
○ 1297
† As a regal knight, crowned, with fleur-de-lis
🙏 Barbers, printers, stonemasons; France

King Louis' genuine devotion, even-handed fairness, and sense of justice made him the most adored of French monarchs.

Louis succeeded to the French throne at age eleven in 1226 upon the death of his father Louis VIII, although his mother acted as regent for the next nine years. He married Margaret of Provence in 1234, and took control of his kingdom in 1235. Renowned as a just and fair Christian ruler, his reign saw the flowering of French Gothic culture, and the creation of institutions such as the Sorbonne. He gave generously, and established hospitals. Louis also founded the exquisite Sainte-Chapelle on the Ile de la Cité to house the relic of Christ's Crown of Thorns, donated by the crusader Baldwin. Louis was not free from the prejudices of the age and, for instance, in 1269 he decreed that Jews should wear a red badge on their clothing to distinguish them.

In 1244, Louis embarked on a crusade, capturing the city of Damietta in the Nile delta, but was himself captured, and then only freed after returning the city to Muslim hands and paying a huge ransom. Undeterred, he launched a further Crusade in 1270 against the Muslims of Tunisia. The venture turned into a disaster after an outbreak of typhoid, from which Louis himself died. His relics were taken back to France by his son, Philip the Bold, and are interred at St.-Denis in Paris.

Despite his inadequacies as a military leader, Louis is frequently portrayed in triumphant martial attitudes.

SAINT LOUIS

Date	Name	Status	Venerated	Life
Aug. 26	Elizabeth Bichier des Ages (1773–1838)	Nun, Founder, Social Reformer ○ 1947	By Daughters of the Cross	Born in France. In early life worked caring for the poor. Encouraged by Andrew Fournet to found a community, the Daughters of the Cross. By 1825 the community numbered 25 nuns. Within a decade, 60 convents opened across France, part of huge spread of orders dedicated to social welfare in 19th century.

AUGUST 27 | MONICA

STATUS Widow

BORN 331, Tagaste, North Africa

DIED 387, Ostia, Italy

GRC ♣

CofE ♣

LCDUS ♣

OTHER Eastern Orthodox churches

○ Pre-Congregation

† Widows' clothes or black nun's habit

⚘ Mothers, wives, various mothers' associations

Monica is important as the mother of St. Augustine of Hippo (Aug. 28, *below*), and it is largely from his *Confessions* that we know of her. Raised as a Christian, she married Patricius, a wealthy but dissolute pagan, and they had three children. Her patience eventually led Patricius to convert shortly before his death in 371. She had less immediate success with her oldest son Augustine, who took after his father, and despite her entreaties refused to be baptized. Argument failing, she set an example of piety through fasts, prayer, and vigils. Augustine left for Rome, and Monica set off after him, catching up with her son in Milan, where she also met St. Ambrose (Dec. 7). Together, through logic and enlightenment, they convinced Augustine to convert, and he was baptized in 387. On the return journey to Africa, Monica died at Ostia, where her relics remain in the church of Sant'Agostino, although they were briefly translated to Arrouaise, where the Austin Canons promoted her cult.

Monica is normally shown wearing a black nun's habit, reflecting her role as a widow.

AUGUST 28 | AUGUSTINE OF HIPPO

STATUS Bishop, Doctor of the Church

BORN 354, Tagaste, North Africa

DIED 430, Hippo Regius (Bône), modern Annaba, Algeria

GRC ♣

CofE ♣

LCDUS ♣

OTHER Eastern Orthodox churches, US Episcopal and Evangelical Lutheran churches

○ Pre-Congregation

† Usually as a bearded bishop, with book, often accompanied by a flaming heart pierced by arrows

⚘ Theologians, printers, brewers; against sore eyes

Despite a late conversion, baptized at 33, largely due to the persistence of his Christian mother, Monica (Aug. 27, *above*), Augustine emerges as one of the towering thinkers and theologians of the early medieval church.

He studied law and rhetoric at Carthage and became deeply involved in Platonic philosophy. He joined the heretical Manichaean sect, which renounced the scriptures of the Old Testament and saw existence as a continuing struggle between the equal powers of good and evil. In 383 he left North Africa to teach rhetoric in Rome. A year later he was appointed professor of rhetoric in Milan. Here he met St. Ambrose (Dec. 7) and under his influence, and that of his mother who had joined him, he came to understand that it was possible to resolve the teachings of the Bible with Platonic ideas. In 386, Augustine retired to live a communal contemplative life with students and his family near Milan. He rejected Manichaeism and within a year he returned to Milan, and under Ambrose's guidance, prepared for baptism.

Augustine returned to Tagaste to set up a monastic community of laymen on his family's estate. In 395, Augustine was appointed bishop of Hippo. Over the next 34 years, he developed the model of an episcopal ministry, being actively involved in pastoral, ecclesiastical, and even lay legal matters. However, it is in his writings that his greatest influence was embedded: more than 200 of his letters survive, and 113 books and treatises, including his autobiographical *Confessions, The City of God*, and *On the Trinity*. These provided strong doctrinal arguments on innumerable issues including the nature of divine grace, creation, and the sacraments, and condemnations of heresies such as Donatism, Manichaeism, and Pelagianism.

Augustine is ranked as one of the four original western Doctors of the Church, along with Ambrose (Dec. 7), Jerome (Sept. 30), and Gregory the Great (Sept. 3).

Augustine's emblem of a flaming heart pierced by arrows represents his religious ardor and devotion after his conversion.

· QVM· M. OBITV BEATI AVGVSTINI AQVAMPLVRIMIS EIVS ANIMA INCELIS COMITANTIBVS ANGELIS FERRI VISA E·T·

By the time of his death, Augustine was a major figure throughout the western Christian world. This fresco of his funeral by Bennozo Gozzoli is in Florence. The dead saint is surrounded by Augustinian monks and many other Church elders.

AUGUST 29   THE BEHEADING OF JOHN THE BAPTIST

There is an enduring fascination about John the Baptist's life (*see* June 24) and his gory fate. Like his protégé Jesus, John fearlessly and fatally courted controversy. The story of his imprisonment and death is told in the Gospels of Matthew, Mark, and Luke. John publicly accused the Jewish ruler Herod Antipas of adultery and incest upon Herod's marriage to Herodias (Herod's niece, and his brother's ex-wife). Herodias demanded John's imprisonment. At a birthday banquet, Herod was enthralled by the erotic dancing of his stepdaughter, Salome, and offered to grant her any wish.

Herodias, seeking yet greater vengeance on John the Baptist, told her daughter to demand John's head on a platter. Reluctantly, Herod complied with her wish.

John's relics, all of dubious provenance, are spread widely, the most important being a fragment of his skull in Würzburg, Germany, and another (apparently entire) skull in Amiens Cathedral, France, purportedly brought there by crusaders in the 12th century. However doubtful these relics might be, the representation of St. John's disembodied head in many forms perpetuates his cult.

Late 19th-century artists such as Gustave Moreau were interested in the erotic allure of Salome's demand for John's head on a platter as a reward for her dancing (above).

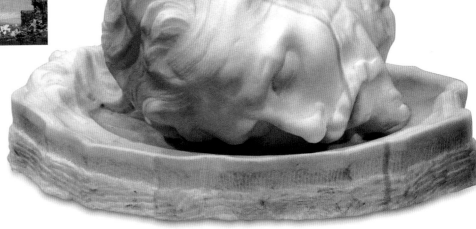

The Severed Head of John the Baptist by Auguste Rodin (1875). Given Rodin's dedication to Realism, this was probably a representation of a guillotined criminal's head.

Date	Name	Status	Venerated	Life
Aug. 30	John Bunyan (1628–88)	Preacher, Writer	CofE By Nonconformists and Baptists	Active in Bedfordshire, England. Fought for Puritan Parliamentarians during English Civil War, then launched career as non-conformist preacher. Frequently imprisoned, especially after Restoration, for preaching without a license. Began his allegorical dream autobiography *The Pilgrim's Progress* in jail.
Aug. 31	Aidan of Lindisfarne (d.651)	Missionary, Abbot ⬤ Pre-Congregation	✝ Stag or torch	Irish missionary who worked initially on Iona, then was invited to evangelize Northumbria. Established egalitarian monastery on Lindisfarne with support of King Oswald, where he trained many other missionaries.

SEPTEMBER

With the gathering of the harvest and the autumnal equinox occurring in the northern hemisphere, September also marks the Indiction, the beginning of the Eastern Orthodox Church year. The Nativity of the Blessed Virgin Mary (or the *Theotokos* — meaning God-bearer — as she is named by the Orthodox churches) is celebrated by most denominations on September 8. The Exaltation of the Holy Cross is observed on September 14, and the following day is devoted to Our Lady of Sorrows.

September 29, known as Michaelmas, is a day of recognition for the actions and achievements of the archangels Michael, Raphael, and Gabriel, the principal messengers of God in the earthly realm. The day was traditionally associated with the payment of agricultural rents and church tithes.

Although angels rather than saints, Michael, Raphael, and Gabriel are celebrated in much the same way. Their lively representation by Francesco Botticini (c. 1446–98) includes the figure of Tobias, with his dog and fish, whose encounter with Raphael is related in one of the books of the apocryphal Book of Tobit.

SEPTEMBER 1 | GILES OF PROVENCE

STATUS Hermit
BORN c.650, Athens, Greece
DIED c.710, Languedoc, France
GRC ○
CofE ♣
LCDUS ○
OTHER Church of Scotland
○ Pre-Congregation
† Arrow, hermitage, hind
🙏 Forests, horses, rams, hermits, beggars; cancer victims, the disabled, the mentally ill, sufferers from epilepsy; Edinburgh

Giles was a Greek hermit, probably legendary, who settled in a forest near Nîmes in the south of France. His only companion was a deer that fed him with milk. Hunted one day by a local king, known as Wamba, the deer took shelter with Giles, who was then wounded by an arrow intended for the animal. Wamba was so impressed by the hermit's humility and sanctity that he built him a monastery, St.-Gilles-du-Gard, where the saint eventually died.

Giles was one of the most venerated of saints in the Middle Ages. St.-Gilles-du-Gard itself became a major place of pilgrimage, not least as a stop on one of the many pilgrimage routes to Santiago de Compostela in northern Spain (*see* July 25). Numerous miracles were ascribed to his shrine. His relics were also claimed to have been widely distributed across Europe. He is also traditionally one of the Fourteen Holy Helpers, those saints invoked for aid against a variety of illnesses. St. Giles' Cathedral in Edinburgh, consecrated in 1243, is the most imposing medieval church in the Scottish capital.

St. Giles and the Hind from an altarpiece (c.1500) by a Flemish painter known only as the Master of St. Giles. Here the king, Wamba, has been elevated to the king of France. St. Giles, an arrow in his right hand, comforts the deer after the king has chased it.

SEPTEMBER 1 | FIACRE

STATUS Hermit
BORN 7th century, Ireland
DIED c.670, Breuil, France
GRC ○
CofE ○
LCDUS ○
OTHER In France
† Pilgrims, spade
🙏 Gardeners, plowboys, taxi drivers, tile-makers; sufferers from venereal disease and hemorrhoids

Fiacre was a hermit in Ireland so renowned as a herbalist and healer that he removed himself to France to escape the increasing numbers of those who came to consult him. It is said that once in France, he asked permission from bishop Faro in Meaux in the northeast of the country to build a hermitage for himself, a chapel in honor of the Blessed Virgin Mary, and a hospice for travelers. Faro replied that Fiacre could have as much land as he could plow in a single day. The

saint miraculously plowed so much land that a woman accused him of witchcraft, a claim Faro instantly rejected but which led Fiacre to ban all women from his hospice and chapel. Though best known as the patron saint of gardeners, he also gave his name to a form of carriage or taxi, a *fiacre*, developed in the 17th century by the owners of the Hôtel de St.-Fiacre in Paris. His cult was among the most vigorous in France well into 17th century. Louis XIV is said to have invoked Fiacre during a particularly severe illness.

A 15th-century statute of St. Fiacre, spade in hand, in the Church of St. Taurin in Evreux, Normandy.

Date	Name	Status	Venerated	Life
Sept. 2	Patriarch John IV (d.595)	Bishop ○ Pre-Congregation	Eastern Orthodox churches	Due to great self-denial, known as 'John the Faster.' First self-proclaimed ecumenical or 'universal' patriarch of the Eastern Christian Church. This title downgraded authority of other bishops in Eastern Church and directly challenged authority of the pope in Rome. Brought him into direct conflict with Pope Gregory I, significantly undermining fragile unity of early Christian church.

SEPTEMBER 2

THE MARTYRS OF PAPUA NEW GUINEA

STATUS Martyrs
BORN 19th/20th centuries
DIED 1901, 1941–45, Papua New Guinea
GRC ⬠
CofE ♣
LCDUS ⬠
OTHER In Papua New Guinea, Australia

Among the many victims of Japan's aggressive Asian and Pacific conquests in World War II were an estimated 272 Christians in Papua New Guinea, which was invaded by the Japanese in December 1941. The exact numbers remain disputed, but it is believed that the dead included 189 Catholics, 26 Methodists, 23 members of the Salvation Army, 20 Lutherans, 12 Anglicans, and two Seventh Day Adventists. Following the invasion, the Catholic bishop of Papua, Alain de Boismeau, and the Anglican bishop, Philip Strong — at this stage clearly unaware of the Japanese attitude to conquered (and thus by definition inferior) peoples — had urged their various missionaries, priests, nurses, and teachers not to flee to neighboring Australia. In the ringing words of Bishop Strong: "We would never hold up our faces again if, for our own safety, we all forsook Him and fled … the church in Papua." It has subsequently emerged that a number of those killed, including an Anglican priest, Vivian Redlich, were killed by Papuans rather than by the Japanese, their motive apparently resentment at their forced conversions to an alien religion. Those executed by the Japanese were mostly beheaded. In 1993, the Catholic Church beatified the native New Britain priest Peter To Rot, born in 1912, who was lethally injected by the Japanese in 1945. His feast day is July 7.

The Church of England also marks this day for several Anglican missionaries killed by native Papuans in 1901.

During World War II, Japanese anti-colonial propaganda frequently played on the themes of Christianity and the supposed depravity of Westerners. In this leaflet, nubile white women dance among the cemetery markers of dead Allied soldiers.

SEPTEMBER 2 & 3

THE BLESSED MARTYRS OF SEPTEMBER

STATUS Martyrs
BORN Mid-18th century
DIED 1792, Paris, France
GRC ⬠
CofE ⬠
LCDUS ⬠
OTHER In France
♥ 1926

The convulsions of the French Revolution included the legal murder by the embryonic republican French state of between 16,000 and 40,000 members of the Ancien Régime between June 1793 and July 1794. This bloodbath was presaged in September 1792 by the deaths of 191 Catholic priests in an outbreak of extraordinary and improbable violence in Paris. Those killed in the 'September Massacres' were already prisoners of the state, arrested after refusing to swear an oath of loyalty passed in July 1790 that effectively stripped the pope of his authority in France. That the Church in France was a natural target of the Revolution was understandable. It enjoyed — and exploited — privileges that placed it at the center of the Ancien Régime. It was believed to be immensely wealthy. For the new apostles of the Age of Reason, it was also a bastion of superstition. None of this entirely explains the savagery that accompanied the killings. Those arrested were held in three main locations in Paris: the Carmelite monastery in the rue de Rennes, the seminary of St. Fermin, and the abbey of St.-Germain-des-Prés. A kind of collective mob frenzy appears to have sparked the bloodletting. Those killed, among them the archbishop of Arles and the bishops of Beauvais and Saintes, were collectively beatified by Pope Pius XI in 1926.

An illustration, published in 1862 in France, of the September Massacres. The Catholic priesthood was not the exclusive target of the mob; many aristocrats were also killed.

IVORIES

Delicately carved ivories were among the most precious devotional items during the Middle Ages. Few have survived undamaged. They usually took the form of elaborate book covers or folding tabernacles, which were designed to be light and portable, allowing the owners to take the tabernacle as a movable altar on their travels.

This well-preserved 10th-century ivory book cover (left) of Gregory the Great (Sept. 3), depicts him writing as the dove of inspiration sits on his shoulder. Below him, scribes copy his words. The substantial buildings in the upper tier represent the rebuilt city of Rome over which Gregory presided.

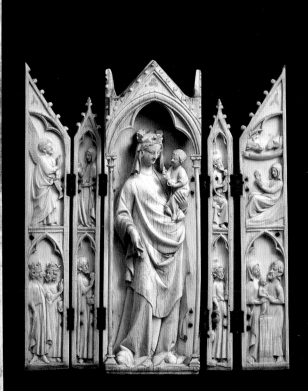

Folding tabernacles, such as these exquisite examples, often celebrated the life of the Blessed Virgin Mary. This 14th-century German example (above) depicts the Annunciation on the top left panel, the Nativity on the top right, and the Adoration of the Magi across the lower panels, framing the magnificent central image of the Madonna and Child. The tabernacle (left) produced in France in the 14th century, although simpler, beautifully conveys the intimate nature of the Holy Family.

SEPTEMBER 3   GREGORY THE GREAT

STATUS Pope, Doctor of the Church

BORN c.540, Rome, Italy

DIED 604, Rome, Italy

GRC ♣

CofE ♣

LCDUS ♣

OTHER Eastern Orthodox churches

○ Pre-Congregation

† Usually shown writing, or with quill and scroll; Holy Spirit in form of dove at his ear

♔ Teachers

Gregory's complex arms represent, in the upper banner, his guardianship of the Roman Church, the three bands below symbolizing his monastic foundations, the primacy of his office, and his reform of church music.

> "I am the servant of all bishops so long as they live like bishops."
>
> FROM GREGORY'S LETTERS.

The medieval Catholic Church, based in Rome, presided over by the pope, was the most powerful and prestigious institution in Europe, whose authority, temporal as much as spiritual, was immense. Even if only nominally, every Christian emperor, king, and prince owed allegiance to it. This was ancient Rome recast, a vast enterprise that critically shaped and determined the nature of what could now properly be called Christendom. Where once it had been Rome's emperors who directed the fate of Europe, in the Middle Ages it was the city's popes. The man responsible for this extraordinary transformation was Gregory the Great.

There was nothing inevitable about any of this. That Gregory, appointed pope in 590, was an exceptionally able administrator was clear: he wrote, directed, and instructed relentlessly, reshaping liturgical practices, setting up elaborate mechanisms for the relief of the poor, dismissing recalcitrant clergy, routing out heretics and schismatics, and dispatching missions to pagan lands. But he became pope at a moment when Italy had suffered well over a century of barbarian incursions that had almost entirely broken down the final remnants of Roman imperial control. Such imperial rule as did exist was based in Constantinople. The imperial court was not merely distant, it was increasingly inward-looking: worldly, sumptuous, and less and less interested in the fate of Rome. It was also the site of an Orthodox Christian Church presided over by a patriarch who, since the near-contemporary rule of Patriarch John IV (Sept. 2), was now proclaimed the 'universal' head of the Church.

The Struggle for Supremacy

Gregory's response to Constantinople's attempt to reassert its authority in Rome was devastatingly effective. He ignored it. He cast himself as the direct heir of St. Peter, the first bishop of Rome, appointed by Christ himself: "I, albeit unworthy, have been set up in command of the Church," he said.

On his own authority, Gregory negotiated peace treaties with the Lombards, the semi-pagan Germanic invaders of Italy, and he appointed a new ruler of Naples when it, too, was threatened by the Lombards. He also oversaw the consolidation of what would emerge as the Papal States, a swath of territory in central Italy, answerable to the pope, which endured until the 19th

Gregory's fame rests significantly on the substantial number of his writings that have been preserved, including 850 of his letters. This 10th-century Anglo-Saxon manuscript illustration is a precise example of a cult that reinforced the notion of Gregory as an indefatigable man of letters.

century. Of equally lasting significance, Gregory, himself a Benedictine monk, presided over an enormous surge in support for monastic communities, which were responsible to the pope alone, in many parts of Europe. He instituted Latin as the liturgical language of the Western Church, and plainsong (the Gregorian chant) as its devotional soundtrack. Perhaps most important of all was his wooing of the emerging Frankish empire in France and Germany. It was a decisive shift away from Rome's historical Mediterranean focus in favor of northern Europe, a trend reinforced by Gregory's decision in 596 to send St. Augustine to England to convert the Anglo-Saxons.

Date	Name	Status	Venerated	Life
Sept. 4	Rose of Viterbo (1235–51)	Nun, Visionary ○ 1457	In Viterbo, Italy	At age three, said to have brought her aunt back to life. At seven, claimed to have been visited by the Virgin Mary, who instructed her to join the Franciscan Tertiaries to preach against the Holy Roman Emperor Frederick III; subsequently banished from Viterbo. In neighboring Vitorchiano, claimed to have banished a sorceress by standing unharmed in a fire for three hours. Once allowed to return to Viterbo, spent rest of her short life in prayer, penance, and fasting. Accurately foretold her death. Her body, paraded every year through the streets of Viterbo on her feast day, found to be incorrupt.

SEPTEMBER 4

ALBERT SCHWEITZER

STATUS Missionary, Doctor
BORN 1875, Alsace-Lorraine, Germany/France
DIED 1965, Lambaréné, Gabon
GRC ☁
CofE ☁
LCDUS ☁
OTHER US Lutheran Church

A middle-aged Schweitzer at his mission in Lambaréné.

Rather like Dr. Livingstone before him, despite Schweitzer's isolation in a remote part of Africa, he became an instantly recognizable, world-famous humanitarian.

Albert Schweitzer could be considered the most startling polymath of the 20th century. He was a musician and the world's leading expert on Bach's organ music; a theologian, author in his 20s of a radical re-evaluation of the historical reality of Jesus; a Lutheran curate; a university teacher; and finally a missionary and doctor in one of the most deprived regions of West Africa. In 1913, at age 38, he opened a hospital for lepers in Lambaréné on the banks of the muddy river Ogooué in French West Africa. Lambaréné was as remote and unpromising a spot as anywhere in Africa – isolated, impoverished, and disease ridden. The hospital's main building was a hastily converted chicken hut. Schweitzer remained there for much of the rest of his long life.

Schweitzer was driven partly by his Christian faith, and partly by what he called "reverence for life," the belief that all sentient beings are worthy of respect. In reality, he often seemed more 19th-century patrician colonialist than 20th-century man of mercy. "The African is indeed my brother but my younger brother," he said. If such seemingly patronizing statements of European superiority jar today, measured against a life given over to such obvious good works, Schweitzer can still reasonably be claimed among the most remarkable of 20th-century Christians. He was awarded the Nobel Peace Prize in 1952.

Albert Schweitzer, seen here in an etching made in the 1950s by Arthur William Heintzelman, became notably crustier as he grew older, given to rapping out peremptory demands to his black workers, parading his sanctity and his wisdom a little too obviously for some.

SEPTEMBER 4

BIRINUS

STATUS Bishop, Missionary
BORN c.600, France
DIED 650, Dorchester, England
GRC ☁
CofE ♣
LCDUS ☁
○ Pre-Congregation
† Shown baptizing a king
⚶ Berkshire, Dorchester

Birinus, sent to England in 634 by Pope Honorius I, played a key role in spreading Christianity across Wessex in the southwest of England, after St. Augustine's initial Christianizing mission to Kent in 596.

Birinus's most notable convert was Cynegils, the king of Wessex, and later the king's son and grandson. Cynegils subsequently awarded Birinus the settlement of

Dorchester-on-Thames as the seat of his diocese. Birinus established a series of churches, particularly at Dorchester itself, where he was buried, and later at Winchester, the capital of Wessex and new seat of the diocese of the kingdom.

A 19th-century stained-glass window of St. Birinus in Dorchester Abbey.

SEPTEMBER 5 | MOTHER TERESA OF CALCUTTA

STATUS Nun, Missionary

BORN 1910, Skopje, Macedonia

DIED 1997, Calcutta, India

GRC ☁

CofE ☁

LCDUS ☁

OTHER By the Missionaries of Charity; in India, Macedonia

❤ 2003

✝ White sari, with blue bands

🙏 World Youth Day

Mother Teresa's determination to embrace the poor elevated her to an iconic status. In reality, she was a much more troubled – and troubling – figure than her popular image allows.

The Blessed Teresa of Calcutta, Mother Teresa to the rest of the world, was born to Catholic Albanian parents in what today is Macedonia, which was then part of the Ottoman empire. She became one of the best-known humanitarians of the 20th century. The Missionaries of Charity, established by Teresa in 1950 in the slums of Calcutta, is today one of the world's foremost charitable foundations. When she died, it boasted 610 missions in 123 countries and over one million volunteer workers. Its goal remains to offer succor to the needy and the sick, wherever and whoever they may be. Teresa's inspiration was simple: "I was to ... help the poor while living among them. It was an order. To fail would have been to break the faith." As knowledge of the diminutive Teresa, invariably dressed in a white sari with blue bands, spread from the early 1970s onward, she was increasingly feted and showered with honors, including the 1979 Nobel Peace Prize 'for work undertaken in the struggle to overcome poverty and distress.' Her beatification in 2003 will certainly lead to her canonization.

Teresa's vocation was evident from at least the age of 12. When she was 18, she joined the Sisters of Loreto, first in Ireland then, as a teacher, in India, where she took her vows as a nun in 1931. At that time she adopted the name 'Teresa' after St. Thérèse of Lisieux (Oct. 1). Her move to Calcutta (modern Kolkata) was a brutal introduction to the horrors of Indian urban poverty, above all during the great Bengal famine of 1943, when an estimated three million people died. She worked there, under an increasing spotlight of celebrity, for the rest of her long life.

A Troubled Sanctity

For all the evident sanctity of Mother Teresa, she remains a controversial figure. As was pointed out even during her lifetime, she was less interested in saving lives than in saving souls. Her insistence that suffering was "a gift of God" and her absolute opposition to abortion, for example, troubled many, especially given the large number of indentured prostitutes in her parish.

Similarly, many of her hospitals were criticized for the often shoddy levels of medical care that they provided, with untrained volunteers expected to act as doctors and nurses, and elementary standards of hygiene routinely ignored. The mission's finances also remain opaque. In addition, whatever her absolute, almost fanatical, support of the Catholic Church, for much of her life she was assailed by a crisis of faith. "Where is my faith? Even deep down ... there is nothing but emptiness and darkness ... If there be God," she wrote, "please forgive me." So candid and despairing a statement was a remarkable testimony for a woman who was alternately decried as a 'fundamentalist' and a 'fraud,' and as often invoked as an indisputable modern saint.

Mother Teresa was a familiar and popular figure on the streets of Calcutta, wearing her distinctive white sari with blue bands and head covering, adapting local clothing to a nun's habit.

Date	Name	Status	Venerated	Life
Sept. 5	Bertin the Great (d.c.709)	Monk, Missionary ◯ Pre-Congregation	In Normandy, France	With two companions, Mommolin and Ebertran, evangelized in northeast France around what today are towns of Calais and Boulogne. Built a series of churches and monasteries, including that subsequently known as St. Bertin's, where Bertin himself was abbot. Said to have lived to age 110.
Sept. 6	Bertrand de Garrigues (d.1230)	Monk ❤ 1881	By Dominicans In France	One of first Dominicans (ordained 1215), and close companion of St. Dominic himself (Aug. 8), with whom he journeyed in southern France in Dominic's crusade against the Albigensians. First head of the order's Priory of St. Jacques in Paris.

THE MARTYRS OF KOŠICE

SEPTEMBER 7

STATUS Martyrs
BORN 1580s
DIED 1619, Košice, Slovakia
GRC ☁
CofE ☁
LCDUS ☁
OTHER By the Jesuits; in Slovakia
♥ 1905
◯ 1995

During the Thirty Years' War, which bloodily divided Europe both religiously and politically during the 17th century, a group of three Jesuit priests – Marko Krizin, a diocesan priest, and two Jesuits, Stefan Pongrácz and Melchior Grodziecki – were working in Košice, today in Slovakia, but at the time under Hungarian rule. Krizin, a Croatian, was the head of the Benedictine abbey of Zeplak outside Košice. Pongrácz and Grodziecki had only recently been sent to Košice, where, like Krizin, they worked assiduously on behalf of the city's beleaguered Catholic majority, who faced persecution by the city's much more numerous and vehemently anti-Catholic Calvinists. All three were arrested in 1619 by

a Calvinist army, imprisoned, and ordered to renounce their Catholic faith; when they refused, they were horribly tortured and then executed. They were beatified in 1905 and canonized in Košice by Pope John Paul II in 1995.

Krizin, born in 1588 near Zagreb, is only the third Croatian to have been canonized. The canonization of all three saints in 1995 was attended by a crowd of 300,000.

ANTOINE FRÉDÉRIC OZANAM

SEPTEMBER 7

STATUS Lawyer, Founder
BORN 1813, Milan, Italy
DIED 1853, Marseille, France
GRC ☁
CofE ☁
LCDUS ☁
♥ 1997

Ozanam, a lawyer, and then a professor of literature at the Sorbonne in Paris, was one of the most important influences on the Catholic Church in mid-19th-century France. It was a period when the Church was still struggling to reassert itself in the face of the bitter anti-clericalism fostered by the French Revolution. Ozanam argued that, whatever its shortcomings, the Church had nonetheless been an overwhelming force for good in the shaping of medieval and modern Europe. Yet he also recognized that it had to adapt if it was to have meaning in an increasingly industrialized world. He was a staunch advocate of papal authority. In 1833, at age only 20, he was a co-founder of the Society of St. Vincent de Paul, an organization dedicated to tackling poverty and want.

Ozanam's health was frail throughout his life. He died of consumption at age 40 on his return from Italy, which he had visited in the hope that its climate would help him counteract the illness.

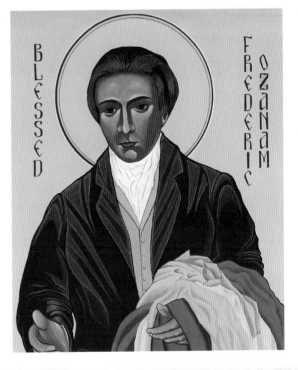

BLESSED FRÉDÉRIC OZANAM

Date	Name	Status	Venerated	Life
Sept. 7	Sozon of Cilicia (d.c.304)	Martyr ◯ Pre-Congregation	Eastern Orthodox churches	Shepherd who converted to Christianity. Inspired in a dream to break off the hand of a gold statue of the Greek god Artemis in a temple dedicated to her, and to distribute proceeds among the poor. Confessed his crime to local governor, Maximian, to prevent punishment of a group of Christians falsely accused. Beaten, chained to a tree, had nails driven into his shoes, and finally flung onto a fire. Numerous miracles ascribed to his tomb.

SEPTEMBER 8 | THE NATIVITY OF THE BLESSED VIRGIN MARY

Important in the cycle of Marian feast days, the Nativity of the Blessed Virgin Mary originated in the Eastern Church, but became established in the West under Pope Sergius I (r.687–01), who also instituted feasts for Mary's Annunciation (March 25), the Presentation at the Temple (Nov. 21), and the Assumption (Aug. 15). The birth of Mary is not recounted in the Bible, and the principal source is the apocryphal 2nd-century *Protoevangelium of James*, which tells the story of her parents, Sts. Anne and Joachim (July 26).

The Nativity of the Blessed Virgin Mary is a popular feast in the Eastern Orthodox churches. This icon depicting the event was painted in Poland in the 15th century.

SEPTEMBER 9 | PETER CLAVER

STATUS Priest, Missionary
BORN 1581, Verdú, Spain
DIED 1654, Cartagena, Colombia
GRC ♣
CofE ◯
LCDUS ♣
OTHER US Evangelical Lutheran Church
♥ 1850
◯ 1888
✝ Usually shown in Jesuit robes ministering to African-American slaves
♪ Slaves, African-Americans, Colombia

Peter Claver was born to a poor family in Catalonia, but aspired to a university education in Barcelona, where he encountered the Society of Jesus. He joined the order in 1602 and moved to the Jesuit college in Majorca. There he was advised to seek his vocation in the New World. He was sent to Cartagena, on the Caribbean coast of Colombia, in 1610, and was ordained in 1616, working under the Jesuit Father Alfonso de Sandoval.

Cartagena was one of the principal slave ports in Spanish America, with some 10,000 souls passing through its markets each year. Peter undertook to minister to the slaves as the ships from Africa arrived, often in terrible conditions, feeding them and treating any wounds or sickness before they were sold on. Peter is estimated to have baptized over 300,000 African-Americans. He also traveled inland to visit his converts on the plantations where they worked, lodging in the slaves' quarters. Peter also visited British and French prisoners of war. He died following four years of illness, neglect, and seclusion.

"The Slave of the Slaves."

PETER'S DESCRIPTION OF HIS VOCATION.

Peter Claver's compassion for the victims of the slave trade means he is still widely revered throughout the Caribbean and the American South.

SEPTEMBER 10 — NICHOLAS OF TOLENTINO

STATUS Friar

BORN 1245, Ancona, Italy

DIED 1305, Tolentino, Italy

GRC ⬭

CofE ⬭

LCDUS ⬭

⬯ 1446

† In Augustinian robes, often bearing bread

⚶ Mariners, mothers and babies, animals, souls in Purgatory; the Philippines

The fame of this Augustinian friar and preacher resides less in his extensive pastoral work than in the many visions and miracles associated with him. Once when ill from fasting, he had a vision of the Blessed Virgin Mary, who instructed him to eat a particular type of bread roll, soaked in water. He later distributed these, and St. Nicholas Bread is still made in Italy today.

Nicholas was said to have raised over 100 children from the dead, been beaten by the devil with a stick, have brought a roasted fowl back to life (he was a vegetarian), and saved the Doge's Palace in Venice from burning by throwing holy bread on the flames.

Nicholas's devotion to the Blessed Virgin Mary means he is often represented bearing her symbol, a lily.

One of Nicholas's most popular miracles involved saving a sinking ship during an Adriatic storm.

Date	Name	Status	Venerated	Life
Sept. 9	Charles Fuge Lowder (1820–80)	Priest, Founder	CofE	Oxford-educated churchman, influenced by Newman and Oxford Movement. Ordained 1843. Founded the Society of the Holy Cross (1855) to bring succor to the poor, homeless, and destitute in London's Soho and East End docklands. Almost prosecuted for Catholic practices, his work for sufferers during cholera epidemic in 1866 earned him sobriquet the 'Father of Wapping.'
Sept. 11	Protus and Hyacinth (late 3rd century–early 4th century)	Martyrs ⬯ Pre-Congregation	Eastern Orthodox churches	Popular in medieval Europe, but little known for certain about these two saints. Possibly brothers, possibly eunuchs in the Egyptian court. Referred to as 'teachers of Christian law' in some martyrologies. Often associated with the Roman widow and convert Basilla, with whom they were said to have been beheaded, probably during persecutions of Maximian.
Sept. 11	Theodora of Alexandria (d.c.490)	Penitent ⬯ Pre-Congregation	Eastern Orthodox churches ⚶ Taming wild animals	Adulteress who repented of her sins, and joined a monastery disguised as a man, under the name Theodore. Her real identity was only revealed after her death. Her relics were regarded as miraculous.

SYNCRETIST RELIGIONS IN THE AMERICAS

The introduction of Catholicism to the New World, with its intrinsic veneration of saints, produced some interesting crossover or syncretist cults. In Guatemala, the country with the highest surviving Maya population in Central America, Catholic saints have been blended with pre-Columbian cult figures. Among the West African peoples who were transported across the Middle Passage as slaves, saints were often fused with traditional African divine beings and practices, producing the Caribbean religions of Voodoun, Santeria, and, in Brazil, Candomblé.

Guatemalan cult figures are dressed in a combination of Western and indigenous clothes and fabrics. Among the most powerful in the Guatemalan canon is Maximón (right), sometimes also called Jesús Malverde, and sometimes San Simón after an early Catholic priest who legendarily helped the native Maya. Offerings are made to Maximón in the form of cash and tobacco.

The cult of Santeria is based in Cuba and is a product of the overlaying of Catholic saint veneration with West African beliefs, mainly originating from the Yoruba tribes of West Africa. Among its pantheon of orishas (deities) are Shango and Ogun. La Santísima (left), also known as Doña Sebastiana or Santa Muerte, is an interesting variation on the theme of the Blessed Virgin Mary and mortality. Santeria is closely linked to the Yoruba tradition of Candomblé.

Perhaps the most notorious of the region's syncretist religions is that of Voodoun, principally based in Haiti, but originating from the religions of the Fon peoples of Benin. Here Christian imagery is almost inextricably entangled with West African magical practices. Lurid tales of possession, sexual frenzy, animal sacrifice, and raising 'zombies' from the dead have done little to diminish its powerful allure as a popular cult. Voodoun amulets and totem figures (above), often combined with Christian crucifixes, feathers, bones, and other materials, are regarded as propitious.

STEVE BIKO – MARTYR FOR RACIAL INJUSTICE

The 20th century saw many fall foul of oppressive regimes. In the fight for equal rights for blacks in South Africa, allegations of terrorist activities cast something of a shadow over Nelson Mandela's reputation, although few doubt his moving dedication to the outcome of his cause, especially as South Africa's first black premier. But, while Mandela was serving out his long imprisonment on Robben Island, Steve Biko (1946–77) was the most high-profile and articulate anti-apartheid campaigner and activist in South Africa, founder in the late 1960s of the Black Consciousness Movement.

In 1977, Biko was beaten to death, repeatedly clubbed on the head, by the South African police. His death – initially claimed by the police to be the result of a hunger strike, the following year ruled by a South African court to have been a suicide attempt – resounded around the world, generating huge headlines and earning South Africa an even greater degree of global opprobrium. In 1997, five members of the South African police admitted that they had killed Biko.

Biko is celebrated around the world as the most prominent martyr of apartheid in South Africa, and also for his pithily memorable assertion that 'black is beautiful.'

The Black Consciousness Movement, directly inspired by Gandhi and by Dr. Martin Luther King, Jr., though avowedly political, and committed to the overthrow of South Africa's white supremacist ruling National Party, was also an actively Christian organization, though the extent to which Biko genuinely subscribed to the doctrine of non-violence is open to doubt. At all events, Biko was a key figure in the Soweto uprising in the winter of 1976. During the uprising, South African security forces gunned down what are estimated to have been between 200 and 600 of the protestors.

By 1973, Biko had already been forbidden to take part in any political activities. After Soweto, he was a marked man. When he was arrested the following August, picked up at a road block, he was beaten and then driven, naked and bleeding, almost 1,000 miles in the back of a police van to a hospital-prison in Pretoria. He died shortly after he arrived, on September 12, 1977.

SEPTEMBER 13 — JOHN CHRYSOSTOM

STATUS Bishop, Doctor of the Church

BORN c.347, Antioch, modern Turkey

DIED 407, Pontus, modern Turkey

GRC ♣

CofE ♣

LCDUS ♣

OTHER Lutheran Church, Eastern Orthodox churches

⊖ Pre-Congregation

✝ Bishop's robes; beehive, white dove

⚕ Educators, preachers; against epilepsy; Constantinople/ Istanbul

John was a towering figure of the early Church, a dynamic preacher, a tireless campaigner against paganism, and a vehement, often controversial, critic of what he considered abuses inside and outside the Eastern Church. His name Chrysostom, apparently bestowed after his death, means 'golden-mouthed.' His influence – and popularity – rested not merely on the potency of his preaching but on its straightforwardness. In 398, having already served 12 years as a priest in Antioch, he was made archbishop and patriarch of Constantinople, but he accepted the position with reluctance. The position not only obliged him to live amid the splendors of the imperial court, but also brought him into immediate contact with those who opposed him. The patriarch of Alexandria, for example,

Theophilus, had long schemed to assert his religious authority over Constantinople. John as frequently clashed with the empress Eudoxia, whose extravagances and high-living John consistently, perhaps tactlessly, deplored. In 403, Theophilus and Eudoxia succeeded in having John briefly banished. In 404, he was banished again, despite the best efforts of Pope Innocent I to have him reinstated. He was eventually exiled to a remote outpost of the Eastern Empire but died en route. John Chrysostom's relics were brought back to Constantinople in 438. In 1204, they were taken to Rome during the Fourth Crusade, when Constantinople was sacked. In 2004, Pope John Paul II had them returned to what had by then become Istanbul.

An 11th-century soapstone relief of John Chrysostom, today in the Louvre, Paris. His criticism of the rich was a consistent theme of his life. "It is not possible for one to be wealthy and just at the same time," he wrote.

Date	Name	Status	Venerated	Life
Sept. 12	Ailbe (d.c.528)	Bishop ⊖ Pre-Congregation	In Ireland	Early Irish saint, probably mythical. Only account of his life dates from eight centuries after his death. Said to have pre-dated St. Patrick (March 17), though the claimed date of Ailbe's death is 70 years after Patrick's. Son of a slave and a king of Munster, who ordered him to be put to death, but executioner gave him to a wolf, who raised him. Later traveled to Rome, where he was ordained a bishop by the pope. In Ireland again, established monastery at Emly. Supposedly baptized St. David (March 1). When Ailbe died, was carried off on a ghostly ship.

SEPTEMBER 14

THE ELEVATION OF THE CROSS

The Elevation of the Honorable and Life-giving Cross, sometimes known as the Exaltation of the Cross, is one of the most important feasts of the Orthodox Christian calendar. First it commemorates the finding of the 'True Cross,' the cross on which Jesus was crucified, by St. Helena (Aug. 18) in the fourth century. More particularly, it marks the recovery (by Emperor Heraclius in 627) of those fragments of the cross that had been removed from Jerusalem by the Persians after their conquest of the city in 614. In 630, Heraclius triumphantly restored the fragments to Jerusalem. When the city fell to the Muslims in 637, however, they were hastily brought to Constantinople. The feast is marked by fasting and prayer.

St. Helena, mother of the first Christian Roman emperor, Constantine, and finder of the fragments of the 'True Cross,' is commemorated in a monumental statue in the crossing of St. Peter's, Rome.

The Orthodox cross is conventionally represented with three bars: at the top, a short bar on which was nailed the mocking notice, 'Jesus of Nazareth, King of the Jews;' the main bar to which his outstretched arms were nailed; and an angled bar lower down on which his feet rested.

EXALTATION OF THE HOLY CROSS

Hagia Sophia ('Holy Wisdom') in Istanbul, Turkey, was built between 532 and 537 by Emperor Justinian, a startlingly potent statement of Constantinople's power and sanctity. For 1,000 years it was easily the largest church in the Christian world. In 1453, the Muslim Sultan Mehmed II converted the basilica to a mosque.

THE GREAT SCHISM

Christianity was a religion whose origins were Middle Eastern. It was in the Middle East, as well as in nearby Egypt and Ethiopia, that it made early headway. Yet, founded at almost the height of the Roman empire, Christianity also rapidly spread westward via Greece to Rome, the capital of the empire. For much of the next millennium, whatever Christianity's claims to universality, the Western and Eastern churches were engaged in an uneasy struggle for supremacy. It climaxed in 1054 in a full schism, or split, that endures today.

Origins of the Schism

The schism's causes were partly political, doctrinal, and cultural, and partly a simple matter of geography. First, the formal division of the Roman empire in the early 4th century into separate West and East Roman empires encouraged the churches in their respective spheres to develop differently. Equally, the disintegration of the Western empire in the late 5th century led to a power vacuum in Italy that only the papacy was strong enough to fill.

By the 8th century, the papacy had decisively allied itself to Charlemagne's new Holy Roman Empire. More and more, the papacy was turning its back on Rome's traditional Mediterranean and eastern focus and seeking to take advantage of emerging powers in northern Europe. In Roman terms, Constantinople was looking increasingly alien and increasingly vulnerable to Persian and Muslim incursions.

The divisions were highlighted by persistent doctrinal differences, above all over the nature of the Trinity – the exact relationship between God the Father and God the Son – and by a growing linguistic divide. The language of the Western Church by now was Latin, that of the Eastern Church, Greek. No less divisive was the bitter argument over iconoclasm in the 8th century. There were also disputes over whether the clergy should be celibate.

The Western Church emerged stronger after 1054. The Eastern Church, by contrast, was from 1453 traumatically subsumed within the Ottoman Muslim world.

SEPTEMBER 15 | OUR LADY OF SORROWS

The feast of Our Lady of Sorrows commemorates the seven most sorrowful moments of the Blessed Virgin Mary's life. Most are connected with the Crucifixion and death of her son, Jesus. If Mary was uniquely blessed by having been chosen as the mother of Christ, she was also uniquely cursed, given that the end point of His ministry on Earth was to atone for humanity's sins by being put to death on the Cross. The Virgin's inevitable fate was therefore essentially sorrowful, encapsulating not simply the unbearable pain of any mother forced to confront the death of a child, but one whose death was preordained from the moment of His birth. The following episodes in Mary's life are commemorated on this date: the prophecy of Simeon immediately after Christ's birth that her son would be sacrificed; the flight to Egypt to escape Herod's command that all newborn children in Bethlehem be killed; Jesus's three-day disappearance at the age of 12, when He was found disputing with elders in the temple in Jerusalem; the meeting of Jesus and Mary on His way to His Crucifixion; the Crucifixion itself; His descent from the Cross; and, finally, His burial.

A 17th-century statue of Our Lady of Sorrows in the Basílica de la Macarena in Seville, Spain, her heart pierced, in accordance with Simeon's prophecy, by seven swords.

SEPTEMBER 16 | CORNELIUS

STATUS Pope, Martyr
BORN Early 3rd century
DIED 253, Civitavecchia, Italy
GRC ♣
CofE ♢
LCDUS ♣
⬭ Pre-Congregation
⚕ Against hearing ailments, epilepsy

Cornelius succeeded Pope Fabian (Jan. 20), who was martyred in 250 during the Decian persecutions. The election of a new pope was postponed until the persecutions subsided (Decius died campaigning in 251), and in the meantime the Church was administered by a council whose spokesman was a presbyter called Novatian. Although Cornelius ruled for little more than two years, he had to contend not merely with a further round of persecutions of the infant Church, but a potentially damaging schism led by Novatian. The split centered on whether those who had renounced their faith when threatened with execution

Cornelius's arms incorporate an unusual variant of the papal crucifix; usually the lower crossbar is wider than the middle one.

could be received back into the Church. Novatian, who declared himself antipope in opposition to Cornelius, maintained they could not; Cornelius argued that true repentance was sufficient. Cornelius was able to muster ample support for his position (including that of Cyprian of Carthage, who shares this feast day, *see below*) and thereafter had Novatian excommunicated. His triumph proved short-lived. In 252, Cornelius was exiled by the new emperor, Trebonianus Gallus. He died the following year from mistreatment during his exile, although other reports claim he was beheaded.

SEPTEMBER 16 | CYPRIAN OF CARTHAGE

STATUS Bishop, Martyr
BORN c.200, Carthage, Tunisia
DIED 258, Carthage, Tunisia
GRC ♣
CofE ♣ (Sept. 15)
LCDUS ♣
⬭ Pre-Congregation

This contemporary of Pope Cornelius (*see above*) was a powerful voice in the many doctrinal disputes that beset the Church in the early 3rd century. He trained as an orator and lawyer in his home city, and was ordained and elected bishop of Carthage, soon falling foul of the Decian persecutions. He fled the city, and in 251 was accused by local pagans of invoking a plague, despite giving succor to the afflicted. Cyprian's compassion and humanity became clear when he supported Cornelius in his dispute with the antipope Novatian concerning his freely readmitting repentant Christians who had apostatized during the Decian persecutions. He later came into dispute with Pope Stephen I (r.254–57) when Cyprian supported the view that repentant heretics and

schismatics need not be rebaptized. Stephen died before a potential rift occurred.

Cyprian was an obvious target during the renewed Christian persecutions under Emperor Valerian. Accounts of his trial reveal a restrained and courteous man; twice he refused to apostatize, and was beheaded, but not before greeting his executioner and giving him a generous gift.

Cyprian's crown of martyrdom is combined with the supposed tool of martyrdom, although swords were more usually employed at the time.

SEPTEMBER 17 | ROBERT BELLARMINE

STATUS Bishop, Cardinal,
Doctor of the
Church

BORN 1542, Montepulciano,
Italy

DIED 1621, Rome, Italy

GRC ♣

CofE ○

LCDUS ♣

♥ 1923

○ 1930

🙏 Canon lawyers,
catechists

Robert Bellarmine, ordained a Jesuit priest in 1569, was among the most distinguished and able of Counter-Reformation theologians. He combined immense learning with an acute appreciation that the authority of the Roman Church had to be underpinned by much greater rigor and discipline on the part of its clergy if it was to withstand the Reformation's challenge. As a theologian, he is best remembered for his *Disputationes*, a vast three-volume work published between 1581 and 1593 that sought to place the doctrinal authority of the Church on a solid legal footing. It was perhaps the most important and authoritative defense of the Church of the 16th century. As a senior churchman, a cardinal, an inquisitor from 1599, and archbishop of Capua from 1602, he became in effect an enforcer of papal authority: in 1616, for example, on the instructions of Pope Paul V, he forced Galileo to renounce the Copernican doctrine that the Earth revolved around the Sun.

In 1931, in recognition of his contribution to Counter-Reformation doctrines, Robert Bellarmine was declared a Doctor of the Church.

SEPTEMBER 17 | HILDEGARD OF BINGEN

STATUS Abbess, Mystic,
Philosopher,
Composer

BORN c.1098, Germany

DIED 1179, Bingen,
Germany

GRC ○

CofE ○

LCDUS ○

Hildegard was among the most remarkable figures of the medieval church: a mystic, herbalist, composer, and author. She was placed in a Benedictine convent at possibly as young as age eight. Here she underwent a regular series of visions, which lasted throughout an unusually long life. In 1136, she became abbess of the convent. In 1150, after a lengthy dispute with the abbot at Disibodenberg, she founded a new convent at Rupertsberg. She opened another such convent at Eibingen in 1165.

In 1141, she claimed she had been ordered by God to record her visions, though they caused her great physical and emotional torment. The result was the *Scivias* ('Know the Way'), an immensely long and vividly illustrated account of 26 such religious visions. She subsequently wrote two further such works. Hildegard is famed, too, as a composer: almost 80 musical works by her have survived. She also wrote widely on the medical uses of plants. By her death, she was among the most celebrated figures in Christendom. Though popularly known as a saint, she has never been canonized.

Hildegard undergoing a vision and dictating to a scribe, in an illustration from the Scivias. *Hildegard described her visions as the "shade of the living light." Her emphasis on this light has led to the suggestion that her visions may have been a form of migraine.*

Date	Name	Status	Venerated	Life
Sept. 16	Ninian (d.c.432)	Bishop, Missionary ○ Pre-Congregation	CofE In Scotland	Converted the Picts of southern Scotland. Since the Middle Ages has been venerated as the 'Apostle of the Picts.' Many churches dedicated to him across southern Scotland, northern England, and on the Isle of Man.
Sept. 16	Edward Bouverie Pusey (1800–82)	Priest, Tractarian	CofE	One of leading figures of Victorian High Anglican Oxford Movement (or Tractarians). Prolific writer and supporter of the daily practice of Holy Communion, confession, and penance, and the revival of the medieval veneration of relics.

SEPTEMBER 18   JOSEPH OF CUPERTINO

STATUS Monk, Mystic

BORN 1603, Cupertino, Italy

DIED 1663, Osimo, Italy

GRC ☁

CofE ☁

LCDUS ☁

OTHER By Franciscans

♥ 1753

○ 1767

† Crucifix, Franciscan habit, levitating

☈ Astronauts, aviators, the mentally handicapped, students

Joseph was from all accounts a simpleton, scarcely capable of even the simplest of tasks, who nonetheless had a profoundly mystical streak that manifested itself most memorably by bouts of uncontrollable levitation. It is said that even the sound of church bells was enough to send him into religious raptures from which it was almost impossible to bring him down to earth. It was this sanctity that led to his being ordained a Franciscan. As news of the 'Flying Friar' spread, he became an object of fascination, drawing ever-larger crowds. The Church, increasingly embarrassed that this vacant figure was rapidly becoming the focus of a cult, did its best to hide him in remote and obscure monastic foundations. For the last 30 years of his life, he was a virtual prisoner. He was much given to self-mortification, fasting, and prayer.

There are many artistic representations of levitating friars. This painting captures the bewildering wonder of Joseph's affliction.

SEPTEMBER 20   THE KOREAN MARTYRS

The Korean Martyrs' deaths were not in vain. Today, though Christianity can scarcely be said to exist at all in Communist North Korea, there are over 5 million Korean Catholics in South Korea, comprising ten percent of the population. The mass canonization in 1984 instantly elevated Korea to fourth in the list of those countries with the greatest number of Catholic saints.

In 1984 in Seoul, the capital of South Korea, Pope John Paul II canonized 103 Korean martyrs, 79 of whom had been beatified in 1925 and a further 24 in 1968. Eleven of them were priests, the majority French. The remaining 92 were lay Catholics. They were no more than a handful of representatives of the 8,000 Christians estimated to have been martyred in 19th-century Korea, chiefly in persecutions in 1839, 1846, and 1866. The first priests to enter Korea, in 1836, were members of the Paris Foreign Missions Society. They were amazed to discover a thriving if small Christian community already active in Korea, converts of lay Chinese Catholic missionaries, who had begun secretly entering Korea from about 1784. Nineteenth-century Korea was an intensely inward-looking, almost feudal society, its rulers determined to resist Western incursions, of which Christianity not unreasonably appeared an early outrider. Equally reasonably, Christianity was almost instantly seen as a direct threat to the country's Confucianism, in which ancestor worship was both a chief tenet and a crucial underpinning of the ruling nobility's claim to legitimacy. Reprisals against Christians were savage and swift.

Among the martyrs are three French priests: Pierre Philibert Mauban, the first priest to enter Korea; Laurent Imbert, the first bishop of Korea; and Jacques Honoré Chastan, all members of the Paris Foreign Missions Society and all tortured and beheaded in 1839. The martyrs also include the first native Korean Catholic priest, Andrew Kim Taegon, who was beheaded in 1846, only 13 months after his ordination, and Paul Chong Hasang, one of the lay founders of the Catholic Church in Korea.

SEPTEMBER 20 · EUSTACE

STATUS Martyr
BORN 1st century AD, Italy
DIED 118, Italy
GRC ◇
CofE ◇
LCDUS ◇
OTHER Eastern Orthodox churches
♥ Pre-Congregation
✝ Bulls, crucifixes, stags
🙏 Firemen, hunters; Madrid

Eustace was a Roman general known as Placidus, who was confronted by a vision of a stag with a crucifix in its antlers. His conversion to Christianity was instant, and upon his baptism he took the name Eustace. His new faith led to the loss of his fortune, the kidnapping of his wife, the death of his servants in a plague, and the eating of his sons by a wolf and lion. He was killed with the rest of his family by being burned alive in a bronze ox during an early Roman persecution. There is little evidence for his existence, but his story was popularized by Voragine's *Golden Legend* (c.1260).

Eustace, transformed into an early Renaissance soldier, prays before the crucifix in the stag's antlers. An engraving by Dürer from c.1501.

SEPTEMBER 20 · SAINTS, MARTYRS, AND MISSIONARIES OF THE PACIFIC

The death of Patteson sparked a renewed missionary effort in the South Pacific. In 1881, a church in Melanesia was consecrated in his memory, shown here in a contemporary illustration from The London Illustrated News.

As early as 1794, a missionary attempt was launched in Tahiti. It was followed by similar efforts in New Zealand in 1814, Hawaii in 1820, and Tonga in 1822. It was a daunting undertaking: the attempted imposition of a wholly alien doctrine over a vast, little-known area, the greater majority of whose peoples had had no contact with the West in any form. A number of organizations, chiefly British and French, Protestant and Catholic alike, spearheaded the attempt.

The challenge of converting a patchwork of remote, insular (and often indignant) cultures was considerable. Several figures stand out in this epic endeavor. One is the ill-fated Marist Peter Chanel (April 28), clubbed to death in Futuna in 1841. John Coleridge Patteson, a high-born Anglican parson, ordained in 1853, was persuaded in 1855 to join the Melanesian Mission. He proved an inspired choice, a cheerful and resourceful figure who embraced his calling with zeal. In 1861, he was appointed bishop of Melanesia. Yet his fate was strikingly similar to his French counterpart's. In 1871, in an act that would provoke outrage in Britain, natives in the Solomon Islands murdered Patteson as a protest against the abduction by white men of a number of islanders, apparently taken as slaves.

Date	Name	Status	Venerated	Life
Sept. 19	Januarius (d.c.305)	Bishop, Martyr ○ Pre-Congregation	GRC, Eastern Orthodox churches ✝ Blood, Mt. Vesuvius 🙏 Blood banks; against volcanic eruptions; Naples	Priest at 15. Said to have been made bishop of Naples at 20. Beheaded under Diocletian after initially being sentenced to be eaten by wild bears. Relics dispersed until reunited at Naples Cathedral (1497). They were famed for the regular liquefaction of his blood (Sept. 19, Dec. 16, and the eve of first Sunday in May); this miracle apparently averted eruption of Vesuvius in 1631.
Sept. 19	Theodore of Tarsus (c.602–90)	Bishop ○ Pre-Congregation	CofE, Eastern Orthodox churches	Greek scholar, calligrapher, and churchman, appointed archbishop of Canterbury (668) by Pope Vitalian. Instituted reform of English Church. In 673, called the Synod of Hertford, which as at Whitby (664), reaffirmed Roman practices over Celtic (Irish) practices. Revived link between learning and the priesthood, opening an ambitious school in Canterbury under Adrian (Jan. 9).

MATTHEW THE APOSTLE AND EVANGELIST

STATUS	Apostle, Evangelist
BORN	Early 1st century AD, Galilee, modern Israel
DIED	Late 1st century AD
GRC	♣
CofE	♣
LCDUS	♣
OTHER	Eastern Orthodox churches
◯	Pre-Congregation
✝	A winged man; with money bags or box; sometimes shown wearing spectacles, or with a quill or pen, book or manuscript; with tools of martyrdom (sword, spear, or halberd)
🙏	Tax collectors, accountants, bankers, customs officials, stockbrokers, security guards; Ethiopia

Matthew was a Jewish tax collector at Capernaum in the employ of the Romans when he was called to become an Apostle by Christ. In his own Gospel, Matthew describes the event pithily: " … [Jesus] saw a man, named Matthew, sitting at a receipt of custom: and he saith unto him, Follow me. And he arose, and followed him." (Matthew 9:9). Later, Christ is described as dining with other tax collectors, who were regarded as sinners by the Jewish authorities. Jesus rebuked them: "I am not come to call the righteous, but sinners to repentance." (Matthew 9:13).

Matthew is referred to as Levi in the Gospels of Mark and Luke, and as the son of Alpheus, and possibly as the brother of James the Less (May 3). Although he appears in all lists of the Twelve Disciples, and it is assumed that he is present when all twelve are involved in Christ's story, he is not associated with any particular event. It is thought that he continued to spread the word in the Holy Land after the Resurrection until the persecutions of Herod Agrippa (AD 42), and then traveled to evangelize in either Parthia, Persia, or Ethiopia. Although there is little early evidence to support his martyrdom, most Roman martyrologies attest to it, but with varying details and locations.

The Gospel

Matthew is regarded as the author of the first Gospel (although there has been some debate that the Gospel of Mark may precede it). It was probably written after Matthew left the Holy Land, and probably before AD 70. It is succinct in style and designed to be read aloud. This tone reveals Matthew as an accurate but modest observer and recorder of the events that unfolded around him. Matthew's Gospel is the principal source for the Annunciation, the Adoration of the Magi, the slaughter of the innocents, Christ's temptation in the wilderness, His recruitment of the first Apostles around the Sea of Galilee, and the Sermon on the Mount. Matthew's description of Christ's Passion and Resurrection has a gripping narrative quality. He describes several parables and miracles with all the zeal of an eyewitness. Matthew's main purpose in writing the Gospel appears to have been to record events and the teachings of Jesus, and thereby to announce that with the coming of Jesus, the Kingdom of God is at hand, and will remain so for eternity — a message aimed at non-believers and converts alike.

The Calling of St. Matthew *uses a setting more closely suggesting a 17th-century tavern of gamblers than a Biblical tax collector's office. It is typical of Caravaggio's frequent use of contemporary settings and dress to convey a sense of immediacy to the scene. This painting and* The Martyrdom of St. Matthew (opposite) *were painted for Cardinal Matteo Contarelli, and can be found in the Contarelli Chapel in San Luigi dei Francesi in Rome.*

Often mistaken as representing an angel, St. Matthew's crest in fact shows a winged man, representing the possibility of divine inspiration for all human beings.

One of a series of intimate paintings of the Evangelists by Caravaggio, The Inspiration of St. Matthew *draws on the central element of Matthew's divine guidance in composing his Gospel.*

"Why are ye fearful, O ye of little faith?"

JESUS TO THE DISCIPLES DURING A STORM ON THE SEA OF GALILEE (MATTHEW 8:26).

The lack of any reliable detail concerning the alleged martyrdom of St. Matthew allowed Caravaggio free scope to create a moving yet violent composition. It is thought that the face in the background, emerging from the shadows behind the executioner, is a self-portrait of the artist.

SEPTEMBER 23 | PADRE PIO OF PIETRELCINA

STATUS Friar

BORN 1887, Pietrelcina, Italy

DIED 1968, San Giovanni Rotondo, Italy

GRC ♣

CofE ♧

LCDUS ♣

OTHER By Capuchins

♥ 1999

◯ 2002

✝ A bearded Capuchin, usually smiling

"Pray, hope, and don't worry."

PADRE PIO.

A young Padre Pio clearly showing the marks of the stigmata on his hands. He often wore mittens to protect them.

Born Francesco Forgione, Pio was ordained a Capuchin monk in 1910. His health was always precarious, but from 1918 he bore the marks of the stigmata for the rest of his life. Despite this, Pio remained unbelievably active; he was said to have heard some 25,000 confessions a year, and his humble but approachable, indeed amicable, attitude made him one of the most popular figures in the Italian Catholic Church in the 20th century. To some extent he reveled in his popularity – no bad thing in a century of turbulence – and in 1956 Pio established the Casa Sollievo della Sofferenza, a center for biomedical research, in the town where he lived and died, San Giovanni Rotondo in the southeastern Puglia region of Italy. The town has now become a major modern pilgrimage center.

MARTYRS OF THE SPANISH CIVIL WAR

The election of a Republican government in Spain in 1931, after decades of extreme political turbulence, eventually provoked the Spanish Civil War (1936–39). The elected leftist Republican, or Popular Front, government saw the Catholic Church as one of the bulwarks of ancien régime control. The war bitterly divided a very traditional society. When the Nationalist rebellion under General Franco began in 1936, Catholic priests became a soft target for the Republicans. Churches and shrines were desecrated, and soon the clergy was openly attacked. In total, over 6,500 priests and over 230 nuns were killed.

The Martyrs of Valencia, priests, friars, and sisters who were slaughtered in the province, were beatified by Pope John Paul II in 2001, with a feast day on September 22. Since then, a further 500 martyrs of the Spanish Civil War have been beatified.

SEPTEMBER 23 | THECLA OF ICONIUM

STATUS Virgin, Martyr

BORN 1st century AD, Iconium, modern Turkey

DIED 1st century AD, Syria

GRC ◯

CofE ◯

LCDUS ◯

OTHER Eastern Orthodox churches (Sept. 24)

◯ Pre-Congregation

✝ With lions or serpents, or by a hand emerging from a cave

🙏 Tarragona, Spain; Este and Milan, Italy

Thecla's story is largely apocryphal, deriving from the 2nd-century *Acts of St. Paul*, with whom she is closely associated. She cancelled an arranged marriage, vowing chastity, and was immediately persecuted: Thecla miraculously survived being burnt, thrown to the lions, torn apart by bulls, and being cast into a pit of venomous snakes. She eventually retired to a cave to avoid further persecution. Only her hand emerged from a fissure in the cave's walls to perform healing miracles. She was widely regarded in the Middle Ages as an exemplar of the highest virtue. Her cult was adopted in Spain during the *Reconquista*.

Thecla managed to avoid several potential martyrdoms by displaying her crucifix. When thrown to the lions, they ceased roaring and licked her feet.

iNo pasarán!

The colorful, but doomed, Spanish Popular Front, combining republicans, radicals, anarchists, communists, and international anti-fascists, also contained a strong anti-clerical contingent.

Date	Name	Status	Venerated	Life
Sept. 22	Thomas of Villanova (1488–1555)	Bishop ◯ 1658	In Spain	Senior Spanish Augustinian churchman, ordained in 1518. Known for preaching skills, integrity, and understanding that charity, especially to the poor, was best served by alleviating the cause of their problems. Lived a personally frugal life, giving own clothing and bedding to the poor. Sent first Augustinian missions to Spanish New World. Bishop of Valencia from 1544, converting Moors, among others.
Sept. 24	Pacificus (Pacifico) of San Severino (1653–1721)	Friar ♥ 1786 ◯ 1839	By Franciscans	Orphaned at age 3. Franciscan monk, ordained in 1678. For half a decade worked as missionary among peasants of Ancona, Italy. Soon developed lameness, and went blind and deaf, but continued his vocation for 30 more years until his death.

SEPTEMBER 24 — GERARD SAGREDO (GELLÉRT OF CSANAD)

STATUS Bishop, Martyr
BORN c.980, Venice, Italy
DIED 1046, Buda, Hungary
GRC ☁
CofE ☁
LCDUS ☁
OTHER In Hungary
◉ 1083
🙏 Hungary

The formidable, evangelizing monument to Gerard now dominates the western end of the Liberty Bridge in Budapest.

A learned Benedictine monk, trained in Bologna and Venice, Gerard determined to make a pilgrimage to the Holy Land. He traveled east overland via Hungary. The king, St. Stephen (Aug. 16), convinced him to remain there, with Gerard tutoring Stephen's son, St. Emeric. Gerard then entered a hermitage until Stephen established the see of Csanad, with Gerard (called Gellért by the Hungarians) as its bishop. Gerard energetically set about evangelizing the divided kingdom, but on Stephen's death he became a target for anti-Christian factions. He was captured in Buda, and cast from the cliffs into the Danube, possibly in a barrel lined with nails.

Gerard was canonized on the same day as King Stephen and Emeric, and with them is a patron saint of Hungary. Gerard's relics were translated to Venice in 1333.

SEPTEMBER 25 — SERGIUS OF RADONEZH

STATUS Abbot
BORN c.1315, Rostov, Russia
DIED 1392, Sergiyev Posad, Russia
GRC ☁
CofE ♣
LCDUS ☁
OTHER Eastern Orthodox churches, US Episcopal Church
◉ 1452
✝ Usually shown as a monk with abbot's staff
🙏 Russia

One of Russia's leading saints and an early mystic, Sergius's greatest achievement was the revival and reform of the monastic (cenobite) tradition. Baptized Bartholomew, as a youth his wealthy family fled Rostov when threatened by the Tartars, becoming farmers at Radonezh, north of Moscow. Upon their parents' death, Sergius and his brother Stefan became forest hermits, but soon developed a community of disciples, building a chapel and, in 1345, a monastery of wooden shelters where they reconstituted the Rule of Theodore the Studite.

Sergius went on to found around 40 more monasteries and his original foundation became the heart of northern Russian Orthodoxy and missionary activity. Today, his foundation, the Holy Trinity St. Sergius Lavra Monastery at Sergiyev Posad (formerly Zagorsk), is a major Russian pilgrimage center. Sergius has been called the Francis of Assisi of Russia, as his love of nature, sympathy for

Sergius blessing the crusade against the Tartars by the prince of Moscow, Dmitri Donskoi, in 1380.

peasants, apparently mystical visions, and overwhelming humanity draw strong parallels with the founder of the Franciscan Order.

Date	Name	Status	Venerated	Life
Sept. 25	Lancelot Andrewes (1555–1626)	Bishop, Translator	CofE	Senior Anglican career churchman, educated at both Oxford and Cambridge. Later master of Pembroke College, Cambridge, and bishop of Chichester, Ely, and Winchester. Supervised translation of the King James, or Authorized, version of the Bible, published 1612.
Sept. 26	Elzéar (1285–1323) and Delphine (1284–1358)	Virgins ◉ Pre-Congregation	By Franciscans	Elzéar of Sabran was a French nobleman who entered a diplomatically arranged marriage to Delphine, already a nun. Couple became Franciscan tertiaries, undertaking vows of celibacy, self-mortification, and charity. Elzéar became important figure in French intervention in Italian affairs, leading an army against Rome. Both buried in Apt in Provence, France.

SEPTEMBER 26   COSMAS AND DAMIAN

STATUS Martyrs

BORN   Mid-3rd century,
        Arabia

DIED   c.287, Syria

GRC   ♣

CofE   ○

LCDUS   ♣

OTHER   Eastern Orthodox
        churches

○   Pre-Congregation

✝   With surgical
        implements

⚕   Physicians, nurses,
        surgeons, dentists,
        apothecaries,
        barbers, the blind;
        against hernias
        and pestilence; the
        Medici family

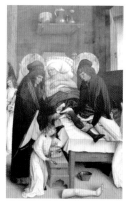

One of the demonstrations of the medical skills of Cosmas and Damian involved Justinian, suffering from a withering leg ailment, who had his leg amputated by them. They miraculously attached a replacement from a black corpse, fortunately assisted by angels.

L ittle is known for certain about Cosmas and Damian. They were brothers, possibly twins, probably born in Arabia, who practiced medicine and refused to accept fees for their services. They are thus seen as the patron saints of doctors, alongside Luke the Evangelist (Oct. 18) and Pantaleon (July 27). They were apparently arrested for their Christian beliefs under Diocletian, and managed to survive execution by drowning, burning, and stoning, but were eventually beheaded.

Despite their medical skills, the brothers fell foul of Diocletian's persecutions, and were decapitated along with their three younger brothers. Fra Angelico's depiction of the event, commissioned by the Medici family of Florence, is particularly gruesome.

Date	Name	Status	Venerated	Life
Sept. 26	Wilson Carlile (1847–1942)	Founder	CofE	Middle-class businessman. Turned to Anglican Church after a slump, becoming ordained in 1880. Keen to evangelize urban lower classes. Organized rallies and founded the Church Army in 1882, which grew to become largest home mission movement in Britain.
Sept. 26	Justina of Antioch (late 3rd century–c.304)	Virgin, Martyr ○ Pre-Congregation	Eastern Orthodox churches	Young Christian, admired by the pagan Aglaides, who recruited the sorcerer Cyprian to beguile her. She resisted all their attempts at seduction, and eventually converted them. Cyprian became bishop of Antioch. All three tortured and beheaded during persecutions of Diocletian.

SEPTEMBER 27 | VINCENT DE PAUL

STATUS Priest, Founder
BORN 1581, Pouy, France
DIED 1660, Paris, France
GRC ♣
CofE ♣
LCDUS ♣
OTHER In France
♥ 1729
○ 1737
† Shown helping the poor
🙏 Charity, lost things, hospitals, prisoners, volunteers, horses, leprosy; Madagascar

Vincent's body is preserved (in wax) in the St. Vincent de Paul Chapel in Paris.

Vincent was born to a peasant family in southwest France and remained an essentially humble man among his Counter-Reformation contemporaries. He studied at Dax and then Toulouse, and was ordained in 1600. While traveling by sea from Marseille on family business, he is said to have been kidnapped by Barbary pirates and enslaved, being released in 1607.

He traveled to Rome, then served as chaplain to Marguerite de Valois, and briefly worked as a parish priest at Clichy near Paris before entering the service of the Gondi family, under whom his vocation for caring for the poor was fostered. In 1622, his experience of enslavement led him to be created chaplain to the galley slaves, and he went on to found the Congregation of the Mission (the Vincentians or Lazarists) and, with Louise de Marillac (March 15), the Daughters of Charity. He was an ardent critic of the Jansenist movement in France.

SEPTEMBER 28 | WENCESLAUS

STATUS Martyr
BORN c.903, Prague, modern Czech Republic
DIED c.929, modern Czech Republic
GRC ♣
CofE ♧
LCDUS ♣
OTHER In the Czech Republic
○ Pre-Congregation
† In armor, with black eagle on his arms or banner
🙏 Czech Republic, Slovakia, Bohemia, Moravia

Wenceslaus ascended to the dukedom of Bohemia at only 15, at a time of religious and civil unrest. Wenceslaus became a figurehead for Bohemian (Czech) independence. He had been raised a Christian by his grandmother, St. Ludmilla, and was said to have been protected in battle by angels. They did little to protect him from his own family, unfortunately. His younger brother Boleslav (a non-Christian) was eager for control and, supported by their mother, was also keen to forge a relationship with the Bavarians who threatened the duchy from the south. When Wenceslaus produced an heir, his mother lured him to Boleslav's castle, where he was cut down in front of the altar by Boleslav. His relics are housed in St. Vitus Cathedral in Prague. Wenceslaus is best known through J.M. Neale's Christmas carol celebrating his generosity to the poor in winter, but this has no basis in fact.

The equestrian monument to St. Wenceslaus in his square in Prague portrays him as a martial figure, a model for successive generations of Bohemian kings.

Date	Name	Status	Venerated	Life
Sept. 28	Lorenzo Ruiz & Companions (d.1637)	Martyrs ♥ 1981 ○ 1987	GRC, LCDUS In the Philippines	Ruiz was a native Filipino, raised a Christian under Spanish colonial rule. Although accused of murdering a Spaniard, joined Dominican mission to Japan in 1636. Upon landing, missionaries (mainly Spanish) arrested and tortured at the 'Mount of Martyrs' in Nagasaki, being hung upside down, having needles inserted in them, and eventually dying through their own weight. Ruiz was first canonized Filipino martyr.

SEPTEMBER 29 | MICHAELMAS DAY

The iconographic meaning of St. Michael's cross is now lost; occasionally it is presented with trefoil ends. The sword of St. Michael has, since the time of the Crusades, been seen as a symbol of the Cross.

Gabriel means 'God is mighty' in Hebrew. His emblem combines a spear with a shield bearing the monogram of the Blessed Virgin Mary, commemorating his delivery of the Annunciation of Jesus.

Raphael's travels on Earth are represented in his emblem, which combines a walking-staff with a satchel. The satchel does not contain food, as one might expect (angels don't eat), but medicinal cures. Raphael is often shown with Tobias, a dog, and a fish.

This day was long associated with the Archangel Michael, but has now become a feast day for the three principal messengers (Michael, Gabriel, and Raphael) sent from Heaven to Earth by God to provide guidance or instruction at critical points in the Christian story. These are the only angels to be mentioned by name in the Bible, and they are also regarded as saints. Michaelmas Day marked the end of the agricultural cycle in the northern hemisphere when, with crops safely harvested, taxes, rents, and tithes would be paid to the Church. The three archangels are also venerated as saints in the Eastern Orthodox churches.

Archangel Michael

The leader of the angels fighting Satan's hordes in the war in Heaven (*see opposite*), Michael is regarded as the guardian of the souls of men, and in the Eastern tradition as guardian of the sick. Michael is frequently represented as a martial figure, clothed in armor and bearing a sword (echoing the Cross) while trampling on a dragon or worm representing Satan. In Iberia especially, Michael was invoked, alongside James the Greater (July 25) and George (April 23), as a champion of the *Reconquista*, with the vanquished satanic figure often acquiring Moorish features. A vision of Michael occurred in the 490s on Mount Gargano, southern Italy, which explains the construction of shrines such as Mont St.-Michel in Brittany, France, at St. Michael's Mount in Cornwall, England, and at Stranberg in Germany.

Archangel Gabriel

Gabriel is principally associated with the Annunciation of Our Lord (March 25), when he visited the Blessed Virgin Mary to inform her of her impending role as the mother of Jesus (Luke 1:26–38). Gabriel first appears in the Old Testament, to the prophet Daniel, explaining his visions (Daniel 8:16–26; 9:21–27). In the New Testament, he also appears to Zachariah in the Temple, announcing the impending birth of John the Baptist (Luke 1:11–20). Gabriel is also often identified as the angel who proclaims the Nativity to the shepherds. He is seen as the most gentle of the archangels. Before the revision of the Catholic calendar in 1969, Gabriel was celebrated on March 24.

Archangel Raphael

A senior archangel, who represents the ineffable power of God the Creator, Raphael only appears in the apocryphal Book of Tobit. His involvement with the adventure of Tobit's son, Tobias, indicates that he is capable of existing on Earth for extended periods. It is Raphael who reveals that there are only seven archangels.

During the Babylonian exile, the elderly and reverent Tobit of Nineveh, blind and seeking funds, sends his young son to collect money he has deposited in a distant city, and hires a traveling companion for him. The pair set off on their journey, accompanied by Tobias's dog. Stopping for the night, Tobias catches a monstrous fish, and the mysterious companion tells him to remove its heart, liver, and gall. They travel on and stay with Raguel, a relative of Tobit's; the companion points out that, under Jewish law, Raguel's daughter, Sarah, should be betrothed to Tobias. It seems, however, that she is possessed by a demon, her previous seven suitors all dying on the wedding night. Raguel agrees to the match, and Tobias's companion advises him to cast the fish's heart and liver on an incense burner to exorcise his bride's demon. It works: Tobit's money is safely retrieved, and Tobias, Sarah, the companion, and the dog all return to Nineveh to Tobias's by now very worried parents. Finally, the companion tells Tobias to smear the fish's gall on Tobit's eyes, and the old man's sight is restored. Tobit advises Tobias to pay the companion half of what he has brought back, at which point the companion reveals himself to be the Archangel Raphael.

THE FALLEN ANGELS

The Book of Revelation, or the Apocalypse of St. John, provides several accounts of angels and archangels, though few are named. Revelation also provides the source for the story of the war in Heaven between God the Creator and the rebel angels led by another archangel, Lucifer (Revelation 19–20). This was later elaborated on by the English poet John Milton in his epic poem *Paradise Lost* (1667).

Following a battle between the faithful angels, led by Michael, and Lucifer's followers, who questioned God's supreme authority, the latter were cast down from Heaven to a lake of fiery brimstone (hell) for the sin of pride. After a thousand years chained to the fiery lake, Lucifer (now called Satan, or the Devil) constructs the infernal palace of Pandemonium in his new domain and, at the first council of the demons, decides to form a new battleground on Earth, intending to seduce God's new creation, mankind, in the form of Adam and Eve.

Satan travels to the Garden of Eden and, in the form of a serpent, lures Eve to taste the fruit of the Tree of Life. She then offers it to Adam – the single fruit God forbade mankind to taste. At this point, Adam and Eve acquire knowledge, mortality, and a conscience – in short, original sin. God expels them from Eden, and the scene is set for the eternal struggle between good and evil.

English mystic artist and poet William Blake (1757–1827) provided some profoundly disturbing images of Lucifer/Satan. This one inspired the suspense novel Red Dragon *(1981) by Thomas Harris.*

Date	Name	Status	Venerated	Life
Sept. 29	Garcia (c.1000–73)	Abbot ◯ Pre-Congregation	In Spain	Spanish fighting monk during the *Reconquista*. Became abbot of Artanza, Old Castile (1039), and counselor to Ferdinand I of Castile.
Sept. 29	Charles of Blois (1320–64)	Founder ◯ 1904	In Blois and Brittany, France ⚚ Prisoners	French aristocrat. Duties overruled his calling to become a Franciscan monk. Military commander noted for humane treatment of prisoners. Founded religious houses; helped the poor and sick. Captured Nantes but was himself captured (1346) and ransomed to the English for nine years. Killed at battle of Auray.
Sept. 29	Luigi Monza (1898–1954)	Founder ♥ 2006	In northern Italy	Ordained 1925. Imprisoned for anti-Fascist activities. Founded Institute of the Little Apostles of Charity (1937).

SEPTEMBER 30 | JEROME (HIERONYMUS)

STATUS Priest, Doctor of the Church

BORN c.342, Stridon, Dalmatia

DIED 420, Bethlehem, modern Israel

GRC ♣

CofE ♣

LCDUS ♣

OTHER US Episcopal Church, US Evangelical Lutheran Church

○ Pre-Congregation

✝ Shown in the desert or in his study, accompanied by a lion; often wearing red cardinal's robes and cardinal's hat, and usually writing; sometimes carrying a stone

🙏 Archaeologists, archivists, librarians, students, translators

The spike at the foot of the Potent Cross may refer to the thorn which Jerome removed from the lion's paw.

Possibly the most famous theologian in Church history, Jerome is one of the Four Western Fathers; the others are Augustine of Hippo (Aug. 28), Ambrose of Milan (Dec. 7), and Gregory the Great (Sept. 3). Jerome seems particularly approachable, despite being difficult, sarcastic, and argumentative. He was born Eusebius Hieronymus Sophronius to wealthy parents in modern Slovenia. He enjoyed an adventurous youth before studying the classics and rhetoric in Rome under Donatus, and then traveled in Gaul and Germany. He was baptized in around 365, and became a monk in Aquileia. In 373 he traveled with three companions to Antioch, visiting Athens and many cities in Anatolia on the way. It was here that he reputedly extracted a thorn from a lion's paw, and the beast is said to have remained his faithful companion.

Jerome is frequently represented wearing a cardinal's robes and broad-brimmed hat.

Father of the Modern Bible

While in Syria, Jerome learned Hebrew, the better to read the original Scriptures, and was ordained in Antioch. He went to Constantinople and studied under Gregory Nazianzen (Jan. 2), where he began to translate Eusebius's *Chronicle* from Greek to Latin, along with some of Origen's works. He returned to Rome and was retained as secretary by Pope Damasus I (r.366–84), who instructed him to produce a new Latin translation of the Bible. The resulting manuscript became the Vulgate Bible, which became the canonical Catholic biblical text, still in use today. Despite this enormous undertaking, Jerome continued to produce commentaries, other translations, and a martyrology. He conducted several debates by letter, and it is from these that something of his cantankerous and argumentative nature emerges.

While in Rome, Jerome became the mentor to a group of Christian widows, including Paula, Marcella, and Eustochium. A scandal blew up, and in 385 Jerome returned to the Levant, first to Antioch, then settling in Bethlehem in a rock-cut cell near the traditional birthplace of Jesus. There, he worked, taught, and entertained visitors.

Jerome died of natural causes and was buried under the Church of the Nativity (as were Paula and Eustochium), but his relics were later transferred to Santa Maria Maggiore, Rome.

> ## "Now we have to translate the words of the Scriptures into deeds."
>
> ST. JEROME.

St. Jerome in his Study (right) by Antonello da Messina (c.1430–79) sees Jerome poised at his writing desk, his faithful lion in the background, while somewhat mysteriously two birds appear to occupy our space: a peacock, an ancient Christian symbol for eternal life, and a partridge, a more subtle reference, probably to Jerome's famed irascibility, as the bird often represents jealous rage.

Date	Name	Status	Venerated	Life
Sept. 30	Ursus the Theban (d.286)	○ Pre-Congregation	In Solothurn, Switzerland	One of the Martyrs of the Theban Legion. Beheaded with his fellows during persecutions of Maximian.
Sept. 30	Conrad of Urach (c.1180–1227)	Abbot	Cistercian Order	Canon of Liège Cathedral. Became Cardinal Bishop of Porto, Abbot of Clairvaux (1214), Citeaux (1217), General of the Cistercians, then a cardinal (1219). While papal legate to France (1220–23), Pope Honorius ordered him to suppress the Albigensians.
Sept. 30	Frederick Albert (1820–76)	Founder ♥ 1984	By Albertines	Italian priest. Founded Congregation of the Vincentian Sisters of Mary Immaculate.

OCTOBER

In October the longer nights draw close in northern climes, and although the weather can still be clement, the year begins to wane as leaves turn gold and night frosts begin. Despite this, some glorious achievements come forward for celebration during the month, including those of the humble Saint Francis of Assisi on October 4, founder of the Franciscan Order and patron saint of all living things, and those of Saint Luke on October 18. The most gentle and contemplative of the Evangelists, Luke was a doctor and the companion of Saint Paul on some of his missionary journeys. The Gospel of St. Luke provides one of the best-loved accounts of the Nativity, and Luke went on to write the Acts of the Apostles. The lesser-known Apostles Simon and Jude are celebrated on October 28.

Giovanni Bellini's painting Saint Francis in Ecstasy *(c. 1480) captures the saint during his retreat in the wilderness in the Umbrian landscape. The ass, bearing the mark of the Cross on his back, reminds us of Christ and the constant presence of God in the natural world.*

OCTOBER 1 | THÉRÈSE OF LISIEUX

STATUS Virgin, Doctor of the Church

BORN 1873, Alençon, France

DIED 1897, Lisieux, France

GRC ♣

CofE ♡

LCDUS ♣

OTHER By Carmelites

♥ 1923

⬯ 1925

✝ Normally shown in Carmelite habit, holding a bunch of roses

🙏 Missions; France

Marie-Françoise-Thérèse Martin, or Thérèse of the Child Jesus, was one of four daughters of a Norman watchmaker who all became nuns. Thérèse, however, was exceptional in her devotion, and was given special permission to enter the Carmelite Order at age 15. She did not undertake the traditional penance regime of self-mortification, did not claim ecstasies or visions, but trod a simple path to faith. Her life was cut horribly short by tuberculosis, and she died after a long but bravely borne illness at only 24.

The Little Flower

The key to Thérèse's fame rests upon her short but moving autobiography, *The Story of a Soul*, subtitled *The Little Flower*, which became a widely translated bestseller after her death. It was first published in a heavily edited and rewritten form. Nevertheless, the book provided a simple and approachable path to faith and spirituality that appealed to modern sensibilities. Its impact was enormous: miraculous cures were attributed due to her intercession, and her cult grew rapidly. A new building was erected at the convent at Lisieux to accommodate the numerous pilgrims. A revised version of her book, based on her original manuscript, was published in 1952, which proved even more successful.

Thérèse was declared a Doctor of the Church in 1997. In 2009, her relics were taken on an extended tour, which included the United Kingdom, drawing huge crowds.

Thérèse's association with flowers arose from the subtitle of her book, probably added when her memoirs were edited and added to after her young death. Her rapid elevation to cult status and canonization had much to do with the large number of miraculous cures and intercessions attributed to her.

Date	Name	Status	Venerated	Life
Oct. 1	Gregory the Enlightener (c.240–326)	Bishop ⬯ Pre-Congregation	In Armenia (June 9) 🙏 Armenia	Son of a Parthian who had murdered Khosroe I of Armenia. As child taken to Caesarea, Cappadocia. Raised as a Christian. Became bishop of Caesarea and returned to Armenia, converting King Tiridates after surviving 12 tortures. Died as a hermit.
Oct. 1	Rémy (Remigius) (c.438–530)	Bishop ⬯ Pre-Congregation	CofE ✝ Bishop with ointment	High-born priest. As archbishop of Reims, baptized the Frankish king Clovis and 3,000 of his followers (496). Known as the 'Apostle of France.'
Oct. 1	Anthony Ashley Cooper (1621–83)	Social Reformer	CofE	Controversial Earl of Shaftsbury. Served under Charles I, then Cromwell, then as High Chancellor under Charles II. Ardent anti-papist, accused of treason when plotting against the succession of Charles II's Catholic brother. Died in exile.
Oct. 2	Leger (Leodegarius) (c.616–79)	Bishop, Martyr ⬯ Pre-Congregation	In France and Switzerland 🙏 Millers; against blindness	Aristocratic Frankish bishop of Autun. Earned political enmity of Childeric II and his minister Ebroin. Captured and blinded, secretly tried, then beheaded for treason.
Oct. 3	Théodore (Theodora) Guérin (1798–1856)	Missionary, Founder ♥ 1998 ⬯ 2006	In USA	French missionary in USA. Founded Sisters of Providence of St. Mary-of-the-Woods, Indiana, and several schools.

A Soul Brought to Heaven *by Adolphe-William Bouguereau (1825–1905).*
The Victorians, obsessed with the dead and with Spiritualism, found great comfort in
the soul's protection, both in this life and the next, afforded by guardian angels.

OCTOBER 2 ✦ GUARDIAN ANGELS

The English novelist Philip
Pullman (b. 1946) provided
his characters with personal
daemons, effectively guardian
angels, in his controversial
His Dark Materials *trilogy*
of novels. The books and the
2007 film version of the first
novel have been condemned as
anti-Christian.

Christianity is not alone in
acknowledging that each of
the faithful has a guardian
angel — a spiritual being who
protects us from harm and guides
our footsteps. Judaism and Islam
have similar traditions, as do many
indigenous religions. For Christians,
there is little theological evidence
for their existence. Personal angels
are obliquely referred to in Matthew
18:10 and Acts 12:15. However, such
beings were long celebrated on the
Roman Calendar on the feast day of
the Archangels (Sept. 29), until Pope
Clement X introduced this dedicated
feast day in 1670, derived from a local
Portuguese cult. It remains on the
General Roman Calendar.

A belief in the omnipresence of personal guardian
angels provides the faithful with a direct channel to
the subconscious — the psychoanalytical id.

OCTOBER 4 ❦ FRANCIS OF ASSISI

STATUS Friar, Founder

BORN c.1181, Assisi, Italy

DIED 1226, Portiuncula, Italy

GRC ♣

CofE ♣

LCDUS ♣

OTHER US Episcopal Church, US Evangelical Lutheran Church

○ 1228

✝ Short stature, bearded, tonsured, in Franciscan hooded robes, with stigmata, often surrounded by birds or animals

🙏 Animals, animal welfare societies, the environment; Italy, Assisi

The emblem of St. Francis combines the brown of the Franciscan habit with the wounds of the stigmata on a cross.

One of the scenes from Benozzo Gozzoli's cycle of episodes from the life of St. Francis, dating from around 1450, captures the saint's famous Sermon to the Birds, and the dedication of his basilica at Assisi, set among the Umbrian hills.

Francis is undoubtedly one of the most popular and well-recognized saints in the history of the Church, Catholic or otherwise, partly because of his renowned love for all living beings, and partly due to the influential mendicant order of friars he founded.

Francis was born to a wealthy Umbrian cloth merchant's family and was baptized Giovanni after John the Baptist (June 24). Francis enjoyed a privileged and dissolute upbringing and fought in various local wars, until his health broke down in 1203. Recovering from a fever, he experienced a revelation: "There is God in everything, but in my heart there is no God." He turned his attention to the poor and underprivileged, even working in a leper hostel, before giving away all his possessions, living as a beggar, and retreating as a hermit to a ruined chapel of the Portiuncula, one of several he helped to restore in the hills outside Assisi. It was this habit of retreat into the countryside that cemented his reputation as a lover of all living beings as manifestations of God's all-embracing creation.

The Mendicant Friars

In 1208, following a further revelation, Francis adopted a hooded brown robe and rope belt, based on a shepherd's outfit, and began to travel, preaching as he did. A group of 12 followers assembled around him, several also from wealthy backgrounds, who became known as the Penitentiaries of Assisi; Francis called them the Friars Minor (*fratres minores*) when he wrote a simple Rule for them, which he presented for papal approval in 1212. Although consent for the new order was not granted until 1223, by then the band of mendicant friars had expanded and were traveling in small groups throughout Italy and beyond, developing into an effective though humble missionary order, living simply, and constantly laboring and preaching. Francis also helped an admirer, Clare of Assisi (Aug. 11), to found the 'Poor Clares.'

It was the time of the Crusades, and Francis himself attempted to travel to the Holy Land at least twice. One tradition claims that he reached Mamluk, Egypt, in 1219 and impressed (but failed to convert) the sultan. Although confronted by many failures (several Franciscan missions to Muslim North Africa came to sticky ends), the Franciscans did become established in the crusader states, and began a tradition of missionary zeal with an ability to appeal to common people of whatever faith that would place them at the forefront of the conversion of Spanish America 300 years later.

Stigmata and Sainthood

Despite the successful growth of the Franciscan Order, and the wide respect that was accorded to Francis himself, he both resisted aggrandizement and bore continual ill health with great fortitude. Much of his thinking was enshrined in his mystical works such as *The Canticle of the Sun* (1225). Although he became a deacon of the Church, Francis refused to be ordained. In 1224, with his strength ebbing, Francis received the miracle of the stigmata — the first on record. It is said the wounds, which Francis welcomed, also contributed to his decline and death. His great friend Cardinal Ugolino, who helped gain papal assent for the Franciscans, also effected the saint's canonization a mere two years after his death. It would be Ugolino, who became Pope Gregory IX in 1227, who would found the basilica in Assisi that remains one of the great pilgrimage centers of the Catholic world, and where St. Francis's remains were translated from the Portiuncula.

OCTOBER 6 — BRUNO OF COLOGNE

STATUS Hermit, Founder

BORN 1030, Cologne, Germany

DIED 1101, Calabria, Italy

GRC ♣

CofE ○

LCDUS ♣

OTHER By Carthusians

○ 1623

✝ Contemplating a skull, with a book and cross; sometimes crowned with a halo of seven stars; Carthusian habit

🙏 Calabria

Born into the prominent Hartenfaust family, Bruno studied at the cathedral school at Reims, before returning to Cologne for his ordination in 1055. He went once again to Reims, this time as professor of theology and head of the episcopal school, and stayed there for the next 18 years, becoming the chancellor of the church of Reims in 1075. He was a highly respected and influential teacher, celebrated for his eloquence. In 1076, Reims was thrown into turmoil when Bishop Manasses was denounced as unfit for the office of prelate. Bruno discreetly withdrew from the city and the violent dissent among its leading clergymen, only returning in 1080 when Manasses was deposed. Bruno was encouraged to take on the role of bishop, but refused, deciding instead to renounce the secular world and pursue the life of a hermit.

Hermit and Monastic Leader

Bruno moved to the Grenoble region with six companions in 1084, under the protection of St. Hugh (April 1), then bishop of Grenoble. With his help they sought out a place for their hermitage at Chartreuse in the bleak terrain of the lower Alps. They built an oratory and individual cells, and lived an austere life of prayer and study. This was the foundation of the Carthusian Order.

Despite his wish for solitude and obscurity, the fame of Bruno's new order spread. In 1090, he was summoned to Rome by Pope Urban II, a former pupil, to act as an adviser on the reformation of the clergy. Bruno was a reluctant recruit to the papal court, and he persuaded the pope, who wished him to remain in Italy, to allow him to continue his hermit's life. He refused the pope's offer of the archbishopric of Reggio, and instead founded the hermitage of St. Mary of La Torre, in Calabria. Here he enjoyed the patronage of Roger I of Sicily, who built a small retreat for himself within the hermitage, and helped to fund the construction of the monastery of St. Stephen nearby. Bruno remained there until his death, and is buried at St. Mary of La Torre.

Bruno in marble at the Carthusian monastery of San Martino, Naples.

The Vision of St. Bruno *by Jusepe de Ribera (1643). Bruno was an influential writer and scholar, whose commentaries on the Psalms and the Epistles of St. Paul demonstrate his eloquence and learning. The Carthusian Order was innovative in promoting the ideals of contemplative solitude, without completely excluding the communal monastic life.*

Date	Name	Status	Venerated	Life
Oct. 5	Maria Faustina Kowalska (1905–38)	Nun ○ 2000	In Poland	Born to a poor Polish family. Entered a convent of the Sisters of Our Lady of Mercy. Said to have experienced visions of Jesus and Mary, but died of tuberculosis at age 33. Recorded her mystical experiences in a diary, which has become a devotional handbook.
Oct. 6	Marie Rose Durocher (1811–49)	Nun, Founder ♥ 1982	LCDUS	Born to Catholic family in Quebec, Canada. Founded the Congregation of the Sisters of the Holy Names of Jesus and Mary, women dedicated to a Christian education, near Montreal. Despite great poverty, and her own sickness, her community flourished.

OCTOBER 6 | WILLIAM TYNDALE

STATUS Translator, Martyr
BORN c.1494, Gloucestershire, England
DIED 1536, near Brussels, Belgium
GRC ◯
CofE ●
LCDUS ◯

William Tyndale passionately believed that the people of England should be able to read the Bible in their own language, and dedicated his life, and his considerable linguistic and scholarly abilities, to printing a Bible in the English vernacular.

Educated at Oxford, Tyndale received his degree in 1515 and was ordained in around 1521. A gifted linguist, fluent in French, Greek, Hebrew, Latin, and Spanish, he earned a living by working as a tutor in the household of a Gloucestershire family, and became increasingly locked in controversy with his fellow clergymen over his radical, and outspoken, religious opinions.

In 1523, Tyndale set out for London, intent on translating the Bible from the original Greek into English, which was strictly forbidden. He sought the help of Bishop Cuthbert Tunstall, but was rebuffed. Tunstall did not accept Tyndale's academic credentials and was uncomfortable with the idea of a Bible in the vernacular. He was to become an implacable opponent of Tyndale.

Tyndale left England for Hamburg in 1524, met Martin Luther in Wittenberg, and completed his translation of the New Testament in 1525. The printed book was smuggled into England, where it was denounced by the authorities and burned.

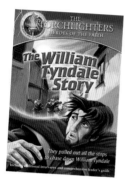

Tyndale was determined to bring the Bible to the everyday reader – even at the cost of his life.

A Clash with the Authorities

The archbishop of York, Cardinal Wolsey, condemned Tyndale for heresy, demanding his arrest. Tyndale remained in hiding in Germany, and began the epic task

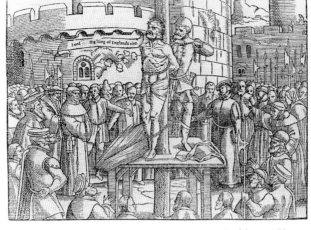

Tyndale's execution was relatively merciful by the standards of the time. He was tied to a stake and strangled, before being burned.

of translating the Old Testament. At this time he wrote *The Practice of Prelates*, which stirred the controversy surrounding him by condemning Henry VIII's divorce.

An enraged Henry VIII requested that Emperor Charles V arrest Tyndale and return him to England. Tyndale was betrayed to the authorities by a fellow Englishman. He was tried on a charge of heresy in 1536, and condemned to death. Despite interventions from Thomas Cromwell, the most powerful man in England after the king, the sentence was eventually fulfilled.

Within four years, four English versions of the Bible, all based on Tyndale's pioneering work, were published in England, and one of them became the basis of the King James Bible, adopted by the Anglican Church.

OCTOBER 7 | OUR LADY OF THE ROSARY

This day celebrates the Blessed Virgin Mary in relation to the method of praying known as the 'rosary.' The rosary itself is attributed to an apparition of the Virgin Mary to St. Dominic (Aug. 8) in 1208.

In 1571, Pope Pius V instituted an annual feast entitled 'Our Lady of Victory' to commemorate the victory of the battle of Lepanto, when troops of the Holy League held back Muslim forces who were threatening

to overrun Christian Europe. The victory was attributed to the praying of the rosary. In 1573, the title of this feast day was changed to the Feast of the Holy Rosary, and it was inserted into the Roman Catholic Calendar, eventually – in 1913 – falling on the fixed date of October 7. In 1969, Pope Paul VI changed the name of the feast to Our Lady of the Rosary.

The Virgin of the Rosary by Ludovico Brea (c.1500). The Virgin is surrounded by saints.

Date	Name	Status	Venerated	Life
Oct. 8	Thaïs (d.c.4th century)	Penitent, Nun ◯ Pre-Congregation		Wealthy courtesan living in Alexandria, Egypt. Was converted to Christianity by one of the desert monks, burned her finery, and retreated to a convent cell for three years, where she performed penance for her sins. When she finally emerged from her solitude, lived for only another 14 days.
Oct. 8	Pelagia (d.c.5th century)	Penitent, Hermit ◯ Pre-Congregation		Actress and courtesan, famous in Antioch. Converted to Christianity when she heard St. Nonnus, bishop of Edessa, preach. Gave up her worldly possessions, left Antioch dressed as a man, and lived life of a hermit in a cave near Jerusalem. Known as the 'beardless monk,' her sex was only discovered after her death.

OCTOBER 9 DENIS (DENYS) AND COMPANIONS

STATUS Martyr

BORN 3rd century, Italy

DIED c.258, Paris, France

GRC ♣

CofE ♣

LCDUS ◌

○ Pre-Congregation

✝ Carrying his severed head in his hand, bishop's miter

🙏 Against frenzy, possession, rabies, headaches, hydrophobia; France, Paris

Denis is usually shown bearing his own head, an unsettling but immediately identifiable piece of saintly iconography.

Denis was sent as a Christian missionary from Italy to Gaul in the 3rd century, reputedly under the direction of Pope Fabian. He set out with his companions, Rusticus and Eleutherius, to Lutetia (Roman Paris) and settled on the Île de la Cité, an island in the river Seine, some distance from the Roman settlement on the Left Bank.

Denis, who became known as the first bishop of Paris, made many conversions among the Gauls, but the pagan priests were alarmed by his success. The three Italians were taken to the highest hill in Paris (now Montmartre) where they were beheaded. It is believed that the name — Mount of Martyrs — derives from this event. According to legend, after Denis's head was severed, he picked it up and walked two miles, preaching all the way. In fact, the bodies were thrown in the Seine and recovered by converts, who buried the remains, and constructed a chapel over the tomb. Dagobert I, king of the Franks (r.629–39), founded the abbey of St.-Denis and a Benedictine monastery at the burial site. In the 12th century, the abbey church was rebuilt by Abbot Suger; it became the burial place of the kings of France, and the first northern Gothic building in Europe.

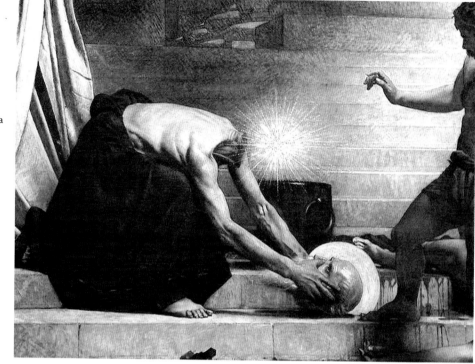

This painting from the Panthéon in Paris dates from the 19th century, a period when the Catholic Church was concerned with re-establishing its presence within a now secular republic. The violent method of Denis's martyrdom had great resonance for those who had witnessed decapitations under the guillotine.

Veneration of St. Denis and his companions began soon after their deaths, and their place of burial became a revered shrine. In time, the phrase "Montjoie! Saint Denis!" became the war cry of the French armies. The feast of St. Denis, celebrated since the 9th century, was added to the Roman Calendar in 1568. Denis is also honored as one of the Fourteen Holy Helpers, and is one of the patron saints of France.

Date	Name	Status	Venerated	Life
Oct. 9	John Leonardi (d.1609)	Priest, Founder ○ 1938	By Jesuits	Priest who was a key figure in the Counter-Reformation, inspired by the reforms proposed at the Council of Trent. With papal approval, founded an association of secular priests, the Clerks Regular of the Mother of God. Co-founder of the Jesuit seminary of the Propagation of the Faith in Rome.
Oct. 10	Daniel and Companions (d.1227)	Missionaries, Martyrs ○ 1516	By Franciscans	Leader of group of Franciscan missionaries who traveled to Ceuta in Morocco to preach the Gospel in 1227. All arrested, refused to renounce their faith, and were beheaded.
Oct. 10	Angela Truszkowska (1825–99)	Founder ♥ 1993	By the Felician Sisters In Poland	Born into Polish nobility. Dedicated herself to religious life, opening her own home in Warsaw to homeless children. With her cousin, founded Felician Sisters (1843), a Franciscan tertiary order devoted to helping the poor, sick, and elderly.

OCTOBER 10 · FRANCIS BORGIA

STATUS Priest
BORN 1510, Valencia, Spain
DIED 1572, Rome, Italy
GRC ☁
CofE ☁
LCDUS ☁
◯ 1670
† Skull, often crowned with an emperor's diadem
🙏 Against earthquakes; Portugal

Two hundred years after Francis's death, the Romantic skeptic Francisco de Goya (1746–1828) could still produce an image of an apparently miraculous event, when Francis's crucifix sprayed holy blood on a dying man, thereby reviving him.

Francis was born the scion of Juan Borgia, the duke of Gandía in Valencia. On his father's side he was the great-grandson of Rodrigo Borgia – the notorious Pope Alexander VI. On his mother's side, he was the great-grandson of King Ferdinand of Aragon. Although he was a pious child who wished to become a monk, his illustrious family sent him to the court of the Holy Roman Emperor Charles V (r.1519–58). Francis accompanied the emperor as equerry on several military campaigns, distinguished himself at court, and married a Portuguese noblewoman, Eleanor de Castro Melo e Menezes, with whom he had eight children. He became marquis of Lombay, and was appointed master of hounds and equerry to the empress, Isabella.

In 1539, the empress died, and Charles V commissioned Francis to accompany her remains back to Granada in Spain for burial. This break from the sophisticated and brilliant life of the court had a profound impact on him. He began to contemplate the vanity of worldly success, and was determined to reform his life and become a perfect Christian. In the meantime, Charles V had appointed him viceroy of Catalonia, commissioned with reforming the justice system, overhauling the administration, and fortifying Barcelona. Francis was a distinguished and able administrator, but when his father died in 1543, and he succeeded to the dukedom of Gandía, he put aside worldly success and dedicated himself to the Church.

Francis Borgia is frequently portrayed with either a skull or an emperor's crown, a reminder of his rejection of worldly power.

Reforming Jesuit

In 1546, Francis was widowed, and he became determined to enter the newly formed Society of Jesus. He put his affairs in order and spent some time in Rome as the disciple of Ignatius of Loyola (July 31), founder of the Jesuit Order. Francis then renounced his dukedom in favor of his eldest son, and was ordained a priest. Despite his protests that he wanted to be no more than an itinerant Jesuit preacher, Francis was offered (and refused) a cardinalship, but his abilities and high birth soon led to his promotion within the order. In 1554, he became the Jesuits' commissary general in Spain and, in 1565, the third father general of the Society of Jesus.

Francis went to Rome, where he founded the Collegium Romanum (which became the Gregorian University), dispatched Jesuit missionaries all over the world, founded missions in Florida, New Spain, and Peru, and was the confidant of kings and emperors. In 1567, he published the Rules of the Society of Jesus, still in use today. Francis's later life was humble and austere.

In 1571, Pope Pius VI asked Francis to accompany his nephew, Cardinal Bonelli, on an embassy to Spain and Portugal. Although Francis was suffering from ill health, he acceded to the pope's wishes. He traveled throughout Iberia, where he was acclaimed as a 'living saint.'

Date	Name	Status	Venerated	Life
Oct. 11	Ethelburga of Barking (d.675)	Abbess ◯ Pre-Congregation		Abbess of one of first religious houses for women in England. Famous for her heroic care of the sick during an outbreak of plague that eventually killed her and most of her community.
Oct. 11	María Soledad (d.1887)	Founder ◯ 1970	In Madrid	Founded small lay community to administer to the sick and poor, named the Handmaids of Mary Serving the Sick. Papal approval awarded 1876. During her lifetime, 46 houses founded in Europe and Latin America. Governed community for 35 years.
Oct. 12	Elizabeth Fry (1780–1845)	Social Reformer	CofE	English Quaker from a banking family. Greatly involved in prison reform, did much to bring the plight of incarcerated mothers to public attention. Founded support groups and refuges.

OCTOBER 12 · WILFRID OF YORK

STATUS Bishop, Missionary

BORN c.634, Northumbria, England

DIED d.c.709, Oundle, England

GRC ○

CofE ♣

LCDUS ○

○ Pre-Congregation

† Fishing net; baptizing, preaching, engaged in theological disputes, landing from a ship

🙏 Ripon, Middlesbrough

The lozenges on Wilfrid's shield might refer to a fishing net (celebrating his reputation as a 'fisher of men,') or the seven hills of Rome, where his allegiance lay.

Wilfrid left his family at just 14 for the court of King Oswy of Northumbria, and went on to study at Lindisfarne. He traveled to Rome, studied under the archdeacon Boniface (June 5), and joined a monastery in Lyon, before returning to England and becoming abbot of the monastery at Ripon, which he placed under Benedictine rule. Familiar with Roman liturgical practice after his journey to Italy, and advocating its adoption in the English Church, Wilfrid's was a powerful and persuasive voice at the Synod of Whitby in 664, and he was subsequently appointed bishop of York.

Unwilling to be consecrated by bishops of the Celtic tradition, Wilfrid went to France to be consecrated according to Roman liturgical practice. In 666, he returned to England, nearly drowning when he was shipwrecked off the Sussex coast. However, during his absence he had been replaced as bishop by St. Chad (March 2). Wilfrid instead retired to his monastery in Ripon until 669, when Chad was persuaded to withdraw from the see.

Exile

Wilfrid became embroiled in power politics when he was sympathetic to Queen Etheldreda, who wanted to move to a convent and separate from her husband King Ecgfrith. Archbishop Theodore of Canterbury subdivided the York diocese in an attempt to diminish Wilfrid's growing influence, but Wilfrid traveled to Rome to appeal the decision, and the pope ruled in his favor. On Wilfrid's return to England, an angry Ecgfrith accused him of buying the pope's favor, and exiled him to heathen Sussex. Mixing his Christian message with expert advice on sea fishing, Wilfrid won many converts, becoming the first bishop of Selsey. During this period he made his peace with Theodore, and when Ecgfrith died and was succeeded by Aldfrith, Wilfrid was allowed to return from exile, and served as the bishop of Hexham, and subsequently York.

Wilfrid once again attempted to consolidate York into a single, powerful see, but was met with opposition. After a series of meetings, synods, rulings, and appeals to Rome, Wilfrid stepped down, remaining the bishop of Hexham and Ripon until his death.

Wilfrid was a prolific builder of churches and founder of monasteries, and initiated the rebuilding of York Minster.

Date	Name	Status	Venerated	Life
Oct. 13	Gerald of Aurillac (c.855–909)	Nobleman ○ Pre-Congregation	🙏 Counts, bachelors, the disabled	Born into Gallo-Roman nobility. Consecrated his life to God, giving away his worldly possessions, taking a vow of chastity, and founding a church and abbey on his estate at Aurillac.
Oct. 14	Pope Callistus I (d.c.223)	Pope, Martyr ○ Pre-Congregation	Roman Catholic Church	Roman slave. Became mixed up in a failed banking project and imprisoned. After his release became deacon to Pope Zephyrinus; succeeded him as bishop of Rome (217). Liberal pope who welcomed repentant sinners into the communion. Probably martyred in a popular uprising c.223.
Oct. 14	Esther John (Qamar Zia) (1929–60)	Evangelist, Martyr	In South Asia Anglican Church	Born to a Muslim family in British India. Moved to the newly founded state of Pakistan (1947). Became Presbyterian missionary against wishes of her family. Found brutally murdered, possibly by a Muslim fanatic.

OCTOBER 12 · EDITH CAVELL

STATUS Nurse, Humanitarian
BORN 1865, Norfolk, England
DIED 1915, Brussels, Belgium
GRC ☁
CofE ♣
LCDUS ☁

This memorial to Edith Cavell stands in St. Martin's Place in central London.

The daughter of a vicar, Edith Cavell worked as a governess in Belgium, subsequently training as a nurse at the Royal London Hospital. She went on to become matron of a newly established nursing school, L'Ecole Belge d'Infirmières Diplômées, in Brussels. She launched a nursing journal, *L'Infirmière*, in 1910, and was responsible for training nurses in three Belgian hospitals.

On the outbreak of World War I, Cavell elected to stay in Belgium, and her clinic and nursing school were taken over by the Red Cross. With the German occupation of Brussels in the fall of 1914, she became actively involved in the underground movement, sheltering Allied soldiers and helping them to escape occupied territory. She was outspoken and showed little regard for her own safety, and soon came to the attention of the German authorities.

On August 3, 1915, Cavell was arrested and charged with harboring Allied soldiers. She was held at the prison of St. Gilles for ten weeks, and court-martialed. The British government insisted that they

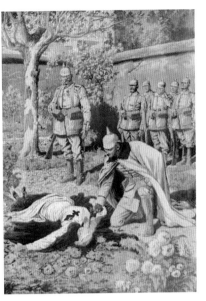

Cavell's story was used as a powerful icon of patriotism in British military recruitment drives and in the propaganda campaign to persuade the United States to enter World War I.

could not help her, arguing that any intervention would do more harm than good. However, the First Secretary of the American Legation in Brussels warned the Belgian authorities that executing Cavell would "stir all civilized countries with horror and disgust."

Cavell was tried for treason, and made no attempt to defend herself. Along with four colleagues she was condemned to death. She accepted her fate with calm resignation: "My soul, as I believe, is safe, and I am glad to die for my country." Despite last minute pleas for clemency, she was executed by firing squad on October 12, 1915.

Cavell's body, buried next to the prison of St. Gilles, was taken back to Britain after the war for a memorial service at Westminster Abbey, London, and finally laid to rest in Norwich Cathedral.

"Patriotism is not enough, I must have no hatred or bitterness towards anyone."

EDITH CAVELL, IMMEDIATELY PRIOR TO HER EXECUTION, OCTOBER 1915.

OCTOBER 13 · EDWARD THE CONFESSOR

STATUS King
BORN c.1006, Islip, England
DIED 1066, London, England
GRC ☁
CofE ♣
LCDUS ☁
◯ 1161
⚱ Kings, separated spouses, difficult marriages, the British royal family

The martlets echo the birds found on coins minted during Edward's reign.

The son of King Ethelred II 'the Unready' and Emma of Normandy, Edward spent much of his early life in exile in Normandy following the Danish invasion of England. He did not return to England until 1041, becoming king the following year. Edward brought with him a retinue of Norman nobles, who were much resented at the English court.

The early part of Edward's reign was particularly dominated by his father-in-law, Godwin, earl of Wessex, who became the effective ruler of the kingdom. Edward's attempts to assert his regal authority came to a head when he appointed the Norman bishop of London, Robert of Jumièges, archbishop of Canterbury, rejecting Godwin's candidate. In 1051, Edward outlawed Godwin and his family, including Edward's own wife, Edith. Two years

later the exiled earl and his sons returned, and Godwin's son Harold (Godwinson) continued to expand the power of the Godwins, securing the succession to the English throne when Edward – who was childless – died in 1066.

Once Edward had named Harold as his successor, he became more dedicated to religious affairs and built St. Peter's Abbey at Westminster in London (now Westminster Abbey, where he is buried). His piety gained him the sobriquet 'the Confessor.'

When Henry II came to the throne in 1154, the cult of Edward was promoted in association with the English royal family. Edward was represented as a holy man, who performed miracles, and healed people by touch. Here he is seen, flanked by Sts. Edmund and John the Baptist, accompanying the kneeling Richard II in the left panel of the famous Wilton Diptych (c.1395).

OCTOBER 15 ✣ TERESA OF ÁVILA

STATUS Mystic, Founder, Doctor of the Church

BORN 1515, Ávila, Spain

DIED 1582, Alba de Tormes, Spain

GRC ♣

CofE ♣

LCDUS ♣

OTHER Lutheran Church

♥ 1614

○ 1622

✝ Book and quill, pierced heart

🙏 Headaches, the sick; Spain, Croatia

Teresa described four stages of mysticism, climaxing in what she called the "devotion of ecstasy or rapture." Bernini's mid-17th-century Ecstasy of St. Teresa in Santa Maria della Vittoria in Rome brilliantly expresses this surrender to overwhelming religious sensation.

Teresa of Ávila was one of the most remarkable saints of the 16th century, a Spanish Carmelite nun and mystic who raised devotion and poverty, centered on absolute obedience to God, to a new and extreme intensity. She not only founded the Discalced (or barefoot) Carmelites, a reform movement of the Carmelites, but also established 17 convents across Spain for them. In addition, she wrote widely, chiefly on mystical theology. In 1970 she was made a Doctor of the Church. At that point, with Catherine of Siena (April 29), she was one of only two women to be so honored. Yet it is as a mystic that she is best remembered.

Visions of Christ

Though Teresa entered the Carmelite convent in the castellated hilltop town of Ávila in 1535 when she was 20, it wasn't for many more years that she had the first of her visions of Christ. They continued for a further six years and led directly to her determination to establish a reformed Carmelite order in order to duplicate the sufferings of Christ. Between 1557 and 1582, she founded numerous convents. In 1568, with St. John of the Cross (March 5), she also established a monastery for what were called the Discalced Carmelite Brethren. Perhaps ironically, piety on this scale did not make Teresa popular. Even before she launched her program of convent opening, she had been accused of being under diabolical rather than divine influence. Her ruthless insistence on extreme poverty and flagellation alienated many in the Carmelites, to the extent that for a number of years she was forbidden from opening new convents. That said, her influence then and later on a highly distinctive brand of Catholic mysticism was enormous.

"Accustom yourself continually to make many acts of love, for they enkindle and melt the soul."

ST. TERESA OF ÁVILA.

Date	Name	Status	Venerated	Life
Oct. 16	Gall (d.640)	Monk ○ Pre-Congregation	In Switzerland	Irish monk; accompanied St. Columban on mission to Europe. Falling out with Columban, settled near Lake Constance, Switzerland, where he is remembered by famous monastery of Sankt Gallen.
Oct. 16	Hedwig of Silesia (1174–1243)	Queen, Nun ○ 1267	GRC, LCDUS In Poland	One of a number of royal medieval saints celebrated for piety. Married to Henry I of Silesia, later duke of Greater Poland. Persuaded Henry to found Cistercian convent at Trebnitz in Silesia (1203). Hedwig settled there upon Henry's death; devoted remainder of life to good works and prayer.

OCTOBER 16 · HUGH LATIMER AND NICHOLAS RIDLEY

LATIMER

STATUS Bishop, Martyr

BORN c.1485, Leicestershire, England

DIED 1555, Oxford, England

GRC ♢

CofE ♣

LCDUS ♢

RIDLEY

STATUS Bishop, Martyr

BORN c.1500, Northumberland, England

DIED 1555, Oxford, England

GRC ♢

CofE ♣

LCDUS ♢

With Thomas Cranmer (March 21), Latimer and Ridley remain the best known of the Marian Martyrs, those Protestants executed by Mary I in her attempt to re-impose Catholicism in England after the Protestant reforms of her father Henry VIII and the efforts of her brother, Edward VI.

Hugh Latimer was bishop of Worcester, one of the most important dioceses in the English church, from 1535, making him a natural target for Mary. Ridley was a proctor at Cambridge in the early 1530s. He stated that "The Bishop of Rome has no more authority and jurisdiction derived to him from God, in this kingdom of England, than any other foreign bishop." He thrived under Edward VI, when he was made bishop of Rochester and then, in 1550, bishop of London. He was a marked man upon Mary's accession in 1553.

Their joint trial in Oxford was perfunctory, its verdict never in doubt. Led to the stake, Latimer urged his companion to "Be of good comfort, Master Ridley, and play the man; we shall this day light such a candle, by God's grace, in England, as I trust shall never be put out." It is said that Ridley's death was unusually protracted, his suffering accordingly the more terrible.

It was a particular refinement of the grim cruelty that Mary I brought to the burning of Latimer and Ridley that the former archbishop of Canterbury, Thomas Cranmer, also imprisoned in Oxford and shortly to suffer the same fate, was forced to witness their deaths. "O Lord Strengthen Them," he is shown as saying in the top right.

OCTOBER 17 · IGNATIUS OF ANTIOCH

STATUS Bishop, Martyr

BORN c. AD 50, Syria

DIED c.110, Rome, Italy

GRC ♣

CofE ♣

LCDUS ♣

OTHER Eastern Orthodox churches

◯ Pre-Congregation

✝ Lions, chains; holding his writings

Ignatius was not merely one of the earliest Christian martyrs, said to have been devoured by lions in the Colosseum in Rome during the persecutions of Trajan, but one of the Apostolic Fathers, those early Christians presumed to have had personal contact with Christ's own Apostles. It is said that St. Ignatius was appointed bishop of Antioch in Syria by St. Peter himself (June 29) and was a follower of John the Apostle (Dec. 27). But his importance lies also in his surviving writings, produced during his arduous overland journey from Antioch to Rome following his arrest

Images of St. Ignatius conventionally depict him either with chains, a symbol of his imprisonment, or, as here, with lions, the beasts that ensured his end – and martyrdom – in Rome.

as a Christian. These deal not only with spiritual matters and forms of worship, but, as important, with the organization and hierarchy of the Church. He was the first person to use the term 'catholic,' meaning universal, to describe the infant Christian Church.

Date	Name	Status	Venerated	Life
Oct. 16	Margaret Mary Alacoque (1647–90)	Nun ◯ 1920	GRC, LCDUS In Burgundy, France	Burgundian nun. From 1673 had series of visions of Christ's heart pierced by a sword, with crown of thorns surmounted by a cross. Became potent devotional symbol. In 1856, Pope Pius IX declared Feast of the Sacred Heart, (19 days after Pentecost), now one of most important feasts in Catholic liturgical calendar.
Oct. 16	Marguerite d'Youville (1701-71)	Founder ♥ 1959 ◯ 1990	In Canada 🙏 Widows, unhappy marriages	Studied under the Ursulines. Briefly married to a bootlegger. Once widowed, founded the Grey Nuns (1737), administering to the poor and sick. Grey Nuns went on to establish schools, orphanages, hospitals in Canada, US, Africa, South America.

OCTOBER 18 — LUKE THE EVANGELIST

STATUS Evangelist

BORN Early 1st century AD, Antioch, Syria

DIED Late 1st century AD, Greece

GRC ♣

CofE ♣

LCDUS ♣

OTHER Eastern Orthodox churches

○ Pre-Congregation

† Winged ox

🙏 Physicians, surgeons, painters, picturemakers

The winged ox representing Luke is probably associated with the notion of Christ's sacrifice for mankind.

Like St. Paul the Apostle (Jan. 25), Luke was born a Greek Gentile, probably in Antioch, and grew up to practice medicine there. It seems that after St. Paul's return to Antioch from his first missionary journey, Luke decided to accompany the Apostle for at least part of his second and third journeys. He traveled with Paul to Rome, and was shipwrecked with him at Malta on the way. Luke is known to us as the author of the third Gospel, and of the Acts of the Apostles. At no point does Luke claim to have witnessed any of the events in the Gospel, and it is likely that he converted as a result of meeting Paul. Several passages in Acts are in the first person plural, and Paul mentions Luke's presence in Rome in his letters to Timothy. Luke probably wrote the third Gospel and the Acts of the Apostles after Paul's death, possibly leaving Rome to write and preach in Boeotia, Greece. Luke was described by a 2nd-century writer as dying unmarried, at age 84. His relics are claimed by both Constantinople (modern Istanbul) and Padua, Italy.

The Gospel and the Acts of the Apostles

Just as Mark the Evangelist (April 25) undoubtedly gleaned much of his material from his sojourn in Rome with St. Peter (June 29), Luke appears to have benefited from the companionship of St. Paul. Both his Gospel and Acts reveal a lively storyteller, showing a closely observed attention to detail, and a concern with linking sacred history to the events and conditions of the profane world at the time. Archaeological research has supported many of Luke's details. His Gospel includes the fullest description of the Annunciations of both John the Baptist and Jesus, and of the Nativity. The Gospel is also the longest of the four, and contains some of the most popular episodes and parables (including the Good Samaritan, the Prodigal Son, and the Supper at Emmaus). Luke tends to stress Christ's compassion, and women feature more prominently in Luke than in the other Gospels.

In Acts, Luke describes Christ's work in the 40 days between His Resurrection and His Ascension, the inspiration of the Apostles at Pentecost, and the first meetings and decisions of the new church under the leadership of Peter. Thereafter, much of the book concerns the missionary journeys of Paul and his various companions, providing a rich source of detail about the establishment of the early church and the various cultures of the eastern Mediterranean.

> " ... I bring you good tidings of great joy, which shall be to all people."
>
> THE ANGEL TELLING THE SHEPHERDS OF THE NATIVITY, LUKE 2:10.

Luke was frequently portrayed drawing or painting the Virgin and Child in both Eastern and Western art, especially in the Netherlands, as in this delicate painting by Derick Baegert, c.1470.

Some later martyrologies include Luke, describing him being hanged in Boeotia, but there is no evidence to suggest that he didn't die from natural causes.

OCTOBER 19 | THE NORTH AMERICAN MARTYRS

A mosaic in the Cathedral Basilica of St. Louis, in St. Louis, Missouri, showing Isaac Jogues, René Goupil, and the Huron saint Kateri Tekakwitha (July 14).

STATUS Martyrs

Jean de Brébeuf	d.1649
Noel Chabanel	d.1649
Antoine Daniel	d.1648
Charles Garnier	d.1649
René Goupil	d.1642
Isaac Jogues	d.1646
Jean de Lalande	d.1646
Gabriel Lalemant	d.1649

GRC ♠

CofE ♡

LCDUS ♠

♥ 1925

◯ 1930

✝ In Jesuit robes

🙏 Canada

This feast was established by Pope Pius XI in 1930, when he canonized eight 17th-century missionaries. It is observed in Canada on September 26.

Isaac Jogues entered the Society of Jesus (Jesuits) in 1624, and in 1636 he was sent to New France (Canada) as a missionary to the Hurons and Algonquins, allies of the French. Here, he penetrated far into the interior. In 1642, Mohawk Iroquois captured Jogues and his companions, a lay brother, René Goupil, and Guillaume Couture. They took them back to their village, Ossernenon (modern Auriesville, New York), where Goupil was hacked to death after blessing a native child, while several of Jogues's fingers were cut off. Forced to live as a slave among the Mohawks, Jogues began to teach them the rudiments of Christianity. He managed to escape after 13 months, and returned to Europe. Pope Urban VIII gave this "living martyr" special permission to say Holy Mass with his mutilated hands — normally only the thumb and forefinger may touch the Eucharist.

But Jogues was undeterred by his terrible experiences, and a few months later returned to Canada where a tentative peace had been forged between the Iroquois and the Hurons, Algonquins, and their French allies. In the spring of 1646, Jogues entered Mohawk country, accompanied by a layman, Jean de Lalande. When sickness and crop failure hit the Mohawks, Jogues became the scapegoat. Jogues and Lalande were clubbed to death and beheaded by their Mohawk hosts, near Auriesville.

Another French Jesuit missionary, Jean de Brébeuf, and his companion Gabriel Lalemant, had met with some success ministering to the Hurons. They achieved hundreds of conversions, and Brébeuf produced the first Huron dictionary. But they fell foul of the Huron war with the Iroquois, and were captured by the latter, scalped, tortured with boiling water and fire, and finally beheaded and partly eaten. The other Jesuit martyrs commemorated on this day are Charles Garnier, Antoine Daniel, and Noel Chabanel.

OCTOBER 21 | URSULA AND THE 11,000 VIRGINS

STATUS Martyrs

BORN Southwest England

DIED 3rd–7th century, Cologne

GRC ♡

CofE ♡

LCDUS ♡

◯ Pre-Congregation

🙏 Students

There is much uncertainty about this anonymous group of virgins, supposedly murdered in Cologne. The legend is that Ursula was a Romano-British princess who set sail, with 11,000 handmaids, to join her future husband, the pagan prince of Brittany. A miraculous storm brought them to a Gaulish port, where Ursula swore she would undertake a pilgrimage to Rome. Returning, she arrived in Cologne, which was being besieged by Huns, and she and her companions were horribly massacred.

The legend of St. Ursula was embellished and elaborated by medieval historians and has been remarkably persistent. The basilica of St. Ursula in Cologne contains the alleged relics of the saint and her virgin companions, although much doubt has been cast on the provenance of the bones. The Order of Ursulines, founded in 1535 by St. Angela Merici (Jan. 27), was dedicated to the education of young girls. It has also helped to spread the legend and cult of St. Ursula throughout the world.

Date	Name	Status	Venerated	Life
Oct. 19	Paul of the Cross (1694–1775)	Mystic, Founder ◯ 1867	GRC, LCDUS By Passionists	Born into wealthy Italian family. In 1720 a vision convinced him that God is found by us in the Passion of Jesus Christ. Dedicated his life to spreading this message; founded the Passionists, a community whose members would meditate on the Passion of Jesus, living lives of penitence, solitude, and poverty.
Oct. 19	Henry Martyn (1781–1812)	Missionary	CofE	Anglican priest and chaplain for the British East India Company. Translated New Testament into Urdu, Persian, and Judaeo-Persic. Traveled from India to Persia as a missionary, but was infected with plague, and died in Turkey on his way home.
Oct. 19	Jerzy Popieluszko (1947–84)	Priest ♥ 2010	In Poland	Charismatic Polish priest. Associated with the Solidarity trade union and staunchly anti-communist. His anti-regime sermons, broadcast by Radio Free Europe, famous throughout Poland. Finally silenced by the authorities when brutally murdered by three Security Police officers.

OCTOBER 22 · PETER OF ALCÁNTARA

STATUS Monk, Mystic, Founder

BORN 1499, Alcántara, Extremadura, Spain

DIED 1562, Ávila, Spain

GRC ♧

CofE ♧

LCDUS ♧

OTHER October 19

⬯ 1699

✝ In Franciscan friar's habit

⚱ Nightwatchmen; Brazil, Extremadura, Spain

Peter's father was the governor of Alcántara, and his mother was from a noble family. At age 14 he was sent to the University of Salamanca, two years later becoming a Franciscan of the Stricter Observance in Extremadura. He was ordained priest in 1524, and was soon intent on reforming the Constitution of the Stricter Observants. His severe and ascetic ideas met with opposition, so he retired to the mountains of Portugal where he intended to live an eremitic life. Soon other friars came to join him, and several small religious communities were established.

In 1555, he started the Alcantarine reforms; the extreme austerity of his interpretation of Franciscan rule was influential throughout Iberia and the Spanish colonies.

Peter was a devout mystic, who frequently entered an ecstatic state. He existed on bread and water, wore only a sackcloth habit and cloak, and only traveled on foot. He was the confessor of Teresa of Ávila (Oct. 15) and was said to have aided her in her foundation of the Carmelite Order of nuns.

OCTOBER 23 · JOHN OF CAPISTRANO

STATUS Priest

BORN 1386, Capistrano, Italy

DIED 1456, Ilok, Croatia

GRC ♣

CofE ♧

LCDUS ♣

OTHER By Franciscans

⬯ 1690

⚱ Jurists, military chaplains

John was a lawyer who was appointed governor of Perugia. When war broke out between Perugia and Sigismondo Malatesta in 1416, John was dispatched as an ambassador of Perugia, but was betrayed and thrown into prison. During his captivity he studied theology under St. Bernadine of Siena. On his release he entered the Franciscan Order, dedicated himself to a life of extreme asceticism, and became an eloquent preacher. He was a passionate opponent of heresy of all kinds, and was especially zealous in his pursuit of the Hussites.

After the fall of Constantinople, Pope Callixtus III sent John to preach a crusade against the invading Turks. His rhetoric inspired a huge gathering of troops, who marched on the city of Belgrade in the summer of 1456, and turned the Turkish troops away.

The Apparition of John of Capistrano to Peter of Alcántara, *by the Neapolitan painter Luca Giordano (1634–1705).*

Date	Name	Status	Venerated	Life
Oct. 20	Mary Bertilla Boscardin (1888–1922)	Nun ⬯ 1961		Born into poor family in Veneto, Italy. Became a nun; sent to learn nursing under direction of her order, the Sisters of St. Dorothy. During World War I her dedicated care for her patients was unswerving, despite hospital being on the front line. Went on to take charge of a children's isolation ward.
Oct. 21	Hilarion the Great (d.372)	Hermit ⬯ Pre-Congregation	Eastern Orthodox churches	Born in Palestine. Converted to Christianity and became disciple of St. Antony of Egypt (Jan. 17). Gave away his worldly possessions and devoted himself to an ascetic life of fasting and prayer in Palestinian desert. Regarded as founder of monasticism in Palestine.
Oct. 23	James of Jerusalem (d. AD 62)	Early Christian Leader ⬯ Pre-Congregation		Early leader of Christian congregation in Jerusalem. Thought to be author of the Epistle of St. James. Revered in early Christian Church. Jewish historian Josephus reports that he was "put to death by his enemies."

OCTOBER 24   ANTHONY MARY CLARET

STATUS   Bishop, Missionary, Founder

BORN   1807, Sallent, Spain

DIED   1870, Narbonne, France

GRC   ♣

CofE   ♧

LCDUS   ♣

◯   1950

Anthony's appeal remains firmly rooted in the latter years of Spain's power as a missionary force, and is marked by sentimentality; the Claretians came into being a generation after Spain had lost most of its New World colonies to independence movements.

St. Anthony Mary Claret.

A memorial card for the Claretian Order.

Anthony was the son of a weaver, and was ordained in 1835. His missionary career flourished in his native Catalonia, and in 1849 he was in a position to found the Missionary Sons of the Immaculate Heart of Mary (the Claretians). This resulted in his immediate assignment to the archbishopric of Cuba. There were at the time vigorous demands for independence in the Spanish colony that, combined with strong religious factionalism arising from local African-American cults such as Voodoun and Santeria, made Anthony's residence in Cuba a difficult one. He resigned in 1857, returning to Spain to become confessor to Queen Isabella II, where he established a number of academic institutions before following the queen into exile in France after the revolution of 1868.

OCTOBER 26   ALFRED THE GREAT

STATUS   King

BORN   849, Wantage, England

DIED   899, Winchester, England

GRC   ♧

CofE   ♣

LCDUS   ♧

OTHER   US Episcopal Church

◯   Pre-Congregation

✝   As king, crowned

♈   The British royal family

King Alfred (r.871–99) remains an important figure in English history, not only as the first ruler of a unified Wessex, and steadfast opponent of Danish incursions from the east, but as a fortifier of the Christian Church in England. Like many near contemporaries (such as Charlemagne in France and Stephen in Hungary) Alfred used Christianity to weld together a robust body politic in his nation state. His support for Church reform, learning, and monastic communities in particular, provided a solid footing for both church and state in Anglo-Saxon England.

Alfred is remembered as one of the first kings of a united England, albeit only the southern and western parts of the modern country, and as a noted lawgiver.

Date	Name	Status	Venerated	Life
Oct. 25	Chrysanthus and Daria (d.c.283)	Martyrs ◯ Pre-Congregation		Chrysanthus's Roman/Egyptian father tried to distract him from Christianity with the help of pagan priestess Daria. They fell in love, he converted her, and they entered a virginal marriage. Converted many others. Eventually martyred by being buried in sand on the Salarian Way, Rome.
Oct. 25	Crispin and Crispinian (d.c.285)	Martyrs ◯ Pre-Congregation	In Soissons, France; Faversham, England ✝ Shoes, cobbler's last ♈ Cobblers, leatherworkers	Twin Christian brothers who fled Rome, reaching Soissons, France. Earned their living making shoes when not preaching. Possibly reached Faversham in Kent. Eventually martyred. Popularity in Middle Ages evinced by 'St. Crispin's Day' speech before battle of Agincourt in Shakespeare's *Henry V*.
Oct. 25	Antônio de Sant'Anna Galvão (1739–1822)	Friar, Founder ♥ 1998 ◯ 2007	In Brazil	Born near São Paulo. Trained as Jesuit, but became Franciscan. Ordained 1762. With Helena Maria of the Holy Spirit, founded community of Our Lady of the Conception of Divine Providence and extended Franciscan missions in Brazil. Brazil's first native-born saint.

OCTOBER 27 FRUMENTIUS

STATUS Bishop, Missionary

BORN Early 4th century, Tyre, modern Lebanon

DIED c.383, Ethiopia

GRC ♧

CofE ♧

LCDUS ♧

OTHER By Ethiopian Orthodox Church (Aug. 1), Eastern Orthodox churches (Nov. 30), Coptic Orthodox Church (Dec. 18)

⬭ Pre-Congregation

✝ Often shown holding a sword

♠ Ethiopia

Frumentius is regarded as the father of the Christian Church in Ethiopia.

The introduction of Christianity to Axum also saw other Mediterranean conventions being adopted, such as minted coinage.

This remarkable saint is venerated as the evangelizer of Ethiopia and the founder of the Coptic Church in the kingdom of Axum. He first traveled down the Red Sea from Egypt as a boy, with his brother Aedesius, under the guardianship of their uncle Meropius. Their ship was hijacked, the crew killed, and the two boys taken to the realm of Axum, an enormously wealthy trading state in northeast Africa. Here they grew up as slaves in the royal household, but were released shortly before the king's death. They remained for several years, helping to educate his young heir. Eventually the brothers traveled north to Egypt, Aedesius returning to Tyre where he became a priest. Frumentius petitioned St. Athanasius of Alexandria (May 2) to send a mission to Axum to establish Christianity there. Athanasius encouraged Frumentius himself to return, and he succeeded in establishing a Christian community in the kingdom. Frumentius was consecrated by Athanasius as bishop of Axum in around 328.

Ethiopian crosses are often much more elaborate in design than traditional Christian crosses.

Date	Name	Status	Venerated	Life
Oct. 26	Cedd (d.c.664)	Bishop, Founder ⬭ Pre-Congregation	CofE	Brother of Chad (March 2), educated and ordained under St. Aidan (Aug. 31) at Lindisfarne. Went on to found monasteries in Northumbria and Yorkshire, including Lastingham. Became bishop of East Saxons, founding further monasteries at Bradwell-on-Sea and Tilbury.
Oct. 27	Bartholomew of Vicenza (c.1200–71)	Friar, Bishop, Founder ♥ 1793	By Dominicans	Educated at Padua, Italy. Entered Dominicans c.1220, serving as prior at several houses. Founded the military order Fratres Gaudentes (Joyful Brothers, 1233) to maintain civil peace at a time of internecine warfare between Italian city states. Accomplished several missions as papal legate. Created bishop of Vicenza in 1256. Wrote extensively.

SIMON AND JUDE THE APOSTLES

Two of the Twelve Apostles of whom little is known, Simon and Jude are referred to as cousins of Zebedee, and may therefore have been fishermen in Galilee before being called to follow Christ. They share this feast day on the slender evidence that they might have been martyred together in Persia *(right)*, or possibly Beirut or Edessa, although their individual biographies provide little evidence to support any of these claims. They are often represented together. Their relics were traditionally believed to have been translated to Rome in the 7th or 8th century, although both Toulouse and Rheims in France also claim their relics.

SIMON

STATUS	Apostle, Martyr
BORN	Early 1st century AD
DIED	Mid-1st century AD
GRC	♣
CofE	♣
LCDUS	♣
OTHER	Eastern Orthodox churches (July 1)
◯	Pre-Congregation
✝	Fish, boat, oar, saw (the instrument of his martyrdom)
🙏	Sawyers, tanners, curriers

The traditional method of Simon's martyrdom was exceptionally gruesome: he was sawn in half, lengthwise.

Simon is often called 'the Canaanite' or 'the Zealot' due to his apparently rigid observance of Jewish law. These sobriquets might also indicate that he was a member of a particular Jewish sect at the time. We know nothing concerning his calling to be an Apostle and, although he appears on all the major lists of the Apostles, he is not associated with any major events in the Gospels, except as one of the Twelve Disciples chosen by Christ.

He is not to be confused with 'Simon called Peter' who is often referred to simply as Simon, despite Jesus renaming him Peter upon his calling (June 29).

Simon's activities following Pentecost are not mentioned in Acts, but he is believed to have preached in Egypt before possibly traveling north with Jude to evangelize Syria and Mesopotamia.

The Spanish/Greek Mannerist painter El Greco (c.1541–1614) painted a series of individual portraits of the Apostles which emphasize their humanity, including Simon (left) and Jude (opposite, bottom right).

OCTOBER 28   JUDE (THADDEUS)

STATUS Apostle, Martyr

BORN Early 1st century AD

DIED Mid-1st century AD

GRC ♠

CofE ♠

LCDUS ♠

OTHER Eastern Orthodox churches (June 19)

◎ Pre-Congregation

✝ Ship, oar; club, axe, or halberd, (the instruments of his martyrdom); often shown carrying an image of Christ

🙏 Hospitals; desperate or lost causes, the unfortunate, those suffering bad luck; Armenia

St. Jude's association with hardship, bad luck, and social ostracism persists today in such works as Thomas Hardy's scandalous final novel, Jude the Obscure *(1895), and Paul McCartney's song 'Hey Jude' (1968), the melancholy but encouraging tone of which did not stop it from becoming* The Beatles' *most successful single.*

This moving portrayal of an aging Jude by Georges de la Tour (c.1615) shows the saint bearing his most frequently depicted tool of martyrdom, a halberd.

Referred to as the Apostle "not Iscariot" (John 14:22) Jude is also referred to as Thaddeus or Lebbaeus. He may be the author of the General Epistle of Jude in the New Testament, in which he identifies himself as the brother of James the Greater (July 25), and would therefore be a cousin of Jesus. This epistle, to the churches of the east (Mesopotamia and Persia), reveals a concern for backsliding among recent converts, and alerts the recipients to the dangers of heresies such as Gnosticism (*see* page 57).

Jude plays little active part in the Gospels, but is the Apostle who, at the Last Supper, asked if Jesus would manifest Himself to the world after the Resurrection. He is believed to have spread the Gospel north and east, preaching in Syria and possibly Mesopotamia and Persia. However, there is another tradition whereby Jude was martyred alone in Armenia, which was then subject to Persia. Armenia was to become the first modern state to adopt Christianity as its national religion, in the 4th century, and Jude/Thaddeus remains the patron saint of the country.

Jude's reputation as patron saint of lost causes may stem from the similarity of his name to that of Christ's betrayer, Judas Iscariot.

> "Keep yourselves in the love of God, looking for the mercy of our Lord Jesus Christ unto eternal life."
>
> THE GENERAL EPISTLE OF JUDE: 21.

Date	Name	Status	Venerated	Life
Oct. 28	Fidelis of Como (c.280–304)	Martyr ◎ Pre-Congregation	In Como and Milan, Italy	Roman soldier executed for helping Christian prisoners to escape during persecutions of Diocletian.
Oct. 28	Abraham (d.6th century)	Archbishop ◎ Pre-Congregation	Eastern Orthodox churches	Archbishop of Ephesus, Greece. Founded monasteries in Jerusalem and Constantinople. Came into conflict with Byzantine emperor Theophilus by refusing to adopt the Iconoclast heresy. His followers called Abrahamites.
Oct. 28	John Dat (1760–98)	Martyr ◎ 1988	In Vietnam	Vietnamese convert, ordained in 1798. Almost immediately arrested, imprisoned for three months, then beheaded.

OCTOBER 31 | WOLFGANG OF REGENSBURG

STATUS Bishop

BORN 924, Swabia, Germany

DIED 994, Pupping, Austria

GRC ☁

CofE ☁

LCDUS ☁

○ 1052

✝ Forcing the devil to help build a church; as a hermit in the wilderness

⚚ Carpenters, woodcarvers; against apoplexy, strokes, paralysis, stomach diseases; Regensburg

Wolfgang was descended from the Swabian counts of Pfullingen. He was tutored at home, later attending the Benedictine school at Reichenau Abbey. He formed a strong friendship with Henry of Babenberg, and went with him to Würzburg to the cathedral school there. When Henry was made archbishop of Trier in 956, he summoned Wolfgang to become a teacher at that cathedral school. After Henry's early death, Wolfgang entered the Benedictine Order at Einsiedeln, Switzerland, and was ordained a priest in 968.

In 955, at the battle of Lechfeld, King Otto I the Great decisively defeated the Magyars of Hungary, who had been making repeated incursions into Western Europe. Converting the heathen Magyars was seen as the most effective way of integrating them into the Holy Roman Empire; in 971, Wolfgang was chosen to undertake the task, and set out as head of a group of missionaries. Just a year later, on Christmas 972, Wolfgang was appointed the new bishop of Regensburg. In this post his intellectual abilities, diplomacy, and piety all came to the fore; he was the highly influential tutor to Henry II (July 13), who went on to become the last Holy Roman Emperor of the Ottonian dynasty. He made reforms to the famous St. Emmeran's Abbey, allowing it a measure of self-governance, which took it outside the flawed control of the diocese of Regensburg.

As a mainstay of Ottonian government, Wolfgang took part in various imperial diets, accompanying Emperor Otto II on his campaign to Paris in 978, and participating in the Diet of Verona in 983, where Italian and German nobles gathered together to elect Otto III the king of Germany and Otto II's successor.

In his old age, Wolfgang withdrew from the world, living the life of a hermit in a solitary region of Upper Austria, now known as the Wolfgangsee ('Wolfgang's Lake'). He died in the Austrian village of Pupping, and his body was returned to the abbey at Regensburg. Many miracles were reported to have been performed at his grave.

Legends from Wolfgang's life are memorably commemorated in the altarpiece panels by the remarkable Tyrolean painter Michael Pacher (1430–98), now in the Alte Pinakothek, Munich. He is shown praying for a miracle (above) and tricking the Devil into helping him build a church (right).

OCTOBER 31 | QUENTIN

STATUS Martyr

BORN Unknown

DIED c.287, Saint-Quentin, France

GRC ⬭

CofE ⬭

LCDUS ⬭

⬭ Pre-Congregation

✝ Dressed as a deacon; with a broken wheel; tied to a chair; with a sword; beheaded; a dove flying from his severed head

🙏 Chaplains, locksmiths, surgeons

"San Quentin, I hate every inch of you!" (Johnny Cash, Live at San Quentin). St. Quentin is one of the few saints with a famous state prison named after him.

Quentin was a Roman citizen and an enthusiastic convert to Christianity who traveled to Gaul as a missionary. He settled in Amiens, and was said to perform many miracles there. But his Christian sermons brought him to the attention of the authorities, and he was imprisoned by the prefect Rictiovarus.

Quentin was subject to brutal torture but refused to renounce his faith. The prefect decided to take the obstinate prisoner to Reims, the capital of Gallia Belgica, where he wanted him judged. But on the way, in the town of Augusta Veromanduorum (now Saint-Quentin, Aisne), Quentin escaped, apparently with the aid of divine intervention, and immediately resumed preaching.

Rictiovarus decided he had no option but to pass sentence himself; Quentin was tortured again, then beheaded, and his body was secretly thrown into the marshes bordering the river Somme.

The Cult of St. Quentin

It is said that some 55 years later, a blind woman named Eusebia traveled from Rome and discovered — by the power of prayer alone — the corpse and head of St. Quentin. As the body was pulled from the marshes, her sight was restored. She buried the body at the top of a mountain near Augusta Veromanduorum, and built a small chapel there. By the mid-7th century the whereabouts of the tomb had been long forgotten, and Bishop St. Eligius set out to find the shrine. After several days digging, he miraculously found the tomb. In the Middle Ages the cult of St. Quentin became well established, reflected in the number of towns named St. Quentin, especially in northern France. His tomb became a place of pilgrimage.

The wide range of tortures to which Quentin was subjected allowed artists a free range in their devotional depictions. Here the artist Jordaens (1593–1678) shows the martyr about to be decapitated after a mauling by a wild beast has failed to kill him.

Date	Name	Status	Venerated	Life
Oct. 29	Narcissus of Jerusalem (c. AD 100–216)	Bishop ⬭ Pre-Congregation	Eastern Orthodox churches	Of Greek origin. Became 30th bishop of Jerusalem. Said to have performed many miracles. During Easter vigil, changed water into oil to supply the church lamps. Falsely defamed by his enemies, retired from Jerusalem for some years, but returned at request of his parishioners. Died while at prayer.
Oct. 29	James Hannington (1847–85)	Missionary, Bishop, Martyr	CofE	Born in Sussex, England. Rural deacon who offered his services to Church Missionary Society. Became bishop of Eastern Equatorial Africa. In 1885, while attempting to open a new route to Uganda with other missionaries, was captured on the orders of King Mwanga II of Buganda and killed.
Oct. 30	Benvenuta of Cividale (1254–92)	Nun, Visionary ⬭ 1765	In Friuli, Italy	A pious child, already practicing self-mortification by age 12. Became Dominican tertiary; subjected herself to rigorous regime of self-flagellation (often thrice daily) that broke down her health. Experienced visions of Sts. Dominic, Peter Martyr, and the Blessed Virgin Mary. After her death, miracles were attributed to her intercession.
Oct. 31	Alphonsus Rodríguez (1532–1617)	Jesuit ⬭ 1888	By Jesuits 🙏 Majorca	Native of Segovia. A 38-year-old widower when he became a Jesuit lay brother. Uneducated and in poor health, became porter at Montesión College in Majorca. Remained there 46 years; finally ordained 1585. Dispensed sympathy and advice, impressing everyone with his spirituality and asceticism.

NOVEMBER

❧⟶⟵❧

November is beckoned in with three major festivals associated with the dead.

November 1, the day after Halloween, is All Saints' Day and celebrates those who have enjoyed a beatific experience of Heaven. Widely observed in the West, in the Eastern churches it is celebrated on the first Sunday after Pentecost. November 2 commemorates those who have passed on, but may not yet have reached Heaven, with All Souls' Day (or The Day of the Dead). November 11, for centuries celebrated as Martinmas, the traditional beginning of winter in the European agricultural calendar, is now better known as marking Remembrance (Veterans) Day, recognizing all those fallen on the field of battle.

On a more joyful note, November often includes the first day of Advent.

The Day of the Dead is a major festival throughout Latin America, when families come together to remember their departed loved ones and ancestors. Revelers build altars, create confectionary in the form of skulls and skeletons, visit graves, and hold parties.

NOVEMBER 1   ALL SAINTS

The cult of sainthood, and the ability to intercede directly with the Holy Trinity, became central to Catholic dogma during the Counter-Reformation.

An important ecumenical feast (a Solemnity in the General Roman Calendar), All Saints celebrates not only every saint recognized by the Church, but also their associates and followers, and indeed all those whose lives displayed demonstrable sanctity. It is also a time to remember all those who have been nominated as suitable for canonization, but whose cases remain under consideration. Further, it reminds us of those en route to full sainthood, who have reached the stage of veneration or beatification, but who have not yet been canonized, or have not been assigned a feast day.

The feast was possibly first introduced in England in the early 8th century (where it was called All Hallows). It became established throughout Europe by the 12th century, and is observed by most Christians around the world, although the Eastern churches celebrate this feast on the first Sunday after Pentecost.

The Solemnity of All Saints, especially in Latin America where the invocation of saints is of particular importance, includes a complex iconography. Here the Blessed Virgin of Carmel gives her instructions to the archangels concerning who should be raised from Purgatory.

NOVEMBER 2   ALL SOULS

All Souls can first be traced to Spain in the 7th century, although it probably had its origin in pagan ancestor worship. The feast was adopted by Odilo, abbot of Cluny, in 988, and became common on liturgical calendars by the 13th century. In the Catholic Church it is formally known as the 'Commemoration of All the Faithful Departed,' and is now linked to the dogma of Purgatory propagated at the Council of Trent in 1545. Catholics specifically direct prayers and celebrate Mass for those whose souls remain in Limbo (Purgatory), and who require the intercession of the living to complete the purging of their sins. However morbid this may seem, it is a singularly popular feast, with family graves being visited and decorated across the Catholic world, and it is commonly known as 'The Day of the Dead.' The Eastern Orthodox churches set aside seven Saturdays in the calendar for this feast.

The vision of the fate of those entering Purgatory after death (literally the 'state of purging') was considerably more frightening in northern Europe, as shown in this 15th-century English woodcut.

A preparatory drawing by the Baroque artist Rubens shows saints interceding on behalf of souls in Purgatory, appealing for their admission to Heaven.

NOVEMBER 3 — MARTIN DE PORRES

STATUS Priest
BORN 1579, Lima, Peru
DIED 1639, Lima, Peru
GRC ♣
CofE ♣
LCDUS ♣
OTHER In Peru
♥ 1837
◯ 1962

Martin took after his mother, a freed black slave from Panama, rather than his father, a Spanish *hidalgo*. He was apprenticed to a barber-surgeon before becoming a Dominican tertiary, entering a convent as a menial lay servant in 1595. He soon became noted for his devotion, spiritual guidance, and considerable healing skills. In 1603 he was appointed lay brother. He humbly referred to himself as a "mulatto dog," but was revered by his fellow priests and patients.

FRAY MARTIN DE PORRES

NEW MARTYRS

The creation of saints in the 20th century accelerated dramatically as a result of global wars and repressive regimes. Both Pope John Paul II and Pope Benedict XVI proved keen canonizers. Spain, Mexico, China, Vietnam, and Korea all added significantly to the 5,000 or so saints listed by the *Catholic Encyclopedia*, but many remain nameless.

Mass canonizations were instituted by the Russian Orthodox Church in the wake of *glasnost* and the effective collapse of Communism. The Orthodox Church remembers the 600 bishops, 40,000 priests, 120,000 monks and nuns, and maybe millions of lay Christians who were persecuted prior to 1989.

Date	Name	Status	Venerated	Life
Nov. 3	Hubert (d.727)	Bishop ◯ Pre-Congregation	In the Ardennes ✝ Stag with crucifix in its antlers ⚊ Hunting, hunters	Succeeded St. Lambert as bishop of Maastricht (modern Belgium). Undertook missionary journeys in the Ardennes to eliminate heathen practices. Died following fishing accident on river Meuse. Had youthful revelation while hunting of a stag with a crucifix in its antlers (suspiciously similar to that of St. Eustace, Sept. 20). Has emerged as patron saint of hunting, at least in Western tradition.
Nov. 3	Winifred (7th century)	Nun ◯ Pre-Congregation	In Wales ✝ Headless, with well	Possibly a niece of St. Beuno. Resisted attentions of Prince Caradoc of Wales, who struck off her head. The earth swallowed him up, and Beuno reattached her head; restored, she retreated to a nunnery. A spring erupted where her head landed (Holywell, Wales) and is still reputed to have healing powers today.
Nov. 3	Richard Hooker (1554–1600)	Priest, Theologian	CofE	Oxford-educated theologian whose *Of the Laws of Ecclesiastical Polity* (1593) was important in establishing legal structure of Anglican Church. Often in conflict with the Puritans. Served at Salisbury Cathedral, the Temple Church in London, Boscombe in Wiltshire. Died in Bishopsbourne, Kent, where he was vicar.

NOVEMBER 4 · CHARLES BORROMEO

STATUS Bishop, Founder
BORN 1538, Arona, Italy
DIED 1584, Milan, Italy
GRC ♣
CofE ◯
LCDUS ♣
♥ 1602
◯ 1610
✝ Usually shown bareheaded and tonsured, barefoot, with a rope or cord, although often in cardinal's robes
🙏 Bishops, catechists, seminarians; against stomach disorders

As a measure of Borromeo's importance, this colossal statue, some 80 feet (23m) high, was created by Giovanni Battista Crespi. It was erected at Arona, on the shore of Lake Maggiore, Italy, in the 17th century.

Charles Borromeo was one of the most important figures of the Counter-Reformation. He was born to a noble family, educated in Milan and Pavia, studying civil and canon law, and entered the clergy at age 12. Under the patronage of his uncle, Pope Pius IV, he rose rapidly, becoming administrator and then bishop of Milan, then cardinal. He attended the final session of the influential Council of Trent (1562–63), where many Counter-Reformation measures were initiated.

Despite his aristocratic background, wealth, and large income, Charles gave most of his money away. He lived frugally and worked actively for his congregation during the plague of 1576. He was determined to re-establish the Catholic faith as a dignified central force in contemporary society. In the face of the Protestant challenge, Charles energetically dedicated himself to implementing the reforms promulgated at the Council of Trent, reorganizing the structure of his diocese, founding seminaries and schools, and imposing strict discipline on his priests. His actions were not unopposed, and he survived an assassination attempt by a lay confraternity in 1569. He founded a society of diocesan priests in 1578, the Oblates of St. Ambrose (now the Society of St. Ambrose and St. Charles, or the Ambrosians), to enforce his reforms.

Charles was widely revered beyond Italy: both Sts. Edmund Campion and Francis Borgia were admirers and colleagues. Overwork seems to have exhausted him, and he died of a recurring fever at age 46. Support for his canonization was immediate, and by 1613 his feast had been added to the General Roman Calendar. His tomb is in Milan Cathedral.

Charles offering the Host to a plague victim. Despite being something of a martinet, Charles was selfless in his devotion to his flock.

Date	Name	Status	Venerated	Life
Nov. 6	Leonard the Hermit (6th century)	Abbot, Hermit ◯ Pre-Congregation	🙏 Prisoners	Almost nothing known of him, but enormously popular in France, England, and Germany, especially during Crusades. Founded St. Leonard monastery near Limoges, France. Numerous miracles attributed to him.
Nov. 6	William Temple (1881–1944)	Bishop	CofE	English clergyman, teacher, and social reformer. Supported working-class movements and economic reform. As archbishop of Canterbury (1942–44) caused controversy with his support for Allied war effort in WWII. Visited Normandy beaches during Operation Overlord. First Anglican primate to be cremated.

NOVEMBER 5 — ZECHARIAH AND ELIZABETH

STATUS Parents of John the Baptist

BORN Mid-1st century BC

DIED Early 1st century AD

GRC ☁

CofE ☁

LCDUS ☁

OTHER Eastern Orthodox churches

⬭ Pre-Congregation

✝ Aged couple, usually attending birth of John the Baptist; Elizabeth sometimes features in figure groups with the Virgin and Child and St. John

🙏 Parents, grandparents

In the Gospel of Luke, Zechariah, a priest in the Temple at Jerusalem, is visited by the Archangel Gabriel (Sept. 29), who announces that Zechariah's elderly and barren wife Elizabeth is expecting a child – John the Baptist (Luke 1:5–25). Disbelieving, Zechariah asks for proof, and in punishment, Gabriel strikes Zechariah dumb, although his speech is miraculously restored following John's birth (June 24), after Zechariah confirms the unusual name of the child in writing. Zechariah then speaks the prophetic lines of the Benedictus (Luke 1: 68–79). Elizabeth also features in Luke 1:42 when she is visited by her cousin – the Visitation of the Blessed Virgin Mary (May 31).

Domenico Ghirlandaio's rich imagining of Zechariah's encounter with the Angel Gabriel was painted in Florence in 1490. The assembled congregation comprises portraits of Florentine worthies of the time, all unaware of the miraculous event.

NOVEMBER 6 — PAUL OF CONSTANTINOPLE

STATUS Bishop

BORN c.300, Thessalonika, Greece

DIED c.350, Cucusus, Armenia

GRC ☁

CofE ☁

LCDUS ☁

OTHER Eastern Orthodox churches

⬭ Pre-Congregation

Paul was a strong defender of the Nicene Creed at a time when the Arian controversy wracked the Roman empire (*see page 12*). He was elected bishop of Constantinople in around 336, some ten years after the Council of Nicaea had condemned Arianism, but just as the emperor Constantius, an Arian supporter, gained power. Paul was rapidly supplanted, but was soon re-elected.

Imperial pressure on the see resulted in a popular rebellion, during which one of the emperor's emissaries was killed. Paul was exiled to the shores of the Black Sea, but once again was reinstated, then once again exiled to the Caucasus region. It is said that he was throttled by Arians in Armenia.

Date	Name	Status	Venerated	Life
Nov. 7	Willibrord of York (d.739)	Bishop, Missionary ⬭ Pre-Congregation	CofE	Benedictine monk from Northumbria. Consecrated bishop of the Frisians and sent to convert pagan tribes of what is now the Netherlands. Built numerous churches and monasteries. Became first bishop of Utrecht. Buried at Abbey of Echternach; many miracles attributed to him.
Nov. 8	John Duns Scotus (d.1308)	Philosopher, Theologian ♥ 1992		Ordained priest and scholar. Born in Duns, Scotland. Studied at universities of Oxford, Cambridge, Paris, and Cologne. Famous for his complex arguments supporting existence of God and Immaculate Conception. Known as 'Doctor Subtilis' due to subtlety of his thought. Also accused of sophistry, leading to origin of the word 'dunce' – one incapable of learning. Founded Scotism. Possibly accidentally buried alive while in a coma.

THE DEDICATION OF ST. JOHN LATERAN

This feast celebrates the foundation in 324, by Pope Sylvester I (Dec. 31), of the first church in Rome, on land on the Celian Hill belonging to the Laterani family. The present basilica was built in the 17th-18th centuries by Borromini and others. It is regarded as the cathedral church of the pope in his role as bishop of Rome.

The pope's church was burned down in 1360 and major rebuilding started in 1586. The main east façade was added in the 18th century by Alessandro Galilei.

LEO THE GREAT

STATUS Pope, Doctor of the Church

BORN c.400, Tuscany, Italy

DIED 461, Rome, Italy

GRC ♣

CofE ♣

LCDUS ♣

OTHER Eastern Orthodox churches

⊘ Pre-Congregation

An influential churchman, Leo was unanimously elected pope in 440, succeeding Sixtus III.

In 445, Leo obtained from Emperor Valentinian III the famous decree that recognized the primacy of the bishop of Rome. The rulings of the pope were to have the force of ecclesiastical law, and any opposition would be interpreted as treason. Leo made a series of moves to assert the authority of the papacy, rebuking errant bishops for deviations from Roman practice. He was also an implacable foe of heresy.

At the Second Council of Ephesus in 449, Leo's representatives delivered his famous *Tome*, a statement of faith in the Roman Church. He went on to convene the Council of Chalcedon in 451 to condemn the heretical teachings of the day.

Rome, meanwhile, was increasingly vulnerable to barbarian threats and incursions from the East. The impending collapse of the Roman Empire gave Leo another opportunity to assert his authority. In 452, the king of the Huns, Attila, invaded Italy and threatened Rome.

Leo was sent to negotiate with Attila at Mantua. The encounter was successful – perhaps because of the large sum of money offered to Attila, or because he recognized that his forces were overstretched – and Attila withdrew. Legend has it that, as Leo spoke, Attila saw a vision of a sword-wielding man in priestly robes who threatened to attack if he did not retreat.

When the Vandals under Genseric finally occupied the city of Rome in 455, Leo persuaded the invaders to desist from pillaging the city and harming its inhabitants. He died in 461, leaving letters and writings of great historical value. His eloquent prose style, called *cursus leonicus*, went on to influence ecclesiastical language for many centuries.

A medieval illumination of Leo the Great pronouncing judgment on the Monophysite doctrine of the archbishops of Constantinople, Antioch, and Alexandria.

This fresco in the Vatican painted by Raphael shows the meeting between Leo and Attila the Hun. It was commissioned by Pope Julius II (r.1503–13), but was only completed in 1514, under his successor Leo X (r.1513–21).

Date	Name	Status	Venerated	Life
Nov. 8	Four Crowned Martyrs (d.c.287–304)	Martyrs ⊘ Pre-Congregation	In Serbia	A group of sculptors (actually five men from Sirmium, modern Serbia), who refused to fashion a pagan statue for Emperor Diocletian. Were buried alive in lead coffins and thrown into the sea.
Nov. 9	Margery Kempe (c.1373–1438)	Pilgrim, Mystic	CofE, US Episcopal Church	Worldly medieval housewife who felt a spiritual calling and committed her life to God. Stories of her pilgrimages all over Europe, and her mystical musings, gathered by her in *The Book of Margery Kempe*, thought to be first autobiography in English language.

NOVEMBER 11 | MARTIN OF TOURS

STATUS Bishop

BORN 316, Savaria, modern Hungary

DIED 397, Candes-St.-Martin, France

GRC ♣

CofE ♣

LCDUS ♣

○ Pre-Congregation

† Man on horseback, sharing cloak with beggar; cutting cloak in half; globe of fire; goose

⚱ Beggars, geese, horses, innkeepers, soldiers, tailors, vintners; against poverty and alcoholism; Tours, Dover, Buenos Aires, Mainz, Rottenburg-Stuttgart, Utrecht, France, Malta

El Greco's St. Martin and the Beggar (c.1597–99) anachronistically shows Martin in 16th-century dress.

Born into a senior military family in imperial Rome, Martin served as a cavalry officer in Amiens. Here, he experienced the pivotal vision that was to shape his life. Encountering a poor beggar at the gates of the city, he cut his cloak in half and shared it. That night he dreamed he saw Jesus, dressed in the half-cloak, saying, "Here is Martin, the Roman soldier, who is not baptized; he has clad me." This vision reinforced Martin's nascent piety, and at age 18 he was baptized. After two more years' military service, he came to the conclusion that his faith prohibited him from fighting. He was imprisoned for cowardice, and when the Gauls sued for peace, he was released from military service.

Martin made his way to Tours, and became a disciple of Hilary of Poitiers (Jan. 13). When Hilary was sent into exile, Martin made his way back to Italy, and for a time lived the solitary life of a hermit on a remote island.

In 361, Martin returned to Gaul under the patronage of the newly-reinstated Hilary, established a monastery, and traveled around western Gaul preaching and converting. He was acclaimed bishop of Tours in 371. Legend has it that — unwilling to accept the honor — he took refuge in a stable filled with geese, whose gobbling soon betrayed his whereabouts. His feast day is still widely commemorated with a roast goose.

Martin immediately embarked on an enthusiastic campaign of burning and destroying all the pagan temples and shrines in Tours, constructing churches to replace them. He also founded an abbey at Marmoutier, on the opposite bank of the Loire from Tours, and frequently withdrew there for the tranquility and asceticism of the monastic life.

This fresco, from the Lower Church of San Francesco at Assisi, painted by Simone Martini in 1321, celebrates St. Martin's renunciation of violence in the battlefield.

The Cult of St. Martin

Medieval veneration of Martin was closely associated with *The Life of St. Martin*, written by his friend Sulpicius Severus. It is filled with accounts of miracles, from raising the dead to casting out devils. Threads from St. Martin's 'sacred' cloak were said to have miraculous powers. By as early as the mid-5th century, crowds of pilgrims were swamping the small chapel built over Martin's grave at Candes-St.-Martin on the Loire, and his body was re-buried beneath the high altar of the new basilica.

St. Martin was adopted as a patron saint by successive royal houses of France. The Merovingians, the effective founders of the French state, credited their success against the Alemanni to the intervention of St. Martin, and their devotion was adopted by their successors, the Carolingians. The shrine of St. Martin of Tours became a major stopping point on medieval pilgrimage routes. In 1453, the remains of St. Martin were transferred to a magnificent new reliquary, which was sacked by Huguenots in the 16th-century wars of religion and completely desecrated during the French Revolution. In 1925 a new basilica was consecrated on the site.

St. Martin was promoted as a military saint during the Franco-Prussian War of 1870-71. His association with militarism was reinforced at the end of World War I when the Armistice fell on St. Martin's Day (November 11), and people saw it as a sign of his intercession in the affairs of France. His feast day also falls shortly after the annual grape harvest, and he is even credited with a prominent role in the spread of wine-making.

Date	Name	Status	Venerated	Life
Nov. 12	Didacus of Alcalá (d.1463)	Lay Brother of the Order of Friars Minor ○ 1588	GRC, LCDUS By Franciscans	Lay Franciscan brother. Became guardian of Franciscan community on Canarian island of Fuerteventura. Traveled to Rome and worked as an infirmarian. Spent his last years in spiritual contemplation in a convent in Alcalá, Spain. Many miracles attributed to his intercession.
Nov. 12	Josaphat of Polotsk (1580–1623)	Bishop, Martyr ○ 1867	GRC, Eastern Orthodox churches	Eastern Orthodox bishop. Supported movement to return to communion with the Catholic Church. Eastern Orthodox faithful in his own diocese of Polotsk (Belarus) turned against him, and he fell victim to an angry and violent mob. First saint of the Eastern churches to be canonized by Rome.

NOVEMBER 13 | FRANCES XAVIER CABRINI

STATUS Virgin, Missionary, Founder

BORN 1850, Lombardy, Italy

DIED 1917, Chicago, USA

GRC ○

CofE ○

LCDUS ♣

♥ 1938

○ 1946

⚭ Immigrants, hospital administrators

Though born in Italy, Frances Xavier Cabrini, the 13th child of a moderately prosperous Lombardy farmer, is the first American to have been canonized. Having run an orphanage in northern Italy for three years after becoming a nun in 1877, in 1880 she founded the Missionary Sisters of the Sacred Heart of Jesus. Her intention was to do missionary work in China, but the pope, Leo XIII, instead requested that she travel to the United States, then already home to millions of Italian immigrants.

Frances arrived in New York in 1889 and immediately began to open orphanages and other institutions, chiefly hospitals and schools. Her first orphanage, the St. Cabrini Home, was in Ulster County, New York. She became an American citizen in 1909. Her work was never restricted to the United States. She traveled widely across Central and South America as well as making numerous return visits to Europe. In all, she oversaw the opening of 67 institutions. The Sisters continue their work today across all parts of the globe.

Although her work extended across the Americas, Frances will always be most associated with New York, and the famous immigrant entrepôt of Ellis Island, lying in the shadow of the Statue of Liberty. By the time she started work in the city in 1889 there were over 50,000 Italian immigrants, often living in dire conditions, in the tenements of Manhattan's Lower East Side.

Date	Name	Status	Venerated	Life
Nov. 13	Brice (Britius) (d.444)	Bishop ○ Pre-Congregation	CofE In France	Successor, in 397, to Martin of Tours (Nov. 11).
Nov. 13	Charles Simeon (1759–1836)	Priest	CofE	Evangelical clergyman. Rector of Holy Trinity Church, Cambridge, UK. Co-founder of the Church Missionary Society and the Simeon Trust. Prolific writer of 'sermon skeletons,' and of the biblical commentary *Horae homiletica*.
Nov. 14	Lawrence O'Toole (1128–80)	Bishop ○ 1225	In Ireland	Influential medieval Irish prelate. Kidnapped at age ten during clan rivalry. Educated at Glendalough Monastery, and elected abbot (1153), then archbishop of Dublin (1162). Notable negotiator and peacemaker following English invasion of Ireland (1170). Appointed papal legate for Ireland.
Nov. 14	Samuel Seabury (1729–96)	Bishop	CofE, US Episcopal Church, Anglican Church of Canada	American-born Anglican polemicist and priest who remained a Loyalist during American Revolution, but contributed greatly to post-bellum restoration of Anglican liturgy in America, based on Scottish Episcopal Rite (under which he was consecrated bishop of New London, Conn., due to his US citizenship).
Nov. 14	Joseph Pignatelli (1737–1811)	Priest ♥ 1933 ○ 1954	By Jesuits	Influential Spanish Jesuit who sustained the Society of Jesus during its period of general repression from 1773 by appealing to Russian branch of the order.

NOVEMBER 15 — ALBERT THE GREAT (ALBERTUS MAGNUS)

STATUS Bishop, Theologian, Doctor of the Church

BORN 1200, Swabia, Germany

DIED 1280, Cologne, Germany

GRC ♣

CofE ♤

LCDUS ♣

OTHER By Dominicans

❤ 1622

⬤ 1931

✝ Dominican robes, miter, books

🙏 Scientists, the natural sciences

Albert was one of a group of enormously literate medieval churchmen and scholars – which included his pupil Thomas Aquinas (Jan. 28) – who had a profound influence on the doctrinal footings of the Catholic Church. This meant that, despite the widespread laxity of much of the clergy (and indeed some popes), Rome was well equipped to meet the challenge of the Reformation some three centuries later. He entered the Dominican Order while studying at Padua, and went on to teach at Hildesheim, Regensburg, Cologne (where he taught Aquinas, and reorganized the Dominican studies there), and Paris. For three years from 1254, Albert was Dominican Prior Provincial to Germany and personal theologian to Pope Alexander IV. He was appointed bishop of Regensburg (Ratisbon), Germany, in 1260, but retired to Cologne after two years. He pioneered the application of Aristotelian principles to theology, seeking the coexistence of science and religion.

Albert's prolific output, some 38 volumes of treatises on subjects as varied as astronomy and botany as well as theology, led him to be declared a Doctor of the Church in 1931, upon his canonization.

NOVEMBER 15 — SAINTS, MARTYRS, AND MISSIONARIES OF NORTH AMERICA

The Pilgrim Fathers celebrating the first Thanksgiving reflects something of the settlers' intention to live peacefully with their native North American hosts. For many decades, however, this proved an uneasy relationship.

The evangelization of North America shadowed both the patterns of European colonization and the levels of resistance by the indigenous peoples to the imposition of a new religion. A cursory reading of the map of North America reflects these patterns.

The first Spanish colonists established an indelible Catholic imprint in the South, the Southwest, and the West Coast, reflected today in the abundance of missions, forts, and associated place names, from St. Augustine in Florida through San Antonio in Texas, Santa Fe in New Mexico, to Santa Barbara, Los Angeles, and San Francisco on the Pacific coast. Most of the Spanish missionaries were Franciscans or Jesuits following in the steps of the conquistadors, and determined to destroy all trace of indigenous religion in the name of the Roman Church. Much of this was achieved inadvertently by the introduction of European diseases to which the natives had no resistance.

French Catholic missionaries entered the North American continent through two axes: the St. Lawrence river and the Great Lakes, and the Mississippi valley. Most missionaries were Jesuits. It was in Canada and the Northeast that the most interesting attempts to convert native North Americans occurred, as priests endeavored to settle among groups such as the Iroquois, the Mohawks, and the Hurons, and gain their trust. Many were turned upon, such as the North American Martyrs (Oct. 19).

The Protestant influence was more varied. The New World provided an opportunity for many Reformist groups to found new communities in a continent free of religious persecution, among them the Anabaptists, Quakers, and Calvinists. These fledgling communities strove to live peacefully alongside the indigenous peoples, but did not tend to proselytize. The Church of England's first 'missions' were aimed merely at supporting the settlers, not converting the natives. However, with the opening of the Midwest and the frontier in the 19th century, itinerant European immigrants often found themselves confronted with vicious resistance from the powerful Plains Indian tribes, who understandably saw the newcomers as a threat to their traditions, lands, and livelihood.

A further admixture resulted from religious traditions that accompanied the millions of black Africans who were transported as slaves across the Middle Passage. Many, in particular the Yoruba peoples, found a way to combine their worship of traditional gods with the saints revered by their white masters, producing new syncretic religious cults such as Voudon (Voodoo) and Santeria.

NOVEMBER 16 — EDMUND RICH

STATUS Bishop
BORN c.1175, Abingdon, England
DIED 1240, Soisy-Bouy, France
GRC ◯
CofE ♣
LCDUS ◯
○ 1246
✝ Archbishop making a vow before a statue of the Blessed Virgin Mary; receiving a lamb from the Blessed Virgin Mary; with St. Richard of Chichester or St. Thomas of Canterbury
⚘ Abingdon, Diocese of Portsmouth

Educated at a monastic school in Oxfordshire, Edmund attended the universities of Oxford and Paris, and became a lecturer in mathematics and dialectics, and the first known Oxford Master of Arts. Pious and ascetic, he abandoned his secular career and was ordained some time after 1205. He received a doctorate in theology, and soon his reputation as an inspirational preacher was widespread. After three years as vicar of Calne, Wiltshire, and treasurer of Salisbury Cathedral, he was appointed archbishop of Canterbury in 1234.

A proponent of independence from Rome, Edmund was opposed to the appointment of foreigners in influential ecclesiastical and civil positions. He asserted these views to King Henry III, and persuaded him — under threat of excommunication — to dismiss his councilors, in particular the bishop of Winchester, Peter des Roches. He visited Rome in 1237 to enlist the pope's support

The pious Edmund Rich rendered in a woodcut from the Nuremberg Chronicle.

for his ecclesiastical reforms. The mission was futile, and on Edmund's return to England he found his authority was seriously undermined. By 1240, he was forced to submit to the pope's demands, paying Rome one-fifth of his revenues. This broke his spirit, and in the summer of 1240 he retired to the Augustinian house at Soisy-Bouy, 60 miles (96 km) from Paris. He died just a few months later. Miracles were said to have been wrought at his grave, but his canonization did not proceed until Henry III lifted his objections.

Edmund's Oxford career was memorialized when St. Edmund Hall was founded in his name. His life inspired the formation of the Society of St. Edmund at Pontigny, France, in 1843, which was dedicated to faithful service and mission work. After religious persecution in France, members of the Society fled to Vermont, where they continue their work to this day.

NOVEMBER 17 — HUGH OF LINCOLN

STATUS Bishop
BORN c.1135, Avalon, France
DIED 1200, London, England
GRC ◯
CofE ♣
LCDUS ◯
○ 1220
✝ A white swan
⚘ Swans, the sick

Hugh's arms refer to a swan that supposedly formed a lasting friendship with the saint and became his constant companion.

When Hugh's father William, seigneur of Avalon, became a widower, he retired to a nearby priory and took his eight-year-old son with him. Hugh adapted well to the monastic life, becoming a deacon at age 19, and eventually rose to become procurator at the monastery of Grande Chartreuse. In 1179, he was appointed prior of Witham in Somerset, the first English Carthusian house, founded by Henry II. The monastery was in a parlous state, with the monks living in wooden huts. Hugh petitioned the king, and in 1182 Witham Charterhouse received a royal endowment. For the next four years Hugh presided over the monastery, which was frequently visited by the king.

In 1186, the canons at Lincoln Cathedral elected Hugh bishop, and he was consecrated five months later. Hugh asserted his independence from the king, refusing to seat one of Henry's court nominees as prebendary of Lincoln, but his diplomatic tact and charm kept the king's anger at bay. He proved to be an exceptionally diligent bishop,

rebuilding the cathedral, endowing many charities, and traveling tirelessly throughout his diocese. When the large Jewish population in Lincoln began to suffer persecution in the reign of Richard I, Hugh became their staunch defender.

In 1199, Hugh undertook a diplomatic mission to France for King John, which ruined his health. When he returned home he consecrated St. Giles' Church in Oxford, but some months later he died of a mystery illness while attending a national council in London.

Lincoln Cathedral was damaged in an earthquake in 1185, and Hugh set about rebuilding it.

'LITTLE ST. HUGH'

In Lincoln, in 1255, the body of a nine-year-old Christian boy, Hugh, was found with stigmata-like wounds and evidence of other torture. Suspicion fell on the Jewish community, one of whom confessed to the ritual murder of the child, explaining that this sacrifice was an annual requirement of his faith. By no means coincidentally, six months earlier, King Henry III had transferred the revenue from Jewish taxation to his brother, Richard of Cornwall, but had retained the right to confiscate property from convicted Jewish criminals. Eventually around 90 members of the Jewish community were arrested and taken to London for trial; 18 were hanged and the rest were released after the intercession of the king and his brother, probably fearful of loss of income from taxation. A number of legends grew up around the miraculous properties of Little St. Hugh's remains, which are lodged in Lincoln Cathedral.

NOVEMBER 17   ELISABETH OF HUNGARY

STATUS Princess
BORN 1207, Pressburg, Hungary (modern Bratislava, Slovakia)
DIED 1231, Marburg, Hessen (modern Germany)
GRC ♠
CofE ♠ (Nov. 16)
LCDUS ♠
⊖ 1235
✝ Roses, crown, basket of food
🙏 Dying children, the homeless, widows, exiles

Daughter of King Andrew II of Hungary, Elisabeth (Elizabeth) was brought to the court of the rulers of Thuringia in the Holy Roman Empire, at the age of just four. It was decided that she would marry Ludwig IV of Thuringia, reinforcing the political alliance between the two courts. She married Ludwig when she was only 14, and he was crowned ruler in the same year, 1221. At this time Elisabeth came under the influence of a group of Franciscan monks, and started to dedicate herself to charitable works.

Konrad von Marburg, a harsh and worldly priest, was appointed as her confessor, and began to exert considerable influence over her.

When, in 1226, her husband was called to represent the Holy Roman Emperor at the Imperial Diet in Cremona, Elisabeth assumed control of the affairs of state. She built a hospital in Wartburg Castle, and distributed alms to the poor. Just a year later Elisabeth was left a widow and she moved away from the court at Wartburg to Marburg.

A Cruel Widowhood

Konrad now began to wield sadistic power over his young charge. Elisabeth swore complete obedience to her spiritual adviser, taking a vow of celibacy, which would prohibit her from remarrying and making a new dynastic alliance. Konrad ruled her household with a rod of iron, meting out physical punishments for transgressions, and ordered her to send away her three children.

Elisabeth became affiliated with the Third Order of St. Francis, a lay Franciscan group, and built a hospital at Marburg for the poor and sick. She died when she was only 24, possibly broken down by Konrad's harsh treatment.

Very soon after her death, there were reports of miracles taking place at her grave. Close examination of these reports led to her very rapid canonization in 1235. Her shrine at the Elisabeth Church in Marburg became a major center of pilgrimage in the 14th and 15th centuries. During the Reformation, her bones were removed from the shrine to discourage pilgrimage. Some of her remains can now be found in Vienna, while other relics have been returned to her shrine at Marburg.

A 19th-century picture by Calderon of Elisabeth taking her vow of celibacy, as the loathsome Konrad von Marburg looks on.

Date	Name	Status	Venerated	Life
Nov. 16	Margaret of Scotland (1046–93)	Queen, Philanthropist ⊖ 1250	GRC, CofE 🙏 Scotland	Member of the Anglo-Saxon ruling dynasty. Fled England after Norman conquest of 1066. When shipwrecked off the Scottish coast, King Malcolm of Scotland took her under his protection and married her. Admired for her personal morality, charitable works, and fidelity to the Church.
Nov. 16	Gertrude of Helfta (the Great) (1256–1302)	Virgin, Nun, Mystic Universal feast day declared 1677	GRC, LCDUS ✝ Lily, taper 🙏 Travelers; the West Indies, Naples	At age 5 joined Benedictine monastery of Helfta in Thuringia. Became expert in literature and philosophy. Had many mystical experiences, including a vision in which Jesus invited her to rest her head on his beating heart.
Nov. 18	Rose Philippine Duchesne (1769–1852)	Nun, Founder, Missionary ❤ 1940 ⊖ 1988	LCDUS	Born in France, convent-educated. Helped found the Society of the Sacred Heart and became a missionary in St. Charles, Missouri. Other foundations followed. Continued her mission work into old age, teaching among the Pottowatomies at Sugar Creek, Kansas.

NOVEMBER 20 | EDMUND THE MARTYR

STATUS King, Martyr

BORN c.841, probably East Anglia, England

DIED 869, East Anglia, England

GRC ○

CofE ♣

LCDUS ○

○ Pre-Congregation

✝ Crowned and robed as a king; holding orb, scepter, arrow, or sword

⚓ Kings, wolves, pandemics, torture victims

Unsurprisingly, arrows feature in Edmund's arms: according to one account, the Danes shot him until his body was "like a thistle covered in prickles."

The story of Edmund's life is mainly derived from the *Anglo-Saxon Chronicle*. He is said to have descended from the previous kings of East Anglia in the Wuffling line, although there is a legend that claims that Edmund was the youngest son of Alcmund, a Saxon king. There is no dispute, however, that Edmund succeeded to the throne of East Anglia, at age 14, in 854. Little is known of his life over the next 14 years, though he is said to have been an exemplary king, who was impervious to flattery and bribery, and treated everyone justly.

In 869 Danish invaders, who had over-wintered in York, marched south toward East Anglia, taking up their quarters in Thetford, Norfolk. Edmund engaged the invaders in battle at Hoxne, and was killed. While it is perfectly possible that he simply fell in battle, legend has it that he died a martyr. It is said that he was beaten with cudgels and tied to an oak tree. He refused to renounce his Christian faith, even when he was subjected to a rain of Danish arrows, and eventually he was beheaded. His remains were thrown into the nearby forest.

Representations of Edmund tend to focus on his martyrdom at the hands of Danish archers.

In the account of his martyrdom written by Abbo of Fleury in the late 10th century, it is said that Edmund's subjects searched the forest day and night for his severed head. They eventually heard Edmund's voice calling out "Here I am!" and found his head in the possession of a grey wolf, resting between its paws. Although the wolf was starving, it had not devoured the head, and it accompanied Edmund's subjects as they took it back to the town, before turning back and disappearing into the forest. The king's body was eventually buried in Beadoriceworth (modern Bury St. Edmunds, in Suffolk). His shrine soon became one of the most popular pilgrimage destinations in England, and the reputation of St. Edmund became emblematic of the English royal family. He features on the Wilton Diptych alongside Edward the Confessor, accompanying King Richard II in his devotions (*see* page 261); a banner bearing his crest was carried into battle at Agincourt (1415); and churches dedicated to his memory can be found all over England. His shrine at the abbey at Bury St. Edmunds was destroyed during the Reformation.

NOVEMBER 21 | THE PRESENTATION OF THE BLESSED VIRGIN MARY

This liturgical feast is celebrated in both the Roman Catholic and Orthodox churches. The feast is associated with the story, recounted in the apocryphal writings of James, of Mary's parents Joachim and Anne (July 26) who, long childless, gave thanksgiving for the birth of their daughter, and took her as a small child to the Temple in Jerusalem to consecrate her to God and to be educated. She remained in the Temple for some years.

The feast originated in the East, in 543, with the dedication of the basilica of St. Mary the New, near the site of the ruined Temple in Jerusalem. The feast spread to the monasteries of southern Italy by the 9th century, and reached the papal court in Avignon by 1372. It had become a feast of the Universal Church by the 16th century. It is celebrated by the Eastern Orthodox churches as one of their 12 Great Feasts.

THE HELFTA CONNECTION: THE MYSTIC NUNS OF SAXONY

Mechtilde of Helfta (sometimes called Mechtilde of Hackeborn, c.1241–98) was born to a noble Saxon family in Thuringia. She entered a convent at age seven, then joined the Cistercian (Benedictine) abbey of Helfta in around 1270, under her sister the abbess Gertrude, a foundation established by their brothers. Musically gifted, pious, and amiable, Mechtilde was entrusted with the care of a younger nun who would become Gertrude the Great (c.1256–1302, feast day Nov. 16). The latter is said to have recorded Mechtilde's ideas in the influential *Book of Special Graces* and went on to compose her own collection of *Revelations*

and *The Herald of God's Loving Kindness*. Mechtilde died on November 19, and was never formally canonized.

Mechtilde of Helfta is sometimes confused with her near contemporary Mechtilde of Magdeburg (c.1207–94), also a nun and spiritual writer at the abbey of Helfta, whose colorful and emotive *The Flowing Light of the Godhead* is now widely regarded as a medieval literary masterpiece.

The influence of the mystic nuns of Helfta traveled far beyond 13th-century Saxony, and may have inspired parts of the descriptions of Hell in Dante's Divine Comedy.

NOVEMBER 22 | CECILIA

STATUS Martyr

BORN 3rd century, Rome, Italy

DIED 176/180, Rome, or possibly Sicily, Italy

GRC ♣

CofE ♣

LCDUS ♣

○ Pre-Congregation

† Flute, organ, violin, harp, harpsichord, singing, roses

🙏 Music, especially church music, musicians, poets; Albi, France; Archdiocese of Omaha, Nebraska; Mar del Plata, Argentina

St. Cecilia was an early Roman martyr who experienced visions of angels, heard heavenly music, and sang to God as she was dying. She has long been revered as the patron saint of music.

It had been generally accepted that Cecilia was a noblewoman of Rome who was martyred, along with her husband and brother-in-law, around 230, under the emperor Alexander Severus. Later research, however, indicates that she died in Sicily between 176 and 180, during the rule of Marcus Aurelius.

The Sound of Music

Legend has it that Cecilia was an ardent Christian who heard heavenly music in her heart as she was married. She went on to convert her husband, Valerian, and his brother, to the Christian faith, and they dedicated themselves to burying Christian martyrs. Following the execution of her husband and his brother, she arranged to have her home preserved as a church.

Roman officials attempted to kill Cecilia by suffocating her in a steam bath; they then attempted to behead her three times, but she would not succumb until she had received Holy Communion. It was three days before she finally died. The skull of St. Cecilia is kept as a relic in Torcello Cathedral, Venice. A church in her honor has stood in Rome since the 5th century.

Cecilia became an enormously popular saint in Rome from the 5th century. Her basilica in the Trastevere district was rebuilt by Pope Paschal I around 820, and again in 1599.

Date	Name	Status	Venerated	Life
Nov. 19	Barlaam (d.304)	Hermit, Martyr ○ Pre-Congregation	Eastern Orthodox churches	From Antioch, apparently martyred after refusing to pay tribute to pagan deities. Sometimes associated with a legendary Josaphat, son of 'an Indian ruler,' King Abenner, whom Josaphat later converted, both also becoming hermits. Barlaam and Josaphat celebrated jointly on Nov. 27.
Nov. 19	Hilda of Whitby (614–80)	Abbess, Founder ○ Pre-Congregation	CofE	Born into Northumbrian royal family, which converted to Christianity under St. Paulinus (627). Chose to live as a nun and learn the traditions of Celtic monasticism. St. Aidan made her an abbess, founding monastery at Whitby in 657. Respected as devout Christian, skilled administrator, and gifted teacher.
Nov. 20	Priscilla Lydia Sellon (1821–76)	Founder	CofE	Dedicated Anglican. Became leader of first Anglican religious community for women, the Society of the Sisters of Mercy of the Holy Trinity (1848) in Devonport, England. Her charitable work took her to schools, orphanages, slums, and battlefields of the Crimean War.

NOVEMBER 23 — CLEMENT I

STATUS Pope, Martyr

BORN Mid-1st century AD, Italy

DIED c.101, Italy

GRC ♣

CofE ♣

LCDUS ♣

⬭ Pre-Congregation

† Often shown writing; an anchor

Clement's letters remain an important source for understanding the status of the early Christian Church in Rome, and established a significant precedent for the development of the papal see.

Clement of Rome is one of the most important of the early popes, possibly appointed by St. Peter himself. He is most noted for his first epistle to the Corinthian Church, dealing with the structure of the Church there. This letter reveals the clear authority of the Roman Church in ecclesiastical matters, and the need for submission to that authority. It also acknowledges the political supremacy of the Roman empire, at the time under the emperor Domitian, a persecutor of Christians, and accords due respect to the secular powers of the empire. Voragine's *The Golden Legend* provides Clement with an unsubstantiated martyrdom under the emperor Trajan, in which he was thrown from a ship with an anchor tied to his neck. The sea immediately receded for three miles, and a marble temple was discovered, containing his sarcophagus and remains, still attached to the anchor.

NOVEMBER 23 — COLUMBAN (COLUMBANUS)

STATUS Abbot, Missionary

BORN c.540 Leinster, Ireland

DIED 615, Bobbio, Italy

GRC ♣

CofE ♢

LCDUS ♣

OTHER In Ireland, in Italy

⬭ Pre-Congregation

† Bear

Columban was one of the outstanding missionaries of the Irish Church. He was probably quite nobly born, and was well educated before becoming a monk against his mother's wishes. He was a disciple of St. Finian, then spent many years in Bangor. Accompanied by 12 other monks, Columban set off for Europe in around 590. They spent their time in various courts of the Frankish empire and, despite their adherence to Celtic rather than Roman rites, seem to have built a substantial reputation as missionaries on the Frankish/Germanic frontier territories in Neustria and Austrasia. Columban also developed a direct epistolary relationship with several popes, who endorsed his endeavors, although the letters reveal Columban's lack of understanding of the wider diplomatic issues at hand. Columban founded several monasteries, and introduced a notably harsh Rule.

It is clear that his mission was something of a problem for the Franks. His company of monks was shuffled from one center to another before finally being ejected. Dissent had already occurred within the mission, with St. Gall (Oct. 16) remaining in Switzerland after the monks had rowed up the Rhine to Lake Constance. Already in his 70s, Columban crossed the Alps into Lombardy in 612, and was granted land near Piacenza where he founded the important abbey of Bobbio.

A pensive St. Columban, bearing an illuminated book of the Gospels.

NOVEMBER 23 | MIGUEL AGUSTÍN PRO

STATUS Priest, Martyr

BORN 1891, Guadalupe, Mexico

DIED 1927, Mexico City, Mexico

GRC ☁

CofE ☁

LCDUS ♣

OTHER In Mexico, by Jesuits

♥ 1988

Pro prayed quietly before facing the firing squad. He forgave his executioners, then adopted a cruciform stance, refusing a blindfold, and shouted "Viva Cristo Rey!" as the firing order was given.

Pro was only one of thousands of Mexican priests who were killed under the savagely anti-clerical administration of President Calles. He had entered the Jesuit novitiate in 1911, but like many of the clergy was forced to flee into exile during the Mexican Revolution, first going to California then to Granada, Spain, to continue his studies. In 1917, the new Mexican constitution was drawn up. The document included numerous limitations and prohibitions of clerical activity, including the banning of monasteries, clerical garb, and public worship, the confiscation of Church property, the disenfranchisement of the clergy, and the secularization of education.

Pro taught in Nicaragua from 1919–22, then returned to Europe to complete his studies in Belgium, being ordained in 1925. He returned to his homeland in 1926, performing his ministry as best he could under the constitutional restrictions. A failed assassination attempt on the ex-president Álvaro Obregón provided the government with a pretext to round up prominent members of the clergy. Pro was given a show trial, and condemned to death.

Pro's execution by firing squad was unwisely photographed in detail (including the coup de grâce). The images were published in national newspapers, intended as a warning to supporters of the Cristero rebels (*see* page 132), but instead they only served to inflame the situation, and provoked international condemnation.

NOVEMBER 23 | ALEXANDER NEVSKY

STATUS Prince

BORN 1220, Pereslavl, Russia

DIED 1263, Vladimir, Russia

GRC ☁

CofE ☁

LCDUS ☁

OTHER Russian Orthodox Church

⊙ 1547

✝ Usually shown in armor

Alexander was the grand prince of Novgorod, Vladimir, and Kiev at a critical time in medieval Russian history. The fledgling Russian Orthodox state was threatened on all sides. Alexander concluded peace settlements with the Tartars of Central Asia, and firmly resisted attempts by western European powers to invade his state. The name Nevsky came from his defeat of a Swedish invasion force on the Neva river in 1240. Two years later he defeated the crusading order of the Teutonic Knights on the frozen surface of Lake Peipus, and subsequently forced a withdrawal of Lithuanian forces from his territory — Lithuania at the time being one of the most powerful states in Europe. Alexander remains an outstanding example of a medieval ruler who combined militant patriotism with a keen sense of Christianity.

The importance of Alexander Nevsky as a Russian national hero was celebrated in Eisenstein's 1983 patriotic propaganda film, with its memorable battle on the ice and a score by Prokofiev.

"God is not on the side of force, but of truth and justice."

ALEXANDER NEVSKY.

NOVEMBER 24 · THE MARTYRS OF TONKIN

Pierre Borie, a member of the Paris Foreign Missions Society, was beheaded in November 1838. On the ground in front of him is a cangue, a kind of portable yoke rather like a ladder, worn by the prisoner around his neck. The cangue Borie was forced to wear is today on display in the Society's headquarters in Paris.

Even more than in other parts of eastern Asia, Christian missionaries and converts in Vietnam were brutally persecuted from the moment the first Europeans reached the country in 1533 and Christianity was declared illegal by imperial edict.

At least 130,000, and possibly as many as 300,000, Christians were executed for their faith; many were tortured beforehand. The killings reached a peak after 1855, when Emperor Tu-Dúc instituted a renewed, even more savage persecution of Christians. It was ended in 1862 when France effectively annexed Vietnam, partly in response to the treatment of French missionaries, which had outraged opinion in France. The promotion of Christianity in Vietnam became a French priority.

Canonization

Sixty-four of those executed were beatified in 1900, eight in 1906, 20 in 1909, and 25 in 1951. All 117 were canonized by Pope John Paul II in 1988. Of them, ten were French, members of the Paris Foreign Missions Society; 11 were Spanish Dominicans; and the remaining 96 were Vietnamese, Andrew Dung-Lac (d.1839) being among those most venerated.

The martyrs had all suffered a variety of appalling fates, of which beheading was perhaps the most merciful. Many were dismembered, others suffocated, some burned alive. Most had the characters *ta dao,* meaning 'false religion,' branded on their faces before they died.

Date	Name	Status	Venerated	Life
Nov. 25	Isaac Watts (1664–1748)	Writer of Hymns	CofE, Lutheran Church, US Episcopal Church	Author of more than 700 hymns and other devotional songs. Known as the 'Father of English Hymnody.' Devotional music had long played key role in Christian worship, but Protestant churches generally held that only works of Scripture – in this case the Psalms – were suitable for singing in church. To substitute new texts veered alarmingly toward heresy. For Watts, what counted was the faith any such hymns sought to convey. Immensely influential in England and America, initiating a vigorous tradition of hymn-singing in almost all Protestant churches.

NOVEMBER 25 CATHERINE OF ALEXANDRIA

STATUS Virgin, Martyr

BORN 3rd century, Alexandria, Egypt

DIED c.305, Alexandria, Egypt

GRC ♠

CofE ♠

LCDUS ♣

OTHER Eastern Orthodox Churches

○ Pre-Congregation

† Book, bridal ring and veil, crown, dove, hailstones, scourge, sword, wheel

🙏 Apologists, lawyers, librarians, milliners, nurses, philosophers, preachers, scholars, teachers, theologians, unmarried girls, wheelwrights; against sudden death

A silver spiked wheel on a blue ground is Catherine's most widely recognized symbol.

The spinning, fiery Catherine Wheel is a staple at firework displays.

An idealized image of an ideal saint. St. Catherine by the early Renaissance Venetian painter, Carlo Crivelli, c.1470.

Even if the historical veracity of Catherine's story is doubtful, her importance in the Middle Ages as an exemplar of beauty, intelligence, learning, sanctity, and chastity made her among the most important and influential of saints whose intercession was widely sought. She was particularly venerated in France after some claimed she had spoken to Joan of Arc (May 30). Her status as a virgin-martyr is unchallenged. She is also one of the Fourteen Holy Helpers.

The facts of her life, whether true or not, are simple. She was the daughter of the Roman governor of Alexandria, and was converted to Christianity before she was 20 by one of the Egyptian desert hermits. She underwent a vision in which she was united with Christ in a 'mystic marriage.' She subsequently attempted to convert the Roman emperor, Maximinus, in the process brilliantly confounding the 50 pagan philosophers he had deputed to argue with her. Many of them instead converted to Christianity, as did the empress, Caecilia Paulina. Maximinus then had Catherine imprisoned and subsequently ordered that she be 'broken' on a wheel (hence 'Catherine Wheel'). When the wheel itself miraculously broke, Catherine was beheaded.

The Cult of Catherine

Angels are said to have transported Catherine's body to Mount Sinai where, in the 6th century, Justinian ordered the construction of St. Catherine's Monastery. It was here in about 800 that her body was reputedly rediscovered, her hair still growing, holy oil seeping from her corpse. It was from this point on that her cult began to develop. The monastery itself, despite its inaccessibility, became a noted place of pilgrimage, especially for women. Catherine's supposed purity would exercise a key influence on the ideal behavior

Depictions of Catherine's martyrdom are relatively rare; she is more usually shown as part of a mystic marriage, or attending the Blessed Virgin Mary. This stirring narrative painting by Pietro de Lignis (1577–1627) links her miraculous escape from the dreaded wheel to her eventual decapitation in the background.

of women throughout the Middle Ages. Her relics were later dispersed across a large number of different locations. Rouen, for example, in northern France, where Joan of Arc was burned at the stake, became the most important center of Catherine's cult in the West, chiefly through possessing her fingers. The English king, Edward the Confessor (Oct. 13) had a phial containing Catherine's oil, which he installed in Westminster Abbey in London. Despite her enormous popularity, Catherine was removed from the General Roman Calendar in 1969 due to a lack of historical evidence for her existence; her legend is probably a combination of various stories connected to the early Christian martyrs.

Date	Name	Status	Venerated	Life
Nov. 25	Moses of Rome (d.c.251)	Priest, Martyr ○ Pre-Congregation		Widely presumed to have been of Jewish origin. Priest in Rome and active supporter of Pope Cornelius in his struggles against heretical anti-pope, Novatian. Reportedly among first Christians martyred during Decian persecution.
Nov. 26	Leonard of Port Maurice (1676–1751)	Preacher, Writer ○ 1867		Italian Franciscan. After early illness, emerged as a preacher and tireless propagandist. Especially successful in his advocacy of the Sacred Heart of Jesus, the Blessed Sacrament, the Immaculate Conception, and, above all, the 14 Stations of the Cross as aids to contemplation and prayer.

NOVEMBER 27 — JAMES THE PERSIAN (INTERCISUS)

STATUS Martyr
BORN 4th century, Persia
DIED c.421, Persia
GRC ◯
CofE ◯
LCDUS ◯
OTHER Eastern Orthodox churches
◯ Pre-Congregation

James, venerated as a martyr in the Eastern Orthodox churches, was a high-born Christian in the Persian Sassanid empire, "a lord of merit ... wealthy, knowledgeable, and virtuous." As a favorite of the emperor, Yezdegeherd, he was showered with honors to the point that, his head turned by his worldly success, he renounced his faith. His mother and his wife, appalled by his apostasy, wrote to him, rebuking James for his fickleness. He at once recognized his foolishness and publicly re-embraced Christianity. His reward was to be put to death by Yezdegeherd's successor, who instituted the second great Persian persecution of Christians in around 420. It was decreed that James be progressively dismembered. One by one, his fingers were severed, then his toes, then his legs, then his arms, then his shoulders. All the while, James gleefully proclaimed his Christian faith. Finally, he was decapitated. "A sweet-smelling fragrance, as of a cypress" was reportedly given off by what remained of his mutilated corpse. His head was subsequently removed to Rome.

In the Catholic Church, James the Persian is known as James Intercisus, meaning literally 'cut to pieces.'

NOVEMBER 28 — CATHERINE LABOURÉ

STATUS Mystic
BORN 1806, Burgundy, France
DIED 1876, Paris, France
GRC ◯
CofE ◯
LCDUS ◯
OTHER In France, by the Daughters of Charity
♥ 1933
◯ 1947
† Miraculous Medal

A prayer appears around the rim of the front of Catherine's medal: "O Mary, conceived without sin, pray for us who have recourse to thee." The two hearts, the stars, and the letter M entwined in a cross, appear on the reverse.

In 1830, Catherine Labouré, an illiterate peasant girl, the ninth of eleven children and a very junior member of a nursing order in Paris, the Daughters of Charity, claimed to have had three visitations by the Blessed Virgin Mary. On the first, in July, she was said to have been summoned at night to the order's chapel on the rue du Bac, Paris. There she encountered "a most beautiful lady," who issued a series of warnings about the imminent collapse of the restored French monarchy. On the second, in November, the Virgin appeared to her shimmering with light emanating from the many rings on her fingers. She stood on a globe. Around her was a glowing oval frame. Slowly the figure rotated. As it did so, 12 stars appeared around it, as did the letter M, the Sacred Heart of Jesus, and the Immaculate Heart of Mary. The Virgin charged Catherine with having a medal made incorporating these devices. Catherine received a final visitation in December. Catherine reported the visitations to the order's priest, Father Aladel, who requested permission from his bishop for the medals to be made. They became instantly popular across the Catholic world. Catherine was buried in the chapel, today known as the Chapel of the Miraculous Medal, where the Virgin appeared to her. Her body, when exhumed in 1933, was found to be incorrupt.

Date	Name	Status	Venerated	Life
Nov. 29	Saturninus of Toulouse (d.c.257)	Bishop, Martyr ◯ Pre-Congregation	In France	A Greek from North Africa. One of seven bishops dispatched by Pope Fabian to Gaul in an effort to re-Christianize the country after persecutions under emperor Decius. Appointed bishop of Toulouse in southwest France. Killed on the orders of town's pagan priests, whose oracles he was said to have silenced. Tied to a bull, which dragged him through the streets until he expired. Re-buried on site of what is now a 14th-century church, Notre-Dame-du-Taur – Our Lady of the Bull.

NOVEMBER 28 JAMES OF THE MARCHES

STATUS Lawyer, Preacher

BORN 1391, Ancona, Italy

DIED 1476, Naples, Italy

GRC ♡

CofE ♡

LCDUS ♡

♥ 1624

○ 1726

✝ Holding chalice from which a snake escapes

🙏 Naples

James was among the most active Franciscan preachers and missionaries of the latter Middle Ages. He traveled widely across Italy as well as across much of central Europe and Scandinavia. He was also active in attempting, unsuccessfully, to reconcile more moderate Hussites with the Church. He similarly strove to bring about closer relations between Rome and the Greek Orthodox Church. He was perhaps best known for his role as inquisitor against the heretical Fraticelli, a breakaway group of Franciscans who, taking literally St. Francis's strictures on poverty, objected violently to the wealth of the Church. With St. John of Capistrano (Oct. 23), he oversaw the destruction of 36 Fraticelli houses and the death at the stake of many of their members. He was himself accused of heresy in 1462, over the divine nature of Christ's blood after His death. Pope Pius II refused to rule on the accusation. James led a life of exemplary sanctity.

DOROTHY DAY – THE ARDENT PACIFIST

Dorothy Day was a relentless activist of a distinctly left-leaning kind, a tireless campaigner for social reform and the alleviation of poverty, co-founder in 1933 with a Frenchman, Peter Maurin, of the Catholic Worker Movement, and editor until her death of *The Catholic Worker* newspaper. The movement's most impressive achievement was the establishment of a series of communities for the dispossessed, 'Houses of Hospitality.' There were more than 30 across the United States by 1941. Today, there are over 100 worldwide. Day was a Catholic convert, joining the Church in December 1927. Hers was nothing if not a practical faith – the Church to her was 'the church of the poor' – but it was no less a profoundly spiritual one.

The striking logo of the Catholic Worker Movement.

As a consequence of her beliefs, Day became a fierce pacifist; during World War II, she remained a patriotic American but was nonetheless wholly opposed to the war. She was similarly opposed to all subsequent American wars and campaigned relentlessly for the abolition of nuclear weapons, spending several brief periods in prison. She was also a vigorous supporter of the Civil Rights movement. Her faith remained her greatest comfort in a world of seemingly arbitrary violence and inequality. "If I have achieved anything in my life," she said, "it is because I have not been embarrassed to talk about God." Day died on November 29, 1980. The Vatican has declared her a 'servant of God' and is considering the case for her canonization.

Day with veteran anti-war campaigner A.J. Muste on a draft card burning demonstration during the Vietnam War.

St. James, characteristically emaciated due to his fasting, and carrying a book as a sign of his great learning, painted in 1477 by Carlo Crivelli and today in the Louvre, Paris.

NOVEMBER 30 ANDREW THE APOSTLE

STATUS Apostle

BORN Early 1st century AD, Bethsaida, modern Israel

DIED c. AD 60, Greece

GRC ♣

CofE ♣

LCDUS ♣

OTHER Eastern Orthodox churches

⊖ Pre-Congregation

✝ Saltire cross, fishing net

🙏 Fishermen; Scotland, Greece, Russia, Ukraine

Andrew's distinctive saltire cross appears to be unknown before the late Middle Ages, but remains an easy way to identify the saint in scenes of martyrdom. It is also the Scottish national flag.

Andrew bears his cross in one of four monumental sculptures of the first Apostles by François Duquesnoy (1597–1643) in St. Peter's, Rome.

A fisherman from the northern shores of Lake Galilee, Andrew was the first of the Apostles to be called by Jesus. He was the brother of Simon Peter, and introduced Simon Peter (St. Peter) to Jesus, although both brothers had formerly also been followers of John the Baptist. He is mentioned among the first four Apostles in all the main lists, and is remembered in the Gospels as one of the disciples involved in the miracle of the feeding of the five thousand.

The Acts of Andrew

After Pentecost, the record of Andrew's ministry and preaching becomes very unclear, and there are a number of conflicting accounts. The apocryphal *Acts of Andrew and Matthias*, compiled in the 2nd century, describes Andrew rescuing Matthias (May 14) from cannibals, while the *Acts of Andrew* tells of him preaching and performing miracles in Greek Anatolia and Greece itself. The Old English poem *Andreas* even saw him visiting Ethiopia. One account cites Andrew as the first bishop of Byzantium, where his relics were said to have been translated from Patras; this would effectively identify Andrew as the founder of the Eastern Orthodox tradition.

There are also several claims as to the site of Andrew's martyrdom. Scythia, on the northern shores of the Black Sea (modern Romania and Ukraine), Kiev, and Epirus are among the most prominent. The most likely is Patras in Achaea, Greece, where Andrew is said to have been crucified (tied rather than nailed), preaching from the cross for two days before expiring.

Date	Name	Status	Venerated	Life
Nov. 30	Zosimus (d.6th century)	Hermit ⊖ Pre-Congregation	In the Holy Land	Palestinian hermit noted for his numerous miracles, earning him nickname 'Wonder Worker.'
Nov. 30	Tudwal (Tugdual) (d.6th century)	Bishop ⊖ Pre-Congregation	In Wales and Brittany	Welsh missionary. Traveled to Brittany at behest of his cousin Deroc, a local ruler. Established monastery near León. Patronized by King Childebert I.
Nov. 30	Joseph Marchand (d.1835)	Martyr ⊖ 1988	In Vietnam	French missionary to Vietnam. Arrested in Saigon. Put to death with red-hot tongs.

"Come ye after me, and I will make you to become fishers of men."

JESUS CALLING ANDREW AND SIMON PETER, MARK 1:17.

Christ calls Andrew and Simon Peter, His first disciples, as they trawl for fish in the Sea of Galilee, in this painting by the early Renaissance Paduan fresco artist Giusto de' Menabuoi, c.1375.

Myths and Legends

Andrew's relationship with Scotland springs from another story. Andrew's cult was well established in both Eastern and Western churches by the middle of the 6th century, and many churches were dedicated to him in Italy, France, and England (where there are over 630, such as Hexham in Yorkshire, Rochester in Kent, and Orwell near Cambridge). This enthusiasm for the first Apostle was endorsed in the 8th century, when St. Rule, a native of Patras, was apparently instructed by an angel to take Andrew's relics to a place in the far northwest. He traveled across Europe, across the English Channel, and continued through Britain to Fife in eastern Scotland, where the angel told him to stop. There he built a church and reliquary; the city of St. Andrews today is the site of a distinguished university.

Somewhat in conflict with this story, the Frankish adventurers on the Fourth Crusade looted Andrew's purported remains from Constantinople in 1204, taking his body to Amalfi in Italy, and his head to Rome, where it became one of the most prized relics of the Vatican. The head was returned to Amalfi in 1988. Meanwhile, Patras still claims to hold Andrew's relics, and Malta remains a cult center, probably due to Andrew's association with fishing.

DECEMBER

Advent marks the start of the Christian year in most Western traditions. Derived from the Latin *adventus*, or 'coming,' the season begins on the fourth Sunday before the celebration of the Nativity of Christ on December 25, occurring on or between November 27 and December 3. As winter closes in, December is a time of hushed expectation as Christmas approaches. The season's traditions are continued far beyond the portals of the church by Advent candles and calendars, full of the promise of treats and joyous abundance to come.

The feast day of the saint most widely associated with Christmas, Nicholas of Myra, remembered in some countries today as Santa Claus, falls some time before Christmas itself, on December 6. The first martyr, Saint Stephen, is commemorated on December 26, and the Massacre of the Holy Innocents by Herod on December 28.

There is a characteristic simplicity and humanity in the early Renaissance painter Giotto's representation of the Nativity (c. 1310) that is far removed from the elaborate narratives we are familiar with today.

DECEMBER 1

JOHN (GIOVANNI) OF VERCELLI

STATUS Monk, Founder
BORN c.1200, Vercelli, Italy
DIED 1283, Montpellier, France
GRC ♧
CofE ♧
LCDUS ♧
OTHER By Dominicans
♥ 1903

Master General of the Dominicans from 1264, John of Vercelli was one of the leading churchmen in a period when faith in Christendom was unquestioned. He was highly learned, having studied and taught law in Paris and Bologna, where he was ordained in 1229. He was successively prior of the Dominican convent at Vercelli, papal legate to Innocent IV, and vicar for Hungary. In 1257 he was appointed Dominican provincial of Lombardy and subsequently master general. In this latter role he traveled across Europe, always on foot, despite a crippled leg, visiting Dominican monasteries in Italy, France, Germany, and England. In 1274, he also played a leading role in the Second Council of Lyon, called by Pope Gregory X, the 'Peacemaker,' to unite the warring states of Christendom. As a direct consequence of this, the pope charged him with the establishment of the Holy Name Society, intended to promulgate the name of Jesus as a means of reinforcing papal authority. He died in the south of France, following a further visit to England and the Low Countries.

DECEMBER 1

CHARLES DE FOUCAULD

STATUS Trappist Monk, Hermit
BORN 1858, Strasbourg, France
DIED 1916, Tamanrasset, Algeria
GRC ♧
CofE ♣
LCDUS ♧
OTHER In Morocco, Algeria
♥ 2005

Charles Eugène, Vicomte de Foucauld, was among the most remarkable of 20th-century holy men: an aristocrat, immensely rich, and an explorer and soldier, forever disdainful of his superiors, who argued forcefully for the French colonization of North Africa (in which he played a key early role). As a young man, Charles was so taken by a rare wine he drank in a restaurant that he bought the entire stock for 18,000 francs (at a time when the average laborer in France received perhaps 2,400 francs a year). But in 1890, in an utter reversal of his early life, Charles became a Trappist monk, devoting himself to an existence that was spartan to the point of almost complete destitution. Between 1890 and his ordination in 1901, he spent time not just with Trappists in France and Syria, but also with an order of Poor Clares in Nazareth. He subsequently lived as a hermit in North Africa, first at Béni Abbès, Morocco, and later in even more remote Tamanrasset, deep in southern Algeria, among the desert Tuareg people. In between his devotions, he compiled a scholarly dictionary and grammar of their language. He was shot and killed by Senussi Bedouins struggling against the imposition of French rule.

By 1902, Charles had reduced his diet to such a degree – bread, some porridge, and tea – that he was on the point of death from malnutrition. He told a group of Trappists who hoped to join him that they could do so only if they were "prepared to die of hunger."

Date	Name	Status	Venerated	Life
Dec. 2	Rafal Chylinski (1694–1741)	Monk ♥ 1991	By Franciscans	Known when young as the 'little monk' due to his piety, Chylinski, though educated by Jesuits, became a cavalry officer. However, in 1715 joined Franciscans; ordained two years later. Renowned for his great sanctity and unwavering ministrations to the poor and sick, above all in last years of his life spent in Lagiewniki in central Poland.

DECEMBER 2 | CHROMATIUS

STATUS Bishop, Theologian

BORN 3rd century, Aquileia, Italy

DIED c.406, Italy

GRC ◌

CofE ◌

LCDUS ◌

◯ Pre-Congregation

Among the many mosaics preserved in Aquileia, secret symbols of Christian allegiance can be found, such as this 'Good Shepherd' motif, signifying Christ.

Chromatius, ordained in about 378, was bishop of the northern Adriatic city of Aquileia from 388. He was a leading theologian of the period and wrote a number of surviving commentaries on St. Matthew's Gospel as well as a series of 38 sermons. Chromatius was in regular contact with many of the most important early Christian churchmen, among them St. Jerome (Sept. 30), who dedicated a number of works to Chromatius, St. Ambrose of Milan (Dec. 7), and St. John Chrysostom, bishop of Constantinople (Sept. 13). He was an active opponent of Arianism (*see* page 12), the most divisive heresy of the age, taking forceful steps to eradicate it in his own diocese. He remains a key figure in the development of the early Church.

A Romanesque fresco from the basilica at Aquileia celebrating the church father Chromatius.

DECEMBER 2 | MAURA CLARKE, ITA FORD, DOROTHY KAZEL, JEAN DONOVAN

STATUS Martyrs

DIED 1980, El Salvador

GRC ◌

CofE ◌

LCDUS ◌

OTHER In USA

Clockwise from top left: Ita Ford, born 1940 in New York; Maura Clarke, born 1931 in New York; Jean Donovan, born 1953 in Connecticut; Dorothy Kazel, born 1939 in Cleveland.

On December 2, 1980, three American nuns and a Catholic lay missionary in El Salvador were raped and murdered by security forces. Their bodies, dumped in a shallow grave, were found two days later. They were Maura Clarke and Ita Ford, both Maryknoll nuns; Dorothy Kazel, an Ursuline nun; and Jean Donovan, a lay missionary. Late in the afternoon of December 2, Kazel and Donovan had picked up Clarke and Ford, returning from a conference in Nicaragua, at San Salvador's airport. National Guardsmen followed them as they drove away from the airport. At about 10 pm, villagers heard machine-gun fire followed by single shots.

It was clear the women had been murdered on the orders of the government of José Napoleón Duarte, then engaged in a bitter civil war against insurgent communist forces. The women had been singled out because the Catholic Church as a whole in Central America was seen to be actively opposed to the government — not least through the support of many clergy for Liberation Theology, in effect an attempt to link traditional Catholic beliefs with Marxism. In attempting to help the innocent victims of a left-right clash, Clarke, Ford, Kazel, and Donovan had become victims of a vicious conflict that was none of their making.

Like Oscar Romero (March 24), archbishop of El Salvador, who had been gunned down on government orders earlier the same year after demanding that the United States stop supplies of military aid to Duarte's government, they were murdered for no greater crime than their humanity.

DECEMBER 3 · FRANCIS XAVIER

STATUS Priest, Missionary

BORN 1506, Navarre, Spain

DIED 1552, Sancian (Sangchwan), China

GRC ♣

CofE ♣

LCDUS ♣

OTHER US Evangelical Lutheran Church

♥ 1619

○ 1622

† Usually shown bearded and youthful; bearing crucifix, flaming heart, torch, or lily

🙏 Missionaries; plague epidemics; Goa; India, Japan, Pakistan, Bangladesh, Indonesia, the Philippines, Mongolia, Borneo

The list of countries of which Francis Xavier is the patron merely scratches the surface of his importance as the greatest missionary the Catholic Church ever produced. He is known today as the 'Apostle of the Indies and Japan.' His career developed at an opportune moment. Rome, under pressure from Reformation movements north of the Alps, was forced to take decisive action to re-establish its authority within Europe; more significantly, Rome seized upon the chance to evangelize and convert as many as possible across a wider world that was increasingly being explored and colonized by European powers.

A Founding Jesuit

A well-born Basque, Francis attended the University of Paris, where he met his close contemporary and fellow Spaniard Ignatius of Loyola (July 31), and with him was one of the seedling group of seven who took their vows at Montmartre in 1534 and went on to form the Society of Jesus – the Jesuits. He was ordained in Venice in 1537. By 1540 he was in Lisbon, and set off to the Portuguese trading settlement of Goa on the Indian coast. While attending hospitals and prisons and teaching children in Goa, Francis traveled throughout southern India, working mainly with the low-caste Paravas. He also evangelized in Ceylon (modern Sri Lanka), Malacca (another Portuguese colony, on the Malay peninsula), and the Moluccas (in modern Indonesia). His letters to the king of Portugal reveal that he was highly critical of the behavior of colonists toward the indigenous populations, but equally had little time for local creeds.

In 1549 he voyaged from Malacca to Japan. Here he made over a hundred converts at Kagoshima, contributing greatly to the Japanese Christian community, which at the time numbered around 2,000 souls.

His next target was the Middle Kingdom of China. Although China was also 'closed,' it was seemingly more open to Western approaches than Japan, but still a massive challenge. The faltering Ming Dynasty, like the Japanese shogunate, was deeply mistrustful of Christian missions, possibly rightly perceiving them as forerunners of European political ambitions. What might have happened if the gifted evangelizer had reached the Chinese mainland, we will never know. Francis Xavier fell ill and died on the island of Sancian, a mere six miles (10 km) off the Chinese coast, attended only by a young Chinese Christian convert. He was only 46. His body was translated to Goa in India, where his shrine remains.

From its earliest years Christianity had looked toward the East – the Orient – as a rich source of converts. The Nestorian Church, founded by Thomas the Apostle (July 3), successfully sent missions across the Silk Road to China, and, via merchant shipping routes, established missions and communities in South Asia and further east.

However, the presence of these Christian communities in parts of Asia pre-dated the explosive growth of Islam in the 7th and 8th centuries, which had the effect of suppressing many of them, and o isolating 'Western Christendom' for about half a millennium. With the European voyages of expansion from the 15th century onward all this began to change. Trading outposts developed by the Portuguese, the Dutch, and the English in the 17th century reintroduced Christianity in coastal pockets, but the established kingdoms and faiths of Central and East Asia were justly aware of the potentially erosive danger of European ideas.

Thus, the process of evangelization in early modern Asia became exceedingly bloody, and produced a huge number of martyrs. Often these were those foolhardy enough to simply defy national authorities in countries such as Japan, China, Korea, and Vietnam. But, equally, Asian martyrs were often the product of local ill-feeling, where being an 'outsider' made one an easy scapegoat, or where simple incomprehension provided a justification for persecution.

The suppression of Christianity in Japan under the Tokugawa Shogunate, involving mass public executions, crucifixions, and beheadings, was an emphatic and bloody statement of Japan's intention to plow its own furrow, remote from the developing worlds beyond its shores. The nation remained in isolation for over 200 years.

THE SURVIVAL OF CHRISTIANITY IN JAPAN

A series of persecutions followed the deaths of Paul Miki and his companions (Feb. 6), notably in 1632 when a further 55 Japanese Christians were put to death. Yet despite Japan's then complete isolation from the wider world – after 1641 all foreigners were banned from the Japanese mainland – and its lack of contact with any formal Christian bodies, a form of clandestine Christianity survived.

When, in 1854, with the Meiji Restoration, Japan was forcibly brought into contact with the outside world, those first penetrating the country were astounded to discover a substantial Christian community in Nagasaki. In 1962, to mark the 100th anniversary of the canonization of Paul Miki and his 25 companions, a museum was opened on the site of their deaths.

The Twenty-Six Martyrs Museum and Monument in Nagasaki, a tribute to the improbable survival of Christianity for more than 250 years, despite sustained attempts to eradicate it by a Japan determined to avoid all contact with the West.

DECEMBER 4   BARBARA

STATUS	Virgin, Martyr
BORN	3rd century, Nicomedia, Turkey
DIED	c.306, Nicomedia, Turkey
GRC	☁
CofE	☁
LCDUS	☁
OTHER	Eastern Orthodox churches
⬭	Pre-Congregation
✝	Chalice, lightning, martyr's crown, palm, tower
🙏	Artillerymen, gunpowder makers, mathematicians, miners, stonecutters, those afraid of lightning, fever; against sudden death

Whatever the doubts as to her existence, the legend of St. Barbara, one of the most popular saints in the Middle Ages and one of the Fourteen Holy Helpers, is among the most appealingly vivid of any saint. She is said to have been the daughter of a pagan, Dioscorus, who confined her in a tower, where in her enforced solitude she became a Christian. Her father discovered her conversion after she had three windows installed in a bathhouse in honor of the Trinity. When, enraged, he attempted to kill her, she escaped after an opening miraculously appeared in the wall. A shepherd who then betrayed her was turned to stone and his sheep to locusts. Though she was tortured, her wounds healed instantly. She was beheaded by her father, who was subsequently struck by lightning.

Barbara and her tower portrayed in a 16th-century French statue.

THE 14 HOLY HELPERS

This group of largely traditional, Pre-Congregational saints became enormously popular in Central Europe and Germany during the Middle Ages. Their intercession was invoked on an almost daily basis for everyday problems, and their cultural legacy remains recognized by most today.

Agathius (May 8)	Headache
Barbara (Dec. 4)	Fever, sudden death, lightning
Blaise (Feb. 3)	Throat ailments, pets
Catherine (Nov. 25)	Sudden death
Christopher (July 25)	Traveling, plague
Cyriacus (Aug. 8)	Temptation on the deathbed
Denis (Oct. 9)	Headache
Erasmus/Elmo (June 2)	Stomach ailments
Eustace (Sept. 20)	Family discord
George (April 23)	Pets
Giles (Sept. 1)	Plague, the infirm, good confession
Margaret of Antioch (July 20)	Childbirth, possession by devils
Pantaleon (July 27)	Cancers and tuberculosis
Vitus (June 15)	Epilepsy, lightning

DECEMBER 4   JOHN OF DAMASCUS

STATUS	Monk, Doctor of the Church
BORN	c.676, Damascus, Syria
DIED	749, Jerusalem, Palestine
GRC	♣
CofE	♣
LCDUS	♣
OTHER	Eastern Orthodox churches, Lutheran
⬭	Pre-Congregation

Though John's life is known only imperfectly (the earliest account of him dates from two centuries after his death), he was a key figure in the Middle East's transition from the last remnants of the Hellenic world to the imposition of Muslim rule. Though some of John's relations were Christians, they were highly placed officials under the Muslims, who had conquered Damascus in 635: his father was responsible for raising taxes for Umayyad caliphs. John himself would later serve as chief administrator to the Muslim caliph of Damascus. He was highly educated in both Greek and Arabic and wrote widely on legal, philosophical, and theological subjects. He was a fierce opponent of iconoclasm, the official banning of images of religious veneration, first introduced by the Byzantine emperor, Leo III, in 726. It was claimed that the emperor, in his fury, implicated John in a plot to topple the caliph of Damascus, who in turn had John's right hand severed. It miraculously re-grew after John prayed to the Blessed Virgin Mary. He subsequently retired to the monastery of Mar Saba, where he was ordained in 735. He devoted the remainder of his life to teaching and to contemplation.

THE VENERATION OF MUSLIM SAINTS

Islam, along with Judaism and Christianity, is one of the 'Religions of the Book.' The three share monotheism, territory, shrines, prophets, and angels. Technically, Islam does not observe saints; any Muslim, however humble, has the power to intercede. Further, the veneration of images is inhibited by Islam's iconoclasm. In practice, however, those who are seen to have possessed the God-given charismatic quality of *baraka* are venerated widely, especially as a source of intercession. Most of the family of Muhammad are thus regarded by both Sunni and Shi'a, but across the Muslim world, notably among the Sufi tradition, there are many whose shrines are visited and whose powers are invoked on feast days.

The tomb of Telli Baba near Istanbul is a popular shrine for Muslim women seeking a suitable husband. The tomb is draped in tinsel, and rich tatlisi cakes are baked to invoke his help.

DECEMBER 5 — SABAS THE SANCTIFIED

STATUS Monk, Hermit
BORN 439, Cappadocia, Turkey
DIED 532, Jerusalem, Palestine
GRC ○
CofE ○
LCDUS ○
OTHER Eastern Orthodox churches, Lutheran Church
○ Pre-Congregation
✝ Monk with abbot's staff

Sabas played a critical role in the early monastic tradition as it developed in the Middle East and North Africa. He founded a number of monasteries, most famously that which bears his name, Mar Saba, outside Jerusalem. Almost his entire life was spent in a variety of monastic communities, having entered his first monastery, in Antioch, at only eight. He subsequently served as a monk in Palestine under Euthymius the Great, then under his disciple, Theoctistus. He spent several years as a hermit until his fame as a holy man grew to the point that he was persuaded to found monastic communities of his own. In 491, the patriarch of Jerusalem, Salustius, appointed him head, or archimandrite, of all of Palestine's monasteries. Numerous miracles were associated with his cult.

Sabas's relics were removed to Rome for safekeeping in the 12th century by crusaders. There, they were buried in the church of San Saba. They were returned to Mar Saba only in 1965 as part of a general attempt to improve relations between Rome and the Orthodox Church.

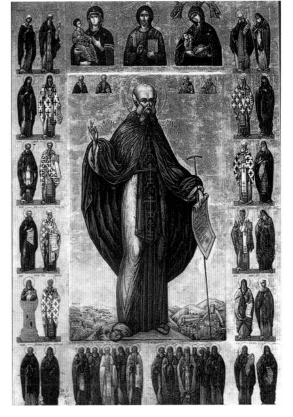

DECEMBER 6 — ADOLPH KOLPING

STATUS Priest
BORN 1813, Kerpen, Germany
DIED 1865, Cologne, Germany
GRC ○
CofE ○
LCDUS ○
♥ 1991
⚒ Apprentices; World Youth Day

Adolph Kolping, son of a shepherd and ordained in 1845, dedicated his life to improving the social and religious lives of Germany's burgeoning 19th-century working classes. Shocked by the conditions of Cologne's urban poor, in 1847 he was made president of the Catholic Association of Journeymen, a body catering to the spiritual and material needs of craftsmen and, above all, apprentices. He fused this with other journeymen associations across Germany to form what became known as the International Kolping Society. Today, it has 450,000 members in 60 countries divided into 5,000 regional groups or 'Kolping families.'

A modern bronze statue of Adolph Kolping in the town of his birth, Kerpen in the Rhineland. He is remembered today as the 'Father of All Apprentices.'

Date	Name	Status	Venerated	Life
Dec. 4	Clement of Alexandria (d.c.217)	Theologian ○ Pre-Congregation	Eastern Orthodox churches	Influential early Christian theologian. Head of the Catechetical School of Alexandria in Egypt, critical in fusing classical Greek traditions of scholarship with Christian teachings. Briefly bishop of Caesarea in Cappadocia (Turkey), where he fled in 202 to escape persecutions under Septimius Severus.
Dec. 4	Nicholas Ferrar (1592–1637)	Deacon, Founder	CofE	Educated at Cambridge. Ordained deacon in Church of England (1626). With close links to the court of James I, was involved with the London Virginia Company (founded 1606) to establish colonies in North America. Briefly Member of Parliament. Remembered for informal religious community he established with members of his family at Little Gidding, Huntingdonshire (1626), aiming to undertake good works in community and to inculcate spiritual discipline.

DECEMBER 6   NICHOLAS OF MYRA

STATUS Bishop

BORN Late 3rd century, Patara, modern Turkey

DIED Mid-4th century, Myra, modern Turkey

GRC ♠

CofE ♠

LCDUS ♣

OTHER Eastern Orthodox churches

⬯ Pre-Congregation

✝ Often shown bearing three moneybags or golden balls; more commonly, since the late 19th century, portrayed as Santa Claus

🙏 Children, archers, sailors, merchants, pawnbrokers; Amsterdam, Moscow

Possibly the most widely known and beloved saint in his role as 'Santa Claus,' or 'Father Christmas,' Nicholas of Myra was an exceedingly popular saint long before the commercialization of Christmas began in the 19th century.

Nicholas was probably born in Lycia in southwest Asia Minor (modern Turkey), and became bishop of Myra, the provincial capital. During the Diocletian persecution he was imprisoned, but was released unharmed. Twenty years later, he attended the Council of Nicaea (325) to denounce Arianism (*see* page 12). He may have been martyred. One legend, which gives rise to the tradition of giving presents (especially to children) at Christmas, involves three girls, to each of whom he purportedly gave a bag of gold as dowries to prevent them from turning to prostitution.

The emperor Constantine built a basilica dedicated to Nicholas in Constantinople, and he went on to become one of the most widely represented and venerated early Christian saints in both the Eastern and Western churches. At some point, the strength of Nicholas's cult in northern Europe appears to have become intertwined with Nordic myths, especially that of Odin, reinforcing his association with the spirit of winter and its attributes such as snow and holly.

Keen to build a reputation as a pilgrimage center, in 1087 the city of Bari in southern Italy endorsed a raid on Myra, and Nicholas's relics were looted from there. A further tradition has it that the relics were later removed from Bari to Jerpoint Abbey, in County Kilkenny, Ireland.

Nicholas's cult in Germany and the Netherlands gave root, in the 19th century, to his present identification as Santa Claus (from the Dutch *Sinterklaas*), a sub-cult that emerged very strongly among the Dutch settlers of New Amsterdam (modern New York). The American cartoonist Thomas Nast (1840–1902) effectively invented the accepted modern image of Nicholas as a rotund Father Christmas in many illustrations; the first was produced in 1863 for Harper's Weekly.

St. Nicholas and the Pickling Jar. One legend, popular in southeast Europe, describes how a butcher murdered three youths, and preserved their bodies to sell as meat. Nicholas discovered the crime, and brought the youths back to life.

Nicholas's generosity in providing dowries to poor girls so that they could marry, rather than face a life of vice, is remembered today in the three gold balls frequently used to indicate a pawnbroker's shop.

DECEMBER 7 — AMBROSE OF MILAN

STATUS Bishop, Doctor of the Church

BORN c.339, Trier, Germany

DIED 397, Milan, Italy

GRC ♣

CofE ♣

LCDUS ♣

◯ Pre-Congregation

† In bishop's robes, with book or miter; with a scourge; with a bee, or beehive

🐝 Beekeepers

As a child, it is said that bees left a droplet of honey on Ambrose's mouth, interpreted as an augur of his future eloquence. The scourge represents his stern treatment of the East Roman emperor Theodosius.

With his contemporaries Sts. Jerome (Sept. 30), Augustine of Hippo (Aug. 28, whom Ambrose baptized), and Gregory the Great (Sept. 3), Ambrose is one of the four Latin Doctors of the Church who lived at a time when Christianity had only recently been adopted as the imperial religion (promulgated under the Edict of Milan in 313 by Constantine). A prolific writer, Ambrose emerged as the most politically astute of his peers in both ecclesiastical and lay matters. Caught up in the Nicene/Arian dispute that dominated the period (*see* page 12), he was a negotiator and persuader rather than a polemicist.

Born to Roman nobility on the northern marches of the empire and extremely well educated, in 370 he was appointed governor of Aemilia and Liguria in Italy, based in Milan. Upon the death in 374 of the Arian bishop of Milan, street fighting erupted between Christian factions, and by popular acclaim Ambrose, whose intercession calmed the mobs, was declared bishop. Although reluctant to accept, he was rapidly baptized and consecrated, and distributed his wealth to the poor, adopting a proto-monastic lifestyle, although he never removed himself from his pastoral duties. His political background made Ambrose an astute advocate of the distinction between Church and State: he advised the emperor Gratian about Arianism, and pointed out to Gratian's successor, Valentinian, that the emperor was part of, but not above, the Church. Ambrose argued against the restoration of a pagan Victory cult, promoted by Valentinian's wife Justina. When Valentinian sought the protection of the East Roman emperor, Theodosius, from the West Roman usurper Maximus, Ambrose demanded public penance (on pain of excommunication) from Theodosius for the atrocities he had enacted in defeating Maximus and his supporters.

Ambrose was a thoughtful promoter of monasticism, nunneries under the Marian cult, the performance of the Eucharist, clerical ethics, and the use of hymns during acts of worship.

St. Ambrose Receiving the Penance of Theodosius *by Anthony van Dyck (1599–1641).*

DECEMBER 8 — THE IMMACULATE CONCEPTION OF THE BLESSED VIRGIN MARY

This is a major feast that celebrates the miraculous creation, free from the taint of Original Sin, of the Blessed Virgin Mary in her mother's womb. It dates back in the Eastern churches to the 7th century. The feast was approved in the West in 1476 by Pope Sixtus IV, and gained importance after the Marian vision of Bernadette Soubirous (April 16) at Lourdes in 1858, when the Virgin announced, "I am the Immaculate Conception."

Date	Name	Status	Venerated	Life
Dec. 9	Juan Diego (1474–1548)	Hermit ♥ 1990 ◯ 2002	In Mexico	Native Aztec to whom Our Lady of Guadalupe reportedly appeared (1531). With his wife, had been among first Aztecs to convert to Christianity, in 1524 or 1525, both taking Spanish names. Thereafter lived chaste, eremitic lives. Following apparitions, devoted rest of his life to caring for the shrine built to commemorate them. Despite central place of Our Lady of Guadalupe in Latin American Catholicism (Diego is thus claimed as first indigenous American saint) – and Juan Diego's canonization by Pope John Paul II in 2002 – significant doubts remain as to whether he existed.

DECEMBER 10

EULALIA DE MÉRIDA

STATUS Virgin, Martyr
BORN c.290, Mérida, Spain
DIED c.304, Mérida, Spain
GRC ☁
CofE ☁
LCDUS ☁
◯ Pre-Congregation
✝ Stake, dove
⚱ Torture victims, runaways; Mérida, Oviedo

Although hidden in the countryside by her Christian mother to avoid the persecutions of Maximian and Diocletian, when Christians were forced to apostatize or face death, Eulalia escaped and presented herself at the court of the Roman governor. She declared her Christian faith, insulted both the pagan gods and the emperor, and dared the governor to martyr her. In spite of the judge's entreaties to the young girl, he was eventually forced to condemn her. Eulalia was stripped, tortured with torches and hooks, and finally burned tied to a cross. Throughout these imprecations she taunted her enemies and continued to avow her faith. When she finally expired, a dove flew out of her mouth, and snow miraculously fell to cover her nakedness.

Eulalia's cult proved very important in Visigothic Spain, and her relics were distributed widely.

Lurid accounts of martyrdoms such as that of St. Eulalia provided popular quasi-erotic subjects for 19th-century paintings, such as J. W. Waterhouse's 1885 depiction.

DECEMBER 11

DAMASUS I

STATUS Pope
BORN c.305, Lusitania, Portugal
DIED 384, Rome, Italy
GRC ♣
CofE ☁
LCDUS ♣
OTHER Eastern Orthodox churches
◯ Pre-Congregation

The emperor Gratian, torn between the Western and Eastern churches.

S. DAMASVS. I

Damasus was elected pope in 366, in an atmosphere of violence and uncertainty. His claims to the papacy were bitterly disputed by Ursinus, deacon to the previous pope, Liberius, who simultaneously had declared himself pope. It was a conflict in which supporters of Damasus were claimed to have massacred 137 supporters of Ursinus. Only in 378, with the exile of Ursinus, was Damasus able to assert his sole authority.

Damasus proved a sturdy champion of the Latin Church, condemning various heretical movements, including Arianism (*see* page 12), and overseeing the translation of the Bible into Latin by his secretary, St. Jerome (Sept. 30). This work, known as the Vulgate Bible, would become the standard Latin Bible. He also restored numerous churches and monuments, particularly those commemorating early martyrs.

Damasus's papacy coincided with the rule of emperor Gratian (r.367–83), a supporter of Christianity but under whom the Eastern Church briefly achieved ascendancy in the West.

Damasus, here depicted in the portico of St. Peter's, was pope at a time when Christianity had only recently become the official religion of the Roman empire. It was a development he successfully exploited, engineering a significant strengthening of the Church.

Date	Name	Status	Venerated	Life
Dec. 10	The Alexandria Martyrs (d.c.313)	Martyrs ◯ Pre-Congregation		Little known of Alexandria Martyrs other than that the emperor Maximinus dispatched a magistrate, Hermogenes, to persuade one of his senior civil servants, Menas Kallikelados – Menas the Eloquent – to renounce Christianity. Upon Menas's refusal to recant, Hermogenes had Menas's tongue cut out. Menas and his secretary, Eugraphus, were once again impeached, whereupon Menas spoke again with a "sweet and beautiful voice." Hermogenes instantly converted to Christianity himself. All three then beheaded.

DECEMBER 12   OUR LADY OF GUADALUPE

> "I am . . . the merciful mother of all of you who live united in this land."
>
> OUR LADY OF GUADALUPE
> TO JUAN DIEGO.

Our Lady of Guadalupe remains one of the most intriguing Marian apparitions. In December 1531, the Virgin Mary appeared three times to Juan Diego (Dec. 9), an Aztec Christian convert, at Tepeyac in central Mexico. She ordered him to instruct Juan de Zumárraga, described as the bishop of Mexico, to build a shrine to her. The woman, Diego reported, appeared to be about 14 and had the appearance of an Aztec princess. She spoke to Diego in a local tongue, Nahuatl. Zumárraga, initially skeptical, was persuaded only after the Virgin's third appearance to Diego, who had told her that the Spaniard had demanded proof that she was the Virgin. She told Diego to gather roses, blooming nearby despite its being mid-winter, and to present them to Zumárraga. She placed them inside his cloak or

An image of Our Lady of Guadalupe as she appeared on Juan Diego's cloak. She is widely known as the 'dark virgin, the little brown one'. It is claimed that after the image was damaged in 1791, when ammonia was spilt on it, it miraculously restored itself. Since 1974, it has been displayed in the new basilica dedicated to the apparition.

tilma. As Diego showed them to the prelate, it was discovered that an image of the Virgin had miraculously appeared on Diego's cloak. Zumárraga fell to his knees in wonderment. The shrine was duly begun.

Historical Veracity

The significance of Our Lady of Guadalupe is hard to overstate. The Virgin Mary, according to Diego, appeared to him only ten years after the Spanish conquest of Mexico by Hernán Cortés. Following this audacious enterprise, the conquest of an entire nation larger than Spain by a force only 600 strong, the Spanish set about converting their newly subject peoples. Surprisingly, the Aztecs proved willing converts, but these efforts received a huge boost after the appearance of the Virgin, with Mexico and, later, Spanish and Portuguese South America as a whole becoming deeply Catholic. It is a unique example of an entire continent embracing a single, hitherto alien, religion. Our Lady of Guadalupe rapidly came to be adopted as the 'Queen of Mexico' and the 'Patroness of the Americas.'

That said, the historical veracity of the entire episode has long been disputed: the first known accounts of the apparitions date from 1648 and 1649. Zumárraga, who in fact became bishop of Mexico only in 1533, made not one mention of the apparitions or of Juan Diego in his voluminous correspondence. In 1995, an apparently contemporary account of the apparitions, the *Codex Escalada*, written on deerskin, was discovered. Its authenticity has never been proven. The suspicion that the apparitions were a Catholic invention of a half-native, half-European figure – designed to facilitate the conversion of Spain's new colonies – remains convincing.

THE BASILICA OF OUR LADY OF GUADALUPE

The original basilica, successively rebuilt between 1531 and 1709, was among the most lavish and imposing buildings in New Spain, a heady, assertive Baroque confection *(below)*. It was abandoned in 1974 as its foundations gradually subsided into the former lake over which it had been constructed, and a new, unashamedly modern circular basilica was begun. This was completed in 1976. It is capable of housing 10,000 people and extra seating in the atrium can take the capacity to 40,000. Over a single weekend in December 2009, the 478th anniversary of the apparitions, six million people visited the site. It remains the most significant pilgrimage center in the Americas.

MEXICAN MYSTICISM

The impact of the Jesuits and the Franciscans on the development of Christianity in the New World, especially in the Spanish colonies, was marked by a profound mysticism, most frequently expressed through the cult of the Blessed Virgin Mary. In Mexico, aspects of devotion and adoration, already deeply embedded in Catholic Counter-Reformation Europe, became magnified to extraordinary proportions.

Some of the enormous wealth which Spain accrued from silver and gold mines in its new colonies found its way into enormously elaborate gilded altarpieces, shrines, and reredos, such as this example in the Church of Santo Domingo in Oaxaca, Mexico, dating from the early 18th century.

The Sacred Heart of Jesus by Juan Patricio Morlete Ruiz (right), dating from the mid-19th century, displays something of the fervor of Mexican devotional art, less than 75 years before religion was effectively outlawed during the Mexican Revolution.

FINIAN (FINNIAN) OF CLONARD

Abbot

Late 5th century

c.549, Clonard,
Ireland

△

△

△

In Ireland

Pre-Congregation

Finian was a follower of Sts. Patrick (March 17), Cadoc, and Gildas. He established monasticism in Ireland and forged strong links with the emerging monasteries in England, Wales, Northumbria, and Scotland. Among his many pupils and disciples were St. Ciaran, as well as the missionaries Columba of Iona (June 9), and Brendan the Navigator (May 16).

He is not to be confused with his near contemporary, St. Finnian of Moville (feast day Sept. 10, d.c.579), who established a thriving monastic school in his native Ulster.

A modern sculpture of Finian from the church at Clonard, County Meath, Ireland.

LUCY (LUCIA)

Virgin, Martyr

Late-3rd century,
Syracuse, Sicily

c.304, Syracuse, Sicily

♣

♣

♣

Eastern Orthodox
churches

Pre-Congregation

Holding a dish
containing her eyes

Peddlers, light; the
blind, sufferers from
diseases of the eye

...mbol of a burning ...ects her enduring ... to Christ.

According to legend, Lucy was born to wealthy Roman parents, but following a pilgrimage to the shrine of St. Agatha at Catania, she wished to give her inheritance to the poor, revealing her Christian beliefs just at a time when the persecution of Christians under the emperor Diocletian was at its height. Threatened with rape by a suitor, she apparently tore out her own eyes rather than submit, offering her eyes to her tormentor. She was tried by the Sicilian governor Paschasius, who implored her to recant, which she refused to do. She was then executed by a sword thrust to the neck. Her relics were taken to Constantinople, but are now claimed by Venice. Lucy has remained an enormously popular saint; the Caribbean island of St. Lucia is named for her, and in Sweden this day is celebrated as the festival of light.

The narrative of Lucy's trial and martyrdom is captured here by an unknown Flemish painter of the late 15th century.

DECEMBER 14 JOHN OF THE CROSS

STATUS Priest, Mystic, Doctor
of the Church

BORN 1542, Fontiveros,
Spain

DIED 1591, Ubeda, Spain

GRC ♣

CofE ♣

LCDUS ♣

OTHER By Discalced
Carmelites; in Spain

♥ 1675

◯ 1726

✝ In Carmelite habit,
barefooted, writing

🙏 Mystics, Spanish
poets

*The arms of St. John of the
Cross combine a number of
features. The white upper
half of the cross represents
his purity, the red lower half
his persecution. The upper
black field refers to his Jesuit
training, the lower quadrants
to the colors of the Carmelite
habit, white and light brown.*

John, born Juan de Yepes, was the orphaned
son of peasants who took to tending the sick
and poor. He was admitted to the Carmelite
Order in 1563 and then studied at Salamanca
University. He was ordained in 1567. Under the
influence of St. Teresa (Oct. 15), John joined
her reform movement, the Discalced Carmelites,
after being trained by Jesuits, and became spiritual
director at her priory in Ávila. Other Carmelites'
opposition to their reforms led to his arrest and
imprisonment in the Carmelite priory in Toledo,
where he was held in dark solitary confinement
for nine months. He was occasionally allowed to
visit the refectory, where he would be abused and
scourged, but here he wrote some of his finest
mystical poetry.

John escaped in 1578, and was appointed
confessor to the Discalced Nuns at El Calvario
near Baeza, where he wrote extensively. His works
from this period include *The Ascent of Mount
Carmel* and *The Dark Night of the Soul*. John was
an advocate of devotional imagery, particularly the
polychromatic statuary typical of Spain, as an aid
to contemplation. He was declared a Doctor of
the Church in 1926.

St. John of the Cross Receiving Divine Inspiration, *by
Domenico Piola, c. 1675.*

Date	Name	Status	Venerated	Life
Dec. 13	Samuel (Dr.) Johnson (1709–84)	Moralist	CofE	Noted critic, lexicographer, and compiler of the *Dictionary of English* (1755). Included in the Anglican calendar as a 'moralist.'
Dec. 15	Mary di Rosa (1813–55)	Nun, Founder ♥ 1940 ◯ 1954	In Brescia, Italy	Italian who cared for the female workers in her father's mill; tended the sick in the 1836 cholera epidemic; founded a school for the deaf; set up a military hospital during the *Risorgimento* wars. Founded the Handmaids of Charity (1840); adopted the name Mary of the Crucifix.
Dec. 15	Mary Frances Schervier (1819–76)	Nun, Founder ♥ 1974	LCDUS In Germany	Well-born heiress from Aachen, Germany. Became a Franciscan Tertiary (1844) and founded the Poor Sisters of St. Francis that aided German migrants to the US, tending to orphans, the poor, and the uneducated. Her order nursed the wounded during the American Civil War.
Dec. 16	Adelaide of Burgundy (931–99)	Queen, Nun ◯ c.1097	In France and Germany	Daughter of Rudolf II of Upper Burgundy. At age 16 was married to Lothair, king of Italy, who was poisoned by one of her other suitors. Briefly imprisoned, she escaped and married Otto (951), who became Holy Roman Emperor (962). After Otto's death (973) devoted herself to converting the Slavs.
Dec. 16	Honoratus Kozminski (1825–1916)	Priest, Founder ♥ 1988	In Poland	Imprisoned in 1846 accused of a religious conspiracy. Entered the Capuchin Order (1848); ordained (1852); founded the Felician Sisters with Mary Angela Truszkowska (1855). Oversaw survival of the Polish Church during the period of Russian repression following the Polish revolt of 1864. Wrote extensively.

DECEMBER 17

JOHN OF MATHA

STATUS Priest

BORN 1160, Provence, France

DIED 1213, Rome, Italy

GRC ○

CofE ○

LCDUS ○

○ 1666

† In white Trinitarian habit with a blue and red cross

🙏 Prisoners

Celebrating his first Mass after his ordination in 1197, John of Matha, a doctor of theology, had a vision of an angel with two captives, one a Christian, the other a Moor. This led directly to his foundation the following year, with a hermit, Felix of Valois, of the Order of the Most Holy Trinity (the Trinitarians). Its purpose was to free Christians from "the captivity they groaned under among the infidels," in other words, to free those Crusaders held prisoner by the Muslims.

The Order, still active today and still ministering to those in prison, expanded rapidly from its first home north of Paris, especially across France, Italy, and Spain. One-third of all its revenues were set aside to ransom prisoners. An initial visit to Tunis in 1201 made by members of the Order saw the release of 186 captives. John himself journeyed to Tunis in 1202 and 1210, returning respectively with 110 and 120 prisoners. In 1655, his relics were transferred to Madrid, Spain.

A painting by Juan Carreño de Miranda from 1666, today in the Louvre, Paris, of St. John celebrating his first Mass. In addition to John's vision of an angel with two prisoners, the Trinity is also depicted, a reference to his Order.

DECEMBER 17

EGLANTYNE JEBB

STATUS Social Reformer

BORN 1876, Shropshire, England

DIED 1928, Geneva, Switzerland

GRC ○

CofE ♣

LCDUS ○

Jebb, though supremely practical and tough-minded, was a convinced pacifist. "All wars are waged against children," she asserted.

Eglantyne Jebb was among the most dynamic and successful social reformers of the early 20th century. As the founder and director of the Save the Children Fund, initially established in 1919 to aid starving children in Austria and Germany immediately after World War I, she was to prove a tireless fund-raiser and an exceptionally innovative and, above all, efficient aid-worker. In its first year alone, Save the Children raised £400,000. By August 1921, it had raised £1m and had 300 branches throughout Britain. She had almost a genius for soliciting the support of the prominent including, in December 1919, Pope Benedict XV. "The SCF pays no regard to politics, race, or religion," she declared. In 1921–23, the immediate crisis in central Europe over, she directed her attentions to those children affected by the famine that accompanied the Russian Civil War, organizing 157 million meals for 300,000 children. In 1923, in Geneva, she issued the Declaration of the Rights of the Child, which the following year was adopted by the League of Nations and, in 1959, formed the basis of the UN's Declaration on the Rights of the Child. Throughout, she was sustained by a fervent Christianity. Ill health, which led to her early death at only 52, dogged her for much of her life. Perhaps surprisingly, she had no children of her own.

DECEMBER 19 — URBAN V

STATUS Pope
BORN 1310, Languedoc, France
DIED 1370, Avignon, France
GRC ◌
CofE ◌
LCDUS ◌
♥ 1870

Urban V, pope between 1362 and 1370, presided over part of the most divisive and destabilizing period of the medieval papacy. Its enforced removal to Avignon in southern France in 1309, effectively on the orders of the French monarchy, was a crushing blow to a papacy that in the early Middle Ages had emerged as the overarching power in Europe. Its claims to spiritual authority, to which all temporal rulers were at least nominally subject, had been buttressed by its growing wealth and political muscle. But this superiority was followed by an increasingly troubled standoff between the rulers of a series of ever-more self-confident Christian states – chiefly France, England, and the Holy Roman Empire. In 1303, Pope Boniface, captured by Philip the Fair of France, became the first, reluctant victim of a newly powerful French monarchy and state. His successor, Clement V, then effectively surrendered papal authority, allowing the papacy to be transferred to Avignon. For 70 years, the papacy became a tool of the ambitions of a succession of French kings. Seven popes in a row were French. All were based in Avignon. Rome, abandoned, became a city of ruins and slums.

Urban V, though French, manfully stood against these trends. He vigorously protested against the luxuries into which the Avignon papacy had sunk. He similarly attempted to resist the ambitions of the German Holy Roman Emperor to dominate Italy. Most straightforwardly, he attempted to restore the papacy to Rome, arriving there himself to what he hoped was acclaim in 1367. He was unsuccessful on all three fronts. Forced back to Avignon in 1370, he died three months later.

The Palais des Papes in Avignon was the largest Gothic palace in the world, begun in 1334 by Benedict XIII and completed under Urban V in 1364. This, the site of the "Babylonian Captivity" as Luther contemptuously called the Avignon papacies, was a building of extraordinary opulence and luxury.

DECEMBER 20 — DOMINIC OF SILOS

STATUS Abbot
BORN 1000, Navarre, Spain
DIED 1073, Silos, Spain
GRC ◌
CofE ◌
LCDUS ◌
⬭ Pre-Congregation
† In abbot's clothing, surrounded by the Seven Virtues
🙏 Captives, shepherds, pregnancy

Dominic became a Benedictine monk and rose to become prior of the monastery of San Millán de la Cogolla in Navarre before being driven out by the king of Navarre, who was determined to annex the monastery's lands. King Ferdinand I of Castile and León then appointed Dominic abbot of the monastery of San Sebastián near Burgos, today the monastery of Santo Domingo de Silos. It was, at the time, impoverished and largely ruined. Today, in large measure due to the extensive renovations begun under Dominic, it is one of the most important and richly decorated Romanesque monasteries in Spain. Dominic made the monastery a major center of scholarship and craftsmanship. He also worked actively for the release of Christian prisoners held by the Moors of central and southern Spain. By tradition, as a saint invoked by pregnant women, St. Dominic's abbot's staff was used to bless Spain's queens as they went into labor. On his death, he almost immediately became one of medieval Spain's most venerated saints. Numerous miracles were attributed to his cult.

The elaborate two-story cloister of the monastery of Santo Domingo de Silos.

Date	Name	Status	Venerated	Life
Dec. 18	Flannan of Killaloe (7th century)	Bishop ⬭ Pre-Congregation		Little known with any certainty, but probably son of an Irish chieftain, Turlough. Thought to have visited Rome, crossing the sea by floating on a millstone. In Rome, Pope John IV made him a bishop. In Ireland, became bishop of Killaloe, today in County Clare.
Dec. 19	Anastasius I (d.401)	Pope ⬭ Pre-Congregation		Pope 399–401. His papacy remembered chiefly for his condemnation of Egyptian theologian, Origen, who held that Jesus, as the Son of God, was junior to His father within the Trinity rather than co-existent and equal. Also had to contend with rise of extreme Christian sect in North Africa, the Donatists.

DECEMBER 21   PETER CANISIUS

STATUS Priest, Doctor of the
        Church
BORN   1521, Nijmegen,
        Holland
DIED   1597, Fribourg,
        Switzerland
GRC   ♣
CofE   ☁
LCDUS   ♣
OTHER   By Jesuits
♥   1864
◯   1925
🙏   The Catholic press;
        Germany

anisius, the first Dutchman to become a Jesuit, was a key figure in the Counter-Reformation, a tireless and resourceful teacher, preacher, diplomat, and, above all, theologian on behalf of what had, for a time, looked a seriously beleaguered Catholic Church. Known as the 'Hammer of Protestantism' and the 'Second Apostle of Germany,' he was the most influential figure in the German Catholic Church in the 16th century.

Canisius was ordained in Rome in 1547, and then helped to establish Cologne's first Jesuit outpost. By 1549, he was teaching theology at Ingolstadt in south Germany. In 1552, he was sent to Vienna, where again he taught theology. His impact was such that a year later he was asked to become the city's bishop. He refused, continuing instead on a near endless series of journeys across central Europe, buttressing Catholic teaching and preaching, and founding four Jesuit colleges.

Canisius's most lasting legacy was a catechism in German, first published in 1558 and issued in 200 editions in Canisius's lifetime alone. When in Fribourg, he claimed he had a vision of the 4th-century saint, Nicholas of Myra (Dec. 6), who instructed him to give up his life of travel and remain in the city. Canisius obeyed, and wrote voluminously for the remaining 20 years of his life.

A miniature of Canisius painted after his death by an unknown artist. Canisius remains one of only two figures to have been declared a Doctor of the Church on the same day as his canonization.

DECEMBER 22   ANASTASIA

STATUS Martyr
BORN   Mid-3rd century,
        possibly Rome, Italy
DIED   c.304, Sirmium,
        modern Croatia
GRC   ♣ (Dec. 25)
CofE   ☁
LCDUS   ☁
OTHER   Eastern Orthodox
        churches
◯   Pre-Congregation
✝   With a martyr's cross
🙏   Housewives, female
        slaves, widows

nastasia is a shadowy figure, about whom numerous legends abound. She nevertheless remains widely venerated, especially in southeast Europe. She is said to have been married to a Roman nobleman, Publius. When Publius discovered that Anastasia was a Christian, secretly baptized by her mother, he ordered her to be treated like a slave. She rejoiced at this opportunity to serve Christ. Publius died on a mission to Persia, and she subsequently devoted her life to ministering to those Christians imprisoned for their faith, performing numerous works of charity.

Despite a number of miraculous interventions during Anastasia's trial, she appears to have been martyred during the Diocletian persecution in 304. In 460, her relics may have been transferred to Constantinople. Uniquely, in the Catholic Church she is commemorated on Christmas Day in the second, or dawn, Mass of the day, while in the Eastern churches she is commemorated on December 22.

One legend tells of Anastasia traveling to Aquileia to tend to the sick, and she is regarded as having healing properties by the Eastern churches.

DECEMBER 23 — JOHN OF KANTY (JOHN CANTIUS)

STATUS Priest, Theologian
BORN 1390, Kanty, Poland
DIED 1473, Kraków, Poland
GRC ♣
CofE ◯
LCDUS ♣
OTHER In Poland
♥ 1676
◯ 1767
✝ Professor's gown, giving clothes to the poor
🙏 Kraków University; Lithuania, Poland

Despite his low birth, John was immensely learned, becoming a professor of theology at Kraków University. He was a man of great sanctity and simplicity with no interest in material goods, giving to the poor much of what little he had. His obvious brilliance combined with long-suffering humility aroused considerable jealousy in some sections of the university. In 1431, these enemies succeeded in having him made parish priest of an obscure Bohemian town. When he was recalled to Kraków eight years later, his parishioners, initially deeply suspicious of John, begged him to stay. He slept on the bare floor and eschewed meat, and made four pilgrimages to Rome — all on foot — and one to the Holy Land. "Fight all error," he said, "but do it with good humor, patience, kindness, and love." He is said to have performed numerous miracles. His cult in Poland after his death was substantial.

The popularity of John of Kanty among Poles made it unsurprising that later Polish communities in North America should have dedicated numerous churches to him.

ABRAHAM HESCHEL – JEWISH ECUMENICIST

Born in the Polish capital, Warsaw, in 1907, educated largely in Germany, and emigrating to America after the rise of the Nazis, Heschel was among the great Jewish thinkers of the 20th century. His spirituality was profound. But what most distinguished him was a concern for mankind in all its manifestations. If in part this was an instinctive response to the atmosphere of Jewish rabbinical studies in which he was raised, it was also deeply colored by his experience of Nazism. In 1938, the Gestapo deported him to Poland. From there he was smuggled to London, and he made his way to the United States, arriving in 1940. Those of his family left in Poland were, in the main, simply exterminated. He never returned to his homeland. "If I should go to Poland or Germany," he said later, "every stone, every tree would remind me of contempt, hatred, murder, of children killed, of mothers burned alive, of human beings asphyxiated."

In time, impeccably liberal, Heschel became a fierce supporter of the Civil Rights movement and later an opponent of the Vietnam War. His influence extended far beyond Judaic teaching and he persuaded the Catholic Church to adopt a notably more tolerant view of Judaism. He remained a beacon of intelligent, tolerant learning to the last, dying in New York on December 23, 1972.

Alabama, March 21, 1965: Heschel, second from right, marches in company with Martin Luther King, Jr. (center). "Racism," asserted Heschel, "is man's gravest threat to man — the maximum hatred for a minimum reason."

Date	Name	Status	Venerated	Life
Dec. 24	Tarsilla and Emiliana (6th century)	Virgins ◯ Pre-Congregation		Two of three paternal aunts of Gregory the Great (Sept. 3), all noted for their piety. The third, Gordiana, eventually married. Tarsilla and Emiliana enjoyed visions, and the former was invited to join him in Heaven by their forebear Pope Felix II. She expired during vigil of Christmas, the skin of her elbows and knees hardened by constant prayer. Some days later, she in turn summoned Emiliana to join her, who died on Jan. 5.

DECEMBER 25   THE NATIVITY

The Nativity is an intensely intimate event, captured brilliantly here by the Dutch painter Geertgen tot Sint Jans (c. 1460–95). The hushed scene is illuminated by light emanating from the baby Jesus. Luke makes no mention of the Three Magi, whose visit is described in the Gospel of St. Matthew.

This very significant day is reserved for the celebration of the birth of Christ to the Blessed Virgin Mary. It has no saints associated with it, other than forming part of the cycle of Marian feast days. It is preceded by Advent, which begins on the fourth Sunday before this date. The Christmas feast starts on the evening of December 24 and continues until Epiphany (January 6, 12 days after the Nativity, or the first Sunday to occur thereafter).

Christ's Birth

The birth of Christ probably occurred in 5 BC, as Herod the Great died in 4 BC. For the Western churches, December 25 was laid down during the revision of the liturgical calendar in the 4th century, as the exact date of Christ's birth is not known. The date may have been chosen to counter various pagan festivals that celebrated the return of the Sun after the winter solstice in the northern hemisphere. In the Eastern Orthodox churches, Nativity and Epiphany were celebrated together on January 6, but December 25 has now become an almost global day of peace, celebration, and meditation, regardless of creed. Much of the symbolism associated with Christmas (decorated trees, Santa Claus – *see* Nicholas of Myra, Dec. 6 – carol singing, and the giving of gifts and cards) derives from early modern German traditions popularized in the 19th century.

The Nativity Story

The story of the Nativity is familiar to most, and derives mainly from the Gospel of St. Luke. Having traveled from their home at Nazareth to Bethlehem in order to enroll in a census, Joseph and the heavily pregnant Mary find no rooms, but are lodged in a stable. Christ is born and laid in a manger, with angels in attendance. Further afield an angel announces the coming of the Lord to some shepherds watching their flocks by night, who will soon seek out and worship the Child.

DECEMBER 26 STEPHEN

STATUS Deacon, Martyr

BORN c. AD 1, Jerusalem, modern Israel

DIED c. AD 35, Jerusalem, modern Israel

GRC ♣

CofE ♣

LCDUS ♣

OTHER Eastern Orthodox churches

◔ Pre-Congregation

✝ Palm of martyrdom, rocks

🙏 Deacons, stonemasons, coffinmakers, horses, sufferers from headaches

Stephen is well known as the first Christian martyr, but little is known of his life. He was born a Greek-speaking Jew in Jerusalem, and he probably converted to Christianity after the Crucifixion. He was one of Seven Deacons appointed by the Apostles to help and serve them, distributing alms to the poor (Acts 6–7). The early Hellenic Christians were instrumental in attempting to divorce Christianity from the Jewish Temple and Mosaic Law, and to open the faith to Gentiles, an initiative which would later be supported by St. Paul (Jan. 25). Stephen advocated this before the Jewish council of the Sanhedrin (Acts 7:2–53), also accusing the Jewish orthodoxy of conspiring in the murder of Jesus. Enraged, the councilors demanded that he be immediately stoned to death without trial. It is said that Saul, later St. Paul, witnessed and may have participated in Stephen's martyrdom.

The martyrdom of St. Stephen, although well known, was not a widely illustrated subject before the Counter-Reformation, when the passion of the subject provided ideal material for painters such as Rubens and Rembrandt van Rijn (below, 1625).

Stephen's emblem unsurprisingly combines three rocks with the palm of martyrdom, indicating spiritual victory over his executioners. Sometimes the palm is replaced with a deacon's robe.

Date	Name	Status	Venerated	Life
Dec. 26	Theodore the Sacristan (6th century)	Sacristan ◔ Pre-Congregation		Sacristan of St. Peter's, Rome. Described by Gregory the Great as frequently seeing angels.
Dec. 26	Dionysius (c.230–68)	Pope ◔ Pre-Congregation	Eastern Orthodox churches ✝ With book, or having vision of the Trinity	Born in Greece. Bishop in Rome under Pope Stephen I; succeeded him in 259. Insisted on Trinitarian doctrine; gave money to Cappadocian churches when threatened by invading Goths; negotiated an edict of toleration with Roman emperor Gallienus. First Pope not to die a martyr.
Dec. 26	Vincentia Maria López y Vicuña (1847–96)	Virgin ♥ 1950 ◔ 1975	🙏 Domestic servants	Spanish nun. Founded the Daughters of Mary Immaculate for Domestic Service (1888).

DECEMBER 27 — JOHN THE EVANGELIST

STATUS Apostle, Evangelist

BORN c. AD 7, Galilee, modern Israel

DIED c.101, Ephesus, modern Turkey

GRC ♣

CofE ♣

LCDUS ♣

OTHER Eastern Orthodox churches (May 8)

○ Pre-Congregation

✝ Eagle (especially when represented as one of the Four Evangelists), chalice with serpent (when offered a poisoned chalice at Ephesus), cauldron (when Domitian attempted to have him boiled), book; often represented with John the Baptist

🙏 Authors and all in the publishing industry, theologians, painters, engravers, art dealers; victims of burns and poisoning

The son of Zebedee and brother of James the Greater (July 25), John worked in the family's fishing business in Galilee, until he and James became some of Jesus's first disciples during the first year of His ministry. They may have been cousins of Jesus, as one tradition says that their mother was a sister of the Blessed Virgin Mary. After a brief return to Galilee, John accompanied Jesus throughout His ministry, becoming known as the 'Beloved Disciple.' At the Last Supper, John asked Jesus who would betray Him, and John was the only one not to desert Him during the Passion, remaining at the foot of the Cross. Jesus appointed John guardian of the Blessed Virgin Mary, and he cared for her after both the Crucifixion and the Ascension. John was also the first disciple to meet and recognize Jesus after the Resurrection.

Missionary Journeys

Jesus called John and James 'the Sons of Thunder,' and both of them played leading roles in the first Christian community in Jerusalem. John became particularly friendly with Peter (June 29), and is often regarded as second only to Peter in seniority among the Apostles. Peter and John were arrested for preaching in the Temple, and they went on a missionary journey to Samaria together.

John made later journeys to Ephesus to establish the Church there, and these produced some apocryphal legends. Journeying by sea, John is said to have made seawater drinkable, before the ship was wrecked. John was presumed to have drowned, but he was washed up on shore two weeks later. At Ephesus he is said to have been challenged to drink poisoned wine by the high priestess of the temple of Artemis; he then prayed at the temple, invoking the fury of her worshippers, who attempted to stone him, but the rocks bounced back and hit them instead. Also, he caused a mighty fire to come from the skies, killing some 200 of the idolaters. John then raised them from the dead, converted them, and cast out the demons who inhabited the temple. A further legend tells

The tondo by Jacopo Pontormo (1494–1557), designed for the church of Santa Felicità, Florence, presents the contemplative, bearded evangelist leaning forward to receive inspiration from the high altar.

> ## "In the beginning was the Word, and the Word was with God, and the Word was God."
>
> THE GOSPEL ACCORDING TO ST. JOHN 1:1.

Date	Name	Status	Venerated	Life
Dec. 27	Sára Salkaházi (Schalkház) (1899–1944)	Martyr ♥ 2006	In Hungary and Slovakia	Born in Kassa, Hungary (now Kosice, Slovakia). Entered the Sisters of Social Service in 1929. From 1941 edited Catholic working women's journal in Budapest, writing anti-Nazi polemics. Provided safe havens for Jews. She and five others arrested (1944). Shot on the banks of the Danube, and their bodies thrown into the water.
Dec. 27	Francesco Spoto (1924–64)	Martyr ♥ 2007	By the Missionary Servants of the Poor	Born in Raffadali, Italy. Became head of the Missionary Servants of the Poor (1959), restructuring the congregation, and leading a mission to Biringi in the Congo. Mission attacked by Simba rebels during civil war. Captured and beaten; died 11 days later.

of the emperor Domitian having John brought to Rome where he was poisoned, beaten, and cast into boiling oil, from which he emerged unscathed. John does, however, appear to have then been banished to the island of Patmos after preaching in Rome, and it is likely that it was here that he undertook most of his writing.

Legacy and Writings

John is regarded as the author of important elements of the New Testament: the fourth Gospel (in which it is suggested that both John and his brother were followers of John the Baptist before meeting Jesus), three Letters (Epistles), and the Book of Revelation (the Apocalypse), which ends the Bible on a thunderous note, and earned John the further sobriquet, 'the Divine.' However, the latter book is often thought to be the work of a different John.

John was the only Apostle not to have been martyred, dying around the age of 94, probably at Ephesus during the reign of Trajan. His grave is said to have produced a scented dust that cured the sick on this day each year.

The Revelation of St. John proved particularly appealing in medieval western Europe; Albrecht Dürer (1471–1528) envisaged the Four Horsemen of the Apocalypse – Death, War, Famine, and Plague – all facts of life in 16th-century Europe.

The Eastern Orthodox tradition tends to represent John either with John the Baptist, or in a format which combines episodes from John's life with images from the Revelation, as here in an icon by the Russian master Andrei Rublev (c.1360–1430) (above).

"And I saw a new heaven and a new earth ... And I John saw the holy city, new Jerusalem, coming down from God out of heaven, prepared as a bride adorned for her husband."

REVELATION 21:1–2.

Mary, and her husband Joseph. More specifically, the day recognizes Joseph's shepherding his new family away from Bethlehem to the safety of Egypt, following Herod the Great's proclamation that he intended to kill all recently-born male children to avoid a challenge to his throne. The chronology of the Nativity story and its aftermath becomes somewhat confused at this point. In the Gospel of St. Matthew, the flight to Egypt occurs after the Adoration of the Magi (the Epiphany, January 6), but it is not mentioned in the Gospel of St. Luke (the most detailed account of the Nativity). Here, in the immediate aftermath of Christ's birth, the Circumcision and the Presentation at the Temple (Feb. 2) are described before the Holy Family returns to Nazareth, having fulfilled their duties under Roman law. The feast is observed by all the major churches.

Arise, and take the young child and his mother, and flee into Egypt, and be thou there until I bring thee word: for Herod will seek the young child, to destroy him."

THE ANGEL TO JOSEPH (MATTHEW 2:13).

nificant emblem of lily, symbolizing as a fleur-de-lis, the Holy Trinity.

The Flight to Egypt, or Rest on the Fli was a popular Renaissance and Baroque art, providing an opportunity to present often exotic landscape. This treatment by colorist and narrative painter Vittore Ca (c.1460–c.1525), set in an Italianate c is unusual in presenting the Holy Fami large scale in the foreground of the comp

DECEMBER 28

THE MASSACRE OF THE HOLY INNOCENTS

U pon hearing of the birth of Jesus, who had been described in Jewish prophecy as 'a governor which shall be shepherd of my people Israel,' the Roman-sponsored King Herod I interrogated the three Magi, asking them to seek Jesus out and report back to him so that he too could worship the Christ Child. They didn't report back, and an enraged Herod determined to slaughter all male children under the age of two in Bethlehem in order to ensure that there was no threat to his rule. Only St. Matthew mentions this, one of the most horrifying events in the New Testament. He describes Joseph being instructed by an angel to take his family to Egypt, only returning after Herod's death (which occurred in 4 BC). No other record of the event is known, and it seems likely that this was a particularly heavy-handed piece of anti-Roman and anti-Jewish propaganda on Matthew's part. Statistically, it is unlikely that there would have been more than 20 male infants in Bethlehem at this date, although the number may have been increased by visitors to the town who, like Joseph and Mary, had traveled there to register. The feast is observed by all the major churches, despite the somewhat problematic chronology.

Peter Paul Rubens' fascination with capturing violent action, movement, and extreme bodily contortions, while at the same time conveying compassion, found the perfect subject in The Massacre of the Innocents *(c.1611).*

DECEMBER 28

THE 20,000 MARTYRS OF NICOMEDIA

STATUS Martyrs
BORN Late 3rd century
DIED Between 303 and 311
GRC ☁
CofE ☁
LCDUS ☁
OTHER Eastern Orthodox churches
⬯ Pre-Congregation

N icomedia was an ancient city in western Anatolia, near to Byzantium (later Constantinople). It was the capital of the Roman province of Bithynia and Pontus, and Diocletian chose it as his eastern capital when he divided the empire in 293. In 303, the imperial palace burned down, and Diocletian's co-ruler Galerius insisted that Christians were responsible. Hitherto relatively tolerant toward Christians, Diocletian unleashed what has become known as the Great Persecution (*see also* page 167). One tradition has it that all 20,000 martyrs of Nicomedia were burned while celebrating Christmas in a church. This feast day is another example of the demonizing of pagans by Christian hagiographers, as 20,000 victims, even spread over several years, is almost certainly an exaggeration. Historians believe it is more likely that between 3,000 and 3,500 Christians were put to death in this period throughout the Roman empire and, although a large number were killed in Nicomedia, many were executed in other Roman provinces, such as Syria, Palestine, and Egypt.

Emperor Caesar Galerius was an ardent advocate of traditional Roman religious worship. He persisted with Christian persecution in the Eastern empire until 311 (the year of his death), when he realized that Christianity could not be eradicated.

DECEMBER 29

THOMAS BECKET (THOMAS OF CANTERBURY)

STATUS Bishop, Martyr

BORN 1118, Cheapside, London

DIED 1170, Canterbury, England

GRC ♣

CofE ♣

LCDUS ♣

OTHER In France

⬭ 1173

✝ Sword, miter, chains of office

⚚ Secular clergy

Black choughs, members of the corvid family, are now rarely found in England. Their red beaks and feet reflect the blood shed by Thomas.

Probably the most significant English saint, Thomas Becket embodies the clash between Church and State, between the sacred and the profane, which was to dominate the English Reformation 400 years later, and which still reverberates down the centuries to us today. Thomas was born to a fairly wealthy mercer and landowner in Cheapside, London, and was educated at Merton Priory in England and in Paris. In 1142 he gained a position in the household of Theobald, Archbishop of Canterbury. Thomas was ordained a deacon, and was sent to study at Bologna and Auxerre, qualifying as a civil and canon lawyer, which reflects his outstanding talents. He was appointed Archdeacon of Canterbury in 1154. In the same year, the 21-year-old Henry II came to the English throne, and made Thomas Chancellor in 1155. They became close friends and confidants despite their age gap, and Thomas lived the privileged life of a courtier and royal favorite; however, he also became aware of Henry's urge toward absolutist royal power. Henry had begun to seek control of Church taxes and revenues from Church properties (tithes), and he pushed for the removal of certain Church privileges, especially its immunity from civil prosecution.

Thomas Becket was slain by Henry II's knights while conducting a service in Canterbury Cathedral during the feast of Christmas. This image is from a German devotional cycle by Meister Francke celebrating Thomas's life and martyrdom (c.1450).

Canterbury Cathedral (left), the seat of the most important Episcopal see in England, was still under construction at the time of Thomas's death, but rapidly became a major pilgrimage center. It was the destination of Chaucer's irreverent travelers in his Canterbury Tales *(c.1380–1400), some of whom appear in a stained glass window in the cathedral (above).*

Church versus Crown

After Theobald's death in 1161, Henry wished to appoint Thomas Archbishop of Canterbury. However, fearing a clash with the king, Thomas resisted until, encouraged by a papal legate, he accepted in 1162. Thomas took high office seriously, living austerely and defending the rights of the Church. Henry's intentions became more pressing and, after a confrontation at a royal council in Northampton, Thomas secretly fled to France and sought papal advice, remaining in exile for some six years.

During this period the Archbishop of York crowned Henry's son, Prince Henry, heir to the throne, specifically defying Thomas's orders and rights as Archbishop of Canterbury. Thomas returned to England and excommunicated the Archbishop of York and other senior clerics involved in the ceremony.

Upon learning this, Henry was enraged, seeing it as a direct challenge to his royal authority. In a drunken moment in Normandy, he is said to have asked, "Who will rid me of this turbulent priest?" On December 29, four of Henry's knights crossed the English Channel and rode to nearby Canterbury: they cut Thomas down as he was performing a service in the cathedral.

An analysis of the intensely personal struggle between Thomas Becket and the king of England became a highly successful play by Jean Anouilh, and an Oscar-winning film in 1964.

The Cult of Thomas Becket

The shocking news of the murder spread rapidly across Europe, and Thomas's tomb in Canterbury became a major pilgrimage center; over 700 miracles are recorded as occurring there in the decade following his murder. Pope Alexander III canonized him almost immediately, and some 80 churches in the United Kingdom are dedicated to him.

The Pope also immediately excommunicated King Henry, whose royal power increased, but his subsequent reign was undermined by a number of revolts against him led by his various sons, both in England and in his territories in France. Upon his death in 1189, Henry was not succeeded by Prince Henry, but by one of the prince's younger brothers: Richard I, the Lionheart.

Date	Name	Status	Venerated	Life
Dec. 29	Ebrulf (Evroul) of Ouche (626–706)	Abbot ⊙ Pre-Congregation	In France and England	Born in Bayeux, France. A married Merovingian courtier. Resigned from court of King Childebert I to become a monk (his wife became a nun) and then a hermit in forest of Ouche. Converted a gang of forest robbers and founded monastery based on harsh regime of self-sufficiency and manual labor in the service of God. The Order spread locally, then to England with the Norman invasion (1066). His cult in England overshadowed from 12th century by that of Thomas Becket.

DECEMBER 30 — EGWIN OF WORCESTER

STATUS Bishop

BORN Mid-7th century, Worcester, England

DIED c.717, Evesham, England

GRC ☁

CofE ☁

LCDUS ☁

OTHER By Benedictines

○ Pre-Congregation

✝ A fish and a key

🕉 Evesham Abbey

Egwin was of royal blood, being related to King Aethelred of Mercia. He was Bishop of Worcester, England (693–711) and founded Evesham Abbey in Worcestershire. His reforming zeal created enemies, and he was denounced to the king and the archbishop of Canterbury and was forced to step down. To vindicate his position in Rome, he fettered his ankles and threw the key into the river Avon. Later, a fish was caught in the river Tiber that was found to contain the key. The Pope absolved him because of this miracle.

Evesham Abbey, founded by Egwin, became an important center for the Benedictine Order in England in the 13th century. The abbey was partly demolished during the Dissolution of the Monasteries under Henry VIII (1540), although the bell tower (right) and the abbey church have been restored.

DECEMBER 31 — SYLVESTER I

STATUS Pope

BORN Late 3rd century

DIED 335

GRC ♠

CofE ☁

LCDUS ♠

OTHER Eastern Orthodox churches (January 2)

○ Pre-Congregation

✝ Chained dragon or bull, miter

Sylvester's pontificate lasted 21 years (314–35) and is one of the longest, certainly in the early years of the papacy. It lay entirely within the imperial reign of Constantine (306–37), and Sylvester benefited from Constantine's introduction of Christianity as the official religion of the Roman empire under the Edict of Milan in 313. However, at this critical and advantageous stage, Sylvester seems to have done little apart from beginning to consolidate the central position of the Church of Rome. In 325, the first major ecumenical conference was convened under the auspices of the emperor, at his summer residence in northwest Turkey; the Council of Nicaea promulgated the important doctrine of Christ's indivisibility from the central substance of God, known today as the Nicene Creed. Sylvester did not attend. Nevertheless, the Holy City gained considerably from Constantine's patronage during this period. Sylvester oversaw the foundation of the first basilica of St. Peter, and of the Basilica Constantiniana, which became the pope's palace and cathedral, now St. John Lateran, the second most important basilica in Rome (*see* Nov. 9). Two myths are attached to Sylvester: that Constantine conferred primacy on Sylvester over all other patriarchs, although the document, the *Donation of Constantine*, proved to be a forgery; and, secondly, that Sylvester baptized Constantine (who was in fact only baptized on his death bed, three years after Sylvester's death. This baptism became a popular subject in art.

Pope Sylvester I being given the Donation *by Constantine. The event proved to be a fabrication, and the document a forgery.*

Date	Name	Status	Venerated	Life
Dec. 31	Zoticus (d.c.350)	○ Pre-Congregation	Eastern Orthodox churches 🕉 Orphans, the poor	Wealthy Roman. Became a priest and gave his money to the poor. Traveled to Constantinople when it became capital of the Eastern empire. Established a hospital and orphanage. Martyred under rule of Arian emperor Constantius by being dragged through the streets by a wild ass.
Dec. 31	John Wyclif (c.1325–84)	Translator, Scholar	CofE	Early English dissenter against the Catholic Church, which he perceived as corrupt. Oxford-educated. Produced first translation of the Bible in English, as means of bringing the Scriptures to the common reader. His followers called Lollards.

GLOSSARY OF EMBLEMS, SYMBOLS, AND ATTRIBUTES

A

Acorns Brigid of Kildare
Alms box John of God
Ampulla Remigius of Reims
Anchor Clement I
Angel (winged person) Matthew the Evangelist
Apples Swithun (with raindrops)
Apron with bread and flowers Casilda
Armor Alexander Nevsky, George, Joan of Arc, Louis, Martin, Wenceslaus. *See also* Soldier
Arrow(s) Edmund, Giles, Sebastian, Canute IV
Axe Alphege (sometimes cleaving skull), Boniface (with oak), Cyprian of Carthage (with crown), Jude, Matthias the Apostle

B

Balls, three Nicholas of Myra
Baptismal font *See* Font (baptismal)
Basket with food Elisabeth of Hungary, Elizabeth of Portugal, John of God, Dorothy Frances of Rome
Bear Columban, Seraphim of Sarov
Bees, Beehive Ambrose (with scourge), Bernard (honey-tongued), Isidore of Seville, John Chrysostom
Bell Antony (with pig), Pedro de San José Betancur, Peter Nolasco
Birds Francis
Blackbirds Kevin of Glendalough
Blood, drops of Rita of Cascia (on forehead). *See also* Stigmata
Boar Quiricus and Julitta
Boat Jude the Apostle, Simon the Apostle. *See also* Ship
Book Often with a pen or quill, generally associated with scholars and writers. Hilary of Poitiers (with quill), Paul the Apostle (with sword). The four Evangelists are usually shown brandishing or writing their respective Gospels, frequently with an indication of divine inspiration, and often accompanied by other identifying emblems: Matthew (with spear, sword or halberd, or moneybags); Mark (with lion); Luke (with ox); John (with eagle, chalice, or snake). *See also* Pen, Scroll
Bowl John of God (two around neck)
Bread Nicholas of Tolentino. *See also* Loaves of bread
Breasts, on a dish Agatha
Bridge Botolph (bridge often represented by a chevron), Swithun
Building Founders of basilicas, churches, monasteries, abbeys, and other institutions are often shown holding a small building. Willibald often shown overseeing construction of a building
Bull Blandina, Eustace, Fermín/Ferminus, Saturninus, Sylvester I. *See also* Cattle

C

Candles Blaise (two, crossed), Brigid of Kildare, Gudula
Cannon Barbara
Capstan Erasmus (Elmo)
Captives *See* Prisoners
Cardinal's hat Bonaventure, Robert Bellarmine, Jerome
Carpenter's square Joseph, Thomas the Apostle (with spear)
Cattle Perpetua and Felicity (heifers), Walston (pair of calves)
Cauldron Vitus
Cave(s) Often associated with hermits. Thecla chose to be immured in one, her hand protruding from fissure
Centurion's uniform Longinus
Chains Leonard
Chalice Barbara, James of the Marches (with snake), John the Evangelist (with snake), Bonaventure (with cross), John Chrysostom (with book). *See also* Ciborium, Holy Grail
Chasuble Ignatius of Loyola
Children John Baptiste de la Salle, Quiricus (as child)
Choughs Thomas Becket
Church *See* Building
Ciborium Bonaventure, Clare, Dunstan, Norbert
Cloak Angela Merici, James the Greater (pilgrim's cloak), Martin (cut by sword)
Club Fidelis (with nails), Gervase and Protase, James the Less (a fuller's club), Timothy (with stones)
Cobbler's last Crispin and Crispinian
Cockleshell James the Greater
Comb Blaise
Coracle Brendan, Maughold
Corn Walburga
Crocodile Pachomius (on its back)
Crosier Often associated with archbishops and bishops, abbots. Augustine of Canterbury, Augustine of Hippo, Benedict of Nursia. *See also* Staff, Shepherd's crook
Cross Appears in various forms as part of the emblems of innumerable saints: Helena, finder of the 'True Cross'; bottony with roundels, Philip the Apostle; inverted, Peter the Apostle; Iona, Columba; Maltese, John, James the Greater, Elizabeth (with withered leaves and heart); red on white, George, Ursula; saltire, Andrew (blue on white), Patrick (green on white); Tau, Antony of Egypt; with rope, Julia of Corsica; with thorns and tears, Joseph of Arimathea
Crown Generally associated with royal saints, kings, queens
Crown of thorns Francis de Sales (with heart), John of God, Louis (with fleur-de-lis), Veronica Giuliani
Crowns (triple) Elisabeth of Hungary, Etheldreda, Eric of Sweden (with waves). *See also* Tiara (triple crown)
Crown with arrows Edmund
Cup Benedict of Nursia (fractured)

D

Daffodil David
Dalmatic Stephen, Vincent of Saragossa
Demons Antony of Egypt
Devil Juliana (winged), Bernard of Montjoux (on chain), Wolfgang (building a church)
Doe, shot by arrow Giles
Dog Bernard of Montjoux, Dominic (with star or taper in mouth), Margaret of Cortona (lapdog), Roche (with bread in mouth), Vitus
Dolphin Lucien of Antioch
Dove Catherine of Alexandria, David, Dunstan, Eulalia, Gregory the Great (perched on shoulder), Joseph (perched on flowering branch or rod), John Chrysostom, Quentin (flying from severed head), Scholastica
Dragon David, Margaret of Antioch (being trampled or with cross in mouth), George, Juliana, Archangel Michael, Perpetua (with ladder), Sylvester I (chained)

E

Eagle John the Evangelist, Wenceslaus (on red banner)
Eggs Swithun (broken)
Epigonation Gregory Nazianzus
Escarbuncle Victor of Marseille
Eucharist Ignatius of Loyola
Eyes, on a dish Lucy

F

Fish Egwin (with key), Simon the Apostle, Archangel Raphael
Fishing net Andrew the Apostle, Wilfrid
Flame Brigid of Kildare
Flaming fire Polycarp, Teresa Benedicta (Edith Stein)
Flayed, flaying knife Bartholomew
Fleur-de-lis Blessed Virgin Mary
Font (baptismal) Birinus, Francis Xavier
Forceps Apollonia (holding tooth)
Fox Boniface

G

Giant/gigantic Christopher
Golden balls Nicholas of Myra
Goose Martin
Greyhound Ferdinand III
Gridiron/griddle Lawrence, Vincent of Saragossa

H

Halberd Jude, Matthias the Apostle, Matthew the Evangelist
Harp Cecilia
Head, severed Denis, John the Baptist, Quentin, Sigfrid of Sweden (usually three in a basket), Winfred (with well)
Heart Augustine of Hippo (often flaming, pierced by crossed arrows), Blessed Virgin Mary (winged, often pierced by sword), Catherine of Siena (with cross in it), Francis de Sales (with crown of thorns), Ignatius of Antioch, Teresa (pierced by arrow), Valentine (with arrow); the most frequent *ex-voto* symbol
Hind Eustace, Giles, Hubert, Neot
HIS Inscription usually associated with members/founders of Society of Jesus (Jesuits), especially Ignatius of Loyola; also Bernardine of Siena
Holy Grail Joseph of Arimathea
Horn Cornelius
Horse/on horseback George, Longinus

J

Jar of ointment Mary Magdalene

K

Keys Egwin (with fish), Peter the Apostle (crossed), Zita (in a bunch)
Knife (flaying) Bartholomew

L

Ladder Angela Merici, Joseph, Perpetua (spiked, with dragon), Romuald
Lamb Agnes, John the Baptist (with shepherd's crook or flag)
Lamp/lantern Brigid of Kildare, Christopher, Frances of Rome, Gudula, Lucy, Nilus
Lance Maurice, Canute IV
Leek David
Levitating John Joseph of the Cross, Joseph of Cupertino
Lightning Barbara
Lily Blessed Virgin Mary and those devoted to or closely associated with her: Aloysius Gonzaga, Anne, Anthony of Padua (with book), Casimir, Catherine of Siena, Francis Xavier, Gertrude the Great, Joseph (with carpenter's square), Kateri Tekakwitha, Margaret of Hungary
Lion(s) Cuthbert (rampant with cross), Denis (rampant with cross), Ignatius of Antioch, Jerome, Mark the Evangelist (winged), Sabbas, Vitus
Loaves of bread Agatha, Anthony of Padua, Mary of Egypt, Philip the Apostle, Sigfrid of Sweden (in fact heads of his companions)
Lozenges Wilfrid (seven)

M

Martlets Edward the Confessor (with cross)
Medicine box Pantaleon, Cosmas and Damian
Millstone Florian
Miter Generally associated with popes, bishops, and other high-ranking church officials. Three miters with a book, Bernard of Clairvaux, or Bernardine of Siena
Moneybags Matthew the Apostle, Cyril of Jerusalem, Nicholas of Myra
Monstrance Clare of Assisi, Norbert, Paschal Baylon
Moon, crescent Blessed Virgin Mary
Musical instruments Cecilia

O

Oak Boniface, Brigid of Kildare (with wreath of acorns)

Oar Jude, Simon the Apostle

Ointment, pot/jar of Mary Magdalene, Rémy, Walburga

Old/in old age A frequent characteristic, denoting sagacity and wisdom. As a specific attribute: Alferius de la Cava

Olive branch Barnabas the Apostle

Oranges/orange branch Frances of Rome

Ox, winged Luke the Evangelist

P

Pallium/Pall Athanasius (with triangle), Augustine of Canterbury (with four black crosses)

Palm Generally associated with martyrdom. Stephen (with stones)

Pens Cyril of Alexandria, Hilary of Poitiers (with books), Justin (with sword)

Pickax, with miter Leo

Pig, with bell Antony of Egypt

Pillar Simeon Stylites, Simeon Stylites the Younger, stylite hermits generally

Pincers Apollonia (holding tooth)

Pitcher Venerable Bede (gold), Florian (containing water)

Plague sores (buboes) Roch

Pomegranate John of God

Prisoners Peter Claver, Vincent Ferrer

Pulpit Vincent Ferrer

Pyx Clare of Assisi

Q

Quills *See* Pens

R

Raindrops Swithun (with apples)

Raising from the dead Lazarus, Stanislaus

Raven Benedict of Nursia, Boniface, Paul the Hermit

Ring Edward the Confessor

Rod Joseph (flowering)

Rooster Vitus

Rope Judas Iscariot (with pieces of silver)

Rosary Aloysius Gonzaga

Rose(s) Blessed Virgin Mary, Barnabas the Apostle, Cecilia, Elisabeth of Hungary, Rita of Cascia, Thérèse of Lisieux

S

Salmon with ring Kentigern

Salt cellar Rupert of Salzburg

Sari Mother Teresa

Saw James the Lesser, Simon the Apostle

Scourge Ambrose, Catherine of Alexandria, Gervase and Protase

Scroll Symbol frequently associated with significant early Church writers such as the Evangelists, the Christian Fathers, and Doctors of the Church, especially Gregory the Great. *See also* Book

Scythe Walston

Shamrock Patrick

Sheep Geneviève (tending). *See also* Shepherd's crook

Shepherd's crook A frequent symbol for an archbishop, bishop, or abbot; also, specifically, Irenaeus, Paschal

Shield Archangel Gabriel (with spear)

Ship Anselm, Bertin, Brendan, Pedro González, Wilfrid. *See also* Boat

Shoes Crispin, Crispinian

Sickle Isidore the Farmer

Skin Bartholomew, often shown carrying his own

Skull Aloysius Gonzaga, Bruno, Francis Borgia (with crown), Odilo (with crossbones)

Slaves Peter Claver

Snake Patrick, Hilda (three, coiled), James of the Marches (escaping from a chalice), John the Evangelist (with chalice)

Soldier Many saints are shown as soldiers, including George, James the Greater, Joan of Arc, Longinus, Louis, Michael the Archangel, Martin, and Pancras

Spade Fiacre

Spatula Pantaleon

Spear Archangel Gabriel (often with shield), Longinus

Staff Generally used (in the form of a shepherd's crook) for bishops, abbots, abbesses, or missionaries and pilgrims. Archangel Raphael (with wallet), Bridget of Sweden, Christopher (with lamp), Francis of Paola (with cloak), Gertrude of Nivelle (with mouse), James the Greater (with pilgrim's hat and cloak)

Stag Eustace, Hubert. *See also* Hind

Stake Eulalia

Star(s) Thomas Aquinas, Bruno (seven)

Stigmata Francis of Assisi, Catherine of Siena, Charles of Sezze, Padre Pio

Stones Stephen (with palm), Timothy (with club)

Sun Thomas Aquinas (Sun in Splendor with an eye)

Surgical implements Cosmas and Damian

Swan Hugh of Lincoln, Ludger of Münster

Sword Generally associated with martyrdom (a sword stroke to the neck was the most common Roman method of capital punishment), or fighting for the Church (often in the form of a cross). Frumentius, Justin (with quill), Gervase and Protase, James the Greater (red, in form of cross), Kilian, Paul the Apostle (crossed, or with book); multiple swords: Felicitas, Archangel Michael, Peter of Verona, Stanislaus

T

Table, with food and drink Martha

Taper Gertrude the Great

Tears Our Lady of Sorrows, Joseph of Arimathea, Mary Magdalene

Thorn Jerome, Joseph of Arimathea (thorned cross)

Tiara (triple crown) Generally associated with popes

Tongs Dunstan

Tonsure Usually indicates a deacon of the Church (such as Stephen, Maurice, or Lawrence), or a friar (especially Franciscans)

Tooth Apollonia

Torch, flaming Aidan, Dorothy

Tower Barbara

Trampling Bernard of Clairvaux

(demons/the devil), Fidelis (heretics), Archangel Michael (the devil), James the Greater (devils, Moors)

Turtle Kateri Tekakwitha

V

Veil Veronica

W

Walking stick Pedro de San José Betancur. *See also* Staff

Waves Botolph, Eric of Sweden (with crowns)

Well Winfred

Whale Brendan

Wheel Catherine of Alexandria, Quentin (broken)

Widow's clothing Monica

Windlass Erasmus (Elmo)

GLOSSARY OF PATRONAGE

A

Abortions, victims of Catherine of Sweden, Vincent of Saragossa
Accidents Christopher
Accountants Matthew the Apostle
Adultery, victims of Elizabeth of Portugal
Advertisers Bernardine of Siena
Advocates Fidelis
African Americans Peter Claver
Agricultural workers Benedict of Nursia
AIDS/HIV sufferers Aloysius Gonzaga, Damien of Molokai, Marianne Cope
Alcoholics John of God, Martin, Matthias the Apostle, Matt Talbot
Alpine travelers Bernard of Montjoux
Amputees Antony of Egypt
Animals Anthony of Padua, Francis of Assisi, Nicholas of Tolentino
Apologists Catherine of Alexandria
Apoplexy sufferers Wolfgang of Regensburg
Apothecaries Cosmas and Damian, James the Greater, Roch
Apprentices John Bosco
Archaeologists Jerome
Archers George, Nicholas of Myra, Sebastian
Architects Thomas the Apostle
Archivists Jerome
Armorers George
Art dealers John the Evangelist
Arthritis sufferers Alphonsus Liguori, James the Greater
Artillerymen Barbara
Astronauts Joseph of Cupertino
Astronomers Dominic
Athletes Sebastian
Authors John the Evangelist
Automobile drivers Christopher, Frances of Rome
Aviators Joseph of Cupertino

B

Bachelors Benedict Joseph Labre, Casimir, Gerald of Aurillac, Pantaleon, Roch
Bankers Matthew the Apostle
Barbers Cosmas and Damian, Louis IX of France
Basketmakers Antony of Egypt
Beekeepers Ambrose of Milan, Bernard of Clairvaux, Valentine
Beggars Giles of Provence, Martin
Betrothed, the Agnes, Valentine
Bishops Charles Borromeo
Blacksmiths Dunstan
Blindness, the blind Cosmas and Damian, Leger, Lucy, Lutgardis, Parasceva
Blood banks Januarius
Boatmen Francis of Paola
Booksellers John of God
Breast cancer sufferers Agatha
Brewers Amand, Augustine of Hippo, Boniface

Brides Dorothy, Elizabeth of Portugal
Builders Vincent Ferrer
Burn victims John the Evangelist

C

Cab drivers Fiacre, Frances of Rome
Cabinetmakers Joseph
Cancer victims Giles of Provence
Canon lawyers Raymond of Peñafort, Robert Bellarmine
Carpenters Joseph, Matthias the Apostle, Wolfgang of Regensburg
Catechists Charles Borromeo, Robert Bellarmine
Catholic lawyers Thomas More
Catholic press, the Peter Canisius
Catholic publishers John Bosco
Catholic universities Thomas Aquinas
Cattle Felicity
Cavers Benedict of Nursia
Chaplains Quentin
Charity, charity workers Elizabeth of Portugal, Vincent de Paul
Chastity Agnes, Maria Goretti, Mary of Egypt
Chefs/cooks Lawrence
Chest problems, protection from Bernardine of Siena
Childbirth Boniface, Gotthard, Juliana, Lutgardis, Margaret of Antioch
Childless, the Anne and Joachim
Children Clotilde, Nicholas of Myra, Pancras; **abandoned** Jerome Emiliani; **adopted** William of Rochester; **choirs of** Dominic Savio; **death of, dying** Elisabeth of Hungary, Frances of Rome, Perpetua and Felicity; **sick/ill** Quiricus and Julitta; **sons, birth of** Perpetua; **with convulsions** Scholastica
Circus people/performers Julian the Hospitaller
Clairvoyance Clare of Assisi
Cobblers Crispin and Crispinian
Coffinmakers Stephen
Comedians Lawrence
Confessors Alphonsus Liguori, Jean-Baptiste Vianney
Construction workers Thomas the Apostle, Vincent Ferrer
Converts Alban
Counts Gerald of Aurillac
Crops, protection Agnes, Walburga
Curriers Simon the Apostle
Customs officials Matthew the Apostle

D

Dancers Vitus
Dauphins Petronilla
Deacons Stephen
Deafness, the deaf Cornelius, Francis de Sales
Demons, against Mary of Egypt
Dentists Apollonia
Disabled, the Gerald of Aurillac, Giles of Provence, Lutgardis
Dogs Roch, Vitus
Dyers Lydia Purpuraria

Dying, the Benedict of Nursia, James the Less, John of God, Margaret of Antioch
Dysentery sufferers Polycarp

E

Earache sufferers Polycarp
Earthquakes, against Francis Borgia
Ecologists Kateri Tekakwitha
Ecumenism Cyril and Methodius
Educators Ignatius of Loyola, John Baptiste de la Salle
Embroiderers Clare of Assisi
Engineers Ferdinand III of Castile, Patrick
Environment/environmentalists Francis of Assisi, Kateri Tekakwitha
Epileptics Antony of Egypt, Apollinaris, Christopher, Cornelius, Giles of Provence, Vitus
Ergotism, against Antony of Egypt
Eucharistic confraternities Paschal of Baylon
Exiles Clotilde, Elisabeth of Hungary, Kateri Tekakwitha, Margaret of Antioch
Eye affliction sufferers Augustine of Hippo, Clare of Assisi, Lucy

F

Fallen women Mary Magdalene
Falsely accused, the Dominic, Dominic Savio, Margaret of Antioch, Margaret of Cortona
Families Eustace, Quiricus and Julitta
Farmers Botolph, George, Isidore the Farmer, Walston
Ferrymen Julian the Hospitaller
Fever sufferers Barbara, Geneviève, Mary of Egypt, Petronilla
Filemakers Theodosius the Cenobiarch
Fire, protection from Florian
Firefighters Agatha, Eustace, Florian, John of God
Fish Neot
Fishermen Andrew the Apostle, Anthony of Padua, Peter the Apostle
Florists Dorothy, Rose of Lima
Forests Giles of Provence
Foresters John Gualbert
Frenzy, protection from Denis

G

Gallstone sufferers Benedict of Nursia
Gamblers/gambling addicts Bernardine of Siena, Cajetan, Camillus de Lellis
Gardeners Agnes, Christopher, John the Gardener
Geese Martin
Gentiles Paul the Apostle
Geometricians Thomas the Apostle
Girls Agnes; **unmarried** Catherine of Alexandria; **teenage** Maria Goretti
Glassblowers Mark the Evangelist
Glaziers Mark the Evangelist
Goiter sufferers Mark the Evangelist
Goldsmiths Anastasius the Persian, Clare of Assisi

Gout sufferers Apollinaris, Gotthard
Governors Ferdinand III of Castile
Grandparents Anne and Joachim, Zechariah and Elizabeth
Gravediggers Antony of Egypt
Guides Bona of Pisa
Gunpowder makers Barbara

H

Hailstorms, protection from Barnabas the Apostle
Handicapped, the Angela Merici
Hatmakers James the Greater
Haymakers Gervase and Protase
Headache sufferers Agathius, Anastasius the Persian, Denis, Pancras, Stephen, Teresa of Ávila
Hemorrhoid sufferers Fiacre
Heresy, fighters against Fidelis
Hermits Antony of Egypt, Giles
Hernia sufferers Conrad of Piacenza, Cosmas and Damian
Historians The Venerable Bede
Homelessness/the homeless Elisabeth of Hungary, Margaret of Cortona, Benedict Joseph Labre
Horses Anthony of Padua, Giles, Martin, Pontian and Hippolytus, Stephen, Vincent de Paul
Horsemen James the Greater
Hospitals Camillus de Lellis, John of God, Jude the Apostle, Vincent de Paul; **hospital administrators** Frances Xavier Cabrini
Housewives Anastasia, Anne and Joachim
Hunters/hunting Eustace, Hubert
Hydrophobics Denis

I

Immigrants Frances Xavier Cabrini
Infants Blaise
Innkeepers Julian the Hospitaller, Martin
Insanity, the insane Margaret of Cortona, Theodosius the Cenobiarch
Insect bite sufferers Mark the Evangelist
Internet, the Isidore of Seville

J

Jurists John of Capistrano
Juvenile delinquents Dominic Savio

K

Kidnapping victims Alphege
Kidney disease sufferers Margaret of Antioch
Knights George
Knights Hospitaller John the Almsgiver

L

Laborers Isidore the Farmer, James the Greater, John Bosco, Joseph
Lacemakers John Francis Regis
Launderers Clare of Assisi, Veronica
Lawyers Catherine of Alexandria, Fidelis, Mark the Evangelist
Lay people Frances of Rome

GLOSSARY OF GENERAL TERMS

A

Anglican Church Is comprised of the established (official) Church of England and the autonomous family of Anglican churches worldwide that are in communion with the see of Canterbury (the Anglican Communion). Professes continuity with the Old Catholics while also having absorbed influences from the Protestant Reformation. Its doctrine and practices differ from the Roman Catholic, Orthodox, and Protestant communions.

antipope An illegitimate pope; a claimant set up as the bishop of Rome in opposition to the legitimately elected pope.

Apostle Usually one of Jesus Christ's Twelve Disciples: Simon Peter, Andrew, James, John, Philip, Bartholomew, Thomas, Matthew, James, Thaddeus (Jude), Simon, Judas Iscariot.

Arianism/Arians A Christian heresy started by Arius (c.250–336), a priest of Alexandria. Arians denied the Trinity, challenging the full divinity of Jesus by saying that the Son of God was a creature, not God's offspring (i.e. created not begotten) and that his title Son of God was given by God only by virtue of his perfect obedience to God.

ascetic A person who practices strict self-denial or self-control, sometimes adopting painful practices for religious purposes.

Augustinian (Austin) Order Christian order of mendicant friars formed in 1256 from several orders of hermits at the instigation of Pope Alexander IV. They based their lives on the Rule of St. Augustine that had been drawn up by one of Augustine's followers. Its chief tenets were union with others in a love of God and of one's neighbor, love of spiritual beauty, abstinence, discretion, and charity.

Avignon Papacy *See* Great Schism

B

Baptists Today one of the largest Protestant Christian denominations worldwide. Baptists affirm their faith and gain membership in their church through adult baptism by total immersion in water. The first Baptists were inspired by the Anabaptists of the 1530s and John Smyth (c.1554–1612), an English Puritan exile in Amsterdam.

beatification Second stage in the canonization of a saint in the Roman Catholic Church, when the pope grants the title of 'Blessed' to a person of exemplary life and faith, and allows his or her public veneration in local churches after death.

Benedictine Order Monastic communities following the Rule of St. Benedict. Their scholarship, teaching, and care in copying manuscripts greatly contributed to the preservation of Classical learning.

bishop/bishopric The highest minister and official in the Christian Church. After election, a bishop is enthroned in a cathedral, which is the chief church of his area of jurisdiction (diocese or bishopric). Bishops are the sole church officials empowered to confer the sacraments of ordination (holy orders) and confirmation.

Black Death (Black Plague) Epidemic of bubonic and pneumonic plague that swept Europe between 1348 and 1350 from the Far East, killing an estimated one third or more of Europe's population.

Blessed *See* beatification

Byzantine empire The Eastern part of the Roman empire following its division into East and West by the emperor Diocletian in 293. It took its name from the eastern capital, Byzantium (later Constantinople, modern Istanbul), and continued in various forms until overrun by Ottoman Turks in 1453.

C

calendar, liturgical The allocation of dates of the year for various religious observances, including feast days of saints. These may vary according to the denomination concerned, the diurnal calendar used, and will vary annually due to the calculation of the date of Easter each year, as a result of which certain observances and feast days might be moved or set aside for a year. *See also* pages 6–7.

Calvinism/Calvinists Protestant movement inspired by the theologian and reformer John Calvin (1509–64). He emphasized the grace of God and the rule of God over all aspects of life, and also the supremacy of the Scriptures as the sole rule according to which faith and life should be practiced.

canonization Final stage of elevation to sainthood of a deceased and previously beatified individual, when a public cult for the new saint is ordained throughout the whole church. This is done by the pope in the Roman Catholic Church, and by a synod of bishops in the Orthodox Church. A long testing of evidence, including the proof of at least one miracle, takes place before canonization.

Carmelite Order Roman Catholic monastic community originating in the late 12th century with the Hermits of Mount Carmel in Israel. They sought the way of life of the prophet Elijah and venerated the Virgin Mary. Their Rule of solitude, abstinence, prayer, and contemplation was written 1206–14 by St. Albert, Latin patriarch of Jerusalem. Known as the White Friars, they flourished as mendicants in Europe. Earlier members specialized in teaching and preaching; those after reforms by St. Teresa of Avila (1562) and St. John of the Cross (1593) in parochial and missionary work.

Carthusian Order Roman Catholic monastic community founded in 1084 by St. Bruno of Cologne at La Grande Chartreuse (Charterhouse) in France. The monks lived by austere eremitic principles based on contemplative prayer, study, manual labor, and silence, gathering just once a day for Mass, a meal on Sundays and feast days, and a weekly period of fellowship.

catechism Elementary manual of religious instruction set in question-and-answer format to teach children and converts the Christian doctrine.

Cathars/Catharism Christian dualist heresy in Western Europe in the 13th and 14th centuries that posed a threat to the Roman Church in southern France (the 'Albigensians') and northern Italy. Adherents believed good and evil existed in separate spheres (dualism); the material world was evil while the spirit was good and had to be made pure. Suppressed in the 15th century.

Catholic League Military alliance (1609–35) of Catholic princes in Germany led by Maximilian I, Duke of Bavaria, to halt the spread of Protestantism.

Celtic Rite/Celtic Church Developed from the original Christian Church of late Roman Britain in the 4th and 5th centuries, but survived the 5th-century Saxon invasions only in Scotland, Ireland, the Isle of Man, Wales, and Cornwall (also Brittany). It then resisted the Roman Christianity of St. Augustine, seeking renewal instead by establishing its own monasteries in remote locations. Characteristics of the Celtic Rite are simplicity in prayer, asceticism, the practice of scholarship and art, and missionary outreach.

cenobites/cenobitic Individuals, originally hermits, living together in a monastic community. The tradition originated in Egypt.

chalice Cup containing wine consecrated in the Eucharist, often made of precious metals and jewels.

Church Fathers/Holy Fathers Name used from the late 4th century for authors whose writings on Christian doctrine were regarded as especially valuable. The Western Church regarded the Fathers as authoritative until the 18th century; the Eastern Orthodox churches continue to consider them so.

Church of England Official state church established on the basis of episcopal authority with the monarch of England as its formal head. It originated when Henry VIII broke with the Roman Catholic Church in 1533–34 and had himself declared supreme head of the church (then Catholic) in England by Parliament.

ciborium Lidded vessel in the form of a chalice containing the Sacramental Bread ('Host') of the Eucharist. Also the canopy on four pillars over the altar in Christian basilicas or churches.

Cistercian Order Mother house at Cîteaux in Burgundy founded by Sts. Robert of Molesme, Alberic, and Stephen Harding in 1098. Known as the White Monks, the order kept a very strict form of the Benedictine Rule based on communal adoration, intercession, silence, seclusion, and manual labor. The order spread extremely quickly, having 700 monasteries by 1300. Their most renowned member was St. Bernard of Clairvaux.

Cluniac monasticism A form of Benedictinism largely formulated by St. Odo in the 930s, although the great abbey at Cluny had been founded in 910 by Duke William the Pious of Aquitaine to reform monastic laxity. It accepted authority only from the pope and kept a tight, centralized control over all its daughter abbeys. There was emphasis on the personal spiritual life, choral offices, and splendor and solemnity in worship.

communism A social or political system based on the ideas of property held in common and equal distribution of wealth with the aim of achieving a classless society. Its origins lie in the ideals of the early religious orders. In recent times it refers specifically to the 20th-century political systems inspired by Karl Marx's *Communist Manifesto* of 1848, and subsequent Marxist-Leninist doctrines.

Coptic Church The national Christian Church in Egypt, said by legend to have been founded by St. Mark the Evangelist when he built a church in Alexandria.

Council of Nicaea The first ecumenical council of bishops of the Christian Church. It was called in 325 by the emperor Constantine to deal with the rise of Arianism and to unify the church in the eastern part of his territory. It succeeded in its aims and also reached a decision on the calculation of the date of Easter.

Counter-Reformation Revival of the Roman Catholic Church in Europe between the mid-16th century and the end of the Thirty Years' War in 1648. The movement was prompted by the desire to oppose Protestantism and to reform the Catholic Church internally.

Crusades Taking place between 1095 and 1270 and at first known as pilgrimages, these were European military expeditions that were sanctioned or instigated by the pope to recover the Holy Land and, in particular, Jerusalem and Christianity's holiest place, the Shrine of the Holy Sepulchre, from Islam.

cult/cultus Set of beliefs or practices associated with one or more gods, spirits, objects, or places.

D

deacon Third-ranking minister below bishop and priest in the hierarchy of the Christian Church.

disciples The followers of Christ as named in the Gospels. Can also refer to Christian believers in general.

Doctor of the Church Title given to Christian theologians of outstanding scholarship and sanctity.

Dominican Order Founded by St. Dominic in 1215 in Toulouse in France, this order spread internationally with much speed and success. Adherents led a life of mendicant poverty and theological study that gave rise to their alternative name: the Friars Preachers. One of their greatest intellectuals was St. Thomas Aquinas.

Donatism/Donatists Schismatic Christian movement formed in 311 in the North African Church. The Donatists held that only ministers of blameless life were fit to confer sacraments or indeed to belong to the church. They also demanded re-baptism of Catholics joining their church.

E

Eastern Orthodox churches Family of self-governing Christian churches originating in the Byzantine empire that accept the patriarch of Constantinople as their honorary head. Their refusal to accept the authority of the pope led to the Great Schism. Their doctrine is strongly Trinitarian, accepting official Catholic Christology.

ecumenical Representing a number of different Christian churches.

ecumenism Promoting unity among Christian churches.

Edict of Milan Declaration made in 313 by the joint Roman emperors Constantine and Licinius to tolerate all religions and give legal status to Christianity.

epigonation Ornamented vestment, usually lozenge shaped, worn on the chest to signify senior rank in the Eastern Orthodox churches.

eremite A Christian hermit or recluse.

eremitic/eremitical Relating to hermits or a hermit's life.

escarbuncle Ornament involving or resembling a complex of fiery red precious stones (rubies, garnets).

Eucharist From the Greek word meaning 'Thanksgiving.' The focal point of Holy Communion, a Christian church ceremony at which bread and wine are consecrated and consumed to commemorate the Last Supper. This is the central act of Christian worship. Also used to refer to the entire service or ceremony, or to the consecrated items, especially the bread ('Host').

ex-voto A votive offering, often placed on an altar or shrine, in gratitude for a miraculous intercession.

F

Franciscan Order The 'Friars Minor.' Founded by St. Francis of Assisi in 1209 as a mendicant community that followed a Rule of complete poverty and focused on preaching and missionary work. The establishment of settled houses as membership grew led to the order dividing into three branches: the Friars Minor Observant (reform communities going back to the order's original principles); the Friars Minor Conventuals (the settled friars); and the Friars Minor Capuchin (more radically austere). The Poor Clares were Franciscan nuns established by St. Clare in 1212.

Frankish empire/Franks The most powerful Christian kingdom in early medieval Europe (centered on modern France and Germany), which dominated Europe from 500–900.

G

Gentile A non-Jewish person.

Gnosticism A heresy of the 2nd and 3rd centuries that arose from a complex mix of Christian, philosophical, mystical, and magical beliefs. Adherents believed in a Demiurge (a lesser creator god) who made the imperfect material world, and in a remote and unknowable supreme divine being of whom Christ was an emissary in phantasmal human guise. The human spirit could achieve salvation by esoteric knowledge (*gnosis*) of the supreme being, and thereby gain knowledge of the cosmic origins and spiritual destiny of humanity.

Great Schism 1. The split between Western and Eastern Christendom in 1054 following long-running doctrinal differences. Subsequent efforts at reconciliation failed irretrievably and formally in 1484, dividing Christianity into the Western Catholic Church headed by the pope in Rome and the Eastern Orthodox Church headed by the patriarch of Constantinople. The mutual anathemas against one another were nullified in 1965.
2. Also the period 1378–1418, when Western Christendom was divided in allegiance between the pope in Rome and antipopes created successively in Avignon and Pisa.

H

hagiography The writing of the lives of the Christian saints.

hagiology The literature or study of the lives of Christian saints and devotional followers.

heathens *See* pagans

heresy Beliefs and practices at variance with accepted Christian doctrine.

hermit A person living in solitude for religious reasons.

High Church Term first used in the 17th century, meaning to follow doctrine and practice within the Anglican Church emphasizing ritual, the sacraments, the authority of the episcopate, the divine nature of authority in Church and State, and historical continuity with the pre-Reformation Catholic Church.

Holy Roman Empire Large complex of European territories ruled by Frankish or German kings, originating in Charlemagne's coronation in 800. Its formation, though, is generally dated from 962, when Otto I conquered Italy and was crowned emperor in Rome. After its 12th-century medieval peak of power, the Holy Roman Empire, as it subsequently became known, experienced conflict with the papacy in the 13th century, and reached its greatest extent (to include Spain and the Netherlands) under the Hapsburg emperor Charles V (r.1520–55). Dissolved by Napoleon in 1806.

Huguenot Name given from the mid-16th century to Protestants in France. They mainly followed Calvinist principles. They suffered severe persecution during the French Wars of Religion (1562–98), the worst atrocity being the St. Bartholomew's Day Massacre in 1572.

I

icon In the Eastern Orthodox Church, a sacred painting or mosaic of Christ, the saints, or the mysteries of the Church.

iconoclasm From the Greek word meaning 'image breaking.' A period of extreme rejection of the veneration of religious images in Christendom in the 8th and 9th centuries.

Immaculate Conception Belief in the Western Catholic Church, dating back at least to the 7th century, that the Virgin Mary lived free from original sin from the moment of her conception. It was made Roman Catholic dogma in 1854 but has never been endorsed by the Eastern Orthodox Church.

indulgence Remission before God of all punishment for a living person's sins after repentance and forgiveness. At first rare, the practice became common in the 12th century and large-scale abuse developed, including the selling of indulgences by 'professional pardoners.' Martin Luther's vehement condemnation of this sparked the Protestant Reformation.

Inquisition A Christian tribunal set up by Pope Gregory IX in 1231 to combat heresy and sorcery. The accused was allowed to confess and be absolved, or, if not, either tried with testimony from witnesses and punished with penance, or handed over to the secular authorities for more severe punishment including imprisonment or occasionally death. The use of torture was authorized by Innocent IV in 1252. The Roman Inquisition was set up by Pope Paul III in 1542 specifically to combat Protestantism. The most notorious abuses were perpetrated by the Spanish Inquisition, which was independent and controlled by the Spanish Crown.

intercession Saying a prayer on behalf of someone else.

Islam/Islamic Monotheistic missionary religion based on the absolute unity of God (Allah), His Word as revealed through his prophet Muhammad in the Koran, and Sunna, a body of custom recording the actions and life of the Prophet and the first four 'Rightly Guided' caliphs. There are two main sects – the Sunni and the Shiites.

J

Jacobites Name given to Christians in Syria who dissented from the official doctrines of Christianity determined at the Council of Chalcedon in 451 and formed their own church with a patriarch in Antioch. They became known as Jacobites after Jacob Baradaeus, a clergyman who was secretly consecrated a bishop for a Monophysite Syrian ruler. A small church has survived, known as the Syrian Orthodox Church.

Jesuits *See* Society of Jesus (Jesuits)

Judaism The monotheistic religion of the Jews. At first its practice was centered on the Temple in Jerusalem. After the latter's destruction by the Romans in AD 70, the family and synagogue became its focus, with the ritual of the Sabbath as the main religious observance. Judaism is founded in belief in the Torah, the law of God as revealed to the Jews. Its main scriptures are the Hebrew Bible; the Talmud, the written collection of oral Torah; and the Halakhah of the medieval period containing the codes of Jewish law and ritual.

L

Lateran Council Name of the five Christian ecumenical papal councils held at the Lateran Palace in Rome between 1123 and 1517. They discussed theological, administrative, and political matters, and church reform. The fourth council, in 1215, was the most important, as it defined the doctrine of transubstantiation in the Eucharist.

Lent The Christian fast of 40 days before Easter. It is a time for penance, special religious devotions, and almsgiving.

Liberation Theology Originated in Latin America in the 1960s through missionary protests against the exploitation of indigenous peoples. It emphasized the mission of the church in helping the poor and the oppressed, with Jesus Christ as the liberator.

liturgy The set form by which a Christian church service is conducted.

M

Manichaeanism A dualistic and gnostic religion based on the opposition of God and matter, light and darkness. Founded in Persia c.240 by Mani (Manichaeus), the Apostle of Light or Supreme Illuminator, who sought a religion that would unite all others worldwide. It taught that although the soul shares the nature of God, it needs to be saved by spirit or intelligence from its fall into the evil and painful matter of earthly life.

Marian cult/apparition Relating to the worship of the Blessed Virgin Mary, often in turn related to a manifestation or apparition of the Virgin.

Marist Brothers Also known as the Marianists, they were founded in 1817 on papal direction by a Marist Father as a Roman Catholic congregation of teaching brothers for the Christian education of young people in France. They have grown to staff academic and technical schools and colleges from primary to university level worldwide.

Marist Fathers Also known as the Society of Mary, they were established in Lyon in France in 1816. They specialized in teaching in schools and missionary work, and were given the western Pacific as their particular territory by the pope. The order spread to Australia, New Zealand, North America, and through Europe.

martyr Person who voluntarily suffers death for his or her religion. In Roman Catholicism, martyrs rank before all other saints (after the Blessed Virgin Mary and the Apostles).

mendicant order Community of friars who renounce all possessions, both individually and in common. However, practicality led the Council of Trent of 753 to permit most orders to hold goods in common.

Mercedarian Order Formally known as the Order of Our Lady of Mercy and also as the Knights of St. Eulalia, they were founded in 1218 as a military order in Barcelona by St. Peter Nolasco and 19 other noblemen to ransom Christian captives from the Moors and tend the sick. They followed the Rule of St. Augustine, and offered themselves as hostages for Christian prisoners in danger of losing their faith.

monasticism In Christianity, a way of life enabling adherents to seek God through prayer and asceticism. Monks and nuns take perpetual religious vows including those of celibacy, usually the renunciation of private property, and sometimes silence. They may live either a cenobitic (common) life or an eremitical (hermit or solitary) life.

Monophysite doctrine/Monophysitism A Christian doctrine that arose out of vehement 4th-century debates over the nature and person of Christ. It held that there is only one inseparable nature in the Incarnate Christ, deriving from the union of God and man. In 451, the Council of Chalcedon upheld the different view that the Incarnate Christ was one Person 'in two natures' (one human, one divine). All those who rejected this were termed Monophysites (meaning 'only one nature').

monotheism Belief in one God, or in the oneness of God. The world's three great monotheistic religions are Christianity, Judaism, and Islam.

monstrance In Christianity, vessel for showing the Blessed Sacrament or Host (consecrated bread in the Eucharist) during a church service or in procession. Monstrances first appeared in 14th-century France and Germany. They usually take the form of a glass cylinder or glass pane held in silver or gold rays through which the Host may be seen by the congregation.

Montanism An apocalyptic early Christian heresy instigated by a self-proclaimed prophet, Montanus, in Phrygia in the second half of the second century. He prophesied that a New Jerusalem would descend imminently in Phrygia in an outpouring of the Holy Spirit. He demanded a severely austere life from his followers, and an enthusiastic acceptance of martyrdom by refusing flight from persecutors. The heresy spread to Rome, but was condemned by the church in both the East and the West around 200.

mortification Deliberate restraint of the needs or desires of the body through spiritual discipline and bodily self-denial, or by infliction of bodily discomforts, in order to gain salvation through faith.

Muslim *See* Islam/Islamic

Mysticism The spiritual quest for union with or direct experience of God, or the gaining of knowledge of the divine not ordinarily knowable. Facilitated by contemplation and usually results in the experience of bliss (spiritual blessedness) or serenity.

N

Nestorian Church A Christian church that grew up in Mesopotamia in the Persian Sassanian empire (modern Iraq) based on Nestorian doctrines. Despite some persecution and a number of martyrdoms in the 4th and 5th centuries, it prospered as a significant minority church, founded monasteries, and sent successful missions to India and China. It suffered under invading Mongols in the 14th century. Small communities survive, mainly in Iraq, Iran, Syria, Lebanon, and the United States. It is now also known as the Christian Church of the East or Assyrian Church of the East.

Nestorianism A Christian doctrine that in the Incarnate Christ there are two separate persons, one human, one divine (at variance with official Christian doctrine that Christ Incarnate was a single person, both God and man). It was named after Nestorius, a patriarch of Constantinople, who was deposed and exiled in 431 for heretical teachings.

O

Oriental Orthodox churches General name given to a group of churches that embraced Monophysitism and broke away from the Orthodox Christian Church of the Byzantine empire. Following the Arab invasions in the 7th century, Armenia, Syria, and Egypt were separated from the Byzantine empire and the Oriental churches grew up independently as the Armenian, Coptic, Ethiopian, and Syrian Orthodox churches.

Oxford Movement Far-reaching and very influential movement in the Church of England that aimed to restore many of the High Church ideals of the 17th century and emphasize its continuity with the early, undivided Christian Church. As a result, the whole Church of England developed more ritual and ceremony, founded new monasteries, and saw a better-educated clergy, pastorally closer to their congregations.

P

pagans People who hold beliefs different from those of the world's major accepted or organized religions.

pallium/pall Decorated fabric band or mantle worn over the shoulders to signify the rank of pope or archbishop.

papal/papacy *See* pope

patriarch/patriarchate Title given from the 6th century to the bishops of the five principle sees of Christendom (Rome, Constantinople, Alexandria, Antioch, and Jerusalem).

Pelagianism A Christian heresy initiated in Rome by the British monk Pelagius from c.380 to combat lax moral standards. He believed in the fundamental goodness of human nature and taught that God gave humans free will to choose between good and evil – human effort was the prime force in attaining spiritual salvation.

penance A voluntary act of repentance, or a Roman Catholic sacrament in which a person confesses a sin to a priest and is given absolution. Also means a spiritual duty or physical action required by a priest in this sacrament to demonstrate the sinner's repentance.

penitent A Christian who repents his/her sins and seeks God's forgiveness. In Roman Catholicism, a person who confesses to a priest and undertakes to do penance. In the 13th century, a system of public penance developed in the Western Church. Penitents were segregated in church, and wore special robes and cropped hair until they were readmitted to Holy Communion. In the Eastern Church they might retain impediments to their purity for life.

Peoples of the Book The name given by Muslims to the Jewish and Christian communities, because they are described in the Koran as "possessing a scripture" and are therefore accepted as having received a revelation from God.

pilgrim Someone who travels to a sacred place for religious reasons.

pilgrimage Journey to a holy place to seek help from God, the Virgin Mary, or a saint, to fulfill vows, give thanks, obtain forgiveness, re-enact a past event, or as a penance. The place may be associated with a religion, or be the site of objects of veneration.

Poor Clares Founded by St. Francis of Assisi and St. Clare in the first half of the 13th century, this is the most austere of the Roman Catholic orders. An enclosed (contemplative) order where the nuns lead a life of poverty, prayer, penance, and manual work.

pope From the Greek word for 'father,' its usage as a title for all bishops appears in the 3rd century and refers to spiritual paternity. By the 6th century it was reserved for bishops of Rome.

Pre-Congregation *See* pages 6–7

predestination Christian belief particularly associated with St. Augustine of Hippo and the Protestant reformer John Calvin. It holds that all that happens is divinely foretold, especially whether or not any individual will receive divine salvation.

Protestantism/Protestant The Christian doctrines professed by those who split away from the Universal Catholic Church during the Reformation to follow the principles of Luther. This now means most non-Roman Catholic and non-Eastern Orthodox churches (the main ones being the Lutheran, Methodist, Baptist, and Calvinist churches). Protestantism stresses individualism and equality in worship; the Bible as the sole source of truth; justification by faith alone (believers are deemed righteous, regardless of personal qualities); participation of lay people in worship; rejection of the doctrine of transubstantiation and of the authority of the pope.

Puritan/Puritanism A Calvinist-inspired movement in England in the late 16th and 17th centuries to 'purify' the Church of England of remnants of Roman Catholicism (or 'popery'). They believed that conversion was necessary to redeem a person's inherently sinful condition. Preaching, not ritual, was central to their faith. In practicing plain living and plain dress, they extended their strict moral and religious outlook to every aspect of their lives. They founded model communities in North America.

Q

Quaker/Quakerism Formally called the Society of Friends, this religious movement was founded by George Fox, attracting the strictest members of the Puritans in mid-17th-century England. It spread rapidly throughout Great Britain and to North America. Quakers believed in peace, and that each person could receive God's 'Inner Light' directly, and so had no appointed clergy, rites, or buildings. Their popular name may come from Fox's direction to 'tremble at the name of the Lord,' or to shaking fits when illuminated by the Spirit.

R

Reconquista Christian campaign (718–1492) to reconquer Iberia from the Moors.

Reformation Revolution in theological doctrine and practice in the Western Christian Church in the 16th century initiated by Martin Luther and John Calvin. It resulted in the emergence of Protestantism and the attenuation of the power and influence of the Roman Catholic Church and therefore of the papacy. It had far-reaching political, social, and economic impacts and sparked civil and international wars across Europe. The Protestant Reformation also prompted reform and a renewed spirit of evangelism within the Roman Catholic Church, known as the Counter-Reformation.

relics Remains of a saint or holy person after death, or objects sanctified by having been in contact with a saint's body during his or her lifetime.

reliquary A container, usually of precious materials, for safeguarding and exhibiting relics. They often took the form of caskets, crosses, rings, purses, or the shape of the body part they contained. In post-medieval times, the glass monstrance form became popular.

Rite The observances held in common that characterize a church, including canon law, liturgy, traditions, and customs. Catholic Christianity is divided into two major rites: the Latin (or Roman) Rite under the authority of the pope – historically in Rome; and the Eastern Rite – historically five independent patriarchates, comprised of those of the Byzantine empire (Constantinople, Alexandria, Antioch) and those of the Christian churches that developed outside it to the east (East Syria and Armenia). The churches that developed in the Eastern Rite are the Eastern Orthodox churches, the Oriental Orthodox churches, and the Nestorian Church.

Rule of St. Benedict Written by St. Benedict of Nursia c.540, this standard of behavior and religious observance was moderate and became fundamental to the development of all Western Christian monasticism. The most important observances were obedience, compassion, stability (a monastery with an elected abbot), the holding of possessions in common, communal divine office (worship), private prayer, study, and work.

Russian Orthodox Church Shares most of its doctrines and traditions with the Greek Orthodox Church. St. Vladimir of Kiev established Greek Christianity as his nation's official faith in 988. Russia's independent church was established by the enthronement of its first patriarch in 1589. It suffered persecutions (1929–30, 1937–38) and the closure of churches and seminaries (1959–64) under the atheist Communist regime (1918–88), but has since seen a widespread revival.

S

sacrament General meaning: a ceremony of the Christian Church. Specifically, in the Roman Catholic and many Eastern Orthodox churches, the seven chief rites: baptism, confirmation, the Eucharist, penance, anointing the sick, ordination, and matrimony. In Protestantism, baptism and the Eucharist. In the Catholic Church, the Blessed Sacrament refers to the bread and wine of the Eucharist, or individually to the Host (bread).

Second Vatican Council An ecumenical council called by Pope John XXIII in 1962 to renew and update the Roman Catholic Church. Completed in 1965 under Pope Paul VI, the Council's work resulted in the biggest changes in the Catholic Church since the 16th century, including:

vernacular replacing Latin in the liturgy; the laity having the right to participate in Communion; freedom of conscience emphasized; deacons being permitted to marry; regular consultation with other churches; and the revision of the General Roman Calendar (completed 1969).

self-mortification The imposition of a regime of mortification upon oneself, often involving fasting or scourging.

simony The buying or selling of ecclesiastical privileges such as appointments in the church, or something spiritual, such as pardons.

Society of Jesus (Jesuits) A highly successful, non-contemplative, male religious order founded in 1540 by Ignatius of Loyola, a Spanish nobleman and soldier turned ecclesiastic. His Rule demanded unconditional obedience and loyalty to the pope, including a vow to go anywhere in the world at the pope's command, while his *Spiritual Exercises* were an essential part of every Jesuit's training. The order's prime aims were religious teaching, and charitable and missionary work.

stigmata In Christian tradition, marks or pains corresponding to Christ's wounds at the Crucifixion that appear on a person's body to show divine favor.

Sulpician Order A community of secular priests founded in 1642 in Paris as the Society and Seminary of St. Sulpice. Its aim was to train zealous priests who would themselves become seminary directors. Members took no religious vows but lived in the spirit of poverty. They shared a common schedule of study, prayer, and work with their students, who participated in parish life and often went on to university.

syncretism The merging of different religions, doctrines, or cultures.

synod In Christianity, a gathering of clergy, or clergy and laity, for decision-making or consultation on church matters.

T

Tertiary In monasticism, a 'Third Order' created in medieval times to allow lay men and women (including married people from 1175) to take part in religious life and to be associated with a particular monastic order, mainly Franciscan, Dominican, or Carmelite.

Thirty Years' War Conflict that engulfed much of central Europe from 1618–48, resulting in a decline of population there from 21 million to 13 million. Beginning as a war between the Holy Roman emperor and some of his rebellious Protestant states, it drew in Denmark, Sweden, France, and Spain (through the Spanish Netherlands) to become a battle for both political and religious dominance.

Trappists Formally, the Order of Cistercians of the Strict Observance. It was founded in 1664 as an austere branch of the Cistercians at the abbey of La Trappe in Normandy. In 1893

they reinstated the original Cistercian mother house at Cîteaux. This became the mother house of a new independent Trappist order, the Reformed Cistercians of the Strict Observance, which then spread worldwide. There are now Trappist nuns.

Trinity The Christian doctrine that arose in the early Christian Church that God exists in three persons, Father, Son, and Holy Spirit, thus preserving the unity of God. It was confirmed as dogma by the Council of Constantinople in 381 and is the central dogma of Western Christianity.

V

Vatican Independent and sovereign papal city state within Rome, created by the Lateran Treaty of 1929, over which the pope has absolute legislative, executive, and judicial powers. As the see of the bishop of Rome, it is the central government of the Roman Catholic Church.

Visigothic empire/Visigoths Western branch of the Germanic Goths who invaded the Roman empire between the 3rd and 5th centuries, sacking Rome in 410. After an agreement with the Romans, they first settled in southwest France. They subsequently lost most of this land to the Franks, and moved into and ruled most of Iberia until overthrown by the Moors in 711.

Vulgate Bible Latin version of the Bible most widely used in Western Christendom. It was mostly the work of St. Jerome (4th century). A revised edition published in 1592 was declared by Pope Clement VIII the authoritative text for the Roman Catholic Church. 'Vulgate' derives from the Latin *versio vulgata* ('version for the public').

INDEX